A Practical Guide to **Producing and Harvesting White-tailed Deer**

Dr. James C. Kroll
Professor, School of Forestry,
Stephen F. Austin State University
Nacogdoches, Texas

FOREWORD by **Ray Sasser**
Dallas Morning News

AFTERWORD by **Gordon Whittington**
North American Whitetail Magazine

With photography by **Mike Biggs**

Poetry by **Kenneth Sutton**

The views expressed are not necessarily those of the Center for Applied Studies, School of Forestry, Stephen F. Austin State University

© 1991, 1992, 1994 by Dr. James C. Kroll
Institute for White-tailed Deer Management and Research
Center for Applied Studies in Forestry
College of Forestry
Stephen F. Austin State University
Nacogdoches, Texas (USA) 75962

All rights reserved, including those to reproduce this book or parts thereof, in any form, without written permission of the publisher.

Third Edition
3 4 5 6 7 8 9

ISBN 0-938361-09-0

Publication also supported by:
    Houston Safari Club,
    Temple-Inland Inc., and
    International Paper Co., Inc.

For Victor D. Rippy,
Hunter, Teacher, Friend

ACKNOWLEDGMENTS

A friend of mine once remarked that great men stand on the shoulders of giants. Well, I do not know whether or not I ever will become great; but if I do not, it will not be because a great number of giants did not offer me a lift along the way! Over the last two decades, I have had the privilege to work with some of the finest people in the world, each of whom is tops in my book. Without their help, this book, and much of my research would not have been possible.

The Scientists: Harry Jacobson, David Guynn, John Stransky, David Kulhavy, Lowell Halls, Gary Kronrad, Billy Higginbotham, Charles DeYoung, Phil Goodrum (deceased), Vic Nettles, Larry Marchinton, Karl Miller, Ben Koerth and Larry Harris.

The Managers: Bill Carter, Tom Bourland, Charles Boyd, Carl Frentress, Al Brothers, Bob Zaiglin, David Whitehouse, Bill Goodrum, Don Dietz, Daryl Stanley, Joe Hamrick, Charles Hamilton, Larry Weishuhn, Horace Gore, David Baggett, Donnie Harmel, Bob Cook, Gary Machen, Johnny Hudman, Skipper Dickson, Oscar Rogers (deceased), and Paul Dickson.

The Students: Randy Tucker, Darrel Evans, Lee Rayburn, Bill Wall, Rodney Green, Rick Braden, Ronnie Bane, Mark Ellett, Randy Browning, Todd Stewart, Charlie Vyles, Robert Skinner, Shawn Coughlin, John Scherer, John Osborne and the many undergraduates who endured my absences from class.

The Friends: Dennis Coffman, Gene Samford (deceased), Eddie Miller, Bill Jones, Gordon Whittington, Ray Sasser, Steve Knight, Steve Vaughn, David Morris, Aaron Pass, Nick Gilmore, Bob Ellett and Jack Cooper.

The Staff: Debbie Corbin, Carol Selman, Betty Morrow, Marcie Conner, and Amy Pearlman.

The Outfitters: Jon Ducharme, John Finegan, Mike Zelman, George Chase, Bob Nunley, Richard Nunley, and Bob Harris.

In particular, I would like to thank Harry Jacobson and David Guynn. Harry has been a good friend, as well as, a source of critical thought and ideas. His advice always will be appreciated. David Guynn is the scientist I hope to be. He is a consummate gentleman and one of the real thinkers of our time. I value his advice and friendship. Bill Carter is an "unsung hero" in my book. With nothing but a grade school education, Bill has come to be one of the foremost whitetail managers in the country. His hard work has served to substantiate many of my original ideas about the biology of whitetails. Tom Bourland likewise is a leader in his field. His ideas concerning people management and the economic development of wildlife resources have been revolutionary; and, have made a significant impact on the way we do business.

Dennis Coffman M.D., as well as, piecing me back together on many occasions, is as good a friend as one would ever want. He is a good listener. Eddie Miller always has been there to lend a hand, and on many occasions, equipment in my quest for whitetails. Gordon Whittington is the best at his trade. He also is a good friend, and the greatest sportsman I know. This book would not have been possible without him. Ray Sasser has served as counselor and friend. Steve Vaughn has made a significant contribution to my research efforts, becoming a good friend in the process.

Debbie Corbin, Carol Selman and Betty Morrow always have given 110% to the effort. I appreciate their professional spirit and hard work. Amy Pearlman has worked, often without compensation, to see this book to its finish.

Jon Ducharme and John Finegan are the two best outfitters in the world, as far as I am concerned. They have given me their knowledge, their help and their friendship over the years. I am grateful. George Chase in a very short time became a close friend, and taught me a great deal about the northern races of whitetails. I offer him my highest compliment. He is a good hunter.

I also would like to thank my Dean, Dr. Kent T. Adair. Not only has he made more contributions to the School of Forestry at SFASU than anyone, he also has not failed to give me total support in my work. A good administrator backs his people; and, as far as I am concerned, he has backed me in every endeavor.

I would thank my wife, Susie, and my daughter, Sydney, for all of those lost hours on the road during the early days when giving talks on whitetails was not in vogue. They sat patiently night after night, listening to the same stories over and over again, in the backs of old schools, camps and courthouses. They endured my absences, as I traveled around the country, lecturing, learning and hunting whitetails. They truly have been the "wind beneath my wings." I also would thank my parents, C.P. and Doris Kroll, and my mother and father-in-law, Bo and Ruby Masters. Bo has been a strength I have needed on many occasions.

David Kulhavy provided invaluable assistance and advice in the preparation of this book. If it had not been for the computer expertise of P. R. Blackwell, this book would never have come to fruition.

This book would be much less than it is without the photographs of Mike Biggs. He truly is the greatest deer photographer of all time. He has the ability to recognize behaviors in whitetails few hunters ever will notice. Additional photography also was provided by two young photographers, William Lea and Robert Skinner. Mike better watch his tracks, as I expect great things from these two men.

My friend Kenneth Sutton graciously allowed me to use his excellent poems. He has the unique ability to express what few hunters can about their sport.

Gene Samford, now deceased, was responsible for the complete turnaround of the

Boggy Slough deer herd. He was willing to give a young biologist his head, when conventional "wisdom" dictated otherwise. He was a respected and fair game warden, biologist and human being. He will be missed.

Charles (Charlie) Boyd is a real unsung hero. He stood up for what was right for deer when those more politically inclined had abandoned the species. He truly is a giant among us.

I cannot express enough appreciation to Ken Kennemer for editing and proofing this book. Also my friend and colleague, Ben Koerth, spent countless hours correcting copy and making changes significantly improving the quality of the third and subsequent printings.

Finally, I would like to thank Aldo Leopold; who, although he long ago departed this earth, continues to influence so many professional wildlife managers. The battles he fought in Wisconsin some 50 years ago are still with us.

...J.C.K.

FOREWORD

It's been nearly a decade since I heard about an East Texas wildlife biologist who was doing some interesting telemetry work with white-tailed deer movements. One phone call to Dr. James C. Kroll convinced me that he was not just another self-proclaimed authority spouting the same tired philosophy gleaned from dusty scientific volumes.

A writer is only as good as his sources and over the years, I came to rely on Kroll for observations about whitetails that were often radical, seldom typical and never boring. Somewhere along the way, maybe as early as our first meeting, the subject of this book arose.

"The Book" has been a standing joke, almost a metaphor for the trophy whitetails we both pursue-- elusive creatures that, like "The Book," are oft spoken of but seldom seen. James' book bears other similarities to a trophy whitetail. It took years to develop. It required genetics (the author's) and nutrition (untold reams of data and personal observations upon which to feed).

Producing Trophy Whitetails by Al Brothers and Murphy Ray, long considered the bible for whitetail managers, receives in this book the credit it deserves. *A Practical Guide to Producing and Harvesting White-tailed Deer* is the new testament, equally as compelling for deer hunters as for deer managers. Simply stated, it is everything you ever wanted to know about white-tailed deer.

Houstonite Bill Carter, a self-taught whitetail expert and a mutual friend of both Kroll's and mine, has a wonderful philosophy about when to harvest a buck, a philosophy adapted from the advertising slogan of a popular winery. Carter says he will shoot no buck before his time. James Kroll has seemingly adopted a like philosophy concerning "The Book." Despite our long-standing joke, James was determined not to publish his whitetail book before its time.

Now is the time.

Ray Sasser,
Dallas Morning News, 1990

TABLE OF CONTENTS

DEDICATION ———————————————————————————— iii

ACKNOWLEDGMENTS ———————————————————— iv

FOREWORD ———————————————————————————— vii

TABLE OF CONTENTS ———————————————————— viii

INTRODUCTION ———————————————————————— 1

PART I: BIOLOGY AND MANAGEMENT

CHAPTER 1   MANAGEMENT: THE FUTURE OF WHITETAILS ———————————————— 7

CHAPTER 2   SPRING AND SUMMER: FEAST AND FAMINE ———————————————— 17

CHAPTER 3   THE RUT: A TIME OF TURMOIL ———— 27

CHAPTER 4   WINTER: A TIME OF TESTING ———— 45

CHAPTER 5   DEER SENSES ———————————————— 51

CHAPTER 6	ANTLEROGENESIS: HOW ANTLERS GROW	67
CHAPTER 7	NUTRITION AND SUPPLEMENTAL FEEDING	79
CHAPTER 8	HABITAT MANAGEMENT AND HOME RANGE	101
CHAPTER 9	UNDERSTANDING DEER MOVEMENTS	133
CHAPTER 10	POPULATION MANAGEMENT: THE BASICS	145
CHAPTER 11	CENSUSING WHITE-TAILED DEER	161
CHAPTER 12	RECORD-KEEPING: THE BASIS FOR SOUND MANAGEMENT	177
CHAPTER 13	INTERPRETING RECORDS: THE FINE-TUNING PROCESS	199
CHAPTER 14	TROPHY MANAGEMENT: SOME PLAIN TALK	211
CHAPTER 15	A BLUE PRINT FOR DEER MANAGEMENT	219
CHAPTER 16	GENETICS AND CULLING	235

CHAPTER 17	CONTROLLING DEER MOVEMENTS ---------------------------------- 250
CHAPTER 18	THE BOGGY SLOUGH STORY ----------- 263

PART II: HARVESTING WHITETAILS

CHAPTER 19	THE ART OF SHOOTING DEER --------- 279
CHAPTER 20	SCOUTING: THE ART AND SCIENCE -------------------------------------- 299
CHAPTER 21	STANDS AND BLINDS: EFFECTIVE USE IN DEER HUNTING------------------------------------- 321
CHAPTER 22	THE SCHOOLING OF A TROPHY BUCK --------------------------- 336
CHAPTER 23	BUCK HABITAT: WHAT IS IT AND HOW DO BUCKS USE IT? ---------- 353
CHAPTER 24	BUCK SANCTUARIES AND TRAVEL CORRIDORS ------------------------- 364
CHAPTER 25	UNDERSTANDING BROWSING PATTERNS -------------------------------------- 389

CHAPTER 26	HOW TO AUTOPSY THE RUT	399
CHAPTER 27	HUNTING THE RUT	408
CHAPTER 28	HUNTING RUTTING SIGN	419
CHAPTER 29	THE TRICKLE RUT: UNDERSTANDING AND RECOGNIZING IT	429
CHAPTER 30	DOES: THE ULTIMATE BAIT	435
CHAPTER 31	TIMING YOUR TACTICS	443
CHAPTER 32	ADVANCED RATTLING AND CALLING TECHNIQUES	453
CHAPTER 33	LUNCH-TIME TROPHIES	463
CHAPTER 34	HUNTING NOCTURNAL BUCKS	469
CHAPTER 35	HUNTING CLEARCUT BUCKS	479
CHAPTER 36	FIVE STEPS TO A LATE-SEASON BUCK	489
CHAPTER 37	TWELVE-MONTH DEER SEASON	497

PART III: SOCIO-ECONOMICS OF WHITETAIL MANAGEMENT AND HUNTING

CHAPTER 38   PEOPLE MANAGEMENT ------------------ 507

CHAPTER 39   IN SUPPORT OF DEER HUNTING ------ 515

CHAPTER 40   TO BE A TROPHY HUNTER -------------- 525

CHAPTER 41   ORGANIZING A HUNTING CLUB ----- 535

CHAPTER 42   GUIDED HUNTS FOR WHITETAILS --- 551

CHAPTER 43   THE ECONOMICS OF WHITETAIL MANAGEMENT ----------------------------- 561

CHAPTER 44   POACHING ---------------------------------- 571

AFTERWORD --- 581

SUGGESTED READINGS -------------------------- 591

INDEX --- 583

INTRODUCTION

You probably are thinking to yourself, "Why do we need yet another white-tailed deer book?" Believe me, I repeatedly have asked myself that question as I suffered the throes of producing this book! Yet, there **is** a need for a new deer book— but a special type of deer book. Over the last two decades interest in deer hunting and deer management literally has exploded. Faced with a decreasing land base and fewer quality deer hunting opportunities, the hunting public has taken new interest in gaining useful information about white-tailed deer.

Most deer books primarily have dealt with hunting techniques and lore. Although entertaining, and often informative, many of these books were written by laymen or popular writers, with little background in the scientific study of whitetails. Only a few books have addressed the principles of deer management, most notable of which is the landmark book by Al Brothers and Murphy Ray, *Producing Quality Whitetails*. Their book probably did more to stimulate public interest in deer management than any other. For the first time, the basic principles of producing deer were outlined in an easily understood manner.

During the late 1980's, the Wildlife Management Institute published a voluminous (some 870 pages) work entitled, *White-tailed Deer Ecology and Management.* This book, written by knowledgeable deer researchers, was aimed primarily at a scientific audience; yet, brought together for the first time state-of-the-art knowledge about whitetails.

About the same time, Dale McCullough wrote one of the most exciting technical books ever written about white-tailed deer. In his *George Reserve Deer Herd*, McCullough explained the complicated population processes exhibited by deer. He clearly demonstrated the concept of sustained yield and its applicability to deer management.

So, again you probably are asking yourself, "Then why do we need another white-tailed deer book?" The answer is simple. All of these books dealt either with the more technical points of deer biology and management, or specific hunting techniques and stories. No book has addressed both the production **and** harvesting of whitetails. Yet today, we are at a crossroads. The general public has reached a level of sophistication which demands an indepth manual aimed specifically at the production and harvesting of whitetails— one written in easily understood language. That is my intent with this book.

A Practical Guide to Producing and Harvesting White-tailed Deer is organized into three sections. Part One presents information I feel you need to know in order to effectively manage and hunt whitetails. Chapters are limited only to those aspects of deer biology necessary to make you a better manager or hunter. For example, unlike previous deer books, there is no chapter on the history of deer and deer hunting. Now, don't get me wrong. It **is** important to know about the history of whitetails; however, other books have more than adequately covered this aspect of whitetail lore. So, there is little need to "re-invent the wheel."

Part One also presents the "tried-and-true" principles I have used successfully to produce large numbers of quality bucks throughout the U.S. My management philosophy will quickly manifest itself. **I firmly believe in the concept of intensive management.** Wildlife management professionals can be divided into two camps. One camp believes in *extensive management,* while the other subscribes to an *intensive management* philosophy. The difference is significant. Extensive management refers to providing the animals' needs over the broad landscape. This philosophy arose out of the days when America had a presumably inexhaustible supply of land and game. Department of Natural Resources biologists often adhere to this philosophy. The goal is to provide hunting opportunities for large numbers of people. This certainly is admirable, but it often is difficult to satisfy both the demands of hunters and deer. Furthermore, since 75% of the deer habitat is controlled by private landowners, state agencies exercise little

Introduction

influence over the long haul. Faced with a large proportion of private land holdings, an ever-shrinking land base and a deterioration in the quality of the deer hunting experience, some biologists have opted for intensification of management on a smaller land base. Under the intensive management philosophy, the needs of deer on each parcel of land are addressed, in order to maximize production of deer and quality hunting opportunities.

For too long now, the word *management* has been viewed as a dirty word. **I contend that management is the salvation of the white-tailed deer**. Hunters want quality experiences, and are willing to participate in the management of deer. Unfortunately, their needs currently are not being addressed by professionals. The public clearly wants help. This need probably motivated you to purchase this book.

It is one thing to grow quality bucks, yet another to harvest them. After successfully producing many trophy-class animals, I became frustrated in my inability to get one of these magnificent animals on some hunter's wall! That is why I became involved in hunter education through magazine articles and speaking tours. It is sad to say that the average deer hunter—excluding yourself, of course-- is inept. He pushes back from his desk or work bench in September, and announces that he is going out to kill "RAMBO with antlers!" The mature white-tailed deer is, without a doubt, the most difficult game animal to kill in the world. That precisely is why the vast majority of bucks harvested are eighteen month old deer. The mature whitetail is one smart cookie! In order to outsmart him, you have to be armed with the proper tools and be prepared to deal with him on his level; not yours. Part Two presents techniques I successfully have used in harvesting quality whitetail bucks. Emphasis is placed on knowledge and preparation, rather than gimmicks and equipment.

Finally, we will come to the most important aspect of whitetail management. As a college professor, I have had the honor of working with some of the finest students any where in the country. But, each student comes to our program with one basic misconception. A young man or lady will come to my office, professing to want to become a wildlife biologist. "Why do you want to do that?" I always ask. "Because I don't like people," too often is the answer. Wildlife management **is** people management! The principles for producing quality whitetails basically are simple. Getting people to believe in these principles is quite another thing. Part Three deals specifically with the people aspects of deer management. Hunting always has been a social endeavor. An understanding of how people think and act in a social setting will significantly improve your ability to achieve management goals. The growing interest in leasing and hunting clubs will demand that people management skills be developed and refined. The biologist only makes recommendations, the hunter is the true manager.

There also is a chapter on one aspect of deer management seldom appreciated by modern managers; economics.

A basic understanding of the true costs and benefits to management often is paramount to a successful management program.

I have spent the last ten years working on this book. It has been a labor of love, as well as, one of the most difficult things I ever have done. It is the culmination of many years of experience and "hard knocks," both on my part and by the dedicated professionals with whom I have had the privilege of working. I hope this book will be of use.

PART I: BIOLOGY AND MANAGEMENT

Chapter 1

MANAGEMENT: THE FUTURE OF WHITETAILS

I just finished one of the most memorable years of my career of working with whitetails. I had the privilege of hunting and studying the species in Canada, the U.S. and Mexico. October found me working with the Cerf-Sau Hunting Camp on Anticosti Island, where the quality both of whitetails and whitetail hunting are seldom surpassed. Later, I hunted New Brunswick, where there are few hunters and monster bucks. January of the same season ended my hunting year in pursuit of big bucks in Mexico. The year served to finally crystalize my thoughts about the "state of the union" and future of whitetails and whitetail hunting.

In order to begin this discussion, it will be necessary to retrace our steps to around the turn of the century. At that time, the whitetail, as with many species, was to the point of being counted down and out. Our best estimates of the population across its entire range suggest that less than 500,000 animals survived the early days of wholesale habitat destruction and heavy market shooting. Then came the wildlife management profession and concerned sportsmen. By the 1940's deer were making a comeback across the continent. Funds from the Pittman-Robertson Act and license fees were being used to restore both habitat and whitetail populations. Advent of the screw worm eradication program in the South gave added impetuous to the recovery of whitetails. As a result, numerous Boone & Crockett whitetails were reported shortly after this period. Texas, for example, founded its reputation on the monster whitetails harvested from its rapidly growing herd. However, the whitetail approached another plateau of population growth.

Much of the existing deer range in the 1960's was open to public hunting. Heavy hunting pressure, especially in the Mid-West, East and South pretty much kept populations at low levels. Game departments considered densities of 6-10 deer per square mile as acceptable under this system. In the South, heavy poaching and dog hunting, in addition to a high proportion of open hunting lands held deer densities at very low levels. Then in the 1970's, new trends in deer management and hunting began to emerge.

North American Whitetail Magazine and other periodicals had much to do with these changes. Clearly, the whitetail was emerging as **the** big game animal of North America. The average hunter was no longer satisfied to harvest a small forked-antlered buck every few years. Hunters were becoming educated about what it takes to produce trophy quality heads, although misinformed on many occasions. Texas led the nation in these revelations about deer management. The publication of Al Brothers' and Murphy Ray's book on producing trophy whitetails was a significant milestone in deer management.

"Texas-style" management became synonymous with quality and trophy hunting. Also, Texas because of its Spanish land-ownership heritage, spawned some new attitudes about rights of landowners in regard to wildlife management. Leasing of hunting rights is now as common as leasing of grazing rights in Texas, as well as, many other states. The leasing movement quickly spread to the Southeast, where the hunting club is rapidly becoming the norm rather than the exception.

Finally, in their efforts to produce larger populations of deer, sportsmen's groups pushed for bucks-only laws. Biologists generally went along with these regulations in an attempt to reestablish both huntable populations and quality habitat. Deer populations in states such as Alabama not only recovered, but became major economic pests to agriculture. Once co-evolving with the wolf, deer populations left unchecked rapidly saturated range after range.

As we approach the next century, white-tailed deer rapidly are increasing throughout the range. Current estimates vary from 15 to 17 million animals in the U.S. alone. Texas reports a population of better than four million animals. Yet, through all of this the overall quality of the hunting experience and of whitetail bucks appears to be on the decline. Hunters are expressing increased dissatisfaction with the quality of bucks and the deer hunting experience. One hunter I met in Canada was from New York state. I asked him why he traveled all the way to Canada to hunt deer. "Well," he replied, "there is absolutely no way that I will ever kill the kind of buck in New York that I can here on Anticosti Island!" I hear this time and time again from sportsmen, and New York is not an isolated case. It is sad to say that this is true over most of the country. Hunters are questioning state wildlife management philosophy.

Anti-hunting groups use my words to condemn hunting. Obviously, they are only hearing what they want to hear. Hunting pressure is only reducing the age structure of the buck population. It is not controlling the population!

Much of the deterioration in quality of deer and deer hunting comes from over-protection, not over-shooting.

MANAGEMENT

The word "management" is not a dirty word! It implies many things to many people. It may be as simple as the issuance of hunting permits, or as complex as maximizing the production of quality bucks. So, do not be overly impressed when the word is applied to the deer herd in your area. White-tailed deer management can be reduced to three options. These are: **trophy buck management, quality buck management** and **deer numbers management**.

Trophy Deer Management

Whenever I talk deer management with landowners and hunting clubs, I always ask the same question, "Do you want trophy bucks, quality bucks or just bucks?" The resounding answer always is TROPHIES! But, when I explain what is involved in trophy management (see **Plain Talk About Trophy Management**), most opt for one of the two remaining choices. Trophy management involves a very intensive program of herd population control, extremely restricted buck harvest, intensive habitat manipulation, and most often, supplemental feeding. You can expect to harvest one trophy buck per one thousand acres. On a three or four thousand acre area, this means that

only three or four guys are going to be able to reap the benefits of trophy management in any one year. This may be acceptable for some rich landowner in South Texas, but for the average hunting club, it just is not practical. The sociological, ecological and economic costs are too high for most. In light of this, I usually suggest that what they really want is quality deer management.

Quality Buck Management
A quality buck is one that best realizes the potential of his age class, living in a quality habitat, and harvested through a quality hunting experience. An example would be one that is two to three years old, sporting an eight point rack with about 15 inches of inside spread. In other words, it is a buck that you can be proud of. You do not have to hide it behind the garage when you skin it out!

Most hunters by now realize some of the rudimentary tenants of quality buck management. Obviously, a whitetail buck never will realize his potential if he is not allowed to mature. Some states are harvesting 70-80% of their buck herd. Heavy buck harvest quickly leads to a herd where the vast majority of bucks out there are yearlings. Also, even if you allow a buck to reach an older age-class, he never will realize his potential if adequate nutrition is not available. The number one cause for lack of adequate food is over-population. I have said on numerous occasions, and somewhat facetiously, that the best habitat management tool I know of for whitetails is the .22-.250!

Mike Biggs

Heavy buck harvest, coupled with over-population, leads to the situation now "enjoyed" by many hunters. On the rare occasions that a buck is harvested, it is most likely to be a spiked antlered yearling. In Texas, outfitters often are amused by eastern hunters who literally shake in their boots at the sight of a forked-antlered buck. Many have never seen such a creature!

In order to produce quality bucks, managers and sportsmen have to work cooperatively to control the herd density and to exercise constraint on the type of buck being harvested. Biologists do not manage deer, the hunter is the true manager. He is the guy pulling the trigger and making the management decision out there in the woods.

Numbers Deer Management

In many areas, state game agencies are faced with a terrible dilemma. They must satisfy a growing number of hunters with a limited resource; i.e., bucks. Some states put as many hunters into the field as they have deer! The solution taken by many states, as one state biologist recently told me, is to set the goal of producing just a deer to shoot. He could care less whether or not there was something on its head— the goal is a deer in the bag, pure and simple.

Under such management programs, populations are manipulated so that they remain at or above the carrying capacity of the range. Some states, particularly those in the mid-west, often try to hold deer populations well below carrying capacity in order to maximize production. As odd as it may seem, you actually can produce more deer for the gun when the herd is around half of the range carrying capacity (see **Population Management**). At this point, the fawn crop is very high. The number of fawns living to take their place in the population is called the recruitment rate. If we desire to hold a deer population at a certain point, it seems logical that we should harvest a number equal to the recruitment rate. When a herd is well below carrying capacity, and producing a large number of fawns, this may translate into at least 35 percent of the herd being available for harvest annually.

Future of the Whitetail

It is interesting to note that a recent survey conducted here at Stephen F. Austin State University showed that most members of East Texas hunting clubs felt that there were not enough deer on their lands. In contrast, Texas Parks & Wildlife data, plus my own, clearly show that the herd is now saturated in most areas of the state. Other states are rapidly following suit, especially those in the Southeast. In the northern portion of the range, deer populations have reached a point where they are a serious liability to agriculture and public safety. Accidents involving deer are on the increase. Depredation on vegetable and fruit crops has prompted state agencies to issue landowners permits to shoot deer. All of this may sound great for the hunter, but is it really? **We are wasting our resource!** What it all boils down to is this. Should we manage for quality or quantity?

Mike Biggs

In answering, I must be loyal to my prime directive as a biologist. In short, I must be loyal to the resource first, and society second. The white-tailed deer is not an animal that can reach a saturation point and then just level off in balance with its world. Deer are well-suited for responding to disturbances such as fire, hurricanes and tornadoes. The American Indian knew this and regularly burned the forest to keep deer herds flourishing. Recent trends in public opinion about clear-cutting and prescribed fire have greatly curtailed much of the positive deer management practices. In addition, protectionism by sportsmen, and ironically anti-hunting groups, have allowed deer populations to reach very high levels in many areas. The high population levels can only lead to disaster. An anthrax epidemic in South-Central Texas recently devastated the deer herd in that region, yet many individuals in the area still feel that there are not enough deer! Various diseases now are being commonly reported—diseases such as hemorrhagic disease (blue tongue) are widespread. The human disease, Lyme Disease, is carried and augmented by whitetails. But, there is an even greater problem.

A few years back, I conducted research on the impact of over-population on the habitat itself. My findings were shocking! Deer characteristically exhibit "boom-crash" cycles over the years. The population increases rapidly over a six to seven year period, over-shoots the carrying capacity and then crashes. After the crash, the habitat and climatic conditions usually improve enough to allow the herd to start the cycle all over. Even though wasteful, it would seem on the surface that this is not all that bad. Not so. We now know that, each time one of these crashes occurs, two things happen. First, the quality of the habitat deteriorates beyond a point of recovery. Species of plants highly favored by deer virtually disappear form the range. Deer have the ability to seriously alter their habitat, even removing various species of trees form the forest. After all, the small woody plants eaten by deer are nothing more than baby trees. Each time the herd exceeds carrying capacity, it is reduced to a lower level. This downward plunge in the past was checked by nature through catastrophic disturbance.

Second, deer themselves change under boom-crash conditions. No where is this more apparent than in the Edwards Plateau of Texas. Deer in this region probably have existed at high densities longer than anywhere in North America. Veteran hunters and area ranchers will tell you that the body size and antler quality of Hill Country whitetails have diminished significantly in the last 25 years. I call it the **bottleneck effect**. Each time a herd crashes, individuals with small body size are favored, since these animals do not require as much nutrition as the larger individuals. They have a selective advantage, survive and reproduce, passing own their genes to the next generation. Subsequent crashes repeat this phenomenon until the average mature animal bares little resemblance to the original deer.

SATISFYING THE NEEDS OF DEER AND MEN

One basic question arises: From a public's agency's viewpoint, can we balance the scales between more deer and bigger deer on a widespread basis? I feel that this is entirely possible, however, in order to accomplish such a goal, agencies will have to greatly alter the way they conduct business. Unfortunately, we are rapidly evolving toward two completely separate forms of deer management. First, there is the type of management practiced by agencies for the general public: i.e., business as usual. Second, many hunting clubs and landowners have lost faith in state agencies, and have become actively involved in management themselves. Some have even hired biologists with expertise in quality or trophy management. This does not have to continue. Here are some suggestions for possible resolution of the problem.

Future deer management probably will involve three situations. First is the **state wildlife management area**, which is either leased or owned by the state for the expressed purpose of producing sport hunting opportunities for its citizens. Second, there are **open lands**, usually privately owned, on which the public hunt under a set of rules established by the state. Lastly, there are **areas on which access is limited either by the landowner or a group of sportsmen**, and managed specifically for deer. In order to satisfy the growing demand for quality deer hunting, states will have to develop programs aimed at each of these situations.

State owned or managed areas could provide high quality hunting experiences. State agencies must realize that it is their job, not to provide an animal to shoot, but rather a quality experience. This demands that access and harvest be strictly controlled. Each state now regulates access to management areas in different ways. Some exercise no control on the number of hunters enjoying this privilege, while others strictly limit access through public drawings, fees, etc. On such areas, agencies could strive to produce reasonable numbers of quality bucks for harvest. The quality of the experience is easily manipulated by limiting the number of hunters at any one point in time. **My surveys suggest that the average hunter requires both a reasonable expectation for success and some exclusivity in order to enjoy the sport hunting experience.** Some states have even designated two different kinds of deer management areas, some for numbers deer management and some for quality buck management. This may be a reasonable compromise. Frankly, I feel that states should establish quality management areas.

No matter how strongly you may feel about the topic, hunting on public lands is just not what it used to be. Buck populations on open lands are often greatly diminished, while hunter-hunter and hunter-non-hunter conflicts are increased. It is extremely difficult to regulate hunters on open lands. Such measures as harvest quotas, tagging programs and buck permits may help, but the real solution is public education. Most states now have hunter safety programs, stressing the need for safe firearms handling. But how many of these programs spend any reasonable amount of time on the ethics of hunting? How many teach the hunter how to maximize the quality of the experience? Public service announcements emphasize the need for safety, but have you ever seen one about letting that young buck walk?

The real salvation for quality deer management is the hunting club. It is my prediction that the coming years will see a tremendous explosion of hunting clubs in areas where traditionally open lands have predominated. This is a hot topic in many states. Hunters view clubs as a direct threat. Wildlife managers assert that hunting clubs will make deer hunting too expensive for the average hunter, and that the sport will become one for the rich. The fact is that none of these fears are well-founded. Deer hunting has, and will remain a common man's sport. I work with hundreds of hunting clubs annually, and only a handful are controlled by the wealthy. Most members are middle-class Americans. The fact is that only about eight percent of the hunter's dollar is spent on privilege or trespass fees. The average membership fee for a club is about $400 annually. I calculate that the average smoker spends more on cigarettes each year than that! If you drink soda pop, you spend even more. Fact is, the hunter is going to have to spend money to enjoy a quality experience, pure and simple.

State agencies should develop programs which address the needs of hunting clubs. These organizations are very much interested in sound management, and are desperate for information. Extension positions within agencies should develop programs which address the needs of hunting clubs. These organizations are very much interested in sound management, and are desperate for information. Extension positions within agencies should be created solely to address these needs. My experience is that the hunting club is a sound management unit. Experience in the Southeast has shown that quality bucks can be produced in reasonable numbers on hunting clubs. Intensively managed clubs often harvest a deer to thirty or forty acres, and a buck to one hundred acres. At the same time, the quality of the hunting experience is maintained.

In spite of my comments and suggestions, I am not a total optimist concerning agency programs to benefit hunting clubs and landowners. That is why I have written this book. Hopefully, the information presented herein will allow the layman, as well as, the professional manager to better manage deer herds on private lands.

SUMMARY

The white-tailed deer faces many problems in the coming decade, and so does the whitetail hunter. Pressures from increased urbanization, anti-hunting groups and a deterioration of quality in the hunting experience will demand that management take a different direction. Sportsmen's groups and state agencies must begin now to prepare for these changes. Public education programs, both from hunters and non-hunters, must be developed which emphasize the need for population control. Hunters must be taught that success is not just killing a deer, but lies in a quality, memorable experience. States must become involved in providing quality hunting experiences, not just animals to shoot. A coordinated program which provides quality bucks to all, whether it be a hunting club member or a public hunter, will assure that the whitetail will remain the magnificent game animal it has been since the founding of this country.

Chapter 2

SPRING AND SUMMER: FEAST AND FAMINE

The first tender shoots of spring bring good times to the woods. It has been a long hard winter, and some of the deer who took part in the fall rut no longer roam the woods. Some have fallen to the hunter's gun, but most of those who died succumbed to the relentless toll taken by scarcity and cold. The spring is a good time to begin our discussion of basic deer biology. It is a time of renewal and of plenty.

Deer arrive at the early spring green-up in pretty poor condition. Although their bodies are well-suited to doing without, the fat stores obligatorily saved in later summer and early fall, long ago have been exhausted. The deer are relegated to a life of reduced activity and recycling. But, alive within most of the does is the new year's crop.

Approximately 200 days after the buck and doe become acquainted, the fawns are born. Inside the mother's branched uterus, the two fawns have been developing since the fall rut. The growth pattern of the fetus is carefully timed to that of the forage. Although growth is very slow during the first two-thirds of the gestation period, the latter part of pregnancy sees an explosive, compound interest growth rate.

The time of birth in each geographic area is exactly timed to fit the best growing conditions for that area. In the Pineywoods of East Texas fawns are born just at the peak of succulent forage production— April and May. To the far north, Canadian deer drop their fawns in May and June, since spring comes later there. To the south, in Mexico, the fawns appear much later, probably to coincide with the hurricane season, with its abundant rainfall. But, wherever deer live, the fawns arrive just in time to be nourished by the bountiful growing conditions.

FAWNING TERRITORIES

Most hunters think of bucks when it comes to fighting. However, the does are just as quarrelsome and just as "territorial" as the bucks. Does travel in complex social groups, made up of several related individuals. Doe groups may contain only two individuals, or as many as twenty. The term *territorial* really is inappropriate, since white-tailed deer, by strict definition, are not territorial. However, groups of does are territorial, in that they actively exclude non-members whenever they can from feeding areas. Furthermore, in the fawning season, dominant does (alpha does) "stake out" and exclude other members of the social group from their fawning area. Several years ago, I conducted a radio-telemetry study on doe movements and home range, concluding that does of the same social group have overlapping home ranges for most of the year, but minimize home

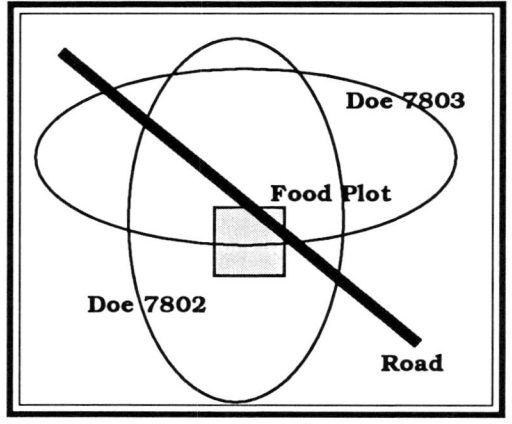

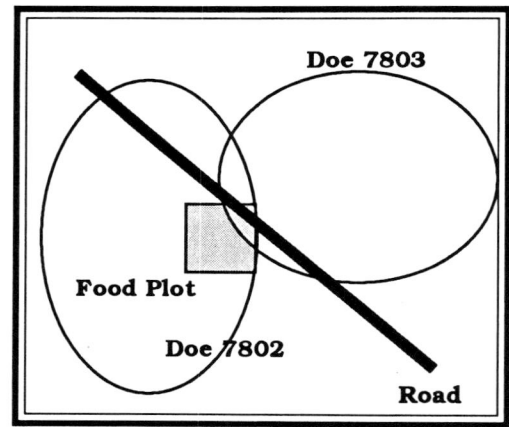

Home ranges of two radio-tracked does in East Texas, before (above) and during (below) fawning. Note the spatial separation at fawning, signifying a brief period of "territoriality."

Spring and Summer: Feast and Famine

range overlap during the fawning period.

The dominant doe commands the best fawning habitat, while her subordinates must seek less than optimum conditions. Fawning habitat is any area where there is adequate food for the doe and screening cover for the fawns.

FAWNING

By the time of birth, does have become pretty much sedentary within their fawning territories. Just as in human females, this is a time of discomfort, and the does really are reluctant to move any appreciable distance. It is amusing to disturb one of these does from her bed. She will stand up slowly, then look back at you as if to say, "You really don't expect me to run in this condition, do you?"

The fawns are born together or singly. In most cases, older does (two years or older) will give birth to twins. Triplets are not uncommon in well-managed herds. As soon as they are born, the doe cleans up the fawns and establishes the identity of each, primarily by smell. Each fawn will be placed in a separate area during the first week or so of life. This makes complete sense, because keeping them separate reduces the chances of a predator finding both fawns. Fawn mortality is quite high during the first week to ten days. In overpopulated herds, this mortality may be very high, as much as two-thirds of the new born fawns! Most of the mortality occurs among fawns of does with lower social status, since they have the poorer habitat, and less experience in rearing young.

One of the problems I have during the fawning period, is the number of calls I receive from folks who have supposedly found an "orphan" fawn. Rarely is there such a thing as an orphan fawn. Since the doe leaves the fawns alone for most of the time, in order to protect them from predators, the lone fawn you find in the woods simply is waiting for its mother to return. If you take him home with you, you not only have done something illegal, but you have interfered with nature. It is far better to leave a fawn in the woods. There is no way to know if it truly is an orphan fawn. If it is, it is better to let nature take its course.

The doe seldom places her fawn in a particular location; rather, the fawn

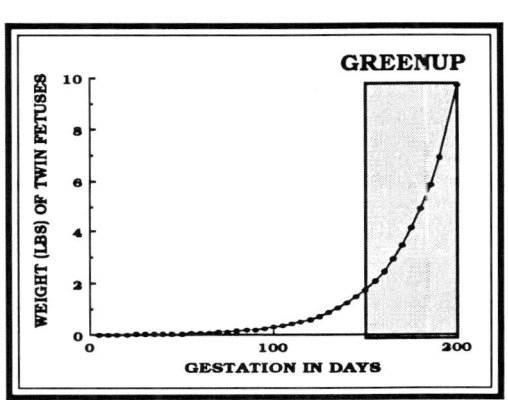

Growth rate of the fetus is similar to compound interest, with the vast majority of growth during the spring greenup period.

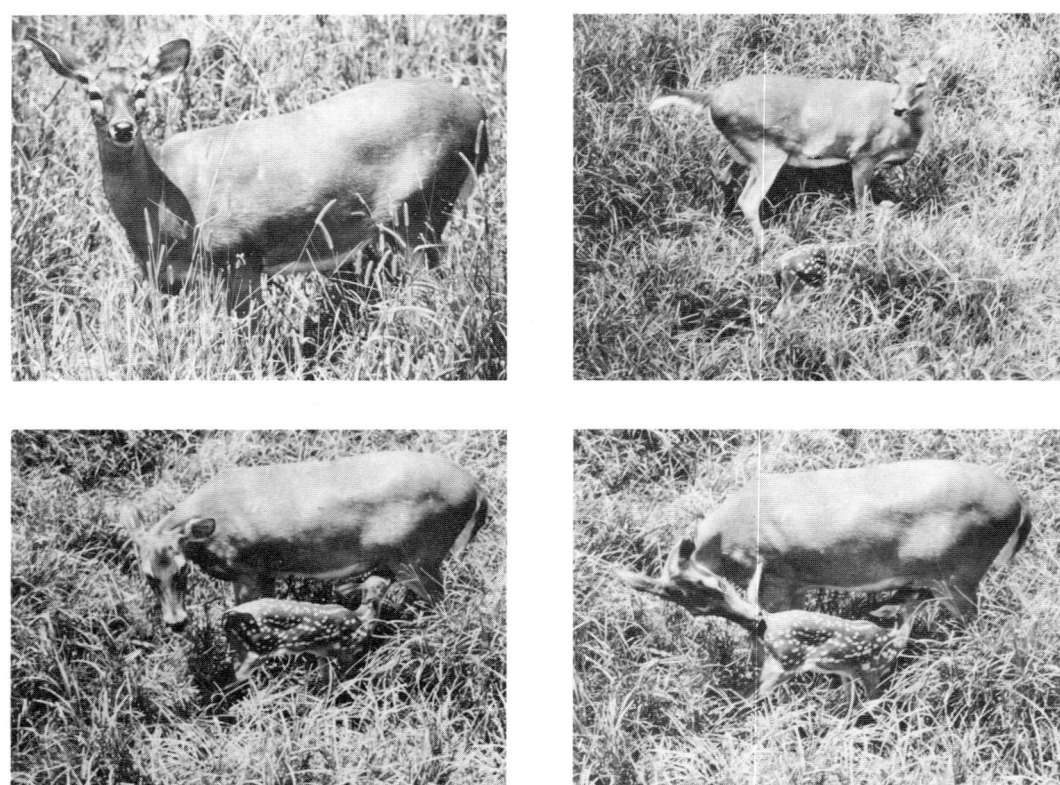

This sequence of photographs illustrates typical doe:fawn behavior at nursing. The doe approaches the general area where she last saw her fawn, and begins calling. The fawn responds, running to the doe. Yet, the doe must identify its fawn before allowing it to nurse. As the fawn nurses, the doe licks the anal region, stimulating the fawn to urinate and defecate. This seemingly repulsive behavior is important, in that it prevents odors from accumulating in the fawn bedding area, reducing the probability of a predator locating the fawn by scent.

itself picks its bedding area. The doe has no idea exactly where the fawn is, only that it is somewhere in a general area. She periodically returns to feed the little fawn. She walks in a circle around the area, calling gently with a grunting sound. This is the only time a doe makes a grunt call. The fawn hears its mother and comes running, making a light mewing sound. As it approaches,

Spring and Summer: Feast and Famine

the doe affirms the identity of the fawn by call and smell. Once the identity is established, she allows the fawn to nurse. The act of nursing only takes a few seconds. If you ever have bottle-fed a fawn you know this. A fawn can drain an eight ounce bottle in fifteen seconds flat!

As the fawn is nursing, the doe reaches around and licks the anal-genital region of its fawn. This stimulates the fawn to urinate and defecate; the doe consuming these waste products. Again, this apparent repulsive behavior is completely logical in analysis. Consumption of waste products by the doe assures that odors do not accumulate in the fawn's bedding area. This reduces the probability of a predator locating the bedding site. The doe also may lick the fawn as part of a grooming behavior, reinforcing the bond between mother and fawn. Older deer in the same social group also exhibit this mutual grooming, presumably to reinforce social relationships.

The doe seldom stays with the young fawn for long, slowly feeding away from its offspring. The fawn then seeks a new bed, and waits for mother's return. In good years, and in well-managed herds, the doe then goes to her second fawn and repeats the process. Does remain to themselves, alternating feeding themselves and their fawns for about two weeks, after which they rejoin the social group.

LIFE IN THE DOE SOCIAL GROUP

When the does once again join their social groups, it is an exciting time. Those does that have been successful return with their fawn(s). Does are very protective of their fawns, and do not tolerate the fawns of subordinates inside their personal distance. However, there are times, as with domestic cattle, that a doe will serve as a "nursemaid," watching over several fawns while their mothers feed. I once saw a doe with eight fawns, each of which she carefully guarded. Their mothers were visible, feeding several hundred yards away.

A doe social group will be made up of several age-classes of does, their fawns, and occasionally a yearling buck or two. Yearling bucks are seldom tolerated during the fawning season. Their mothers generally cast them off just prior to fawning. This also may happen with daughters, as well. A cast-off yearling buck may begin to roam about, greatly increasing his chances of mortality. For example, this spring I radio-collared a yearling buck just prior to fawning. He had a relatively small home range until fawning occurred. Then, he began running all over the place! Two months later, he was killed by coyotes. Mortality is high in yearlings for this reason.

Does fight just as much as bucks, although they do not have antlers. An average fight involves both individuals standing on their hind legs and "boxing." A doe can hit another with a terrible force. In fact, some tame does will exhibit this same boxing behavior with humans, resulting in injury to the hapless owner. Another typical aggressive behavior is the leg kick. The dominant doe will walk over to a younger

Does, as well as bucks, fight to establish social position. Here a dominant doe attacks a doe decoy in an effort to assert dominance.

deer or a subordinate, flipping the foreleg upward in a stabbing motion. This does not appear to be as painful a reminder, but it is effective. Other, more subtle mannerisms and behaviors are used to intimidate subordinates. A direct stare, with ears laid back, definitely is an aggressive posture. Dominant does and their fawns are the first to feed in a good area, the subordinates waiting their turns.

BUCK SOCIAL GROUPS

During all of this the bucks also have arranged themselves in social groups. They have come out of the winter in much worse condition than the does. The rut has exacted its toll, with very high winter mortality observed for bucks. As soon as the rut subsides and winter draws to a close, however, bucks

Spring and Summer: Feast and Famine

Bucks also fight with their front legs. Here two bucks settle a dispute over social position. Other, more subtle postures help a dominant buck intimidate another.

begin to drift back to their spring and summer feeding areas. Those that have survived renew old social relationships. Dominance hierarchies are well-established by summer. As with does, bucks kick, bite and box their way to intimidating rivals.

Bucks traditionally occupy the poorest ranges, bowing to the does in order to assure maximum survival of their offspring. This has been demonstrated in many species of birds and mammals, and is thought to be just another mechanism to guarantee successful procreation.

A buck social group may, as with does, contain just a few or many individuals. This summer, I observed a buck social group on a managed property that contained some eighteen individuals! A little observation clearly identified the dominant buck, even in such a large social group. His behavior left no question as to who was the top animal! These social groups will remain loosely associated until the pre-rut period, but the number of individuals within a social group may vary. One group I have radio-tracked for some time now has from three to six individuals. Apparently, this group centers around a dominant seven year old buck, with younger bucks leaving and joining the group erratically.

Dominate bucks use body language to intimidate younger bucks.

Although I will discuss home range and movements in detail later, it is interesting to note here that spring and summer home ranges of bucks are smaller than either fall or winter. Abundant food supplies allow the bucks to satisfy their daily requirements without having to travel great distances, especially in the spring and early summer. Bucks have very similar nutrient requirements to does during this time. Although there is no fawn to nourish, the demands placed on the buck by antler growth are very similar. Again, this phenomenon is carefully timed to coincide with abundant food. Antler growth is characterized by the same growth curve as presented for the developing fetus. Antler growth begins slowly, but accelerates in a compounding fashion later in the growing season.

LATE SUMMER STRESS

Depending on the geographic region, the late summer can be a very stressful time both for bucks and does. This is a time when forage growth is complete, with very little succulent vegetation available. Prolonged dry periods reduce both the availability and quality of foods. In the warmer climates, late summer sees more deer mortality than the late winter. Excessive demands placed on does by fawns and on bucks by developing antlers increase the chances of malnutrition. Poor condition leads to increases in parasite loads, as well as the chance for disease. This is a time when some of the more virulent diseases, such as blue tongue, take their toll.

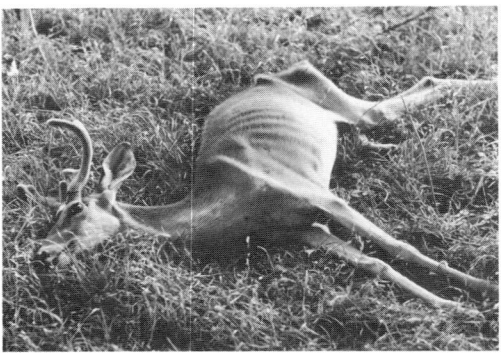

Mike Biggs

Summer is a particularly stressful time for whitetails. Most hunters do not realize that there often is high mortality during this time of the year.

Home range size in most areas is smallest at this time. There are many physiological changes taking place in both bucks and does. Coupled with a lower quality food supply, these demands cause deer to reduce activity in order to prepare for the coming rut.

By the end of the summer, bucks must accomplish several things, all in the proper order. Among these are: shedding of the reddish summer coat, growing of the grayish winter coat, mineralization of antlers and storing of fat. Does also must molt and grow a new coat, as well as store fat for the coming winter. Fat storage in deer is obligatory; even a deer in poor summer condition will store some fat. I often am amused by landowners who claim their deer to be in "excellent condition," because they have body fat when killed. Actually, fall body fat tells us far less than the amount of summer fat.

SUMMARY

The spring brings a time of abundance for both bucks and does. A time for rearing of fawns, and for antler growth. Does are loosely organized in social groups for most of the spring and summer, separating only to stake out fawning territories. Fawning is carefully timed to coincide with the best growing conditions. The dominant or alpha doe takes the best fawning habitat, with subordinates taking appropriately lower quality areas. Dominant does tend to have higher fawn survival. Once the fawns are of sufficient size, the does once again come together in social groups.

Does become antagonistic toward their yearling offspring just prior to fawning, causing an increase in movements, especially by the yearling bucks. This is a time of dispersal and high mortality for young bucks.

Bucks also travel in social groups, ranging in size from two to as many as twenty individuals. Social position is established, as with does, by kicking, boxing and intimidation.

By late summer, both bucks and does are preparing for the rigors of the coming rut and the hard times ahead. In some regions, late summer is a significant stress period, with a considerable portion of the annual mortality occurring at this time. In order to prepare for the rut, deer must shed their summer coat, grow a new winter coat, and in the case of bucks, mineralize their antlers. All of these activities require a tremendous amount of nutrients, often scarce in late summer.

The storing of fat by deer in the late summer and early fall is an obligatory process, even with deer in generally poor condition.

Mike Biggs

SUMMER EVENING

Across the meadow at twilight,
Behold, it was quite a sight.

From the forest they came, single file,
Upon my face grew a great big smile.

All males with antlers almost mature,
Which one was largest I wasn't sure.

All season I knew they were there,
I knew, but just didn't know where.

Its nice to see them in late July,
This fall I'll give them another try.
...K.S.

Chapter 3

THE RUT: A TIME OF TURMOIL

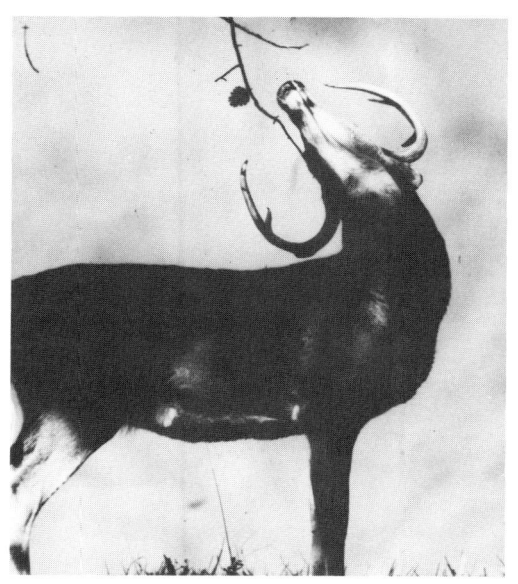
William Lea

The rut probably is the most written about, yet poorly understood, aspect of whitetail behavior. However, it is the one time that trophy bucks let their guard down to satisfy instincts stronger than personal survival. Animals are driven by the need to procreate. The "name-of-the-game" in survival-of-the-fittest is getting your genes into the next generation. By this I mean that, in order to be successful from an evolutionary sense, animals must pass on their traits to offspring, who in turn successfully reproduce. Whether or not a buck dies in the process may be a personal tragedy, but he still is genetically successful. The more offspring a buck produces, the more successful he is. Understanding this need to procreate not only is important to effective population management, but also to the efficient harvesting of deer.

BASICS

In order to understand the rut, it is necessary to examine the role whitetails play in the forests and brushlands. The white-tailed deer evolved primarily as a forest animal, probably in the eastern U.S. The first records of deer are from the early writings of the Old World explorers. They reported deer in abundance in what is now New England and the Atlantic Coastal states. Deer were the primary source of food for the early settlers, and had already become an important part of the Indian's lifestyle.

In order to find mates, animals of all species have evolved specialized mechanisms that allow them to get together.

William Lea

Whitetails evolved in the forest, probably at low population densities. Consequently, deer have a highly developed scent communication system. Chemical odors are deposited on vegetation and left as signals to other deer.

This may range from elaborately colored plumages, in the case of some birds, to the piercing calls of tropical monkeys. Each adaptation is designed to facilitate finding a female in a reasonable amount of time. Such is the case with white-tailed deer. However, whitetails faced special problems in the pristine environment of pre-Columbian America. It is a common misconception that deer were literally crawling all over the woods at the time of first settlement. This may have been true in some localized areas, but our best estimates are that about seven deer per square mile was more common. For, you see, deer do not thrive under virgin forest conditions. (See **Habitat Management**). They do best when there is a constant source of disturbance to keep vegetation, primarily browse and weeds, within easy reach. Such disturbances took the form of hurricanes, tornadoes, ice storms and fires during those times. So, early deer were faced with finding mates, often in old growth, densely stocked stands with low density populations.

One of the best ways to find a mate under such conditions is to develop a system that announces to whomever passes that you are in the area and available for mating. Animals living under similar situations have developed many techniques, but two seem to be most effective for whitetails. First, you can leave a scent deposited on the ground or on vegetation that attracts the opposite sex. Second, you can leave visual signposts that are readily seen at a distance. Since deer are not noted for their vocalizations, except elk and moose, these first two cues probably evolved at a higher level of importance for communication relating to reproduction. Deer evolved a system of scent and visual cues that we know collectively as the rut.

White-tailed deer, both bucks and does, must annually go through a series of physical and behavioral changes that prepare them for the upcoming rutting or breeding period. The timing of these changes is critical and is triggered by several environmental conditions. There are many myths perpetuated by "sage" veteran hunters about the rut. Some of them are the right observations, but the wrong interpretations; while others are downright fabrication. You would be amazed how many of these stories I hear from hunters that claim to have seen some bizarre behavior first hand, when I know good and well that the whitetail is totally incapable of such behavior. In order to give you a more informed knowledge base about the rut, let's begin where we left off in late summer.

PRE-RUT

Summer, as I noted in the last chapter, is the time to develop the body and, in the case of does, to feed growing fawns. Most hunters think that the winter is the most crucial stress period, but in many portions of the range the late summer is equally stressful. This is a time when vegetation has become too woody to digest, weeds dry up in the heat, and mast such as acorns and berries are non-existent. A whitetail often enters the early fall in pretty poor

Mike Biggs

Both bucks and does must annually go through a series of physical and behavioral changes that prepare them for the upcoming breeding season or rut.

condition. And, there is a common rule of nature, your body and personal survival take precedence over reproduction. For you always can wait until next year, if you survive that long, to reproduce. Hence, the whitetail is faced with getting into breeding condition in a very short time, usually from late August to early October. Depending upon where you are, this is a time when several species of plants start to produce fruits which are high in energy and fats. I have seen a buck put on a additional thirty percent of his body weight during early fall on nothing more than American beautyberry fruits. Acorns also begin to fall in October, and areas with grapes are attractive at this time.

Bucks and does face entirely different situations in preparation for the rut. Bucks have expended a great deal of energy and body nutrients such as calcium and phosphorus in growing their antlers, while does have used this same ability to mobilize nutrients to nurse their fawns. But time is crucial to the buck. He must, 1) grow his antlers, 2) shed the velvet, 3) molt his summer coat for a more insulating winter coat, and 4) develop his muscles for the approaching combat period. There is absolutely no way that a buck can do all of these things at the same time. During the summer, much of his resources are shunted into growing antlers. The minerals and protein needed for antler development come from the bones of the body and from high quality forages. In addition to final formation of the antlers, other necessities such as molting the summer coat have to be attended to. You would be amazed at how much energy it takes to molt and regrow hair, not to mention the high protein requirement. Shedding must take place before the animal begins preparation for actual rutting activity. That is why you will see bucks in the fall with gray winter coats, while does may still have their reddish summer coats. The does have a longer period of time to shed their summer coats, since there are no antlers and pre-rutting activity to worry about.

Over just a few days, the velvet-covered antlers change dramatically. The "burr" begins to form around the base, choking off the vital blood supply to the velvet. In addition, a process similar to hardening of the arteries occurs within the antler. In a matter of hours, the velvet "dies" and falls off in shreds. Many hunters think this phase takes days, but the vast majority of my penned bucks have taken less than two hours to shed their velvet.

Once the velvet is shed and the winter coat is obtained, the buck can then place its energy into more important matters, namely preparation for the rutting rituals and combat. There are a whole host of interesting physiological and anatomical changes taking place at this time. This inactivity is why you suddenly see very few bucks. It is a time when hunters become very nervous

Mike Biggs

Shedding of velvet is accomplished in a short time span, and is caused by loss of blood flow to the antlers.

William Lea

Antler rubbing during the pre-rut serves several functions, most notable of which is strengthening of the neck muscles.

about the prospects for the coming season; not to mention biologists. The period between velvet shedding and actual rutting activity is called the **pre-rut period**. During this time, the mature bucks as I noted above move very little and prefer to stay in and around their summer sanctuaries. These areas are usually associated with a thicket adjacent to a stream bottom. The yearling bucks often do not have such areas and may even begin to roam. Early in the fall, yearlings attempt to become associated with buck social groups, and hopefully, work their way up the peck order over the years. Younger bucks may start socializing with other young bucks in the summer, staying with these young bucks throughout much of their life.

The Rut: A Time of Turmoil

Most of the initial rutting sign occurs in and around the summer core area or sanctuary. The buck needs two things for the combats ahead, body size and antlers. His age and nutrition have supplied the body size, but the buck does have to work on his strength. Like an athlete in training, the buck starts to exercise the important muscle groups used in combat. At the same time, male hormones are beginning to exercise their influence and the buck becomes more and more belligerent. It must be like going through puberty every year! The buck takes out his frustrations on the nearest vegetation, usually small saplings. There is a definite preference for tree species. My studies have indicated a preference for resilient species such as cedars, pines and willows. One ornamental nursery lost a considerable amount of shrubs to a rather large, trophy-class buck. The damage was in excess of $50,000! That made a pretty

William Lea

Sparring matches often occur during the pre-rut, serving to establish the "peck" order of younger bucks.

expensive buck.

Many hunters think that the swollen neck of a rutting buck is due to glandular enlargement. However, this is not the case. The constant rubbing and sparring with vegetation produces the enlarged neck muscles. Later, more spirited mock combats with larger trees also develop the shoulder and ham regions.

Bucks, especially older ones, often have a favorite tree which they mark each year. These trees may be as large as twelve inches in diameter, and

William Lea

The instinctive need to make scrapes manifests itself during the pre-rut period. Scrapes are not made by all bucks, and even does have been known to make them.

George Chase

Signposts can be quite large, and usually occur adjacent to a bedding area.

usually are species that have a light colored underbark. I have designated these trees as **signposts** and their presence often is useful in locating rutting whitetails. Sign posts generally are located near the primary bedding spot, but there are other types of sign posts which I will discuss later. Sign posts satisfy one of the ways I indicated that a forest animal can signal its presence. It has been my experience that the more open the country, the

The Rut: A Time of Turmoil

Mike Biggs

Scent rubbed on signposts can come from the forehead gland and/or those picked up by forehead rubbing against the tarsal gland area.

fewer signposts and rubs are utilized as territorial markers.

Scent communication is critical to whitetails. Unfortunately, we know very little about it, in spite of what scent manufacturers may indicate. We are only recently coming to understand the complexity of scents in the communication of one deer with another. Landmark studies are being conducted by Drs. Larry Marchinton and Carl Miller at the University of Georgia. The body is covered with many glands and gland-like areas that serve various presumed purposes. The scent communication most commonly encountered by hunters, and I might add most commonly misunderstood, is scraping. Scraping is a way in which a rutting buck can let everyone know that: 1) he is in the area,

and 2) he is in breeding condition. The scrape serves as much as a territorial marker as an announcement to does. Scraping begins early in the season, sometimes as early as mid-summer. Some of my penned bucks will make scrapes when their antlers are barely half formed. This is especially true if an older buck is involved. But there is a paradox about scraping that has not as yet been solved. Not all bucks make scrapes. And, it apparently has little to do with social position. I have seen dominant bucks that never have made a scrape in their lives. It may also have something to do with the type of habitat that a particular deer lives in. For example, I have not seen the degree of scraping in the Hill Country of Texas that I have in the Pineywoods regions. Why this is so I do not know, but it may have something to do with the openness of the Hill Country. Perhaps Dr. Marchinton soon will educate us on this matter.

I have seen many a hunter find a scrape early in the year and think that he has the buck patterned. Weeks of sitting on the scrape produce nothing but a back ache. Just because you find a scrape does not mean that you have the buck figured out, especially early in the rut. During the pre-rut, bucks often make countless "mock scrapes" for nothing more than just practice. At this time, they really are not as yet interested in the first, and are just constructing scrapes out of instinct. There may be a second function I will discuss later. These early scrapes often are the ones found by hunters out scouting early in the year. They occur

Scent deposited by dominant bucks on rubs and signposts may have a suppression effect on subordinate bucks.

around the summer sanctuary all right, but the buck will probably not be there once the full rut begins.

It's during the pre-rut that mock combats and sparring may occur between bucks, especially younger individuals. These probably are the "fights" seen and reported by some hunters out scouting the pre-season. Although serving just as practice matches, social position can be reaffirmed through these matches.

A WORD ABOUT SIGNPOSTS

Signposts can either be rubs or scrapes. At this time I now feel that there is more than one function for signposts. I feel that they serve both to suppress the breeding activity of subordinate bucks and to prime the does

William Lea

The influence of testosterone during the late pre-rut period makes bucks extremely aggressive. A mature buck literally will walk around the countryside spoiling for a fight.

Bucks communicate aggression by laying back their ears and elevating their hair. Bucks appear to change color as they approach a challenger.

Mike Biggs

for estrus. This is not without precedence, since sheep and goats are known to have estrus primed by the odors produced by males. This also would partially explain why herds in good physical condition and a balanced sex ratio tend to have a more pronounced rut than those with skewed sex ratios.

LATE PRE-RUT

The late pre-rut period occurs during the last few days prior to the actual rut. Bucks by this time have become extremely aggressive and agitated. It takes very little to trigger a full-scale fight between similarly matched individuals. A real buck fight is something to behold! If you ever have observed one, it long will be remembered.

The two contestants approach each other in a slow, stiff-legged fashion. The intent is obvious. Each has its ears laid back and the hair standing on end. Bucks actually appear to change color and become darker as they approach each other. The initial attempt is to present a broadside to the opponent. This apparently serves to make the challenger look larger.

The bucks slowly circle each other. One or both bucks will issue a rattling hiss, called a **snort-wheeze**, which again signals intent on fighting. The snort-wheeze also is used to intimidate younger bucks, but it only serves to infuriate older, more equally matched opponents. Through body language and an increase in tension, the fight begins with a violent coming together of antlers. In sparring matches, bucks simply will engage their antlers and begin

Mike Biggs

pushing each other around. In a fight, however, the contact is much more violent. The duration of a fight is highly variable, ranging from a few seconds to several minutes. The longest fight I personally have witnessed was forty-five minutes. Two tremendous ten pointers came together in a sendero (cleared strip in South Texas), and fought for almost an hour.

There has been much written about buck fights. Oddly enough the winner of these fights seldom is the buck with the biggest set of antlers. Rather, it is the buck with the most experience and the largest body. Apparently, once a buck has enough antler to engage his enemy, he is ready to participate in fights. Yet, it is his own physical condition and experience that will determine his success. Often, I have seen mediocre eight pointers become dominant, when there were many ten and twelve pointers, with larger antlers in the herd.

The fight breaks off as quickly as it starts. Through some unseen signal, the loser breaks away and flees the field. The victor pursues with vigor, often damaging the defeated buck. On one occasion, my friend David Whitehouse and I rattled up two bucks who got into an impressive fight. After some time, one buck tried desperately to escape his tormentor, only to be stabbed repeatedly in the side and rump by the victor. The defeated buck was mortally wounded in the process. This is not uncommon in areas with high buck populations. In a single year, for example, I removed more than twenty carcasses of mature bucks from a managed area, where fighting had become excessive. David reports similar observations from his managed herds. As I will discuss later, this can become quite a problem to the manager, and makes me question the wisdom of intensive trophy management programs.

RUT

Although fighting continues well into the rut, most of these severe combats have taken place by the start of the full rut. The full rut begins in response to light conditions. Weather is often implicated by hunters, but light is the real key. I often have said that "light cocks the pistol, and weather pulls the trigger." As the rut comes into full swing, the mature bucks begin an ever-expanding zone of activity that moves farther and farther away from the summer core area. The buck I have been monitoring for some time now begins scraping and rubbing within a few hundred feet of his bedding area in late October. But by the first week of November, on the other hand, the buck has expanded his activities to a ridge line along his home creek drainage. His scrapes are almost always located within the same general area, sometimes even in the exact same spot as the previous season. By December, he has expanded his scrape line a full mile to mile and a half along the drainage. Then, in late December the buck changes drainages altogether, moving some five to seven miles away to another drainage system. Why does he do this?

The breeding structure of whitetails is almost identical to that of mice. There are female social groups that occupy specific areas and are, for the most part, related to each other. I have followed several such doe groups over the years, observing that the dominant or **alpha doe** is usually most successful in raising her fawns to maturity. Her daughter occupies the lower social structure, along with a few lesser related does that may have joined the social group. Yearling bucks and some does often are forced out of the group and have to find their own social group. If bucks were not vagrant, travelling around the country, there would be a tremendous inbreeding problem with deer. Indeed, in grossly over-populated ranges, there are so few bucks that there is no need for them to move much. Consequently, inbreeding is quite common, which leads to all sorts

A buck constantly is checking the status of his rubs and scrapes to monitor reproductive activity in the area.

William Lea

of problems.

Vagrant bucks have a set route they travel in visiting their doe social groups. Each time a buck moves to a new area, it sets up a line of scrapes which I have dubbed a "trotline." The term for the buck's behavior is the **full scrape sequence**, made up of several activities organized in set sequence. The buck paws out a depression in the ground beneath a bush and urinates in it. The urine carries with it male secretions that apparently signal to other bucks that a new buck is in the area, and to the does that he is ready to receive company. Does may be able to judge the physical condition of bucks by smelling the urine in scrapes, but this is not fully documented at this time.

He may also establish or re-work an old signpost as an additional signal that the buck is about. As I noted earlier, I now am of the opinion that the signpost serves an additional function. It may serve to suppress the activities of subordinate bucks. Substances left on the signpost from the forehead gland and/or tarsal gland secretions deposited on the antlers and forehead may be picked up by subordinate bucks by licking and smelling. Subsequently, these chemicals may help dominate a buck of lesser social status. These are as yet unproven observations, but there is a growing amount of evidence in support of this hypothesis.

A rutting buck works scrapes just like you would a series of trotlines. He concentrates his activities in areas that are producing results, constantly re-baiting his hooks. However, once an area becomes unproductive, the buck

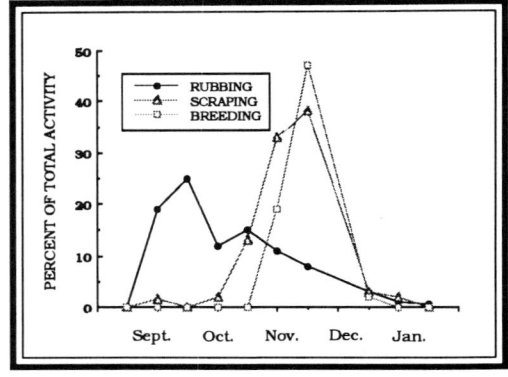

This graph shows the general sequence of three different rutting activities: rubbing, scraping and breeding. Notice that the three activities peak at different times; hence, each is carefully timed to lead into the next. To obtain a similar graph for your area, you should move the curves either earlier or later, depending on exactly when your rut occurs. (Data modified from Kile and Marchinton, 1977).

either moves on to other scrapes or establishes a whole new line of scrapes. I have found that there is no set time of the day during which a buck works his scrapes. Late-morning often is a good time to find a mature buck moving about, but in areas that are heavily hunted, bucks may become totally nocturnal. The only consistent observation I have on the subject is that bucks are more likely to be moving about when there are does in heat. Does within a particular social group are likely to come into estrus at about the same time, provided they are in good physical condition. This is a time when you are most likely to see increased buck movements.

In well-managed deer herds, or those with low population densities, you can expect two to three distinct peaks in the rut. The first and strongest peak occurs early in the season and involves the vast majority of does. The second or secondary rut peak occurs about 25-30 days later and involves those does that did not become pregnant during the primary rut, plus the younger yearling does that are just then coming into physical condition to breed. A very small third peak may also occur in some ranges when a few of the fawn does come into estrus. Up to forty percent of fawn does have the capability to reproduce their first year in well-managed herds or low population densities.

BUCK:DOE BEHAVIOR

There is much debate over the mechanisms for buck:doe communication during the rut. There is little doubt that scrapes play an important role in getting the two sexes together; however, how these chemical systems work still needs clarification. Apparently, bucks have the ability to trail does for some distance. I have seen bucks with their noses to the ground, like hound dogs hot on the trail. Most researchers now think that does may use scrapes to

William Lea

Chemicals produced in the vaginal area of does give close-range confirmation as to her reproductive state.

William Lea

The doe often aids the buck in copulation by elevating her posterior. A buck may copulate several times during the attendance period.

locate bucks, and remain in the general vicinity waiting for the proper suitor. Whether or not does choose specific bucks has not been scientifically demonstrated but I do feel that, under natural conditions, does will show a definite preference for a dominant buck in good physical condition.

The role of pheromones (chemical communicators) in the courting process has been the subject of countless articles and considerable commercial activity. I feel that sexually exciting chemicals are produced by the female that serve more in close-range communication. Laymen often are confused about the source of these chemicals. I have seen hunters religiously collect the urine of a doe for use in luring a buck into gun range. Further, several manufacturers claim to collect urine from estrous does for this purpose. However, it is certain that the source of sex pheromones is not the urine. Rather, these chemicals are produced in the vaginal area, and may become mixed with urine which serves as a carrier only. Hence, collecting urine from estrous does will not isolate the attractive source. In the presence of unfamiliar deer, does often rub-urinate just as do bucks. Does also make scrapes.

Visual cues often are overlooked in the literature. I feel that signposts and rubs are useful in reproductive communication. These structures are carefully located so that they are most easily seen from a distance. My research has shown that rubs seem to be located more in open understory habitats or on edges where they obtain higher visibility. Rubs also may serve the buck:buck communication function I discussed earlier. In addition, postures and movements both by bucks and does serve to stimulate both sexes.

Once a buck finds a doe, the resultant behavioral patterns are interesting. The buck approaches a doe with a great deal of ceremony. He may strut with his antlers high, and walk stiff-legged. Or, he may come running in like a puppy, with his tail wagging. Seldom will a doe be ready to mate on first approach. What often happens is a show to rival the best quarter horse working a calf. The buck tries to move a doe to a more open habitat, so that he can keep her in sight. Of course, the doe initially is not too willing to cooperate. Apparently, this chasing and coy behavior serves to further stimulate the participants.

This also is a time when vocalizations are important. Dr. Harry Jacobson of Mississippi State University studied deer vocalizations pertaining to courtship, and was one of the first to draw attention to the grunting call made by bucks. As the buck approaches the doe, he emits several pig-like grunts. This has been likened to similar sounds made by fawns as they approach their mothers. My experience has been that grunts are extremely variable in pitch and delivery. Some are very much like the grunt of a pig, while others are more high-pitched. At this point, I am uncertain as to the exact function of these calls. However, they have to affect the doe in some way. Although bucks are highly attracted to grunt calls, it does not make ecological sense for grunts to serve this function. Why would a buck want to attract competition?

Contact established, bucks stay in attendance for one to two days, during which time mating occurs. Once the doe decides to mate, she really is quite shameless about it. She will position herself to more easily facilitate copulation. I have seen does even get down on their knees to better present a target for the buck. Mating may take place several times over the short attendance period. I never have heard a doe make a grunting noise during the courtship process, and neither have my colleagues. So, a doe grunt call is a man-made device!

At this time, little is known about the actual number of does serviced by a particular buck. In pen studies, bucks have successfully bred as many as twenty does during a season. However, I feel that these artificial conditions mean little to interpreting what wild deer actually are doing. It is possible that a buck will breed a large number of does, but I feel that six to eight does probably is more appropriate. But, this is only conjecture at this point in time.

POST-RUT

As the rut winds down, the instinct for survival begins to take precedence over the need to reproduce. Bucks that have survived to this point have become increasingly wary, spending most of their time in their sanctuaries. Movements are pretty much limited to times when hunters are not about, and may be totally limited to the night time

William Lea
The post-rut period often finds the buck in pitiful condition. This is a time when there is considerable buck mortality.

or pre-dawn hours. This has to be the most difficult time to kill a mature whitetail buck.

This also is the most difficult time for buck survival. Bucks, as I will note several times in this book, lose a large portion of their weight and fat reserves during the rut. This leaves the buck without reserves for the remainder of the winter. Indeed, much of the mortality observed in bucks comes during the post-rut period. In areas with a high winter kill, such as the northern United States and southern Canada, as much as 40% of the buck population may be lost in any one year. This is significant mortality! Does, on the other hand, do not experience this high level of mortality, primarily due to a lower level of rutting activity.

During the post-rut, bucks not only reduce activity, but also seek out high carbohydrate and high fat foods. In good acorn production years, bucks tend to have a higher survival rate than in poor years. Also, areas with supplemental agricultural crops, such as corn and winter cover crops, tend to have higher post-rut survival.

Finally, again in response to light conditions and breeding activity, the bucks begin to lose interest altogether in rutting. Loss of male hormone causes a breaking layer (abscission layer, see **Antler Development**) to form between the antler base and the skull. The antlers fall off either singularly or as a set. The process begins anew. But, bucks may even continue making scrapes during the post-rut period, mostly just out of habit. The single spiked increase of testosterone in the early Spring also serves to stimulate bucks to scrape at strange times.

SUMMARY

The rut is a complicated series of events and behaviors that vary from area to area, and buck to buck; however, a basic understanding of the rutting process can greatly increase your chances of harvesting a quality buck, as well as aid in the management of the species. The timing of the rut is dependent on many factors and has a great impact on the reproductive success and antler quality later in life. As we will see in later chapters, when these cues go awry, the rut becomes less defined and creates problems both for the manager and the hunter.

Chapter 4

WINTER: A TIME OF TESTING

It is winter now, and most hunters are back home, watching the Super Bowl in the comfort of their living rooms. Yet, the deer still are out there, battling the environment just to stay alive! Throughout much of the range, this is a time of extreme hardship and scarcity for the deer. In this chapter, we will examine how deer have learned to cope with the unique problems imposed by this harshest of seasons.

ADAPTATIONS FOR WINTER

As I noted in the last chapter, deer have evolved physiological mechanisms which prepare them for the winter. The dense, hollow coat put on in the late summer now becomes important. Deer must face, in some parts of their range, temperatures as low as -50°. Generally, the hair of whitetails of northern races is considerably longer than that of southern races. A cold deer will elevate its hair, giving a somewhat "scruffy" appearance. This is more than a discomfort posture. It increases the amount of air between the skin and the external environment.

Whitetails have white fat distributed

Mike Biggs

Winter is particularly hard on bucks, since they emerge from the rut in poorer condition than does. The author's field studies in Canada confirmed that greatest mortality occurs in bucks and fawns. This buck died from post-rut mortality.

---

within their body cavity and along the back, which is quite different from the yellow fat seen in domestic cattle. In addition, there is fat within their long bones (marrow fat). Fat deposition in whitetails, as I noted earlier, is obligatory, meaning that it occurs even when growing conditions are below optimum, and often in spite of the animal being stressed. Energy reserves also are in the form of animal starch or glycogen in the liver. Biologists use a **Kidney Fat Index (KFI)** as an indication of herd health. The KFI is the ratio of kidney weight to the weight of fat surrounding the kidney—it is expressed as a percentage figure. In the past, some managers looked at kidney fat in the fall as an indicator of health. This is a mistake, for reasons given above. It is best to look at KFI in the summer stress, which gives us a much better indication of the overall condition of the animal. Dr. Harry Jacobson of Mississippi State University notes that examination of KFI late in winter also is useful in evaluating condition. This would give an indication of the impact of winter conditions.

Another adaptation for winter survival involves a modification in metabolic systems which allows the deer to reduce feed intake. We see this even in penned deer with plenty to eat. Normally, food consumption declines by as much as 40% during the winter. Highest consumption rates occur during the growing season. There is evidence that deer have the ability to recycle the urea and nitrogenous waste products in their blood.

In northern deer, we also see a serious reduction in activity during the winter. In these areas, deer have the interesting habit of "yarding." Yarding occurs in areas with suitable insulating cover such as evergreens. Whitetails may move great distances from their spring and summer feeding grounds to these yards. Aldo Leopold, the Father of Wildlife Management, wrote extensively during the 1940's about the importance of yards in Wisconsin. These also are the areas where winter die-offs occur. When I was hunting on Anticosti Island, I often found large piles of deer bones beneath dense conifer cover. Winter kill is significant in these areas, and I will discuss this at length later in this chapter. Obviously, yarding opens the door for various social stresses, as well as disease and parasite transmission.

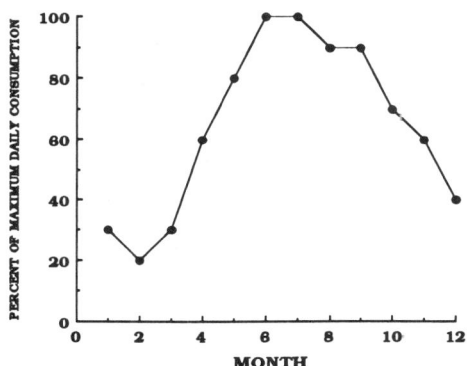

Overall food consumption declines from spring and summer to fall and winter. This is an adaptation for coping with scarcity.

The impact of deer on the yarding habitat is significant. Although yards may contain less than optimum feeds, deer consume large quantities of low quality browse, just to maintain the flora and fauna within their complex digestive systems. Often, every limb and twig within a deer's reach are gone by spring, seriously reducing the quality of the area for the next winter.

Throughout the range, the highest impact of overpopulation on habitat quality occurs in the winter. Consumption of 50 percent or more of a plant's growth will result either in stunting of the plant or death. Areas with chronic overpopulation are characterized by the total disappearance of quality browse plants. That is why we conduct browse surveys (see **Record-Keeping**) during

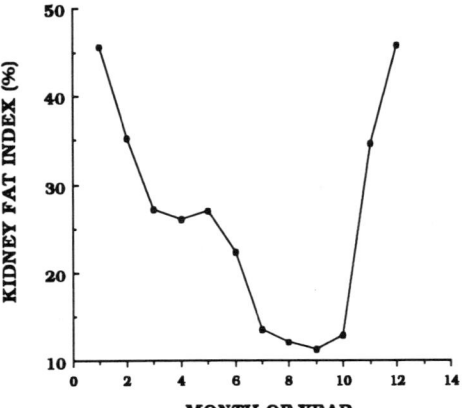

Kidney Fat Index (KFI) is highest in fall, and lowest in the summer. Unfortunately, laymen view the presence of fat in the fall as an indication that the deer is in good condition. To the contrary, fat storage occurs even in deer on poor ranges. Here is a typical KFI pattern for a southern deer. (Data adapted from "A Field Guide to Spring-Summer Deer Herd Health Evaluation in Mississippi by Steve Demarais and Harry Jacobson.)

---

this time to obtain an indication of herd density. Unfortunately, the so-called browse-line is becoming more common as the deer herds of America increase exponentially.

Snow is a significant problem to deer. Their feet are not adapted to traversing snow and ice; hence, snow is an impediment to movement. Also, deep snow not only impedes travel, but also covers the very foods needed for energy. Furthermore, cold and frozen vegetation adds terribly to the energy demand, since food taken into the rumen must be heated in order for digestion to take place. The heat of fermentation within a ruminant's stomach often is quite high. This is yet another reason why deer consume low quality forages during the winter. This keeps the rumen flora alive, plus helps generate some heat.

Deep snow gives a significant advantage to predators also. The deer yards attract a great deal of attention from predators, especially wolves. In the few areas where they still exist in any numbers, wolves have a dramatic impact on wintering deer. Lately, however, coyotes have invaded areas vacated by wolves, and themselves have become an important predator.

In the South, deer behave much differently in the winter. Whereas northern deer curtail activity during this time, their southern cousins tend to increase activity. My radio-telemetry studies show a marked increase in movements during the winter months. This presumably is an attempt either to maintain body temperature (given the lighter winter coat), and/or to acquire high energy foodstuffs. Generally, the winter is not the major stress period in the South.

WINTER— THE KILLER OF DEER?

In the North, excessively harsh winters exact a heavy toll on the herd. My examinations of yarding sites in Canada suggest that much of this mortal-

Predation often is higher during the winter, due to increased crowding in yards and poor physical condition.

ity occurs among fawns and bucks. Fawns have smaller body size, which has a significant effect on metabolism. A small-bodied fawn loses heat more quickly than a large-bodied adult. In addition, fawns cannot reach as high as adult deer. Deer yards provide much of the winter foods, and quickly are eaten to "deer height." The little fawn cannot reach above this level, even standing on its hind legs. Also, studies have shown that fawns deplete fat stores more quickly.

Bucks, although generally larger than does or fawns, also fall prey to prolonged cold weather. This is particularly true for mature bucks who have rutted heavily. After the rut, bucks seldom have fat and energy reserves to withstand long periods of cold weather. It is the cost of procreation, but once breeding is accomplished there is little tragedy in a buck's death— he has served his purpose.

Winter kill may be as high as 50 percent in some areas and years. On the extreme northern limit of the range, this may be a significant factor in preventing overpopulation. That is why the Canadian provinces of Alberta, Saskatchewan and Manitoba remain trophy buck hotspots. My Anticosti Island (eastern Canada) hunt, although one of the most enjoyable of my career, unfortunately came shortly after a severe winter-kill. This reduced the number of older bucks in the herd. My two year-old buck was typical for that year.

Yarding of deer during the winter can lead to serious habitat damage. Here an American holly tree, a low choice browse plant, has been completely stunted by over-browsing.

WINTER— THE FRIEND OF DEER?

All of this may seem bad on the surface, but the winter can be a friend to the northern whitetail. As I noted above, winter-kill often keeps the population at an acceptable level. In fact, severe winter weather probably is the major limiting factor to northern whitetails. To the south, this seldom is the case, and it is in the South that we see the greatest number of overpopulation-related problems.

In spite of the tremendous losses from winter-kill experienced over the last century, the general public has not been willing to do what is necessary to manage deer herds in these regions. Aldo Leopold endured severe criticism toward his stand on herd control in Wisconsin. Even visits to deer yards, where the frozen bodies of deer had been piled high, failed to elicit concern on the part of hunters. Some forty years later, landowners and hunters throughout the range believe that more deer is better. Yet, the wintering habitats slowly but surely are degrading. The annual toll amounts to a waste of millions of pounds of venison annually, and diminishes the quality of life for the deer. It is a shame that we must rely on death by starvation to control our herds in these regions!

SUMMARY

Winter is a time of testing for whitetails. It is a time for which deer prepare all spring and summer. Complex physiological and social adaptations allow deer to survive the harshest of weather conditions. Deer obligatorily store fat and animal starches as reserves against severe weather conditions. They also reduce food intake, recruiting physiological mechanisms such as urea recycling to make up the difference between body needs and nutrient availability. But, often these adaptations are not enough. In the North, winter-kill is a significant limiting factor to population growth. But, unfortunately, it occurs only after damage has been done to the habitat. Previous attempts by resource professionals to ameliorate this damage by herd control have met with public resistance. Hence, winter-kill has become as much an ally as an enemy of the whitetail manager in the North.

In the South, winter commonly has less impact on deer. The primary stress period in this region occurs in late summer. Only in very overpopulated herds do we see significant winter mortality in the South.

Chapter 5

DEER SENSES

Mike Biggs

It was November 17, 4:15 p.m. and I was sitting in one of those "pill box" deer blinds that seem to dot the Central Texas landscape during the season. Before me casually grazed six does, assorted fawns and one yearling spike buck. It was one of those lazy kind of Hill Country days. The sun was already starting to set and a light breeze was blowing in my face. The deer were about 75 yards from me, busily devouring the small winter grasses beneath the live oak trees. I just knew that any minute a big buck would come charging in to visit one of those cute little does. But then, I did something stupid! I knocked my gun over against the side of the blind. It hit with a loud thud. "Well, that's the end of that," I thought to myself. But, you know what? One of the does raised her head, looked leisurely in my direction and then went right back to feeding. Now, that was too much for me. Being a scientist I just could not resist seeing exactly what I could get away with. I completely lost interest in shooting a trophy buck and started to experiment.

First, I tried a light tap against the side of the blind. There absolutely was no response. That was followed by a louder tap. Again, no response was observed. Over the next several minutes, I tried a variety of noises at different levels of intensity. Slowly but surely, I worked my way up to a loud whistle. Then I got cocky, and opening the door of the blind, stood straight up. The deer continued to feed. It was not until I stood up, whistled and waved my arms that the deer spooked.

Ten days later, I was sitting in the top of a live oak overlooking a small creek bottom. I had cut the top out of the tree during the previous summer and had nailed a small board on top of the main branch of the tree. It was a perfect spot about twenty yards from a well-used deer trail. Just before dark, a nice little buck came slowly down the trail. He was walking at such a relaxed pace that I just knew I had him. I drew back on my bow and waited. This was a perfect setup. The wind was in my face and I was well camouflaged in the top of the tree. "Easy shot," I thought. But then, everything went bad. The buck suddenly stopped in his tracks about 60 yards away. He sniffed the air and began rotating his ears in all directions. There was no way the buck could have seen or smelled me. I had even approached the stand from the downwind side and had avoided walking anywhere near the trail. But still he seemed to know. The buck just backed up and skirted around me until he got my scent. He snorted and was gone.

Two different days and two entirely different reactions by deer. Was it because in the first case just does and a yearling were involved, while the second dealt with an older buck? Probably not. Although there is an abundance of literature on white-tailed deer senses, we still know very little about how deer use them and how good their senses really are. In this chapter, I will examine each of the deer's senses, and evaluate the effectiveness of each.

First of all, let's examine the niche that the whitetail fills in the world. You can find whitetails throughout North, Central and South America, but the

Ray Sasser

The sounds made by whitetails are generally low-pitched. The advantage of low-pitch sounds is obvious, once you consider the type of habitat in which deer evolved. Low-pitch sounds travel better through dense vegetation, while high-pitch sounds are best used in open habitats such as grasslands.

deer probably evolved in one habitat, possibly the eastern deciduous forest. Much of what we know about the whitetail's behavior supports this hypothesis. If you are a forest animal, it is necessary to develop sensory defenses that are cued to that environment. The principle predators of deer are the cats and wolf-like animals. The cats hunt by an entirely different means than wolves and coyotes. Their bodies are adapted to kill prey by a sudden surprise attack, usually from above. Dog-like predators, on the other hand, try to trail and chase their prey until the animal tires.

Deer also are faced with the problem of finding each other in the forest. This may include a doe looking for one of her fawns or a buck attempting to notify the female society that he is available, and vice versa. In the forest, visual displays probably are of little use; especially since deer were probably not as abundant in old growth forests as many writers and researchers would have us believe. On the average, there probably were about seven to ten deer per square mile in the pre-Columbian forest.

Finally, as with many prey species, deer primarily are crepuscular in their movement pattern (see **What Makes Deer Move**). Consequently, they must be able to see adequately in low light conditions. In order to do so, they have to possess different visual systems than man, a daylight species. Some say that deer can see 100 thousand to one million times better in low light than man!

So, what does all this technical stuff mean? It means that, in order to understand what senses deer use and how they use them, we must realize that we are dealing with an animal that: 1) is preyed upon from both the air and the ground, 2) must communicate with each other primarily by some other means besides visual displays, and 3) has the ability to see in low light conditions. The white-tailed deer has the same five senses that humans use every day: viz., hearing, sight, smell and taste. Touch probably is not that important in avoiding predators.

SOUND

I have a nice drop-tined buck mounted

Mike Biggs

A deer's head contains the most important senses: hearing, sight and smell.

on my den wall. The buck means a great deal to me, since I harvested it from one of the areas I have been working with for many years. It also means a lot to me because, under my direction, the taxidermist mounted it with one ear cocked back and one ear pushed forward. But the mount has caused me considerable frustration. Every time a new acquaintance comes into the house, he scrutinizes the mount and then proclaims, "I never saw a buck do that! Why did you have him mounted so crazy?" At first I was patient, but lately I have become a bit sarcastic. "You probably haven't," I now reply, "The average hunter only sees a buck for about three seconds before he shoots it!"

The ears of whitetails are marvelous machines with the ability to rotate independently in all directions. It is fascinating to watch an alarmed or suspicious deer stand erect with those "radar antennae" in motion. Because their ears are essentially cone-shaped, as well as highly mobile, deer can pinpoint the exact location of a particular sound. You too can do this if you cup your hands over your ears and rotate your head.

Nowhere is this more evident than in horn rattling. I once had the occasion to rattle up a buck from a great distance, and had the good fortune to see him from the time I started rattling until my father-in-law, Bo Masters, shot him ten yards away. It was one of those perfect days, Thanksgiving to be exact. We had just finished a fine turkey dinner and Bo turned to me with a smile. "Let's go to the ranch," he said with a smug look, "and be sure to bring those horns of yours." Well, I was dressed in a suit and was certainly not ready for a deer hunt. For some time, Bo had made it obvious that he really did not believe in all that horn rattling stuff. So, we loaded up, me in my suit, and headed for Bo's ranch.

We positioned ourselves on the top of a hill overlooking what had to be at least a mile of South Texas brush. It was a relatively still day with a light breeze. I stomped the ground and began rattling. I really felt kind of silly dressed as I was! Almost immediately, Bo said, "Keep rattling, keep rattling!"

He was looking way into the distance through his binoculars. I looked in that direction and could make out a buck standing in a prickly pear flat some thousand or so yards away. I had to look myself. Through the binoculars, I could see the buck clearly. He was moving his head from side to side. I rattled again, and this time the buck turned his head in our direction. With reckless abandon, the big buck ran a zig-zag pattern straight at us. He obviously knew exactly where we were. At 75 yards he disappeared below the crest of the hill. We waited. Suddenly, the buck roared over the crest right into our laps! Bo barely had time to shoot. I was looking through the binoculars at the time, and all I could see was gray hair. Bo squeezed off the 7 mm at ten yards. The buck skidded into the brush and lay dead not twenty yards away.

Deer probably have a better sense of hearing than humans. Leonard Lee Rue has suggested that the upper hearing limit for whitetails is somewhere around 30,000 cycles, but may be even higher. Human response tops out at around 20,000 cycles. So, a deer also is tuned to the higher pitched noises. However, it is the lower pitched noises that serve most in communication. In order to understand what a deer hears and how it interprets such sounds, let's again examine the deer's natural world.

As far as a whitetail is concerned, there are only two types of sounds—those that emanate from day to day occurrences and those that spell danger. The whitetail's world is filled with all sorts of sounds. Birds are calling, the wind is blowing through the leaves and

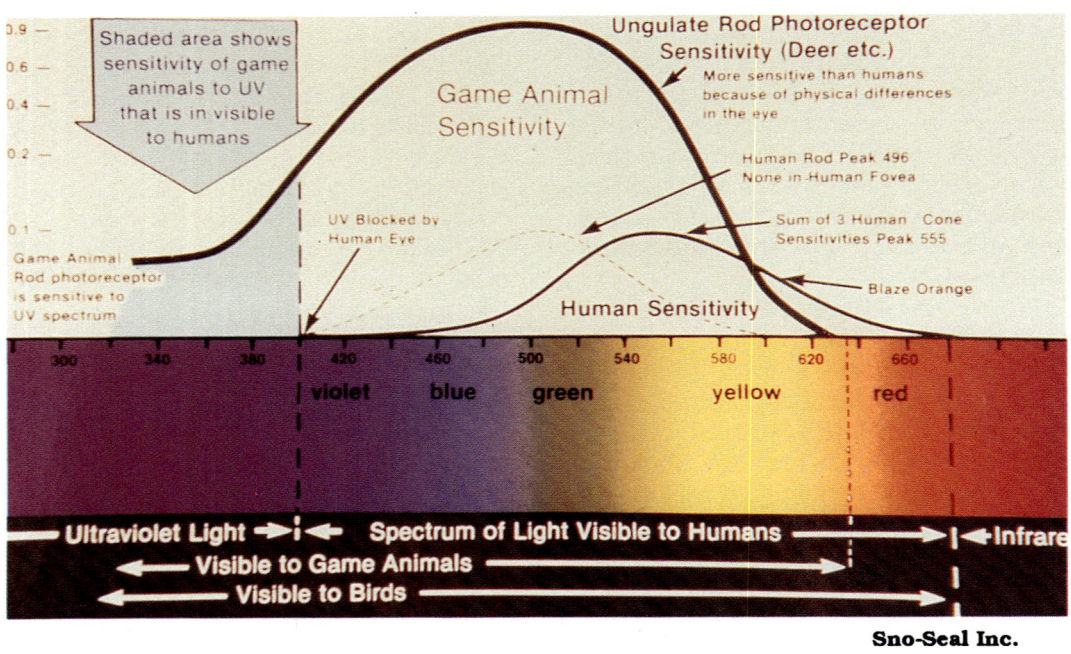

parts of trees may even fall to the ground with a thud. These sounds, although constantly monitored, probably are accepted as completely normal. It is the strange, out-of-place sounds that alert the deer. Footsteps and objects brushing against the vegetation are reasons for concern. When a deer hears something that seems out of place, it immediately goes on the alert. The degree of alertness depends on the seriousness of the sound and the current state of the deer itself. The source is quickly pinpointed and a decision is made about an appropriate action. That action may involve fleeing or further investigation. Some noises seemingly go unnoticed, but no sound is dismissed. If it seems natural, it receives little thought. A good friend of mine, for example, uses a gimmick to accustom deer to movement and sound in a tree stand, located near a feeder. He nails a feed sack up in the tree so that it regularly blows in the wind. The deer become accustomed to the noise.

How Deer Use Their Senses

Deer seem to be able to hear another deer approach at a great distance. For example, I have had numerous occasions to watch deer on green food plots. Each doe social group enters the plot by a different trail. High in a tree, I have watched doe groups approach food plots. On still days, deer usually appear to hear another's approach about 100 yards away. I cannot hear their approach at 20 yards!

How do you combat a deer's sense of hearing? The wind seems to be the number one enemy to the deer's ability to perceive sound. On very windy days, deer just do not seem to want to move about. Wind appears to affect sound waves by two means. First of all, sound seems to travel less effectively upwind. Second, movements of vegetation caused by wind muffles or confuses the sound. So, days with any wind are a more opportune time to stalk deer. Recently, however, some South Texas researchers have reported that deer move frequently in very high winds. I just cannot believe that this is anything but a spurious observation. It does not make sound ecological sense!

Clothing is often critical in making a silent approach. Notice I said quiet and not silent. There is no such thing. Two things make noise when you stalk, your footsteps and your clothing. Deer make little noise in walking around, primarily due to the difference between their feet and ours. The surface area of contact for a deer is significantly smaller than the human foot. I like to wear a pair of those rubber bottomed boots that you see in almost every outdoor catalogue. Although they supply little arch support, and I often bruise my feet on rocks and sticks, these boots provide the quietest approach. Clothing is very important. There is nothing I hate more than those water-proof parkas and coveralls worn by many hunters. They are usually made from synthetic materials that sound like four thousand people whispering in the woods. Just walking along makes a great deal of noise. I prefer the more natural materials such as cotton, wool and moleskin. The soft textured surface

Recently, scientists have learned that some fabrics are treated with UV enhancers, which make these garments literally "glow in the dark." (Photograph courtesy of Sno-Seal Inc.)

provides less abrasion against vegetation.

SIGHT

Now we move to an area perfected by whitetails. Deer generally are classified as crepuscular; meaning that they move about under low light conditions. Again, this is logical since they are predominantly woodland creatures. Even when they are active in the midday, deer try to stay in subdued light, either along an edge or in the shadows. Their eyes are well adapted to such conditions. Most hunters will tell you that deer are color blind. This really is not true, because deer have some limited color vision. There are two types of cells in the eyes of mammals; rods and cones. Rods primarily are responsible for receiving light and dark signals, while the cones perceive the more subtle colors. To understand the role of black-and-white and color in interpreting what an animal sees, let's take the average outdoor magazine as an example. It is printed in the four color process. As the paper passes through the printing press, four different "colors" are laid down in sequence. Three of these pigments are the true colors, magenta, cyan and yellow. When combined, they give all the subtle hues that you enjoy as color. The fourth pigment, however, is black. If this color is omitted from the final printing, the pictures you enjoy would not be sharp and well-defined as you have come to appreciate. Black adds contrast to the photograph.

So it is with the ability to perceive color and black-and-white, although the primary colors are a little different. The ability of an animal to perceive these two visual categories affects how it interprets its environment. It is ludicrous for humans to assume that deer see their world as we do. In fact, once the facts are known, deer see things very differently from the way we see them. Total color vision is not of much use in low light conditions. Just try to take a quality color photograph at dusk. Other than sunset pictures, you have little color saturation! High dependence on color vision reduces the ability to discriminate in low light. High dependence on black-and-white vision, on the other hand reduces ability to discriminate subtle differences in objects. The whitetail is such an animal, except that it takes advantage of certain intensifications of color perception. It has many times more rods (black-and-white receptors) than cones (color receptors), but it can perceive some colors, especially in the upper and lower portions of the spectrum. Whereas humans are trichromatic, perceiving red, blue and green wave lengths, whitetails are dichromatic. The middle wavelengths related to green are not perceptible to deer. Furthermore, the vast majority of color vision lies in the lower wave lengths of 350 nm (nanometers) or less.

Hence, whitetails possess the unique ability to recognize the ultraviolet portion of the spectrum. Dr. Jay Neitz of the University of California (Santa Barbara) has studied vision in ungulates for some time now. He has concluded that deer have extreme difficulty in discriminating between the

How Deer Use Their Senses

colors green, yellow, brown, orange and red. Since deer have only the long wave length and short wave length sensitive cones, these colors would be perceived only as shades of yellow! But why would such a system develop?

Humans, unlike deer, are predominantly diurnal creatures. This means that we, along with our primate relatives, prefer to move about in the daylight hours. Our trichromatic vision allows us the ability to discriminate between many components of our environment. But, in being a daytime ani-

The whitetail's body is covered with specialized glands, used to communicate with other deer in many ways. In all there are seven known glands: frontal (F), nasal (N), preorbital (PR), tarsal (T), metatarsal (M), interdigital (I) and preputial (P). Of these seven, the function(s) of preorbital, metatarsal and preputial glands have not been demonstrated.

Mike Biggs

mal, we must deal with the harmful ultraviolet rays. Our eyes contain a lens which is pigmented to combat ultraviolet light. This yellowish lens prevents the entrance of these wave lengths into our eyes. Since the ultraviolet portion of the spectrum is highly diffuse, a large amount of ultraviolet in the human eye would result in loss of visual acuity. Also, too much day time ultraviolet would seriously damage our retina.

Whitetails much prefer to move about in low light conditions. Under these conditions, the highly refractive and diffuse ultraviolet becomes the friend, not the enemy, of the deer's eye. Since whitetails are perhaps a million times more sensitive to ultraviolet, this gives them a vision advantage far beyond our capability. "To an animal with dichromatic color vision, a sportsman wearing garments that strongly reflect short wave length light would stand out against these backgrounds (sic. green, yellow, brown, orange and red) like a ripe red tomato on a green vine," asserts Dr. Neitz.

There is one additional difference between the eyes of deer and man. Many animals that venture out at night have a highly reflective membrane behind the retina, called the **tapetum lucidum**, which serves to reflect light back through the retina. In so doing, the deer "reprocesses" the light to give the rods and cones another chance to be stimulated by the light.

Dr. Neitz offers the following contrast between the eyes of deer and man:
1. the deer's eye is larger;
2. the deer's pupil is capable of opening much wider than humans;
3. the UV filter in the lens of humans is not present in deer, allowing them to utilize UV much more efficiently;
4. deer have more rods than man, and the ratio of rods to cones is greater; and,
5. deer, as with many animals, have a tapetum lucidum which allows more efficient utilization of light.

In spite of this high visual efficiency, vision probably is the easiest sense to confuse in whitetails. Deer are good at detecting movements, but have a very poor ability to pick out detail. Their one advantage lies in their ability to, 1) see in low light, and 2) pick up any object that reflects UV. Unfortunately, many of our modern fabrics either have dyes or are washed in soaps that have UV enhancers. One company even makes a wash additive that destroys the UV enhancing effect of detergents.

Camouflage also is an interesting subject to me. It seems that some hunters cannot live without having everything they own in camo pattern. I once was told by a sporting goods manufacturer that product sales could be greatly enhanced by packaging a product in camo pattern. The European hunter rarely uses camouflage, relying on muted colors and shades such as gray, forest green or brown. These colors all are viewed by deer as slightly different shades of yellow! This is not, however, to say that I am opposed to using camouflage. Rather, it probably is more the color combinations than the specific pattern that is effective. As far as I am concerned, one could be as well concealed with a camouflage made of various sized and configured blotches of yellow, brown and green, as with the most sophisticated modern camouflage. Recently, I attended the SHOT Show in Las Vegas. SHOT stands for Sporting, Hunting, Outdoor Trades Show. At each show, there are marvelous new products to tempt the prospective sporting goods dealer. One of these products was aimed, as noted earlier, at destroying the UV enhancing effect of modern detergents. Under UV light, for example, treebark camouflage which had been washed in a popular detergent literally glowed! What is the use of wearing this clothing if all you do is heighten the deer's ability to see you?

Whether or not you use or rely on camouflage patterns is up to you, but the best way to remain undetected is to remain motionless. This is something with which most hunters have the greatest difficulty. I really do not blame them either. Sitting completely still for hours at a time is one thing that I seldom relish. But, you can reduce the impact of having to move.

I try always to anticipate the direction of movement by a buck. I sit, stalk or align my stand in such a manner that I have the sun at my back. If you have ever tried to photograph a back lighted subject, you know exactly why I do this. The resulting picture is just a silhouette of the subject. I also arrange to have something at my back.

Never sit on the top of a hill. You will stick out like a sore thumb. I often sit against a tree or an embankment, but I really prefer to get well above the deer. That is another question I often am asked. How high up in a tree should you climb? I usually reply, "As high as your nerves will allow." Last year I hunted New Brunswick, where I often hunted 60 or more feet in the air. There is an old wives tale floating around that deer do not look up. Nothing could be further from the truth. Deer do look up, and do that regularly. Remember, one of the their predators is the cat, and where do cats like to ambush their prey? However, there is a lesser probability that you will be seen if you can get above 15 feet. Simple physics suggest that a deer would really have to stretch its neck to look up at that angle.

SMELL

Now we come to the sense of smell. This probably is the real topic of interest to hunters. An incredible amount of verbiage has been published over the last few years about deer scents. There are many products on the market nowadays that make claims to do everything from lure deer right to you and cure baldness at the same time! Let's try to make some sense out of scents.

The deer's sense of smell is many times more sophisticated than our own. First of all, the nose is greatly elongated so as to house many convoluted structures (conchae), covered with tissues sensitive to odors. As with vision, the number of sensory cells determines the sensitivity of the particular receptor.

Man, with his short nose, has very few conchae and is poorly adapted to detecting smells in a sophisticated manner.

The whitetail probably depends more on its sense of smell than any other. Again, it is logical in light of where deer evolved. In the woods, especially when deer density is low, sight and sound really is not a good way for deer to get together. Forest animals often depend on smell and calls for communication in dense vegetation. This is the case with deer. The scientific literature reports four basic glands in a deer's body that produce chemicals for one purpose or another. These are the tarsal gland, interdigital gland, metatarsal gland and preorbital gland. The tarsal gland is located on the inside of the hock, and probably is most familiar to hunters. When I first started hunting whitetails as a kid, I was told that if I did not remove this gland within a few seconds of the kill, the meat would be tainted forever. Of course, this is utter nonsense, but the gland does smell horribly in rutting bucks. But, it also has an odor in does. When a strange deer is encountered, bucks, does and some fawns pull their legs together and urinate on these structures. The long hairs provide an evaporative surface to signal other deer of the buck's breeding condition. The hairs of this gland are specialized to hold scent. The interdigital gland is located between the toes and probably serves as a trail marking mechanism. Deer may be able to determine direction of travel and individual identification from these secretions. The metatarsal gland is located on the outside of the lower leg and probably serves little function in whitetails. In mule and blacktail deer it serves an alarm function. The preorbital glands are located just in front of the eye and also have a reduced activity in whitetails.

There is one additional glandular area that seldom is discussed in the literature, and I feel it more important to rutting bucks that any other. This gland is what I refer to as the **frontal gland**, and is located on the forehead. It probably is a dispersed gland; i.e., the glandular cells are not concentrated in any one grouping. Bucks also rub their facial and forehead region against the tarsal gland area. This probably deposits tarsal secretions on the forehead. I have noticed a marked difference in the color of the frontal gland area in bucks. Dominant bucks have a much darker appearance than subordinate bucks. Dominate bucks appear to use the frontal gland to mark their territory. I have some excellent videotape of a dominant buck on Bill Carter's Sombrerito Ranch rubbing his frontal gland on a signpost, apparently checking it periodically for the right amount of scent with his nose. I feel that much of the so-called antler rubbing reported for bucks is actually forehead rubbing to deposit scent. I have also seen this behavior in mule deer.

Some of my recent observations in Canada suggest that there may be an additional function for the forehead secretions. On several occasions, I have seen subordinate bucks licking the rubbed surface after it is worked by a dominate buck. Some of us feel that these secretions may serve to reduce the libido of subordinate individuals. Time will tell on this one, but it is an ecologically attractive thought.

Does also use scent communication, especially during the rut. Finding a dominant buck's scrape, the doe urinates in it and lays down a trail for him to follow. I have seen and photographed bucks trailing receptive does like a blood hound.

Now to the question for which I know you are dying to have an answer. What about the use of commercial scents and how effective are they? I could really get into trouble on this one! Let's look at it logically. There are three basic types of products available; 1) those that mimic communication scents, 2) those that mask human scent, and 3) those that neutralize human scents. The first types are usually made from or are synthesized from chemicals presumed to affect deer behavior. The **presumed** is critical here. At this point in time, there absolutely is no evidence that any of the commercially available scents do indeed elicit the response espoused.

The first, and most common type, is designed to smell either like a receptive doe or a rutting buck. Over the years, I have found a number of these products to be useful in hunting trophy whitetails. Such products can be used in various ways. The products designed to simulate a doe in estrus should be used to treat active scrapes or to stimulate scraping activity. Last season, for example, I literally led a buck to me by making mock scrapes near his early season sanctuary. I used a combination of doe and rutting scent to make mock scrapes along a buck's travel corridor. Observing the buck from a distance, I found it really drove him crazy. He would approach such scrapes, sniff the earth and vegetation and then tear up the ground in the scrape itself. This buck regularly reworked every one of my scrapes. But, before you go running off to buy some scent, let me offer two comments. First, the scents I was using were taken from freshly killed deer and frozen in an ultra-freezer. Second, the chemicals that end up in your hands may be something entirely different from that presented. Some have identified everything from rabbit urine to water in some commercially available scents. At this time there is no way of knowing what you are buying.

I also use scents that mimic rutting bucks when horn rattling, especially during bow season. I keep a supply of frozen tarsal glands just for this purpose. I place some of the scent or a tarsal gland on the ground upwind about forty yards from my vantage point. I try to get a friend to rattle near the scent station, so that when the buck comes in, he will look to that spot instead of where I am hiding. I have found this tactic to be quite effective.

Masking scents take a variety of forms. I was first exposed to such products when I began trapping deer using drop nets. I would excise scent glands from skunks found dead on the highway. My wife was not too happy to have me around during the trapping season. Later, I switched to commercially prepared scents such as fox urine or various kinds of natural scents (apple, earth, evergreen, etc.). Whatever form you use, they all work similarly. Here is an explanation of how these products work.

If you are carrying on a conversation with a radio playing in the background, your ability to hear what is being said depends on the volume of the radio. At some point, the noise from the radio becomes so distracting that you no longer pay attention to what is being said. The conversation is still there, you have just lost your ability to discriminate from it and the background noise. So it is with masking scents. Your odor is still there, it just is being overridden by the masking scent. Whether or not this is a good tactic may be debatable and certainly depends on the type of scent being used. My philosophy is this. If a deer can smell it, it has to mimic something occurring in the day-to-day life of the deer. Any unusual odor will do nothing but draw attention to your location and cause the deer to employ some of its other senses to check you out.

The neutralizing scents represent a very good idea. These chemicals attempt to destroy the odor itself. I have had considerable experience with these products, and have found them to be useful. This last season, I had a nice seven point buck walk less than ten yards from me downwind in a 15 or more mile per hour wind without even noticing my presence. I was using a liberal amount of odor neutralizer at the time.

I have seen hunters go to incredible lengths to neutralize their odors, or at least think they have. Some never eat red meat, while others bathe and wash their clothes in baking soda. When asked about such tactics, I always reply that if it seems to work for you, then go for it! Quite frankly, when I am seriously trying to harvest a trophy buck, I will twirl a chicken around my head if I think it might work! But seriously, all these chemicals may be useful, but I think any of the manufacturers will agree that they do not substitute for the most lethal weapon of all, your brain. Proper position is everything in trophy deer hunting. If you keep downwind from the buck, there is little chance that he will smell you. When seriously hunting trophy bucks, I always am aware of my position in relation to the wind. I learned this many years ago while working with South American Indians. They often carry a small fungus around with them, puffing away to monitor the wind.

TASTE

I will not spend a great deal of time discussing taste. Deer use taste interchangeably with smell, especially bucks. Bucks will lick branches on which scent is deposited or lick the ground where a doe has urinated. As I noted earlier, bucks lick the rubs of dominate bucks, and in so doing may have their behavior and/or physiology influenced in some way. The **Flehmen** behavior (lip curl), often observed in bucks and other male hooved mammals, is an attempt by the buck at placing the odor in his Jacobson's organ in the roof of the mouth. Apparently, this serves as a feedback system

The flehmen behavior involves "tasting" of doe estrous scents in order to prime the buck's reproductive system. Some individuals think that the function of the flehmen response is to tell the buck if the doe is in estrus. This is totally false. The vomeronasal organ is innervated by a completely different portion of the brain, than is the nose.

to help physiologically prepare the buck for breeding. Some individuals have written in the popular literature that the function of flehmen is to tell the buck whether or not the doe is in estrus. This is totally false.

THE SECRET SENSE

There is one last sense about which, as a scientist, I am reluctant to mention. Deer seem to have a sixth sense that cannot be explained organically. The buck that skirted my bow stand was using this sense, I am convinced of that. It must be a "feeling" they get when danger is eminent. We humans sometimes share this unique sense. On numerous occasions, I have become aware of a buck's presence long before my normal senses have become activated. I really do not know the cues for this sixth sense, for all I know they may be just a subconscious recognition of the other five senses. I do know that prey often move about happily near a predator that has no intention of making a kill. Later, that same predator's presence will send terror through the same prey group.

SUMMARY

Whitetails evolved in the forest where it is important to be able to communicate indirectly. Consequently, deer have evolved specialized sensory mechanisms that enable them to not only communicate with each other, but also enables them to avoid predators.

Sounds used by whitetails are primarily lower-pitched, which allows sound to travel through dense vegetation. The ears of a deer are enlarged cones which aid in trapping sound waves.

The eyes of whitetails are finely tuned to function in low light conditions. This is particularly manifested in the ability of a deer to receive ultraviolet light. This wave length is abundant under low light, hence deer have evolved mechanisms which allow them to receive the lower wave lengths; perhaps a million times better than man.

Smell is perhaps one of the most important defenses of deer. They are capable of smelling odors at the molecular level.

Taste is used primarily to supplement the sense of smell. The Flehmen behavior of bucks is designed to prime other portions of the brain for reproduction, and does not involve the sensory pathways used by the sense of smell.

The most difficult sense to confound is the sense of smell. The other senses can be fooled by the hunter, especially in light of modern technology. Confounding the deer's sense of smell has not, as yet, been perfected.

Chapter 6

ANTLEROGENESIS: HOW ANTLERS GROW

Antlers! They are the stuff dreams are made of. Men have spent their lives and fortunes in pursuit of trophy-class antlers, and they bring out the best and worst in hunters. But what are antlers, and why do some people desire them so? How do they develop? And what determines their quality? In this chapter, I will discuss the annual growth cycle of antlers, the physiological and hormonal phenomena associated with antler development, and what goes into the production of a trophy-class set of antlers.

Antlers are made up of very unique body tissue. They exhibit one of the fastest tissue growth rates known to science. The only growth phenomenon reported to rival antler growth is that of certain cancers. That is why the National Cancer Institute is so interested in antler-growth studies. Antlers also are the focus of incredible amounts of misinformation often put forward as "fact" by sportsmen.

THE NATURE OF ANTLERS

Antlers really are nothing more than modified bones. Structurally, they are almost indistinguishable from normal bone. Although many writers call them "horns," they are not technically so. Horns are permanent structures found on members of the cow family. Horns grow throughout the animal's life, and are never shed or replaced. Antlers, on the other hand, are temporary structures found only in the deer family (Cervidae). Deer must develop a new set of antlers each year, with each rack being shed after the breeding season.

Antlers begin developing very early in a buck's life. Buck fawns that are just a few months of age already have bony projections on their foreheads. These are the precursors to antlers. In order to produce antlers every year, the buck must have a permanent base on which to grow them. These bases are projections of the frontal bone of the skull, forming what are called **pedicels**. Although there are some notable exceptions, fawns rarely produce more than a small set of pedicels covered with skin. Fawn bucks often are called "nubbin" or "button" bucks for this reason. During the first 12 to 18 months of life, however, the young buck experiences physiological changes that set into play forces that will cause antlers to be developed.

Last March, one of the landowners with whom I work on a management program called me, all excited. It seems that he had found a rather large scrape that still was being worked by a buck. Because he felt that this had to be a monster buck, he decided to watch the scrape, in order to capture a glimpse of the deer. He was shocked at what he saw. A "doe" came up to the scrape and began working it! Now, does do make and use scrapes, but this was not the case. He was surprised, to say the least. However, he was in for an even greater shock. Upon close inspection with binoculars, he discovered that the animal actually was a large-bodied buck that had dropped its antlers several weeks prior to the man's discovery of the scrape.

But this is not all. The following December brought further excitement. The landowner was behind in his doe harvest, so he decided to conduct a special doe hunt at the end of the season. To his total frustration, six of the antlerless deer harvested were mature bucks that already had dropped their antlers! These two observations represent the beginning and the end of the antler cycle, and are fully explained by our current knowledge about the biology of whitetails.

Because antlers really are just modified bones, their composition is very similar to that of bone. The accompanying drawing shows the basic structure of a developing antler. As with all other bone, the buck's body first grows a protein framework, composed primarily of cartilage covered by the skin of the frontal portion of the skull. The skin contains small hairs— hence, the term "velvet." This is a time when protein is very important to the buck, for it is the amount of protein available in the diet that ultimately will determine how much of the buck's antler-growth potential is realized.

But, what makes antlers begin to develop? For the answer to this question, I return to the seemingly odd

Antlerogenesis: How Antlers Grow

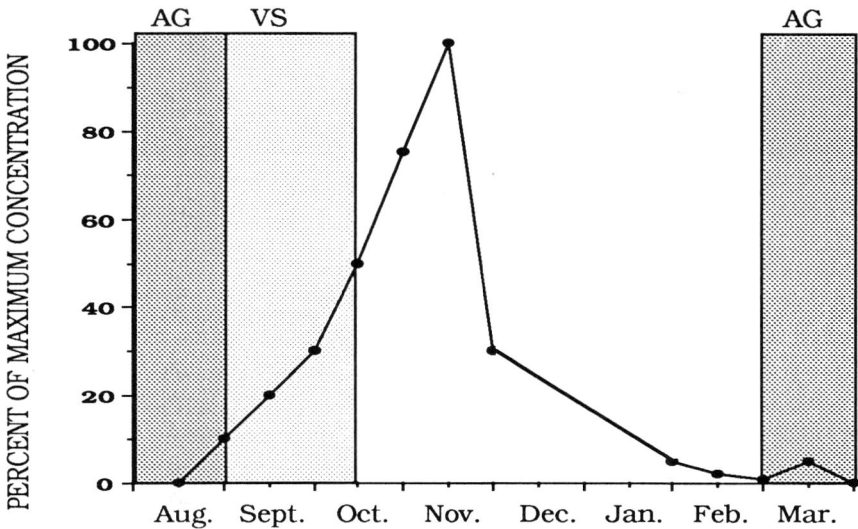

Blood levels of testosterone, a male sex hormone, show two peaks during the antler-growing cycle. The first (March) is relatively small, but enough to stimulate antler growth (AG). The second (late August-October) causes velvet shedding (VS).

---

observation of an antlerless buck making a scrape. For years, researchers proposed several possible explanations for factors which initiate antler development. Biologists monitored the blood level of several suspect hormones for clues. Because antler development, except in reindeer, is pretty much a male phenomenon, it seemed logical to examine the role of sex hormones in antler development. Male and female sex hormones were monitored in several buck deer throughout an annual cycle. Testosterone was most abundant during the rut, so many researchers felt that its role in initiating antler development was minimal. Testosterone is the major male hormone produced by all mammals, originating in both the testes and adrenal glands. Scientists expected testosterone to be low after antler shedding. This was not the case. Just prior to the initiation of antler growth, there is a sudden increase in blood-testosterone level. It is not as dramatic as the increase during the rut, but bucks do exhibit elevated levels of this hormone. Apparently, the small increase in serum testosterone is just enough to stimulate the onset of antlerogenesis (the growing of antlers). Increased testosterone production probably is caused by a response of the brain to longer day length, measured indirectly by sensing the length of the night. The rise in serum testosterone also temporarily affects the buck's behavior. Although the buck no longer is in rutting condition, the hormone triggers innate behavior patterns typical to those of the rut. One of these behaviors is scraping, and that is precisely what the landowner was observing: the onset of antler development.

This development begins almost immediately after shedding (casting) of the old set of antlers. The scar produced on the surface of the pedicel quickly heals over, and within a few weeks, a small antler "bud" appears. The growth rate of antlers is very slow at first. Apparently, several complex phenomena taking place within the buck's body prohibit rapid development of the new antler. First, bucks come out of the rut and winter in terrible physical shape. Many die just after the rut from a condition I call "post-rut mortality." This phenomenon was discussed at length in the chapter on Winter. For example, I once observed a mature buck in South Texas that sported a tremendous set of antlers measuring 23 inches inside spread. He obviously was the dominant buck in the area, and I often saw him chasing does over a 7,000-acre area. A good friend photographed the deer in February and showed the photographs to me. Compared to November, the animal looked to be a mere "shell" of himself! Later, a ranch hand found the buck's remains. This deer had paid a heavy price for successfully reproducing.

Bucks must spend the early spring recouping some of the losses sustained during the rut. This is a time when protein is critical to bucks. A minimum of 16 percent protein in the diet is necessary to produce the best set of antlers a given buck can grow.

Once the buck has replaced body tissues lost during the rut, he can direct his physiological processes toward growing antlers. Apparently, the future appearance of the antler set is pre-coded into some portion of the brain, for it is the nervous system that seems to direct the building of antlers. Antler growth progresses from the tip of the antler bud, which contains unspecialized cells that develop into cartilagelike tissue. This growth is very similar to that of the bones in children. That is, bones are first formed as soft cartilage, which later is replaced by hardened bone. In deer, the developing antler bud often has an enlarged, bulblike appearance, especially when the developing antler begins to differentiate into tines, antler growth has sped up dramatically. Reports of growth rates of one to two inches per week are not unusual. In fact, if we plot antler growth rates over time, the curve looks very much like compounded interest figures (See graph).

During the time of antler development, bucks usually travel in social groups of various numbers. Although technically the bucks are physiologically "neutered" at this time, there is

Antlerogenesis: How Antlers Grow

MAY 1

MAY 14

JUNE 7

JUNE 30 Duncan Dobie

JULY 30

SEPTEMBER 2

Duncan Dobie

quite a bit of social posturing. Bucks are very much aware of the size of developing antlers in other individuals, and this probably affects the social hierarchy. In fact, there is some evidence now that social position greatly affects the size of antlers. Removal of a dominant individual can result in an enlargement of the next set of antlers in a subordinate.

Once antler growth is completed, day length again is having its influence on the physiological condition of the buck. Several complex things are happening in proper sequence. Because it takes a great amount of energy and nutrients to grow antlers, the buck cannot shed his summer coat until antler growth is complete. Once completed, however, the buck first sheds its summer coat, replacing it with the typical grayish winter coat. Once this transition is accomplished, the buck's body now turns to the matter at hand: shedding the velvet.

Just prior to the pre-breeding period, the newly formed, velveted antlers begin to change. First, the soft framework is replaced with minerals from the bones. These probably are minerals deposited during the previous growing season, and include calcium and phosphorus. That is why these minerals are so important to deer managers, as well as to deer. This process, called **mineralization**, is completed just prior to velvet shedding.

We are not totally certain of the exact mechanism(s) that initiate velvet shedding. Some researchers feel that the formation of the "burr" at the base of the antler shuts off the blood supply to the antler and its velvet. Others believe that the deposition of minerals in the antlers causes a condition similar to hardening of the arteries in humans. I personally feel that it is a combination of both. At any rate, one thing is certain:

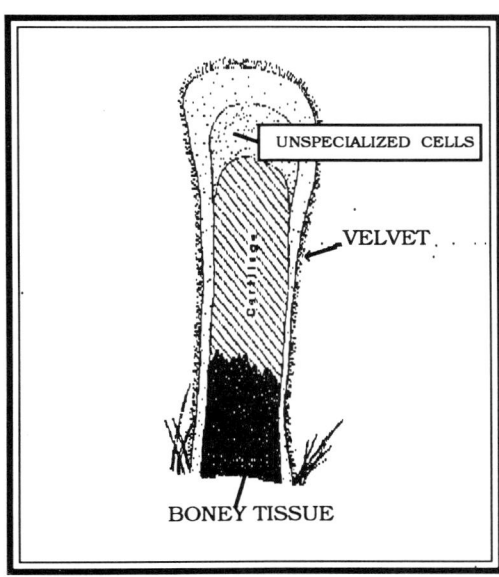

The actively growing tip of an antler is made up of unspecialized cells that eventually turn into cartilage. This cartilage later is replaced by boney tissue, in much the same way children's bones harden.

The velvet begins to "die" from lack of blood supply. This whole process once again is caused by an increase in serum testosterone levels. Sensing shorter day length, the brain signals the testes and adrenals to produce this hormone in larger and larger quantities.

Once velvet shedding begins, the entire process only takes a few hours. Many hunters think that bucks rub the velvet for days or weeks, but this is not the case. One of my penned bucks, for example, takes about 90 minutes each year to completely shed his velvet. Some bucks, especially younger individuals, may take longer to complete the process.

The death and shedding of the velvet produces large quantities of blood from the deteriorating blood vessels. This blood stains the antlers and produces their characteristic color. Some sportsmen think the stain on antlers comes from rubbing against vegetation, and indeed some of it does. But, for the most part, the staining arises from spilled blood. Once velvet shedding has occurred, the buck experiences a need to rub his antlers against small saplings and trees. This probably results from a combination of the effects of increased male hormones and some itching from the "dying antler." (Once the velvet shedding process is complete, the vast majority of the antler is non-living tissue. Some portions in the base may be alive, but most of the tissue is now inert). Increasing amounts of male hormone in the buck's blood completely changes his personality. He is now pugnacious, and he takes out his frustrations on any suitable tree that offers resistance.

The pre-breeding period also is characterized by sparring matches between bucks of similar status. This serves two functions. First, it allows the buck to subtly improve his social position, just like young boys playing sports. They learn who is the strongest in this manner. Second, it provides daily exercise of the neck muscles, which allows the buck to increase his shoulder and neck strength. These muscles will be used in future combats during the rut, when more serious fights occur. Many hunters tell me that the enlarged necks of rutting bucks are due to glandular development in the neck region. One prominent outdoor writer even espouses this theory. However, this is untrue.

Because antlers are the source of contact between bucks, they often are in pitiful condition by the end of the rut. I recently hunted Mexico, on a ranch with a low deer density and very high buck:doe ratio. By the end of the rut, virtually every buck harvested had broken tines from fighting. However, this does not cause any pain to the buck, because the antler is not alive at this time.

As the rut wears on, the buck begins to lose testosterone, either through breeding or normal changes in physiology. It has been my experience that dominant bucks that breed many does usually show lower hormonal levels in their blood. It also is the dominant bucks that often are the first to shed their antlers. The process of antler casting is quite fascinating. A thin layer of tissue destruction forms just above the pedicel. This layer is called the **abscission layer**, and readily can be seen in a cross-section of the antler and skull. Once the abscission layer is formed, the antler may drop off at any moment. Sometimes this may occur at the most inopportune time. For example, my uncle Spencer Johnson once killed a buck near Fredericksburg, Texas, on the last day of the season in early January. He was walking along and spied a medium-sized buck hiding in the grass about 20 yards away. My uncle whirled and fired, dropping the buck on the spot. Upon approaching the buck, he was horrified to discover that the animal had no antlers! There were two neat little bloody pedicels on its forehead, but no antlers. A frantic search yielded both antlers, lying near the buck's body. We tied them to one of the buck's legs and took the prize home for all to see.

No one knows exactly how antler casting takes place in the wild. It is my suspicion that each antler just falls or pops off as the buck walks around the countryside. I rarely have found both antlers in the same location, and feel that such an occurrence would be quite rare. Several individuals licensed to keep penned bucks have told me over the years that they often grab the bucks by the antlers, only to have them pop off in their hands.

Once antler casting has taken place, the whole process begins anew. The bloody patch left by the discarded antler quickly heals over, and the newly forming antler bud develops over the next several weeks.

TIMING OF ANTLER GROWTH

The actual timing of antler development is remarkably consistent across the geographic range of whitetails. The variability comes with the timing of the rut. Depending on its timing, dates of velvet shedding and antler casting vary greatly. I will begin with most variable portion of the antler cycle: antler casting.

Casting of antlers is directly related to the timing of the rut. In some areas, such as portions of Florida, the rut may take place as early as August or September, while in other regions, such as Mississippi, it may occur as late as February. Apparently, antler casting is influenced by the nervous system and the level of male hormone in the blood. Once male sex hormones (mostly testosterone) are depleted in the blood, the abscission layer forms rapidly, and antler casting occurs shortly thereafter. I regularly see bucks with shed antlers as early as the last part of December in East Texas; yet, Dr. Harry Jacobson of Mississippi State University notes that his deer cast as late as the last week of March. I have seen antlered bucks in Mexico as late as the middle of April. Whatever the time of casting, the regrowth of new antlers appears to be somewhat consistent from one geographic region to the next, although individual bucks may be exceptions.

The appearance of a noticeable antler bud usually occurs in the period from March 15 to April 15. As noted, antler growth initially proceeds at a snail's pace, then accelerates in later stages, similar to compound interest (See graph). By the first part of May, antler growth begins to show acceleration. A noticeable bud now extends well above the pedicel and is somewhat enlarged and bulbous at its tip. This bulb will give rise to the brow tines, also called "dog catchers." The brow tines develop during June. It appears to me that each pair of tines is well developed before development of the next pair reaches completion. By the end of June, the brow tines are well established, and the growing beam produces a new set of bulbs which will become the primary tines. During July, some of the

> **Antler casting occurs when the abscission layer forms at the base of the antler and the pedicel. This process occurs fairly rapidly.**

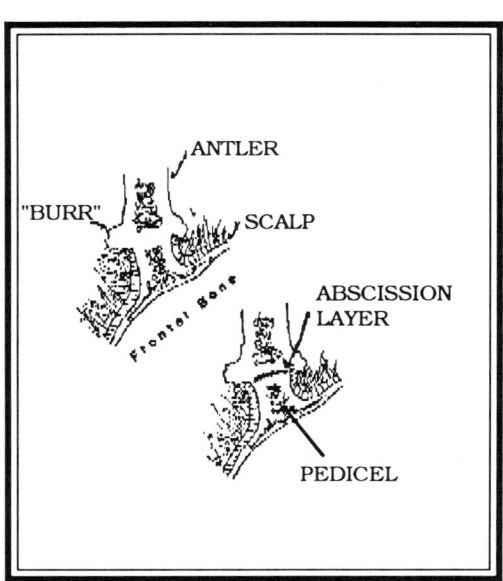

ornamentation that often occurs at the base of the antler begins to develop. These are such traits as extra points and bifurcation (branching) of the brow tines.

August brings completion of brow tine development and the establishment of a well-defined primary tine. Antler growth really begins to accelerate by this time. By the end of August, the secondary tine bulbs have formed and developed into tines and any extra points from the primary tines have begun to form. These extra points go under many names, some of which are "kicker" and "stickers." It also is at this time that the rarest of all points, the drop tines, may begin to make their appearance.

The first week in September usually finds the antler near completion, especially in younger bucks. It appears to me that antler growth is completed earlier in young bucks than in more mature ones.

The velvet-shedding process also is highly variable in timing from one portion of the whitetail's range to the next. In Texas, for example, velvet shedding occurs sometime in mid- to late September. Therefore, early October finds the bucks in hardened antler. It could be a bit earlier or later in your region, depending upon the breeding dates. We now have come full circle in antler development.

ANTLER QUALITY

The demand for trophy antlers and trophy management is so great that millions of dollars are spent annually in an attempt to produce large numbers of such bucks. A great deal of recent attention has been paid to the genetics of whitetails, with certain researchers proposing some rather bizarre management schemes which are "guaranteed" to produce results. The truth is that we know very little about the genetics of whitetails, in regard to trophy-antler production.

Dr. Jacobson knows more about whitetail genetics than any other individual, in my opinion, and he will be the first to tell you that he knows very little about the subject! After years of research and hundreds of breeding experiments, Dr. Jacobson feels that two points hold true in antler potential. First, there is absolutely no way to look at a yearling buck and predict form his first set of antlers what he will produce as a mature buck. I recently viewed a commercial videotape in which the producers show yearling buck antlers "with" and "without" trophy potential. This is ludicrous at best, given Dr. Jacobson's findings. Second, he feels that the doe contributes at least as much to antler quality as the buck does! If this is so, and I believe it is, then it is almost impossible to produce trophy antlers by currently accepted "culling" techniques. In a later chapter, I will discuss culling at length.

In addition to Dr. Jacobson's finding, I have noted that, although non-typical antlers may result from genetics, some of the strange antler formations we see in outdoor magazines may be as much the result of injuries as genetics. Indeed, some researchers have shown that deer exhibit a phenomenon known as "trophic memory." I have seen this phenomenon in whitetails. Apparently, a substantial injury to the antler during the velveted growing period can initiate a feedback message to the nervous system. The following year, this system directs the antler to attempt a repetition of the malformation or an over-compensation for it. In the laboratory, I have grown drop tines on bucks by altering their antler-bud development, but given the mania for drop tines, I will not divulge how I did it.

SUMMARY

Once you dismiss genetics as a serious consideration, *the real factors that determine antler quality are age and nutrition.* Each year, the buck grows a larger set of antlers until, at some point, quality (size) peaks. This point varies geographically. In the Hill Country of Texas, bucks often peak in the wild at 4.5 years, while bucks in northern states may not peak until 7.5 or 8.5 years. Because most of the bucks harvested in the U.S. are considerably younger than these ages, few bucks ever realize their true antler potential.

Nutrition is critical to antler production. Again, bucks require a high protein diet during the antler development period. If this level of protein is not available, a buck's true genetic and age-related antler potential will not be realized. Also, because antlers are a form of bone, bucks must have adequate levels of calcium, phosphorus and vitamins A and D to produce large antlers. Many of our ranges do not supply adequate nutrition. Therefore, the sportsman will either have to accept the limitations of his hunting territory to produce large antlers, or become actively involved in habitat management and/or supplemental feeding.

What all this means is that, of the three factors that determine antler quality-- age, nutrition and genetics— we can do more about the age and nutrition factors than genetics. An understanding of the factors that determine the quality of a buck's antlers should help you better appreciate just how marvelous the white-tailed deer is, and hopefully dispel some of the old wives' tales often associated with antlers.

TWINS

I saw them first in early spring,
They both were just such tiny things.

Snow white spots and legs so fragile,
How could something be so agile.

By fall they had grown quite a lot,
Solid brown and not a spot.

One a buck, the other a doe,
It was lots of fun to watch them grow.

A button buck that might someday be,
Another trophy who will outsmart me.   ...K.S.

Chapter 7

NUTRITION AND SUPPLEMENTAL FEEDING

When you consider the broad range of habitats occupied by whitetails, it is no wonder so many laymen are confused about the nutritional needs of deer. In this chapter I will first examine the feeding requirements of whitetails, the specific nutritional needs and then attempt to develop some efficient and economical recommendations regarding supplemental feeding of deer.

Over the years, I have discussed many times the three basic factors that influence the quality of antlers. These are: nutrition, age and genetics. Of these, nutrition perhaps is the most easily manipulated factor for producing trophy antlers. White-tailed deer management has enjoyed increased public interest of late, primarily in response to the growing sport of deer hunting. No doubt, the whitetail is and will remain the number one big game animal. Hence, I only see more emphasis being placed on deer management in the future.

Whitetails are extremely adaptable creatures, and to characterize their specific preferences for individual plant species would take many volumes. Further, discussions on food habits by geographic area may serve only to confound the misconceptions about feeding preferences of whitetails. It is better to discuss the various nutritional needs and foraging strategies that appear consistently throughout the range.

Recently, I was presenting a talk on deer management to a mixed crowd of landowners and hunters. During the question and answer session, one strange fellow roase from his chair and queried, "How would you respond to the statement that the chain saw has destroyed more whitetails than the automobile or gun?" Obviously, this rather obtuse question was a slam at the forestry practice of clearcutting. "Since you obviously are worried about the cutting of trees, specifically oaks," I responded, "have you ever seen an oak in South Texas?" For those of you unfamiliar with that region, oaks are rarer than hen's teeth in South Texas. Deer thrive in regions where many hunters never would venture. The coastal islands of the Gulf of Mexico is an excellent example.

WHAT IS DEER FORAGE?

White-tailed deer are very different from other deer species such as elk, moose or mule deer. These species are more generalist feeders, preferring to remain in one place and take in large quantities of food stuffs. To the contrary, whitetails are more specialized feeders, preferring to range widely, stopping here and there to select specific feeds in order to satisfy their unique nutritional requirements. Therefore, whitetails are more specialized feeders than their cousins.

In order to understand deer nutrition, we first must understand the term **forage**. Deer forage can be divided into the following categories: 1) grasses and grass-likes; 2) forbaceous plants (weeds); 3) browse (leaves and twigs of woody plants); 4) hard and soft mast (fruits of woody plants); and 5) mushrooms.

The old farmer in the bib overalls spat a long stream of tobacco juice, hooked his thumbs in his overall straps, and began to philosophize. "You biologists don't know what you are talking about," he said, "We don't have too many deer. There's plenty of grass and stuff out there on my place for deer to eat." This incredibly ill-informed statement epitomizes the general public perception of deer nutritional needs. Just because there is "green stuff" in the woods does not mean that there are quality foods available for deer. Deer forage is like a can of mixed nuts at a party. In an hour or so you are left with a bowl of peanuts! Someone has stood there and eaten every pecan and every cashew, and who eats the Brazil nuts I will never know. Hence, what we often see in the woods is nothing more than peanuts. The idea that all green stuff is deer food is ludicrous. If that were so, we could just buy ourselves a can of green spray paint and make plenty of deer food!

Seriously, very few of the plants occurring on a deer range are suitable for deer. Grasses certainly are a case in point. Improved grasses such as coastal bermudagrass offer little to whitetails. As I noted earlier, whitetails are de-

Nutrition and Supplemental Feeding

Mike Biggs

The quality of forage available greatly affects both antler quality and the fawn crop.

---

pendent on the more easily digestible plants and these are sparsely scattered over the landscape. Most studies on feeding habits report only a small proportion (usually 5% or less) of grass in the diet. Grasses and grass-like plants such as sedges have high fiber contents, making them difficult to digest. The highest grass use occurs during late winter and early spring, a time when the newly developing grass shoots are most digestible. The exceptions to this rule are the cereal grains. Plant varieties such as wheat, oats, rye and ryegrass are highly nutritious and palatable species which significantly can improve nutrition. I will discuss the usefulness of cereal grains in the second part of this chapter.

In virtually every portion of the whitetail's range, deer prefer forbs over all other forage classes. Weeds generally are highly nutritious and easily digestible. The fact that weeds have been under-reported in deer feeding studies reflects more a problem with rapid digestive rates of these plants than low preference. Weeds simply are digested so quickly that they are difficult to find in the deer's stomach (rumen).

Weeds are characteristically ephemeral in that they occur only during short periods of time, usually during and after the wetter portions of the year. Weeds provide high levels of protein and phosphorus, as well as vitamins, to deer. In my feeding studies, I have recorded as much as 35% protein in some weed species.

Browse is the mainstay of most deer. The most notable exception may be the Avery Island race found along the coasts of Texas and Louisiana, where weeds and grasses predominate. Although often of lower nutritional quality than weeds, browse is more dependable in availability. Which woody plants are taken by deer depend on many factors, among which are the growth habits of the plant, its digestibility and its defense mechanisms. There are two basic types of woody plant growth, determinate and indeterminate. In determinate plants, growth occurs during one or two seasons, usually spring and fall. At this time, growing stems and shoots are highly nutritious and palatable. Second, many trees and shrubs have indeterminate growth, regulated by periodic rains. These plants produce palatable shoots only after significant rainfall.

It also is interesting that browse plants of the same species may have different growth habits dependent on their topographic position. Upland plants tend to leaf out, grow and fruit at different times than lowland plants of the same species. Whitetails realize this, and adjust their movements to take advantage of this phenomenon.

Mast is the hard and soft fruit of woody plants. Acorns, pecans, blackberries and grapes are excellent examples of mast. Obviously, availability of mast is seasonal, but you would be surprised to learn that there often is some type of mast available during almost any month of the year. For example, blackberries and dewberries are available in late spring or early summer, while raspberries come into production later in the summer. Grapes begin to ripen in mid- to late summer. Acorns begin falling in later September and are available in good years until late winter.

Mast, due to its highly variable availability, cannot be counted on by deer. Mast should be looked upon as a windfall supplement to the diet. In well-managed herds, availability of mast has less importance to the population than in herds held at saturation level. In the Hill Country of Texas, for example, the deer herd has been allowed to hang precariously at the saturation level for many decades. As a result, years of good mast production will be followed by a higher fawn crop than those following poor mast years. Further east, well-managed herds such as the Brushy Creek population (Champion Paper Inc., Groveton, TX) are little affected by poor mast years.

Mast provides the often needed energy required by deer during the colder portions of the year. Foods such as acorns are high in fats and carbohydrates, but are low in protein. Hunters often use corn as a deer bait, since deer are attracted to this feed by its high carbohydrate level. Other baits such as apples and carrots also are attractive to deer during poor mast years.

Mushrooms often are critical to whitetails, especially in phosphorus-poor soils. Much of the range is deficient in phosphorus, and mushrooms have a very high phosphorus content. Unfortunately, however, mushrooms occur during the wetter portions of the year. Winter normally is an excellent time for mushroom production.

MEETING THE NEED WITH NATIVE FORAGE

The nutritional needs of whitetails coincide with the specific activities taking place at any point in time. For example, a common statement often made by biologists is that deer need at least 16% protein for maximum antler and fawn production. This certainly is true, but not for the entire year. I recently heard a biologist tell a crowd of landowners that deer need this level of protein year-round. A little common sense would question this statement. I have spent a good portion of my career monitoring protein levels in native forages. Generally, protein levels are highest in spring and again in fall, and lowest in summer and winter. Of course, this is determined by the specific climate involved. For example, forages in the northern portion of the range tend to be more nutritious during summer

Acorns seldom are a reliable food source. (Robert Skinner)

Mushrooms often provide needed phosphorus, and are primarily available during the wetter portions of the year.

months than their southern counterparts. Deer have compensated for this seasonal availability of protein by developing conservation mechanisms to recycle proteins. One notable adaptation is the recycling of urea in the blood. hence, deer are adapted to doing without high protein feeds for portions of the year.

Protein is important in that its availability during the growing season does affect antler quality and fawn production. Both antler growth and fetal development coincide with the seasonally high level of available protein. In most of the range, antler and fetal growth is complete by early summer, when protein levels fall below optimum.

Available energy often determines whether or not deer survive the winter. This especially is true for bucks. Bucks come out of the rut (post-rut period) with badly depleted fat reserves. Consequently, availability of digestible energy may determine whether or not that young buck you passed up this season survives to realize his genetic potential. Fully 25% of mature bucks never make it through the winter. Winter survival depends on one or two factors. First, the amount of fat stored by a buck prior to the rut greatly affects his survival prospects. Bucks spend a great deal of time seeking high energy, high fat foods during late summer, early fall. Bowhunters often take advantage of this by waiting in ambush at mast production areas. Second, the availability of emergency high energy foods after the rut can be critical to over-winter survival. This is a time that can be quite limiting to whitetails, and is a

Mike Bigg

Over-winter survival for bucks can be influenced by the availability of high energy foods.

time when the manager can take advantage of supplemental feeding.

Antlers are pre-formed as cartilage, composed primarily of protein. During the mineralization phase of antler production, the cartilagenous antler matrix is replaced by calcium-phosphorus compounds. Calcium seldom is lacking in deer forage, but phosphorus is more often scarce than abundant. Areas with high rainfall and/or acid soils traditionally are low in phosphorus. High rainfall leaches phosphorus from the soil, and high acid content makes phosphorus unavailable. Dr. Harry Jacobson of Mississippi State University recently showed that body size of bucks was correlated to available soil phosphorus. Phosphorus is in high demand by both bucks and does. In fact, the ability of does to assimilate phosphorus will determine not only the size of the buck fawn dropped and milk production, but ironically, the ability of her buck to produce large antlers later in life. Anti-hunting critics often say that trophy hunting and management select for non-adaptive traits. This is nonsense. Selecting for big antlers may subsequently affect the doe's ability to produce healthy fawns of proper weight. A healthy fawn will later become a large antlered, healthy buck.

High phosphorus feeds such as mast and mushrooms are highly attractive to whitetails. The importance of mushrooms in particular is an often overlooked factor in deer management. Some forestry practices, such as logging and burning, actually increase mushroom availability. Where mast is an important component to quality deer habitat, sound forest mangement practices which encourage oaks greatly can benefit deer.

The white-tailed deer is a highly adaptable creature capable of surviving throughout a broad range of habitats. Yet, in spite of this, whitetails are "picky" eaters that match feeding habits to specific physiological needs. Meeting these needs may involve exploitation of acorns and fruits in areas where these feeds are abundant, or total independence from mast in the drier climates. Deer also adapt to the quality of forage by adjusting their body size and reproductive rate to compensate for poor nutrition. In some portions of Florida, for example, deer are diminutive and seldom develop large antlers. These deer also have a much earlier rut than any other whitetail. This area is notorious for producing low quality feeds. Fortunately, as I noted early in this chapter, the most easily manipulated factor in producing quality antlers is nutrition.

SUPPLEMENTAL FEEDING AND FOOD PLOTS

Perhaps no other aspect of deer management is as easy to sell to the general public as supplemental feeding. Most sportsmen and landowners want to take an active and visible role in deer management, and are easily at-

Mike Biggs
Antler quality is determined primarily by availability of protein and phosphorus.

tracted to the more showy aspects of management. Over the last decade, food plots and supplemental feeding generally have been viewed as a panacea for quickly producing large numbers of good bucks. For example, much of the Southeast recently was caught up in an American jointvetch mania. This plant, researched and promoted by a few university scientists, was touted as the magic elixir that would not only improve antler quality and fawn production, but cure "prickly heat and acne" at the same time! The result was a diversion of public thought from the sound management principles discussed earlier. But, in spite of these negative aspects, supplemental feeding by feeds and/or food plots do have a place in deer management programs, especialy intensive management programs. This section presents sound supplementation strategies which I have used to substantially improve herd vigor and production.

Ray Sasser

Supplemental feeding is best used in regions where there is inadequate rainfall to support food plots.

Nutrition and Supplemental Feeding

SUPPLEMENTAL FEEDING CONCEPT

Although the layman often is confused on the subject, the term "supplemental feeding" is quite clear. It means that an attempt is made to augment or supplement the quality, and perhaps quantity, of native forages available to the herd. Supplemental feeds were never intended to be regarded as replacement feeding. Rather, these programs should be thought of as a means to bring seasonal or periodic deficiencies in forage quality into line with the current physiological needs of deer. Unfortunately, the recent interest in deer management and trophy production has made it possible for some pretty unsound practices to gain the attention of the public. It seems that the layman constantly searches for a "magic bullet" for trophy deer production. For example, the spike buck research conducted in Texas suggested that removal of spikes may have a positive impact on antler quality. A veritable stampede of spike buck persecution followed over the country. One fellow in Florida, where in some areas nutrition severely limits yearling antler quality, completely annihilated an age class of bucks by shooting spikes! The jointvetch craze is yet another example of the public's desire for a "quick fix" to deer management, but alas, there is no such thing. Hopefully, this section will eliminate some of these misconceptions.

There are four basic dietary constituents which demand the manager's attention: protein, energy, phosphorus and calcium. In most cases one or more of these requisites are lacking during part or all of the year. The basic question to be asked by the manager is: Are any of these factors lacking in my deer's diet? When one is lacking, it is said to be limiting. It can be limiting by curtailing reproduction or by adversely affecting antler production. Even when population growth is under control, a herd may not realize its true potential as a result of limiting factors. Hence, the role of supplemental feeding is to ameliorate the negative impacts of limiting factors. If this is your motivation, and you are adequately managing population numbers, then supplemental feeding definitely has an important role in the management of your herd. If, on the other hand, you are not actively managing both the habitat and the population, then any supplementation program is the proverbial "spit in the wind!" I make it a rule not even to discuss supplemental feeding until the landowner or club has demonstrated a serious commitment to basic population control.

Supplemental feeding is an important part of the fine-tuning process in herd management. Once the manager has realized maximum potential from the native habitat, nutritional supplements can be used significantly to increase herd production. The important question revolves around the most efficient and economic means of supplementation. Basically, there are three means of supplementing a deer's diet; viz., 1) feeding, 2) food plots, and 3) mineral supplements.

SUPPLEMENTAL FEEDS

Over the last decade, a number of supplemental feeds were developed for deer. A brief list of these is presented at the end of this section. The average layman, however, pays little attention to the need to supply critical nutrients at a critical point in time. Instead, deer often are given feeds which do little to improve the nutritional plane. Too often lately, I have the unpleasant task of removing a pet deer which has been illegally held in captivity by some well-meaning citizen who found an "orphan" fawn. We refer to these deer as "dog run" deer. The name comes from the fact that most end up being kept in an abandoned dog run.

In an effort to supply high quality feed, the owner often feeds either corn or horse-and-mule feed (sweet feed). Unfortunately, these feeds do not supply the high level of nutrition required by white-tails for early body development. The result is a stunted animal that never will realize its true potential. One of these deer (see photograph) remained a spike over its entire life, and never exceeded eighty pounds of live weight!

Many landowners feed corn throughout the year. Corn is relatively low in protein (7-9%) and high in carbohydrate. Corn also is often deficient in certain amino acids. Deer readily will feed on corn due to its sweet nature, but in so doing, can significantly reduce body growth. Corn can be used as a good supplement when carbohydrates and fats are needed; i.e., the late fall and winter. A good friend feeds his deer year-round. In the late winter, spring and fall, he uses a high protein, high mineral pelleted ration. He then shifts to corn as a carbohydrate source fall. By early winter, however, he again switches to a mixture of corn and protein pellets. My experience indicates that bucks tend to seek out the protein pellets earlier than does, possibly to replenish body tissues torn down during the rut.

Analysis of Typical Deer Grower Pelleted Ration

Crude Protein- not less than 16%
Crude Fat- not less than 3%
Crude Fiber- not less than 16%

Ingredients:

cottonseed meal	copper oxide
wheat middlings	cobalt carbonate
ground corn	manganous oxide
alfalfa meal	iron sulfate
rice bran	ethylenediamine dihydriodide
bentonite	iron carbonate
ground limestone	magnesium oxide
salt	zince oxide
natural flavor	sodium selenite
calcium phosphate	Vitamin A and E
calcium sulfate	deactivated animal sterol
roughage= 20%	cane molasses

Nutrition and Supplemental Feeding

The prepared feeds are the best approach to deer supplementation in drier climates, where food plots are chancey at best. Although feeds are marketed under various brand names, most contain a similar analysis. Prepared rations usually are high in protein (in excess of 16%), have a 2:1 calcium:phosphorus ratio and various types and amounts of essential nutrients and vitamins. Energy sources such as carbohydrates and fats are added in sufficient quantities to supply normal body demand for energy. Recently, some feed producers have attempted to better match dietary needs with specific feeds. For example, one manufacturer recently developed a synthetic acorn substitute which may show promise for over-wintering deer.

How, when and where supplemental feed is supplied is critical to efficaceous utilization of this management tool. Most of the prepared, pelleted feeds do not stand up to normal weather conditions. The most important attributes of good feeders are that they: 1) provide a dry storage reservoir for the feed, 2) do not limit access (especially by bucks), and 3) reduce the possibility of spoilage or contamination. In regard to criterion one, I prefer feeders that reduce the frequency of servicing. However, too large a storage reservoir may lead to spoilage or pest problems. I suggest that you select a feeder with a 500 to 1,000 pounds capacity. A good friend uses an open trough for his supplemental feeding program. He can afford to do this in that a ranch hand distributes feed daily to each trough. In inclement weather, the hand omits the feeding or removes spoiled feed. Unless you have a great deal of money or surplus time, I suggest you avoid this type of feeder.

Access to the feeder is critical for bucks. Remember that one of the goals of your program hopefully is to produce large antlered bucks. During the growing season, bucks are highly reluctant to stick their heads into anything that might damage the growing velvet. Also, many deer do not "like" the idea of sticking their heads into a closed box. It

Mike Biggs

Timed feeders are excellent for baiting deer, but usually are of little service in long-term feeding programs.

certainly sets one up for attack! Hence, I have had great success using an open feeder that allows the deer to see while feeding. Distance from the top of the trough to the bottom of the roof should be at least three feet, with sufficient roof overhang to prevent a driving rain from entering the feed box.

Feed can become spoiled or contaminated in a number of ways. By contaminated, I refer to either the invasion of fungi (often toxic) and/or the introduction of disease organisms into the feed by an infected animal. I prefer to drill drain holes in the bottom of the trough in case water does enter the feed box, as well as line the box with sheet metal. Periodically, I also wash the box with disinfectant (bleach will do). This can be done when the deer are little using the feed, mostly during the active growing season.

The use of timed feed dispensers is excellent for baiting deer for harvest, but these feeders often cause problems when pelleted feeds are involved. They

Mike Biggs

You should carefully plan the distribution of your feeders and food plots so that a maximum number of deer benefit from the supplemental feeding program.

seldom dispense an adequate amount of feed. Any amount of moisture in the feed reservoir will not only spoil the feed, but also clog the feed dispensing mechanism. Timed feeders are best used to dispense grain-type feeds during the time that a high carbohydrate diet is needed. Several feeder manufacturers are listed at the end of this section. Should you decide to use timed feeders, I suggest that you select one of the solar powered models, as cost of batteries and maintenance is often prohibitive.

The timing of feeding programs is extremely important, as already discussed. Deer will not uniformly use supplemental feed throughout the year. Rather, use will greatly depend on the quality of native forages available at a specific point in time. Several researchers have demonstrated that supplemental feed utilization is directly related to the particular growing conditions on the range. For example, during a study with my graduate student, Billy Higginbotham, use of supplemental feeds in summer diminished after a significant rainfall. Rain often stimulates wee (forb) growth, and deer prefer these highly digestible plants when available. After the flush of plant growth subsides, however, deer once again return to supplemental feed.

Too often, hunting clubs and landowners only feed during the hunting season to increase harvest efficiency. In states where baiting is legal, I have nothing against the use of bait to improve harvest, especially in the antlerless harvest, but such programs can do more harm than good if discontinued after the season. Cool season feeding becomes critical long after the hunters have left the woods. Supplemental feed should be available during the late winter stress period.

Improperly distributed feeders will reduce any positive benefits to a supplemental feeding program. Research has clearly demonstrated that deer will not move their home ranges to include a new food source. Occasionally, there are exceptions, but I have found this to be the rule. Therefore, a well-planned supplemental feeding program provides sufficient supplement distributed properly over the entire management area. The proper distribution will depend on the seasonal home range size of the deer. In most cases, one feeder per 160 acres will produce adequate results. Less than one feeder per square mile (640 acres) will produce poor results. All feeders should be located adjacent to travel corridors and protected areas so that deer will not have to expose themselves to inclement weather or predators in order to feed.

The cost of feed supplementation is quite high. Hence, you must ask yourself whether or not your management goals are economically satisfied using supplemental feeds. Costing $200-$300 per ton, feeding can generate a rather large feed bill! You can count on a deer eating about 4-6 pounds of feed per day. Of course, this is just a ball park figure and may vary with geogrpahic region and weather conditions. But, using a modest 5 pounds per day, that means that each deer will consume around a thousand pounds of feed each year (allowing for a 210-day feeding period). That means a cost of around $150 per animal per year! A hundred deer brings your investment to at least $15,000, not including labor.

FOOD PLOTS

I have found that, principally east of the 35-inch annual rainfall line, a more intelligent approach to supplemental feeding is to use food plots. When properly managed and distributed, food plots can be a cost effective means of supplementing the deer's diet. The key here is the phrase "properly managed and distributed." Properly managed food plots have: 1) plant species matched to the particular climate and soils, and 2) soil adjusted for both pH and nutrients (N,P,K). The attached table presents a listing of recommended plant species by locality and season (warm and cool).

As I noted earlier, the zeal of many individuals to participate in deer mangement has made it easy to sell one "panacea" or another to the general public. Food plot plant varieties are no exception. After two decades of research on supplemental food plots, I have come to the conclusion that there is no one single plant variety that can serve in every management situation, or in every year! My advice is to avoid any variety that is touted to 1) grow over a broad range of conditions, and 2) solve all your deer nutrition problems.

Choice of plant species centers around several criteria. First, you must ask yourself whether or not supplemental feeding is a year-round requirement for your herd. In some areas, the stress period(s) for deer occurs in the late summer months, while in others, it occurs in winter. This dictates that you select a planting that will provide the most nutrition during the major stress periods. There are two basic types of plantings; viz, warm season and cool season. Warm season refers to the spring and summer months, while cool season refers to the fall and winter months. Of course, there is some overlap between these two seasons.

Dr. Higginbotham and I developed some criteria for selecting a specific group of plants. In order to be selected, a planting during any time of the year should provide adequate nutrition when it is needed. It does absolutely no good to have high quality forage peak at a time when deer are adequately satisfying their needs with native forage, or to have a forage not available when it is needed most. A good planting should provide at least 16% protein, a 2:1 or better calcium to phosphorus ratio and be at least 50% digestible. Digestibility values as high as 70% are possible with some plantings.

Timing of production is critical. Some of the white clovers have good potential for providing summer forage, but are not in peak production at the time needed. For example, some of the ladino clovers reach peak production in May and June in the South, a time when native forage competes heavily with plantings, no matter what the quality. In the South, the peak need for supplemental forage is the period July-September, while further north, this period occurs in August-September. Obviously, any planting that thrives

Nutrition and Supplemental Feeding

during the earlier portion of the spring and summer, but not during this period, is of little use to the manager. I suggest that you ask for month by month yield figures before deciding on a particular forage variety.

Another important selection criterion should be cost of establishment. There are some plant varieties on the market that, on the surface, sound great, but under close scrutiny are not economically feasible. Varieties costing $3-5 per pound of seed should be examined closely before launching into a planting program. Likewise, even if a planting is economically feasible, the species involved may not be competitive with native vegetation. I have examined many species of warm season plants that have excellent potential for providing high quality forage, but just cannot compete with native weeds. Jointvetch, for example, often requires the use of herbicides in order to maintain plantings. At a cost of $35 or more per acre, herbicide application can greatly increase your investment, both in time and money.

I have had excellent success using combination plantings of cereal grains and legumes for cool season plantings in the South and Mid-West. Selection of specific plant varieties and species will be determined by the soil type and climate. There is no such thing as a single species that will grow in all soils and climates. Beware of any claim to the contrary!

Southern managers have discovered that plantings of arrowleaf clover, rye grass, oats and elbon rye do well in most upland clay to sandy loam sites.

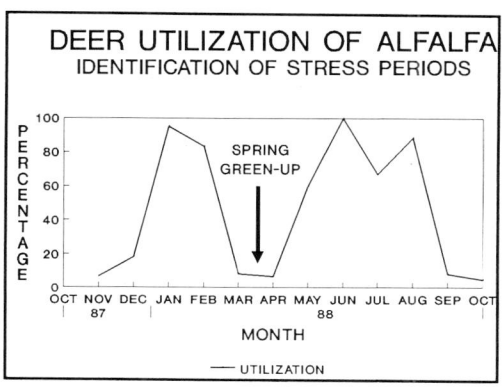

Utilization of supplemental forages often coincides with nutritional needs. These two graphs illustrate how deer use supplemental forages to augment their natural diet. (Data from Higginbotham and Kroll, in press.)

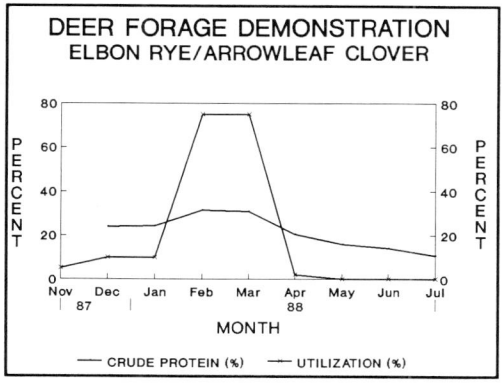

Bottomlands, on the other hand, seldom will support good stands of these species. Hence, I use a mixture of white dutch and wheat in bottomlands. My research has shown that very high yields (ca., 5-7 tons) of high quality forage are possible using cool season plots.

In more northern climates, however, many of the clovers are best planted for spring and summer use. The more cold tolerant grain species such as Bonel rye and winter wheat are best in these areas. In Kentucky, I had good success with a mixture of wheat and red clover on the Grassy Lake management area. In western regions, triticale, wheat and alfalfa plantings have shown promise. In all cases, proper fertilization at time fo establishment and a followup top dressing are critical to realizing the true productive potential of cool season plots. Also, innoculation of legumes with nitrogen-fixing bacteria is mandatory.

There is quite a bit of misinformation concerning the winter hardiness of cool season plantings. My 15 years of research and experience have shown that seldom do combination plantings of cereal grains and legumes suffer excessive winter kill. During the last decade, I have had signicant damage to food plots only twice, and in both cases food plot species recovered adequately to not require re-establishment. Hence, I would not worry about losing cool season plantings in much of the range.

In areas where the late summer is stressful, managers have tried several types of food plots with limited success. Recently, researchers in Louisiana reported high success with American

Field peas are highly preferred by whitetails, but as you can see in these two photographs taken just a few days apart, peas are consumed quickly. Any positive benefit is lost in the process. Plantings of field peas are recommended only when large plots of ten or more acres can be planted.

Billy Higginbotham

jointvetch. Highly publicized reports of the success of jointvetch produced a virtual stampede to the local seed store for jointvetch seed. Unfortunately, however, most mangers discovered that the seed not only was expensive, but that the plant often was difficult and costly to establish. Clearly, jointvetch was not the magic bullet hoped for by deer managers. To be fair to jointvetch, it is indeed a good plant for deer. My research has shown that in some cases jointvetch can be useful in a summer food plot program, but once again in combination plantings. The truth is that no one plant can be used in all situations, especially during the warm season.

Recently, my graduate student, Billy Higginbotham and I completed a comprehensive study in the South on warm season food plots. We examined more than a dozen species of plants, all of which had been highly recommended by professionals and laymen alike. The results of these experiments were enlightening.

One of the most commonly planted varieties is the common field pea. Coming under several varietal names such as red ripper, black-eye, purple hull, catjang and iron-and-clay peas, these plants have the potential to produce large yields of highly nutritious forage. Unfortunately, however, we soon discovered that these varieties were substandard for use in deer mangement in most situations. Two major problems arose. First, in dourght years, der never allowed the peas to produce significant vegetative growth. Food lots planted to field peas were wiped out in a single night. Second, in favorable years, deer allowed peas to reach maturity and then consumed the entire plot in just a few days. Although one could argue that, for a short while, deer received high quality nutrition, the sad truth is that deer benefitted from the plantings only over a short span of time. After heavy deer browsing, the peas never recovered.

Summer clovers and clover-like legumes appear to offer the best warm season food plots. The type of legume will depend on the particular geographic region. For example, we have found that in the South, mixed plantings of alyce-clover, sweetclover, red clover, alfalfa (Baron variety), jointvetch and white clover (ladino) offer the best selections. I particularly am impressed with sweetclover and alyce-clover. One dealer currently sells a combination of these species, plus jointvetch, for summer plantings. These plantings have high adaptability and offer heavy resistance to over-browsing. Alyce-clover has one drawback in that it is susceptible to nematodes, but I understand that there now is a nematode resistant variety available. Once thought not to grow well in the humid climate and acid soil conditions of the South, alfalfa can be used in some cases to produce year-round quality foragea. The Baron variety has shown particular promise in limed and fertilized plots. Jointvetch continues to be an excellent forage in moist soils, but does not hold up well to dry conditions and competition. The best stands are produced using pre-emergent herbicides. But, in combination with more robust plants, jointvetch can be a welcome addition to a mixed planting. Sweetclovers often out-produce summer legumes in both protein content and yield. These species also are excellent reseeders.

Some of the more highly touted summer white clovers are very useful, but often are limited in production to May and June in the South and June and July in the North, both periods when deer normally receive adequate nutrition from native forages. We did not see a marked preference for white clovers over mixed plantings of alyce-clover, jointvetch and sweetclover.

In the North, many species of clovers that only grow during the cool season further south thrive throughout the summer. Red clover and white clover are excellent summer forages. I have no experience with sweetclover or alyce-clover in the North, but I have had excellent success at Grassy Lake (Kentucky) with red and white clovers. I suspect that alyce-clover may not do well in northern climates, but this species should be studied.

I recently visited landowners in Wisconsin. They favored summer plantings of corn to provide forage, and as a carbohydrate source in winter. Frankly, the low price of shelled corn makes me opt for a higher protein summer forage planting, with shelled corn being provided using feeders.

Currently, I am conducting research on possible combination plantings of cool and warm season varieties for a one-time fall planting. If feasible, such plantings would greatly reduce the cost of food plot establishment. Several combinations at this time appear feasible.

Cost of food plot establishment appears to be fairly constant from one geographic region to another. I suggest hat you budget a per acre cost of establishment ranging from $60 to $100, depending on species selected. Subsequent maintenance cost will depend on the plant varieties selected, but should run in the range of $15 to $45 per acre per year. In order to better understand the cost effectiveness of supplemental plantings, let's examine a typical southern food plot combination planting (rye grass, elbon rye and arrowleaf clover).

The initial cost of establishment for an acre of slightly acid soil will be: liming ($25); fertilization ($40); seed ($27.50) and labor ($15). This amounts to a total establishment cost of $107.50, which seems pretty high on the surface. However, if properly maintained (i.e., mowed each fall), the second year cost would be: fertilizer ($20); seed ($20) and labor ($15). Our cost is now reduced to $55 per acre. Seed cost and labor can be reduced further by selecting species with a tendency to reseed, such as arrowleaf clover. For example, I have some food plots that are now eleven years old that were originally planted to arrowleaf clover and elbon rye. Both of these species have a tendency to reseed. By proper timing of my mowing, I have been able to maintain these plots in high quality forage for the entire eleven year period for only $25 per year. Assuming a modest five ton production, my cost per ton of forage is only $5 per year! This certainly seems cost-effective to me. Even if you have to replant each year, the total maximum tonage cost would be $21.50. A one-acre cool season food plot conservatively will support approximately 1,000 deer-days, at a maximum cost of 2 cents per pound You can see why I favor food plots over direct feeding. However, it not always is possible to use food plots, especially in low rainfall areas.

I often divide a food plot in half, planting cool season mixture in one half and warm season in another. By doing this, I have been able to provide high quality forage for every day of the year. This method certainly increases labor, but remains cost-effective.

SELECTING A FOOD PLOT FOR YOUR SITUATION

Before you go running off and plant something, take a few minutes to read this section. I suggest that you make several small plantings during your first year of management in order to narrow your choice of plant species. Use some of the varieties suggested or talk with your local Soil Conservation Service representative. I have included the names and addresses of some reputable food plot dealers at the end of this Chapter, but make the test plantings first before buying large quantities of seed. When I test a particular species or variety, I try to make several plantings on the same property on various soil types and topographic locations. In this way, I rule out species which are not adapted to uplands or lowlands, or identify species that are universally adapted to my area.

No planting should ever be made without soil testing. Take a number of samples from each plot and have your local soil scientist analyze them for fertility and soil pH. This is no place to cut corners. Do exactly as the soil analysis suggests. It takes a little more time, but the payoff is substantial.

For each trial planting, and in all food plots for that matter, I construct a small wire exclusion cage to give me a good indication of the extent of utilization of the food plot. The difference in height between the plants outside the cage and those inside is an excellent indicator of the acceptability of the planting.

GRANULAR MINERAL SUPPLEMENT
General Analysis

Ingredient	Min.	Max.
Calcium	16%	19%
Phosphorus	8%	
Salt	18%	20%
Magnesium	1.6%	
Potassium	.16%	
Sulfur	.48%	
Iron	.7%	
Zinc	.1%	
Manganese	.1%	
Copper	.01%	
Cobalt	9.35ppm	
Iodine	49ppm	
Selenium	2.56ppm	
Vitamin A	120,000 IU/lb	
Vitamin D	50,000 IU/lb	
Vitamin E	50 IU/lb	

MINERAL SUPPLEMENTATION

A number of years back, I became interested in natural mineral licks. The literature clearly states that deer are attracted to natural mineral licks, and prob ably receive minearal supplementation from these deposits. Hence, I analyzed one of the more heavily used mineral licks on my study area, finding that there were significant quantities of common table salt, phosphorus, calcium, metals and trace minerals. Working with some commericial feed manufacturers, I formulated a granular mineral that has not only worked effectively throughout the country, but has been commercially successful.

Hunters and landowners often ask about using salt as a bait and supplement. Alabama prohibits the use of feeds as bait, yet allows hunters to distribute salt for this purpose. I strongly discourage hunters and landowners from using salt blocks for deer. As with humans, salt in large quantities is not a healthy food supplement. Minerals should be limited to no more than 35% salt in order to be effective. It is not sodium chloride (table salt) that benefits antler production; it is the proper proportion of phosphorus and calcium! Further, use of blocks is not recommended. Deer seldom lick salt blocks, rather they have to wait for the blocks to melt under normal rainfall. Supplements provided in granular form are far superior to salt blocks. There now are several brands of granular minerals on the market. These are provided at the end of this Chapter. One such mineral with which I am familiar is the **Buck Chuck Deer Mineral**; however, most brands are quite satisfactory. Some of the products do have an alarmingly high rate of selenium.

Mineral is best supplied in a small trough, either open to the air or covered by a small roof. I seldom have had problems with deer taking mineral from these structures, once they discover the contents. Some managers recommend just digging a hole in the ground and pouring granular mineral into it. I do not recommend this practice unless it is absolutely necessary, as it promotes the spreading of pathogens and parasites. A mineral trough that is periodically cleaned is the proper vehicle for mineral supplementation.

SUMMARY

Supplemental feeding has its place in deer management, provided the population is being maintained in line with the productive capacity of the range. Supplemental feeding is not to be regarded as replacement feeding or as a panacea to producing monster bucks. There are no magic bullets in deer management. However, a well-planned, well-distributed supplemental feeding program, tuned to your particular situation, can significantly increase the quality of forage and of bucks on your property. This is no idle statement. Herds such as the Boggy Slough and Brushy Creek populations in Texas, and the Grassy Lake herd in Kentucky clearly demonstrate that supplementation can be used in the production of large numbers of quality bucks.

Nutrition and Supplemental Feeding

Recommended Cool Season Plantings for Whitetails.

Soil Type / Plant Variety	Recommended seeding rate (lbs./ac.)
Deep, Excesssively Drained Soils	
Rye	60
Ryegrass	15
Oats	60
Wheat	80
Hairy Vetch*	15
Big Flower Vetch*	15
Crimson Clover*	15
Austrian Winter Peas*	20
Well Drained Soils	
Rye	60
Wheat	80
Oats	60
Ryegrass	15
Arrowleaf Clover *	8
Red Clover*	20
Ladino Clover*	8
Hairy Vetch*	15
Austrian Winter Peas*	20
Wet Sandy Soils	
Ryegrass	30
Tall Fescue	15
Singletary Peas*	25
Ladino Clover*	8
Arrowleaf Clover*	8
Red Clover*	20
Austrian Winter Peas*	20
Wet Clay Soils	
Ryegrass	30
LA-S1 Clover*	4
Ladino Clover*	8
Hairy Vetch*	15
Singletary Peas*	25

*Denotes varieties that have to be inoculated prior to planting.

Selected Warm Season Forages for Whitetails

Soil Type Plant Variety	Recommended Planting Rate (lbs./ac.)
Excessively Drained Soils	
Mung Bean *	12
Iron & Clay Pea *	50
Red Ripper Pea *	50
Sorghum-almum	15
Bicolor Lespedeza	Planted Seedlings
Well Drained Soils	
Alyce-Clover*	20
Iron & Clay Pea*	50
Red Ripper*	50
Catjang Pea*	50
Kobe Lespedeza*	30
Re-seeding Soybean*	25
Soybean IV*	60
Soybean VI*	60
Mung Bean*	12
American Jointvetch*	10
Browntop Millet	25
Alfalfa**	15
Sweet Clover**	15
Sunflower	12
Wet, Sandy Soils	
All of the above varieties plus,	
Japanese Millet	20
Browntop Millet	20
Sorghum-Almum	15
Wet Clays	
Japanese Millet	20
Browntop Millet	20
American Jointvetch*	10
Alyce-Clover*	20
Catjang Pea*	50
Sweet Clover*	15
Iron & Clay Pea*	50
Red Ripper Pea*	50

*Denotes varieties that have to be inoculated prior to planting.
**These varieties should be planted in the fall along with cool season varieties.

Chapter 8

Habitat Management and Home Range

No other aspect of deer management is as critical as habitat manipulation. Yet it is the one component which receives the least amount of attention. It seems that planting a food plot or thinning a stand of timber is not as exotic and showy as shooting does or culling bucks. So, the landowner often neglects this component of deer management.

As a good friend of mine once noted about ranching: "There are a whole lot of good animal husbandrists, but very few range managers." What he was trying to say is that it is very easy to understand the day to day physical needs of livestock, but it takes a great deal of experience and natural savvy to really understand how the livestock-range ecosystem works, not to mention being able to manipulate it for man's benefit. So it is with whitetail habitat management.

HABITAT COMPONENTS

There are three basic habitat requirements of whitetails: **brush, cover** and **water**. Unlike modern man, the American Indian understood well the habitat needs of whitetails, regularly manipulating the natural world to favor deer. For example, he knew that deer thrive on disturbance. Events such as tornadoes, wild fires and hurricanes, all of which we routinely consider catastrophic, are viewed by whitetails as manna from heaven. He also understood that deer favor the early stages of forest growth, for it is these stages that bring the one habitat component held in common throughout the range— brush. Although there are a few exceptions, whitetails and brush are one in the same. The old growth forest, with its deep shade, provides neither brush nor cover. It takes sunlight to produce brush; the more the better. And, sunlight comes to the forest floor only after disturbance. The practicing manager will argue that there are other components to deer habitat, and this is true, but throughout the range the common thread runs through brush, cover and water. In this chapter, I will discuss these basic habitat requirements of whitetails, the concept of home range, and outline ways in which the manager can manipulate natural processes to produce large numbers of deer.

Brush

It is now time to change terminology. Although the term "brush" is quite descriptive, whitetail managers prefer to use the word **browse** interchangeably. Wildlife management texts will inform you that white-tailed deer primarily are browsers, and this certainly is true. But, whitetails would rather feed on the more palatable and nutritious weed species. There is just one problem. Weeds (**forbs**) seldom can be counted on throughout the year. Weeds are ephemeral in nature, meaning that they may be abundant today, yet totally absent a week from now. Research has shown that weed production is tied strongly to rainfall. So, weeds are to be considered, with the exception of food plot species, as a windfall rather than a mainstay. Browse, on the other hand, is always present. The nutrient content may not be up to par, but deer can

Mike Biggs

Deer are "picky" eaters who select specific plant species in order to optimize their diet. Although whitetails prefer herbaceous vegetation due to higher palatability, browse is their mainstay.

Habitat and Home Range

count on woody plants as a consistent source of food. Hence, the importance of browse to deer is obvious. But, what is browse?

Browse is nothing more than "baby trees" and shrubs. As I noted in the chapter on nutrition, deer are quite adept at picking and choosing among forage items to provide optimum nutrition. The quantity and nutritional quality of browse available to deer is determined by many factors, among which are plant species, time of year, soil and soil moisture, age of plants and amount of light reaching the vegetation. Many of these factors can be manipulated by the manager to increase forage quality and quantity. Strategies aimed at increasing browse also may serve to increase availability of other foods such as weeds, fruits and hard mast (acorns and nuts). In general, at least one-third of the deer's home range should satisfy browse needs.

Browse and Natural Succession

The actual amount of food available on any given acre of ground, as I noted earlier, can vary in response to many factors. Yields can be as low as a few pounds per acre or as high as several thousand pounds per acre. No other factor can influence forage yield as greatly as the process of **natural succession**. Succession has been defined by many authors using several interpretations. **I define succession as the stepwise, unidirectional process in which one ecological community prepares the way for and is replaced by another.** What this definition means is that succession, first of all, occurs according to a finite set of predictable steps. In the eastern deciduous forest, for example, the destruction of an old growth forest sets into motion a more or less predictable sequence of events, in which invading **pioneer species** (weeds and grasses) give way to more permanent woody species. At each step in this process, a community of plants and animals prepares the way for the next.

Suppose a forest is completely destroyed by a tornado. This is not uncommon from a historical standpoint. It has happened countless times over the millennia. What is left after such a catastrophic event are twisted, torn trees and bare ground. Invading pioneer species, either highly mobile or lying dormant in the soil, quickly take advantage of the rich growing conditions provided by the disturbance. Both nutrients and sunlight are no longer limiting to the smaller, less competitive weed species. But, although less competitive, these species are very hardy. The early pioneers who settled this country were extremely hardy individuals. Men such as Daniel Boone, Jim Bridger and Davy Crockett are synonymous with toughness and resiliency. But, alas, the early pioneers could not cope with city life and the competition brought on by increasing urbanization. Although their fate was predetermined early on in our country's history, these early pioneers served a vital function. They paved the way for the ultimate taming of the wilderness. So it is with natural succession. Destruction of the forest certainly makes

nutrients available, but the site becomes a very inhospitable place to live. Soil temperatures on bare ground often are excessive, well above the upper limit of many plant species. Since the invading pioneers can handle these extremes, their presence significantly improves the site. For example, shading from weeds and grasses protects the tender shoots of woody plants, giving them time to become established. But, what do the pioneers get in return for this service? The same thanks afforded the early American pioneers by their more urbanized cousins! By paving the way for their successors, the pioneers destroyed their world. Forest and brushland succession proceeds in similar manner. Weeds prepare the way for grasses, grasses pave the way for short-lived trees and shrubs, and these give way to the more efficient **climax species**.

A key-word is **unidirectional**, meaning that succession proceeds in only one direction. I often have likened succession to a windup car. If you let it go, it will run into a wall. You can pick it up and carry it away from the wall, but each time the result is the same—it runs into the same wall. The only option you have is how far away from the wall you move the car. So it is with succession. A disturbance, depending on its intensity, can set back succession, but the ecological community immediately strives to return to a point called **climax**. Climax may be a mixed hardwood forest or a chaparral shrubland or even a grassland savannah. Climax generally is thought of as a more stable ecosystem, in which nutrients and energy (sunlight) are in short supply and competition for these commodities is intense. An old growth forest has many of the site's nutrients tied up in wood fiber, far above the whitetail's reach. Shade from the dense canopy gives little opportunity for plant growth to develop on the forest floor. Vegetation above "deer height" is of little use to whitetails. What goes on above five feet is of no concern to whitetails, although it certainly affects them.

The whole process from disturbance to climax may take hundreds of years, but the time frame in which whitetail populations thrive is quite short. This is not to say that deer disappear from old growth forests, rather the ability of later successional stages to support deer is diminished. Depending on geographic location and rainfall, this may be as short as five to seven years. Indeed, whitetail population biology is geared to rapid growth during this general time period. Whitetails are fully capable of saturating their habitat in seven years! Given these facts, any

---

Facing Page. After a disturbance, the forest undergoes a predictable, natural succession which progresses from disturbed site to weed-grass (A), brush (B), young timber (C), intermediate age timber (D) mature forest (E), and climax forest (F). Whitetails occupy all stages of succession, but thrive during the earlier, more productive stages (Robert Skinner).

Disturbances, such as this tornado damage to a mixed conifer-deciduous forest, are commonplace in the deer's world. However, whitetails thrive on disturbances, which release nutrients and rejuvenate the natural ecosystem.

habitat management strategy developed for whitetails necessarily will involve planned disturbances and manipulation of successional processes.

Cover

The common public perception of whitetails is that they are shy and timid creatures, and in many ways this is true. Deer seldom venture far from protective cover during daylight hours. The importance of cover is dependent on several factors, including hunting pressure, non-human predators and climate.

Much of my research revolved around the reactions of deer to hunting. Although whitetails have had some 2.5 million years to adapt to predators, man has an interesting impact on the species. Throughout much of the range, whitetails venture out into openings and fields only under the protective cover of darkness. Until then, they prefer to remain hidden within the protection afforded by early successional communities. Since these communities are dominated by brush, they afford both food and protective cover.

In the more northern climates, dense stands of conifers, some even as old growth forest, provide a life-saving protective cover for deer. The famous deer yards of Wisconsin and Michigan are nothing more than protective windbreaks against the extreme winter conditions common to these regions. Further south, whitetails inhabiting the brush country of South Texas and Mexico must have the protective shade mercifully provided by mesquite and huisache. Therefore, cover is an important component of whitetail habitat. At least 30 percent of the deer's home range should provide adequate escape cover.

Water

There is some debate over the significance of water to whitetails. Most researchers feel that, on the average, a deer requires about a half gallon of water each day. This water is important to the digestive process. In some areas, water sources such as ponds and streams are in high demand, while in others free-standing water is of little consideration. The problem is that water may be available in many forms. Free-standing water is highly attractive in the arid portions of the range. To the more mesic east, deer derive much of their daily water requirement from succulent vegetation. Yet, even in the wetter areas a droughty year will significantly increase the importance of ground water.

Range managers long ago learned that presence of readily available and evenly spaced water sources can improve utilization efficiency of range forage. It is my experience that a similar provision for whitetails, even in the wetter climates, also can improve forage utilization. Unfortunately, agencies such as the Agricultural Stabilization and Conservation Service seldom afford pond construction assistance to landowners wishing to improve forage utilization by wild animals.

It generally is thought that deer need a reliable source of water within a mile of their center of activity. However, **I prefer to make water available within a half mile of any point on the property.**

ARRANGEMENT OF COMPONENTS

Before we proceed, it is important to discuss some of the structural and arrangement aspects of deer habitat. Possibly the two most important concepts in deer habitat management are **edge** and **interspersion**. To understand these two concepts is to understand the day-to-day needs of whitetails.

Edge

The edge concept has been bandied about by wildlife biologists ever since Aldo Leopold, the father of Wildlife

Management, made this statement:

> "Game is a phenomenon of edges. It occurs where the types of food and cover which it needs come together, i.e., where their edges meet. Every grouse hunter knows this when he selects the edge of a woods, with its grape tangles, hawbushes, and little grassy bays, as the likely place to look for birds. The quail hunter follows the common edge between the brushy draw and the weedy corn, the snipe hunter the edge between the marsh and the pasture, the deer hunter the edge between the oaks of the south slope and the pine thicket of the north slope, the rabbit hunter the grassy edge of the thicket."..A. Leopold.

Although recently coming under criticism by practitioners of wildlife management, the fact remains that some **game animals, whitetails included, depend heavily upon edge for their existence.** Studies on other deer species, including mule deer, sambar, elk and moose, all have shown similar demand for edges. But, what is an edge, and are there different types of edges?

An edge is a point where two different habitat types meet. The zone created where a forest meets a pasture certainly qualifies to be an edge. However, there are three different types of edges to be considered. First, in many of the undisturbed forests and brushlands there occur **inherent edges.** These represent the natural transition between different habitat types. For example, the transition from an upland forest community to a bottomland community represents an inherent edge. The edge would be there, whether man was present or not. Other examples include the interface between forest and lake or stream, natural elevational changes and areas where soil types change dramatically.

The second type of edge is called an **induced edge.** This edge type usually occurs after the actions of man have changed the forest. A clearcut adjacent to an uncut forest is an excellent ex-

An inherent edge is one that occurs naturally. The interface between a bottomland and an upland pine forest represents such an edge.

Robert Skinner

An induced edge occurs as a result of man's activities, either by accident or by design. The wildlife manager often uses induced edges in game management.

The soft edge is a form of induced edge, with plantings to "soften" the abrupt change from one habitat type to another. This edge type is highly preferred by whitetails.

ample of an induced edge. These also are the types of edges many wildlife managers seek to increase game species. Many primitive peoples also manipulated the forest to produce induced edges for game production.

A special type of edge is the **soft edge**. This edge type represents an overlap between two completely different habitat types. It is true that an edge exists where an upland and a bottomland community are juxtaposed, but there seldom is a point along the interface where one can say: "This is the edge." Rather, upland species tend to slowly fade out, while bottomland species slowly fade in. The result is a highly diversified community, sharing the attributes of both communities as well as a few characteristics unique to this type of edge. Managers attempt to create soft edges by using shrub plantings between forest and fields.

I feel that whitetails are indeed an edge species, and the amount of edge present greatly affects both the density

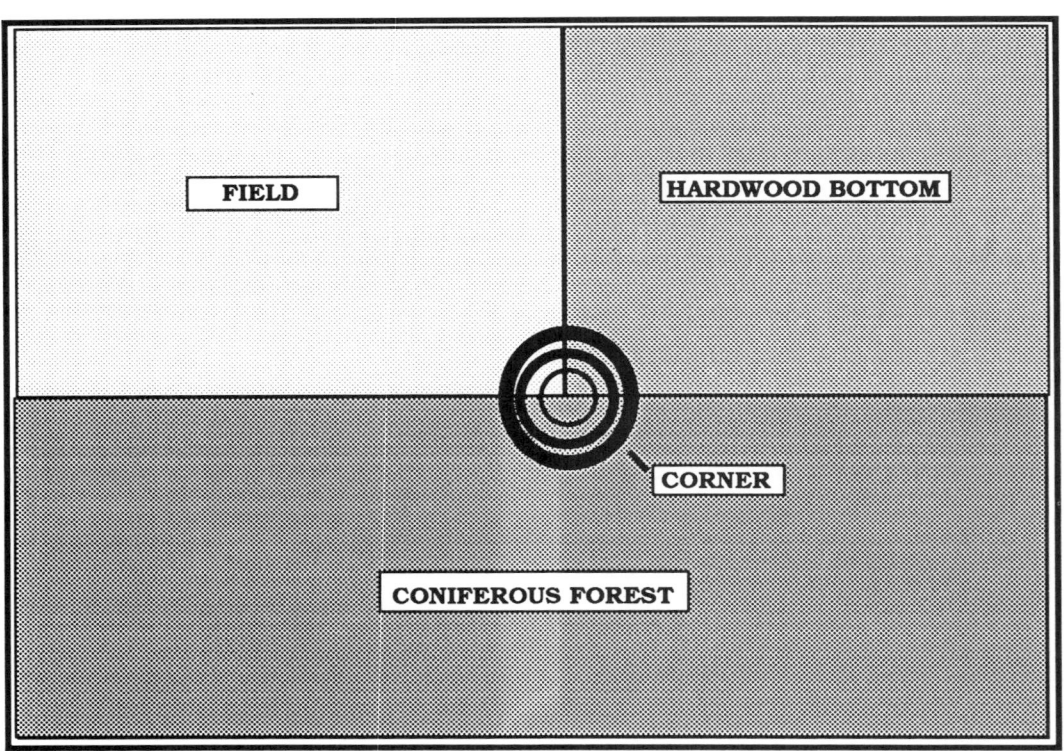

Corners or coverts occur where three or more habitat types meet. The corner probably is the best place to hunt, as it has the highest probability of use.

and quality of deer on a particular piece of property. Any intensive management program for whitetails must consider the amount and location of edges. I am firmly convinced of this fact. But, in order to arrive at an estimate of how much edge is needed, we must examine two additional concepts.

Interspersion

An equally important concept to consider is interspersion, or how the habitat types are arranged on the landscape. More and more, ecologists are coming to think of habitat as a landscape. Just as with humans, deer and other animals have preferred landscapes or "yards." Just as you would organize your yard for maximum visual impact and comfort, a deer tends to select habitat mixes that optimize its daily needs. The trick, of course, lies in determining how the various components of deer habitat are to be arranged. The implications of interspersion will be discussed later.

Corners or Coverts

A companion concept to interspersion is that of corners or coverts. The two terms often are used interchangeably, but I prefer to use the name "corner." A **corner** is a point on the landscape where three or more habitat types meet. An excellent example would be the point of intersection of a mature forest, a clearcut and a young pine plantation. **Although I will discuss the use of corners in hunting deer later in the book, I will say here that the number one place to harvest a deer is at a corner.** This really is not surprising. Humans also conform to the corner concept. Any place that satisfies the most of your daily requirements will receive the greatest number of visits. Think about your work place. Where would you go to intersect the most people?

Openings

There is a wealth of data suggesting that openings are important habitat components. Openings provide high quality forbs and cool season grasses, as well as edges. The primary question regarding these features revolves around the optimum size, distribution and shape. Openings greater than five acres in size probably are less attractive. Of course, this is dependent on the shape involved. A long, narrow open-

Robert Skinner

Permanent openings, such as power or pipeline rights-of-way, are important habitat features. About 10% of the area should be maintained in openings.

ing such as a pipeline or powerline right-of-way is heavily used, no matter the total acreage involved. I prefer to limit permanent openings, other than rights-of-way, to the five acre limit.

Openings should be constructed so that they are rectangular or irregular in shape. The maximum distance across any opening should not exceed 100 yards. Deer are reluctant to venture much beyond this distance in daylight hours, reducing the effectiveness of the opening.

Ten percent of the management area should be maintained in permanent openings. I prefer to mow openings annually (usually during late summer), and top-dress with a balanced fertilizer in early spring and ammonium nitrate in mid-summer. The role of fertilization will be discussed below.

STANDARD HABITAT MANAGEMENT PRACTICES

I already have discussed the importance of nutrition to whitetails in the previous chapter. I also presented some information on the use of supplemental food plots, supplemental feeds and minerals in augmenting the quality and quantity of native deer foods. But, supplementation does not a deer management program make! In order to properly manage deer habitat, it is necessary to manipulate the successional forces that control the basic habitat elements. As I noted earlier, deer are creatures that thrive on disturbance. Hence, planned disturbances are an important part of deer habitat management. Among these disturbance strategies are: 1) fire, 2) mechanical disturbances, and 3) herbicides.

Fire

There are two basic types of fires; wild and prescribed. Wild fires are those that occur either through man's carelessness or from naturally occurring phenomena such as lightning. Recently, I helped battle a wild fire on the Nail Ranch in West Texas that apparently was ignited by a piece of quartz in the sun. No one to date has developed a workable system to accurately predict or plan wild fires, hence we will leave these out of our management program. The use of prescribed fire, on the other hand, is one of the least expensive, yet effective management tools available to the wildlife manager. Considering the alternatives (i.e., herbicides and/or mechanical treatment) fire is very cost-effective. Average per acre costs of $5 or less are typical. Hence, a well-planned, coordinated burning program is critical to producing quality wildlife, wildlife habitat and quality hunting experiences. However, the phrase **well-planned** is important.

Too often forest managers misapply

Prescribed fire probably is the single-most efficient and cost-effective means of managing deer forage.

fire to the forest. Concerned solely with a single product (i.e., timber) managers often burn at too frequent intervals or at the wrong time of the year. Likewise, range managers recently have rediscovered fire as a management tool, but tend to use it to produce plant communities more suited to grazers than browsers.

With one exception, all prescribed burns should be conducted during the late winter or early spring in order to minimize impact on vegetative communities. Summer burns are devastating to wildlife plants, as well as to wildlife itself. Summer burns should only be employed when a dramatic response (e.g., removal of high shrub species) is desired. The single exception is the brush country of South Texas and Mexico. These areas most commonly are over-run with invading woody species, and must be burned in late summer. Naturally occurring fires apparently took place during summer. Woody plants such as mesquite are difficult to kill back using winter fires. However, extreme care must be taken in using summer fires, as such burns can become quite dangerous. Care also must be taken in spring burning not to carry burns into the nesting season of turkeys or other ground nesting birds. No burn should be conducted after spring green-up.

In most cases, backfires are preferable to head fires, since the latter will serve to kill more beneficial species. A **backfire** is one that is ignited so that it backs into the predominant wind direction, thereby producing a slower, cooler burn. A **headfire**, on the other hand, is ignited in such a manner as to allow the wind to carry the fire at a fast pace. Such fires burn many times faster and hotter than a back fire, but may actually do less killing than a backfire due to a short exposure to intense heat. Often, the manager uses a hybrid version of these two techniques called a **strip head fire.** In this method, the manager ignites a backfire, then sets several succeeding headfires a short distance away from the backfire. This gives the benefits of a headfire, without the potential hazards inherent to this technique.

The interval required between burns is greatly dependent on the climate and soils. Dryer climates are characterized by much slower succession rates; hence, it is unnecessary to burn at frequent intervals. Likewise, the wetter portions of the whitetail's range often have rapid rates of succession, requiring a more frequent burn. In some areas of the South, dry sandy soils respond poorly to fire, favoring herbaceous species. Foresters use a measure of a soil's ability to grow trees called **site index**. In general, it is a prediction of the expected height of a tree planted today at some time in the future. A site index of 50 for loblolly pine (base age 50 years), means that you can expect a pine seedling planted today to be 50 feet tall in 50 years. A nearby site may have a site index of 80, making it 60% more productive. Site index is primarily determined by the amount of available soil moisture. The rule-of-thumb is that bottomland, well drained soils have higher site indexes than do dry upland soils. The general sequence of

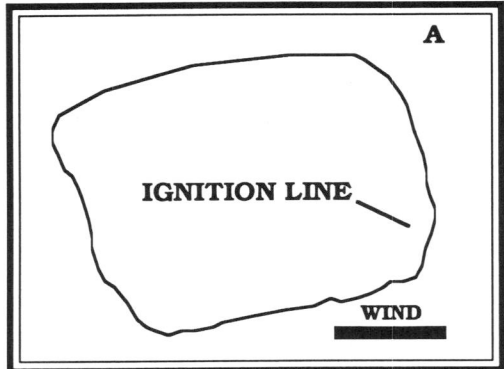
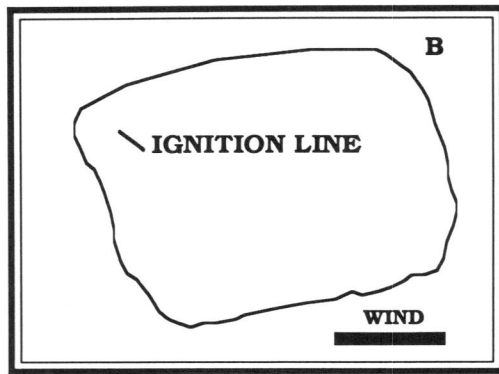
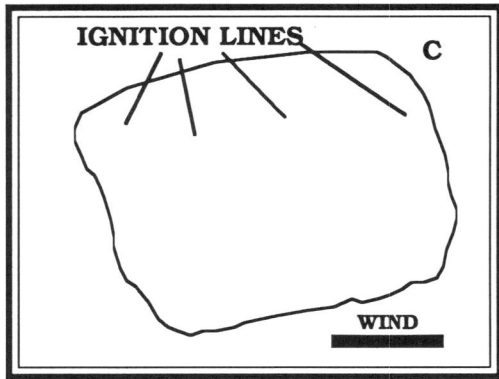

A backfire (A) is one that is ignited so that it backs into the predominant wind direction. A headfire (B), on the other hand, is ignited in such a manner as to allow the wind to carry the fire at a fast pace. A strip head fire (C) is a blend of the two methods, taking advantage of the benefits of both methods.

productive soils is loam, clay and sand, with intermediate types falling between these general types.

If a soil type has a high site index for trees, it also has a high site index for forage production. The site index 50 soil above would naturally produce less forage annually than the site index 80 soil. Consequently, soils with higher forage production potentials must be burned more frequently than those with less potential. Since all of this may be confusing, I suggest that you use these two basic rules:

1. **never burn at an interval less than every other year.**
2. **when in doubt, burn when the woody vegetation is between four and six feet in height.**

No prescribed burn should ever be conducted without the use of fire breaks for control. A **firebreak** is a cleared area completely around the area to be burned. The width of a firebreak is variable, but normally is about 12 feet. I use a bulldozer to clear fire lanes, followed by a tractor outfitted with a disc. **Firebreaks should never be constructed across the contour or**

Habitat and Home Range

across drainages! This will promote soil erosion, which degrades the site and produces environmental problems. Bottomland types should not be burned anyway.

Permanent firebreaks are useful to your supplemental feeding program. I recommend planting firebreaks to a cool season mixture annually. This provides both forage and fire control while intersecting a maximum number of deer home ranges. Rather than disturb firebreaks each year, I recommend that they be mowed in fall, top seeded

Robert Skinner

Firebreaks are easily constructed using a small bulldozer. They should be established as permanent management features and planted to cool season forage species.

Immediately after a fire, woody plants produce highly nutritious sprouts which are relished by whitetails.

with cool season plants, and fertilized appropriately. On the average, a 12 feet wide, one mile long firebreak contains only 1.5 acres, so cost is not prohibitive.

Numerous studies have shown that regular prescribed burns not only keep vegetation in the reach of deer, but also release nutrients and enhances nutrient cycling. Basal sprouting of shrubs following a fire produces highly nutritious and succulent shoots. Even less palatable species are relished by deer during the resprouting period following a burn.

The location of burns is also an important consideration. It is a good idea not to burn an adjacent stand in less than two years. If adjacent stands are burned at the same time, it often limits interspersion and diversity. Burns should be limited only to upland plant communities. Bottomland species are not normally resistant to fire.

Site Preparation and Intermediate Treatments

Often, due to age of the stand, stand density or past management practices (viz., over-grazing, fire protection, etc.), no amount of burning is going to alter the current habitat structure. Also, in many portions of the range, timber management is an important land-use. Mechanical disturbances resulting from companion land-uses can be turned to the manager's advantage; provided, of course, that they are well-planned. If we were to manage solely for whitetails, I would favor techniques that stimulate a mix of browse and weeds. Only fire and chopping offer this option, although herbicides can be used creatively to enhance whitetail forage. Techniques which set back succession to the weedy stages probably should not be used.

Once a timber stand or brush community has been established, there almost always develops a need for **intermediate treatments**, which are treatments aimed at maintaining forage or cover production as succession proceeds. Among these are prescribed burns, thinnings and herbicidal treat-

These photographs illustrate response of a forested habitat to prescribed fire: (A) first year, (B) second year, and (C) third year.

Robert Skinner
Clearing of residual vegetation using a bulldozer is a common forest and range management practice which can benefit whitetails. Succession is set back, producing abundant woody and herbaceous forage.

ment.

Prescribed burns, as I noted above, probably offer the most cost-effective means of maintaining quality deer habitat. However, public sentiment against burning, albeit quite natural, may eventually lead to severe restrictions. Problems with smoke management near metropolitan areas and highways can seriously confound management goals. Also, burning is beneficial only if there is adequate sunlight reaching the ground level, hence burns often must be combined with other treatments for maximum effectiveness.

Thinning of timber to improve wood production has been an accepted management practice for many years. However, thinnings can also increase the amount and quality of forage. The amount of overstory shading influences understory plant growth. **Removal of some of the overstory will allow sunlight to penetrate the canopy.** The question arises as to how much of the overstory must be removed? Forest wildlife biologists have concluded that basal area must be maintained at around 70-80 ft^2 per acre in order to optimize timber and forage. **Basal area** is a forestry term representing a measure of the total area within an acre covered by the trunks of trees. For a basal area of 70, this means that, out of some 43,560 ft^2 in an acre, 70 ft^2 of this area is covered by tree trunks. This may sound like a very small proportion, but trunks are connected to much larger crowns which in turn shade the ground. To put this into perspective, many intensively managed timber stands have basal areas of 150 ft^2 or more! At this density, there virtually is no forage in the understory!

Species composition of the stand is another important factor. There is concern among laymen for hardwoods in mixed stands. However, research has shown that hardwoods can be both good and bad. Because of their canopy structure, hardwood species intercept more light than a pine or a fir. In two stands with the same basal area, one with hardwood and the other with pine, the hardwood stand would produce less forage than the pine. In upland areas, managers routinely remove some of the non-mast producing hardwoods to increase forage production. Removal is either by harvesting or by herbicide injection.

The most commonly used thinning methods include row thinning (plantations) and D+ thinnings (natural stands). Row thinnings are used principally in plantations, where the trees are planted in easily manipulated rows. In these cases, the standard is to thin every third row, beginning at a point where tree growth slows due to crowding. This varies with geographic area, ranging from 15-18 years in the South to 25-30 years in the far North. Thinnings are repeated every few years to encourage tree growth and maintain forage production until time of harvest (=**rotation age**).

D+ thinnings are used in natural stands, where there are no rows on which to base a thinning interval. The most frequently used method is the D+8. In this method, the diameter of the average tree at breast height (4.5 ft.) is calculated. Then, this value is added to 8 to produce an average distance between trees after the thinning. For example, if the average diameter is 10 in., the manager will mark the trees so that there is 18 feet (10+8) between trees. More liberal thinnings are D+10 and D+12.

In brushy habitats, such as South Texas, we certainly are not concerned with timber production; yet, the impact of a closed canopy is still an important consideration. Roller-chopping or herbiciding of narrow strips through the brush will greatly reduce plant density, and increase forage production and quality.

Robert Skinner

Thinning of stands can greatly enhance forage production. Here a young pine stand is presented before (above) and two years after (below) a row thinning. Note the dramatic difference in forage availability.

Robert Skinner

Mast Production and Wildlife Stand Improvement

Hunters and sportsmen erroneously think that just because a stand is composed of hardwood species that it is good for wildlife. This may or may not be the case. Some hardwood species provide excellent food and cover for many species, while others tend to dominate a stand and be less than optimum wildlife species.

Even if a stand is composed of species, all of which are beneficial to whitetails, the distribution of individuals among species may promote a situation in which mast (fruits of woody plants) production is sporadic or unreliable. Factors which determine the consistency of mast production from year to year are:
1) **the diversity of mast producing species;**
2) **the age of the stand;**
3) **the density of trees;**
4) **site fertility and index; and,**
5) **recent fruiting habits.**

Diversity of species and how the individuals are distributed among species (evenness) probably are the most important factors to producing a reliable mast crop. For this reason, each hardwood stand should be sampled to determine the species composition. Different species have varying fruiting habits. Red oaks traditionally fruit one year after setting fruit, while white oaks flower and fruit in the same year. For this reason, white oaks tend to respond to favorable conditions immediately, while red oaks delay response until the second year. An even distribution of red and white oaks and other mast producers will guarantee adequate fruit production year after year.

Most mast producing species do not come into production until age 25, with maximum production at approximately 60-75 years. Older trees tend to decline in fruit production. Hence, very young or very old stands do not produce as well as intermediate age stands. It is well-documented that a high production of mast during one year will seldom be followed by another bumper crop the next. Trees just lack the vigor necessary to produce large mast crops in two consecutive years.

Crown diameter can greatly influence the amount of hard mast produced. Crowded stands usually have small crowns and reduced acorn production. Manipulation of crown diameter through **Wildlife Stand Improvement (WSI)** can significantly increase mast production. Wildlife stand improvement is a modification of the timber stand improvement used by timber managers. Normally, silviculturalists use herbicides to remove competing hardwoods in conifer stands. This may be accomplished either by direct injection or spot treatment with herbicides. In wildlife stand improvement, the goal is not to remove competing hardwood vegetation, but rather to adjust the distribution of individual trees, as well as manipulate species abundance and evenness. Proper treatment not only will increase species diversity, but also will allow individual trees to expand crown diameter. Crown diameter is important in mast production.

Acceptable herbicides include 2,4-D, Tordon and Velpar. Basal injection with either 2,4-D or Tordon can easily remove specific individuals from the stand **without** damaging adjacent trees. Spot treatment with soil active chemicals such as Velpar can accomplish the

Wildlife stand improvement (WSI) is a useful tool in manipulating hardwood stands for maximum mast production. Here is a stand before (above) and five years after (below) selective herbicide treatment. The preferred species have already begun crown expansion, a factor critical to fruit production.

same goal at less cost, provided proper care is taken to avoid killing non-target individuals.

Once species composition and evenness have been adjusted, it may also be desirable to plant additional species to increase the richness. Addition of "food plot" plantings of oaks such as sawtooth or live oak, or soft mast producers such as cultivated apples and pears, can also increase mast production. However, these trees should be planted in small "orchards," fertilized, pruned and maintained similar to a grove of fruit trees. Other plots of soft mast producing species such as red mulberry, hawthorn, crab-apple and autumn olive can enhance production.

Fertilization

Recently, researchers and managers have come to the conclusion that applications of fertilizers to native vegetation can have a significant impact on forage quality and production. This especially is true for phosphorus and nitrogen. Applications of these essential elements, according to soil test, will increase forage concentrations of phosphorus and nitrogen. However, in some areas soils are so acidic or basic that no amount of phosphorus fertilization will improve the availability of this nutrient. This again makes the simple soil test paramount to a proper management. Costing less than $20 in most areas, the soil test is one of the most cost-effective management tools available. Most forages do best at a soil pH range of 6.5 to 7.5. Soil pH can be adjusted using lime (increase pH) or sulfur (decrease pH). Ammonium sulfate is an excellent way to provide nitrogen, as well as reduce soil pH.

I use fertilizers in two ways. First, I

Billy Higginbotham
It is a simple matter to fertilize native forage. Research has shown that this will significantly improve the nutritional value of native plants. These "natural" food plots should be well distributed within the basic management unit.

apply fertilizer to plants along roadsides. This probably is the easiest way to apply nutrients, as it is a simple matter to drive a spreader truck down a road. Second, I make two fertilizer applications to permanent openings as discussed above. When coupled with mowing, this enhances forage quality, while eliminating competition from woody plants.

Now that you are introduced to the basic components of habitat, it is important to determine the proper mix of these components. In order to do so, we must examine the range over which a whitetail can be expected to roam. We already have discussed what makes deer move. Now it is time to learn about normal distances and areas inhabited by deer on a daily and seasonal basis.

THE STREAMSIDE CONNECTION

For many years now, I have been writing about the strong affinity whitetails have for drainages. **After some twenty years of research, I remain convinced that whitetails evolved in association with drainages**. Drainages are attractive for many reasons. First, drainages make excellent landmarks along which to travel. The early American pioneers regularly used rivers and creeks not only for "highways," but also as landmarks for travel. I was amused by the writings of one explorer, who after becoming lost from his party for more than a month, proclaimed: "I have now given up hope of seeing my party again, but it is comforting to realize that I am only 1,500 miles from St. Louis!" The fellow was not being facetious. He knew that rivers could be counted on to lead one safely across the landscape. So it is with deer. Drainage systems provide safe corridors along which deer can move from one habitat type to the next.

I conducted a radio-telemetry study in the Pineywoods of East Texas, in order to determine whether or not deer are attracted to drainages. For each radio-location, the distance to the nearest stream was recorded, and compared to randomly selected points within the deer's established home range. The results were most illuminating.

Deer tended to remain closer to drainages in summer and fall, but ranged further away during spring and winter months. In all cases, there was a significant difference between the actual distance to a drainage and a corresponding random point in the deer's home range. What all this means is that deer are indeed drainage animals. This will be the topic of many of my later discussions on hunting techniques.

In addition, my research and that of others has suggested that deer evolved in association with drainages. In fact, the recent invasion of whitetails into traditional mule deer range has been via drainage systems. Each drainage has one or more doe social groups, who range out from the associated bottomland. A drainage may be as simple as a small, ephemeral upland stream, to a raging river. Bucks tend to use the drainage systems to move from one doe social group to the next. Hence, as I noted earlier, drainages represent both food and travel corridors to whitetails.

Again, a change in terminology is in order. Managers refer to drainages as **Streamside Management Zones (SMZs).** These zones are invaluable to the wildlife manager. It often is necessary to mitigate the negative impacts of intensive forest or range management on the natural community. Intensive agricultural activities should be conducted in the uplands, with SMZs managed for plant and animal diversity. This is true even for the dry brushlands of South Texas and Mexico.

SMZs should be treated as separate management units. The term "management zone" is important. Often, sportsmen and nature enthusiasts feel that no management is the most beneficial approach to wildlife management. Seldom is this the case in modern times. As I noted in the previous section, the hardwood component of SMZs is infrequently perfect in composition or mast production. SMZs can be managed for both timber and mast production, provided careful attention to stand composition and vigor is applied. The number of mast producing species and the evenness of species distribution should be manipulated, using WSI and plantings, to maximize species diversity of important mast species.

I often am asked about the recommended width for SMZs. Although some timber managers designate set widths for these management features, I find it difficult to make such recommendations. I feel that the width of an SMZ should be determined by the drainage itself. A wide, meandering stream necessarily would command a much larger SMZ than a narrow, straight channel. Hence, I establish the boundaries of SMZs along the contour where the upland breaks into the bottomland. This may be only a few yards, or several hundred yards. The width you choose will be determined by other land-uses on the property. In some states, there already are "Best Management Prac-

Habitat and Home Range

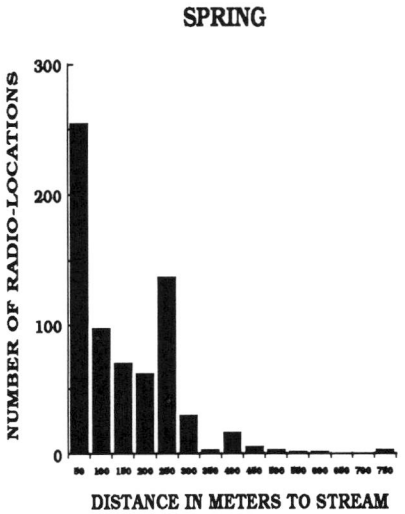

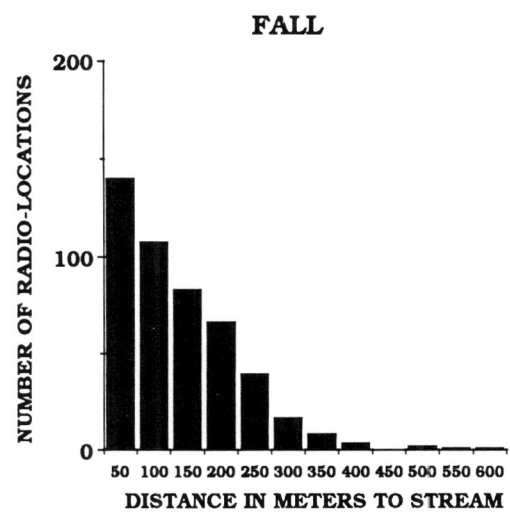

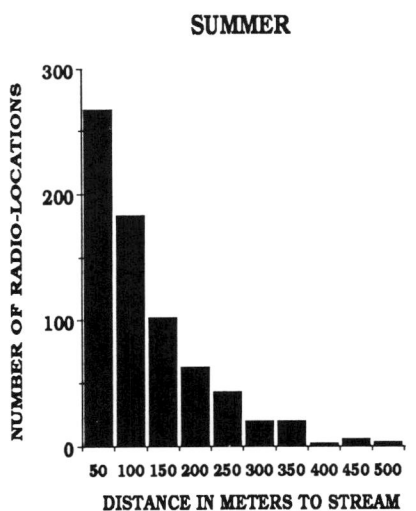

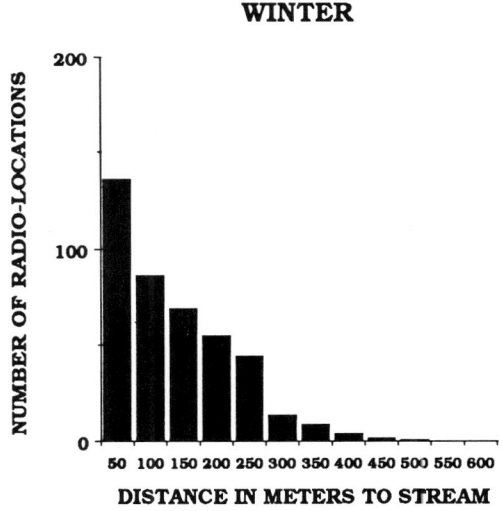

The author's radio-telemetry studies have shown that deer are indeed strongly attracted to streamside areas. Whitetails evolved in association with drainages, and use these habitat features for travel corridors, as well as foraging areas. Presented here are the results of a recent study in which the distance from each radio-location to the nearest stream channel was measured.

Retention of Streamside Management Zones (SMZs), can greatly enhance deer habitat, whether the land-use is timber, range or agriculture.

tices," which by law must be considered. No doubt such legislation will eventually govern all land management activities in all states.

HOME RANGE AS THE BASIC HABITAT UNIT

Home Range Estimates

The concept of home range is one that needs considerable clarification. In order to understand the term, let's take a look at **your** activity pattern. No doubt, you live in an apartment or house, either in the city or country. You rise each morning, dress, eat and travel to your workplace. This trip may be only a few hundred yards, if you are a farmer, or may be many miles for the urban commuter. If we keep track of your movements over a twenty-four hour period, and draw a line around the extreme locations, a pattern would emerge. This well-defined area would be the **core** of your activity range. However, you may take periodic trips outside this core area, possibly to visit family or to take a vacation. Hence, our calculation of your home range over a normal work day may be very much different than one calculated for the entire week. Likewise, as time passes, our estimate of your home range would continue to increase. In these modern times of high mobility, your home range over a lifetime may be the entire earth! Therefore, the calculation of home range size for a deer may be confounded by many factors. Perhaps one of the most confusing factors is how we calculate home range.

In our example, we just connected all of the extreme points and measured the area encompassed by the perimeter. Two methods commonly used by wildlife biologists to calculate home range are referred to as the **convex polygon and concave polygon methods**, terms derived from the appearance of the resulting figures. These are the simplest methods for calculating home range, and we see them most often in the scientific literature. However, accuracy is closely tied to our ability to catch the animal moving at the periphery of its range, and it is susceptible to being influenced by spurious movements. For example, in calculating your home range, what would happen if you suddenly were called out of town? You can see how sampling error and methodology can greatly influence our estimate of home range size! Consequently, researchers have resorted to more sophisticated statistical procedures in obtaining a more reliable estimate of home range size.

The most commonly used statistical techniques are the **bivariate normal methods**, which calculate a confidence limit for home range, resulting either in a circle or an ellipse. The ellipse proba-

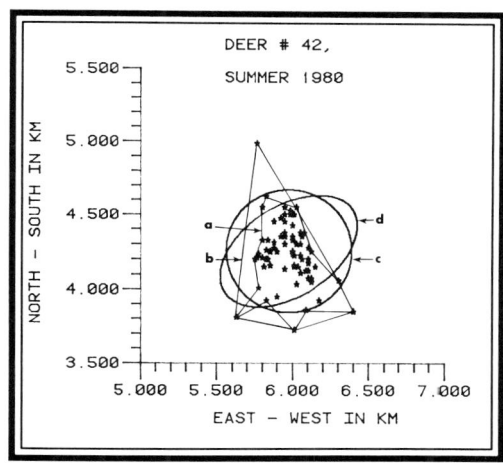

There are many ways to estimate and define the limits of home range. Among these are the concave polygon (a), convex polygon (b), bivariate normal circular (c) and bivariate normal ellipse (d). Obviously the method selected will affect the calculation of home range size, which accounts in part for the disparity in published values.

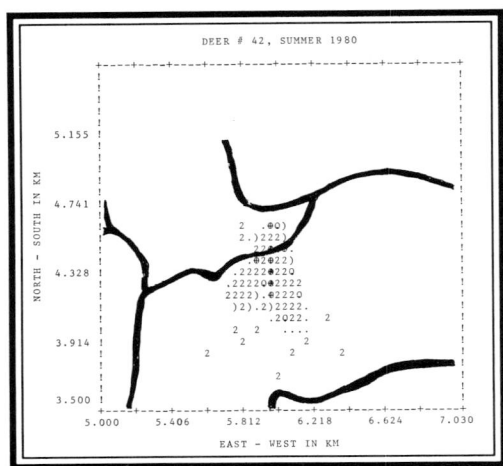

The grid method of home range estimation relies on a system in which a grid is placed over the area, and the number of grid squares visited by a deer summed to give an estimate. This method allows for error in the telemetry system, but does not permit probability calculations.

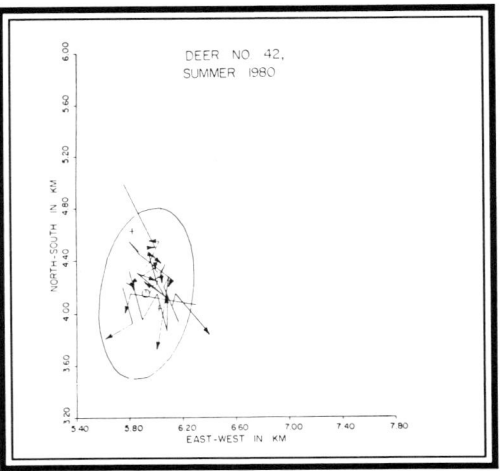

The Multivariate Ornstein-Uhlenbeck Diffusion Process Model is preferred by the author for making home range estimates. Although the name is quite formidable, it is based on the physics of particle movements, and allows valid statistical comparisons.

bly is more appropriate, since home ranges of most species tend to be elliptical or elongated in nature. Usually, elliptical home range estimates tend to be much larger than those calculated using the convex polygon method.

These methods do allow us to establish probability limits to our estimates. Most researchers use the 95% probability level, meaning that we establish a limit that will include 95% of all ex-

pected movements of the animal. But, bivariate normal methods present some real problems due to statistical assumptions, most of which are violated by the methodology. For example, one assumption is that each location is independent of and not influenced by a previous location. Obviously, where a deer is now is influenced by where he was an hour ago. Hence, the locations obtained by radio-telemetry or other means are not independent of each other. Clearly, we need a more reliable statistical technique.

The method I have used most in estimating home range size comes by the terrible name, **Multivariate Ornstein-Uhlenbeck Diffusion Process Model**. This is an elliptical procedure that simultaneously takes into account all movements, instead of individual locations. Without going into a great deal of confusing and unnecessary statistical discussion, the model looks at the direction a deer moves, and the varying speed at which it moves, in order to establish home range probabilities. The method was developed from the physics of atom movement. If you shoot a bullet into space, it will travel in a set direction, and initially at a set velocity. However, as the bullet gets further and further from the muzzle, its velocity begins to slow. If we fire hundreds of bullets from the same gun, we can develop a pretty good statistical model predicting how far we can expect the average shot to travel. So it is with monitoring a deer's movements. There is a core area from which a deer tends to range, and often a preferred direction. As a deer moves further and further from its familiar core area, confidence begins to wane. It is moving in unfamiliar territory. The tendency is for the deer to be reluctant to travel far from its core area. If we examine many of these trips, we not only can identify the core area, but we can place confidence limits on the normal home range.

Some researchers have thrown all of these methods out the window and opted for a more simplified approach. For example, we can impose a gridwork of squares on an area and just record which grid square is currently occupied by the deer in question. This method is called the **grid-mapping method**. The size of each square is determined by the reliability and precision of our equipment, which often is most poor. We seldom know exactly where a radio-collared animal is located, as most telemetry systems have two or more degrees of error. At a mile, this may result in several hundred yards of potential error! Home range is estimated using the grid mapping method by summing the number of grid squares with locations and multiplying by the size of a square. Whatever home range estimate method we choose, there is yet another consideration.

The next source of variation in home range estimates lies in the period over which the calculation is made. There is a possible daily home range calculation, as well as a weekly, monthly, seasonal, annual and lifetime home range. As with our example, the common trend is for these estimates to increase from daily to lifetime. Hence, before you accept a researcher's estimate of home range size, you should ask: By what method was the estimate derived and over what time period does it cover? Since multiple methodologies and time intervals have been reported in the literature, it is no wonder that there is confusion as to what is the normal home range of whitetails. But, then there is yet another confounding factor— habitat quality.

My research here in East Texas has

indicated that home range size is greatly influenced by the quality of the habitat. In mixed pine-hardwood forests, home range sizes of both does and bucks declined as the habitat became more "patchy." This is an important term, and much of my habitat management recommendations are based on it. Most habitats are not homogeneous, they are broken up into various sized patches, representing different habitat types and stages of succession. Very few animal species depend on a single habitat type; most use a combination of types. Theoretically, the more complex or patchy the habitat, the better it is for that particular species. For example, bobwhites need herbaceous vegetation, escape cover, and bare ground for dusting and drying off. Without one of these components, the ability of the habitat to support quail diminishes. So, the quail manager strives to maximize the interspersion of habitat types in an optimum mix. The trick lies in determining the optimum mix, and so it is with whitetails.

Home Range Size

The literature is full of estimates for the home range size of whitetails. These estimates range from about 100 acres to several thousand acres. The above discussion on the sources of variation in home range size estimates should explain some of the variation. Although published accounts are quite confusing, we can make some generalizations.

In almost every study to date, annual home range size is larger for bucks than for does, often twice as large. For example, my twenty years of radio-tracking whitetails here in East Texas has suggested an average mature buck home range of 1,258 acres, 443 acres for adult does and only 257 acres for fawns of both sexes. Published reports range from 365 acres to more than 5,000 acres. Since many of these studies used varying methodologies, it is virtually impossible to make comparisons.

On a seasonal and age related basis, we again can make some generalizations. For the most part, home range size tends to maximize for bucks during the fall breeding season, while does have larger home ranges in winter,

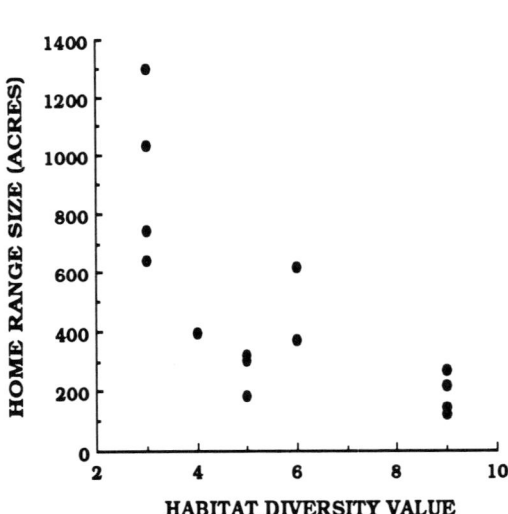

Home range size is a function of habitat diversity. The author has found that the optimum habitat patch size for whitetails is approximately 20-25 acres.

Habitat and Home Range

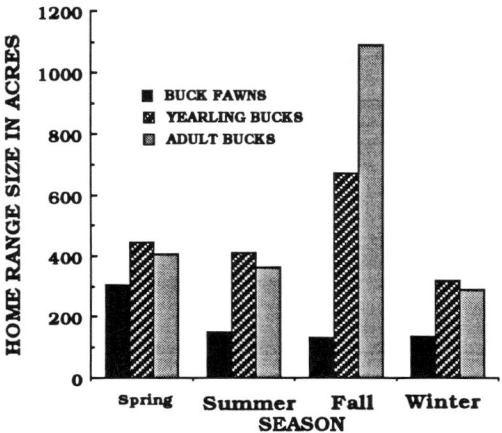

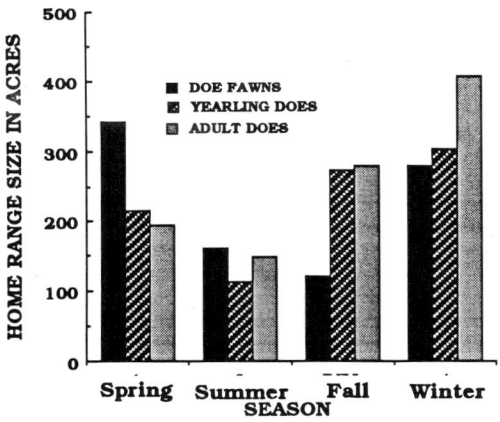

Home ranges vary with sex, age and season. Buck and doe home range trends are quite different, especially for adults. Bucks exhibit the largest home range during the fall rut, while maximum home range for does is in winter, when food is less available.

presumably when food supplies are scarce. In all cases, the smallest home ranges occur in spring and summer, when growing conditions and food supplies are optimum.

Home ranges tend to increase with age for both bucks and does. As with humans, animals become more confident about making exploratory trips as they gain experience. Bucks, in particular, often make trips outside their home ranges for the purpose of exploring new territory. Since deer are reluctant to leave their established home range, these trips are entirely necessary to home range development. Maximum home range size appears to be achieved by four to five years of age, although disturbances may cause shifts in home range size and location.

The Basic Home Range

The most important question in habitat management centers around the minimum acreage necessary to effectively manage whitetails. In order to answer this question, two different concepts must be considered. First, there is the question of the minimum home range size. I already have noted that home range estimates vary with methodology, sex, age and geography. However, in spite of the confusion, I can say with confidence that I never have observed a home range smaller than 125 acres. This appears to be the minimum home range size of whitetails. Consequently, we can build a habitat management program on this basic home range size. Since most land measurements are based on Anglo-Saxon standards, it might be easier to increase the minimum unit size to 160 acres. This really is arbitrary on my part, but I find it useful. Management recommendations are based on this management unit size.

Second, it is important to determine the minimum acreage necessary to control the majority of the bucks on the property. I recently conducted some simulations, using an average home range size of 1,500 acres for bucks, in order to estimate the area required to maintain control over a maximum number of bucks. To my surprise, the results suggested that at least 10,000 acres are needed to effectively manage the buck segment of the population! However, this is not to say that you cannot impact the herd on a smaller acreage, only that this size tract is needed if total control is desired. **The land area required to manage deer is dictated as much by your management objectives as by the deer themselves**. I have effectively managed deer on tracts as small as 500 acres. In fact, it is possible to make even a 100 acre tract quite attractive to deer.

APPLICATION OF HABITAT MANAGEMENT PRINCIPLES

Considering the vast array of management options, one easily can become confused about which strategies are appropriate for a specific parcel of land. Although wildlife management should be considered more an art than a science, I can present you with some generalizations that apply in most situations.

I already have noted that, under an intensive management program, the basic management unit size is the quarter section or 160 acres. Within this area, every life requisite of whitetails should be made available. I attempted to give some guidelines for each habitat component, in regard to the proportion of land area required for each. Now, let's put each of these into the overall habitat management picture.

In the previous chapter, I suggested that 1 to 5% of the area be maintained as food plots, both warm and cool season. The actual percentage you select will depend on the intensity of management and competing land-uses. Obviously, a forest that is managed primarily for timber production will require more food plot area than a less intensively managed forest. In general, one acre of food plot will produce forage equal to 50-100 acres of native woods. For purposes of this discussion, we will set aside two percent of the area in food plots. Permanent openings will take up an additional 10% of the total area, bringing our dedicated acreage to 12%.

Cover is an important habitat element, especially in the northern portions of the range. At least 30% of the management unit should be managed for cover requirements. The specific management strategy will be determined by the need for cover. If screening cover is needed, early successional stages can be maintained which supply both cover and food. If, on the other hand, protection from extreme cold and snow is desired, older stands of conifers should be managed for maximum insulation. In hardwood forests, dense stands of young saplings will provide protection, but it is more desirable to make plantings of conifers for this purpose. Most state forestry agencies offer a variety of conifer species for this very purpose. Pines, firs, spruces and cedars are excellent choices.

Our total acreage at this point accounts for 42% of the land base. The remainder should be dedicated to food production. This may entail timber or range management strategies that optimize forage and fiber, or the designation and management of mast production areas such as SMZs. If forage is the objective, care must be taken to provide a sustained yield of forage within reach of deer. Well-planned clearcuts or selection cuts can easily satisfy this need. Such cuttings should be limited to less than 25 acres, and no two contiguous stands treated in less than 7 years. Harvest and site preparation areas should be limited to 25 acres or less. Prescribed burns should be conducted on a frequency that permits maximum forage production, without allowing the vegetation to exceed deer foraging height. Normal burn intervals range from 3 to 7 years, depending on site index and growing conditions.

Hardwood management areas should be manipulated to provide maximum mast production. These activities include: 1) wildlife stand improvement, 2) manipulation of species diversity and evenness, and 3) stand vigor. Since crown diameter is an important determiner of mast yield, spacings between trees should be manipulated to optimize timber and fruit production. Planting "orchards" of oaks and soft mast producers is a desirable strategy.

Although water requirements have not been established across the range, a year-round ground water source should be provided within each management unit. Ponds should be constructed so as to provide protective cover and a well-screened travel corridor.

All of these activities can only be carried out if there is a detailed plan of activities. One of the many themes of this book is the utility of aerial photographs and maps. Before initiating a management program, you should acquire the necessary resource information in order to make intelligent habitat management decisions. **As far as I am concerned, you cannot have too much information about your land.** I recommend that you acquire soil surveys and infra-red aerial photography of your land. Soil surveys are easily obtained from the local Soil Conservation Service, which often has aerial photography of their district. Additional photographs can be obtained from the U. S. Geological Survey at a nominal cost. From these materials, I prepare a detailed plan of operations, with specific habitat patches and management units designated on a master map of the area. I will discuss the planning process at length in a later Chapter.

SUMMARY

There are three basic components to deer habitat: browse, cover and water. How these requisites are distributed greatly affects the number and quality of deer on the property. Proper mixing of habitat types within a basic management unit of either 640 or 160 acres (extensive vs. intensive managment) will allow maximum production of deer. Browse and herbaceous forage production can be assured by implementing practices that provide an adequate supply of sunlight and moisture to understory vegetation. Timber management practices favorable to deer forage production include: 1) moderate site preparation, 2) intermediate treatments (thinnings and prescribed burns), and 3) wildlife stand improvement. Beneficial range practices include: 1) strip clearing, 2) mowing, 3) well-regulated grazing, and 4) conservative herbicide treatment.

Intensive whitetail habitat management should be based on the minimum management unit size (160 acres). Every life requisite, including food, cover and water should be supplied within each unit. Normally, 2% of the area should be reserved for food plots, 10% for permanent openings and 30% for cover. The remaining landbase can be used to produce forage, primarily browse and mast. Supplemental plantings of fruit producing species also can be developed within this portion of the property or in association with the food plot acreage.

No habitat management program should be implemented **without** a detailed management plan, including a schedule of activities and map of the property. Soil surveys and aerial photographs are important sources of information about the land's available resources.

Chapter 9

Understanding Deer Movements

The fellow at the back of the meeting hall raised his hand. It was one of my deer hunting and management workshops. "Yes," I said confidently. With the chaw of tobacco wedged tightly in his cheek, he began to speak in a long, drawn out manner. "All this biology stuff is well and good," he offered, "but, what makes deer move?" I swallowed hard and tried to compose myself. That is the one question I hate the most in these meetings, primarily because I have to give one of those answers that biologists give all too often. "That depends," was my answer. You can imagine the response I got. That was several years ago. Since then I have concentrated much of my work on answering that very question. The answer probably is still the same, but I now understand deer movements a whole lot better than I did then. In this chapter, I will outline what we **do** know about deer movements and what makes them move, and then critically analyze the concept of solunar tables and how you can take advantage of what we do know about what makes deer move.

There are two basic things that make deer move, intrinsic and extrinsic factors. Intrinsic factors are most easily understood, since they are things within the deer itself that make it move. Extrinsic factors are much more difficult to understand, involving things that happen outside the deer's body. Deer obviously have little control over extrinsic factors.

INTRINSIC FACTORS

As an animal behaviorist, I learned that in most cases the single most important factor influencing daily activity patterns is **light**. Whether it be the nesting season of pheasants or the rutting activity of whitetails, the amount of daylight present each day greatly influences what animals do. The length of each night is carefully measured by the brain (sort of an indirect, but effective way of measuring day length). Daily activity patterns are called **circadian rhythms** by animal scientists. The typical activity patterns of each species are described in various ways and names. White-tailed deer are generally considered as being **crepuscular**, meaning that they are primarily active during low light hours; i.e., early in the morning and late in the afternoon. As I noted in Chapter 5, the eyes of whitetails are well adapted to this lifestyle. They have a highly reflective membrane in the back of their eye (**tapetum lucidum**) which helps them see under low light conditions. Many a poacher has taken advantage of this characteristic over the years. My radio-telemetry studies have shown that this generally is true for deer, but activity patterns change dramatically with season. For example, in the summer deer have the typical activity pattern for crepuscular animals. This is completely logical since the hotter portions of the day, especially in the South, are no time to be out and about in the woods. As the cooler months arrive, however, deer often adopt a more generalized movement pattern, centered around the warmer portions of the day. I have noted on many occasions that the vast majority of record book bucks were taken between mid-morning and early afternoon.

Now that I have described the "typical" built-in behavior pattern of deer, let's explore some of the things that alter the general pattern. There are several physiological factors that influence what a deer does on any one day of the year. Body condition can often over-ride instinct. For example, if a deer is in poor physical condition, resulting from over-population or food shortages, it will often be found moving around at all hours of the day and night. I first noticed this when I began wondering what happened to orphaned fawns after the doe had been killed. I discovered that their activity patterns were often quite different from other non-orphaned fawns and adult deer. They just spent more time feeding. There is one particular pair of fawns that come to mind. On one of my management areas, a hunter harvested a doe that had twin fawns, a buck and a doe. Over the period of the next year, these two fawns were inseparable, and could be found almost any time of the day on a green food plot. They behaved abnormally when compared to the other deer.

Understanding Deer Movements

They were seen throughout the day, and seldom left the green plot. I have seen the same thing happen in the Hill Country of Texas.

Nothing influences deer movements in the fall more than the rut. Over the years, I have come to believe that any amount of movement or any behavior is possible for a rutting whitetail. I have seen bucks that were sedentary throughout the entire year get up and move incredible distances, and at unusual times of the day. Does are also not immune to such strange movements, although I seldom have seen the kind of movements in does reported for bucks. Who knows exactly what determines whether or not a buck is

Many factors, including weather, food supply and hunting pressure, affect the amount of time whitetails spend on or off their feet. However, the variables are forever changing.,

Mike Biggs

going to change its home range and movement pattern? But, I have made a number of observations that may shed some light on the internal factors that motivate bucks to move. Some of these factors I will discuss later.

As serum testosterone begins to increase in the buck's blood, several dramatic changes take place in his overall appearance and mental state. Younger bucks are particularly affected by these changes. As I have noted on many occasions, yearling bucks probably are the most likely to completely change their activity patterns. Work by Dr. Larry Marchinton at Georgia also confirms this fact.

Early in the fall, they begin making exploratory trips, and appear to be wandering aimlessly over the landscape. This wandering may occur earlier in the summer, just after fawning. There probably is no organized movement pattern during this time. Yearling activity patterns may persist into the winter. As for adult bucks, it is interesting to see the high variation in mature buck movements. There seems to be an internal motivation in some bucks to wander. Again, with such a buck it is almost impossible to predict when he will be moving about. Even during the summer months, deer have been shown to make random movements during unusual times of the day.

EXTRINSIC FACTORS

When we speak of extrinsic or external factors that affect deer movements, we move into an area that is considerably less predictable than for intrinsic factors. In order to simplify the discussion, I have classified these factors into four categories: 1) deer-deer interactions, 2) deer-predator (hunter) interactions, 3) weather, and 4) food.

Deer-deer Interactions

Deer usually are highly social animals, especially the does. They like to travel around in loosely organized social groups, ranging in size from two to twenty. The social structure within such a group is often rigid, with a dominant doe (**alpha doe**) and various levels of subordinates. Bucks also have similar social groups, and, except as fawns and yearlings, seldom mix with the doe groups. Social pressures often make deer behave in unusual ways, and are often implicated in strange deer movements. For example, I radio-tracked one doe for several years. She was an alpha doe and pretty well had the run of her social group's territory. Her daughter was the next in line of succession. Suddenly one year, the old doe changed her home range and movement pattern. I feel that her younger, stronger daughter had displaced her from dominant status. Field observations of these deer substantiated that this probably was the case.

Social pressures on bucks often initiate or change movement patterns. Again, yearling bucks are literally looking for a home, and often are socially unacceptable to buck groups. They may roam for some time before joining a buck social group. This explains why I have heard so many stories about pet bucks wandering off and being seen several miles away. In fact, back when

I believed the old literature about deer movements, I would argue vehemently that such movements were old wive's tales. Boy was I wrong. Several years of study have changed my mind.

Often a dominant buck will be displaced by fighting, and start to wander. Each and every member of the buck group is looking to better himself in the social hierarchy. The moment a dominant buck shows any weakness, lesser bucks will not hesitate to attack. I have found mature bucks lying in the woods, just barely alive— their whole bodies punctured by a "mass attack" by lesser bucks.

The rut and previous breeding experience are also greatly implicated in daily activity patterns and gross movements. Some bucks are sedentary and seldom move more than a mile or so, while others may habitually move for greater distances. This often is the case, even though the buck is a dominant individual. Pre-rut scouting trips by bucks of all ages are not uncommon. One particular buck comes to mind, that as far as I am aware, is still very much alive in East Texas. He regularly abandons his typical behavior pattern and home range, even swimming a large river. His rutting territory covers several thousand acres, involving two counties!

Deer-predator Interactions

Deer-predator interactions, especially when hunters are involved, are perhaps the most interesting factors in deer movements. Deer have spent several million years learning to avoid predators. They are marvelously adapted to do just that. Hunters often make the mistake of thinking that deer are just dumb animals, and if you wait long enough, one will blunder by. That is the farthest thing from the truth. Activity patterns of deer are greatly influenced by hunting. The presence of hunters in the woods, especially when they have not been there previously, is a sure cue for deer to alter their normal pattern. One Boone-and-Crockett buck I recently examined from the Davy Crockett National Forest of Texas moved freely about the woods during the day. On the day it was shot, it obviously had been out there among the hundreds of public land hunters, and had gone unnoticed, except for one hunter who did his homework. Under heavy hunting pressure, I have seen deer become totally nocturnal (discussed later in this book), or limit activity to just the mid-day hours. They may not like to be moving around in the bright daylight, but they will do this if it reduces the probability of encountering a human.

Weather

The effect of weather on deer movements is often kicked around in hunting camps and clubs around the country. There are some pretty bizarre theories floating around in such conversations, most of which have never been shown to hold water. For example, ask the average deer hunter what is the best kind of weather for deer hunting, and he will tell you almost without fail that the colder the better. This simply is not so! No deer in its right mind, except maybe a starving animal, would travel

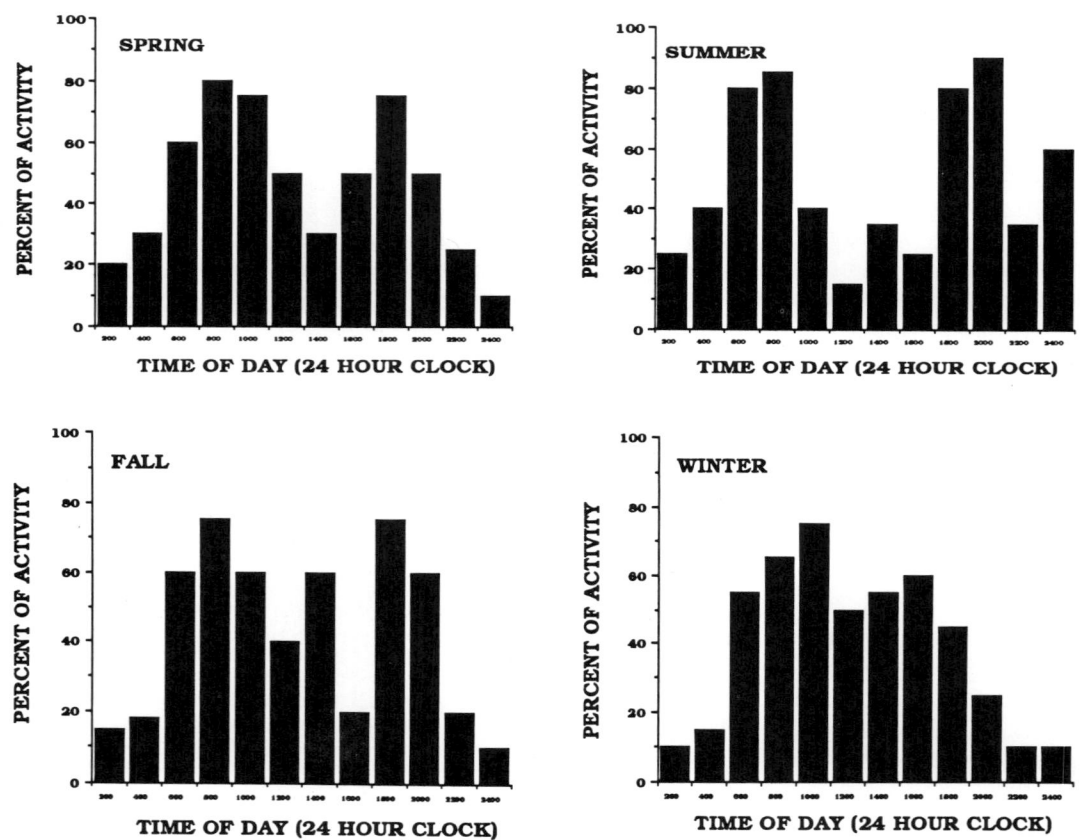

The activity patterns of whitetails change seasonally. Unfortunately, however, hunters first see deer during the summer, when they conform to the typical diurnal pattern.

around in adverse weather conditions, especially in the winter when fat stores are minimal. But, other researchers and myself have found some plausible implications of weather in deer movements. Probably the single most important weather variable is temperature. Whether you are talking about the upper peninsula of Michigan or the South Texas Plains, temperature plays a key role in mediating deer movements. In the northern climates, low air temperatures greatly affect deer activity. It has been found, for example, that distances moved may be shorter, yet actual activity within protective cover may increase with lower temperatures. The presence of snow greatly impedes the movement of deer, especially the heavier bucks. Deer tend to limit movements under deep snow pack conditions to areas already beaten down by yarded deer.

In the South, the name-of-the-game for whitetails is heat. There are times of the year that are quite difficult for deer to handle physiologically. For example, Dr. Jack Inglis of Texas A&M University has pointed out on numerous occasions that shade is everything to South Texas whitetails. I have found this to also be the case in the Pineywoods region. On warmer days, deer prefer overcast conditions. In fact, summer activity often is greatest on such days. Deer move more at moderate temperatures than for either extreme. So, the idea that excessively cold or hot weather conditions will make deer move more is false, and should be discounted. However, let me caution you on one thing. There are subspecies of whitetails, each of which is adapted to its particular geographic area. What may be unbearable to a southern whitetail may be balmy to a northern individual. You have to apply good sense to making decisions about what are "moderate" temperatures.

Deer movements are influenced by relative humidity as well. Several studies have shown that deer are more active on days with low relative humidity. For a generalized model, I have found that deer prefer days with cool to moderate temperatures, little wind, less than fifty percent cloud cover and no more than sixty-seventy percent relative humidity. What I am describing here is a fine fall day! The kind of day that you yourself prefer to move around; after all, you too are an animal.

Windy conditions usually impede deer movements, although some researchers in South Texas recently presented data to the contrary. Since deer rely heavily on their senses of smell and hearing, windy days cause deer to either modify their normal activity pattern, or limit activity to protected areas where wind velocity is not so great. If you ever have watched a deer walking on a windy day, you know exactly what I mean. They literally are as "nervous as a cat," walking gingerly along and looking in all directions. The slightest sound is enough to send them scurrying.

Finally, moon phase seems to be the one factor that hunters trust most. In regard to deer movements, I am probably asked more often about the effect(s) of moon phase than anything else. This is a very difficult question to answer. The position and phase of the moon may have little or no effect on movements one time, and then have a profound effect another. It is certain that deer will use moonlight to feed, especially when hunting pressure becomes excessive. On one of my management areas, the resident caretaker once informed me that we had killed all the deer! The doe harvest I had recommended had been a mistake, and the herd would never recover. I loaded him in a truck and took him to the nearest green food plot. It was about 11:30 p.m. As our headlights spread over the food plot, we could see at least ninety deer feeding. They looked up at us casually and went back to eating. "There are your deer," I said. The issue was dropped from that day on. But, the presence of the moon is not always necessary. One of the biggest bucks I have ever seen ran a doe across the road in front of me on a pitch dark night. It was around 2:00 a.m., and the moon had been down since sunset.

I hope by now that the picture I have been painting tells you that there are **many factors** which influence when and how much deer move. I recently completed some extensive research on factors affecting deer movements. I was particularly interested in usefulness of solunar tables in predicting deer movements. In the next section I discuss these results.

WHAT CAN WE PREDICT ABOUT DEER MOVEMENTS?

It seems that every deer hunter is in search of the "magic bullet", that "something" which will bring the buck to the gun as quickly and painlessly as possible. But, alas, it does not work that way. The very best weapon you have against a really wary trophy buck is your **brain.** It also is the weapon a mature buck fears the most. He is a pure survival machine. Trained by three or more years of constant interaction with humans, he will use any trick in his repertoire to avoid detection. But, he has weaknesses. First, contrary to any conclusions you may have reached, he is not smarter than you are! He may be more woods-wise than you, but he is certainly no match for the human intellect when that intellect is properly applied. (Notice I said **properly** applied.) Secondly, no matter how smart a buck becomes, he has to move sooner or later. It may be in response to many factors, but he will move. The trick is to know in advance when this will be, and where to be when he finally makes that move. That is where knowledge about deer behavior and movements really pays off. In the earlier sections of this chapter, I noted that there are two basic categories of factors that make deer move: intrinsic and extrinsic. In order to understand how each of these factors comes into play, let's examine a typical whitetail hunter's attitudes and behavior. I have noted throughout this book that the average hunter is doing everything he can to avoid being in contact with trophy bucks! (Trophy bucks, of course, simultaneously are doing everything they can to avoid the hunter.) Here's an example.

Joe Matthews is a mythical person, but he certainly could be any of several thousand deer hunters I have met over the years. He has purchased every known gimmick that gives any promise of helping him to harvest a trophy buck. But, Joe is lacking in one piece of equipment: He is not thinking like a deer. Joe arrives at his favorite hunting area in mid- to late September. Dove season is open in his state, and he might as well kill two birds with one shot, if you will pardon the pun. While on the property, Joe begins to search for a place to hunt deer later. He spends his early-morning hours looking for deer and his midday hours looking for birds. It has been a long summer, and

Understanding Deer Movements

the cool mornings are refreshing. He sees several deer feeding in a pasture every morning, and decides this is where he will hunt opening morning.

As deer season nears, Joe is filled with anticipation. He arrives a few days ahead of opening day and erects a rather impressive stand on the edge of the field where deer earlier were seen with regularity. Opening day finds him sitting in that stand well before daylight. He fidgets and squirms into the morning and decides to give up around 8:30 a.m. He goes back to camp and exclaims, "The moon is not right," or, "It isn't cold enough," or, "The rut already is over." He gives up and goes home.

By midseason, Joe is pretty frustrated. He has decided the local acorn crop is so good no tactic will be successful this season, because the deer don't need to move much. But then, the day arrives. A strong cold front is predicted to blow in by daylight, so Joe puts on his heaviest pair or coveralls, arms himself with plenty of coffee, and heads for his old stand. The pasture long since has died back from the frost, and there is little for the deer to eat there. Besides, deer do not eat grass anyway— unknown information to Joe. But, he is determined. "The deer have to move today," he proclaims to his fellow hunters.

Nightfall finds a nearly frozen, depressed Joe heading back to camp. He has seen not a single deer the whole day!

By now, Joe may be sounding pretty familiar to you. But, it does not have to be this way. Joe could have helped himself immensely if he had done a little more work and used a lot of reasoning. Let's analyze this situation in light of the factors discussed earlier.

First, Joe made the fatal mistake that most hunters make: He waited until just before hunting season to pattern his deer. Whitetails are well known to be crepuscular during the warmer portions of the year, they are active in the early and later portions of the day. But, deer usually change this pattern during the cooler seasons. Probably the single most important extrinsic factor deer use to determine their movements is day length. These light cues not only tell the deer when to move, but also dictate when the rutting season will begin. Joe may have stated that the rut already had occurred, but I will bet you he had absolutely no idea when it really occurs in his area. And, the rut is critical to harvesting a trophy deer, for it is the one time that you have him at a real disadvantage.

Joe also hunted at the wrong time of the day. The average mature buck in my radio-telemetry studies becomes active for a short time just before daylight, then becomes inactive again until midmorning. I have seen countless bucks running does before there was enough daylight even to see movement. Then, at midmorning there is another flurry of activity, as bucks either feed, remain in attendance with a receptive doe or search for a new one. About noon, the big buck takes a short break, then continues his activity until midafternoon— about the time Joe typically returns to his stand. The final movement period is sometime between 9 and 11 p.m., a period of no use to a legal hunter.

As an example, I recently examined a Boone-and-Crockett buck that was shot on one of the most heavily hunted portions of a national forest in Texas. The buck was taken in the afternoon as he returned to his sanctuary on private land. He apparently had been snooping around public land while most of the hunters were having lunch or taking naps! The hunter who got this huge buck was not lucky—he had done his homework.

Weather is the next extrinsic factor. I now have studied deer for better than 20 years, spending a great deal of recent effort trying to sort out what weather factors influence deer movements. It is not as clear-cut as I once thought. However, there are some definite trends beginning to emerge from my studies. First, temperature is the single most important weather cue to deer movements. In the summer, deer move at times when air temperature is more moderate. This may be only at night in some areas. They do not like hot weather. Of course, exactly what a "moderate" temperature is depends on where you happen to be.

In the fall and winter, heat is more critical. A whitetail must live through much of the cold season on the energy reserves developed during late summer and early fall. Exposure to cold causes deer to waste these valuable energy reserves, so they try to avoid such exposure. The best time of day to avoid the cold is during midday, provided the sun is shining, of course. But, as any meteorologist will tell you, there is more to cold than simply the air temperature. Humidity also is involved. Higher relative humidities suppress deer movement in cold weather. Wind is equally important. Most weather reports now include the "chill factor," a measure of how cold it really is next to your skin. The higher the wind velocity, the higher the chill factor. A deer tries to avoid exposure to high winds, even under somewhat moderate temperature conditions. Besides, windy days render the deer's hearing sense almost useless.

Next, Joe said the moon was not "right." Well, he probably is both right and wrong on this one. I have tried for years to correlate deer movements to moon phase, but to a large extent I have been unsuccessful. Recently, however, I have stumbled onto something that may prove very useful to hunters. I just completed some preliminary research on possible correlations between deer movements and one of the "moon" tables on which many hunters and fishermen often rely. I randomly selected Dan Barnett's Feeding Times (1997 Tuxedo Ave., N.E., Atlanta, Ga 30307; 404/373-7151) and compared its predictions to the actual distances moved by a radio-collared mature buck and doe. Now, I must be honest. I really was biased against such tables, and I secretly hoped that no relationship would surface. Unfortunately (or fortunately, depending on how you looked at it), there did emerge some definite relationships. Dan's "Best" and "Good" classifications showed greater movements than those predicted to be "Fair" and "Poor." Likewise, his major and minor feeding times showed some promise. However, these differences were not statistically significant; they could be classified only as "greater." Also, there was no real difference between "Best" and "Good," suggesting to me that there really should only be three categories: "Good," Fair" and "Poor." I am encouraged enough by the results thus far that I will be analyzing more data from several thousand deer movements, representing some 15 years of study, in an effort to test further the reliability of such tables. Although moon phases are not the only variables involved in the compilation of these tables, they do play a major role, it seems.

There also is some merit to Joe's assertion that the acorn crop may have been responsible for his lack of success. But, if that is true, why was he hunting a frozen pasture? I have found that food availability does affect deer movement patterns. As noted, deer must make it through the winter on the stored resources acquired during late summer and early fall. If the berry and acorn crops are poor, and agricultural crops are absent, you pretty well can bet the deer will not be in good shape to face the winter.

Acorn production is highly unreliable, and is affected by many climatic variables. During a recent year in East Texas, for example, we had a very dry summer. Because many of our counties are saturated with deer, I was concerned that we would experience a die-off during the coming winter. But, the acorn crop came to our rescue. We had one of the best acorn crops in modern times— great for the deer, but horrible for hunting. The region's buck kill was off during the previous year, primarily due to the tremendous availability of acorns. The deer were in excellent condition, and they needed to move only short distances to feed. The movement pattern was there, but it was abbreviated. Our hunters did not know what to do. Most took stands on green food plots or overlooking openings, and the deer never appeared. The acorn crop was so good that I found sound

Robert Skinner

In order to be successful, the wise deer hunter will match his stand location to the current activity of whitetails. Placing your stand adjacent to a pasture late in the season will give poor results.

acorns into spring! Although some of the scientific literature reports that whitetails curtail their movements when in poor physical condition, I have often found the opposite to be true. Hungry deer are more likely to display aberrant behavior than are deer in good physical condition.

If it had snowed considerably, Joe could have added that the snow was so deep the deer were unable to move about. That could have been true, because research has shown that deer retard their movements in deep snow. Whitetails walk around on tiny hooves that concentrate their weight. Thus, they break through the snow more readily than do men, and they generally try to avoid traveling far under deep-snow conditions. Again, it takes energy to walk through deep snow, and energy must be conserved at all times.

Joe could have made one last excuse: He was out there, and every mature deer in the area knew it! He made little effort to conceal his movements to and from his stand, but there was an even greater sin. Joe used that impressive permanent stand. In my opinion, there is little, sort of standing out in the clearing each day and singing, that can better guarantee failure than the use of a permanent stand (see chapter on stands). It may be comfortable, but it seldom will get you a trophy buck. On one of my management areas, we have used permanent stands for many years, and my radio-collared bucks regularly avoid them like the plague.

SUMMARY

I hope by now that you have come to the conclusion that the factors affecting deer movement are so complex that they almost defy analysis. Whether or not a specific deer moves is determined by many compounding probabilities, including such things as physiological condition, social position, food availability, previous experience with hunters and weather. Each deer has arrived at a successful survival strategy drawing on one or all of these factors. The problem is: which ones? However, deer movements can be predictable, provided you have spent an adequate amount of time in the field learning about **your** deer. If there is a single theme to this book, be it management or hunting, it is record-keeping. The successful manager maintains detailed records on his deer, in order to develop a consistent picture of what the deer may be doing at any point in time and for a specific set of conditions.

Chapter 10

Population Management: The Basics

Although it probably is not the most palatable of subjects, a basic understanding of the population growth processes of whitetails is important to the efficient management of the species. In this chapter I will present a primer on the principles of population management, as well as, outline the ways in which you can manipulate whitetail populations to achieve specific goals. In a later chapter, I will present a blue print for deer management, incorporating both population and habitat management.

THE BASIC MODEL

The Theory of Population Growth

In order to understand how deer populations behave, I first must present a brief discussion on the basics of population ecology. It is a very complex subject, but the basics are not that difficult to understand, even for the layman. We shall begin with the concept of growth.

If I were to deposit $100 in a passbook savings account in a local bank, paying 10% interest, how much money would I have at the end of one year?

The answer is simple. You multiply 0.1 times $100, obtaining the answer $10. Now add the $10 back to the principle ($100), giving a total account of $110 at the end of the first year. Now that I have made it, what can I do with this money? I basically have two options, either spend the interest or leave it in the account to accumulate. I can spend up to $10. But, if I spend more than this amount, I will be reducing the principle, and will receive less money the following year. If I continue to remove more money than is generated in interest, the outcome surely will be bankruptcy! If, on the other hand, I remove only what I generate in interest each year, I will be able to spend $10 on a **sustained basis** for the rest of time. If I decide to let my interest compound, the money will behave in a predictable manner (see Graph). The equation for calculating the value of money over a long period of time is,

Eq. 1 $N_t = N_o e^{rt}$, where

    N_t is the expected value at time, t;

    N_o is the amount of money at the beginning;

    r is the rate of increase;

    t is the amount of time; and

    e^{rt} is the base of the natural logarithm raised to the **rt** power.

It is amazing how few individuals understand the concept of compound interest. Here is a brief explanation. At first, the amount of money builds very slowly from $100 to $110 to $121; however, by year 20 I have a whopping $672.75! As time passes, the percentage of growth remains the same, but the principle slowly but surely increases. The more time passing, the larger the principle. Ten percent of $100 is only $10, but the same percentage of $672.75 is $67.28. Projecting this trend on out to 50 years really shows how compounding begins to accelerate growth. At that point my money would increase to more than $11,000. The resulting growth curve

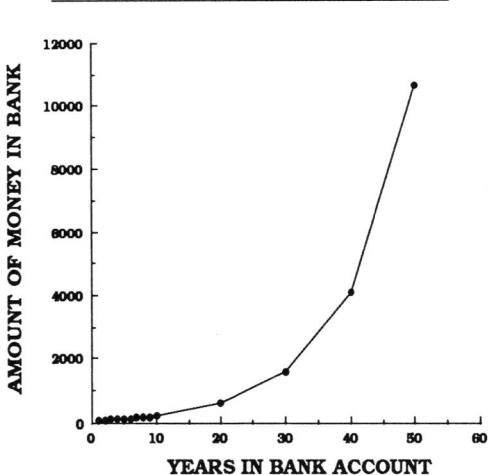

It often is amazing to the average person the growth potential of money earning compound interest. At first, money grows at a rather slow rate, but as time passes, the realized growth accelerates rapidly. This is no different from the kind of growth seen for some animal populations.

Population Management: The Basics

resembles a "J," hence the commonly used term, **J-shaped growth.**

But, we have not been talking about money. We have been discussing the basic principles of population growth. The interest rate used in the above example is called the **intrinsic rate of natural increase (r)** by population biologists. In other words, every species has a "built-in" rate of increase. On several occasions, I have noted that the name-of-the-game in natural selection is "getting your genes into the next generation." The fact that a buck dies from rut-related stress really is no tragedy, provided that he successfully reproduced in the process. The drive to procreate is quite extraordinary among individuals of a species. Each species has evolved reproductive strategies and rates which assure that their efforts pay off genetically.

Although species often have a set reproductive rate, the realization of this rate is determined by many factors. Returning to the bank account example, at some point way in the distant future, your money would be expanding at the speed of light! Obviously, this cannot happen. No bank has that much money. So it is with animal populations. Something must eventually happen to retard population growth. That something is a whole host of events, called **limiting factors.**

A limiting factor is one that impinges directly upon the organism. Availability of essential nutrients, climate, water, disease and other animals all are limiting factors. Limiting factors are of two types, **density independent** and **density dependent**. Density independent factors are those that exert an influence on the population uniformly at all levels of population growth. Climate is perhaps the best example of a density independent factor. If a tornado destroys a local population of animals, does it matter how many happened to be present? But, in the case of density dependent factors, the number of individuals present certainly affects the outcome. Disease and parasites are perhaps the best examples of density dependent factors. The magnitude of the impact of these factors on a population is directly determined by the number present. A densely packed population makes the spread of disease much easier than a sparsely distributed population. That is why most of the influenza outbreaks occur in large cities.

J-shaped Growth

Species such as the bobwhite typically exhibit J-shaped growth over a period of a few years ("booms"). However, density independent factors such as climate sooner or later will exert a devastating impact on the population, causing a dramatic "crash" period. In fact, some ecologists call this type of population behavior, a **boom-crash population growth cycle**. Such species often are difficult to manage, since in a poor year the very best of habitat management efforts will go unrewarded. But, such species make excellent game animals, in that there often is a surplus for harvest. They are called **r-strategists** by ecologists, because they have adopted the reproductive strategy of producing many times more offspring

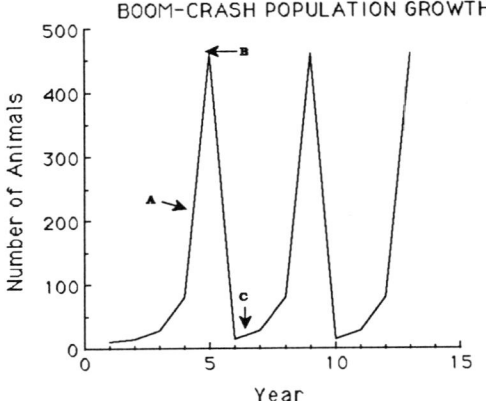

Exponential population growth, also called "J-shaped" growth, is characterized by three distinct phases: A, rapid exponential growth; B, maximum or peak population point; and, C, depression (crash) phase.

than will possibly survive. The salmon is an excellent example of this type of reproductive strategist. The salmon lays thousands of eggs in the "hope" that at least two survive to reproductive age. No parental care is given to the hatchlings. Success is assured by the large number, not by parental care. It may seem wasteful, but it works quite nicely. In good years, the large number of offspring is excessive, while in poor years this amount is barely adequate. But it all balances out.

S-shaped Growth

There yet is another type of population growth, which at first resembles the J-shaped growth strategy. When the population reaches some point at the top of "J," it has two options. It can crash as discussed above, or it can level off, more or less in balance with the ability of the habitat to support the population (see Graph). This type of population growth is called **S-shaped growth**. The previous equation must be modified to allow for a leveling off. The most commonly used equation is,

Eq. 2 $\quad N_t = K/(1 + e^{r/K - rt})$

where,

N_t is the predicted population size,

Logistic population growth, also called S-shaped growth, is used to describe the behavior of a population growing in a limited environment. K-adapted species conform more or less to this growth pattern.

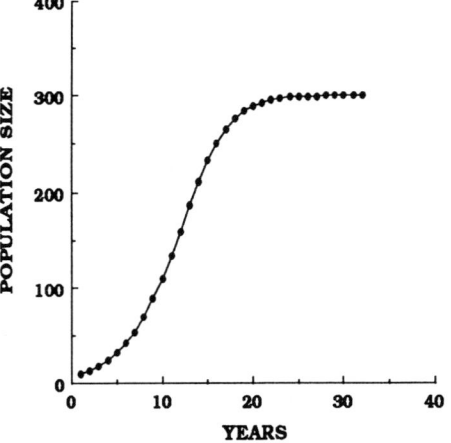

Population Management: The Basics

K is the carrying capacity,
e is the base of the natural logrithym,
r is the rate of increase, and
t is the amount of time passing.

If the population "chooses" the latter path, the realized reproductive rate must not exceed the death rate. In other words, the rate of increase is zero. In order for this to happen, births must be equal to deaths. The actual number of individuals added each growth period can be calculated using the simplified version of the equation,

Eq. 3 $\Delta N = rN((K-N)/K)$, where
ΔN is the change in population size.

Let's examine what must be happening at the leveling off point. Consider a night out on the town with your favorite date. If you select a fine restaurant, you no doubt will have to wait an extended period before being seated. The length of wait is a good indication of the quality of the restaurant. There you sit, all dressed up and cooling your heels, until two people leave the establishment. It is no different with populations at the saturation or leveling off point. In order for an individual to join the population, one must leave it. This is accomplished either by death or by migration. The number of individuals that successfully join the population after each reproductive period is called **recruitment**, and the percentage of new individuals added is the **recruitment rate (%)**. The capacity of the habitat to support a finite number of individuals has been called the **carrying capacity (K)**, a more or less useful term. The concept of carrying capacity has been questioned by myself and other researchers.

Returning to the restaurant example, the length of time you have to wait is determined by the timing of your visit. If you decide to meet at 5:00 p.m., for example, you either will have a short wait or none at all. If, on the other hand, you arrive at the peak of business, say 8:00 p.m., you are guaranteed a long wait. The percentage of individuals seated immediately upon arrival declines as the seating is exhausted. Again, the analogy is appropriate for S-shaped population growth. Unlike the intrinsic rate of increase, the recruitment rate changes over time. Early in population growth, many new individuals are successfully recruited, yet at the point of saturation, very few new individuals are added. The turnover rate of new individuals is quite long at this point. Resources (limiting factors) become very scarce, and competition is intense.

Species exhibiting the typical S-shaped growth are called **K-strategists**. K-strategists tend to maximize competitiveness, and are strongly influenced by habitat quality. To put it more succinctly, these species tend to produce fewer offspring, but expend a great deal of effort seeing to it that their young survive to reproductive age. Humans are perhaps the best examples of K-strategists. According to recent reports, the average American child remains under parental support for at least 20 years!

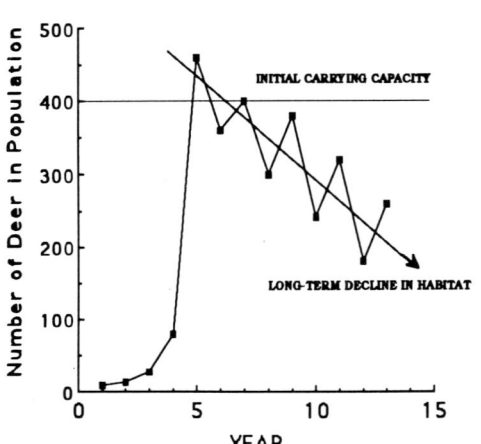

Without periodic disturbances, K-adapted populations would eventually deteriorate to the point of extinction. The concept of a static carrying capacity is theoretical at best!

What you have just read is the textbook explanation of S-shaped population growth. Every undergraduate wildlife biology student during the last 20 years has been tortured with these principles. Unfortunately, however, this explanation is only good for textbook examples. In the real world, seldom will you find populations strictly adhering to this model. They are based on one big, erroneous assumption— a stable ecosystem. The real world is not static, it is dynamic! Although ecosystems try desperately to stabilize themselves and reach a balance, nature periodically reaches in and "stirs the pot." Further, populations do not always behave in a discrete manner, especially since man has come on the scene. Reproductive periods often are protracted over time, and population responses occur only after a reasonable passage of time. Most populations are incapable of responding instantly to positive conditions. This delayed response is called **lag-time**.

The textbook example of a K-adapted population reaching carrying capacity, then leveling off in balance with the ability of the habitat to support the population is ludicrous at best. What actually happens is that the population experiences a rapid growth period, in which recruitment rate is maximized. As the population approaches the calculated carrying capacity, however, it does not level off. Rather, it over-shoots K significantly. The resulting negative impact on the habitat significantly reduces the ability of the range to support the population. A "mini-crash" follows the over-shoot period. Unfortunately, the original K is adversely affected to the point that a new carrying capacity must be established.

Once the population crashes below K, the habitat is given time to recover somewhat, due again to a lag time in population response. Subsequently, a series of booms and crashes follow, each of which degrades the ability of the habitat to support the population. The result is a downward slide of the population, not the "dynamic equilibrium" portrayed in textbooks. In short, a balance of nature seldom occurs.

But what keeps populations from

Population Management: The Basics

going extinct? The answer is simple—**disturbance**. Periodically, nature benevolently disturbs the system. Disturbances such as hurricanes, tornadoes and wildfires were common occurrences in the pristine, natural world. Animals seldom view a disturbance as a catastrophe, rather as a bonanza. Many species are marvelously adapted to exploiting these disturbances.

CONCEPTS OF SUSTAINED YIELD

These population models, although fraught with problems due to statistical assumptions, can be quite useful in developing a workable sustained yield harvest model. In order to understand the concepts, considerable explanation is in order.

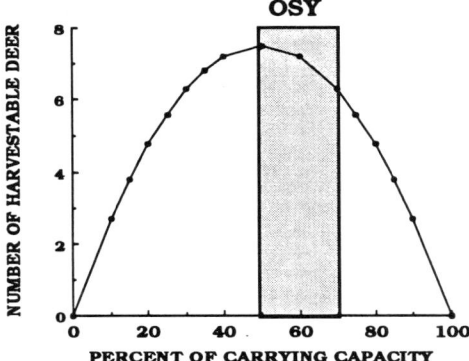

The point of maximum sustained yield (MSY) occurs at 50% of carrying capacity (K). Optimum sustained yield, which optimizes both yield and human benefit, occurs at 50-70% of K.

Back once again to the interest example, what could we do each year with the money earned on the principle? We could reinvest it as discussed, or we could spend it. As long as you do not spend more than the amount of interest, you can be guaranteed of having the same amount available year after year. In other words, you will have a **sustained yield** of money generated, theoretically, forever! At each point in time, there is a corresponding sustained yield, the amount of which is influenced by the size of the principle. Obviously, the larger the principal, the more interest we will enjoy. In this model, we see a variable principle, but a constant interest rate. But, what if the interest rate were not constant? And, in addition, what would happen if the interest rate diminished as the principal increased? This complicates the issue tremendously. **The value of r does not remain constant, rather it changes with population density.** In other words, there is a density dependent effect.

The number of new individuals added to the population increases to some point on the growth curve, then diminishes after this time. Let's take an example. Suppose we have a range which will support 300 animals. Through our research, we have learned that the maximum r-value for this population is 10%. The current population size is estimated to be 50, well below the saturation level of 300. Using Eq. 3, which allows both for population growth and the effect(s) of density dependent factors, we can learn some important facts. For example, if there were no density dependent effects, we would expect this hypothetical population to increase by rN_0 (50 X .1) or 5 individuals. But this does not allow for the negative impact the existing population may have on the habitat. Every time an animal takes a bite from the vegetation, something has been removed. In this case, however, there is little impact since the population is well below the saturation level. To obtain an estimate of recruitment we must multiply 5 by (300-50)/300, or 0.83. The real recruitment would then be 4 (rounding the answer, 4.17 to the nearest whole number). So, even at the relatively low population size of 50, there is a density dependent impact on recruitment. Repeating this process, substituting increasing values for N_0 is most enlightening. At a population density of 100 individuals, the total recruitment is 7, certainly higher than that for a population of 50 individuals. So it is with 150 individuals, yielding a net recruitment of 8. But, once we exceed 50% of the saturation level, the recruitment rate drops as a mirror image of the previous values (see graph), and the resulting curve is dome-shaped. For example, at a population size of 250, the net recruitment is only 4!

This is one of the most difficult concepts to get across to the layman. In essence, we can harvest more individuals from a smaller population than we can from a large population near saturation. In essence, if you want the grass to grow, you have to mow it!

What this discussion boils down to is that there are three levels of sustained yield. First, there is a possible yield from almost any population size. Certainly, at each of the changing values of recruitment for the above example, there is a corresponding sustained yield. Who would argue that you could not harvest, on a sustained yield basis, 4 individuals each year when the population size was 50 individuals or 250 individuals? The yield is the same for both the small (50) and large (250) populations. **But, if we desire to maximize harvest, the population must be maintained at 50% of K, or 150 individuals.** This level is referred to as the **Maximum Sustained Yield (MSY)**. This is the most difficult concept to get across to anyone. When you tell a landowner that he can harvest more deer by having fewer deer on the range, you get some pretty odd looks!

Now, before you go off shooting every deer on your property, let me discuss one very important point. In all of my years of deer management, I only have achieved MSY once. I have tried very hard on numerous occasions, but the fact is that it is very difficult to achieve this harvest level under legal hunting conditions. Why? There are two basic reasons. First, as I have said many times, hunters are basically inept when it comes to killing older deer. The modern sport hunter is not the efficient killing machine that the animal rights advocates would have the public believe. Second, whitetails adapt very quickly to heavy harvest conditions, even the does. On intensive management areas, does are just as difficult to kill as most bucks.

When you take into account problems associated with achieving MSY, you very quickly realize that this probably is not what the average hunter or landowner is after. Instead, I often suggest that a "medium ground" approach be adopted. This approach to population management is called **Optimum Sustained Yield** or **OSY**. OSY can be defined as that population density that best maximizes both deer harvest and hunter satisfaction. My experience has shown that this level occurs at around 60-70% of K. At this population density, hunters still see plenty of deer, but the population being held well below K allows for a high sustained yield of deer for harvest.

Both MSY and OSY harvest strategies can be applied to whitetails. Later in this book, I will outline steps necessary to achieve each of these goals. But, first it is necessary to give you an understanding of how whitetails function as K-strategists.

WHITETAILS AS K-STRATEGISTS

Although there rarely are examples of pure r or K-strategists, whitetails generally have been considered to be more K-adapted. They indeed are regulated by habitat quality and density dependent factors. A doe will only produce one or two offspring per year, and certainly takes excellent care of her fawns. However, does are known to live up to 20 years, producing at least one fawn per year after the yearling age class. Hence, over a period of years, the whitetail doe has a reproductive potential of at least 19 fawns!

Whitetails probably inhabited the pristine forest in various numbers

Mike Biggs

Within the normal range of whitetails density dependent factors, such as disease and parasites, exert a controlling influence on population growth. This buck was photographed on a ranch where deer populations are allowed to oscillate around the saturation level, a questionable practice.

during the pre-Columbian period. Several predators, as well as aboriginal man, depended heavily on whitetails for subsistence. For the most part, whitetails have outlasted most of its predators, including primal man.

Population estimates for the period prior to white men coming to this continent are highly variable, but generally considered to have been from 14 to 34 million. I feel that there are approximately 20 million deer currently inhabiting the range; hence, whitetails probably are nearing the original population density. Much of the difficulty in estimating deer populations prior to the 1500's probably results from the dynamic and unpredictable nature of the habitat-environment complex.

Although occurring throughout succession, whitetails are predominantly a subclimax species (see Habitat Requirements and Management). Population biology is closely tied to periodic habitat disturbances. The American Indian was well aware that deer were a subclimax species, responding to both natural and man-caused disturbances. For example, Indians of several tribes regularly used fire to set back forest succession. In addition, there are many records of large scale, natural disturbances (i.e., tornadoes, hurricanes, etc.) throughout much of the whitetail's range.

In order for you to understand the population behavior of an animal adapted to exploiting disturbance, let's develop a model based on what we know about whitetails. Dale McCullough, working with Michigan deer, has proposed some of the most plausible explanations for deer population behavior. Apparently, whitetails do not respond immediately to disturbances—there is a time lag effect. **A time-lag effect, as noted earlier, is one in which there is a delayed response to habitat improvement.** Disturbances can occur at any time of the year, and it takes both the habitat and the population time to react. Population eruptions by deer basically occur under two situations, 1) creation of new habitat by some form of disturbance, and 2) introduction of a population into an unoccupied range. The sudden protection afforded deer by leasing of previously open range is similar in effect to an introduction.

At first, recruitment rate is quite high, producing a growth rate which is J-shaped in nature. At the same time, the population is approaching carrying capacity, natural successional processes, coupled with density dependent habitat destruction, are reducing carrying capacity. The stage is therefore set for population over-shoot. Habitat conditions deteriorate to a point where the population crashes to a level well below K. There is then a subsequent recovery period for both the habitat and the population. However, since the population crashes well below K, the habitat recovers at a faster rate than the population. The cycle is then repeated. Additional habitat disturbances during this recovery period further confound the model. Hence, from a historical perspective, white-tailed deer have probably experienced countless population irruptions and crashes in response to a changing environment, reaching an equilibrium only on a broad geographical scale. McCullough eloquently noted that:

> **" It is theoretically possible to achieve an equilibrium state between vegetation and deer in which succession is halted, with the subsequent deer population at a higher level than it was prior to the**

creation of new habitat. However, such an equilibrium is difficult to achieve, particularly if rate of succession is rapid. If the deer population is increasing at the same time K carrying capacity is decreasing because of succession, achieving equilibrium at the intercept of these two variables with opposite signs is unlikely, even with management."

WHITETAILS AND PREDATORS

There is considerable confusion in regard to the role predators play in whitetail ecology. Although wolves are considered to be the major historical predator, coyotes, bobcats and mountain lions are now more common throughout the whitetail's present range. Elaborately contrived theories have been established which often overstate the impact of these predators on some deer species; yet, serious population reductions by predators are more the exception than the rule. Predators have more commonly exerted a dampening effect on whitetail populations. Although David Mech noted several localized cases where wolves over-exploited deer populations, McCullough reported that neither predation by wolves nor by aboriginal man tracked normal population age structure. Wolves, and probably other predators, usually select individuals that are very young, very old or infirm.

The one exception may be with wolves. Wolves and deer are brothers! Each depended on the other for survival. The wolf fed extensively on whitetails, fairing well when deer populations were in an expansion stage, and less favorably when succession reduced deer numbers. The deer, on the other hand, received many genetic and natural selection benefits from the wolf's predation. Many of the deer's senses that annually frustrate hunters were derived from millennia of wolf-deer interactions.

There is some evidence that, in the few areas where wolves are abundant, they have a tremendous impact on the deer population; yet, in a very interesting way. Once again, wolves seem to have preadapted deer to deal successfully with man. In areas with high wolf populations, Dr. David Mech tells me that deer exist primarily in the "seams" between wolf territories. These "sanctuaries" probably serve the same functions as those I repeatedly have written about in deer hunting.

In spite of the mixed information about the role of predation in the whitetail's biology, one fact stands out. There seldom are wolves to exert their magic on modern deer populations. And, no matter how much we wish for it to be different, there is little hope that wolves once again will be a significant player in the whitetail's world. But, what about the coyote?

Again, we see mixed results concerning the role of coyotes in deer mortality. One study by Dr. Sam Beasom on the Gulf Coast of Texas indicated that coyote control resulted in a significant increase in deer populations and survival. Yet, a different study by Dr. Charles

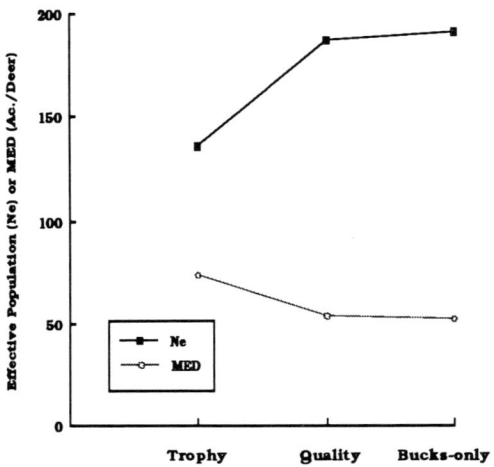

Results of Dr. Wall's "average case" scenario for three management strategies. Notice (above) that highest Ne and MED occurred for the Bucks-only model; however, the %Ne calculation (below) showed quite a different story. %Ne was highest for the Quality Management strategy.

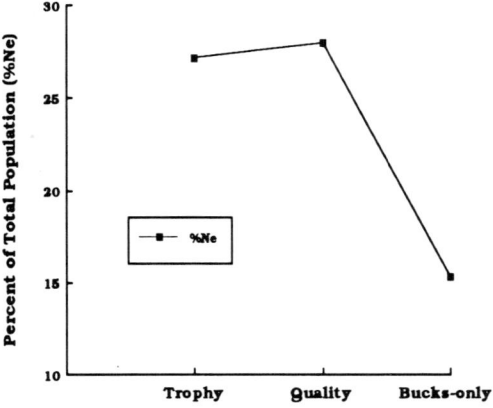

DeYoung in South Texas showed completely contradictory results. Although there probably were confounding factors (which I will discuss below), it appears that coyotes will not be the salvation to deer population control. The fact is that man now has the sole proprietorship on deer population management; and, in spite of what anti-hunting forces may assert, he has not emerged as a significant control agent.

THE HIDDEN DEER HERD

There actually are two herds on any range: 1) the total number of deer actually present, and 2) the deer that are actively involved in reproduction. The values of these two parameters seldom are the same. **This statement really leads to a great deal of confusion.**

The hunter judges the quality of the management program by the number of deer seen on any one day in the field, as well as by the number of deer in the bag. In addition, the biologist should also evaluate the success of his/her management program by the relationship of the total population size to the actual breeding population size. Here is an explanation, using cattle as an example.

The bottom line in cattle production is the number of calves produced for market. The decision to keep or sell a particular cow often is based on her reproductive performance. If she does not produce a calf on a regular basis, she contributes little or nothing to the operation, while at the same time consuming valuable resources. The successful rancher, over a period of years, culls his herd so that at least 90% of the cows are productive. A pasture full of cows means little to the ranch manager. Rather, it is the number of productive mother cows on which he judges the success of his program. So it is with a deer herd.

The fact that the hunter or landowner sees plenty of deer means little to the manager, other than the illusion of success. I once tried to work with a hunting club that refused to control its deer population. On the area was a large green food plot which was referred to as their "sanctuary." The fastest way to lose your membership in the club was to kill one of the many does that daily shared the plot. The idea behind this was that it provided a protected central core of does for breeding. Unfortunately, however, it never occurred to the members that only about 25% of the one hundred or more does on the plot had fawns with them. The remainder seldom contributed anything to the population. The actual breeding population amounted to only 25 does! The remainder were nothing more than excess baggage, putting a real drain on the ability of the range to support deer.

Ideally, the perfect deer herd would be one in which all males and females contribute equally to the reproductive effort. However, this is not possible, as does must reach a certain age to reproduce, bucks have dominance hierarchies, and there is fawn mortality at all population densities. Even though at low population densities, a small percentage (ca., 15-25%) of doe fawns come into reproductive condition, the majority do not breed until the following year. Again, there is a lag-time.

The concept discussed above has been examined at length by population geneticists, but is little known to whitetail managers. It is known among these scientists as the **Effective Population Size** or **Ne**. There are many ways to calculate Ne, but the most commonly accepted equation is:

Eq. 4 $1/N_e = .25(L_m M_{br} K_m l_m) + .25(L_f F_{br} K_f l_f)$

where,

Lm and **Lf** are the generation length or the mean age of all males and females that reproduce in a stable population;

Mbr and **Fbr** are the number of breeding males and females that reproduce in a stable population;

Km and **Kf** are the number of young born to males and females per year; and,

lm and **lf** are the probabilities that a newborn male or female survives to the average age of reproduction and successfully breeds.

Although there are many assumptions concerning this equation, it first provides us with an excellent way of estimating the effective population size of the managed herd.

There are modifications of this statistic which are even more useful in population study. Dividing the area size by the effective population size, Ne, yields a useful expression, the **Effective Population Density** or **MED.** This allows us to make comparisons between areas of different size acreages. Finally, a valuable statistic can be calculated by dividing the actual estimated population size into the calculated Ne. This figure produces an estimate of the relative size of the effective population **(%MNe)**. One management strategy may produce more breeders, due primarily to area size, but the actual percentage of individuals taking part in reproduction may at the same time be quite small.

A cursory examination of the basic equation suggests that several population parameters will affect the values of Ne, MED and %MNe. Among these are: 1) adult sex ratio, 2) average age of breeders, 3) number of fawns produced, and 4) the probability that a fawn will live to average breeding age and take part in breeding. Varying any one of these will affect the value of each of the parameters.

My former graduate student and colleague, Dr. William A. Wall, used these equations to evaluate the effectiveness of three management programs for the Pineywoods of East Texas. He compared three theoretical management options: 1) bucks-only exploitation, 2) quality buck management, and 3) trophy buck management. His results were enlightening.

A theoretical 10,000 acre area was established, with varying population densities of one deer to 8 acres (bucks-only), 15 acres (quality buck management) and 20 acres (trophy management). Under average conditions, both the quality buck and bucks-only management systems produced the highest Ne. However, when we examine the %Ne figures, the quality and trophy management programs yielded the best results. The bucks-only system yielded approximately one-half the %Ne estimated for the other two systems. On the other hand, MED estimates were almost identical for bucks-only and quality buck management systems. I conclude that the quality management program, except when intensive trophy management is desired, is the best population management approach.

What this all boils down to is that there **are** two completely different herds, both genetically and reproductively, that potentially exist on the same piece of land, the **total population** and the **effective population**. As with the cattle analogy, those individuals not involved in breeding only take up space and deplete resources, while those that do take part impact the genetic makeup of the herd. The larger the percentage taking part in breeding, the more diverse the herd; and, **it is diversity that affects such important parameters as reproductive success and antler quality.**

PERIPHERY VERSUS TRADITIONAL RANGE

We in the wildlife business often have a tendency to make far-reaching statements based on limited data. You would be amazed at the number of "sound" management principles that actually have been derived from one or two-year studies in specific geographical areas. So it is with deer population management. The modern whitetail biologist now travels about the countryside, espousing the doctrine as if it were written in stone. Fact is that it is not! My above discussion applies only to the deer living within the traditional range of the species, the mesic forests and brushlands. When dealing with deer on the periphery of the range, say South Texas or Mexico or Canada, or even in areas within the traditional range with serious site limitations, a whole new set of rules apply.

We only recently are discovering that deer populations do not behave the same in areas where density independent factors come into play. For example, Dr. DeYoung's study on coyote predation in South Texas is a watermark piece of research. He has suggested that predator control in highly variable environments has little, if any impact on survival of adults or fawns. His companion study on population control further suggests that we do not see the dramatic increase in fawn production (=compensatory response) when the population is adjusted to 50-60% of K. My own experience in this particular geographic region further supports this hypothesis. **In Canada, I discovered that weather related mortality was density independent** in many cases, with annual mortality rates of 40% common. Hence, on the periphery of the range, whitetails appear to behave more as r-strategists than K-strategists. This heretical view, I am certain, will be borne out by the scientific process.

Given the published mortality and fecundity (birth) rates for such areas, it is clear that %MNe for a herd on the periphery of the range is much smaller than for one within the traditional range. %Ne is genetically critical, especially in trophy management. What this means is that relatively fewer individuals are taking part in the breeding. This, in turn, has some far-reaching consequences in regard to genetic diversity. Genetic considerations will be the topic of Chapter 16.

When compared to a traditional portion of the range, herds on the periphery must be maintained at a higher density in order to accomplish what can be done with a lower density elsewhere. Hence, we should be very careful in applying "one-size-fits-all" population management to whitetails. On the periphery of the range, it may not even be necessary to control the population. Excessive harvest of antlerless deer may have far-reaching and detrimental impacts on the herd. Again, I will address these issues in Chapter 16.

SUMMARY

Whitetails are primarily a K-adapted species, whose population processes are controlled by the quality of the habitat. Reproductive performance declines as the herd approaches saturation. Maximum Sustained Yield (MSY) occurs at approximately one-half the saturation level, while Optimum Sustained Yield (OSY) occurs at some point above this level, say 60-70% of K. Although OSY does not maximize production, it often is the preferred management strategy, especially when hunter satisfaction is considered. At this population level, the hunter or landowner sees more animals than at MSY. This has been shown to be an important criterion used by hunters in judging the success of management. Also, having more deer on the range allows for an increase in hunter success. Although parameters such as reproduction and antler quality are not maximized, OSY management satisfies more individuals than trophy management.

For each deer herd, there are two components: the breeding and non-breeding populations. Although a high population density, often with a seriously skewed sex ratio, gives the appearance of management success, such herds have a small %Ne which may have long-term genetic implications. The relationship between the total population size and Ne is a good indicator of the effectiveness of the management program. Although the equations currently in use to calculate these parameters are somewhat crude, I feel they provide an excellent basis for making management decisions.

One must be careful in applying general population information over the entire range of the whitetail. On the periphery of the range— Canada and Mexico— deer populations behave much differently from those within the traditional habitats. Herds in these regions seldom reach saturation densities, and the traditional tenets of population management (population control) may not be as critical as elsewhere.

Chapter 11

CENSUSING WHITE-TAILED DEER

Hunters always ask me about the validity of the census techniques we use in white-tailed deer management. The average hunter doubts the veracity of such counts. "Just how accurate is one of those spotlight counts?," a fellow will say with a knowing grin. "Well," I replay, "they are not very accurate. They usually **under-estimate** how many deer you have by about fifteen to thirty percent!" The fellow's face usually will drop. He was obviously hoping to show that deer censuses **over-estimate** population size. The fact is that there is much distrust and misunderstanding about censuses and their use in wildlife management. Herein, I will discuss the various options open to you in censusing whitetails, which techniques to use, how to use them and when.

A census is **not** an absolute count of all deer on the property. It is an index to what is going on in the population. For example, it we go down to the local grocery store on July 4th at 9:00 a.m. and count everyone we see down four aisles, we have an index to how many people shop there on that date. The number we obtain means absolutely

Mike Biggs

Spotlight counts probably offer the most cost-effective means of deriving a reasonable population estimate.

nothing by itself. If, however, we return to the same store and aisles on the next July 4th, we can obtain a second number that then will be useful. When compared to our first index, we can then make inferences about what is going on with customers at that point in time. If the count is lower, then we either can assume that the number of shoppers is down or that there was some inherent error in our counting procedure. One year does not tell us all that much. But, if we continue the process for several years, and the count continues to decline, a definite trend is emerging. The management of the store should be alerted and some decisions should be made. This exactly is the way we use census in managing white-tailed deer.

We conduct an initial census just to obtain an idea of what is going on in the deer herd. And, quite frankly I often conduct censuses just to make the landowner or hunting club happy. Remember that the wildlife manager is

Censusing White-tailed Deer

no different from the average family practitioner. If you do not feel well, he will take several diagnostic tests including such things as temperature and blood pressure to help him make a final decision about the nature of your illness. No single diagnostic test can be used to make this decision. The censuses we conduct are one such diagnostic test. Other tests will be discussed in other chapters.

The first question to ask when considering a census is, do you really need one? In some cases, other diagnostics can provide better information about the herd. I usually recommend a census when there is little or no information available about the herd. In this case, you have to start somewhere, and a census probably is the best place to begin. The next question is what kind of census(es) to use?

Although there have been many novel approaches to estimating deer numbers, there remain only five useful techniques. These are:

    1. spotlight counts;
    2. track counts;
    3. change-in-ratio;
    4. aerial counts;and,

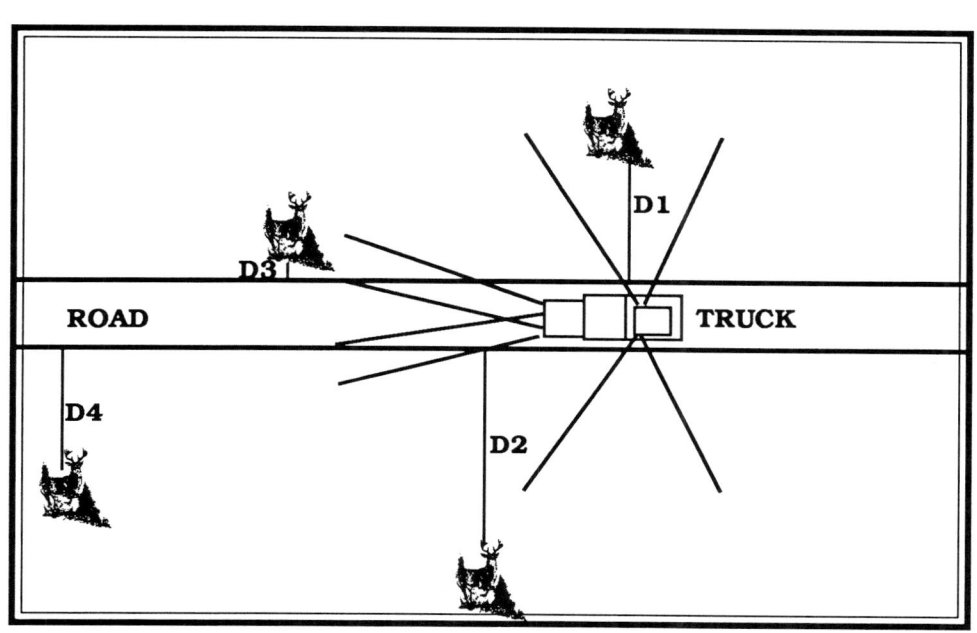

Spotlight counts are based on the concept of estimating a series of visibility distances (D1+ D2 + D3 + D4= AVD) and calculating an average visibility distance (AVD/4) for the entire transect line.

5. guesses.

Spotlight Counts

Spotlight counts have emerged as one of the best methods for acquiring an index to deer density, provided there are adequate roads available on the area. In addition, spotlighting gives information that is valuable in making decisions about the herd. For example, the observer also gets a pretty good idea about the overall condition of his animals, as well as, the potential quality of bucks to be harvested. Reliability of such counts depends on the observer's ability to accurately judge distance. There are considerable differences in abilities of observers to estimate distances at night. Prior to any spotlight count, I recommend that you and your colleagues spend a good deal of time learning to estimate distance in the dark. I set up a course with known stations and distances and have my assistants practice estimating these distances. Only when I feel that they are proficient in distance estimation, do I allow them to conduct spotlight counts. It may also help to purchase a good rangefinder to improve accuracy.

Accuracy vs. precision.— Before we go any further in this discussion, I used a word above that is crucial; viz., **accuracy.** Herein we need to establish the difference between accuracy and precision. It may be a tired old analogy, but it works very well to compare these two terms to developing a fine shooting load. Accuracy in shooting is measured by how close you come to the bull's eye. For example, you may set up your rifle to shoot two inches high at one hundred yards. Where that first shot hits the target gives you some idea of the accuracy of the rifle. But it is the second and third shots that tell you something about the **precision** of your shooting. Precision is the grouping of your shots, while accuracy is how close you come to the target. If you are lucky enough to acquire the mythical minute of angle, all three of your shots will be in an area that can be covered with a quarter. This obviously is high precision. If, however, you are unlucky enough to purchase a rifle (as I once did) that had a pitted barrel, your first shot may well be near the bull's eye, while your second and third shots may be all over the paper! Consequently, the precision of such a rifle is so poor that it may not be counted on to kill a deer. This is the case with any census technique. It is one thing to develop accuracy, but quite another to establish precision. Ironically, we can often have more influence on precision than accuracy, because the true measure of accuracy is how close we come to estimating the correct herd size. To my knowledge, no one has ever demonstrated the true accuracy of census techniques under "wild" conditions. Recently, some researchers in South Texas have done a study on aerial counts within an enclosure, but it is yet uncertain if the results would have been similar for a wild population.

Now back to spotlight counts. What are the factors that influence both accuracy and precision in spotlight counts? First of all, the fact that spotlight counts are conducted along roads means that the distance traveled, configuration of the road system, and the location of the roads will influence the outcome of the census. Roads usually are placed on ridges. It is a completely logical place to put them, since you do not want to be bogged down all the time when you travel across the property. Unfortunately, this greatly influences our census results, especially during the summer months. A portion of your habitat will go un-censused and this will affect results. The number one criticism of deer census still lies in the possibility that a particular deer may be observed more than once during the census. Consequently, the configuration of the road system can cause such an event to happen. Roads that double back upon themselves should be avoided, unless there is more than a mile between the segments in question. This will assure that no deer will have time to travel from one road segment to the next. The distance you travel in spotlight counts is critical. I try not to sample areas with roads less than five miles in length. For smaller tracts, you may want to include the surrounding landowners to obtain a more precise estimate. We have been spotlighting on North Boggy Slough Hunting and Fishing Club for over fifteen years now. Our spotlight count line runs for better than fifteen miles on the approximately seven thousand acre area. We are sampling about five percent of the area with this sampling scheme.

Spotlight counts also are affected by the movements of deer. Ideally, they should be conducted when, 1) deer have the most stable home range, and 2) when deer are most active within that home range. For these reasons, I have found that in most areas of the country, late summer is the ideal time to census by spotlighting. In some areas, early fall is also a good time. This is a time when a deer's home range is most stable. As to the time of night to conduct such censuses, this is influenced by weather and moon conditions. Dr. Charles DeYoung (Texas A&I University) recommends that spotlight counts be run after mid-night. He feels that he achieves about 85 percent accuracy in doing this on areas with vegetation cover of less than 40 percent. A number of years ago, I had great success in determining when to census deer by using a modified track count. I simply dragged a road before dark and then patrolled it at two hour intervals through the night. I noted the number of new tracks for each time period, and from these data determined the best time to run my spotlight counts of that week. Catching the deer moving about is important to obtaining an accurate count. Deer that are bedded down are very difficult to see even with a spotlight.

Conduct of count.— Assuming that all of the above criteria have been satisfied, you should begin your count just prior to peak activity. I often am asked whether or not to use two spotlights or one. An excellent study by Texas Parks & Wildlife Department showed that the results of spotlight counts are not affected by the number of spotlights used. I use two spotlights, one from each side of the vehicle, so I can see more deer. This helps out with some of the other diagnostic features discussed later.

In spotlighting, you can be as sophisticated or as simple as you wish. I prefer to use a pickup truck with either a specially designed rack on the back or just a tool box. You can spotlight with as few as two people or as many as four. More than four usually turns into a "circus" and I strongly discourage trying it. Whenever possible, I use four people— one driver, one observer/recorder, and two spotlighters. Before starting the count, be sure and designate each person's duties, and admonish each to stick to his or her duties. I have seen spotlight counts totally deteriorate because people were trying to do someone else's job!

The type of spotlight you use is not all that critical, as long as you have at least a 200,000 candle-power light or larger. We use both 500,000 and 750,000 candle-power lights with excellent success. Since you will be holding the light for some time, often as long as four hours, I suggest that you purchase one of the types that has a handle.

Although record forms are not really necessary, I strongly suggest that you develop a standardized form to be used year after year. As we begin the count, the recorder writes down the beginning time, road number and beginning mileage. There is a place for tallying the number of adult bucks and does, fawns and unknown deer. There also is a place where visibility distances can be recorded for each tenth of a mile traveled. The driver should proceed at no more than five miles per hour and no less than three. A good driver is hard to find, as most quickly become bored and try to drive faster as the night wears on.

There also is a tendency for drivers to begin looking for deer, which can cause you considerable problems. Remember that the driver has a completely different angle on the deer and may see an animal that you do not. This may seem to improve accuracy of the count, but becomes a problem when the driver attempts to see the deer that one of the spotlighters has found. Drivers often will pull forward or backup to see the deer himself, thereby obscuring the counter's view. The driver should be instructed to tend to the driving, and spend little time looking.

The driver also must call out "mark" at each tenth mile interval. Upon this signal, one of the two observers, or the single observer, will call out the distance at which a deer could be seen at that precise moment in time. If two spotlighters are used, I suggest that you alternate between the two, since except on small areas you really do not improve precision with both estimating visibility at the same time.

My research has shown that the probability that a deer will be observed decreases as the visibility distance increases. For example, on a recent spotlight count, better than seventy-five percent of the deer recorded were seen within one hundred yards of the truck. This does not mean that there were no deer past that point, only that they become more difficult to see. Observers often become paranoid about not being able to see every deer on the property. Most hunters who accompany our counts are shocked to discover that they see so few deer. This is not at all surprising, since we only are sampling a narrow strip through the area. The grocery store analogy is again helpful. Notice that we only sampled certain aisles in the store, and did not obtain a total count of all people in the store. This was done to save time, and to eliminate the effect of people moving while we were counting. The trick is to determine how many aisles and which ones. Ideal census lines best represent the proportions of habitat in the area. For example, if thirty-five percent of the area is in bottomland hardwoods, then theoretically the spotlight route should have about thirty-five percent of its total length in that habitat type.

The number of samples also affects the outcome of a census. Some researchers have suggested that the number of spotlight counts necessary to give an accurate estimate of the population density be determined statistically. Now, I am probably as statistically inclined as any wildlife biologist in the country today; however, I also have some experience in the field, and know that it often is difficult to conduct the number of counts necessary to achieve high precision. Usually, statistical analyses of spotlight counts indicate that as many as ten counts are necessary to achieve precision. This often is impractical. But, what is a good number to shoot for? I have found that at least three counts, all during the same week, will give you an adequate index to population density. Five counts would be better. The number of counts you make will entirely depend on you, and be dictated by the amount of time and resources you have.

The count should proceed at an orderly and controlled pace. There always is a tendency, especially with bucks, for observers to want to spend too much time looking at a deer. Remember that you have many miles of spotlight line to run, and proceed accordingly. Spotlighters should stick to their side of the vehicle, providing aid to the opposite side when asked. Whenever you move the spotlight from one side to the other, however, remember that you have a very powerful light in your hand. So avoid blinding the driver and recorder in your zeal to see a deer.

At each tenth of a mile, the driver

Mike Biggs

When a deer is seen, remain calm and quickly determine the sex and relative age.

should call out "mark" in a voice loud enough to be heard outside of the truck by the recorder. If you really want to get fancy, I often use a set of wireless, voice activated headphones that allow easy communication between the recorder and the driver. This system also is useful for giving directions to the driver to either pull forward or backward when a deer is seen. Upon the "mark" signal the observer on the right side of the vehicle calls out his estimate of visibility at that very moment. This prevents bias from the observer waiting until he can see further. Why the right side of the vehicle? That was completely arbitrary. You can start with the left side if you wish. The next "mark" should see the person on the left calling out the visibility distance. Alternating sides simplifies the procedure and, as noted earlier, does not differ significantly in accuracy from both observers calling out the visibility simultaneously. However, some managers prefer to do this. It makes the final calculation a bit different.

When a deer is seen, remain calm. I have seen new spotlighters beat the top out of a truck in an attempt to get the driver to stop. Remember the inside of the truck is like being in a drum, so have a little pity. A pre-arranged signal is adequate. A light tap on the window or roof should serve to alert the driver. Again, the headphone arrangement works fine for this. As noted above, take an adequate amount of time to identify the sex and relative age of the deer, but do not take too long. Also, do not guess at the identity of the deer. If you do not know, then put it down as an unknown.

Calculating deer density.— In order to estimate deer density for any one count, it is necessary to make a few simple calculations. Now I know that many people pale at the thought of performing mathematical computations, but I assure you that it really is quite easy.

There are two things you need to know in order to calculate a deer density estimate, which is presented as acres per deer. First, you need to know how much territory you have covered in your count. This is accomplished by totaling all visibility estimates for a particular spotlight route. Divide this number by the total number of visibility estimates, giving you the average visibility from one side of the truck. Next, if you alternate sides, you have to calculate the area sampled by multiplying the average visibility by two (since there are two sides of the vehicle). Now multiply that number by the distance of the line in yards. You are probably telling yourself at this point that I lied when I said it was simple. But, it really is. Let's take an example.

Suppose that you conducted a count using both sides of the vehicle. The average visibility was calculated to be 35 yards. We multiply 35 by 2 to give the average census strip width. Now, we turn to the total distance traveled on the census line. In this example, we traveled a total of five miles. In order to obtain the total distance, multiply five times 1,760 (the total yards in a mile), to yield a total distance of 8,800 yards. It probably is a good time to convert all of this to feet, so now multiply both 35

Robert Skinner
Track counts are perhaps the easiest census method to conduct.

and 8,800 by 3. This results in an average census width of 105 feet and a total distance of 26,400 feet.

We now multiply the two dimensions to arrive at a total area sampled of 2,772,000 square feet. Since there are 43,560 square feet in an acre, we now divide this figure into the total area sampled, giving an estimated 63.6 acres sampled. You are safe to round off your area estimate to the nearest acre, so we sampled 64 acres on this census.

A total of five deer were seen on the census line. Hence, the estimated density for this particular census and line was one deer to 13 acres. This figure might be broken down further into acres per buck or doe, provided sufficient observations were obtained to allow this refinement.

There are two methods commonly used to arrive at the most precise estimate using spotlight counts. Some managers take an average of all counts, while others use only the count with the largest number of deer. Again, unless you are going to statistically analyze these data, I suggest that you pick a technique and stick with it.

Since spotlight counts usually under-estimate deer density, I use the maximum count for my computations, especially when I have limited counts. I also calculate two different densities; viz., total deer density and adult deer density. The adult deer density is more reliable and stable, providing information about the stability of the population that total deer density masks. Some managers really split hairs! They calculate not only deer density, but also adult density, doe density, fawn density and buck density. These estimates can be useful provided, as I noted earlier, adequate data were obtained to give a reliable estimate.

Track Counts

Track counts were used by whitetail managers for many years, and in so doing, generated considerable mistrust with the hunting public. Statements such as, " I watched an old doe walk back and forth across a track count line, and that biologist counted a different deer each time she crossed the road!," are common fare around hunting camps. The fact is that track counts do have some real limitations in estimating deer population trends. But, when used properly, track counts can be extremely useful. I find myself using track counts more and more in my work.

I conducted a study a few years ago, comparing spotlight count estimates with track counts on the same area. To my surprise, I found track count population estimates did not differ significantly with those of spotlight counts. For example, clearcutting and pine regeneration are common forestry practices in the South. During the first five years of growth, visibility remains very high in these regeneration areas. After this time, however, visibility becomes less than five yards in many cases. The manager is forced to adopt a new census technique or eliminate the area entirely from his census. This is why I conducted the study comparing spotlight and track count estimates. Since visibility remains poor for about ten years, I switch my census technique to track counts during this period. I also use track counts in some of the brushy habitats outside of the forested regions.

Conducting a track count.— Track counts are relatively easy to conduct, and do not require the equipment and expertise needed for spotlight counts. However, there are obvious trade-offs. There is no way to obtain buck-doe ratios from track counts. Hunters may claim they can discriminate between sexes by tracks, but the fact is that this is not possible. Fawn tracks sometimes can be distinguished from adult deer, especially in areas where does are particularly large.

As with spotlighting, roads are useful in track count censuses, although other topographic features such as rights-of-way and fire lanes can be used. The same criteria as used in spotlight counts for road selection apply to track counts. The track count relies on the premise that a deer has a stable home range during the time of counting, never traveling beyond a certon distance. That is one of the reasons biologists conduct radio-telemetry studies on deer. Over several years, we are able to predict just how far the average deer will travel in an average day. This distance (cruising radius) varies with season and geographic area. For example, it is generally thought that a deer never travels more than a mile from its place of birth. My research has shown that this is more often untrue than true. Deer will travel long distance during certain portions of the year, especially young deer. However, for the most part, the late summer period finds most deer sticking to a relatively stable home range of around 600-700 acres, giving an average cruising distance of one mile. But, before you use this figure for your area, I suggest you contact your state biologist for the figure most appropriate for your deer.

Twenty-four hours prior to counting, the road is cleared of all existing tracks using a drag similar to the one pictured. This requires that the road or right-of-way be in a condition that will allow disturbance of the surface by the drag. Roads that are extremely rocky, paved roads and heavy clay roads are difficult to drag. I suggest that such conditions either be avoided or the road or roadside disced prior to dragging.

You should time your line drag so that you will be able to return exactly twenty-four hours later to count tracks. In order to count tracks, you either can walk the line; or if you are less inclined toward such things, you can ride on the front of a truck and call out the tracks to an assistant. I prefer to walk, but when you have many track lines to count, it may be better to drive.

There is an art to counting a track line. In order to avoid the problems discussed earlier, only deer that have completely crossed the line should be included in your count. This is where common sense is important. If a deer obviously crossed the line several times, do not count the deer more than once; however, if there is some question, go ahead and count the total number of crossings.

Calculation of a deer density estimate is quite simple. Once you have an idea of the average daily cruising distance of the deer in your area, that is your base distance. For example, suppose you are working in the South

Mike Biggs
The change-in-ratio method is based on changes in proportions of a recognizable segment of the population such as bucks and does or does and fawns.

where the cruising distance often is one mile. All you have to do is divide the distance of the track count line in miles by the cruising distance. In this example, a five mile track count line will yield a total sample area of: 5 (distance of line in miles) X 1 (cruising distance of deer)= 5 square miles of area. Since a square mile contains 640 acres, the total area sampled is 5 times 640 acres or 3,200 acres. If a total of twenty tracks were observed, then the estimated population density will be one deer to 160 acres, a pretty thin population! Track counts are often very useful under such conditions, as hours of spotlighting will be unfruitful at low deer densities.

The above procedure can be modified for any cruising distance. If the distance is found to be two miles, then you simply multiply the track count distance by 2. If it less than a mile, use the fraction of a mile; e.g., one-half mile equals 0.5 times distance. As with spotlighting, the more times you repeat the procedure on the same management area, the more precise your estimate. An average of ten counts should theoretically be more precise than a single count; provided, of course, that you run the counts in a reasonably small period of time (within thirty days).

Change-in-Ratio

Next we come to a procedure that is perhaps the most mathematically complicated and taxing procedure, but one in which I have a great deal of faith. This technique often is referred to by managers as the CIR technique. It requires a great deal of work and knowledge on the part of the manager, but CIR can be mastered by most individuals seriously interested in deer management. Here are the particulars.

This technique, known by many names, is based on the theory that, if we have an estimate of the sex ratio before and after the removal of animals by hunting, then we can calculate the pre- and post-hunt population density. Now relax! That may sound complicated, but let me give you an example. Let's take a five thousand acre area. Suppose we spend a goodly amount of time on the area, recording the sexes of each deer we see. from these observations, we estimate that the buck:doe ratio is 1:4. Therefore, our estimate of the proportion of does in the population is estimated at 80 percent (4/5). Then we remove 40 does and 25 bucks during the hunting season. A detailed census immediately after the hunting season suggests that our buck:doe ratio has changed to 1:3, changing the proportion of does to 75 percent. In order to estimate the pre-hunt population, you need to perform the following calculations:

- **P1**= 0.80 (the proportion of does prior to hunting),
- **P2**= 0.75 (the proportion of does after hunting),
- **C1**= does removed during the hunt,
- **C2**= C1 + bucks removed during the hunt.

Then,

Pre-hunt population = C1-P2(C2) divided by P2-P1.

In this example,
P1= 0.80,

Robert Skinner

Helicopter counts are popular with wildife biologists, but are expensive and are no more accurate than other techniques.

$P_2 = 0.75$,
$C_1 = 40$,
$C_2 = (-40)+(-25) = -65$.;

therefore, the pre-hunt population is calculated as,

$-88.75 / -.05 = 1,775$

animals or one deer to 2.8 acres. Likewise, the post-hunt population can be calculated by subtracting the total number of deer removed by hunting, in this case 65. This is sort of an after the fact estimation technique, but it gives us an idea of where we stand each year. If you have good data on reproduction (to be covered later), you can then estimate the following year's pre-hunt population. Note that in both C_1 and C_2, the sign is negative since the numbers represent removals. There is one big assumption to this method; i.e., there is little or no mortality between the beginning of the hunting season and the beginning of your post-season data collection, other than hunting mortality. This may or may not be the case.

As to timing, I suggest that you obtain your pre-hunt sex ratio during the late summer and early fall prior to the rut. Once the rut commences, increased buck activity will greatly bias your buck:doe ratio estimation. You should follow up the season as soon as possible with the second ratio estimate, preferably after the season and rut.

Aerial Counts

For some reason or another, wildlife biologists love to use aircraft in their work. I really do not know if it is because it is an exciting thing to do or what, but aerial counts of game populations have increased in popularity during the last few years. This also is evidenced by the increased numbers of obituaries in the professional wildlife journals for biologists killed in the "line of duty." Although aerial counts give the added dimension of allowing the observer to estimate the relative number of trophy class animals, I have serious questions regarding either the increased precision or accuracy of such techniques over other methods, especially in light of the cost. Recent studies by other deer researchers tend to agree with my somewhat biased assertion. Some managers firmly believe in them, and I will not argue the point. But, if you are interested in conducting aerial counts, the procedures are simple.

First of all, you need to ask yourself whether or not an aerial count is possible on your property. If you have very dense vegetation, especially evergreens, I doubt seriously whether or not such a count will be feasible. One study by the Texas Parks & Wildlife Department in South Texas, suggested that accuracy was greatly influenced by vegetation density. Other considerations include cost, which I will discuss for all census techniques at the end of the chapter. Aerial counts are very useful in areas where there are insufficient roads for track or spotlight counts, and for extremely large tracts of land. However, roads are paramount to a quality deer management program; a fact which I will discuss later in this book.

Aerial surveys can be conducted either with fixed-wing aircraft or by helicopter, although I have found helicopters to be the most useful in game counts. Whether you use fixed wing or helicopter surveys, the basic principles are the same. Deer are counted by one of two basic methods. First, the observer flies a series of strips at a fixed altitude. The number of strips flown will depend on the desired precision and the cost of the census. Several researchers have shown that precision increases with the number of flights. In order to determine the area sampled, you need to perform some basic geometry. If you fly at a known altitude, and have two known points of reference on the wing or canopy, then you can calculate the area covered on the ground by solving for the base of a triangle. The second method uses either a 100 percent coverage of the area or marked strips on the ground. A fence marked with white poles is most commonly used.

Aerial surveys tend to under-estimate deer density, even when so-called total counts (i.e., 100%) are conducted. How much error depends on the number of transects flown and the percentage of the area sampled. A recent study by Texas Parks & Wildlife Department and Texas A&I University suggested that accuracy may vary from seventeen to sixty-five percent of actual population; and, averages about thirty percent of true population density. Using this information, it is possible to adjust your census figures accordingly. However, there is one additional consideration. Just as in track and spotlight counts, there is the ever-present problem of counting a deer more than once (duplication rate). The South Texas study suggested that about fifteen percent of the counted deer will be observed more than once during the count. This percentage may vary with area and habitat type. In South Texas, Synatzske used correction factors adjusted for duplications of nineteen to forty-four percent; i.e., dividing the population estimate by the correction factor gives an adjusted population estimate. Charles DeYoung found similar results, suggesting an average adjustment of thirty percent. However, both of these studies, and those of other researchers were conducted with marked animals on specific areas. Hence, utilization of these correction factors may gain you little accuracy.

There is one plus to aerial counts, in my opinion. They allow the manager to get a good look at a cross-section of bucks available on the property in a short period of time. Consequently, the manager can make better decisions as to management direction earlier in the program than from incidental observations. It really is up to you whether or not you employ this census technique.

Guesses

On the surface, it may seem silly to suggest guesses as a reliable population estimate; yet, this is not always the case. I would much rather have the opinion of a manager who spends most of his time on the property than the results of some census technique. Experience is a difficult thing to beat! Whether you hunt whitetails or manage them, there is no substitute for spending a great deal of time on the property. Actually, I like to use several diagnostic tools in herd management, one of which is my own "gut" feeling about the status of the herd. Guesses probably are derived from subliminal analyses of observations by the manager.

ECONOMICS

There are other census techniques that I did not discuss here. Some of them, such as cruise lines and pellet counts, are questionable at best, and I would give them little consideration. This statement will draw criticism from those who are practitioners of these methods, but it is a defensible statement.

I suggest that you pick a technique and stick with it as long as possible. Consistency is the key. It often is difficult to compare "apples to oranges." Unfortunately, however, it also is often necessary to switch census techniques in response to changes in habitat or other conditions. Dr. DeYoung found that it was necessary to use spotlight counts in areas where the canopy cover was forty percent or less, and aerial counts when cover was less.

I conducted an economic analysis on track and spotlight counts, while Dr. DeYoung volunteered some cost information about aerial censuses. On North Boggy Slough (East Texas), it takes fifteen man-hours to conduct each spotlight count. Depending on the salary level, this will amount to $60 to $150 per census. Since North Boggy is approximately 7,200 acres, the cost per acre per census is no more than two cents per acre. Track counts, on the other hand, require twice the amount of time for a spotlight count, resulting in a per acre cost of four cents for each census. This certainly is economical in light of the information obtained. According to Dr. DeYoung, helicopter time currently is averaging about $200 per hour, with a mileage fee (ca., 50 cents per mile) and/or a three hour minimum. He suggests that approximately 2,500 acres can be censused per hour, yielding a minimum per acre cost of eight cents. Of course, this cost does not include the manager's time, but this still is fairly reasonable. A good friend recently contracted a helicopter count in Mexico, at a cost of about $2,000 for a 3,000 acre ranch. This amounted to a per acre cost of 67 cents!

SUMMARY

In this brief discussion of census techniques, I hope that you have come to realize that a census is just an index to what is going on in the population, and by itself should not be the sole criterion for making management decisions. Remember, census is just one of the many diagnostic tools we use in whitetail management. Population density estimates can be useful in making decisions, as long as you are aware of the costs, as well as the benefits.

Chapter 12

RECORD-KEEPING: THE BASIS FOR SOUND MANAGEMENT

In the previous chapter, I outlined the basic methods for estimating the population density of your herd. In this chapter, I will discuss the methods that I feel give the manager a much better understanding about what is going on in the herd, and allow correct decision-making. There absolutely is no way to manage a deer herd without keeping adequate records. At the bare minimum, you need to know something about,

 1. reproductive performance,
 2. age structure of both bucks and does,
 3. antler quality,
 4. body condition, and
 5. forage utilization and condition.

REPRODUCTIVE PERFORMANCE

There are several ways to obtain information about the reproductive performance of your herd, some of which are quite technical in nature. These would include collection of reproductive tracts, followed by gross and microscopic analysis for ova and embryos. But, there are several easier methods

Mike Biggs

Incidental sightings over a season can give us a good estimate of the sex and age structure of the herd.

you can use to obtain a reasonable estimate for herd reproductive performance. First, there is no substitute for spending a great deal of time on your property. That seems to be a recurring theme in this book! You should develop some record cards (see example at end of chapter) for recording each and every deer you see while traveling around or hunting the property. The cards I use are conveniently sized to fit in my shirt pocket. Whether I am driving the roads or sitting in a deer blind, I record every deer I see. You will be amazed at the large number of sightings you obtain over a year's time. My research has shown that you can obtain a random sample of your herd in this manner, even for older bucks.

In East Texas, I usually conduct my doe:fawn ratio census during the period July-September. For other regions, it may be necessary to adjust this period, since fawning varies geographically. At the end of the period, total up all of your sightings of does and fawns and calculate the doe:fawn ratio. For example, if you make 345 sightings of does and see a total of 100 fawns, the estimated doe:fawn ratio is 345/100 or 3.45:1. This equates to what is often called a 29% fawn crop, which means that there are 29 fawns produced for every 100 does.

An additional estimate of reproductive success can be obtained during the hunting season, provided you are harvesting does. Hopefully you are, since **I know of few deer herds for which a buck-only harvest can be justified.** Each doe harvested should be checked for evidence of lactation. Lactation is a technical word for "in milk." When I first began working with hunting clubs in deer management, I included a column in my record form for lactation. After having several bucks killed and recorded as "lactating," I decided to use the term **doe in milk** instead.

It is not difficult to determine whether or not a doe has been nursing during the summer. If you cut into the udder or "bag" of a doe that has been nursing, either milk or a brownish liquid will ooze from the wound. On occasion, you may also strip the teat and obtain milk.

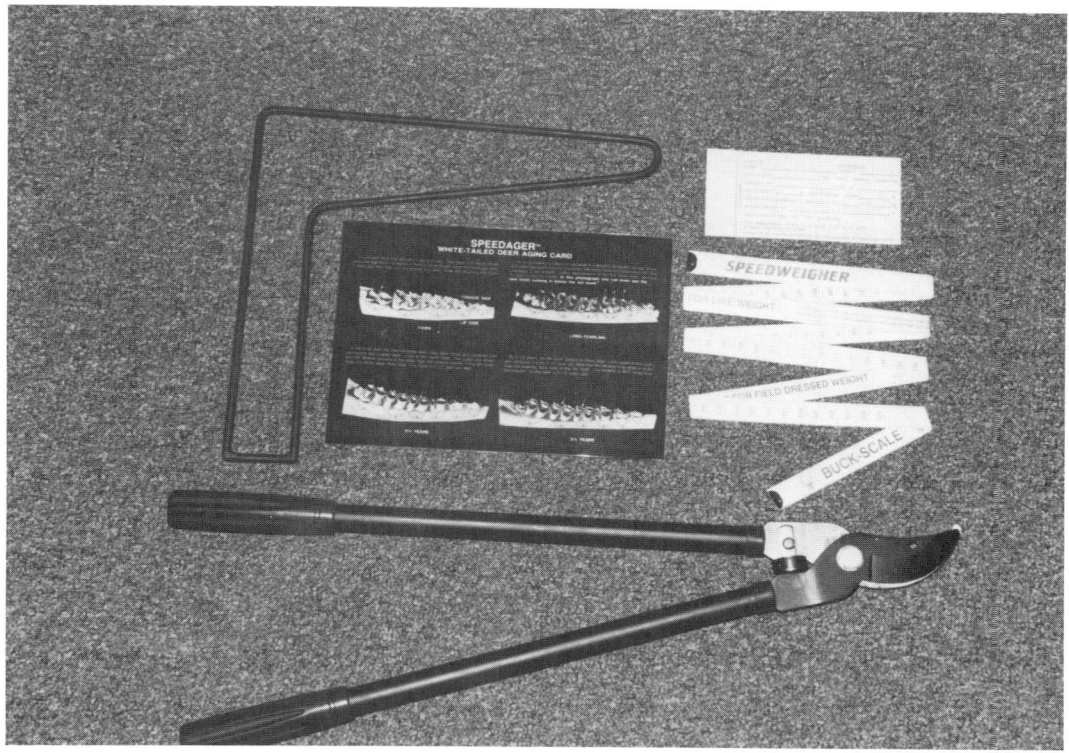

The "tools of trade" for the whitetail manager are record forms, jaw spreader, shears, scales or weight tape and aging chart.

Now if you find milk, do not get upset. This does not mean that you have doomed some poor fawn to starvation. Fawns are fully weaned by the hunting season in most areas, and capable of fending for themselves. I have seen other does in the social group "adopt" a fawn under such conditions. The doe will continue to produce some milk for quite a while after she has weaned her fawn(s). A sample record form is included at the end of this chapter. Simply record "yes" or "no" under the column "doe in milk" for each doe harvested.

A final check on reproduction can be obtained by removing the reproductive tracts of does; however, this requires some expertise. I suggest you ask a biologist to show you how to find and remove the tracts. Reproductive tracts should be removed, tagged with the doe's identification number, and stored in a 10% solution of formalin. Later, you either can have the tracts checked by a biologist or learn to evaluate them yourself. This probably is more than you will care to do, but it will give you one more diagnostic tool. The presence of embryos, especially early in the season, is often difficult to detect without some practice. At the bare minimum, I suggest you record incidental observations, and follow up with lactation records.

AGE STUCTURE OF THE HERD

Age is important to two aspects of whitetail management. First, and perhaps of greatest interest to hunters, age is one of the two most important factors determining antler size. Many clubs tell me that they have experienced a deterioration of genetic quality when the real problem is over-harvest of bucks. The bucks being harvested have small antlers simply because they are young bucks! Second, **it is important to know the age structure of your doe herd in order to assess: 1) the impact of a population control program, and 2) the potential reproductive performance of the doe segment.**

Hunters often assert that it is too difficult to learn to age deer. This is utter nonsense, since I teach hundreds of individuals annually to age deer with a good degree of accuracy. I even have developed a full color aging card (see photo) to help in aging. There are just a few simple principles to follow in order to develop your proficiency.

A checkstation should be constructed at a readily accessible location on the property. All materials should be available for use by hunters.

The method I commonly use to age deer is called the "tooth wear and replacement" developed by Drs. Severinghaus and Cheatum some time ago. There are other techniques, usually involving complicated and expensive laboratory procedures, that are no more accurate than this technique. Recently, some researchers have challenged the use of tooth wear and replacement, but their evidence against the technique is not very strong. How accurate is the method? Once you get past the yearling age class, you can expect an error of plus or minus a year— not really all that bad considering.

The method centers around the fact that deer only have two sets of teeth during their life. Teeth are designed to acquire and process vegetation. The two activities involved in this activity are biting and mastication. For the first activity, deer have sharp incisors on the front of the lower jaw. The upper portion is completely devoid of incisors. I often am amused by hunters who tell me they killed an old buck because he had no teeth in his upper jaw. For this reason, deer acquire vegetation by pinching it from the plant. Deer feeding sign is easily recognized by the characteristic "pulled off" appearance of the plant stem, as opposed to a sharp cut produced by rabbits and rodents. Chewing is accomplished by two sets of jaw teeth (premolars and molars).

A deer is born with three jaw teeth (milk teeth), and over a one to two year period, the first three teeth are shed, replaced by three additional permanent teeth. Three additional molars are subsequently added behind them. Hence, the full jaw teeth complement is six.

Whitetails are aged in one-half year increments, since they are born in the spring and harvested in the fall. The full complement of six teeth is achieved by 2 years of age. The three temporary milk teeth are shed between twelve and eighteen months of age. The milk teeth again confuse hunters in that they are very soft, becoming quickly worn by one year of age. I have looked at many bucks, reported to be old patriarchs, that turned out to be yearlings with well-worn milk teeth. But, how can you make sense of all of this? I suggest you follow my simple rules and use the aging card provided. Aging is difficult to describe, but easy to demonstrate.

It is difficult to look into a deer's mouth, even when freshly killed. If it has been dead for two or more hours, you will really have a problem, as *rigor mortis* has set in by this time. For this reason, I suggest that you acquire a jaw spreader, shears and a flashlight. The jaw spreader is easily made by a welder for a modest price.

Aging

First of all, if you look into a deer's mouth and it has less than six teeth in the lower jaw, you can pretty well be assured that it is less than one year of age. It should be classified as a **fawn.** This is the age-class with which I hope you have the least amount of difficulty in aging. Hopefully, your deer herd is in good enough condition that fawns are easily distinguished from adults without ever having to look at the teeth. However, should you decide that the deer is not a fawn, then the next clue lies in the third jaw tooth. In yearlings, the third tooth is unlike any other, containing three cusps (see photograph). Therefore, if you look into a deer's mouth and the first three jaw teeth are worn, look carefully at the third tooth. If it has three cusps, then it is a yearling. This age-class is also referred to as a **long-yearling**, because the deer actually is eighteen months of age.

On the other hand, if the deer has six jaw teeth and the third tooth does not have three cusps, then the animal must be older than a yearling. The first three teeth are replaced with permanent jaw teeth containing the normal two cusp structure. **Since the fourth tooth is added prior to shedding of its three front neighbors, this tooth is the oldest tooth in the mouth, and will remain so throughout the life of the deer.** This is the tooth to examine next.

The jaw teeth of deer, and for that matter all mammals, are composed of two layers. There is an inner core of brownish dentine, covered with a hard white layer of enamel. As the deer regularly chews its food by grinding between the upper and lower jaws, the teeth become increasingly worn. Since the cusps are shaped like cones, as the point of the cone wears down, more and more of the dentine is exposed. We use the relative amount of dentine showing as an indicator of age in older deer. For example, if you look into a deer's mouth and the third tooth has only two cusps, you immediately know that it is not a yearling. Therefore, you look to the oldest tooth in the mouth, the fourth tooth. Closely examine the cusps on the tongue side of the jaw, comparing the relative widths of dentine (brown) and enamel (white). If the dentine is not wider than the enamel, then wear has not progressed very far. I would classify this animal as a **2-1/2 year old.**

If, however, we look into a deer's mouth and the fourth tooth shows considerable wear, we know that the animal is older than 2 1/2. We now look to the next oldest tooth, the fifth tooth. Again, we examine the relative widths of dentine and enamel on the tongue side cusps. If the enamel layer is as wide or wider than the dentine, then the animal should be classified as a **3 1/2 year old.** The fourth tooth is being worn down at this point. This method progresses with each tooth. If the dentine of the fifth tooth had been wider than the enamel, we would have examined the sixth tooth by the same criteria. If the tongue-side cusps are sharp, with enamel as wide or wider than the dentine, then the deer would be **4 1/2 years of age.** If not, then the deer is at least **5 1/2 years.** But now we have run out of jaw teeth to examine! We must go back to the oldest tooth in the jaw, the fourth tooth. Ask yourself if the tooth has become so worn that the enamel is totally absent from the middle of the tooth. If not, then the deer is 5 1/2 years. If it is, then I classify the animal in the **6 1/2+ year** category. It is possible to age a deer beyond 6 1/2 years; however, I have never found it necessary to do so. A little practice and study, and you should become proficient at aging deer with an accuracy of plus or minus one year. **Most decisions can be made by examining three age categories, fawn, yearling and 2 1/2+.** The accuracy for these age classifications is quite high.

SEX RATIO

Knowing something about the sex

ratio is important to meeting your management goals. To obtain a reasonable estimate, it is necessary to obtain as many deer observations as possible. I recommend no one technique. Rather, I suggest that you use every opportunity to obtain sex composition data from your herd. My experience has been that spotlight counts usually do not provide sufficient observations to allow an accurate estimate of sex ratio. There are those, however, that feel that aerial observations do provide quality data on sex composition, and I will be the last to argue the point. But, there is no substitute for large numbers of observations.

Again, I prefer to use the pocket observation cards discussed above for doe:fawn ratio estimates. The average hunting club of 2,000 acres will acquire more than 1,000 individual observations over the summer and early fall. Surprisingly, these observations have been shown to provide a random sample of your deer, and a reliable estimate of sex ratio. Every time you go to your club or property, you should record the sex and relative age of every animal you see, provided of course that it can be correctly identified. Calculation of the sex ratio estimate is made by simply dividing the number of does seen by the number of bucks. For example, if you see 800 does and 200 bucks, then you have a buck:doe ratio of 1:4. Interpretation of these results will be discussed later.

HEALTH INDICES

I have said many times that I can learn more about a deer herd by looking at its reproductive performance and health index, than by any census you may perform. There are several indices to the general health of your herd. Among these are dressed weights, age-specific antler development, parasite loads, lactation rates and stored fat estimates.

Dressed weights, especially of yearlings, are excellent indicators of overall herd condition. Both live and dressed weights should be recorded for every deer harvested from your property. For this purpose, I suggest that you acquire either a good spring scale or a heart-girth tape. A check station can be set up at a convenient point, such as your club house, a road entering and leaving the property or someone's home. **Every check station should include: a scale or tape, hoist, jaw spreader and shears, and a record book.** An optional dressing trough is handy. Do not succumb to the "get-it-later" temptation. I have seen many a hunter leave the property with his deer, fully intending to record the data at a later time, only to lose the records from the deer. Do it now, not later!

Antler measurements for each age-class are critical to determining the progress of your management program. After all, it is antlers we are after! On numerous occasions, I have heard a hunter say, "You can't eat horns!" This is totally ridiculous. What he really is saying is that he cannot kill a buck. You run a buck and a doe by that same fellow, and I will bet you he shoots the buck! So, let's be honest here.

There are many schemes to judge the quality of antlers. The most notable of these are the **Boone-and-Crockett System** and the **Burkett System**. There also is the **Pope-and-Young System** for bowhunters. In addition to these, hunting clubs and "big buck" contests often develop some pretty novel means of judging antler quality. One Boone-and-Crockett buck killed in East Texas scored second in such a contest! I prefer simple measurements, representing antler size and mass.

I suggest that you acquire the following antler measurements: number of points, inside spread, beam lengths of both right and left antlers and beam circumferences of both antlers. Number of points usually is a hotly debated item around hunting camps. It seems that the quality of the buck is tied to the number of points it has, rather than the size of the antlers. I know some hunters who would be more statisfied with a ten point yearling than an eight point mature buck, in spite of the fact that the eight pointer had massive antlers. The question, "What is a point?," invariably comes up. Some people say that a point is any protuberance on which a ring will hang. I prefer to classify a point as any protuberance that is longer than it is wide at the base.

All antler measurements should be made to the nearest eighth inch. A small, flexible tape is useful in obtaining measurements. I use a small metal, six-foot pocket tape. Inside spread is a pretty straightforward measurement; however, hunters often stretch the measurement a bit. I suggest that spread be measured as given in the illustration. Measure the widest straightline distance between main beams. Beam length is measured from the base of the antler (="burr") to its tip. This takes two hands, especially if the beam is very long. The small, flexible pocket tape is well-suited to this measurement. Official Boone-and-Crockett scorers use a metal wire and two clamp forceps, and then lay the

Yearling buck dressed weights is perhaps one of the best indicators of overall herd health. Under-weight yearling bucks commonly occur on over-populated ranges.

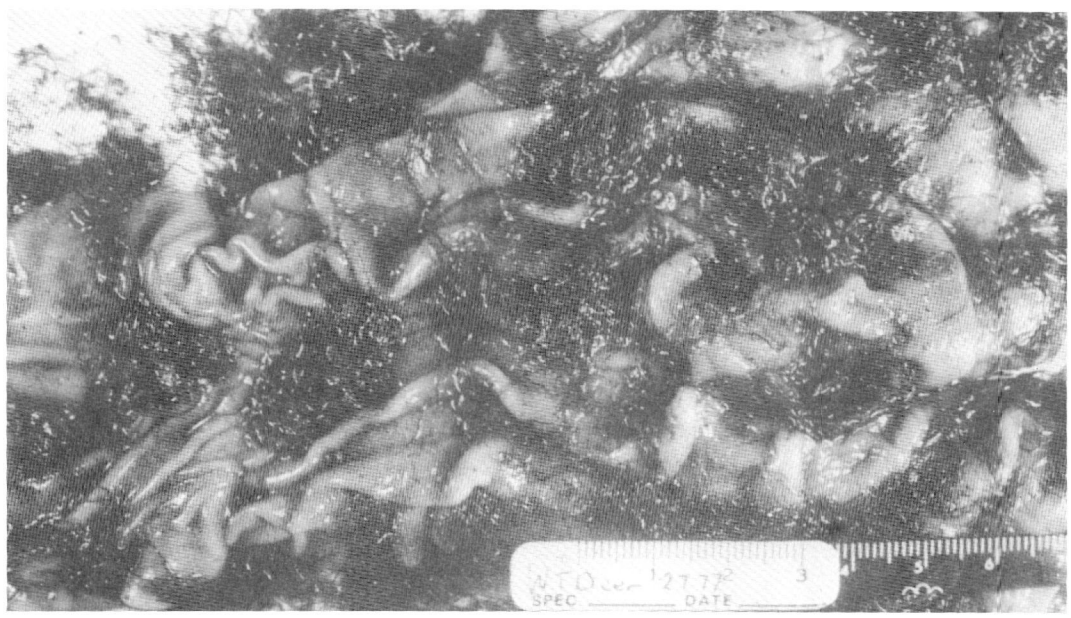

Abomasum from a fawn white-tailed deer massively infected with the stomach worm, *Haemonchus contortus*. (Photograph courtesy of Vic Nettles, Southeastern Cooperative Wildlife Disease Study.)

wire along a measuring stick. Finally, beam circumference should be measured just above the base, avoiding any basal points or odd protuberances. These measurements will be useful in making management decisions. Additional measurements such as length of each tine also are useful. I include tine length whenever possible.

Parasite loads are good indicators of the health of your herd. Parasites include both ecto- and endoparasites. Ectoparasites include mostly ticks and lice while endoparasites are represented by a host of internal worms and flukes. The relative abundance of stomach worms has been shown to give a reasonable estimate of population density. I feel that ectoparasite loads also give a good indication of population condition. For the layman, it is difficult to employ internal parasite indices. Therefore, I suggest that you stick to recording the relative ectoparasite load for each deer harvested. This is quite a subjective evaluation, and I suggest that you classify your deer as either being lightly, moderately or heavily infested with parasites. In order to give you a general idea of these classifications, I would classify an animal as heavily infested with parasites that has ticks and lice over the ears, legs and belly. Moderate loads would find parasites on the inside of the belly, especially the groin area. A light parasite load would be indicated if you have difficulty finding any parasite on the body. If, however, you are interested in internal parasites, you might enlist the aid of a veterinarian or experienced biologist. At any rate, you should examine the internal organs for any unusual conditions.

Liver flukes are easily detected, even by the layman and their presence should be recorded. There is one internal parasite of particular note, the bot fly. Hunters are horrified to find one of these large, maggot-like worms either inside the nose or even crawling out of the deer's nose. These animals occur regularly in many deer herds, and other than recording its presence, I would not be concerned. It may look bad, but it will have no effect on meat quality. However, there are disease conditions for which you should be on

Hemorrhagic disease manifests itself in many ways. The most commonly encountered symptom is the presence of lesions on the tongue and roof of the mouth (Photograph courtesy Vic Nettles, Southeastern Cooprative Disease Study).

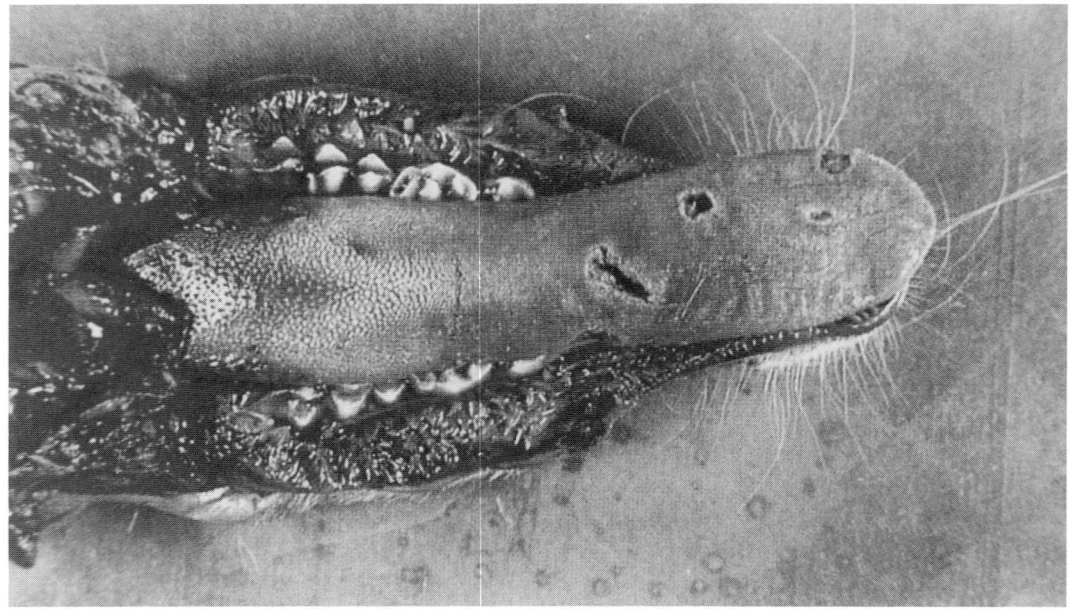

the lookout.

The most notable of these are the **hemorrhagic diseases** such as EHD and bluetongue. These are diseases that can have a dramatic impact on the herd, either chronically or acutely. The organisms which cause these diseases are transmitted by biting gnats, who usually transmit the disease from domestic livestock in which it has little or no effect. The effect on deer, however, is catostrophic! Epizootic hemorrhagic disease (EHD) and bluetongue attack the animal in several locations, most notable of which is the mouth and stomach lining. The hooves also begin to slough off as the disease progresses. The presence of lesions on the nose and inside the mouth, a hemorrhagic appearing stomach lining, or sloughing hooves are indicators that the animal may be infected with the disease. Also, there is a tendency for deer to be found dead adjacent to ponds and streams, presumably where they go in response to fever conditions. Although a badly infected animal may look terrible, the meat is presumed at this time to be wholesome. But, presence of EHD should cause a much greater concern than whether or not the particular animal can be eaten. Hemorrhagic diseases occur in small proportions (=chronic level) in many deer herds, especially in the South. A high incidence of the disease, however, can lead to massive die-offs (=acute level). For example, one landowner in Louisiana recently lost about ninety percent of his deer herd in one year! He had both cattle and deer in the woods, and his deer herd had been hovering on the brink of danger for many years. Any sign of EHD should be recorded and reported to a local biologist or the Cooperative Wildlife Disease Unit at Athens, Georgia.

Browse Surveys

For years now, southern managers have successfully used a technique to assess herd health called **deer range appraisal.** This method was developed and made popular by Dan Lay, a Texas Parks & Wildlife Department biologist in the Pineywoods of East Texas. The

Browse or range evaluations give useful information about the condition both of the range and the herd.

Robert Skinner

technique is simple and easily mastered, even by a novice in the field. It requires that you learn the top twenty or so browse plants eaten by deer in your area. This number may vary with geographic area, so you can make the appropriate adjustment. I have included a list of common browse plants by general geographic region at the end of this chapter. For more specific information, I suggest that you contact your local biologist or state game agency.

Most areas can adeqauately be sampled using 25 to 100 sample plots. I suggest that you establish permanent transect lines on your property, the number of which best samples the extent of diversity on the area. Then, the number of plots desired can be allocated according to the number of lines established. For example, if you have ten lines, you could designate ten sample points along each line. The distance between sample points should be arbitrary, but fixed in distance. I use 100 feet between sample plots.

At each sample point, I establish an approximately 12 feet radius, which defines a plot about 1/100 acre in size. Within the plot, you should estimate the extent of utilization for each preferred browse species. Utilization should be ranked by the classifications: 0, 5, 30 and 70%. It takes a little practice, but is easily accomplished even by a novice.

Browsing sign, as noted earlier, is differentiated from rabbit foraging by the "pulled off" appearance produced as the deer uses its lower incisors to pinch off the vegetation.

This green briar has been excessively browsed to the point (greater than 50%) that it probably will not recover.

For each transect line, you should select the species that occur in 20% or more of the plots, and calculate the average utilization for these species. Confused? Here is an example.

Suppose you put in ten sample plots along a transect line. Species A occurred on eight of these plots, with utilization figures of 5, 5, 30, 70, 5, 30, 5 and 30%. To obtain the average utilization for species A, add the eight numbers to give a total of 180. Now, we divide by 8, yielding an average utilization of 22.5%.

Do this for all species occurring in 20% or more of the plots, then add up the average utilization for all of these species, and divide by the total number of species. Again, here is an example.

Suppose we have five species that occur in 20% or more of the plots. The average utilization figures for these five species were: 22.5, 35.8, 12.7, 59.3 and 38.5. The total utilization for all species would then be: 22.5 + 35.8 + 12.7 + 59.3 + 38.5= 168.8. Dividing this number by 5 (the number of species), gives an average utilization of 33.8%.

Now, what does this number mean? There are several evaluation schemes, including the one developed by Lay. Most involve classification of browse plants into preference categories, most commonly first, second and third choices. However, I feel that you also can learn a great deal just by examining the extent of utilization of preferred browses.

It is a good "rule-of-thumb" that you should never have more than 50% utilization of preferred browse plants. Excessively high utilization figures of 50% or more throws up some red flags. You then need to look at the other records discussed earlier. These will be covered in depth in the next chapter. A form for conducting a range appraisal is included at the end of this chapter. The usefulness of the range appraisal is similar to that for a census. By itself, the average utilization does not tell us a great deal, although more than a census. But, when conducted on an annual basis, it gives us a point of comparison for establishing trends.

SUMMARY

Record-keeping is paramount to a managed deer herd. You do not run a business without knowing your inventory or financial situation; unless, of course, you do not plan on staying in business long. So it is with a deer herd. I know of no situation which will allow you to properly manage a herd without keeping adequate records. These records should be annually reviewed and appropriate actions taken. In the next chapter, I will discuss how you can interpret these records to achieve your management goals.

INCIDENTAL DEER OBSERVATION FORM

Club: _____ Observer: _____
County: _____

DEER SIGHTED

Date	Does	Fawns	Bucks*	Unknown	Remarks

*Record whether spiked or forked

Browse Utilization Survey Form for: _____ Plot: _____
Date: _____

PLANT SPECIES	Utilization Rating(%)			
	0	5	30	70

Record-keeping: The Basis for Sound Management

SEASON: 19___-___
HUNTING CLUB: _____

CONTACT PERSON: _____
PHONE: AC ____ - ____

© 1987 Wildlife Heritage Inc.

Deer #	Date	Sex	Age	Weight (pounds)		Points	Antler Measurements (Inches)				Doe in Milk (Yes/No)	Hunter	Comments
				Live	Dressed		L. Beam Circum.	R. Beam Circum.	L. Beam Length	R. Beam Length	Inside Spread			

PREFERRED BROWSE SPECIES FOR FIVE ECOLOGICAL REGIONS WITHIN THE WHITETAIL'S RANGE

EASTERN CANADA

Common Name	Scientific Name
FIRST CHOICE	
Beaked Hazel	*Corylus cornuta*
Northern White-cedar	*Thuja occidentalis*
Ground Hemlock	*Tsuga canadensis*
Alternate-leaf Dogwood	*Cornus alternifolia*
American Mountain-ash	*Sorbus americana*
SECOND CHOICE	
Mountain Maple	*Acer spicatum*
Striped Maple	*Acer pensylvanicum*
Saskatoon Serviceberry	*Amelanchier alnifolia*
Yellow Birch	*Betula alleghaniensis*
Red Maple	*Acer rubrum*
THIRD CHOICE	
Balsam Fir	*Abies balsamea*
Speckled Alder	*Alnus rugosa*
Black Spruce	*Picea mariana*
White Spruce	*Picea glauca*
Tamarack	*Larix laricina*

NORTHEASTERN UNITED STATES

FIRST CHOICE

Greenbrier	Smilax spp.
Blackberry	Rubus spp.
Japanese Honeysuckle	Lonicera japonica
Alternate-leaf Dogwood	Cornus alternifolia
Northern White-cedar	Thija occidentalis

SECOND CHOICE

Staghorn Sumac	Rhus typhina
Sourwood	Oxydendrum arboreum
Sassafras	Sassafras albidum
Red Maple	Acer rubrum
Downy Serviceberry	Amelanchier arborea

THIRD CHOICE

Eastern Hophornbeam	Ostrya virginiana
Blueberry	Vaccinium spp.
Eastern Redbud	Cercis canadensis
Black Tupelo	Nyssa sylvatica
Carolina Buckthorn	Rhamnus caroliniana

SOUTHEASTERN UNITED STATES

FIRST CHOICE

St. Peterswort	*Ascyrum stans*
Alabama Supplejack	*Berchemia scandens*
Carolina Jessamine	*Gelsemium sempervirens*
Japanese Honeysuckle	*Lonicera japonica*
Greenbrier	*Smilax spp.*, except *S. pumila*

SECOND CHOICE

Red Maple	*Acer rubrum*
American Beautyberry	*Callicarpa americana*
Flowering Dogwood	*Cornus florida*
Red Mulberry	*Morus rubra*
Smooth Sumac	*Rhus glabra*

THIRD CHOICE

American Hornbeam	*Carpinus caroliniana*
Eastern Redbud	*Cercis canadensis*
Sweetgum	*Liquidambar styraciflua*
Hickory	*Carya spp.*
Blackjack Oak	*Quercus marilandica*

MIDWESTERN UNITED STATES

FIRST CHOICE

Quaking Aspen	*Populus tremulodies*
Downy Juneberry	*Amelanchier arborea*
Common Snowberry	*Symphoricarpos albus*
Alternate-leaf Dogwood	*Cornus alternifolia*
Redstem Ceanothus	*Ceanothus sanguinueus*

SECOND CHOICE

Skunkbush Sumac	*Rhus aromatica*
Sasktoon Serviceberry	*Amelanchier alnifolia*
Bearberry	*Arctostaphylos uva-ursi*
Creeping mahonia	*Mahonia repens*
Common Pockberry	*Phytotacca americana*

THIRD CHOICE

Rabbitbush	*Chrysothamnus nauseosus*
Buffaloberry	*Shepherdia argentea*
Myrtle Pachistima	*Pachistima myrisinites*
Common Persimmon	*Diospyros virginiana*
Bur Oak	*Quercus macrocarpa*

SOUTH TEXAS AND MEXICO

FIRST CHOICE

Catclaw	*Acacia greggii*
La Coma	*Bumelia celastrina*
Guajillo	*Acacia berlandieri*
Granjeno	*Celtis pallida*
Blackbrush	*Acacia rigidula*

SECOND CHOICE

Lime Pricklyash	*Zanthoxylum fagara*
Huisache	*Acacia farnesiana*
Berlandier Wolfberry	*Lycium berlandieri*
Bluewood Condalia	*Condalia obovata*
Lotewood Condalia	*Condalia obtusifolia*

THIRD CHOICE

Texas Colubrina	*Colubrina texensis*
Rockbrush (Kidneywood)	*Eysenhardtia texana*
Ceniza	*Leucophyllum frutescens*
Texas Lantana	*Lantana horrida*
Mexican Persimmon	*Diospyros texana*

SPEEDAGER™
WHITE-TAILED DEER AGING CARD

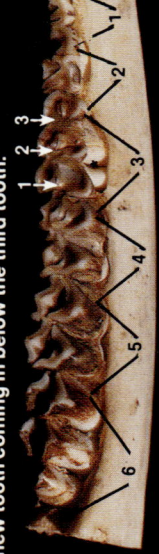

TONGUE SIDE / **LIP SIDE**

FAWN

You should have little difficulty aging a fawn. Their body size alone usually gives the age away. However, if there is some doubt, count the lower jaw teeth. If there are less than six, the animal is a fawn. Note the erupting fifth tooth.

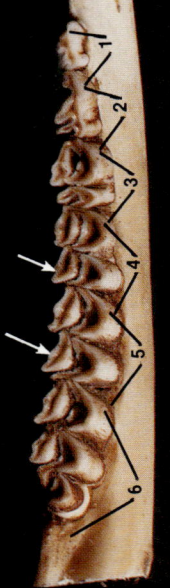

LONG-YEARLING

The long-yearling is called so because it is around 18 months of age. It has all six lower jaw teeth, but the first three milk teeth have not been shed yet. The giveaway is the smooth, chalky appearance of the first three teeth, and the three cusps on the third tooth. **In this photograph you can even see the new tooth coming in below the third tooth.**

2½ YEARS

In the 2½ year old, the first three teeth have been shed and replaced with permanent two-cusped teeth. Look at the fourth tooth. The cusps are sharp and the dentine (brown) is not wider than the enamel (white). If the fourth tooth does not show wear, then stop. You have a 2½ year old deer.

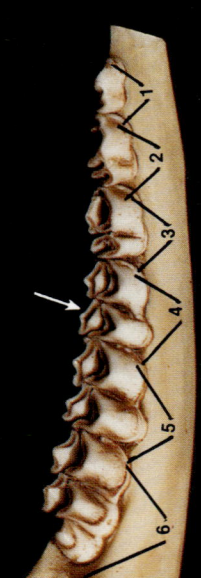

3½ YEARS

By 3½ years, the fourth tooth begins to show wear. Look again at this tooth and compare it to the 2½ year old. Note that the dentine is as wide or wider then the enamel. Now, look at the fifth tooth. The dentine is NOT wider than the enamel, so the deer is 3½ years old.

Record-keeping: The Basis for Sound Management

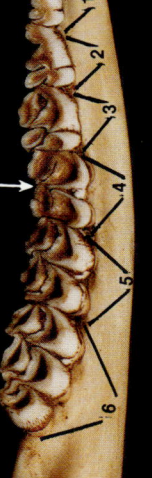

At 4½ years, wear has spread to the fifth tooth. Notice that the dentine is wider than the enamel in both the fourth and fifth jaw teeth. Now look at the sixth tooth. The dentine is NOT wider than the enamel, so it is 4½ years old.

4½ YEARS

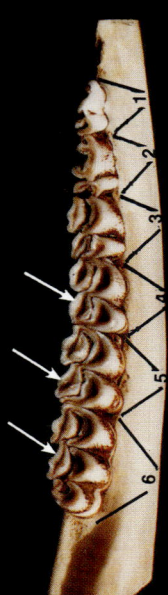

Since deer are usually mature at 6½ years, we do not normally age beyond this point; hence, the age 6½ +. Look at the fourth tooth. At this age, the enamel is completely gone. The fifth and sixth teeth should have only a small amount of enamel left in their centers. **In older deer, all six teeth may be worn smooth. If the fourth, fifth, and/or sixth teeth are worn smooth, place the deer in the 6½ + age class.**

6½ + YEARS

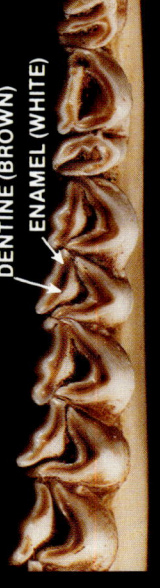

Wear has spread over all six jaw teeth by 5½ years. The dentine is wider than the enamel on all teeth, including the sixth tooth. Since the fourth tooth is the oldest, it will wear out earlier. Note that only a small amount of enamel is left in the middle of the fourth tooth — a sure sign of the 5½ year old.

5½ YEARS

INSTRUCTIONS FOR USING THE SPEEDAGER™

This card is the result of years of effort to acquire the best representatives of the various age classes of white-tails. The jaws were collected from known aged animals, painstakingly photographed and printed for top quality color and clarity.

To use the card, all you have to do is open the right side of the deer's jaw and hold the card next to it. Follow the instructions on each panel and match up the jaw that fits your deer.

DENTINE (BROWN)
ENAMEL (WHITE)

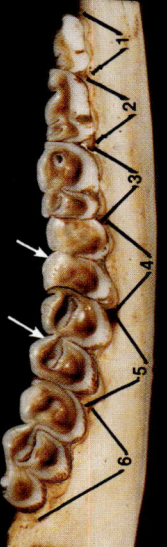

It is only necessary that you learn to recognize two parts of the tooth — the enamel and the dentine. Both are shown vividly in this photograph. Enamel will appear as whitish in color, while dentine will usually be brownish.

© Wildlife Heritage Productions 1984

THE DOE

After the raging storm last night,
I come to graze at dawn's first light.

With my newborn fawns at side,
Coming forth and filled with pride.

Spring is here, danger gone,
No hunters nearby to harm my own.

Peace is here for all to enjoy,
Spring flowers for my new born's toys.

All is well I'll have to say,
Wish it were this way every day.
...K.S.

Chapter 13

INTERPRETING RECORDS: THE FINE-TUNING PROCESS

Proper collection of records on a deer herd is important to making sound management decisions. Unfortunately, most landowners and even some biologists maintain poor records on their herds. As I have noted many times, you do not run a business without adequate records, and so it is with a deer herd. Careful attention to this less exciting aspect of deer management can mean the difference between realizing your goals and total frustration and failure. Once records have been collected, it is time to make interpretations that shed light on the progress of your program. So far, we have collected data on incidental sightings, buck and doe age-structure, reproductive success and body measurements. This chapter deals with the correct interpretation of these data.

During the last decade, I spent a great deal of time developing diagnostic tools which readily can be used by the landowner or hunting club in managing the deer herd. As much as it may hurt my ego to admit it, deer herds, as with cattle herds, can be managed by the layman without the benefit of a professional biologist in most cases. It is only the more fine-tuned aspects of production deer management that require the expertise of an experienced professional.

FAWN CROP

The "name-of-the-game" when it comes to deer management is fawn crop. The number of fawns you produce will determine the number of bucks available for harvest later in your management program. A doe that is not producing fawns is contributing little to the management program. In fact, she probably is taking away quite a bit from the habitat!

The previous chapter discussed some of the types of data which tell us most about the reproductive success of does on the range. Although it is meaningful to collect does during the gestation period (summer) for determining *in utero* fawn counts, this means little to management. As I noted earlier, even herds in poor condition will have a relatively high *in utero* fawn count. By the time a decline shows up, it often is too late to take appropriate action. Your incidental sightings tell us quickly what the true fawn crop situation is. It is the number of fawns that survive until fall that really counts.

By early fall, you should have accumulated a rather tall stack of observation cards. Simply add up all of the doe and fawn sightings, dividing the total fawns by total does to get your first approximation of recruitment. Remember, recruitment is the number of fawns that are assimilated into the population. A summer estimate of recruitment rate will be higher than the real fall rate, but should alert you early on as to impending problems. Doe:fawn ratios of 35-40% are unacceptable to quality deer management. Your ratio, as determined by incidental sightings, should be 80% or better. Should the first estimate of recruitment rate be much below 80%, a substantial doe harvest may be indicated. How much? Remember that a deer herd is not managed, it is "fine-tuned." This means that dramatic steps are seldom made in deer herd management. Rather, you make small adjustments and then monitor the reaction of the herd. As a rule, I often suggest a doe harvest of at least one doe to fifty acres, no matter the habitat type. In some areas this is a gross under-harvest, while in others it may be just right. If the response is positive (increased lactation) the following year, then you increase the harvest a little more, until negative trends (reduced recruitment) dictate that you have overshot your goal.

Some of the best data on deer herd condition are lactation rates. As discussed earlier, this is the percentage of does that are in milk at time of harvest. I have included a diagnostic graph for interpretation of your doe lactation data. In order to maintain quality, you should have at least 80% of your does that are 2.5 years or older lactating. This means that 80 out of every 100 does has produced at least one fawn. Hence, lactation rate is a conservative estimate of the recruitment rate. Once a fawn reaches the fall season, probability of survival is greatly enhanced past that point in time. You may lose another 10% during the winter. The only exception to this is in grossly overpopulated areas, or along the extreme limits of the deer's range, where high winter kill is not uncommon. In these cases, winter mortality is a density independent factor.

So, what all this means is that your harvested does (2.5+ years) should at least have an 80% lactation rate for quality management. Should the rate be less than this figure, you should increase your antlerless harvest the coming season. Should the figure be greater than 80%, keep your harvest the same until it begins to decline.

But, you may be asking: What will happen if you have set your harvest too high to begin with? That really is not a problem in that, after the first harvest year, you have a good idea of the reproductive success of the herd. Total harvest is directly related to deer density. A low population, due to hunter inefficiency, leads to a small harvest. Should the lactation rate be 80% or greater, you have the luxury of backing off the doe harvest until lactation rates suffer. If lactation rates do not increase with doe harvest, you probably have a herd that is affected by density-independent factors such as climate or forage quality. I will address this problem later. That is where doe age structure comes into the picture.

DOE AGE STRUCTURE

Once a doe exceeds 4.5 years, she contributes little to herd production thereafter. She is an obligation, rather than an asset. I once radio-tracked a doe during her entire life. She became a dominant doe at age 2.5 and remained dominant until 4.5 years, after which her daughter took over as matriarch. Over the next four years, she became less productive and had a less than stable home range.

Any positive genetic selection benefits are more quickly expressed in younger doe herds. For this reason, I suggest that you examine another diagnostic, doe age structure.

Fifty to 60% of the does harvested should be 2.5 years of age or less. The total age structure is determined by the intensity of the harvest. Often, I am asked by hunting clubs how to select does for harvest. During the initial phases of deer management, there is no need to try to select specific does for harvest. Unlike bucks, does cannot be aged generally by sight. Rather, the way to lower the average age of does in the herd is to increase the harvest intensity. Since the annual adult mortality rate in many herds is approximately 10%, the number of individuals in older age classes diminishes in pyramidal form. A uniform harvest, therefore, produces a larger proportional reduction in older age classes. Hence, unless you are in an intensive trophy management program (discussed later) I suggest that the first doe that presents herself be harvested without prejudice for age. I have included a diagnostic chart for long-term record-keeping of doe age structure.

BUCK:DOE RATIO

A great deal has been written about

the necessity to maintain balanced buck:doe ratios; however, the mythical 1:1 ratio is seldom attainable in real life situations. A 1:2 or 1:3 ratio is adequate for most herds. In order to derive a reasonable estimate of this ratio, we return to the incidental sightings record cards. Several studies have shown that ratios derived from these data are reliable estimators of the true herd ratio. Again, I have included a long-term diagnostic chart for these data. The quality zone lies in the 1:3 or better range. Should your data suggest that the ratio is much higher (too many does), then look carefully at your doe age structure, lactation rates and average age of bucks (discussed later). A substantial increase in doe harvest is indicated. Remember that buck:doe ratio is adjusted in two ways; viz., doe harvest and the fawn crop.

AVERAGE AGE OF BUCKS

Since most managers are interested primarily in the quality of bucks harvested, careful attention always must be given to this segment of the population. The average age of bucks harvested is an excellent indicator of the harvest intensity on males. The diagnostic chart provided allows for two different management strategies. First, in most cases managers and clubs opt for a quality buck program. I already have discussed the characteristics of such a program. In order to maintain a quality buck program, the average age of bucks harvested should exceed 2.5 years. Therefore, the quality zone includes average ages of 2.5 or better. If, on the other hand, you are more interested in trophies, you should strive for maintaining average ages in the 3.5+ trophy zone. Should average age drop below either figure, a reduction in buck harvest should be effected immediately. However, if the average age of bucks harvested lies well into the quality zone, you have the option of increasing buck harvest. As with the other diagnostics, you are in a fine-tuning situation which may take several years to perfect. On most of my management areas, the average buck age drops out of the quality zone at a harvest intensity of one buck to approximately 100 acres of deer habitat. This figure will vary with habitat type and geographic area. With time, you should be able to establish your own harvest rate specific to your land.

YEARLING SPIKE RATE

Although there has been considerable disagreement and many public misconceptions about the cause(s) of spiking in whitetails, most researchers agree that nutrition plays a large role in spike frequency. Hence, the yearling spike rate is a good indicator of herd density. The quality of the food on the range is directly related to the number of mouths present.

Spike rate is an excellent diagnostic if bucks are harvested without prejudice. This means that in clubs where bucks are harvested randomly, the percentage of spiked yearlings is quite useful. In clubs that tend to avoid harvesting spikes, or in clubs that have decided to wage war on spikes, these data are meaningless. A 15% yearling spike rate is considered the cutoff point for the quality zone (see diagnostic chart). This chart can be used successfully only if bucks are harvested at random. If this be the case, a high yearling spike rate alerts you to possible population problems. Then, you should look at the lactation rate and doe age structure diagnostics to confirm that there is a problem.

YEARLING BUCK DRESSED WEIGHT

Other than lactation rate, the average dressed weight of yearling bucks is one of the most useful diagnostics in deer management. Herds with inadequate nutrition due to habitat quality and/or overpopulation will habitually produce under-weight yearling bucks. The quality zone in the accompanying diagnostic chart has been adjusted for geographic differences in deer body weights. In much of the South, the 80-pound (dressed weight) threshold serves to alert the manager of population problems. In the Mississippi Delta or in the northern races, however, we must adjust the threshold upward to at least 100 pounds. In either case, if average dressed weights fall outside of the quality zone, a serious nutritional problem is indicated. Look carefully at the lactation rate, doe age structure and, where appropriate, the yearling spike rate diagnostics to confirm possible problems.

ANTLER QUALITY

I have included a diagnostic chart which can be customized to examine antler quality. Unlike the previous diagnostics, there are many geographic differences in acceptable antler quality levels. For this reason, I suggest you use a standardized measure of antler quality and graph the average score of bucks on the chart. I use a rather simplified scheme developed here at SFASU.

Calculation One= average main beam length (in.) + average inside spread (in.);

Calculation Two= Calculation One X average circumference of antler bases (in.); and,

Calculation Three= Calculation Two + number of points.

For my purposes, I use a quality level of 125 for quality buck management and 135 for trophy buck management. As I noted earlier, you can set your own quality level, based on **your** specific goals and expectations.

My experience has shown that the antler quality score is only weakly related to average age of bucks. In well-managed herds, you can have a relatively high antler quality score, while maintaining a young buck population. Since nutrition is involved, herd control and a good habitat management program can greatly affect antler quality. I try to increase my buck harvest until antler quality shows a decline below the quality limit. Then, I back off buck harvest in steps until the score returns to the cutoff point.

BROWSE UTILIZATION

As I noted in the record-keeping chapter, monitoring of utilization of preferred browse can tell you a great deal about the relative stocking rate on your range. I also have included a diagnostic chart for evaluating your browse utilization. The quality zone lies in the 50% range for most ranges; however, I have broadened this range to include 50-60% utilization to allow for an optimum sustained yield management goal. In a trophy management program, you may want to drop below the 50% level, realizing of course, that this means fewer deer on the range and a lower potential harvest rate.

SUMMARY

There are no "magic bullets" in deer management. Herds do not deteriorate overnight, and neither do they quickly improve. Deer herd management is a fine-tuning process involving adjustments in both population-habitat dynamics and the desires of the hunters involved. The key is good record-keeping, without which you never will realize your goals.

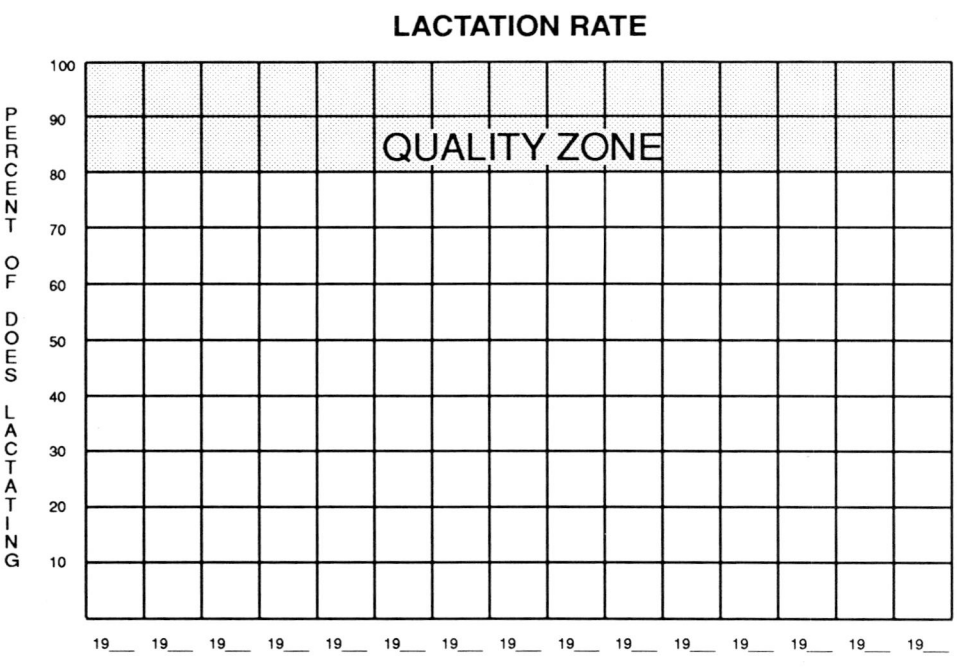

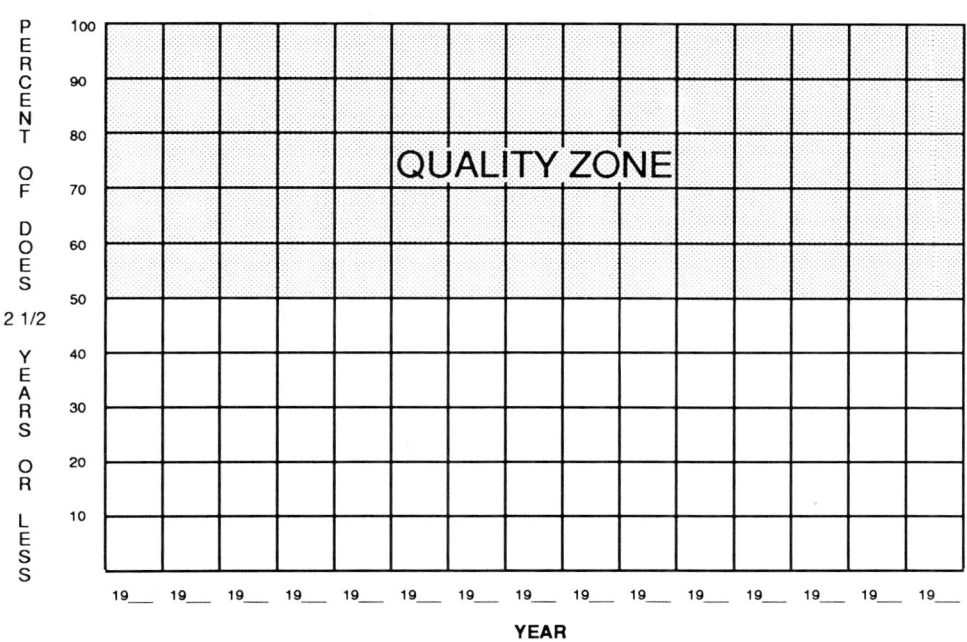

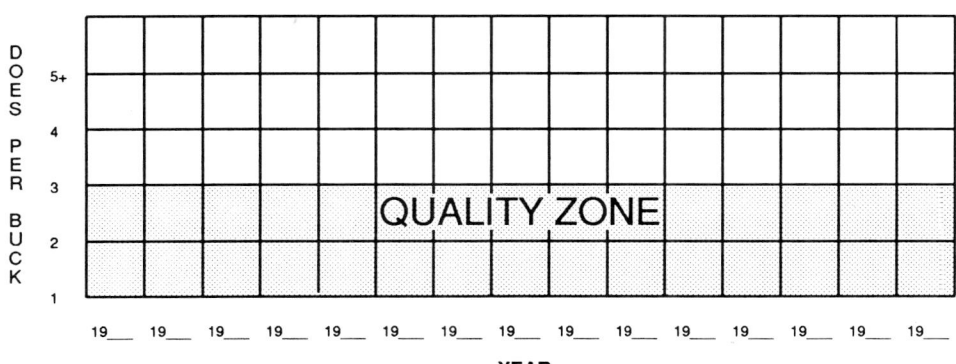

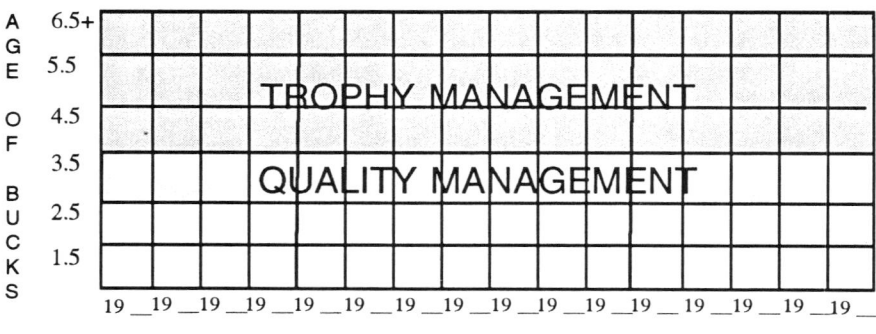

Interpreting Records: The Fine-Tuning Process

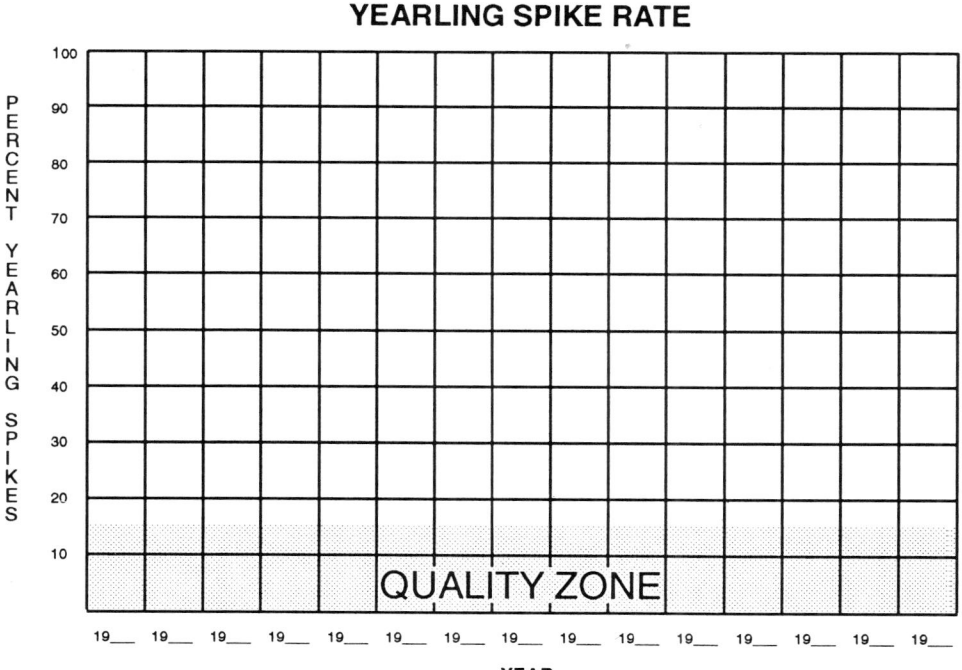

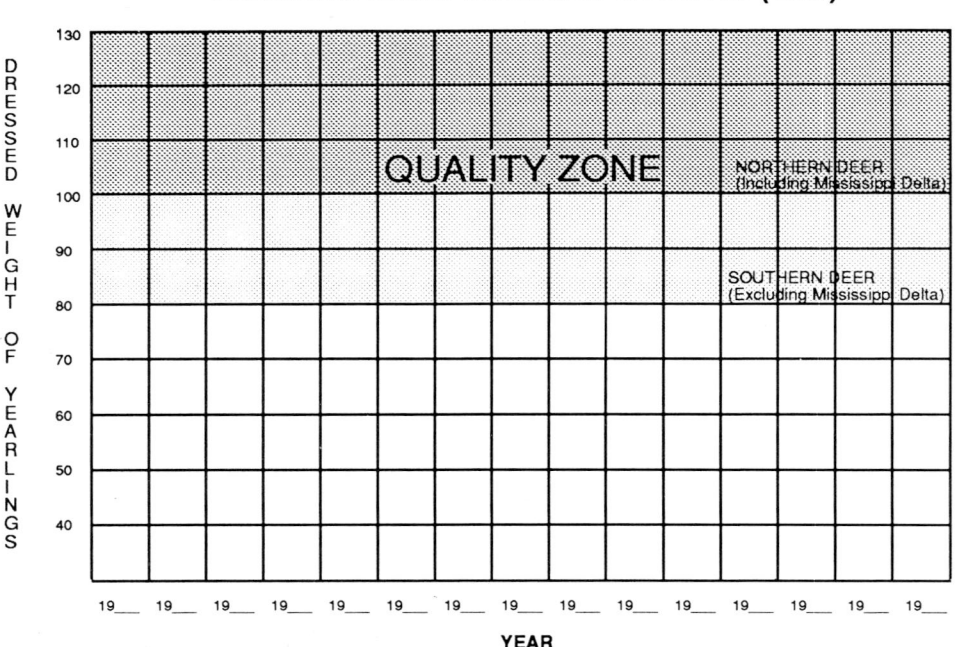

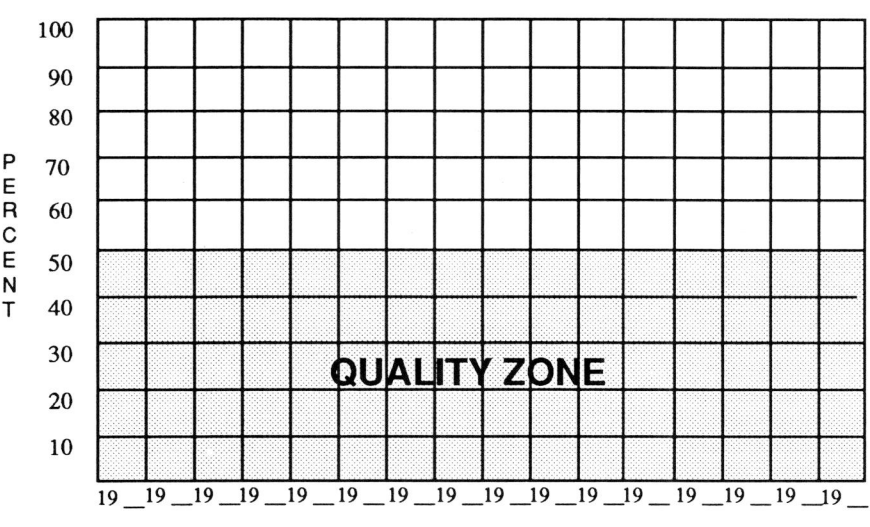

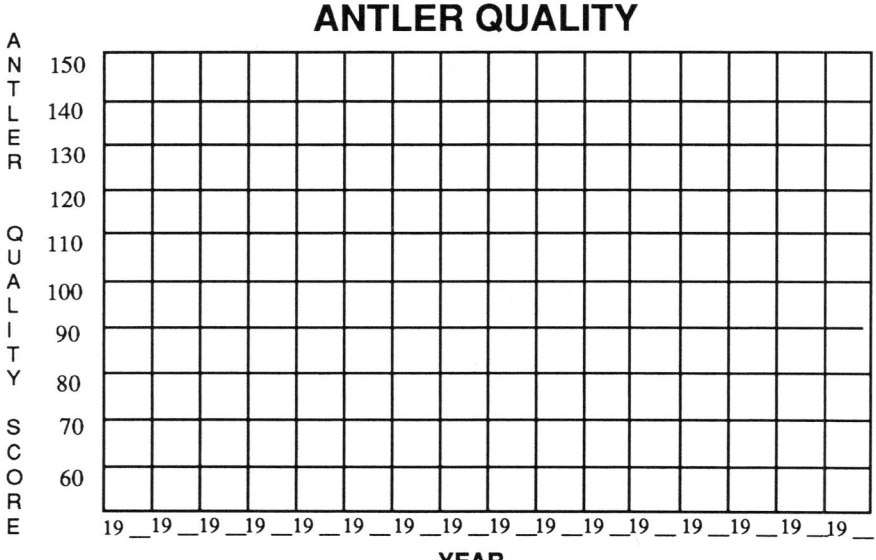

Note: In this diagnostic chart, you must set your own quality zone, depending on the productive capabilities of your land and your personal goals.

Chapter 14

TROPHY MANAGEMENT: SOME PLAIN TALK

You can hardly pick up an outdoor magazine nowadays without reading an article about trophy whitetail management on some South Texas ranchlands surrounded by high fences and managed with the single goal of providing a few trophy-class animals for the landowner or his guests to shoot. Biologists and outdoor writers alike tend to look at these "laboratory" examples as standards of whitetail management. Yet over-zealous, improper application of such practices may lead to frustration for the landowner and even less credibility than we already have experienced in the wildlife management profession. There is far more to trophy whitetail management than shooting does and spikes. Trophy management is a complex, costly, and long-term undertaking.

I have been actively involved in white-tailed deer management over the last two decades, working throughout the whitetail's range. It did not take me long to find out that, with little effort, I could make my hunters and landowners think I was the greatest thing since night baseball! It really does not take much of a biologist to go into an area where bucks have been mercilessly harvested for years, to cut back on the buck harvest, to increase doe removal, and in a few years, have bucks running all over the place.

So, what is wrong with that? Nothing really, if in so doing I have not given the landowner the unreal expectation that his land is going to produce a record-book animal. Now, let's take a look at the problems associated with trophy management, and then take a realistic approach to the management of white-tailed deer. In the next chapter, I will present a blueprint for one of three possible goals. One of these goals **is** trophy management. I am not saying that trophy management is not feasible, only that you must understand the costs and benefits of this type of management goal.

THE PROBLEM

The first problem lies in the definition of a trophy. Webster is of absolutely no help: "A specimen or part, often mounted, preserved as a token of successful hunting." In short, the quality of a trophy, as with beauty, lies in the eye of the beholder. Obviously, any buck taken may be a trophy to someone.

Trophy, as with beauty, is in the eye of the beholder. There is no doubt that the buck on the right is a trophy; yet, the buck on the left also is a trophy to some hunters.

Mike Biggs

The landowner must decide exactly what he wants. It is the job of the biologist to honestly say whether or not such a goal is realistic and attainable. For the purposes of this chapter, however, I propose that a trophy-class whitetail is one that realizes the true genetic and environmental potential of a particular deer herd, and scores 150 or more inches B&C. With this in mind, let's proceed to the problem at hand.

Although there are unique problems associated with each land-holding, any trophy management program must deal with four basic problems:
1. **Increase buck abundance**
2. **Improve buck age structure**
3. **Achieve maximum productivity**
4. **Improve genetic quality**

The deer herds on most ranges, whether in South Texas Brush Country, the southern Pineywoods, or the Upper Peninsula of Michigan, were derived by years of over-exploitation of bucks and over-protection of does. What resulted was young bucks and old does. In addition, some herds may have experienced genetic degradation both from over-harvest and over-protection. In order to increase the abundance of bucks, the harvest rate can be slowed or stopped completely for a number of years. The process can be speeded up by the removal of does. But, how many does should be removed? It certainly seems simple on the surface. For example, if we want a 1:1 sex ratio, and we have 400 does and 100 bucks, we just need to remove 300 does. Can you imagine what it takes to legally remove 300 does? And, if it is not accomplished in a single year, we still have too many does to contend with the next year.

Buck:doe ratio is one of the first topics of discussion among trophy hunters and biologists. A 1:1 or 1:2 ratio has been suggested by several practicing whitetail managers. However, most of these individuals either operate within enclosures (high fences) or on tremendously large land areas. Buck:doe ratio certainly can be improved in a free-ranging herd, but in many cases, a management objective of a 1:1 ratio is **unrealistic.** The fact is that bucks, especially yearlings, migrate. Recent studies have shown that buck:doe ratio can be influenced by deer population density, especially buck density. Seventy percent of yearling bucks annually migrate distances ranging 3 to 10 miles. At the same time, around 30 percent of the does also establish new home ranges. The old statement that a deer dies within a mile of its birth, as I noted earlier, is not always true. It has been my experience that such migrations are more pronounced in herds with greater numbers of mature bucks. Without a high fence, this leak cannot be stopped. You could shoot does until "the cows come home" without reaching the magic ratio, unless of course, you are working with a tremendously large land mass. And, even then, you would only affect the herd at the center of the property.

Just about everyone now knows that antler quality improves with age. Maximum number of points, spread and antler mass are probably achieved around 5.5-6.5 years of age. This antler maturity age varies geographically, and may range as much as 5.5 to 10.5 years! All you have to do to produce reasonably good bucks is let them reach maturity. I have been working with one landowner for several years. He has a high fence around a 10,000 acre area and did not shoot mature bucks for five years. To my surprise, very few bucks over 4.5 years of age showed up in the first or second mature buck harvests. You can imagine my surprise. Unfortunately, we have little information about buck survival rates. My work, as well as that of Dr. Charles DeYoung in South Texas, suggests that annual mortality rates may reach 25-30% in some years. During the rut, bucks generally are off feed and literally run themselves to death. By February, older bucks are in poorer condition than does, and probably are more susceptible to natural mortality agents. My experience throughout the range has been that for every 100 yearling bucks, no more than 24 will live to maturity. This figure probably is optimistic because it excludes harvest mortality, poaching, etc. This is not to say that trophy management is not feasible. I offer this information to make you aware of the realities of the situation. In a later chapter, I will discuss how you can manage for trophy bucks, provided you are willing to "pay the price."

Since the buck mortality problem is not normally tied to habitat quality, the manager must take extraordinary steps to improve survival of older age-class bucks. **A harvest of one trophy-class buck per 1,000 acres under extensive management, and one buck to 300 acres under intensive management, are realistic goals, given these realities.**

Even if we were able to remove the recommended number of does, increase buck abundance and age structure, there is a more important consideration to all of this— **carrying capacity.** The concept of carrying capacity, as I noted earlier, makes defining *trophy* child's play. Few biologists agree on exactly what carrying capacity is, much less how to use the concept. Many feel that carrying capacity is the saturation point; the greatest number of animals that can be sustained on a piece of land for a long period of time. In other words, the herd is just getting by. The number of deer added by births each year is equal to the number removed by death or harvest.

The concept of a harvestable surplus is a myth! Several of us have come to what I feel is a better concept. The **optimum sustained yield (OSY) concept** discussed at length in the Population Management chapter is the only tenable approach, given the true facts about whitetail population dynamics. Under optimum sustained yield management, the manager tries to achieve a population level which will allow him to harvest the most animals and/or the most trophies, given the specific set of management conditions, on a sustained yield, annual basis. It is like finding the highest money market interest rate and living off of the interest, without touching the principle. The real trick is finding the highest interest rate.

Most hunters feel that the same number of fawns (interest) are produced

Trophy Management: Some Plain Talk

each year. They are appalled to discover how few fawns actually survive most years. The North Boggy Slough herd (discussed later in this book) is an excellent example. Remember that the herd only produced 37 fawns for every 100 does when the population density was one deer to 8 acres; while the same herd produced 110 fawns for every 100 does when we reduced the population to one deer to 20 acres. We were getting our highest "interest" rate (=recruitment) with fewer deer on the range. Body size and antler quality also were higher. We decided to maintain our herd at around one deer to 15 acres, since this was the compromise density for optimum sustained yield. This population level is equal to about one half the saturation level for this habitat

---

Most deer ranges share a common problem: too many does and too few harvestable bucks. The product of management is bucks-- not does.

Mike Biggs

type.

When the first deer walks around your property and takes its first bite, it has negatively impacted the habitat. Something has been removed. As long as there are not too many deer, the negative impact can be recovered each year. Hence, the availability of nutrients such as protein, calcium, phosphorus, etc. diminishes as the herd grows. The probability of producing a mature buck that realizes its true genetic potential also diminishes as the population grows. In the southern Pineywoods, we have found that buck quality begins to decrease once the herd exceeds one adult deer to 50 acres. This precisely is why larger bucks are harvested from areas which have been stocked recently or from those with traditionally low population densities.

Trophy management has a high cost. I keep repeating myself. Since fewer deer must be carried on the range, fewer mature bucks can be harvested; and due to their rarity, such bucks will be more difficult to kill. The landowner may become discouraged by the fact that he seldom sees a deer.

Now, let's proceed to genetics. The first thing sportsmen ask is whether or not they should bring in "new blood." Perhaps one of those big South Texas bucks or one of those Missouri bucks will upgrade herd quality. My answer always is an emphatic NO! It is not that these races cannot be reared successfully in other geographic regions. The question lies in the impact such a stocking will have on that specific herd. In most cases, such efforts are a complete waste of time and money. Everyone wants the magic bullet— the one-size-fits-all solution. But, there are no simple solutions.

The genes that once produced quality antlers will not have disappeared entirely from even the most abused herds, even though their abundance may have been greatly reduced. The deer in a particular area will have become well-adjusted to survival at that particular time and under existing environmental conditions. This is the raw material with which you must work.

A basic understanding of population genetics is necessary for effective trophy management. In the chapter on genetics and culling, I will outline what we currently know about whitetail genetics and genetic manipulation; and, that is not a great deal! It is a complex science, but the basics are simple. Remember that the occurrence of some characteristic, say length of index finger, is most commonly normally distributed in a population. Although there will be individuals with extremely long fingers and unusually short fingers, most will have fingers of average length. This is because that appears to be the most advantageous length for us to have. It takes some extraneous factor (natural selection) to move this distribution in one direction or another.

The spike buck experiments by the Texas Parks & Wildlife Department and by the Mississippi State University Department of Wildlife and Fisheries Sciences is an excellent example of the confusion fostered by current genetic thinking. Factors that produce spikes encompass far more than genetics.

A few years back, I attended the Southeast Deer Study Group meeting in Florida. We were met at the airport by a man who was anxious to talk with the Texas contingent. He had heard of the spike buck work and had immediately set out to improve his buck quality by killing every spike he saw. The man was frustrated because he had not improved buck quality at all. The vast majority of these spikes were yearlings. **His problem was overpopulation and poor habitat quality, not genetics.** I have seen landowners and managers eliminate an entire age class of bucks by killing yearling spikes. In healthy herds, living in quality habitats, spike yearlings are rare. But even in these herds, a poor growing season will be followed by numerous spikes, no matter what the genetic potential is! Efforts would be better spent, in these cases, on removing does and improving the habitat.

Now, let's take a more realistic approach to whitetail management. The key word in management is **harvestable deer.** Herds can be managed to meet one of three basic goals. First, you can manage for maximum numbers of trophy-class bucks. Second, the herd can be managed for a sustained yield of quality bucks. And lastly, you can manage the population for a sustained harvest of just deer. Each of these goals carries with it peculiar costs as well as benefits. One cost of trophy management is that fewer mature bucks can be harvested, often one per 1,000 acres. In addition, trophy management requires strict control over population growth, sex ratios, and genetics. Decisions must be made as to whether or not each buck lives or dies, and these are not committee decisions. As in Europe, the herd must be under the control of a single individual. Consider the ramifications of this socially and otherwise.

SUMMARY

When faced with the realities of trophy management, most landowners and sportsmen opt for a quality buck man-

In properly managed herds, yearling bucks should, for the most part, have forked antlers. Spike yearlings appear more often as the result of over-population rather than genetics.

agement program. A quality buck is one which best represents the potential of its age class, harvested in a high quality habitat, and taken via a high quality hunting experience. It is a buck that can be displayed proudly. Most hunters are quite happy to harvest a 2.5 or 3.5-year old buck. Quality management programs provide greater flexibility. Few trophy class animals are harvested, but maximum sportsman satisfaction is achieved. And, isn't that what it is all about?

In the next chapter, I will discuss how each of these three management goals (trophy, quality and numbers) can be achieved. Although I obviously am not an avid proponent of trophy management, I have been successful in the past in producing trophies for those individuals willing to pay the price to produce these magnificent animals.

Chapter 15

A BLUE PRINT FOR DEER MANAGEMENT

I hope by now that you have come to the conclusion that the management of whitetails is site specific. Each management plan must be tailored and fine-tuned to match, 1) the productivity of the habitat, 2) the genetic potential of the herd, and 3) limitations imposed by socio-economic factors. However, we **can** take a diagnostic approach to deer management which will allow you to begin the long, yet enjoyable pathway to meeting your goals.

GOAL-SETTING

The single-most important decision to be made in deer management involves goal-setting. The number one cause for failure of a management program arises from the inability of the landowner or club to clearly establish management goals. In Chapter One, I outlined the three basic options available to the manager: *trophy management, quality buck management* and *numbers management.* I have written numerous pages so far about the various advantages and disadvantages of each. The decision entirely is up to you, but you must take into account the realities of the situation. For example, although most individuals would like to manage for trophies, it makes absolutely no sense to attempt to produce monster bucks on 320 acres of land, unless of course you are willing to high-fence the property. Or, you may have a large enough tract of land (ca., 5,000 acres), but it is grossly dissected by numerous public access roads. Take some time and ask yourself some important questions about **your** expectations.

The next question to consider is the extent of involvement, both time-wise and monetarily, you can afford to invest in the management process. Earlier, I noted that, once you decide on the type of management, there are two approaches from which to choose. First, there is the extensive management approach, which centers around management of deer across the broad landscape. This approach is, 1) suitable for state and federal agencies, 2) large private landowners wishing only to produce a limited number of bucks, and 3) those individuals not wishing to invest large amounts of time or money. Intensive management, on the other hand, centers on maximizing production from each acre of land. This approach should be taken by, 1) small landowners, 2) large landowners wishing to produce large numbers of bucks, and 3) those with the time and money commensurate with their management desires. Intensive deer management is an expensive, albeit rewarding endeavor. You should understand this from the outset.

THE BASIC APPROACH

When I was twelve years old, I worked on weekends mowing lawns for spending money. At that time, one could expect to earn from $3.00 to $4.00 for mowing a lawn— a big difference from what the commercial yard services charge today!

I checked out a book on hamsters at the library. In those days, hamsters were relatively new to the pet scene. In not time at all, I had fallen in love with these creatures, in spite of the fact that I never even had seen one. After considerable discussion with my folks, they finally agreed to let me purchase a pair from the local pet store. At $12.00 per pair it took me an entire month of mowing lawns to raise the money to buy my first pair of hamsters. As a young, budding entrepreneur I already had calculated the amount of money I could generate from a single pair of hamsters.

Finally, the greatly anticipated day arrived. My dad drove me to the pet shop, where I carefully selected my breeders: a lovely buff-colored female and a standard male. The pet shop attendant carefully placed the hamsters in a box for me and we started for home. "By the way son," my dad asked, "where are you going to keep those animals of yours?" I felt the blood ebb from my face. "Well, I guess I need to build a cage," was my reply.

We stopped by a local market and acquired a wooden apple box. (In those days all apples and most fruits came in wooden boxes.) It would be a simple matter to take some of my old rabbit netting and cover the top of the box. A little litter, food and water; the hamsters should have a fine new home in my room. I scarcely could sleep that night, thinking of my little animals and the many hours of enjoyment that lay ahead. But, I did finally succumb to sleep.

The next morning brought a terrible shock. During the night, the hamsters had chewed their way out of the box and were nowhere to be found. After hours of searching, and a great deal of tears, I gave up the search. It would be many years before I once again possessed a pair of hamsters. And, I still cannot forget the valuable lesson those hamsters taught me at the age of twelve— **you do not get your hamsters before you get your cage!**

What does this story have to do with deer management? Too often in resource management, be it deer, livestock or crops, the producer fails to realize that you do not get your hamsters before you get your cage. In deer management, all activities are based on a single commodity, *habitat*. So, before you go worrying about what to do with your deer, you would be better off developing a comprehensive habitat management plan.

DEVELOPING A HABITAT MANAGEMENT PLAN

You probably are tired of reading my admonitions about the importance of maps, aerial photographs and recordkeeping. But, you cannot manage deer without these. Consequently, the first step in developing a habitat management plan is to acquire **recent** aerial photography, and topographic and soils maps of your area. Although almost anyone can learn to interpret these diagnostic aids, you may want to secure the services of a professional resource manager during the initial phases of plan development. Agencies such as the U.S.D.A. Soil Conservation Service, your agricultural extension service or the state forestry service all have expertise available for your use. However, these agencies often are under-staffed and over-worked; so if you want immediate attention, you may want to secure the services of a paid consultant.

Whatever the approach, you should develop a detailed habitat type map, including each habitat type present, all roads and physical features (buildings, fences, etc.), water resources and developments and soils. **A habitat type is an area that is sufficiently different (viz., tree composition, age, etc.) from adjacent areas to require separate management activities.** For example, two adjacent timber stands may be considered as different habitat types, because one is twenty years old and the other 50 years old, in spite of the fact that both stands are pure conifer plantations. The minimum size to be included as a habitat type will depend on the level of management selected. Habitat types as small as one-half acre are not uncommon. Even if you opt for the extensive management approach, I suggest you develop a habitat type map with a high level of resolution. If nothing else, it will aid in developing a harvest strategy for your herd (discussed later). This is the point where we lose the communality between the two management approaches; extensive or intensive management.

Extensive Habitat Management Approach

As I noted in Chapter 8, the basic management unit for extensive whitetail habitat management is the section or 640 acres. Now, I fully realize that seldom does a parcel of land allow itself to easily be partitioned into convenient 640-acre squares. This is a point where common sense must prevail. On your map, delineate (draw a line around) each 640-acre management unit to best approximate a block; a little more or less is acceptable.

Remember that you must supply all of the life requisites— food, cover and water— of whitetails within the confines of the management unit. Approximately 10% (64 acres) should be in permanent openings, 30% (ca., 190 acres) should be in cover, and the remainder in forage production; however, since forage and cover areas often are one and the same, these areas may overlap. A permanent water source should either currently exist or be developed within the management unit. The water source should be located near the center, but the realities of land capability may dictate otherwise. A perennial stream, lake, pond or livestock watering facility all will satisfy this requirement.

This is not the point to discuss supplemental feeding. The need for supplementation is determined by several criteria, each of which will be discussed in a later section.

One of the most critical aspects of forage management lies in the timing of activities such as prescribed burns (where appropriate), timber harvest and intermediate treatments, rotational grazing, planned habitat disturbances and brush clearing and management. The key to a sustained yield of forage is well-planned disturbances. The interval between disturbances is governed by the ability of the land to respond. In the South, for example, I often have said that habitat management amounts to a veritable "war against vegetation;" meaning that vegetation responds so quickly that the manager must expend a great deal of energy to control rapid plant growth. In northeastern Canada, on the other hand, the climate effects a much slower plant response, requiring longer intervals between planned disturbances. Furthermore, in the Pineywoods of East Texas, I regularly conduct prescribed burns at three to five year intervals, while in South Texas and portions of Florida, I seldom burn more than every ten years!

Within the management unit, you should delineate both forage and cover production areas. Each of these areas is termed a **management subunit**, and is treated as a separate entity in regard to planned activities. Several habitat types can be combined to form a single management subunit; but once so designated, the entire subunit must be managed uniformly. Here is an example.

Blue Print for Deer Management

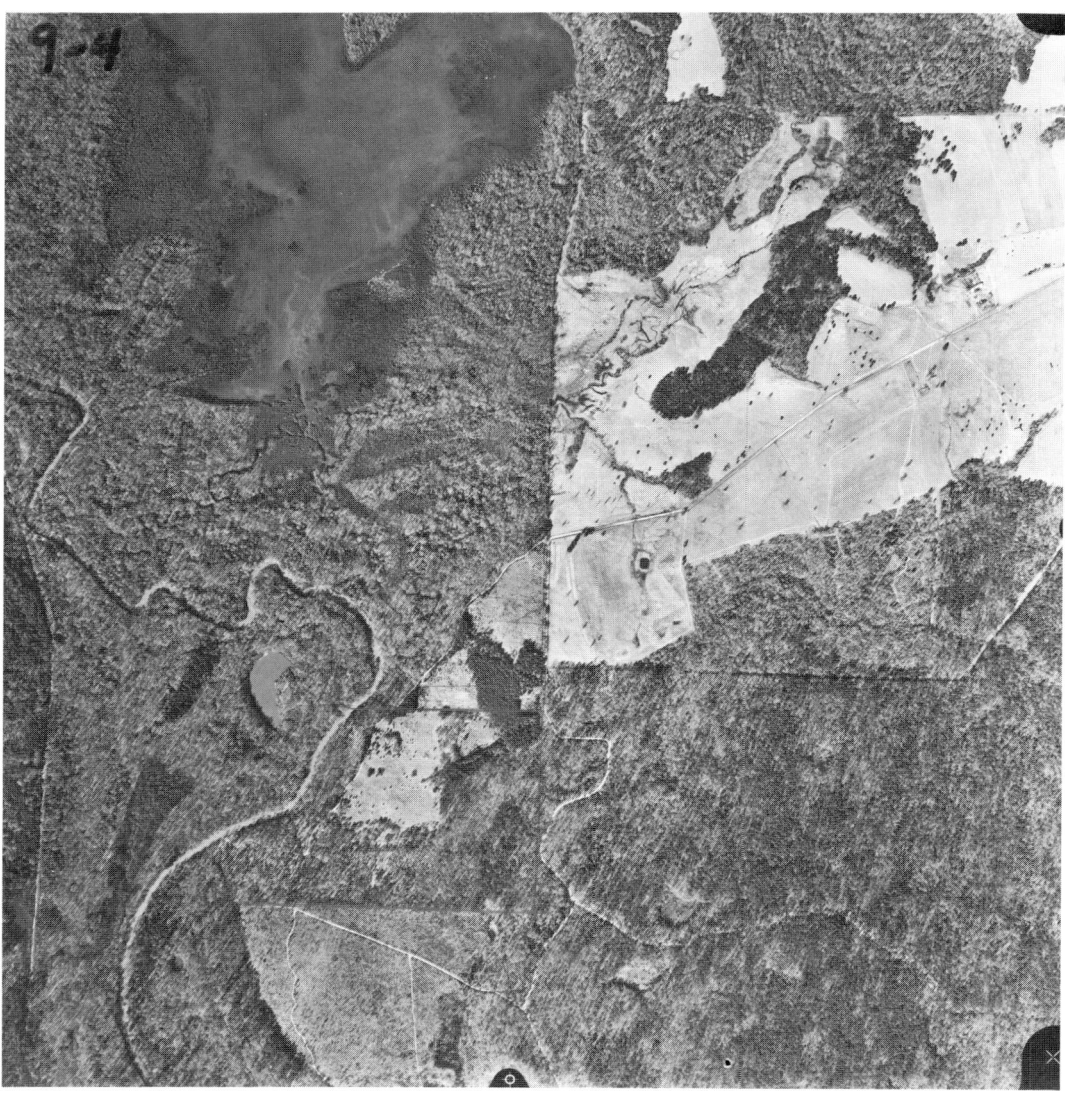

The first step in developing a habitat management plan is to acquire recent aerial photography of the property. Photography is available from the U.S. Geological Survey, Soil Conservation Service or your state forestry service.

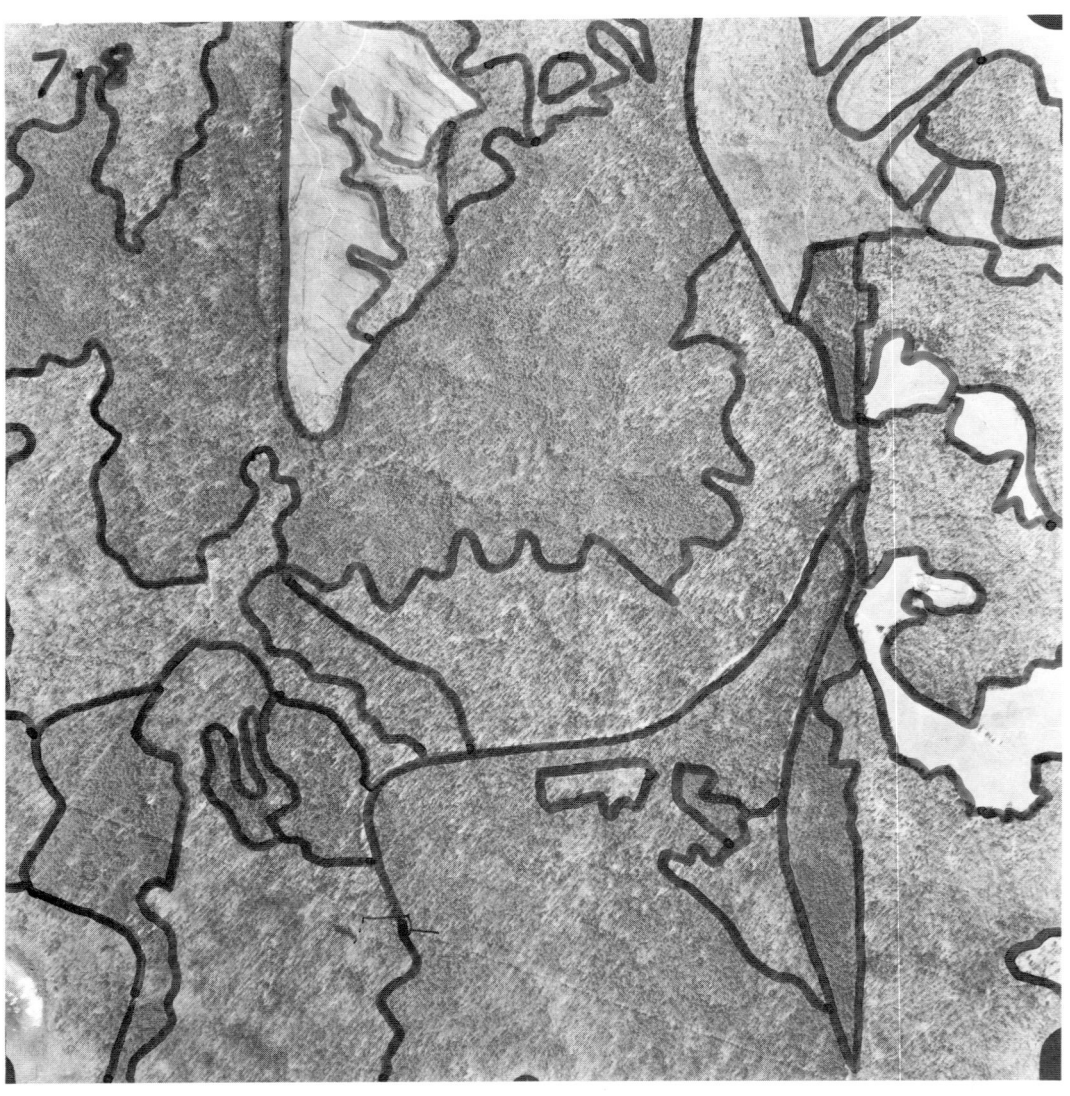

A habitat type map should be prepared from your aerial photograph, which delineates (draws a line around) each different habitat type. From this map, an extensive or intensive management plan can be developed.

You may decide to combine three timber stands, representing three different stand ages, into a single subunit. You then might prescribe burn all three stands at the same time, effectively eliminating the uniqueness of each stand.

Intensive Habitat Management Approach

The basic habitat management unit for intensive management is the quarter-section (160 acres). Again, all of the life-requisites of whitetails must be provided within this smaller unit, significantly increasing the cost and intensity of management over the extensive approach. Once again, you should delineate each habitat type on your map and/or aerial photograph. Unlike extensive management, habitat types are managed as individual units, provided they are around 20 acres in size (excluding food plots, rights-of-way, and special features). Again, this minimum management subunit size is an approximation, and good judgement in delineating subunits certainly applies. Ten percent (16 acres) of the area should be in permanent openings, 20% (32 acres) should be in cover, and the remainder in forage production. As with extensive management, forage and cover areas may overlap.

The positioning of each subunit will have to be based on an arrangement that allows no two contiguous subunits from receiving a treatment in the same year. For example, you may have two brush-dominated subunits, each approximately 20 acres in size. You may burn one brush area this winter, and the other the following winter. This will allow you to maximize habitat diversity **and** forage production, while at the same time providing adequate escape cover.

A water source should be designated or developed for each 160 acre unit. As with the extensive approach, a detailed, long-term plan should be developed for each management subunit, which allows for maximum production of food and cover. This would entail prescribed fires (where appropriate), timber harvest and intermediate treatments, controlled grazing, selective use of herbicides (=wildlife stand improvement) and physical management of brush.

MANAGEMENT OF STREAMSIDE ZONES

Whether you opt for extensive or intensive management, I strongly urge you to delineate all streamsides on the property as special management subunits. This would be appropriate throughout the range, even in the South Texas brush country. I often am asked how wide to make SMZs. My advice is to let the natural topography establish this distance. I construct permanent fire lanes along the topographic break between the upland and the bottomland. This may only be a few feet in the upper reaches of the drainage, or perhaps a mile or more in the large river bottoms.

In areas with mast producing oaks and other hardwoods, the next step is to develop a plan to maximize fruit three. Manipulation of species composition by selective removals and plantings can assure a more even flow of mast production. Wildlife stand improvement can be used to regulate species composition, as well as, the density and crown size of individual plants. Time only can supply the age factor.

Even in areas where you do not expect to conduct upland prescribed fires, SMZs are best separated by cleared breaks. Pushing of breaks with a bulldozer and disc improves the amount of

Streamside management zones are areas adjacent to drainages which are managed as separate habitat subunits. Fire breaks should be constructed along the interface between upland and bottomland, even if prescribed fire is not a part of the management plan.

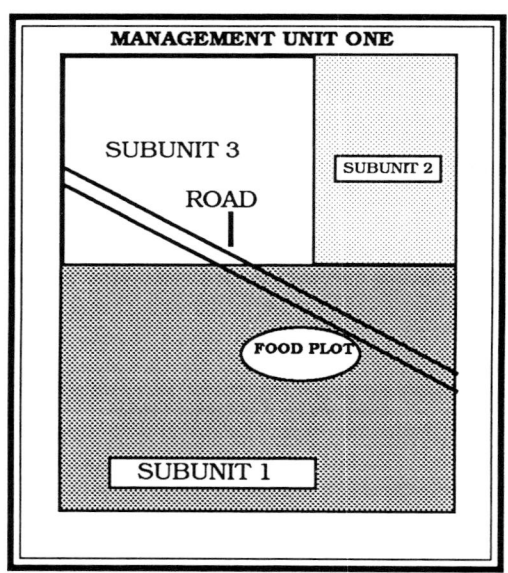

Within the management unit, areas to be managed uniformly are designated as habitat management subunits. Each is delineated on the map.

production. As noted in Chapter 8, the major factors which influence mast production are, 1) the diversity of mast-producing species, 2) the age of the stand, 3) the density of trees or shrubs, 4) site fertility and site index, and 5) recent fruiting habits. Of these, there is little you can do as a manager about points 4 and 5; however, there is a great deal you can do about the first edge and access to these areas both by hunters and the deer. **Fire never should be allowed in the SMZ.**

ACQUIRING BASELINE DATA

Once you have developed a preliminary habitat management plan, it is time to acquire as much baseline data about your herd and habitat as possible. The best approach is first to examine how the existing forage is being utilized. I recommend that you conduct a browse survey (see **Record-Keeping**) during the first winter. This will give you a good indication of the current stocking level (light, moderate or heavy). Use of first-choice browse species perhaps is the best indicator of stocking intensity. No more than 50% of the current year's growth of preferred browse species should be consumed. A reasonable rule-of-thumb for determining stocking rate would be, 1) light, 10% or less; 2) moderate, 10-50%; and 3) heavy, 50% or more. Remember, this is only one of many diagnostics to be used in interpreting the condition of your herd.

The next step would be to acquire age, weight, sex ratio and antler development data. The record-keeping and diagnostic forms provided earlier in this book will be of considerable benefit from this point on. Beginning in mid-summer, you should obtain as many incidental sightings as possible. These data will allow you to make an approximation of the sex and doe:fawn ratios. Harvest records will round out the baseline data base.

One of the most difficult questions to answer is: "How many does and bucks do I harvest the first year?" My response always is that you should harvest approximately the same number of deer you harvested last year; unless, of course, no does were harvested last year. **You must harvest some does during the initial phases of herd management.** These records will tell you a great deal about the condition of your herd, and cannot be neglected.

The number of does harvested will vary; but obviously the larger the number, the more confidence you will have in the results. A small sample size could lead to misinterpretations due to sampling error.

The diagnostic forms supplied in Chapter 13 will be invaluable in making further management decisions. Your response to the first year's data will be guided by these charts, as they relate to your management goals.

MANAGING THE HERD

Whether you opt for numbers management, quality buck management or trophy management, your basic approach will be the same for each. Once the habitat management plan is in effect, it is time to consider management at the population level.

The "name-of-the-game" in deer management is fawn production. Without a high level of production, it is difficult to achieve most management goals. Hence, **the singlemost important diagnostic aid would be an estimate of reproductive success.** Fawn-at-heel and lactation rates, because they are obtained late in the year, give us the best approximation of recruitment. A lactation rate for mature (2.5+ years) does of less than 80% **suggests** a potential problem with population density. This can be confirmed by examination of doe age structure, yearling buck dressed weights and yearling spike rate. If each of these diagnostics also suggests a high population density, then a herd reduction is in order. If, on the other hand, they do not suggest a population density problem, the problem may lie more with low habitat productivity and/or density independent factors. Herds in some portions of Florida, for example, characteristically exhibit poor recruitment, even at low population densities. Likewise, in South Texas, recruitment during some years is due more to density independent factors than high population density. Hence, these concerns must be addressed **before** considering a herd reduction. If you live on the periphery of the whitetail's range, you should be made aware of the potential for greater influence of density independent factors. Excessive herd reductions, in such cases, may adversely affect effective population size, leading to a possible collapse of the population.

When in doubt as to the cause of low recruitment, I suggest that you make a conservative herd reduction, monitoring the resultant reproductive response. Remember that I have said many times that a herd is not managed in dramatic steps, it is "fine-tuned" over time. If repeated herd reductions have little or no effect on recruitment, then it is best either to accept the limitations of the habitat and climate (extensive management) or turn to other means such as supplemental feeding (intensive management). Supplementation can either be supplied using food plots or feeds. Criteria for selecting the type of supplementation program were presented in Chapter 7.

As with herd reductions, the impact of supplemental feeding on recruitment can be determined using the appropriate diagnostic charts. If over an extended period, recruitment increases with supplemental feeding, then this approach may be appropriate. If, on the other hand, supplementation produces little or no increase in recruitment, then you must accept the limitations of the environment, and modify expectations accordingly. This would apply to economic limitations, as well. If supplementation is indicated, I suggest that you either plant 1-2% (extensive management) or 3-5% (intensive management) of the area, provided of course that food plots are indeed feasible in your area (eg., 35 inches or more of rainfall annually). Food plots should be well-distributed, ranging in size from one-half to 3 acres. Pipelines and rights-of-way should be planted whenever possible, along with roadsides.

In areas where food plots are not feasible, supplementation can be supplied using feeder stations. Feeder stations should be positioned at the rate of one per section (extensive) or one per quarter section (intensive). Under both management scenarios, I suggest mineral supplementation using a small trough-type feeder, positioned at this same density. Although there are areas where mineral supplementation is unnecessary, some years may alter this requirement. Remember that you are supplementing the deer's diet, not substituting for it!

At this point, it is time to examine the specific management principles to effect each option; numbers management, quality buck management and trophy management.

Numbers Management

The primary goal in numbers management is to produce as many deer for the gun as possible. Little consideration is given to the age of bucks harvested. This is a completely legitimate management option, provided the herd is not over-harvested in the process. **Numbers management is not the same as bucks-only management.** There seldom is room for a bucks-only harvest strategy.

The success of numbers management lies heavily in fawn production. Under this option, the goal is to produce as many fawns as possible, subsequently harvesting as many bucks and does as possible. Once the fawn crop and recruitment are optimized, **the most important diagnostic tools are the average age of bucks harvested, acres per buck harvested and doe age structure**. Once again, the diagnostic charts supplied in Chapter 13 will be of considerable use. In areas where there are few density independent factors operating, you should strive for a population that has 50-60% of the doe population as 2.5 year-olds or less and an average age of bucks harvested ranging 1.5 to 2.5 years. In density independent-controlled herds, especially in the very cold north, the age structure often approximates this level without management.

The third diagnostic, **acres per buck harvested**, is important to the fine-tuning process. Remember that, for any given herd, there are many solutions to developing a sustained yield. In order to develop an optimum sustained yield for your specific situation, you must fine-tune the herd over time. Monitor the trend in buck harvest, adjusting your harvest recommendation accordingly. For example, suppose you have a herd from which you are harvesting a buck for every 200 acres, and these bucks average 2.8 years of age. You may wish to increase the harvest to one buck to 150 acres, monitoring the impact on average buck age. If the average age of harvested bucks declines, then you may want to hold the harvest at that level for some time. (Even under a numbers management program, I feel that it is inadvisable to let buck age fall much below 2 years.) This may result in some behavior and genetic problems. If there is no further decline in average age, then you may again want to increase the buck harvest. At the same time, you should keep a check on doe age structure, where appropriate adjusting harvest rate accordingly.

The numbers management option can be implemented both on an extensive and intensive basis. Intensive management lends itself well to numbers management, allowing a higher return on your investment of time and money (see **Economics of Deer Management**).

Quality Buck Management

As I noted several times previously, quality buck management is the singlemost common form of deer management in operation today. **A quality buck is one that best realizes the potential of his age class, lives in a quality habitat and is harvested through a quality hunting experience.**

As with numbers management, the first step to producing quality bucks is to optimize fawn production and recruitment. Optimization refers to balancing the yield of fawns with the need of hunters to see deer. Obviously, we can achieve a maximum sustained yield at a lower population density, but hunters will see fewer deer; often degrading the hunting experience.

In a quality buck management strategy, you should strive for an average age of bucks harvested of 3 years. A three-year old buck will more than satisfy most hunters, and present a challenge for harvest. However, this also allows for the production of a few true trophy-class animals for the hunter desiring a greater challenge.

Age of bucks harvested and acres per buck harvested are the most important diagnostic criteria for quality management. Again, adjust your harvest recommendation according to the long-term trend in harvest density. If average age of bucks falls appreciably below 2 years, then you must reduce the buck harvest accordingly. At the same time, you should track the antler quality rating to assure that there are no emerging problems in antler development. If bucks are harvested in a random fashion, I see few potential problems in this area. **There is no place for culling in quality buck management.** The best approach is to use peer-group pressure (see **People Management**) to regulate the types of bucks harvested. Hunters easily are manipulated using this technique.

Trophy Buck Management

We now turn to one of the most difficult aspects of whitetail management. Although there has been much verbiage concerning the production of trophy whitetails, few

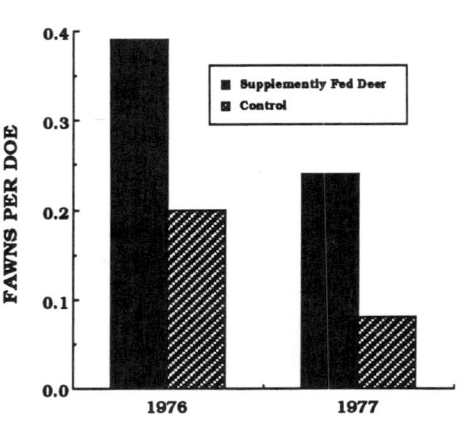

Supplemental feeding can significantly increase fawn production and survival. Presented here are the results of a study conducted by Zaiglin and DeYoung in South Texas, which clearly demonstrate the importance of supplementation. However, supplemental feeding can be expensive.

managers have achieved a documented production of large numbers of trophy bucks. Again, a trophy buck is one that scores 150 or more inches by the Boone and Crockett system. Even under the most intensive of management schemes, these bucks are scarce as the proverbial "hen's teeth." However, it is possible to produce these animals on a sustained basis, provided of course you are willing to pay the price.

The first step to producing large numbers of trophies is to achieve the actual point of maximum sustained yield. Whereas, both numbers and quality buck management revolve around an optimum sustained yield (60-70% of saturation), **trophy management must operate at the MSY level.** This is the point where we are producing the maximum number of fawns, as well as, genetic diversity.

Although trophy management can be implemented both on an extensive and intensive basis, I feel that it is best conducted intensively, maximizing both recruitment and habitat productivity. If, however, your goal is to produce a few trophy-class bucks, without regard for economics or yield, then the extensive approach is appropriate.

Since the goal of trophy management is to produce as many trophy-class bucks as possible under the limitations of the management situation, **the two most important diagnostic criteria are average age of bucks harvested and antler quality.** A third diagnostic, acres per trophy buck harvested, also is useful.

Once you achieve a maximum sustained yield of fawns, the next step is to, 1) increase the average age of bucks harvested, and 2) improve the genetics of the herd. The number of bucks harvested annually must be carefully adjusted to allow an optimum number of animals to reach maturity (6+ years). But, this does not mean that no harvest should take place. I often am amused by an individual that comes to my office all excited over having leased a property that "has not been hunted in ten years." This means little to me as a manager, other than the herd probably has reached saturation, with a concomitant decrease in buck quality. Just like your lawn, a herd should be "mowed" periodically to maintain vigor. Properly implemented harvest is one key to trophy production.

In Chapter 16, I will briefly discuss the realities of whitetail genetics and culling. We still are in the infancy of knowledge about whitetail genetics. What we recommend today may change entirely over the next decade, so I only can offer my best opinion. The use of a "slot limit" to produce genetically superior bucks is ludicrous at best. Under such schemes, you simply are removing the source of genetic variability (culling yearlings), while at the same time selecting against the best animals (shooting trophy bucks). Such systems are doomed from the outset to guarantee mediocrity. In order to produce large numbers of trophy bucks, which are presumed to be genetically superior, it will be necessary to implement a program that may take decades before an impact is observed.

The first step is to decide what kind of bucks you truly desire. I previously discussed some of the criteria for judging quality and conformation in bucks. At this time, I feel that antler conformation probably is the most predictable antler trait. Other characteristics, such as antler mass and spread, are much less predictable. Bucks possessing the selected conformation should be favored, and given "brood buck" status. The brood buck never should be harvested unless, of course, he is to be replaced by a better animal. The culling scheme, both for bucks and does, outlined in Chapter 16 should be carefully followed; but, it should be mediated by the realities of your situation. If your herd lies on the periphery of the range, or in an area with serious site limitations, pay particular attention to the section on doe harvest.

The diagnostic, acres per trophy buck harvested, will aid you in determining the point of maximum sustained yield. When combined with the other diagnostics, this will allow you to fine-tune the herd for maximum trophy production. Increase buck harvest intensity until antler quality and age begin to decrease, then reduce the harvest until these diagnostics improve.

There always is a place for supplemental feeding in trophy management. Even in the best of ranges, there will be years in which optimum growing conditions just are not available. Studies in the fabled South Texas brush country show that, in years with poor rainfall, and even in certain portions of the year, forage quality falls below optimum. A well-balanced, year-round supplement easily can augment the quality of native forage.

A WORD ABOUT HARVESTING DEER

All of the above discussion is aimed at meeting your management goals. In most cases, these goals cannot fully be realized if the proper numbers of deer are not harvested. This applies both to population regulation and hunter satisfaction. It makes little difference to the average hunter that a trophy buck is out there on your property. What is important to the average hunter is the head on his wall! Therefore, a significant portion of this book is devoted to harvesting techniques. One of the most effective harvesting techniques lies in the manipulation of habitat to increase harvest. I refer to this as increasing the "shootability" of the property. Here is an example.

I manage a large tract (3,500 acres) for a private landowner. The goal of this management program is trophy-class bucks. One of my first considerations was to develop a habitat management plan that would both increase production and the ability of the landowner to harvest his deer. I implemented a forage management program in the uplands based on periodic prescribed burns. The burn interval in this case was three years, as this area exhibits rapid plant response to disturbance. But, I carefully designed a fire break system that gives protection to the SMZs. I also left unburned or undisturbed areas adjacent to these SMZs to serve as buck sanctuaries. Now, the bucks are forced to move to and from their sanctuaries (which never are hunted) along the drainages. Since the vegetation in the uplands seldom exceeds "deer height," the shootability of the property has been greatly enhanced. This program has been quite successful, and I strongly urge that you give the same consideration in the development of your management plan.

SUMMARY

Deer herd management is a site-specific affair, with management activities and strategies matched to the productive potential of the range, genetic potential of the herd, and the unique socio-economic characteristics of the landowner-hunter. In general, there are three management strategies and two management intensities. Herds can be managed for a maximum number of deer harvested, for quality bucks and for trophy bucks. Each of these options can be applied either extensively or intensively. In all cases, the basic goal is to produce an optimum number of fawns. The primary difference between the three management options lies in the age at which bucks are harvested. Numbers management opts for bucks averaging 2 years of age, quality management aims for bucks averaging 3 years, and trophy management strives for a sustained yield of older (5+ years) bucks.

Whereas numbers management and quality management strategies maintain the herd at 60-70% of saturation, trophy management demands that the herd be held to 50% of K. The result is fewer deer seen, but a much higher average nutritional plane and maximum production of fawns. Culling strategies should favor "brood bucks," which are retained to effect changes in antler conformation. Implementation of "slot limits," which cull yearlings and older bucks, may have a serious genetic impact on the herd, and should be avoided.

Since harvest is an important component of deer management, the habitat should be manipulated to improve harvest efficiency. This is called improving the "shootability" of the property.

ANOTHER SEASON HAS COME AND PASSED

Another season has come and passed,
Now I can rest at last.

He has done it to me again,
And still holds the upper hand.

I got to see him once again,
As usual it wasn't from a stand.

He's every bit as large as I thought he would be,
I'll have to admit he's smarter than me.

Oh well! I know he's still there,
All I can do is say a little prayer.

That he survives another winter,
In order that he and I might enter
  another duel early next fall.
At that time I'll give it my all.
       ...K.S.

Chapter 16

GENETICS AND CULLING

No other aspect of whitetail management has created more controversy, both among laymen and management professionals, as the practice of culling to improve genetics. And, without a doubt, this has been the most difficult chapter to write! I pondered the consequences of discussing what we **do** know and **do not** know about whitetail genetics for many months. No matter what I write, I surely will alienate someone in the process. However, I would be remiss if I did not cover this important topic. The material presented arises from personal experiences, as well as, the limited amount of published research on the subject.

It seems, whether we are talking about special varieties of clover or shooting spikes, the public is looking for a "magic bullet" for deer management. Since the general public, and even some biologists, are poorly informed about the principles of genetics, it is easy to sell new concepts and ideas; in spite of the fact that most have not stood up to rigorous testing by the scientific method. In this chapter, I hope to present you with the facts, as we know them, about factors affecting antler quality, and present some strategies I personally have used to produce record-book bucks.

WHAT FACTORS AFFECT ANTLER QUALITY?

As whitetail populations increase, we are seeing a boom in the number of Boone-and-Crockett qualifying bucks. Many of these deer come from areas where deer traditionally have been in short supply. It seems, however, that a frightening trend is emerging. Back in the 1960's, Texas gained a mythical reputation among American hunters as the trophy producing area of the world. These were boom times for Texas whitetails. Changing landuse and control of the screw worm had made conditions for population growth optimum. Coupled with a climate that periodically disturbs the habitat via droughts, abundant high protein forage plants, and large land-holdings, the factors necessary for producing trophy bucks came to fruition. But today, although we still see big bucks coming out of the region, the total number of qualifying bucks killed each year is well below the previous levels.

Today, we see increased outdoor press about other portions of the range. Kansas, Ohio, Indiana, Iowa, Wisconsin and Alberta have become the trophy hotspots of the 1990's. But, as these herds (possibly with the exception of Alberta) reach the saturation level, they too will see a deterioration in quality. Often, the trophy hunter must constantly move ahead of overpopulation in order to find reasonable numbers of trophy animals. In an earlier chapter, I discussed density dependent factors which regulate population growth. These same factors have an impact both on body size and antler quality. Let's examine what factors affect antler development.

Nutrition

As far as I am concerned, nutrition plays the single-most important role in antler development. You may have the genes of an NFL fullback, but if you do not receive the proper nutrition, you never will realize your true potential. Likewise, whitetails are greatly influenced by the quality of their diet. A deer raised on poor nutrition never will realize its true potential. For example, bucks harvested from the Sombrerito Ranch near Laredo, Texas showed a definite impact of rainfall on antler mass. Rainfall affects the quality of forage eaten by deer. A study conducted on the Kerr Wildlife Management Area in Texas clearly demonstrated the role dietary protein plays in antler development. The study, conducted by Donnie Harmel, Dr. John Williams and Bill Armstrong, concluded that both body weight and antler quality (viz., beam length, circumference, weight and spread) respond directly to the quality of a deer's diet. They pointed out that, by 3.5 years, bucks continuously fed a high protein diet were far superior to those on a low protein diet. Hence, much of the variation in antler quality may be due to dietary quality.

On my management areas, serious reductions in population density, combined with a well-planned habitat

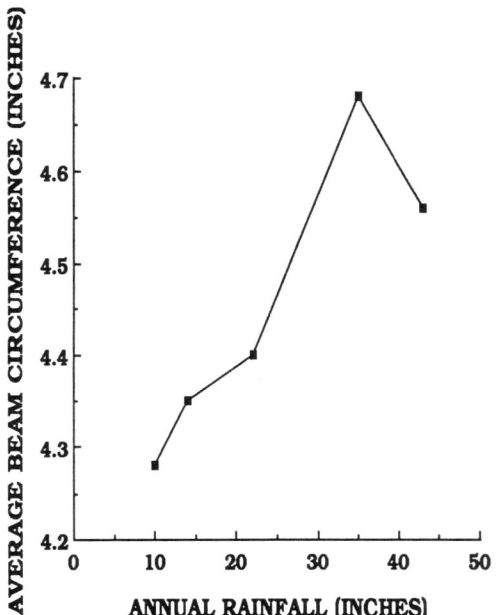

Relationship between average beam circumference, a measure of antler mass, and total annual rainfall for Bill Carter's Sombrerito Ranch, near Laredo, Texas. Note the striking relationship between growing conditions and antler quality.

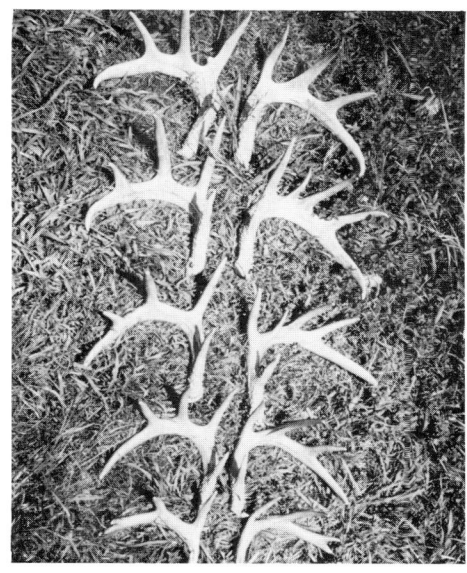

These antlers, all from the same buck over his lifetime, clearly demonstrate the importance of age in determining antler quality.

and supplemental feeding program, led to significant increases in antler size of all age-classes, particularly yearlings. In grossly overpopulated herds, I often see a yearling spike rate of 100%. After reducing the herd to the productive capacity of the range, however, yearling spike rate drops to less than 20%. This all can be accomplished **without** removal of so-called "cull" yearlings. In fact, At Boggy Slough (see The **Boggy Slough Story**), we seldom have made yearling spike removals, yet have consistently produced some of the largest deer in the South!

Age

Earlier in this book, I pointed out that the second most common factor influencing antler production is age. Antler growth is age specific, with trophy-class antlers not appearing until at least 3.5 years of age. However, there also is an age factor involved in the quality of a yearling buck's first set of antlers. In many herds, the birth period may take place over as much as a three month interval. Obviously, fawns born early in the spring will have a much different set of growth conditions than those born later in the season. I recently examined several yearling bucks in the same enclosure in Alabama. These bucks represented ages ranging from twelve to twenty months of age, in spite of the fact that they all were classified as "yearlings." As would be expected, the older yearlings had forked antlers, while the younger bucks had spiked antlers. The difference lay in their birth date, not their genetic makeup. In overpopulated herds, birth dates chronically are spread over a very long period, resulting in fawns being born at a suboptimum time. Even in well-managed herds, maintained below saturation, the younger does breed later, resulting always in some late fawns. These bucks naturally will not produce a first set of antlers equal to fawns born earlier in the growing season.

But, the question arises: Are the bucks born later in the year still inferior to those born earlier? Will these bucks ever catch up to those born earlier? For an answer, I turned to Dr. Harry Jacobson, of Mississippi State University. Harry probably knows more about the genetics and growth processes of whitetails than anyone. "I do not feel that fawns born later in the year should be considered as inferior animals. We are not seeing anything to support the idea that, given a good nutritional plane, these younger bucks do not catch up to

Mike Biggs

Social position can have a dramatic effect on antler quality. Older bucks tend to intimidate subordinate individuals, inhibiting sexual activity.

their older counterparts." He feels, and has the data to support his assertion, that late fawns have every bit as much potential of producing trophy-class antlers.

Social Position

An individual buck's social position also can greatly affect the size of his antlers. Earlier, I discussed how dominant bucks use chemicals deposited on signposts, as well as body language and intimidation to suppress the breed-

Genetics and Culling

ing activity of subordinate bucks. This certainly is of benefit to younger bucks, allowing them to concern themselves more with body growth than reproduction. However, suppression of male hormone also may significantly affect antler size.

Dr. Charles DeYoung, of Texas A&I University, recently demonstrated on an intensively managed trophy buck area that many of the bucks which would have been judged as "up and coming" young bucks actually were older animals. Dr. Bubenik, in Canada, has shown that social position does affect antler size in many deer species. This would explain why some bucks seem to suddenly explode in antler development after many mediocre years. My observations have suggested that such bucks exhibit this antler improvement after achieving social dominance.

This raises an important question. Is the culling of "inferior" bucks a good practice, and does it increase or decrease the genetic variability of the herd? A buck may have superior genetics, but does not realize his potential due to social limitations, rather than dietary deficiencies.

HERITABILITY OF ANTLER TRAITS

No aspect has caused more controversy between whitetail managers and researchers as the nature of spiked yearlings. Today, there are two "camps" with highly differing opinions. The first, represented by Texas Parks & Wildlife Department's Kerr Wildlife Management Area research team, reports strong data to support the idea that there is high predictability between a buck's yearling set of antlers and his ultimate antler quality later in life. The other group, represented by Dr. Jacobson's team, asserts that there absolutely is no predictability. This schism fathered a great deal of confusion on the part of the hunting and lay public; and, I might add, seriously hurt the credibility of whitetail biologists. Why the disparity in findings?

There are many possible explana-

Dr. Harry Jacobson, of Mississippi State University, is one of the pioneers of deer genetics and nutrition research. His landmark studies soon will shed light on our most perplexing questions about the genetics of whitetails.

Dr. Harry Jacobson

Here are four sets of antlers produced by different bucks at the Mississippi State deer pens. The yearling set of antlers (bottom) range from spikes to five points, yet the fifth antler sets cannot be distinguished, based on quality. In fact, the best antler set arose from a spike.

---

tions for the differences in the two projects. There may be differences inherent to the populations selected for study, or there may be significant differences in experimental design. I feel that the latter is most likely. The Kerr project involves a relatively few number of sires and less attention to dams than the Mississippi study. Only 9 sires were used in the Kerr study. Dr. Jacobson has examined many sires, randomly selected from various geographic regions. The Kerr study centered around the role of bucks in genetics, while the Mississippi study investigated the role the male (sire) and female (dam) play in genetics. A single forked antlered buck (Big Charlie) was used in Texas as the

Genetics and Culling

sire for the fork line, with eight remaining spiked antlered bucks used as the spike line sires. The Mississippi study involved many spiked and forked antlered sires, with controlled breeding of dams. Although, this section may read as if I have a strong bias in favor of the Mississippi study, I still am uncertain which camp is correct. But, admittedly, at this time I do favor the Mississippi results; primarily arising from my own management experiences. Both camps do, however, strongly suggest that nutrition plays an extremely important role in antler development, and is the singlemost important element.

Here are the antlers produced by the best and "worst" yearling bucks at the Mississsppi State deer pens. Under some "culling" programs, the buck on the left would have been removed from the herd. Yet, no one could question the quality of his antlers later in life.

Dr. Harry Jacobson

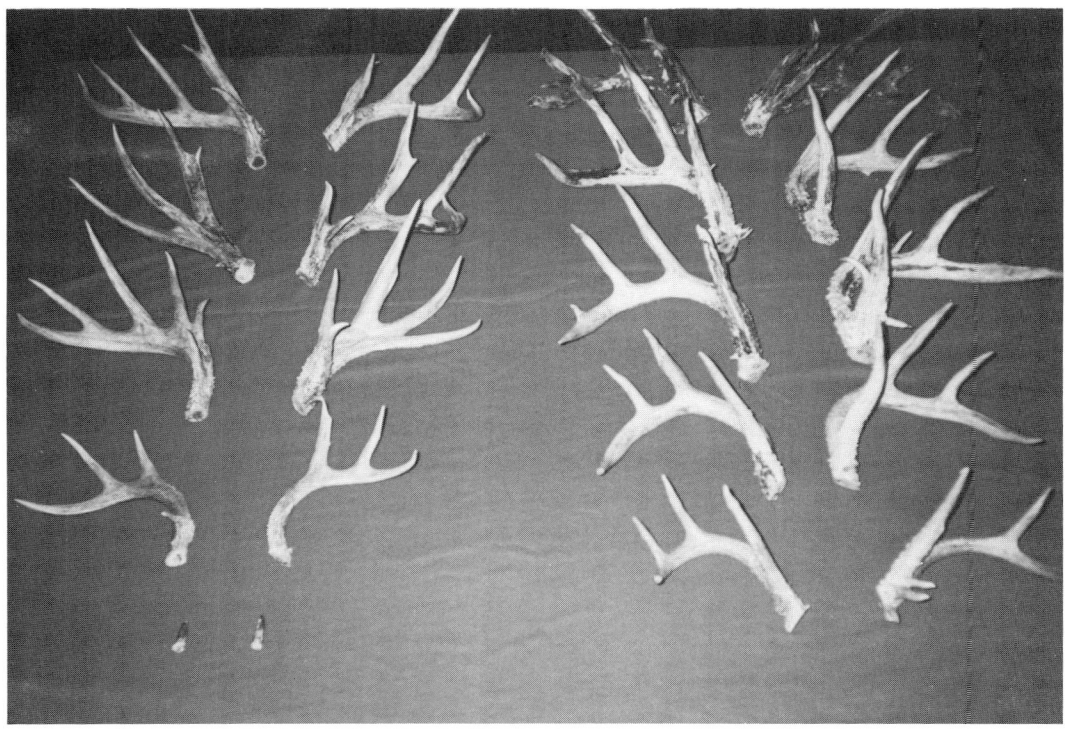

At this point, I feel that the genetics of whitetail antler production cannot be modeled by simple mendelian genetics. For those of you not familiar with this term, it relates to the father of genetics, Gregor Mendel, a monk who studied the inheritance of traits for the common garden pea. His studies led to the development of modern genetic thought: but since that time, we have learned that not all genetic processes can be reduced to simple single gene representations. Mendel found that there were dominant and recessive genes which determined such characteristics as seed color and seed coat texture. Luckily for Mendel, he chose a species that exhibited simple genetic phenomena, or else we probably would have waited many more years for advances in this field.

The factors that produce quality antlers probably are complex, involving many gene combinations. For example, I feel that the dam contributes much to the ultimate antler size of her offspring. The ability of the dam to efficiently mobilize nutrients may be passed on to her son, and manifests itself in his ability to grow antlers. If this is so, then several gene systems, each affecting the physiology of the deer, must be involved. It is ludicrous to think that a simple breeding experiment ever could unravel this complex relationship.

Some managers avidly assert that they have indeed affected the genetic composition of their herd by selective removals of "inferior" bucks. I seriously question these assertions, since most management programs hardly have been in effect for more than one or two generations! How long did it take to develop the common barnyard varieties of pigs? How many selective breedings and generations did it take to produce the Hereford bull? I recently conducted a research project with my colleague, Dr. Bill Wall, on the impact of intensive management on genetic diversity of whitetail populations. **Our research did not show a significant change in heterozygosity (genetic diversity) of a herd after ten years of intensive management.** Furthermore, the Anticosti Island herd of Canada all descended from a handful of animals stocked around the turn of the century. In spite of the high potential for inbreeding and fixation of characters, I did not find any indication of lost antler type diversity in this herd.

In spite of all this, I do feel that there may be a place for genetic manipulation of deer herds to produce high quality animals, provided the manager takes a realistic look at what should be done, factors to be considered and the timeframe required to effect changes in genetics. No program ever will be successful that ignores the important contribution the dam plays in determining antler quality. In fact, I predict that the day will come when a proven breeding doe will command a much higher price than a monster breeding buck! The dam's role is that crucial.

But, all this rhetoric still does not answer the basic question: Is the heritability of antlers predictable? To some extent, the answer is "yes." I feel that antler conformation probably is the most heritable trait. Too often I have seen sons and grandsons with antler conformations strikingly similar to the original sire. Apparently, the buck contributes the basic framework on which the female "sculpts" the final product. Dr. Jacobson soon will add light to this relationship, and I do not wish to "steal his thunder."

"CULLING" WHITETAILS

The practice of culling is not one I would recommend for the vast majority of management situations. It is an as yet unproven practice which has a place only after the herd has been finely tuned to realize its production and antler potential. However, for those of you who feel that you are indeed at the management crossroads, I would offer the following suggestions. But, remember that the following discussion is based on one important assumption: *You have achieved control of your herd.*

A Word About Spikes

As I travel around the country, I run into some pretty bizarre schemes concerning removal of spikes. "We only shoot those goat-horn spikes," bragged one fellow recently. Some clubs have rules, such as spikes above six inches may be shot, while smaller individuals may not. The assumption in both cases is that the longer the spike, the more inferior the buck. This is ridiculous! As I noted earlier, the size of the yearling set of antlers is greatly determined by the timing of birth. A younger buck will tend to have smaller spikes than an older buck. When you shoot longer spikes and leave shorter ones, you actually are removing the animals born in a more optimum time of the year. Again, it is a population and nutrition problem, and culling of these animals will do absolutely nothing to remedy this situation.

Culling to Regulate Production

Ironically, most individuals think in terms of the buck when culling is discussed. But, **culling involves both does and bucks**, and the doe aspect probably is equally important. Now, before you think I am talking about the culling of does with inferior antler genes, please take the time to read further. The removal of does to control population growth now is a universally accepted management practice. If and when you remove antlerless deer from the herd, however, is determined by many factors, among which are, 1) nature of the population regulatory processes in effect, and 2) your specific management goals. Generally, there are two management situations to be considered.

As I noted in Chapter 10, herds should be manipulated to produce a sustained yield of animals. In some areas, deer conform to traditional concepts of density-dependent control; while in others, density-independent factors play a more important role in regulating population growth. Areas such as the South Texas brush country, Canada and areas with site-limiting problems characteristically show a different population ecology than areas within the original range of the whitetail. Consequently, we must develop two completely different culling strategies for these two situations.

Within the traditional range, where density-dependent factors control population growth, culling should be aimed at maintaining genetic diversity and removal of non-productive individuals. In herds maintained below the saturation level, does without fawns should be removed. There is no reason to believe that deer are much different from cattle in this respect. A good cattleman removes the less productive cows from his herd, favoring the proven producers. Although there seldom is a true barren doe, a doe without a fawn is either less thrifty, or of a lower social position, reducing her chances of success. Once you have the population at a sustained yield level, you should strive to maintain a herd of proven breeders. Every attempt should be made to bring the effective population size as close as possible to the actual population size. After the proper population density is achieved, you may want to remove does with buck fawns. It has been demonstrated that buck fawn survival is significantly increased after orphaning; apparently because the doe casts off her yearling son at fawning time.

In herds which are controlled by density independent factors, large removals of does from the herd probably is a questionable practice. A rather large buffer must be maintained between what probably is an ever-changing effective population and the real population. As I noted earlier, herds on the periphery of the range, or those with serious site limitations, must be managed on a "worst case scenario" basis. Cattlemen in the arid regions have successfully used this approach to realize a profit for many years. They manage their herds for the worst range conditions, even in years with above normal growing conditions.

Herd reductions should only be effected during periods of above normal growing conditions, in order to keep the herd from exceeding the productive capacity of the range. When a herd

The doe has just as much, or perhaps even more, impact on antler quality as the buck. The author feels that thriftiness of the doe, regulated by complex genetic processes, allows her to "sculpt" her son's antlers. Bucks contribute conformation to the genetic equation.

Mike Biggs

reduction is in order, I suggest you either remove doe fawns or does with fawns. Why does with fawns? Current research suggests that, in such areas, does may successfully reproduce only in alternating years. Often it takes two years, even in well-managed herds, for a doe to reach peak breeding condition. Hence, it makes good common sense to retain does without fawns, as they have the highest probability of successfully reproducing during the coming year.

Let me offer one caution. **All herd reductions on the periphery of the range should be carefully evaluated before implementation.** In these situations, a doe without a fawn does not mean that she is inferior, only that she probably reproduced earlier and must regain adequate reserves to once again reproduce. Excessive removals of does from these herds may have long-term negative impacts on the population dynamics and genetics of the herd. Again, we manage deer herds by fine-tuning the population to the productive capacity of the range and the management objectives.

"Culling" To Improve Antler Quality

In the vast majority of cases, there is no need to cull bucks from the herd. Both for numbers management and quality buck management, the principles of population and habitat management presented in this book are adequate to allow you to achieve your goals. But, if trophy management truly is your management goal, and you are willing to make an extremely long-term commitment to your program, then culling may be feasible. However, culling programs should only be implemented when you feel the true genetic potential of your herd has been reached.

There have been numerous culling schemes proposed over the last decade or so. Some biologists, based primarily on the Kerr study, assert that "inferior" yearlings should be removed. Others feel that bucks should be culled at the middle-age classes. I am afraid that both approaches may lead to problems. Shooting of "inferior" yearlings and "superior" mature bucks amounts to nothing more than a slot-limit, similar to that used by fisheries biologists in largemouth bass management. In a slot-limit management scheme, the idea is to protect the middle age classes, removing younger animals to control the genetics, and older animals for trophies. Deer are not bass! The bass slot-limit scheme involves a situation in which both sexes have equal trophy value. Fishermen make little distinction, although females are larger, between one sex or another. **Imposition of a slot-limit strategy on a deer herd surely will guarantee the ultimate production of an average buck, and we now are seeing this on some of our oldest trophy management areas**. Removal of yearlings (no doubt in large numbers under a strict culling program) would seriously reduce the genetic variability so necessary to trophy production. Ironically, we are attempting to increase, not decrease, variability in trophy buck production.

A more reasonable approach would be one that has shown great promise to

Dr. Harry Jacobson

Non-typical antlers tend to show up later in life, even though a buck may have been typical for most of his life. This may be the result of many factors. Brood bucks should be chosen from mature, dominant animals.

this point. It is based on the idea that we want to produce as many yearling bucks as possible in order to maximize genetic variability. No attempt should be made to cull yearlings, only to maintain the herd at a high nutritional plane by population control and supplemental feeding.

A pre-established proportion of older bucks (I suggest 10 percent) is removed annually from the herd. Selection simply is on a random basis, without regard to antler quality. Hunters remove bucks on a random basis in most cases. Again, this maintains the genetic variability of the herd. But, the manager selects so-called "brood bucks," which are mature, dominant animals in the herd. In well-managed herds, these bucks will emerge as the primary breeders, and should be protected as such. No matter how tempting it is to kill one of these animals, designation as a brood buck commutes the animal's death sentence for life! A brood buck only should be removed if another, more desirable buck should appear.

The number of brood bucks for a particular parcel of land will be determined by the deer themselves. Each dominant buck will stake out a breeding "territory" of varying size. Within his territory, he will be responsible for most of the breeding, effectively suppressing the subordinate bucks. This obviously requires an intimate knowledge of the bucks on your property, and this often is difficult. Again, this is one of the many factors that make trophy management so extremely difficult.

Does this culling scheme work? My good friend, Bill Carter, has been actively managing trophy whitetails for many years; and probably has produced as many monster bucks "on purpose" as anyone I know. He also feels that the slot-limit approach is a mistake. Needless to say, his ideas— especially coming from a layman— do not set well with established deer managers. His Sombrerito Ranch lies in the heart of the arid brush country near Laredo, Texas. **He successfully has combined a limited doe harvest system with a very effective brood buck program to produce some of the finest bucks I have seen anywhere**. He allows hunters to take good bucks, but jealously protects his brood bucks from harvest. He knows almost every buck on his property, even assigning names to some. "I'm convinced our brood buck program is working," Bill asserts "and we now are seeing positive results on the overall quality of *all* our bucks." I have visited Bill's ranch, and can attest to the high quality of his "average" buck.

Although not strictly a "brood buck" management program, the management regime in effect on the Boggy Slough Hunting and Fishing Club in the Pineywoods is quite similar to that used on the Sombrerito Ranch. However, this herd lies in the more traditional portion of the range, with concomitant density dependent effects, and must be controlled by substantial antlerless harvest. No attempt ever has been made to selectively cull yearling bucks, yet the area has consistently produced record-book bucks (see **The Boggy Slough Story**).

Selecting Brood Bucks

Since antler conformation probably is the single heritable trait, this obviously is the only criterion on which to base our selection. Conformation refers to two basic attributes. The first involves the overall shape of the antlers. I have divided antler conformations into five categories: 1) circle, 2) ellipse, 3) square, 4) rectangular, and 5) diamond (see drawing), relating to their appearance when viewed from the front. Second, bucks have a tendency to have antlers which are either typical or non-typical in nature. (Non-typical is defined as having fifteen of more inches of abnormal points.) A buck may have typical antlers for most of his life, then turn non-typical later in life. So, as the saying goes: "It's hard to judge a book

ANTLER SHAPES

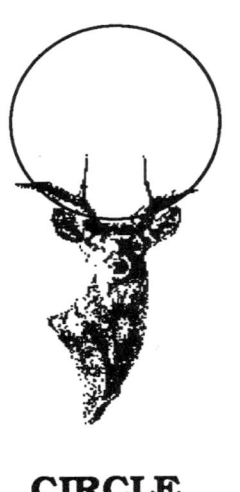 　　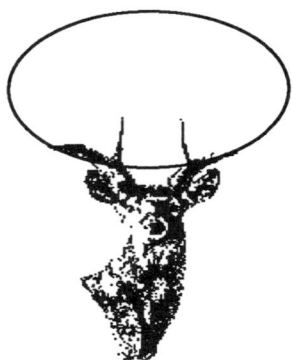

CIRCLE　　　　　　　　　**ELLIPSE**

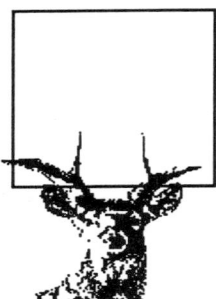 　　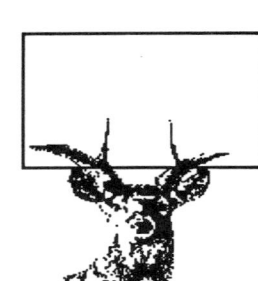

SQUARE　　　　　　　　**RECTANGLE**

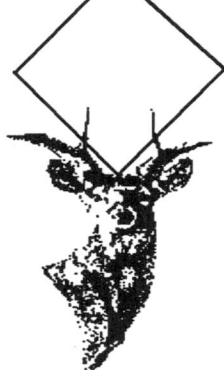　　

DIAMOND

by its cover." A third criterion, number of basic antler points, may be a poor selection criterion, since bucks may only add points once dominance is achieved. Therefore, brood bucks can be selected on the shape and nature of their antlers; but, they are best selected at maturity.

Someone once said that "beauty is in the eye of the beholder." This never was more true than with whitetail bucks. Some hunters think that a non-typical, diamond antlered buck is the most beautiful creature on the face of the earth, while others would not give such a deer much consideration. The types of bucks you select for breeders will depend entirely on you, but I suggest that you select several different types of animals. This will guarantee a diversity of antler types. There could be nothing more boring than to have a deer herd with bucks giving the impression of being "stamped out with a cookie cutter!"

SUMMARY

There are few situations which justify any consideration of genetic manipulation of the herd. Our current knowledge base is, at best, confusing. Attempts to "improve" the genetics of the herd should only be made after many years of intensive management; and, **after** little additional improvement in antler quality is observed.

Trophy management is an expensive and labor-intensive affair. Once the decision has been made to effect a change in the genetics of your herd, you must be willing to accept the fact that changes come very slowly. The whitetail appears to be an innately diverse creature, capable of sustaining many years of inbreeding without serious degradation of heterozygosity.

If you decide to embark on a culling program, you should consider both the female and male segments of the population. In herds with density dependent controls, less productive does should be removed from the herd, favoring proven breeders. Genetic diversity of does, in these herds, can be guaranteed by keeping the population productive, and reasonably young. Culling of bucks using a slot-limit approach is strongly discouraged, along with the culling of yearling bucks. There are serious questions about the predictability of a mature buck's antler traits based on his first set of antlers.

The approach which seems most feasible at this time is the designation of dominant "brood bucks," which are never harvested, and allowed to breed within their established territories. These brood bucks can be selected primarily on antler conformation (the nature and shape of the antlers); but, are selected more on personal preference than any other criterion. Care should be taken to assure the genetic diversity of the herd.

The coming decade should see the answers to many of the questions raised in this chapter. As far as I am concerned, the jury is still out on this one!

THE OLD BUCK

Ray Sasser

Was early spring,
The birds began to sing.
The woods were quiet,
And I could sleep all night.

No hunters to bother us,
But soon there would be dust.
The drought will take it's toll,
Especially among the old.

They came with tractors to plant,
In order that they might grant.
A place for them to sow,
So the newborn would have a place to grow.

In the summer I had grown,
A trophy set of antlers of my own.
I knew the hunter wanted them,
But I also knew I was smarter than him.

When the cool winds of autumn came,
He thought he could put me to shame.
He thought he could catch me unalert,
If he did I knew I'd be hurt.

Instead of mating and feeding by day,
In my warm bed I'd stay.
I could hear them come and go,
But not a glimpse of me I'd show.

In the distance I could hear shots ring,
To me they didn't mean a thing.
When the season finally ended,
I had accomplished what I intended.

I'd made it through another year,
Without having any fear!

...K.S.

Chapter 17

Mike Biggs

CONTROLLING DEER MOVEMENTS

Often it is desirable, due to limitations imposed by the configuration of the property or socio-political problems, to control the movements of deer. The use of "deer-proof" fences probably began in the Hill Country of Texas back in the 1950's. That is when the economic importance of whitetails really came to public attention. The landowners who understood the economic value of deer, soon began to manage their herds for leasing and commercial hunting. Unfortunately, however, adjacent landowners often took advantage of their neighbor's hard work. Since the home range of whitetails is highly variable, exceeding several thousand acres in some instances, a buck grown on one property may be killed on another landholding.

In an effort to keep deer from leaving, ranchers would erect eight feet high, netwire fences along the property line. Later, the idea arose to completely surround the property with a high fence. But, in those days, the cost of fencing a parcel of land was relatively inexpensive. Today, this is far from the truth. Costing $10,000 to $15,000 per mile, deer fencing has reached a cost prohibitive state in many areas.

During the last decade, we have seen high fences show up in some pretty unlikely places. The number of fenced enclosures in Michigan alone is impressive. Areas such as *The Sanctuary* have gained prominence among trophy hunters as **the** places to kill a monster buck. But, what are the realities of deer fencing? When is a high fence necessary? And, what are the fencing options available to the landowner? This chapter will attempt to answer these questions.

WHY FENCE DEER?

There are many misconceptions about the function of "deer-proof" fences. Notice that I have place quotation marks around the term. The reason for this is that seldom have I seen a fence that is totally deer-proof. On numerous occasions, I have seen my radio-collared deer magically appear on the wrong side of a fence. How they manage to get over the fence is a perplexing problem. I have seen deer that were pushed jump an eight feet high fence with little effort. I also have seen deer crawl under a fence; and, go right through a fence! (When struck at the proper angle, many brands of netwire will momentarily separate, allowing the deer to slip through.) The wire stays spring back into place, and you would be hard put to find the spot where the animal penetrated the fence.

Deer fences serve as much to keep unwanted deer out, as they do to keep wanted deer in! One of the paradoxes of deer management is that, no matter how hard you try, the population cannot be reduced to an optimum sustained yield or maximum sustained yield level. For example, I once managed a ranch near Ulvade, Texas. It contained 3,000 acres of excellent brush habitat, but was configured as a long rectangle. Try as we would, no amount of antlerless harvest would ever reduce the number of deer on the property. As soon as we would remove a doe, another one would come in from the adjacent property to take her place. It was a "no win" situation. Hence, one justification for constructing a fence would be to allow the manager to maintain control on the herd.

A second reason deals with the movement of bucks. My research, and that of other biologists, clearly demonstrated that bucks may move many miles during the rut. Movements as great as twenty miles are not uncommon, especially in the North. A fence can significantly increase the number of mature bucks on the property.

Third, it often is desirable to maintain control over the genetic composition of the herd. In a trophy management program, it seems foolish to embark on a culling or genetic manipulation program, when no control on the breeding stock is maintained.

TYPES OF FENCES

Traditionally, deer have been confined within standard high fences constructed from netwire. In earlier times, this entailed the use of two panels of either sheep-and-goat wire or hog wire. Panel width most commonly was forty-seven inches, bringing the total height almost to eight feet (the recommended height). Addition of one or two strands of barbed wire at the top, brought the fence to full height. But recently, the popularity of deer fences, as well as, the advent of deer farming in this country, has encouraged commercial manufacturers to produce fencing specifically designed for deer. Some of the New Zealand companies, in particular, have developed single panel fencing ranging from 6.5 feet to 8 feet in height. This obviously greatly reduces the cost of erection. This fencing also is of better construction than traditional netwire.

Eight feet tall, netwire fences have been used successfully to control deer movements for many years. These fences were first developed to prevent deer from moving from the landowner's property to an adjacent, uncontrolled area. Later, landowners began fencing the entire property in order to maintain complete control over the herd.

High electric fences have been used successfully in New Zealand to confine several species of deer. Here, it is obvious that this whitetail buck is reluctant to encounter the high voltage-high amperage fence.

The vertical and horizontal stays are wrapped in such a way as to make it impossible for a deer to go through the fence as described above.

Netwire fences are not the only option now available for deer fencing. Again, New Zealand deer farmers have paved the way in fence technology. For many years, farmers and ranchers have used electric fences to control livestock, with varying degrees of success. You may be familiar with the electric fencing and chargers sold commonly in mail order catalogs such as the Sears Farm and Ranch Catalog. But, these chargers (energizers) were developed to produce relatively low voltages and amperages, with safety an important consideration. Consequently, they often did not deliver the force necessary to control wild animals. Or, there was insufficient amperage to overcome a significant amount of vegetation coming in contact with the wire.

Several New Zealand companies overcame these problems using a high voltage-high amperage, short duty cycle energizer. Delivering voltages as high as 7,000v. at 30 amps, these new generation energizers suddenly made it

The three-strand offset fence is an inexpensive, yet effective way to deter deer movements. These fences should not be used, however, as perimeter fences.

feasible to power many miles of wire. And I might add, with a considerable "bite" in the process. These potentially lethal currents are mediated by a very short (1-3 msec.) duty cycle (the time in which the current is switched on). When supplied over a heavy 11-gauge, high tensile wire, the New Zealand configurations offer new flexibility in deer fencing.

Electric deer fences have been developed for several purposes. First, there is a very popular fourteen wire, 8 feet tall fence, primarily used both for perimeter and cross-fencing. The wires often are alternated positive-negative, with 7 "hot" wires and 7 ground wires. The first 6 wires are spaced at 6 inch intervals, and the remaining 8 wires on an 8 inch spacing. These fences are suitable for areas with adequate ground moisture to support the flow of current. More xeric regions really are not suitable for electric fences.

A second electric fence-type is useful either for interrupting the emigration of deer or for protecting certain crops. The concept is based on the idea that deer would rather go through a barrier than over one. This type of fence is constructed as a fence within a fence. That is, two fences are erected approximately 38 inches apart. The outermost fence has a single strand of wire, positioned 24 inches above the ground, and is positively charged. The idea is for the wire to contact a deer at the nose to mid-chest level. The second fence has two wires, one at 18 inches, and the other at 30 inches. Both wires are positively charged. Hence, this fence provides a wide barrier to deer movements. I have successfully used this fence to deter 95 percent of deer movements in the forest.

There have been several modifications of electric fences proposed over the years, with varying degrees of success. One such fence is a "slant fence," in which 6-8 wires equally spaced on posts that slant outward. This approach presumably provides a horizontal barrier to the deer, again taking advantage of a deer's desire to go through, instead of over a barrier.

Hybrid versions of netwire and electric fences also have been used successfully. In most cases, a single panel of netwire is erected on the bottom 4 feet, with 6-7 strands of electric wire spaced above the panel to a height of 8 feet.

The type of fence you select will depend on several factors, among which are cost, soil conditions and extent of control desired. I have had success with netwire, high electric and three-strand offset fences. I use netwire and high electric fences as perimeter fences; and, three-strand offset fences to protect crops and to prevent deer from entering or leaving a property via a specific direction.

FENCE SPECIFICATIONS

Rights-of-way

Landowners seldom give adequate consideration to right-of-way preparation, yet this is the second-most common factor contributing to high maintenance costs. The greatest cause of fence failure lies in poor construction and materials. A good rule-of-thumb in right-of-way establishment is to clear at least a 50 feet wide area. Some managers prefer to clear a distance away from the centerline of the fence equal to the height of the tallest tree. This can create a very expensive fence in areas with trees of 100 feet or more in height. I suggest that the best compromise is to clear a 50 feet wide right-of-way, and "hazard-rate" the trees adjacent to the fence. This means that you walk the fenceline, marking all trees for removal that are, 1) leaning, 2) obviously diseased (fungal bodies, etc.), 3) partially dead or hollow, and 4) of poor crown diameter. Removal of high risk trees will significantly reduce maintenance costs. Electric fences can be constructed with a more narrow right-of-way, since they seldom are seriously damaged by falling trees and branches. The high tensile nature of the wire allows resiliency, without breaking. Netwire, on the other hand, is seriously damaged by falling trees and must be replaced in most instances.

Netwire High Fences

In order to get the most for your money, I suggest that as much care as possible be given to the proper construction of fences. When properly installed, netwire fences should last from 15-25 years, depending on the climate and materials used.

One of the major sources of fence failure lies in the improper installation of corners and braces. All corners should be constructed from 14 feet tall, 6-8 inch top diameter treated posts. Either creosote or *Walmonize* posts are suitable; however, be sure that all posts are **pressure treated**, as dipped posts will last only a short while. The corner post should be anchored in cement, and be at least 4 feet in the ground. Cross-braces should be 8-10 feet in length and tied to corner and line posts with a wire strainer. Simple physics dictates that these dimensions be strictly adhered to, as a shorter brace distance will cause the posts to lean and/or fail when pressure is applied.

Stand H-braces should be positioned in the line at a maximum distance of 330 feet. Shorter intervals are required

Controlling Deer Movements

where topographic relief is severe, and at all water crossings. Line posts should be spaced at 10 feet intervals between H-braces, and can either be metal 10 feet tall T-posts or 4-6 inch top diameter treated posts.

A single strand of barbed wire should be placed at the bottom of the fence to provide an anchor for the netwire and to retard digging by predators and other animals. Two strands of either barbed wire or electric wire should be placed above the netwire to add height and to prevent animals and people from climbing over the fence.

I recommend the single panel deer fencing currently on the market. This greatly will reduce labor costs. However, if two panels are used, the top panel should be fastened to the bottom panel with "hog rings." This will prevent a deer from striking the fence at this

The materials and construction of corners will greatly affect both the quality and life-expectancy of any deer fence.

Robert Skinner

point and escaping between the two panels.

If there are streams entering and leaving the property, there always is the potential for problems resulting from flooding or highwater. A log or even debris can rip through a netwire fence, causing loss of animals and/or expensive repairs. For this reason, I suggest that you construct watergates at all stream crossings. These are simply constructed from treated lumber and galvanized metal roofing material. The gate is hinged on a cable extended from one streambank to the next, so that it will swing with the flow of water, then drop back into place as the water recedes. Some of the watergates I have constructed have withstood 12 inch rains over a 6-hour period! These structures increase initial expense, but pay off in the longrun in reduced maintenance costs.

Here is some added advice about wire. Too often there is the temptation to purchase a lighter gauge (13 or 14 gauge) wire to save money. This is a serious mistake, as the lighter wires just will not hold up over the long run; and, you may be faced with loss of animals and increased maintenance and repairs. You can avoid these problems by using a heavy gauge wire from the outset.

High Electric Fences

The specifications presented for the corners of netwire fences also apply to high electric fences. Perhaps even more than netwire fences, the corners of electric fences are extremely important. Excessive pressures (ca., 250 lbs/in^2) are common-place for the high tensile wires used in electric fences. Hence, a poorly designed corner will result in fence failure. Specifications for H-braces also are identical for electric and netwire fences. But, spacings and types of line posts used are quite different. First, I suggest that you use a 3-4 inch top diameter treated post at 100 feet intervals, and metal T-posts or fiberglass stays at 33 feet intervals.

High electric fences should have 14-16 strands of 11-gauge, high tensile wire positioned either in alternating

In high electric fences, insulators are placed in various configurations, usually alternating with ground wires afixed directly to the post.

High tensile, heavy gauge wires are stretched using strainers, tightened with either a torque wrench or a hand tightener.

positive-negative, or have the bottom three strands as positive and the remaining wires alternating positive-negative. The rationale for the latter configuration is that an animal contacting the bottom portion of the fence no doubt will have its feet firmly planted on the ground, thereby establishing a solid ground contact.

Wires are pulled tight using unique strainers developed specifically for electric fences. These strainers come in several makes and models, all of which are more than adequate for properly stretching the wire. Straining is accomplished using a torque wrench-like or simple strainer handle. The high-tensile nature of the wire guarantees that, once the wire has been stretched to the desired pressure, there is little need for future tightening of the wire, even at high air temperatures.

Insulators should be used for connecting "hot" wires to the posts, except in the case of fiberglass stays. There are many types of insulators, ranging from ceramic "doughnuts" to plastic tubing. I prefer to use the plastic tubing to make direct wooden post connections, and clip-on or nail-on connectors for treated and T-posts, respectively.

Water crossings can be handled as given for netwire fences, or by using galvanized chains attached to the bottom electric wire in such a manner as to hang down to near ground level. An electronic device, floodgate controller, is available which will turn the current off of all wires grounded out by high water. When the water recedes, current once again is returned to the affected wires.

One problem with electric fences is the potential for a lightning strike damaging the energizer. You always should use a lightning arrestor to prevent damage.

One of the most common causes for failure of electric fences to control deer results from improper grounding. The energizer should be adequately grounded using copper rods. As many as 6 rods often are necessary to accomplish proper grounding.

Development of high voltage-high amperage energizing systems in New Zealand have allowed managers to control deer movements at less cost. However, these systems must be properly grounded.

Three-strand Offset Electric Fence

Since this type of fence is less than four feet tall and involves only three wires, there is considerable savings in materials. However, this fence serves more to deter than to control deer movements. I would not recommend this fence for confining deer, rather as a deterrent to their movements.

The same principles for corner posts also apply to offset fences; however, a 7-8 feet tall, 6-8 inch top-diameter treated post is adequate for corner posts. However, since this configuration amounts to a fence within a fence, you must erect two braced corners, with a 38-inch distance between the two corner posts. Four to six inch top diameter line posts are spaced in pairs at a 100 feet interval. There is no need for stays or additional posts between these.

ECONOMICS OF DEER FENCING

As I noted earlier, deer fencing can be quite expensive, depending on the type of fence selected and the nature of the terrain. In general, high netwire fences will cost about $5,000 per mile for materials and an equal amount for labor. This does not include right-of-way clearing. High electric fences normally cost about $3,000 per mile for materials and about half this amount for labor. Three-strand offset electric fences cost about $1,000 per mile for materials and again about half this amount for labor.

The cost of right-of-way clearing can vary considerably, but most often approximates $750-$1,000 per mile. Cost of watergates is not included in these cost estimates, as they vary with width of crossing.

From a depreciation standpoint, I noted earlier that most fences will last from 15 to 25 years, depending on climate, construction materials and type of fence. In calculating depreciation or in conducting financial analyses, I suggest you use a 15-year period.

SUMMARY

So-called deer-proof fences are an expensive means of controlling deer movements. Careful consideration should be given to the management goals and the economic realities of the situation **before** embarking on a fencing program.

There are several fence configurations available to the manager, among which are: 1) high (8 ft.) netwire, 2) high electric, 3) slant electric, 4) three-strand offset, and 5) hybrid netwire-electric. The type of fence selected will depend on soil conditions and the extent of control desired.

Cost of fence construction will vary from $10,000-$15,000 per mile for netwire to $1,500 per mile for the offset fence.

Mike Biggs

OFF SEASON

Deer hunters never say die,
All they want is another try.

An entire season has just passed,
It's memories will have to last.

Nine months with nothing to do but dream,
Trying to hatch an evil scheme.

A way to bag that trophy buck,
Will still have to have lots of luck.
                                        ... K.S.

Chapter 18

THE BOGGY SLOUGH STORY

Two men sat on a bench overlooking a lake at North Boggy Slough Hunting and Fishing Club, belonging to Temple-Eastex Inc. Temple is a name well-known to the East Texas Pineywoods region. For it was the founder of the company, T. L. L. Temple, who first came to the area to start a timber company. Later, through his grandson, Arthur, the Temples were to build one of the major timber companies in the U.S., owning some 1.5 million acres alone in East Texas.

Boggy Slough is a well-known entertainment area for the Company. It has a long and rich history, dating back to the first part of this century. Originally made up only of a few hundred acres, it now contains nearly 20 thousand acres. By the turn-of-the-century, most of the deer herd around Boggy had been extirpated. The pure pine and hardwood, old growth forests had been cut-over by 1930, and it was said by an R. E. Minton that only a single doe and fawn survived the wholesale slaughter.

In 1913, a Mr. Gilbert hired Captain J. J. Ray to manage a ranch of 640 acres. Captain Ray was a lover of deer, and resolved to protect what was left of the original herd. The local people were used to having their way, both with the game and for their livestock, especially hogs. Night-hunting using torchlights was common practice, since there were no game laws to protect the deer. When the deer herd had become sparse, the locals had turned to hunting deer with hounds, to ferret out the last remaining individuals. It was truly a dark day for the whitetail. Ray fenced the property and actively excluded both wild hogs and hunting hounds. He protected the small herd with vigor, sometimes risking life and limb in the process.

One of the men sitting on the bench that day was a tall, ruddy-complexioned man, Gene Samford, who was the Director of Wildlife for Temple. The other was me. "You know, James," Gene said with his characteristic southern drawl, "Mr. Temple is committed to making this the best-managed deer herd in the state, and so am I." This comment was spawned by yet another disappointing year for the club. The biggest buck harvested during the previous season was a ten-inch six-pointer!

The year was 1978, a time when deer management was only beginning to gain a foothold in the region. I had been traveling around the Pineywoods for several years, literally a "voice crying in the wilderness." My ideas about controlling herd growth by shooting antlerless deer and restricting buck harvest, did not exactly meet with resounding public approval! In fact, at some of my talks, I understood what one famous country singer had said earlier. "When I first started out," he confided, "they used to put up chicken-wire in front of the band stand, to catch the beer bottles that were thrown at us." Believe me, I understood how he felt. To go into an area, where deer had been non-existent for fifty years, and try to explain the need for population control was a bit risky, to say the least. I was desperately seeking a large landowner who would allow me to implement my brand of management. This clearly was my chance!

I swallowed hard, and began laying out the blueprint to achieve this lofty goal. We first should stop all buck shooting for at least two years. The herd had been heavily harvested for bucks for almost fifty years. Next, we should implement an effective antlerless deer harvest. The population had experienced several die-offs over the years, the first as early as the 1950's. During the previous year (1977), I had recorded a total loss of some 600 deer! Third, we needed to change the way food plots were being managed. In the past, they simply had been planted to oats to bait the deer in. I have nothing against oats, but there are several better plantings (see **Nutrition and Supplemental Feeding**). We would plant a mixture of cereal grains and arrowleaf clover. Lastly, we should hire professional biologists to oversee the management program. Gene thought a minute, then said: "Well, if that's what we have to do, then that is what we are going to do. I'll talk to Mr. Temple."

Gene was a man of his word. The next few years saw all of my recommendations implemented. Bill Goodrum and Don Dietz, both second-generation bi-

Second generation biologist, Bill Goodrum, shows off some the fine bucks produced through Boggy Slough's quality deer management program.

---

ologists, were hired to oversee the program. Bill's dad, Phil Goodrum, was one of the first wildlife biologists ever hired in the State, while Don's father, Don Dietz Sr., is well-known for his work on deer nutrition and management. These fellows did an excellent job of executing the plan.

The first year was not an easy one. As I already have noted, most of the hunters at Boggy are invited guests; important people in one way or another. These guys, for the most part, were used to having their own way. How could we ever tell them what they could or could not shoot? Gene did not bat an eye, though, informing the hunters that there would be no bucks harvested that year. The three biologists carefully explained to the guests the reasons for this decision; and ironically enough, they went along with the program to a man. During the first year, only a handful of does were shot. But, in succeeding years, more and more does were removed by the hunters. Their enthusiasm was fueled by the growing number of bucks they saw each season.

Later in the program, it became necessary to teach the guest-hunters about what bucks to shoot. In the past, any buck that "tickled their fancy" was an acceptable buck. Now, it was not acceptable to shoot a yearling buck. A two-year old also was on the protection list. But, how do you educate grown men, many of whom have hunted all their lives, about which bucks should be shot and which should not? The answer was quite simple. Although I will discuss our methods in depth later in this book (see **People Management**), the solution lay in peer-group pressure. We simply gave talks the evening before the hunt about what we were trying to do, and which bucks we would like for them to shoot. In addition, *every* hunter had his picture taken with his buck. That picture ended up on a prominent bulletin board in the guest lodge. In no time at all, this led to a significant change in attitudes.

The food plot program proved to be quite effective in improving the nutritional plane of the herd. The cereal grain-clover combination was highly attractive to the deer, providing high quality nutrition well into the summer. But, again, this created a problem. Most of the hunters had grown used to hunting out of box blinds on the food plots. Since these blinds had been hunted for many, many years, the deer knew good and well that there were hunters lurking inside these structures. Bill developed a plan, whereby he would move stands around. He also alternated the hunting from a particular stand. The hunter no longer was being patterned by the deer. The result was a significant increase in the number of trophy-class bucks killed. Fully two-thirds of all trophy bucks killed from 1981-89 were taken from newly relocated stands.

The Boggy population, as I noted earlier, had a history of oscillating about the saturation level, with periodic die-offs. Our goal was to dampen these oscillations so that we could better predict the annual harvest, as well as hold the herd at the productive capacity (Optimum Sustained Yield) of the range. The population continued to oscillate violently, until 1986, when the

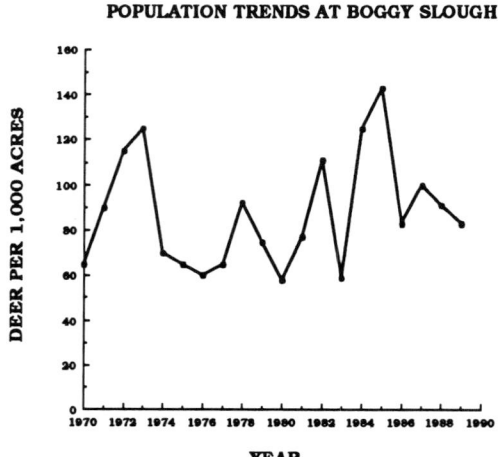

The Boggy Slough Story

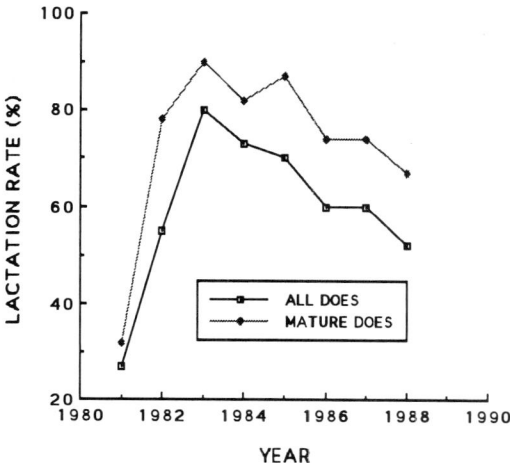

Above. Initially, the lactation rate (an estimate of recruitment) increased dramatically at Boggy Slough after antlerless harvests. But later, lactation rates dropped off, possibly due to observer error or a younger doe herd. (Below) Although average live weight of bucks continues to climb, it was not until later in the program that doe weights also increased.

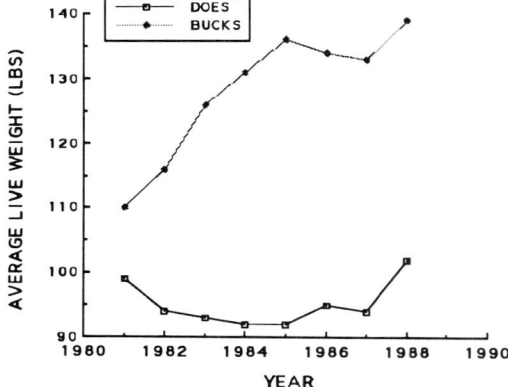

herd began to show signs of a dampening effect. At this writing, the herd is being held at around 80-85 deer per 1,000 acres; a level I feel is equal to 67% of the saturation level, satisfying the definition of OSY.

One of the most interesting aspects of the Boggy Slough story is the impressive response in reproductive performance. Earlier, I discussed the principles of population management; pointing out that, in herds with density-dependent effects, significant herd reductions would lead to increased recruitment. By 1983, lactation rates for mature does (2.5+ years) exceeded 80 percent. Since that time, however, the lactation rate for mature does has dropped below the target of 80 percent. However, fawn-at-heel observations suggest that recruitment actually has stabilized. Part of the reduced lactation rate is due more to mistakes being made in recognizing lactation. The peak of the rut has shifted a full 25 days to around the first of November, putting fawns on the ground in April. Allowing for a sixty-day nursing period, this means that does harvested in November and December may have ceased nursing some six to seven months earlier.

As I noted in the chapter on interpreting records, two other diagnostics, in addition to lactation rate, for monitoring management progress are dressed weights and antler scores. Average live weight of bucks showed a continued increase throughout the project (1981-88); while live weight of does did not increase until the latter years. The goal for antler rating score (see **Record-Keeping**) was set at 125. By 1984, the

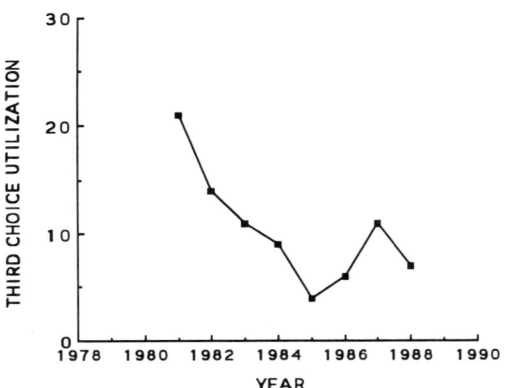

Over the years, control of the deer population at Boggy Slough, has led to lower utilization of low quality (third choice) browse.

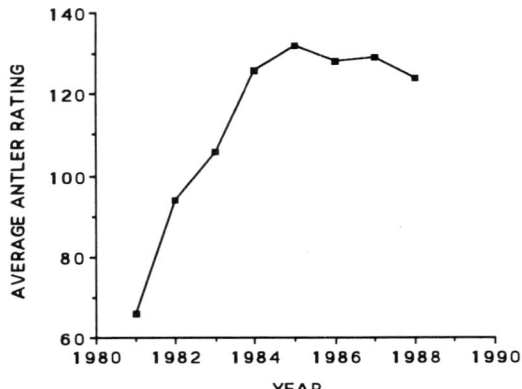

One important diagnostic for monitoring management progress is antler rating. At Boggy Slough, antler rating has leveled off around the predetermined goal of 125.

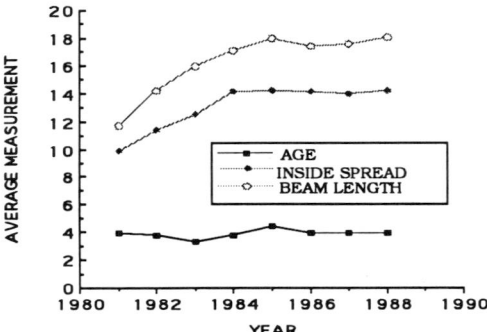

At Boggy Slough, antler quality measurements increased, while average age of bucks remained relatively constant.

average score exceeded this minimum. Since that time, the average score has remained at or above this level, in spite of a relatively heavy harvest intensity (ca., one buck per 125 acres). During this time, the average age of bucks remained fairly constant at about four years. Clearly, we achieved our goal of an optimum sustained yield of bucks.

Probably the most notable change in the harvest was the small percentage of younger (1.5 years or less) bucks killed. The education and peer-group pressure program obviously had a tremendous impact. Interviews with guest-hunters indicated that they were very pleased with the program, but that they had to see at least seven deer per day,

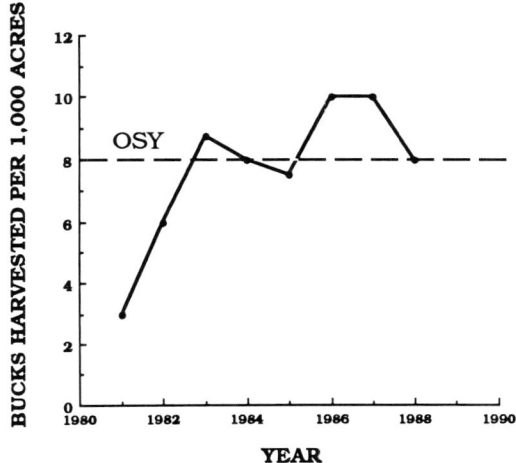

The long-term goal at Boggy Slough was to achieve an optimum sustained yield of bucks. That point, the author believes, is at a harvest intensity of one buck per 125 acres.

in order to be satisfied. Seeing deer obviously is an important motivator to the hunter. There is no doubt in my mind, that if Gene, Bill and Don could accomplish this dealing with guest-hunters, that the average hunting club could achieve far more.

Gene retired after the program had begun, and was replaced with an equally capable man, Darryl Stanley. Darryl initiated a hunting club assistance program within the company. My original idea of taking an East Texas hunting club, implementing a quality buck management program, then using this program as a demonstration for other clubs, seems to be working nicely. We now have numerous biologists operating in the area, with little resistance to population control or the other tenets of deer management. The Pineywoods Region now is looked upon as a trophy producing "hotspot" throughout the south. In the next section, I will discuss one of the most memorable experiences of my life— the hunt for the Ghost of Boggy Slough.

THE GHOST OF BOGGY SLOUGH

In 1982, I was concentrating my efforts on documenting the impact of years of overpopulation on the deer herd and habitat. Some 25 years earlier, a local biologist named Dan Lay had had the good judgment to establish several fenced areas to monitor the impact of deer and cattle browsing on the forest (see **Habitat Management**). Although the study had long since been completed, most of the fenced enclosures were still in place. The result of so many years of overbrowsing was staggering. Inside these enclosures, the forest was completely different from that of the surrounding area, which was open to deer foraging. Clearly the deer had drastically altered their habitat, and that of such animals as squirrels and songbirds, as well.

During September of that year, a yearling buck made quiet a nuisance of himself in my study area. To my frustration, young saplings within the study plots began dying from excessive rubbing. Each time I visited the plots, new damage had been done to the trees!

One day I arrived at the study plots to find the culprit busily rubbing yet another tree. And, was he ugly! He had malformed antlers, yet a rather large body for his age. In most of the so-called buck "culling" programs now in operation throughout some regions, he surely would have been removed from the herd. Instead, I just cussed him and proceeded with my work.

The following year, he was right back in my plots, destroying a new set of saplings. It was during this time that my theories about buck sanctuaries began to take shape. My telemetry research clearly showed that bucks preferred areas hunters seldom frequented, traveling to and from such areas by travel corridors. As a matter of fact, I wrote about this particular buck in several magazine articles of that vintage.

This particular buck had adopted a very successful strategy. He lived in a virtual "no man's land" between North Boggy Slough and South Boggy Slough. By gentlemen's agreement, this area was not hunted, to avoid conflicts between the two clubs. The buck was to stay in his sanctuary for many years to come.

The buck's travel pattern was quite characteristic of the sanctuary/travel corridor concept. He spent the daylight hours in the swamps of the sanctuary, venturing into a nearby upland to feed at night. There was a stand located not more than a quarter-mile from his sanctuary, yet no hunter ever had reported seeing such a buck. Each year the buck's tell-tale rubs were right back in the same area. And, each year, I became more and more attached to this buck. Those pathetic antlers grew to enormous proportions, with prominent drop tines appearing by the fourth year. Each season, I secretly rooted for him to make it through the year, and each year my hopes were rewarded. One year I even rubbed mud on one of his rubs next to a road so that no one would discover my "pet."

But, in '86 the feeding area adjacent to his sanctuary was harvested for pine timber. Now, I am not an opponent to clearcutting. My research and that of others has shown that timber harvest is critical to whitetail management. However, the first year of so after a timber harvest finds most bucks avoiding clearcuts like the plague. That year, I could not find the buck I by then was calling "The Ghost." At 5 years of age, he either was dead or had moved to a new area.

Then came '87, and some exciting reports from Bill and Don. One of the foresters had found a shed antler about a mile to the west of "my" buck's sanctuary. The single right antler scored very high as a typical B&C buck. As a matter of fact, I felt that the buck in '87 certainly would be a new state, if not world, record. (The long-standing Texas typical record is 196 4/8, taken by Tom McCulloch in Maverick County in '65. The world record, of course, is James Jordon's 206 1/8, taken in Burnett County, Wisconsin, in '74.) Thoughts about "The Ghost" long since had faded, so I secretly hoped for a chance at this new monster.

Apparently, the buck had the same pattern as "The Ghost." (We now feel

The Boggy Slough Story

The author's monster buck, scoring 190 3/8 non-typical B&C, is one of the largest bucks ever harvested at Boggy Slough. It gives testimony to the effectiveness of the management program.

that the two bucks were related, if not brothers.) The shed antler had been found in the Cochina Creek bottom, which had already produced B&C bucks. I feel that this area, protected by Capt. Ray, contained remnants of the original Kansas whitetails, which once inhabited the region. The creek was upstream from the old sanctuary. I knew that such a buck would not venture anywhere near one of the many permanent blinds located on the club. Bill long since had learned that hunting success increases greatly when he moves his stands. Each season the two biologists make conscious effort to reposition their stands for this very reason. Most of the stands are located adjacent to drainages which serve most commonly as travel corridors for bucks.

The nearest possible sanctuary for this buck would be a 10- to 12-year-old pine plantation along the slopes rising from the Cochina Bottom. Two lesser drainages rose steadily from the bottom and penetrated the plantation. In my mind, the big typical had to be using the plantation for a sanctuary, traveling into the bottom via one or both of the small drainages. It was a classic case. This certainly was the perfect condition, and there was no doubt about the buck! The stage was set—yet, I first would have to get an opportunity at the buck.

I was invited to hunt Boggy during the second week of December, well into the Texas gun season. But, this really did not concern me, as the rut had been terrible up to this point. The previous spring had been characterized by a late freeze which had destroyed much of the acorn crop. The spring and summer had been very dry, seriously reducing forage quality to the point at which deer were in poor shape when fall arrived. Luckily, the deer of Boggy Slough had suffered less than their counterparts beyond the clubs' boundaries. Yet, the poor weather did have its effect on our rut. We clearly were into a "trickle rut" situation, with the breeding period being longer than usual and without a clear peak. In addition, weather and moon conditions during this time were terrible. The first two weeks of the season, normally the best time to hunt, had produced little in the way of trophy-class animals, so my anticipation was at a peak when I arrived late in the evening at Boggy.

As dinner came to an end, Bill presented a fine slide and video presentation on the management program at Boggy. Then, he ended the program by showing everyone the shed antler from the huge typical. The conversation immediately switched to the big buck. Several hunts already had taken place this season, but none had produced the buck. Some speculated that he probably was dead of old age by now, while others asserted that such a buck likely was unkillable. I fell into the latter category.

The quiet, cold morning air provided a welcome greeting as I eased out onto the porch with a hot cup of coffee in my hand. The air was completely calm. I could not have hoped for a better day. Surely, this weather would stimulate a visible secondary rut. But, one small obstacle still lay in my way.

Temple-Eastex goes out of its way to assure that all guests have an equal opportunity at the best hunting territories. However, there are few poor areas on Boggy. Most hunters have an excellent opportunity to harvest a good buck, and Boggy sports one of the best hunter success (greater than 60%) rates I ever have seen. Stand locations are assigned by a lottery system, in which hunters draw numbers from a hat. The lowest number gets first choice, while the highest receives the last. To my frustration, I drew one of the highest numbers, which meant that I would have to sit by while the vast majority of guests made their selections. I felt that only a couple of choices would be suitable for a chance at the big typical. To my surprise and delight, however, these choices remained untaken by the time my turn came. I swallowed hard and called out my stand preference. I had no intention of hunting the stand itself, but it did put me very close to where I knew the buck had to be located.

One of the guides, Oscar Rogers (now deceased), kindly agreed to drop me off near the stand. I did not want the presence of a vehicle to spook the buck, so the plan was for him to drive quietly by the area and drop me off as he went. As we turned the corner along an old tram road, his headlights caught the reflection of the marker indicating the stand's presence. He quietly wished me good luck and disappeared into the darkness.

Stumbling through the dark woods was one thing I did not intend to do, so I waited nervously for enough daylight to find my way to my vantage point. I reasoned that the big buck probably would be bedded down in the pine plantation. My only hope was that he did not have some lovely little lady with him, for if he did, no amount of coaxing would lure him out of his sanctuary. An earlier hunter had gotten a glimpse of a large buck near the intersection of one of the drainages with the bottom. Although this drainage was located upwind from the sanctuary, I decided to make my stand there. There are a lot of gimmicks on the market today, but the best gimmick is your own brain. Here was my thinking: The primary rut long since had taken place, so horn rattling was absolutely the wrong thing to do. One tickle of those antlers and all of my work would be down the drain. (*Note: The timing of tactics will be discussed at length in a later chapter.*)

It was possible that a secondary rut was about to take place, and hoping that the buck was without companionship, I decided to take a different approach. The plan was to simulate a rutting buck tending a receptive doe. Taking out two bottles of a home-made odor neutralizer concoction, I completely covered myself with the liquid. I use a modified spray bottle borrowed from my wife's cosmetic cabinet to apply the liquid. Carefully, I rubbed the remaining contents of a bottle in my hair and beard.

I then proceeded up the steep slope adjacent to the drainage. I had gone only a short distance when I encountered a fresh rub line. Doubts began to enter my mind, as each rub was carefully constructed on rather small (less than 2 inches in diameter) saplings. Some researchers had reported that rub size indicated the size of the buck. I have found this to be only partly true. A large-diameter rub does indicate a large buck, but a small rub only indicates the presence of a buck. He may be big or small.

Arriving at the best vantage point, I sat down to wait for good light. The tight cover made it mandatory to have good light. If he came in, I would have but a single opportunity to make a good killing shot. I nervously fingered the safety on the Ruger 7mm magnum and waited.

At approximately 7 a.m. I prepared for my stand. Reaching into my pocket, I produced two critical ingredients of the deception about to take place. First, I got out a bottle containing an extract of a rutting buck's tarsal glands, a friend of mine and I had recently made. I had stored it in a freezer up until this time. This chemical would tell the buck that a really serious opponent had invaded his territory. Next, I pulled out a grunt call given to me by Eli Haydel. I had successfully used the call earlier in Canada to call in and harvest a nice 7-pointer. It was time to use it again on Texas bucks.

I quietly chambered a round into my 7mm. Pouring an entire bottle of the buck extract onto the ground in front of me, I raised the grunt call to my lips. I took a deep breath and issued two quick "Who, Who" grunts. I waited a few seconds and repeated the performance.

Suddenly, a monster buck roared out of the plantation and was on top of me before I could react! At 40 yards, there was no doubt about the quality of the buck. The mass was incredible, and points seemed to go everywhere. I gave little thought to the fact that this was **not** the typical buck. My cross hairs quickly found the shoulder, and I squeezed off a round.

It seemed as though time was proceeding at a snail's pace. All of those hours of practice shooting with a small-caliber rifle now paid off. The 7mm shattered the morning air as the buck turned to escape. The bullet caught him squarely in the shoulder, breaking his leg and continuing on into the chest cavity. At that close range, I feared that much of the bullet's momentum would be lost due to high velocity.

In spite of the fact that the buck had a broken leg and a shattered heart, he managed to disappear into the protective cover of the thick pines. I decided not to push him and waited nervously for 30 minutes or so. Two hours later, I walked up on the monster, lying next to one of his own rubs. The interim had produced some anxious moments, certainly challenging my tracking ability. Incredibly, "The Ghost" had lived up to his name. Even with a lethal wound, he had managed to climb up the slope for several hundred yards before finally dying among the young pines that had provided sanctuary for so long.

As I approached him, I could not believe my eyes. The buck lying before me was the great buck who so long ago had caused problems in my study plots. Apparently, when the timber had been harvested he had moved his sanctuary to this new location. It was a sober moment as I stood gazing down at my old friend. I had mixed emotions; I did not know whether to jump for joy or cry. Our two lives had spanned years of hard work and commitment by so many people. Surely, this was a fitting end for a tremendous buck.

At first, we thought this massive non-typical might be big enough to make Boone and Crockett, but after the mandatory 60-day drying period, he came up just a little short. Official B&C measurer David Whitehouse taped him at 190 3/8, scoring him as a basic 8-pointer. The bases are 8-inches in circumference, and the mass is held way out onto the beams and through the tines. He may not score the magic 195 points needed to make the book, but he still is a great trophy, one for which I always will be grateful. And who knows? Maybe that world-class typical is still out there!

PART II: HARVESTING WHITETAILS

Chapter 19

Bill Goodrum

THE ART OF SHOOTING DEER

The young man was still sitting in his portable tripod deer stand as his guide (Bob) and I approached. We had placed him there prior to daylight with the hope that he would get a shot at a monster buck that had a travel corridor within thirty yards of the stand. At about 8:30 a.m., we had heard him shoot, with the tell-tale thud of a bullet striking home. Bob smiled and said, "Well, he got him! I bet he's excited." We waited about an hour to give the hunter time to enjoy the moment. But, as we approached his stand, the fellow was plainly visible still perched atop his tripod. Unless this fellow was a pretty cool customer, I knew right away that something was wrong. The hunter carefully unloaded his gun, slowly climbed down from the stand and started toward our vehicle. Bob scratched his head and questioned his hunter. "Was that you that shot?" The fellow nodded affirmatively. Bob scratched his head again. "Well then, did you hit him?" The young man was already in the vehicle when he finally responded to our questions. "Naw, I missed him clean," he asserted. Twice Bob politely asked whether or not he was positive that it was a clean miss. Each time the response was the same. So, Bob started up the Suburban and began to drive away. We had gone only a few yards when I asked the fellow what the buck had done when he had shot. "Well," he said, "he just kind of humped up and then ran off." I looked at Bob, who already had put on the brakes, and was backing up. Although I knew exactly what he was thinking, he remained completely calm. We left the hunter sitting in the vehicle and started walking in small circles. "Where was the buck when you shot?," Bob queried back at the hunter. He showed us exactly where the buck had been standing, yet continued to protest that he had missed the buck. He also noted that the big buck had been running from left to right, and that there had been two other bucks with him. In the opposite direction from that indicated by the hunter, my worst fears were confirmed. One small spot of brownish blood on a rock told me that the buck had indeed been hit and that it was a gut shot. A few yards further, I found a small piece of tissue and some rumen (stomach) contents. It was only then that the hunter realized that he had hit the buck. Well, to make a long story short, we searched for several hours. The trail was one of the most difficult I have ever followed. We found where the buck had laid down, but we finally were forced to give up. Bob later found the remains of the buck, and mailed the antlers to the hunter. Unfortunately, this is an all too often occurrence now days. As a whitetail manager and hunter, I see too many hunters go to the field ill-prepared to make a clean killing shot, or improperly outfitted for the job In this Chapter, I will discuss the equipment and preparation you will need for the moment of truth, and then discuss the fine art of actually making that shot and finding your buck I make a note here that I am writing this Chapter, not from the perspective of a firearms expert; rather, as one who has killed and/or OBSERVED the killing of several hundred deer. My thoughts are those resulting from countless observations of missed or wounded deer, and scientific analyses of the cause(s) of these occurrences.

PROPER EQUIPMENT

As a professional whitetail manager, I am amazed by the variety of firearms, calibers and bullet types used by deer hunters. I have seen hunters show up at the gate with everything from riot guns to semi-automatic, Viet Nam vintage small caliber rifles. I also have seen what these weapons can do in the field. Therefore, I have some pretty strong opinions about not only the proper use of firearms in deer hunting, but also the most suitable calibers and makes of rifles and shotguns. Although I run the serious risk of alienating quite a number of hunters, I will discuss the relative merits and proper uses of guns, ammunition and support equipment.

Choice of Firearm

There are almost as many different opinions about which guns to use as there are deer hunters. If there were not, some of the gun magazines would

There are three basic firearms from which to choose: bolt action (above), lever action (middle) and semi-automatic (bottom). Of these, the bolt action is the superior firearm for whitetails. (Courtesy of Maverick Arms, Nacogdoches, Tx)

be out of business. The choice of firearm in deer hunting involves many things, but one consistent truth always must be considered. **The function of the firearm is to quickly and humanely kill the deer.** This is particularly true in these days of anti-hunting sentiment. Any firearm that does not allow the hunter to dispatch a deer in such a manner always should be avoided. Instead of discussing the relative merits of every firearm known to man, let's characterize the perfect deer gun, and then discuss a range of firearms that meet these criteria. Remember, my major consideration is use of a weapon that best kills deer, not one that satisfies personal preference or ego. Fact is that a white-tailed buck that has survived years in the woods does not deserve to end his days as a cripple or by starvation. With this in mind, I begin my analysis. The perfect deer gun is relatively light weight, capable of being used at both short and long-range distances, and comes in a readily available caliber which will deliver enough force to cleanly kill the animal. It must also be capable of delivering a second, finishing shot in a reasonable amount of time should the shooter be off the mark or the animal respond in an unpredictable manner. When you consider these criteria, some of the more popular weapons are quickly discarded. You can immediately remove the shotgun from consideration. But wait a minute. I am stepping on a lot of toes here! Although I am fully aware that some states prohibit the use of anything but a shotgun, it is not a reliable deer hunting firearm. In those states requiring its use, I must concede to the hunter safety factor. In other regions, that pretty much leaves the rifle as our choice. Next, there are three basic types of rifles— the **single shots**, **doubles** and **magazine rifles**. By its very nature, the single shot rifle cannot meet all of my requirements. Hence, it also must be excluded from consideration. The double rifle has seen years of faithful service in Africa, and meets the second shot criterion. However, these guns are not available in readily available calibers, and fail when long shots are necessary. That leaves us with the magazine rifles. These weapons come in three basic styles, **bolt action, lever action** and **semi-automatic** (autoloading). All three types meet the criteria for the perfect deer gun. Your choice of which type of gun you will use depends on many things. However, as always, I have my opinions! I recently discussed deer hunting with a guy I met in Mexico. He was an amiable fellow, and very enthusiastic about trophy deer hunting. One thing about the guy bothered me, however. "All of my friends call me ole five shot," he proclaimed proudly. "I have an 'automatic' 30-06, and I shoot five times at a deer whether he needs it or not!" That is precisely the problem with an autoloading rifle. It gives the shooter the false security of multiple shots in quick succession. I have seen more deer wounded by hunters using autoloaders than any other rifle. Most gun experts will agree that the autoloader is not as accurate as either the bolt action or lever action rifle. Also, the thought of that third, four and fifth shot being available often changes the thinking of the hunter. He will take "chancey" shots. Jon Ducharme of Dolan Creek Ranch refers to these types of guns as "wound-o-matics." For these reasons, I prefer the bolt action rifles for deer hunting. Now, don't get upset. If you have had good success using an autoloader or a lever action rifle, go right ahead with what you are using.

A small, but significant, consideration in rifles is trigger pull. There is nothing more distracting to me than an excessive trigger pull. I have noticed this in some of the recent editions of popular firearms, probably as a result of lawsuits from shooting accidents. On the other side of the coin, too little trigger pull will result in premature

The Art of Shooting Deer

firing and probably a missed buck. A three and one-half to four pound pull is optimum for deer shooting.

Choice of Caliber

This topic is almost as controversial as choice of firearm. Hunters argue for hours about the relative merits of this or that caliber. When the facts are rationally considered, however, your choice of caliber must satisfy the following criteria. First, the bullet weight must be sufficient to deliver enough momentum to cleanly kill the deer. Second, the bullet must be traveling at a velocity which will allow it to cover a reasonably long distance in as short a time interval as possible, and have

Calibers ranging in size from .270 to .300 are optimum for whitetails. Bullet weights should be in the 140 to 180 gr. range in order to provide the knock down power required to make a clean, humane kill. Pictured here are (l to r): .222 Rem., .243 Win., .30-.30 Win., .270 Win., .308 Win., .30-06 Win., 7 mm Rem. mag., and .300 Win. mag. (Courtesy of Maverick Arms, Nacogdoches, Tx)

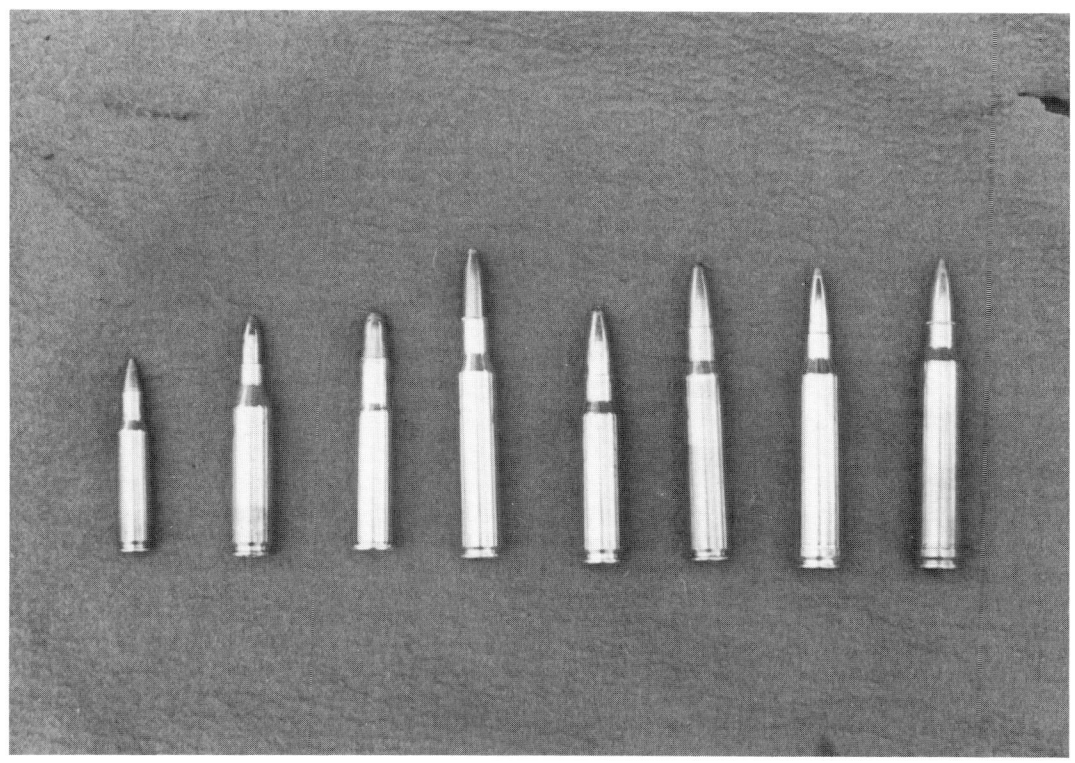

enough residual velocity to mean something on its arrival. In considering the first criterion, I even must alienate myself on this one! I commonly shoot a .243, with a bullet weight of 100 grains. I have been shooting this caliber for years, mostly because I do a great deal of shooting, and prefer not to be punished too severely in the process. But, quite frankly, I am "under-gunned" with this light caliber. After seeing hundreds of deer shot, I am firmly convinced that a bullet ranging in size from .270 to .300 caliber, with weights of 140 to 180 grains, is optimum for whitetails. I would rank calibers such as the .250 and .257 as acceptable, but marginal for killing trophy class bucks. The heavier bullet weights available in the larger calibers often mean the difference between a trophy head on the wall and regrets. On trophy bucks, I now use a 7mm magnum with bullet weights of either 145 or 150 grains, especially when there is a possibility of a shot greater than 200 yards. This may seem a bit large, but I have a little trick which I will discuss later in this chapter. Although preferred bullet velocity can be argued all day, I feel that a muzzle velocity of around 3,000 fps is optimum for most deer calibers. Some hunters prefer to use hand-loads that achieve much higher velocities, but I really think you are "splitting hairs" at that point. If only the shooter was as good as his pet load! Remember, the thing that kills a deer is momentum. Without getting too technical, momentum is calculated by multiplying the mass of the projectile by its speed. The effect of mass and velocity on momentum are best illustrated with the following example. Suppose we give a push to a wagon on a level driveway towards a brick wall. As long as we do not put any weight in the wagon, it will strike the wall with little force, even when we push it with considerable effort. On the other hand, should we put a large amount of weight in the wagon, the resulting impact could be quite devastating to the wall. Conversely, we could put a large amount of weight in the wagon, give a minimal push and the damage would again be minor. The extent of damage is related to the amount of weight in the wagon, as well as the speed at which it is pushed. Once you get the wagon going, it is much harder to stop it if there is a larger quantity of weight. However, if you put too much weight in the wagon, it is very difficult to achieve an adequate speed, and it may pass through the wall so quickly that little damage is done. That is exactly the way modern bullets behave. The amount of energy transferred to the game is directly related to the bullet velocity at point of impact and the cross-sectional density of the bullet. But, do not be fooled into thinking that a large caliber bullet will always deliver sufficient energy to cleanly kill an animal. Just as the heavily loaded wagon will do little damage if not given an adequate push, the 30-30 bullet, for example, has a relatively slow muzzle velocity and delivers minimal impact energy beyond 100 yards. For this reason, I must exclude this caliber from consideration. Also, the heavy weight bullets of 200 grains or larger are too big for

Terry Westmoreland

Telescopic sights are best. A 6X-power scope probably is the best for all-around whitetail shooting.

whitetails. The problem is that the bullet passes through the deer's body without transferring sufficient energy. Again, 140-180 grains is optimum.

Iron or Telescopic Sights?

On this topic, I am reminded of the television image of Davy Crockett making incredibly long shots with his trusty old black powder rifle, Betsy. Although there are shooters who can place a bullet with exceptional accuracy using iron sights, I seriously question the validity of using them on trophy whitetails. No matter how good a shot you may be, the margin for error at longer distances is greater. However, there are situations, especially in very close cover, in which the open sight can give you a distinctive advantage. But, in the vast majority of shooting situations, the telescopic sight offers the highest reliability. Telescopic sights are available in a variety of models and powers. There are basically two types of scopes on the market, fixed focal length and variable focal length. At the urging of my good friend, Dr. John Stransky, I recently test fired my rifle using a variable scope. I fired three shot groups at progressively higher magnifications; and, to my surprise the higher magnifications gave larger groupings. Many hunters assume that the accuracy of a variable scope will remain constant. Apparently, this is not the case. Hence, I feel that the fixed focal length scopes are probably preferable when high variation in shooting conditions is likely. I hunt throughout the whitetail's range, and recently have discovered that, although I often use a variable scope, I seldom change the power adjustment. To my surprise, I always find the scope set on 6X power. Should you opt for a variable scope, I suggest that you not exceed an upward limit of nine power. The reason for this limit will become apparent later. A fixed focal length of four to six power is quite adequate for most situations.

PRACTICE MAKES PERFECT?

A few years back, I took part in a "Skillful Sportsman" series here at Stephen F. Austin State University. Young men and women from Texas took part in the program, designed not only to make them safer hunters, but also to make them better hunters. Part of this program was hands-on shooting at our rifle range. The participants ranged in age from twelve to eighteen. One young man made quite an impression on the other participants when it came time to shoot. At one hundred yards, he consistently had a one-inch, three shot grouping. The other students afforded him great adulation. The young man became a bit "cocky." But, all of the shooting was done from a bench rest. Taking the rifle from the lad, I suggested that he try the same thing off-hand from a standing position. After three attempts, his best grouping could not be covered with a pie plate! It may have been a humbling experience, but the young man learned a lesson that all too many deer hunters never learn. **Once you have your rifle sighted in, it is time to sight in the hunter.** Contrary to popular belief, the average trophy whitetail buck is not shot from a bench rest! It is shot usually from an awkward position, off-hand with your heart racing at about 190 beats per minute. Under such conditions, no amount of bench rest practice will guarantee success. Time and time again, I have had hunters show up prior to the season with their rifle in its case, make three shots on the range, smile to themselves and drive off ready for the hunt. That is precisely the wrong thing to do, and that is how countless trophy bucks are missed or crippled. Why not take a different approach, and have some fun in the process? Bill Carter of the Sombrerito Ranch taught me a valuable lesson in deer hunting. "The average deer hunter fails to make the most of the recreational experience," he notes. "Deer hunting is a year-round activity involving

Developing the ability to shoot off-hand, not from a bench rest, will pay off in trophy whitetail hunting. Normally, you will have about three seconds to make up your mind and shoot! It is best therefore to always take a rest.

developing a reliable load and practice under field conditions. That way the hunter can spread the enjoyment throughout the year, not just for a few days during the season." Bill has given us the formula for successfully shooting deer. Practice makes perfect. I suggest that you begin today to make yourself a better shot by implementing a three phase program.

Phase I.—A shooter is an athlete. Just as physical training can improve your golf or tennis game, proper exercises can greatly improve your shooting skill. **There are two physical demands in making a technically good shot, strength and breath control.** In order to hold a rifle steady, even a light weight model, requires good upper body strength. I have a regular weight training program designed solely to improve my ability to hold a rifle steady. The muscles involved in holding a rifle are the triceps, biceps, forearm and shoulder muscles. Exercises either with weights or Nautilus machines that build strength in these muscles will greatly improve your shooting ability. I personally improved my off-hand three shot grouping at one hundred yards from three inches to one and one-half inches using weight training. I also have developed an exercise program that is designed to improve my cardiovascular ability. I never have been the type of person who enjoys running; however, I have never found a reasonable substitute for cardiovascular training that rivals running. If running is not your cup of tea, brisk walking in varied terrain or swimming for an hour or more is probably a good second choice exercise. I am lucky enough to live on the same land where I conduct much of my research, hunting and shooting. I have worked out a two-mile jogging course that begins and ends at my rifle range. First walking, and later running, I have worked up to covering the two-mile course at a brisk pace. I wear lightweight, standard jogging clothes throughout the run, but on arrival back at the range, I slip on the upper portion of my fall shooting clothes. There is a difference between the feel of the rifle in lightweight versus heavy clothing. I then shoot three shots each

Developing upper body strength will greatly increase the accuracy of your shooting.

Terry Westmoreland

Flinching can be prevented by practicing with a lighter caliber rifle in identical make and model. I use two Ruger M-77's, one in 7mm Mag. and the other in 22-250. Obviously, I practice with the smaller bore gun!

in rapid succession in the standing and sitting positions. This prepares me for those times when I am either excited by the sudden appearance of a monster buck or when I suddenly encounter a buck after a brisk walk. Try it, it will make a difference

Phase II.— One of the greatest causes for missing that all important shot, is flinching. Flinching or jerking the trigger is most often caused by a subconscious anticipation of recoil. Obviously with the higher caliber rifles, especially the .300 and 7mm magnum, the amount of recoil and muzzle blast is considerable. Most of the recoil aversive reaction is caused, not by the actual recoil of the rifle, but the loud muzzle blast. There is just enough time between the report and the physical feel of the recoil that the brain begins to anticipate what is about to happen. On several occasions, I have secretly substituted an unprimed cartridge in a hunter's gun who claims not to be flinching. In almost every case, the shooter will anticipate the recoil by jerking back on the trigger. Some shooters in this sham situation will even grunt in anticipation of the recoil. Why put yourself in that situation? I have a very good solution to this. I purchased two identical rifles, one in .22-.250 and the other in 7mm magnum. The 7mm magnum is excessive, but I do a lot of shooting in South Texas and Mexico where long shots are common. Everything is exactly the same, except I only practice shooting with the smaller caliber rifle. The only time I shoot the large bore gun is when I am checking the sighting point of the scope. Then, I am careful to use shooting muffs to prevent my brain from becoming inadvertently trained to flinch. When it comes time to kill that buck, I will guarantee you that you never will feel the recoil! The adrenalin will be too high for that.

Phase III.— There is an old story about a young man in a hurry to get to Carnegie Hall for a concert. Unknown to him, he stopped a violin virtuoso on the street and hurriedly asked him how to get to Carnegie Hall. "Practice, practice, practice," the old violinist replied. That may be a cliche' but it is a universal truth. Once you have that light caliber gun, use every opportunity to practice. And, I am not talking about shooting from a bench. Practice shooting from the standing, sitting and prone positions. Try shooting off balance (something you would never do with a big bore gun), and around obstacles, especially if you shoot from a tree stand. Remember, the name of the game in shooting deer is shot placement. Actually shooting from a tree stand is a good idea, provided you have a safe backstop. Practice "snap" shots, much in the way that law enforcement personnel are trained. Set yourself up in "shoot, don't shoot" situations. Finally, a white-tailed buck will seldom walk out there exactly one hundred yards from you. You have to develop the ability to judge distance. As a guide, I have developed some little tricks that have helped me over the years. Again, Dr. John Stransky has taught me much about shooting under field conditions. I like to use duplex scope reticles, since they give me a reference for size at a distance. One manufacturer even includes instructions for proper use of duplex reticles as range finders. John showed me a little trick that he uses successfully on pronghorn antelope. He uses a cardboard cutout, exactly the size of the animal, and practices estimating distances by sighting on this silhouette. Commercially available rangefinders are totally impractical under actual shooting conditions. No trophy buck in his right mind is going to stand there while you calculate his distance! Remember, I am writing this series from the viewpoint of a professional whitetail manager and hunter. My opinions and recommendations are based on countless observations of deer either being shot, missed or unfortunately crippled.

MAKING THE SHOT

So far, I have discussed the basic principles of acquiring the proper equipment to shoot trophy white-tailed deer;

and, some common mistakes made by hunters in preparing for that moment of truth. Most hunters spend considerable time getting their equipment ready, but little time getting themselves ready. The average trophy whitetail is not shot from a bench rest. It usually is shot offhand under a great deal of mental and physical stress. For this reason, the hunter must prepare himself well in advance of the hunt through hours of practice and physical training. Once you are ready for the hunt, thought must be given to making the proper bullet placement and following up the shot. In this section I will discuss some common causes of missed or wounded deer from the standpoint of the hunter, as well as give you some tips on making a clean kill. When I think about making a clean kill, numerous bad experiences come to mind. It has been my good, or perhaps misfortune, to see many of the problems that can arise in shooting whitetails. One typical case comes to mind. I was working a check station at one of the hunting clubs with which I work. The biologist in charge, Bill Goodrum, and I went out to pick up one of his hunters. He was walking in little concentric circles in the middle of the road when we approached. He was carrying one of those semi-automatic (autoloader) rifles in .223 caliber without a scope. He looked a might confused, so Bill asked him if he had shot a deer. "Well, I think so," he replied. Bill politely asked him where the deer had been standing, the direction in which it fled after the shot, and the sex of the deer. Unfortunately, the hunter could not answer any of these questions. All he knew was that it had been a deer. There was absolutely no blood trail to follow, so we opted to look for tracks. It did not take long to find the tell-tale sign of a deer pushing off in the soft sandy soil. We followed the trail until it entered the thick brush. Luckily, there was a well-established deer trail through it. About seventy-five yards down the trail lay a very dead buck fawn! It was shot clear through the stomach, and had apparently died of shock. We pulled it back to the truck, congratulated the hunter and returned to camp. This hunter had committed just about every "sin" I can think of when it comes to shooting deer. Pulling the trigger on an animal is a serious business that should not be considered lightly. A frivolous shot can mean the loss of a great deal of work on your part, and unnecessary suffering on the part of an animal as magnificent as a trophy whitetail buck. There are several decisions that have to be made by the hunter before he ever pulls the trigger.

Decision One

The first thing you must consider is whether or not you want to shoot a particular deer. That may seem strange to some of you, especially in light of the fact that the average hunter just looks to see if it is a buck; and if it is, shoots it. But, do you really want that buck? The difference between a trophy whitetail hunter and just a deer hunter is that one decision. The trophy hunter may look at several bucks before taking the shot. I often am amused at a hunter who, after hours of begging on my part, finally passes up his first

The Art of Shooting Deer

buck. It is fascinating to watch the changes that take place. First, he obviously regrets his action. He knows good and well that the buck will be shot by another hunter. After a little thought and some discussion with his fellow hunters, however, he switches to an attitude of pride in his action. If I just once can convince a hunter not to shoot a young buck, I have a convert for life! Soon, he will be evangelizing to his fellow hunters to do the same. Hunters often ask me how to decide whether or not a buck is a trophy. Don't worry. If there is any question about it, it's not! If you decide that you do want the buck, it is time to get down to serious business. Big bucks often are missed because the hunter becomes too excited by the impressiveness of the antlers. Once you have made the decision to shoot the animal, the time for admiring its antlers is over. Never look again at the antlers.

Decision Two

The next decision you have to make is whether or not a clean shot is possible. Just because you want the buck is no reason to make a hasty or futile shot. I have several rules that I strictly follow, and I demand that my hunters also follow. These rules are "set in cement" and, if violated, can lead to dire consequences. First, I never shoot at a running buck. I am fully aware that some of you probably have made some pretty fantastic shots on running deer. But, how many deer are wounded in the process? One notable outdoor writer even has a chapter in his book on how to shoot running whitetails. A trophy buck does not deserve that kind of treatment! The variables are too many to take a chance. Even the best of shots could be off just enough to wound the animal. It is already alerted and probably has adrenalin pumping through its circulatory system. I have tracked bucks wounded in such a manner for more than two miles. And, some of them were shot through the heart! Second, never make excessively long shots. The average buck is killed at less than one hundred yards. Most of the hunters with whom I work cannot hit a pie plate

A buck obscured by brush offers a poor opportunity for a shot. It would be better if you wait for a better shot.

Mike Biggs

off-hand at two hundred yards, much less four or five hundred yards. A buck may be so magnificent that you are tempted to take a long shot, but remember the consequences if you wound the buck. South Texas deer hunters are probably the worst offenders of this rule. In that region, the common hunting technique is to sit perched atop tall stands overlooking large openings or down cleared strips called "senderos." I have seen hunters not give a second thought to making five or six hundred yard shots. But, how much energy is left in a bullet at that distance? Light calibers such as the .243 and .257 can produce some sad results at long distances. Even with the magnum calibers, the probability of making a mistake is great. Remember, if you pass up a shot, it still can produce some pleasant memories. A bad shot never will be forgotten. Third, be reluctant to shoot off-hand. I know that I said that the average buck is not shot from a bench rest, and there will be times when you will have to make an off-hand shot. But, I try to take a good rest whenever possible. Even a small tree limb will provide a more secure support than an off-hand shot. I recently conducted some computer experiments here at the Institute for White-tailed Deer Management and Research. In my computer simulation, I "shot" a 180 grain soft point bullet from a 30-06 magazine rifle more than one thousand times. To my amazement, just a quarter inch of barrel movement, in an off-hand shot at one hundred yards, produced a grouping more than thirty-six inches across! I followed up this experi-

Here is a barrel tracing for a shooter with a heart rate of 150 beats per minute. Notice that the general movement is in an up-and-down direction. Translate this movement to 100 or 300 yards and this means a tremendous amount of variation in shot placement.

ment with one of my own. I placed a marker in the barrel of a gun and asked a hunting companion to hold it steady against a piece of white paper. Then, I had the fellow repeat the experiment after jogging in place. The accompanying "aim point tracings" may make an impression on you. At 150 heart beats per minute, the barrel moved more

The Art of Shooting Deer

than an inch. It also was interesting to note that the barrel moved pretty much in an up and down direction, apparently in response to either the weight of the gun or a beating heart. These experiments have done much to better make me understand why that hunter last season missed such an easy shot.

Decision Three

Shot placement is everything when it comes to shooting trophy whitetails. I am amazed at the false beliefs of deer hunters. The most notable of these is the neck shot. Time and time again, I have overheard hunters asserting that

---

There are three shot placements located in front of the diaphragm: head, neck and the point of the shoulder. The head shot has the highest probability of crippling, followed by the neck shot. Hence, the only place to shoot a whitetail is at the point of the shoulder. This gives you a large margin of error.

Mike Biggs

a neck shot is excellent because "if you miss, you miss clean, and if you hit, you are certain of killing the buck." This is utter nonsense! First of all, the area within the neck available for a clean kill is incredibly small. You either must hit the carotid arteries and jugular veins, or the spinal cord. That is only an area about two inches across, leaving an additional four to five inches of non-lethal area. The head shot is even worse than a neck shot. Even when struck in the brain, a deer will often run for a considerable distance. The brain cavity is only a small portion of the total head area. The head shot has the highest probability of wounding. Over the years, I have seen some pretty graphic illustrations of this fact. One particularly sickening case comes to mind. I was hunting the Texas Hill Country, slipping quietly along one of those beautiful clear streams that seem to be everywhere in that part of the world. Suddenly, a large buck ran out of the brush and splashed his way into the middle of the stream. It was one of the most pitiful sights I ever have seen in my years of deer work. There was a magnificent ten pointer, scoring about 150 B&C, trying to get a drink to cool his fever. His entire face was shot away! I ask you, what kind of hunter would consciously make the decision to head shoot such a magnificent animal? A trophy buck that has spent years surviving predators and hunters does not deserve to receive that kind of treatment. Fortunately, I was able to put him out of his misery. There absolutely is no reason to make either a head or neck shot on a trophy buck. Your chances of missing or wounding the animal are high, and with many calibers, the trophy may be destroyed. In spite of what some hunters may claim, you are not hunting trophy bucks for meat. Many a buck has been lost because some hunter was trying to save some meat by shooting at the neck or head. That only leaves two suitable aiming points, the shoulder and chest. For years, I favored a high lung chest shot. This produced reasonable results, but some deer ran excessive distances and required tracking after the shot. The name-of-the-game when it comes to shooting trophy bucks is to drop him in his tracks. That way, he does not suffer and you do not have to trail a wounded deer. Therefore, I strongly urge that you use the point of the shoulder as your aiming point whenever possible. This will deliver enough force to kill the animal, probably will break his shoulder so that he is incapable of running away, and allows a great deal of latitude for a poorly placed shot. Refer back to our experiments on barrel movement. Ask yourself this question: "If I were really excited, where on a buck's body could I afford up to three feet of error?" A shoulder aiming point is the only place on a buck's body that is forgiving. If you are a little too far forward, you probably will hit the neck. In the opposite direction, you will be in the chest cavity. You also enjoy the luxury of considerable vertical movement, the direction you are most likely to move the barrel.

Decision Four

One aspect of shooting trophy bucks

that seldom receives consideration is when to shoot. Hopefully, you have managed to see the buck without being seen in return. If so, do everything you can to keep the buck from realizing your presence. An alerted buck will behave entirely different after the shot. If he sees you, or is aware of your presence, he will do two things. First, his heart rate will increase and adrenalin will be released into his blood stream. Second, he will more than likely take in a deep breath of air. These two events will guarantee you that the buck will run a tremendous distance if the shot is improperly placed. Just because a buck is shot through the heart does not mean that he will run only a short distance. I once trailed a heart-shot buck for more than a mile, before finding him dead. A lot of things can happen in a mile. You could lose the trail.

Once I decide to kill a buck, I wait until he stops walking. I also prefer for bucks to be either looking away from me or busy doing something like feeding, antler rubbing or working a scrape. Hopefully, the buck never will know what hit him! These may not be very pleasant things to discuss, but if you are to be a good sportsman, you have to consider them. During a recent season, I violated some of the above rules. Luckily, I managed to come out pretty well in spite of my poor judgment, harvesting a high-scoring buck near Del Rio, Texas. Since outdoor writers too often write about what we do right, rather than the things we do wrong, let me relate this experience to you.

I was hunting with my friends Jon Ducharme and John Finegan of Dolan Creek Ranches. We used slingshots to force a particularly nice buck from his canyon sanctuary. He ran up the canyon and stopped about 450 yards from me. I was shooting my Voere .243 which has given me great service over the years. I sight the rifle in "dead on" at 100 yards. I prefer to do this since most of my shots are so close that precise bullet placement is an important factor. Fortunately for me, I have shot the rifle for so many years, having virtually memorized the ballistics of my handload, that I can compensate for bullet drop at larger distances. But, this distance was excessive. in spite of the fact that I had no rest, I decided to make the shot anyway.

The buck was one that I really wanted, perhaps too much. My first distance estimate was 400 yards, so I raised my point of aim to compensate for that distance and squeezed the trigger. The bullet fell short, just beneath the buck's feet. To my surprise, the buck only jumped a few feet and stopped to look around. He obviously had no idea of the source of the irritant. By this time, I had a better idea of the distance. The bullet drop at that distance was some fifty-eight inches! The next shot fell true, but I spent some tense moments wondering whether or not I had wounded that canyon monster. He still ran deep into the canyon and it took us two and one-half hours to get him out. I was a lucky man on that day. I was lucky (not a good shot) to have hit him at that distance with a light caliber. I also was lucky that I did not leave a wounded animal in field. I also shoot a 7 mm magnum, but in retrospect, I would never take that shot again even with a magnum load.

FOLLOWING UP THE SHOT

As many bucks are lost after the shot as during the shot. Now, I know that killing a buck, especially a trophy buck, is not like swatting a fly. I have no use for a hunter who has lost the excitement of shooting a big buck. But, try to remember the following rules.

Rule One

Keep both eyes open when you shoot. You will need to immediately determine whether or not the buck has run away. If he has, try to calmly determine the direction in which he fled. It is a common joke among professional deer guides that you look for a buck in the opposite direction from where the hunter said the buck ran! Funny, but often true. I try to mark a spot where the buck was last seen.

Rule Two

If the buck did not run, but is obviously wounded, shoot until he is dead. Even if there is some doubt or the animal appears to be mortally wounded, shoot until he falls. I have seen countless "dead" bucks run off!

Rule Three

If the buck runs off, even though you may think you missed him, mark the spot where you last saw him. This may be difficult when more than one deer is present. In the excitement, you easily can lose sight of your buck. Pick some distinguishing characteristic of the vegetation or terrain and memorize it.

Rule Four

Pay attention to the buck's behavior after the shot. Often times a buck will give you clues as to the location of the wound through his behavior. However, this not always is the case. There seems to be quite a bit of folk lore about this matter. Some hunters say that a wounded deer will not flag. This is not true. I have seen countless mortally wounded deer flag as they ran away. Over the years, I have catalogued various behaviors of deer shot by me or in my presence. Few shot placements have a characteristic behavior. I can, however, narrow down the possibilities from a description of the deer's behavior. For example, a heart shot deer often will buck or kick out its hind feet. A deer shot in the forward portion of the body often will try to back away from the injury.

Rule Five

Do not move from your position until you absolutely are sure that the buck is dead. Some experts say twenty to thirty minutes is adequate to assure that the animal is dead. I suggest that you either wait at least fifteen minutes or, if he is lying close enough, try to look at the buck's ribs to see if he is breathing. Any movement should be regarded as suspect.

Rule Six

Even when you are convinced that the buck is dead, approach him as though he were not. This means having your rifle ready for a finishing shot. If there is any doubt on approach, make a second shot just to be sure. African hunters call this "insurance." Whitetails certainly are not dangerous game, but you do not want to have him run off either. There are countless stories around the hunting camps of bucks lost in this manner. A good way to determine that the animal is dead is to touch his eye with your barrel. That way, if he reacts you are pointing your rifle in the proper direction for a second shot. A buck that is still alive will usually blink to the touch.

Rule Seven

If the buck is wounded, and has run, give him at least forty-five minutes to settle down. It is also a good idea to remain near your stand and be as quiet as possible. You can quietly go to your point of last sighting and mark it. I carry flagging for that very purpose. I also mark the place where I first saw the buck (why will become obvious later).

Rule Eight

A blood trail should be followed by no more than two individuals, and should be followed at a slow pace. Do not talk. Use pre-arranged hand signals. Mark the trail with small pieces of flagging or tissue. This will give you an idea of the general direction of travel. Bucks usually will try to circle back in the direction from which they came. That is why you should mark the spot where the buck was first seen. If a deer approached your area from a certain direction, it probably will feel that there is safety in the known direction.

Rule Nine

If you lose the trail, try one of two things. First, return to your last flag and check to see that you did not overlook the trail. Second, begin walking in small circles around the point where the trail was lost. You can also look back at your marked trail to get a better idea of where to look ahead.

Rule Ten

This last rule is perhaps the most important of all. **Never give up the search until all possible effort has been expended.** Then, search a little longer. For example, Bill Goodrum of North Boggy Slough Hunting and Fishing Club last season had two hunters wound good bucks on the same morning. One hunter looked for his buck for about an hour and gave up. The other spent several hours looking, went in to the clubhouse to get something to eat, then returned to search again. Appropriately, he found his buck lying in a stream not ten feet from the first hunter's buck. His perseverance not only found his buck, but the other man's as well.

SUMMARY

I know of no more noble sport than hunting trophy whitetails. They are the most difficult game animal to hunt in all the world. In order to be successful, the hunter must have a good understanding of animal behavior, hunting techniques and firearms. He must also understand his own abilities in these matters, and appreciate his strengths and weaknesses. The only way to be successful consistently is to spend as much time as possible developing expertise in all of these areas.

Unfortunately, many hunters shortchange themselves in this regard, and miss out on a lot of fun in the process.

Chapter 20

Mike Biggs

SCOUTING: THE ART AND SCIENCE

I have the same feeling as when I wrote the chapter on travel corridors and sanctuaries. Although there now are countless gimmicks and technological aids for harvesting trophy whitetails, the one "frontier" of deer hunting lies not in technology, but in the realm of scouting. The three most commonly asked questions are: 1) "How do you find good places to hunt trophy bucks?," 2) "How do you recognize good buck habitat when you see it?," and 3) "How do you go about patterning individual bucks?" Having the consistent ability to locate and pattern bucks is one of the most important aspects of trophy hunting. It is surprising how many hunters offer to pay me just to name THE trophy hotspot! Of course I turn down such offers, but it is somewhat amusing as to the extent of frustration experienced by modern deer hunters. Most hunters have the ability to kill a monster buck **once** he is located, but seriously lack the ability to find the buck in the first place. In this Chapter, I once again will be giving away some of the "keys to the kingdom," so to speak. You will be sharing the thought processes I go through each season in selecting a place to hunt, and in patterning trophy bucks.

There only are so many days in the deer season, even for someone who hunts throughout the whitetail's range as I do. Hence, I can ill-afford to make a mistake in selecting the right places and the right bucks to hunt. I begin to locate new hunting territories soon after the season is over. January and February are important months in my annual planning process. When most hunters are back home holding down the couch and watching basketball on television, I spend my time judiciously talking and traveling potential new hunting territories.

RELIABLE SOURCES OF INFORMATION

I spend a great deal of time visiting with taxidermists. Taxidermists are the "mother confessors" of hunting, for a hunter will tell his taxidermist things he never will reveal to a fellow hunter. Hence, over the years I have struck up many a fine relationship with taxidermists all over the country. Besides, I like the guys! Being a fanatic about records, I maintain a notebook in which I record every observation, every conversation and every buck (dead or alive) seen. Over the years, I have accumulated a wealth of information concerning potential trophy hotspots. For example, last season I hunted on the Nail Ranch in the prairie country of west Texas. Now, no one ever would have believed that this prairie country would produce the kind of monster buck dreamed about by hunters. But, this particular geographic area, and more specifically this ranch, have consistently produced some braggin' sized bucks.

I first learned of the Nail Ranch and Shackleford County from a taxidermist friend who asked me what was going on in that part of the country? "Why do you ask," I replied. "A couple of my clients keep bringing in big bucks from that area," he offered. Reaching into a large pile of tagged antlers, he produced a shockingly large set of ten point antlers! They had better than six inch bases and around 25 inches of main beam

Bucks like this bruiser taken by the author on the Nail Ranch in West Texas often are the reward for diligently searching for big buck territory.

Johnny Hudman

length. Clearly, I was impressed.

Later, I talked with Ray Sasser of the Dallas Morning News. He had alluded to this particular geographic region for some time, and I knew that he had the lowdown on the Ranch. "James, to be honest with you, the Nail Ranch has some of the best bucks I've seen," he confided. To make a long story short, the next opening weekend found me hunting on this very ranch. To my surprise, my hunting partners turned out to be Ray Sasser, Gordon Whittington and Larry Weishuhn, all of whom had come to the ranch in similar manner. Oddly enough, I again ran into Ray on another ranch in Webb County (Texas) later in the season. This ranch probably has more Boone-and-Crockett bucks than any one property.

Landowners also are an excellent way to speed up the scouting process. One prominent whitetail writer has developed an effective "scouting network" using landowners. He travels the country visiting with farmers and ranchers. Those landowners have become his eyes and ears in several states. He has such a good rapport with his landowners that the minute they spy a good buck, they do not hesitate to give him a call. This hunter also keeps the meticulous records I recommend.

Newspaper accounts of monster bucks also are heavily used by successful trophy hunters. Unlike magazines, which have a six to nine month publication delay, newspapers publish the news as it happens. In other words, a big buck killed this week in New York will more than likely show up in the local newspaper within a day or so. For this reason, I maintain an outdoor writer network which keeps me informed on the latest big bucks harvested. However, a single kill does not draw my attention. Rather, an accumulation of big bucks harvested from a specific area throws up a red flag. Too often a single monster buck is harvested accidentally from an area that could no more produce large numbers of big bucks than a parking lot. Last season, for example, a Boone-and-Crockett qualifying buck was killed near Tyler, TX. This area has one of the highest buck harvest rates in the state, with over 70% of their bucks being harvested. What this particular buck was doing in that region, and how he evaded harvest for six years is beyond me! But, you can count on me not hunting that area next season.

The photographic sections of major publications also is a great source for big buck locations. Keep track over the years where bucks are taken. I keep a large map on which I pin big buck kills. This aids me both as a hunter and a biologist in monitoring trends in buck harvest.

Biologists, both government and private, are an excellent and reliable source of information about trophy white-tails. These guys, by nature, keep good records on their geographic area. Most can tell you where the big bucks are consistently produced. Biologists working with the U.S.D.A. Soil Conservation Service particularly are of benefit to me. SCS personnel develop excellent working relationships with landowners, and usually can tell you not only where good bucks can be found, but also which landowners to contact. State game biologists and wardens occasionally are useful for these purposes.

WHAT MAKES A BIG BUCK AREA?

It always seems that the Europeans are far ahead of us here in the U.S. in every aspect of game management. Many of the "new" concepts in trophy deer management were common practice in Germany at the turn of the century. So it is with methods of picking trophy buck areas.

In Forestry there is a system whereby we rate a specific area's potential for producing timber. It is called **site index.** Put simply, site index is an estimate of the expected height of a tree planted today at some time in the future. For example, a site index of 70 (base age 50) for loblolly pine means that if we plant a loblolly pine seedling today on that specific soil type, we can expect the tree to be 70 feet tall in 50 years. It is an excellent way to rate various soils.

In American wildlife management, we only now are learning that soils are the most critical factor both for the quality and quantity of game produced. After all, wildlife is a crop no different from corn to soybeans! A number of years ago, a German wildlife biologist named Ueckermann developed a site index for the Roe Deer, a diminutive cousin of the whitetail. He found that the heaviest body weights and largest antlers occurred on soils with a parent material of shell-limestone, while the poorest body weights and antlers occurred on sandy plains and alluvial valley sands. We have long understood the need of deer for calcium and phosophorus in antler development (see **Nutrition and Supplemental Feeding**). Normally a 2:1 calcium to phosphorus ratio is required for adequate nutrition. Hence, an important part of my annual scouting program centers around the soils within a particular area. Again, I make a visit to my local SCS office. For each county, there is a published soil survey report which clearly, and in layman's language, discusses the productive potential of all soil types within the county. Accompanying each report are a series of aerial photographs which also are useful in picking good hunting territory.

In addition to soil and habitat quality, the extent of management on a particular property greatly affects trophy buck production. Most states have data available as to the number of hunters by county, the annual buck and doe harvest, and the estimated age structure of the area. In my home state of Texas, the Department of Parks and Wildlife does an excellent job of documenting these data for all counties and ecological regions. When considering a specific county, I depend on these reports to assess the probability of there being a sufficient supply of mature bucks for harvest. I shun areas in which buck harvest rates exceed 50% with 30-50% being optimum. Also, I tend to avoid regions in which the herd is at or near saturation level.

The number of deer on a range greatly affects buck quality. Unfortunately, hunters too often feel that more deer is better. Recently, we have experienced resistance to doe harvest as a result of these attitudes. Fact is that more deer is **not** better. Once the herd exceeds 60% of carrying capacity (see **Population Management** chapter), buck quality begins to deteriorate, no matter how old the bucks become. I work with a ranch that has an excellent buck:doe ratio and buck age structure. Unfortunately, however, once a buck reaches three years of age on this ranch, antler quality stagnates! This herd is nowhere near reaching its potential, simply because adequate nutrition is not available. What this all means is that I favor areas with expanding herds. Once a herd crashes from overpopulation, you can forget getting me to hunt there. I sincerely believe that once a herd has crashed, its trophy potential is lost, or at best greatly reduced.

Using these methods, I have identified several potential trophy hotspots. In short, several areas in which there are highly productive soils, expanding deer populations and excellent genetic potential are identified. One of these areas is the Ohio River valley of Kentucky and Indiana. This area traditionally has maintained low deer populations due to local hunting traditions and lack of management (control on buck harvest). Recently, some of these areas have come under management, and show tremendous potential for trophy production. I work closely with Grassy Lake Farms, a commercial hunting resort near Cairo, Illinois. Last season, we harvested young bucks that already were in the 130-140 B&C class! One buck was sighted which easily could have scored in the record book classification. The area clearly combines all of the criteria outlined above; viz., good soils, low deer density and quality habitat.

MAKING THAT IMPORTANT CHOICE

I only have so many days a year in which to harvest a trophy buck. Consequently, I am very leery of making a decision to hunt a new place, **unless** I absolutely am sure of a high probability of success. In making a similar decision, you must consider some important factors.

First, you must have some idea concerning the amount of time you will have to hunt next season. This greatly affects your choice of hunting territory. If you are the kind of person who only has the weekend or afternoons to hunt, you hardly would opt for a far-distant area. Travel time can really hurt a hunter on a limited time budget. Your time often is better spent scouting in the area selected. If, on the other hand, you either are willing to take some vacation time or have the free time to devote to proper scouting, a new hunting area in another state or even country may be appealing. If you do have the time, I suggest that you budget it accordingly to allow summer scouting time, as well as fall hunting time.

Second, try to narrow your selection down to one or two locations by spring or early summer. Indecision can be devastating. A good friend of mine spends most of his year procrastinating over which area(s) to hunt. By the time the season begins, he has no firm idea of where he will be at the sound of the opening gun! The result is that he seldom harvests a trophy buck, and has become increasingly frustrated over the years.

Third, you must decide what type of buck you are willing to accept. Remember that buck quality, as with beauty, is in the eye of the beholder. Many hunters declare early on that they are only going to harvest a true trophy buck, then quickly settle for a medium-sized buck on opening day.

You also may be the kind of hunter who traditionally has hunted an over-harvested buck population. A fork horn may be a trophy to you. I see this a great deal here in Texas where we annually entertain hunters from the more heavily hunted Northeast. Show one of these hunters ten or twenty eight-pointers in a day's time, and he thinks he "has died and gone to heaven!"

A few years back, a young hunter called me up with a really sad story. Seems that he always harvested the biggest buck on his hunting club, but the bucks always fell short of his expectations. "Where can I go to harvest a real honest to gosh trophy," he begged. I suggested a few places that were within his time and financial constraints. He

Mike Biggs

One of the first steps in developing a workable scouting plan is to decide what kind of deer you are after. Trophy quality, as with beauty, is in the eye of the beholder.

called me after the season, bragging on a fine trophy he harvested in Mexico. He since has killed bigger bucks, but my tactic got him started on scouting monster bucks across the range of the whitetail, instead of within a small isolated geographic area.

If you decide to seek a real trophy, there are some realities to accept. As I noted earlier, the real trophies rarely come from heavily hunted and/or densely populated regions. Most are taken from expanding deer herds where population densities are well below the magic threshold required by most hunters. Hunters traditionally must see many deer each day to maintain their enthusiasm. This strange trait reared its ugly head last season throughout much of the south. Following a droughty summer, we experienced a very mild fall and, in some areas, an unexpected heavy acorn crop. The result was that deer did not move in a "normal" manner, with the kill being considerably below previous years. The resulting outcry from the public demanded a reduction in the doe harvest, solely because the average hunter saw fewer deer than normal.

In trophy territories, you seldom see large numbers of deer. I now am averaging one buck per twelve hours of hunting. This makes for some pretty boring times. A few seasons back, Gordon Whittington (North American Whitetail Magazine) and I hunted Mexico together. A good friend, Joey Smith, hunted with us. This particular area has a very low deer population, probably less than a deer per 100 acres. (Most well-populated deer ranges have a deer to 20 acres or less.) Joey hunted three straight days on the same portable stand overlooking a travel corridor. On more than one occasion, Joey was ready to give up and move his stand, but Gordon and I suggested otherwise. On the third day, Joey harvested a braggin' sized 20-inch buck! His perseverance paid off.

THE BEST TRACT OF LAND

There is both art and science to finding the right place to hunt monster bucks. The art comes in the ability to ferret out places that either have re-

The real trophies rarely come from heavily hunted areas.

Ray Sasser

mained unnoticed by your fellow hunters or which have relatively new populations of deer. Hence, it is important to develop reliable sources of information concerning areas which have the potential to produce trophy bucks. These sources include: taxidermists; up-to-date written accounts of big bucks; landowners; and, government resource managers.

The science of scouting centers around your ability to do some scientific detective work within specific geographic areas. In general, trophy buck hotspots usually: 1) occur in areas with expanding deer herds; 2) have high-quality soils; 3) have land-uses that favor quality forage production; and 4) have the genetic background to produce big bucks. In this section, I will discuss some techniques you may find useful in selecting that one particular hunting location, once you have homed in on overall big-buck territory.

Once I have located several potentially suitable hunting areas, I conduct two basic analyses. The first revolves around people, the second around the relative quality of deer habitat involved.

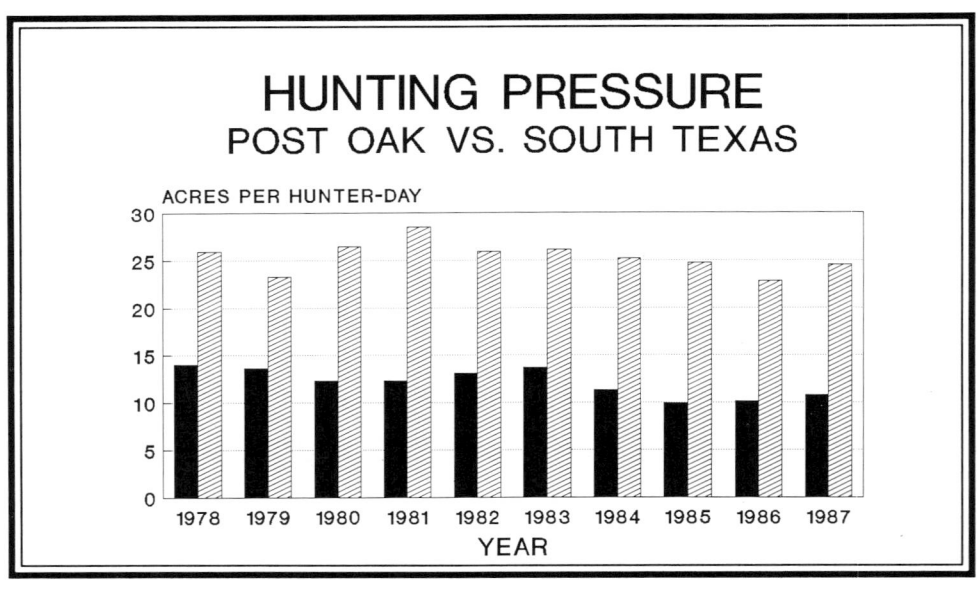

Many states keep excellent records on the deer harvest and hunting pressure by county or ecological region. Note here that hunting pressure for the Post Oak Savannah Texas (dark bars) is much greater than the traditional trophy producing South Texas Brush Country (cross-hatched bars).

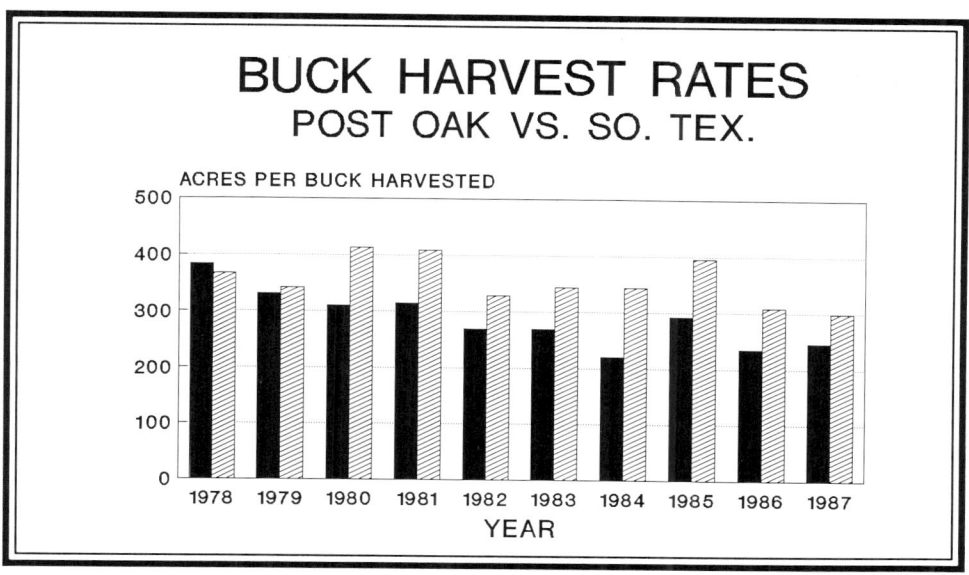

Buck harvest rates are another good indicator of your potential for harvesting a trophy buck from a specific region. Here, harvest rates for South Texas (dark bars) indicate that you have a much better chance of killing a buck there than in the Post Oak Savannah (cross-hatched bars).

Hunting pressure has as much to do with trophy potential as any other variable. In much of the whitetail's range, hunting pressure is excessive, especially on the buck segment of the population. Game agencies often attempt to satisfy large numbers of hunters with just any buck, rather than a quality buck hunted in a quality setting. This condemnation may be hard for some to swallow, but it is a truthful analysis. Fortunately, however, most state and provincial agencies maintain excellent records on the extent of hunting pressure by geographic region. Some even extend these records to the county level.

Data are made available to the public via reports required by the Pittman-Robertson Act. In case you never heard of this legislation, it is the act which mandated U.S. excise taxes be levied on commodities such as rifles and ammunition. Every time you purchase hunting supplies, you pay tax monies which are earmarked specifically for wildlife restoration and management. So-called P-R reports are issued on every project funded with these monies. Over the years, these reports have served me well in making sound decisions about deer management and hunting.

For example, recent P-R reports by the Texas Parks & Wildlife Department highlighted population and harvest trends throughout the state. Because I hunt a great deal in the Pineywoods of East Texas, let's use this geographic area as an example. This particular area is composed of some 27 counties, totaling better than 11 million acres of deer habitat. This one region is as large as the total deer habitat of some states, so it is of little benefit to possess this information alone. However, some additional information is enlightening.

The Pineywoods Region represents 15.6 percent of the total deer range available in the state. Because the deer population for the same area represents approximately the same percentage (15.9 percent) of the statewide population, I can safely assume that this area is now saturated with deer. The next step is to examine specific areas and counties within the region. Although the area in general is now saturated, this is only an average figure, with some areas having more than enough deer and others have fewer than the saturation level. Remember, it is the population that has not yet reached saturation we are after.

Examining the Pineywoods on a county basis reveals several potential trophy-buck hotspots. One such county is Sabine, located along the Texas-Louisiana line. The estimated 1987 deer population density for this county was one deer to approximately 90 acres. In contrast, Houston County, to the southwest, has a comparative density estimate of one deer to 14 acres. Now this is useful information! The next step is to decide on several such areas and make more detailed analyses.

In studying a low-density area, one of the first questions that comes to mind is, "Why is the deer population low?" In some areas, deer populations are held low due to heavy either-sex hunting pressures, while others have abnormally high poaching rates. Others have poor-quality habitat. Traditionally, public hunting areas have lower deer densities than do those with mostly private lands. Hence, the next step is to gain information concerning the hunting pressure for the area in question. Again, P-R reports and talks with **knowledgeable** game biologists will prove fruitful.

Returning to our Texas report, I find that Sabine County experiences a hunting pressure of one hunter per 216 acres, and a five-year average kill rate of one deer per 602 acres. This may be a good harvest rate, but in Texas it is extremely low. By contrast, Houston County had a 1987 hunter density of one hunter per 70 acres and a five-year average kill rate of one deer per 233 acres. Obviously, both the deer population and the hunting pressure are lower in Sabine County.

Whether or not you select such an areas for your hunt will depend on many things, however. Among these are your own abilities as a hunter. Houston County has produced some braggin'-sized bucks, but most bucks harvested are rather small, due to high deer densities and heavy hunting pressure. If you are the kind of fellow who has to see deer every time out, then you would opt for Houston County. (If you are from the area, do not take offense. I hunt there every year.) But, on the other hand, if you are truly seeking a trophy whitetail, you may want to limit your hunting to such areas as the Sabine County example.

Certainly, these principles apply across the range of the whitetail, and are not limited to Texas. But, there is another question to be answered before you go booking a ticket to East Texas— or anywhere else, for that matter. Again, we must return to the quality of the habitat and the deer themselves. Just because an area has a low deer population density does not automatically mean that it will produce a monster buck. There are countless examples of areas with both low deer densities and low buck quality. For example, some portions of Florida have such poor soils and habitat that only small, inferior quality bucks ever will be produced. That is where your detailed notes taken from conversations with taxidermists and accounts of trophy kills come into play.

You do not have to be an expert on genetics to pinpoint likely trophy buck areas. All it takes is a little advanced scouting— not of deer, but of people. Starting in midsummer, I spend a good deal of time driving around several likely areas, talking with local hunters and landowners. This probably is the most enjoyable part of trophy hunting— certainly for one who must adopt a solitary existence during the season. Surprisingly enough, there are older hunters and landowners who can visually demonstrate the trophy potential of an area. Nailed to the walls of barns, garages and even bars are graphic histories of local deer herds. Areas that do not show a decline in quality over time demand further attention. An area about which conversation continues to return to the "good ol' days" should be shunned.

At this point, we have narrowed our search to one or more areas. The next step is to determine the potential for "unhunted bucks," a term that should be added to your vocabulary. It denotes a buck that seldom is faced with the prospect of encountering a hunter. There is only one way this can happen, and that is for there to be few if any hunters visiting a specific area. I usually return to my topographic maps and aerial photographs on this one. As noted earlier, in time I discovered that hunters seldom venture far from roads and rights-of-way in pursuit of deer. Consequently, I mark off a 1,500 to 1,700 feet **hunter influence zone** (see **Travel Corridors and Sanctuaries**) around every road and right-of-way in a county or hunting area. If there appear to be reasonable numbers of areas without hunter influence, I concentrate my scouting in these areas.

But, even when such "hunterless" areas are identified, pinpointing that bruiser buck still is like looking for a needle in a haystack. That is where a rudimentary knowledge of what makes quality deer habitat comes into play.

Although white-tailed deer probably are the most resilient game species in North America, occupying a broad range of habitat conditions, some areas feature better habitat quality than others. Long ago, the wildlife management profession defined areas with high-quality habitat. The components to quality habitat include: 1) a large amount of "edge;" 2) a diversity of habitat types; 3) presence of some form of agriculture; and ,4) high-quality soils.

I have discussed the edge concept many times in this book. Edge now is a relatively well-known concept. **An edge is any place where two different habitat types meet.** Exhaustive studies clearly have demonstrated that the numbers of individuals and species in a specific area are tied closely to the amount of edge. I can significantly alter a deer hunter's chances of success by moving him to an edge. That deer are edge animals cannot be refuted, even in the big woods of the North.

The diversity of habitat types also is of great importance to evaluating the trophy potential of an area. Deer require a diversity of foods and conditions in order to thrive. Recently, in one of my research studies, I demonstrated that the home-range size of a buck is directly related to the complexity of his habitat. **The more complex the habitat, the smaller the home range.** This certainly is important when patterning a specific buck.

Agricultural operations, such as soybean, corn and wheat farming, also can significantly affect the quality of bucks. Most regions lack adequate nutrition to produce maximum antler growth during some portion of the year. Consequently, high-quality forages, such as cereal grains and legumes (clovers, peas, beans, etc.) can make the difference between mediocre antlers and trophy racks. However, not all forms of agriculture are beneficial to deer. Large expanses of such crops as cotton and milo often have the opposite effect. Even large timber plantations are detrimental to deer. As a rule of thumb, I seek out areas in which the croplands are relatively small, less than 50 acres per field if possible.

Lastly, we come to the single most important component to locating a potential trophy hotspot: **soils.** As I reported earlier, the German scientist Uekermann found that for roe deer, soil quality is significantly related to body size and antler quality. But, what makes quality soil, and how do you go about locating these areas?

A quality soil is far more than just a fertile medium in which to grow forage. Basically, there are two components to quality soil: soil moisture and fertility. Soil moisture determines the volume of plant material to be produced each year. The volume of plant material produced and the succulence of that forage greatly enhance the productive capacity of the deer range. However, there is one drawback. **Do not confuse soil moisture with abundance of rainfall.** In some geographic areas, vital nutrients, such as phosphorus, are leached out of the soil by excessive rainfall. Consequently, the range often produces large quantities of low-quality forage. The ideal situation is an area with moderate rainfall.

Bottomlands are a critical component to the trophy equation. A bottomland may be nothing more than a shallow draw in the brush country of South Texas, or a Missouri creek drainage. A small difference in topography plus "tight" bottomland soils assure adequate soil-moisture retention to produce high-quality forage. Obviously, the more lowland soils an area has, the better— unless, of course, the lowland happens to be on the banks of a major river! Such areas have the tendency to flood during the hunting season, a phenomenon which may put you out of business. I prefer to hunt smaller drainages leading to large rivers or streams.

Soil fertility information is easily acquired. Again, we return to our friendly Soil Conservation Service agent for help. They have readily available information on the various soils and productive capacities for any location in a county or township. Published soil surveys are free for the asking, and they map the most fertile soils in easy-to-understand form. It is a simple matter to color in all of the high-quality soils within your hunting territory.

NARROWING YOUR CHOICES

In summary, the best places to find trophy bucks have the following characteristics, all of which can be pinpointed by research. First, trophy hotspots occur in areas where deer populations and hunting pressures are below normal. Expanding herds have both the genetic diversity and available nutrients to produce trophy antlers. Overpopulated deer herds characteristically are genetically inbred, with relatively little genetic diversity. **The amount of genetic diversity in a population dictates survival, as well as trophy quality.**

In herds with population numbers well below the saturation level of the range, there is a surplus of vital nutrients. Herds may be held below the saturation point temporarily, as after recent stocking or protection, or due to heavy poaching pressure. Hunters behave much as predators do. There is a rule in ecology that states that predators are not likely to seek a prey species that is not abundant. As prey become more scarce, predators switch to other species or areas in search of easier "pickings." So it is with whitetail hunters. Most prefer to hunt in areas where the probability of seeing a deer is relatively high. Hence, lower-population areas seldom attract heavy hunting pressure.

Next, trophy bucks occur in high-quality habitats. A high-quality habitat is one that has a large amount of edge, a diversity of habitat types, beneficial agriculture practices and high-quality soils. Soil quality is determined by the amount of moisture available during the growing season, and availability of crucial soil nutrients.

Armed with this information, you now should be able to arrive at a decision concerning one or more potential hunting areas well before next season arrives; or if you are contemplating the acquisition of land for purchase or for a hunting lease, you can use these criteria in making your decision.

The next and last step is to learn to recognize buck habitat and to pattern

312   *Producing and Harvesting Whitetails*

trophy bucks, and that is the topic of the next section.

FINDING THE RIGHT BUCK

Scouting is a full-time enterprise that knows no season. I continually scout, even as I hunt. What are the logical steps to scouting for specific bucks? Where do you begin? How do you use your time effectively? In this last section I will discuss tested methods for locating and patterning bucks.

I try to have two or three well-scouted areas from which to pick each season. I also like to add one or two areas each year, to serve as potential backups for coming years. Take care not to have more areas to scout than time will allow, however. A close friend of mine always has difficulty making up

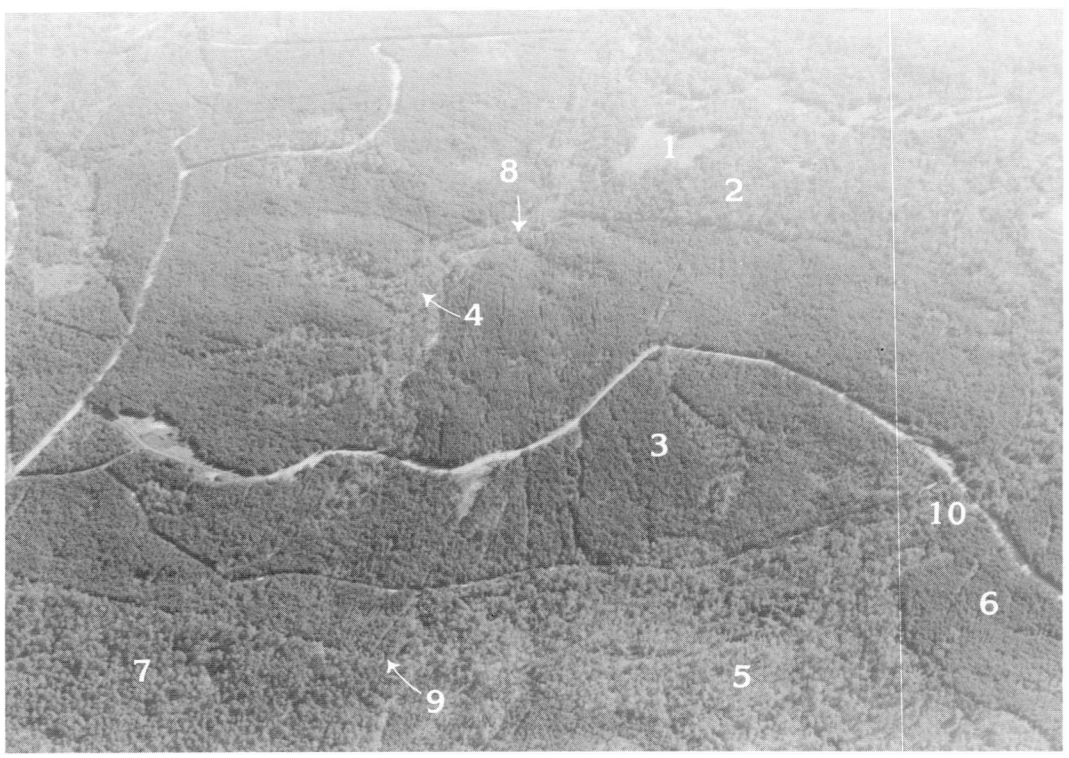

Although the Big Woods may seem homogeneous on the ground, an aerial inspection shows great habitat diversity. The numbers indicate features discussed in the text.

his mind where he will be on opening day. One area looks good one day, another the next. Each year he asks for my advice on making his selection. Always I give the same answer. "Just pick one area and become as familiar as you possibly can with it. There always is a bigger buck somewhere else! Be satisfied with shooting the biggest buck a particular property has to offer." But alas, he never listens, and seldom harvests a good buck.

The first step in scouting a new area is to return to the aerial photograph. Long before I ever take my first step on a property, I have studied every available photograph and topographic map, in order to identify potentially good scouting locations. For the purposes of this discussion, I have included aerial photographs of three typical habitat types. The first is a so-called big-woods situation. Many areas within the whitetail's range include large expanses of wooded habitat. No habitat type causes more confusion and fosters more questions about scouting than this. On the ground, the big woods is an awesome place to be. The general perception is that it is just a homogeneous patch of trees. This most commonly is not the case.

From the air, the big woods turns into a mosaic of several forest types, consisting of different species and ages of trees. Within any big woods habitat there are potential bedding areas, summer and winter feeding areas, and natural funneling features (travel corridors). In addition, even the flatwoods (wooded area with little elevational change) situations, streams still provide the most commonly used travel corridors.

My second example is a large river-bottom area with open pastures and large blocks of bottomland hardwoods and upland conifers on the slopes. Again, this situation lends itself well to analysis, with numerous opportunities for travel corridors and feeding and bedding areas. Large, cleared bottomland pastures and fields provide barriers to daytime deer movements, producing several unique opportunities.

Lastly, many hunters hunt trophy whitetails in regions with large amounts of agricultural lands. Although providing less dense cover and large expanses of open fields, the same critical habitat components, albeit more limited, are easily identified form aerial photographs. Let's examine each of these three examples, and then discuss some methods to work out deer movements on the ground.

BIG WOODS

The first example is a large block of mixed pine-hardwood, pure pine, pure hardwoods and cutover brushland. On the ground, the property is an impenetrable tangle of trees and thick underbrush. From the air, we easily can identify some important features that will require closer examination on the ground.

There are numerous stands of pure conifers, dissected by hardwood drainages (see photo). Although there are roads, several large areas remain unpenetrated by roads. To the northeast is a small field (No. 1 in photograph) located within a hardwood bottom (No. 2). This field, and the surrounding bottom, serve as a feeding area for deer throughout the year.

The conifer stands (No. 3) are quite dense, and function primarily as escape cover. Deer travel to and from the escape cover via hardwood drainages (No. 4).

To the southeast, there is a large cutover area (No. 5), which was planted to pines. Another dense conifer stand lies to the east (No. 6) of this area.

Finally, there is a rather large mixed pine-hardwood stand located to the southwest (No. 7). These areas make up what is, on the surface, a confusing array of habitat types; yet, they can easily be interpreted using a little basic knowledge about whitetail biology and behavior.

I have indicated the stand locations with the highest probability of success. Location 8 is perhaps one of the best setups on the property. Each of the drainageways leading away from the primary drainage offer travel corridors to deer using the pines as sanctuaries. It makes little sense to hunt one of these minor tributaries. Rather, it is better to intercept the bucks at a common travel point (8) where all deer move from bedding to feeding areas (1&2).

The next likely location is 9, where there is a corner. At this point, brushland, pure pine and mixed pine-hardwood meet. This is a prime location.

One last, lower probability location is 10, at the point where the cutover area connects to another hardwood bottom. Since there are potential sanctuaries to the North and South of this connection, there is an excellent opportunity for a travel corridor.

After locating these areas, you should go to the area and check for sign on the ground.

RIVER BOTTOMS

In the river bottom photo, it is logical to assume that bucks will not cross the large, open pasture (No. 1) during daylight hours. Any attempt to cross the pasture likely would involve the thinly wooded field border (2) bisecting the field. The small clump of upland mixed pine-hardwood (3) provides an excellent sanctuary and is connected to another upland stand by a narrow neck of timber (4). This is an excellent spot to begin your ground checking.

The river (5) is a meandering stream, with many oxbows and sloughs. Although such features do not significantly inhibit deer movements, bucks do tend to skirt these features in making their daily rounds of scrapes. The narrow neck (6) between the large slough, located to the Southeast and the stream meander is an excellent location for a potential setup.

Finally, location 7 occurs at the curve of the river, and is connected to a small stand of hardwoods by a narrow strip of brush. This again would be an excellent location for a setup. As with the Big Woods example, the next step would be ground-checking of these locations.

AGRICULTURAL AREAS

The photograph of the agricultural

River bottom habitats offer a unique mixture of good soils and habitat diversity. Bucks tend to use the smaller drainages adjacent to river bottoms as travel corridors. The numbers are discussed in the text.

property suggests several potential hunting locations. First, there is an SMZ (No. 1) in the central portion of the property, which would make an excellent travel corridor leading from the block of woodland (2) to the various fields. Since the farmer plants field 3 to winter cover crop, location 3 would make a great setup.

Finally, the small block of woodland marked 4 might well be a sanctuary. A buck could move from this area to the SMZ via one of two pathways (5 & 6). Both of these pathways are easily watched from a distance using binoculars.

ON THE GROUND

Now that we have completed the first

phase of scouting, it is time to go into the field for study. The locations discussed for each of the three areas only serve as starting points for ground scouting. It will be necessary to hit the woods to make a final decision on where to be on opening day.

Given all options, I prefer to begin scouting during early winter. This is the time when there will be a maximum number of rubs and abandoned scrapes. Some bucks even continue to scrape well into the spring. For example, during the last week of March I found an active scrape in the east Texas pineywoods, some five months after the rut!

The trick is to learn to recognize old buck sign. Although most hunters have little difficulty in recognizing a fresh scrape or rub, most have considerable problems detecting rubs that are 2 or 3 years old.

READING THE WOODS

The first thing to look for on the ground are the various ages of rubs. **No other feature tells us more about the movements of bucks than rubs.** In my opinion, hunters spend too much time trying to locate scrapes, when the bucks are more than willing to tell you where and when they travel about. Unless something dramatic happens to cause a buck to make serious adjustments to his movement pattern, he will continue to use the same travel corridors throughout most of his life. Up to the age of 3 or 4 years, he will attack larger and larger diameter trees. However, recent research suggests that after this time, the buck may or may not continue to use the larger rubs.

Basically, there are two types of rubs: exercise rubs and signposts. The exercise rub is used for daily workouts of the neck and shoulder muscles. Several hundred rubs may be used by a single buck during the pre-rut period. Signposts, on the other hand, are larger diameter trees used both for exercise centers and to advertise the buck's presence. Signposts are more difficult to locate, occurring most commonly within a few yards of a buck's bed/sanctuary.

In most cases, I can work out a buck's complete travel path in two or three days of ground scouting. First, I walk to an area identified on the aerial photograph and begin searching for old rubs. Recognizing the accumulation of several rubbing years is not that difficult. Here are some keys to look for.

When bucks repeatedly rub small saplings, the young trees often die back. This type of old rub is the most commonly encountered, yet seldom is noticed in the woods. The presence of a dead stem with green sprouts emerging around it is the best clue in recognizing this type of rub.

I always carry a roll of blaze-orange flagging tape in my pocket when scouting. When I find a rub, I tie a piece of the material to the nearest tree to mark its presence. Then, I proceed along the natural contour of the land in search of another rub, each time tying a new piece of flagging to the newly located rub. At the same time, I record each rub's location on my photograph or map of the area.

A signpost rub may have been visited

Scouting: The Art and Science

Agricultural areas are similar to clearcuts when it comes to scouting. Most agricultural areas have the ridges cleared for planting and the drainages retained in woody vegetation. The numbered areas are discussed in the text.

one or more times by the same buck or buck group. Whereas the small sapling type often is rubbed completely around, these larger-diameter rubs usually are rubbed on a single side the first year. The side rubbed indicates the general direction of travel by the buck. (That's the direction from which the buck approached the tree.) Again, I record the rub's location on my map.

During the growing season following rubbing of a large-diameter tree, the plant makes an effort to heal over the damage. Seldom are trees able to completely cover the scar, leaving a large, circular area of exposed inner wood. Oddly, the following season bucks are reluctant to rub these trees in the same spot. Rather, a buck moves slightly around the tree or above the previous year's damage to rub. These repeated visits to the same rubbing tree give you a good indication of the age of the deer. Normally, two or three repeated scars on the rubbing tree indicates that the buck is at least 4 years of age.

Occasionally, bucks will rub overhanging branches or leaning trees. The buck walks up under the tree and pushes upward on it. This strengthens the muscles of the back of the neck. My experience is that only mature bucks will exhibit this behavior. It is, however, difficult to locate this type of rub, because the damaged portion of the tree is directed downward, making it difficult to see at a distance.

This signpost is one of the most important signs to search for in the woods. Located adjacent to or within the buck's sanctuary, the signpost usually is a large-diameter tree with multiple rub wounds. The signpost also has a depression adjacent to it where the buck repeatedly pushes against the ground as he leans into the tree. This sign has a scrape-like appearance.

Recently, I patterned a rather large buck along a deep woods drainage system. The buck had a rub line that extended as two loops, each extending more than a mile. At the center of these two loops, I found a thicket around which were five large signposts. Clearly, this situation indicated that I had stumbled onto his bedding area! Indeed, I returned with a ladder stand to watch for the buck. Late in the morning, a 10-pointer that easily would have scored in the 160 B&C class came slowly along the rub line. As he approached the area, he meticulously went to each of the five rubs and pushed vigorously against them. He then walked into the small hawthorn thicket and lay down. I was so close to the buck that I had to wait several hours before I dared to leave the spot.

As the pre-rut begins, I suggest that you return regularly to your flagged line of rubs to search for scrapes. Carefully record the location and date of each scrape. This will allow you to

Learning to recognize old buck sign is a valuable asset in scouting. Here, a buck has rubbed the same sign post for several years. Note the healed-over scars.

Mike Biggs

develop a chronology of each buck's rutting sequence. Unless disturbed, the buck will repeat this sequence each year. Using this method, I have been able to pattern and keep track of several young bucks that I harvested when they matured.

Once you have acquired sufficient rub and scrape locations, it is time to sit down with your photograph and/or map to recreate the buck's lifestyle. For example, a rub line that extends from a bedding area to a slope adjacent to an oak flat obviously represents the buck's movements in a good acorn year. A rub line extending from one drainage to another indicates late-season movements and searches for estrous does. Areas that have active rubs and scrapes year after year are common-use areas that demand your attention.

Observations of sign only gives you an indication of the buck's age and habits. Whether or not he is a "shooter" can only be determined by direct observation. For this reason, I try to get a look at several bucks long before the season starts. However, you must take care not to force the buck to move. As with the bedding buck above, it is better to wait several hours to leave an area than to waste several weeks of work.

Recently, some high-tech methods have been developed to record the size of bucks using a particular area. One manufacturer now sells passive infrared-triggered cameras that can photograph a buck as he passes along a trail or works his scrape. These devices are expensive, but seem to be effective. Similar devices can be fabricated using local electronics store parts, if you are so inclined. No one knows at this time whether or not being photographed will alter the buck's movement pattern. I use a more simple device, just to get an idea of the time and direction of a buck's movements. Laying a light thread across a trail, approximately 12 inches above the ground, clearly demonstrates the buck's travel direction. The thread will be carried in the buck's travel direction without his being aware of its presence. A whisk broom also is useful for this. Clear a small patch along the trail, and then return to see which way the tracks point. I try to return at six-hour intervals, so that the general time of travel can be determined without disturbing the buck.

I also monitor the location and relative abundance of whitetail foods. Acorn production is not consistent from year to year. A periodic check of the number of acorns on sample trees will tell you a great deal about the upcoming acorn crop. Also, pay attention to the planting activities of farmers. What is an alfalfa field this season may be a fallow field next. The former certainly is more attractive to deer, especially in a poor acorn year.

SUMMARY

This chapter by no means has exhausted the subject of scouting. Frankly, to give fair treatment to scouting techniques would require an entire book! Hopefully, through this chapter I at least have given you some new ways of looking at scouting. The techniques presented may not always fit your situation, but you can modify them or develop new techniques to fit your needs.

In order to be successful, the modern whitetail hunter must rely more and more on scouting to harvest a trophy-class animal. The edge goes to the hunter who hones his scouting skills and does his homework **before** taking to the woods.

Chapter 21

Stands and Blinds: Effective Use in Deer Hunting

The sun reflected from the morning frost as I sat perched precariously on top a small board nailed to the top of a live oak. It had been a particularly good acorn crop, and the bucks were coming regularly to feed on this high energy source. Although I already had killed many bucks at my young age, I nervously fingered my Bear recurve. I had decided to try my hand at bowhunting.

I had not been on my eagle's perch for more than a half-hour when two young bucks appeared out of a nearby creek bottom. They walked directly to my tree and began feeding. The setup was perfect. The wind was in my face as the two bucks fed contentedly less than ten yards away. Their feeding frenzy was so intense that neither noticed as I slowly drew back on the skimpy 40 pounds of pull. It seemed that the world was proceeding in slow motion. One buck looked up suddenly! I froze, daring not to let my breath out. He looked away. The next few moments are some of the most memorable of my life. The bowstring twanged as I sent the short little arrow to its mark behind the shoulder. The three-edged broadhead glued to the cedar shaft drove home with a loud thud.

The buck jumped straight into the air and ran wildly back into the creek bottom. His companion, somewhat dumb-founded by the whole thing, stood off a few yards for a while, then pursued his companion. It was only then that I dared to let the air out. How I kept from falling from the tiny board I never will know. I had made my first bow kill. It was the early 60's, a time when few had even heard of compound bows, high technology deer stands and aluminum arrows. Today, it is a different story indeed, with a vast array of hunting aids. During the last decade, hunting stands and blinds also have changed dramatically.

There probably have been as many articles written about hunting stands and blinds and their use as there have been about "horn" rattling and the rut! Yet, few hunters really are proficient in the use of stands.

With better than one hundred models to choose from, how does the hunter decide which equipment to use? Quite frankly I never have read an article that gave much practical advice on stands and stand hunting to the average hunter. The basics of stand hunting are important to trophy whitetail hunting. The type of stand you use and where you decide to use it will determine the outcome of the hunt. This chapter first will discuss the types of stands and blinds available to the hunter, and then give some hints on using these devices.

TERMINOLOGY AND BASICS

For our purposes, we will distinguish between stands and blinds— there is a difference. First, **a STAND can be defined as any portable contrivance, usually elevated and non-enclosed, used to shoot deer**. The term "stand" probably came from the days when hounds were extensively used to harvest whitetails. The hunting party would position "standers" along some natural break in the habitat (often a road), and then drive the deer with hounds across this opening for the standers to shoot. **BLINDS**, on the other hand, **are enclosed structures located either on the ground or elevated on legs**

One of the most simple, yet effective stands available to the hunter is a tree limb or board nailed on a tree.

Robert Skinner

Ladder stands are very popular, especially among southern hunters, and may be homemade or commercially constructed.

which are used to observe and/or to harvest whitetails. They usually are more permanent in nature. Blinds have been used for centuries; many of the European hunting and game management books present construction plans and recommendations for the use of blinds.

Stands

There are five basic types of stands. The first type, and most simple, is the use of a **board**, nailed to a limb to provide a secure perch for the hunter. As I noted earlier, this type of stand was my first experience with stand hunting whitetails, and I have some pretty fine and unusual memories resulting from their use. Even today, I often use simple boards nailed on tree limbs in hunting specific bucks, or just sit on a limb high in a tree.

The second type is built from either wood or metal and resembles a ladder; hence, the commonly used term **ladder stand.** Ladder stands may be homemade or purchased from one of the many supply catalogues or sporting

Tripods offer greater mobility than a ladder stand, but also are difficult to transport. These stands are great for quickly moving in on a specific buck.

So-called "self climbing" stands are lighter, and more mobile than either ladder or tripod stands. Most easily conform to weight limitation, but can be dangerous. These types of stands are responsible for a large number of accidents annually.

goods stores. The more sophisticated models break down into two or more manageable pieces.

The third type of stand is the **tripod stand,** although it may have four legs. Tripods are free-standing and do not have to be erected on a tree. Tripod stands may be quite simple or have blinds attached.

The fourth type comes under several names, most commonly the **self-climbing stand.** This is a misnomer in that the stand does not climb by itself. **You** have to supply the power. The hunter uses the stand to climb a tree or pole. Self-climbing stands are more portable than either ladder or tripod stands; however, they must be erected on a tree.

Other than simple boards, perhaps the most versatile stand is the **hanging** or **"lock on"** stand. These devices are lightweight, usually less than twelve pounds, and easily carried and erected on trees. The only drawback to hanging stands is the fact that you have to carry and install steps in order to hang and reach the stand. Most hunters carry the small screw-in steps offered by several manufacturers.

Weight of stands range from about ten or twelve pounds for self-climbing stands to better than a hundred pounds for some tripod and ladder stands. Obviously, the term portable is subject to interpretation!

Blinds

Blinds are enclosed boxes of various dimensions. I have seen blinds designed for as many as six persons. Hunters can build some pretty unusual blinds.

Robert Skinner

Blinds come in many models, as simple as homemade boxes on legs (left) or products of space age technology (right). Blinds are useful in observing whitetails and in herd reduction, but seldom can be used effectively for hunting mature bucks, except on a blind rotation basis.

Probably the most notable of these was a blind I once saw in the Texas Hill Country that was a two story structure for six men. It resembled a church with a steeple on top. The blind was located on the ground adjacent to a large wheat field, with the "steeple" rising about twelve feet into the air. I suppose that the guys would sit down in the bottom playing cards until a deer was sighted. Then, someone (presumably the card winner) would crawl up into the tower to shoot the deer.

Blinds generally are designed in one of two ways. First, there are ground blinds, usually positioned to overlook a feeding area, baited area or travel corridor. Second, and most common, is the blind erected on legs to various heights, ranging six to sixteen feet.

What Type of Stand or Blind Do You Use?

In spite of the notably humorous stands and blinds discussed above, these structures are useful both for harvesting trophy deer, and for population management involving either-sex harvest. When selecting a stand or blind, you need to ask yourself what kind of hunter you are. Be honest! If you are the type of person who cannot sit still perched on top of a small ladder or way up in a tree, then stands are not for you. If, however, you are the type that can literally sit still for days without either getting bored or your legs going to sleep, the stand is perfect for you.

Habitat type also will influence your decision. If you are hunting the South Texas brush country for example, a ladder stand or self-climbing stand obviously is of no use. The density of the vegetation also can make a ground blind useless. A tripod stand or elevated blind will be more successful in this situation. The physical features of your hunting territory also will influence stand selection. If there are few, if any, roads available, use of heavy stands or blinds will not be practical, unless you have an army of helpers. Stands and blinds that break down into manageable parts are easier to move long distances, especially if the parts can be consolidated into a back pack.

You probably have noticed that I have very carefully avoided using brand names or recommending a particular product or products. Although I have my preferences, I prefer to leave it that way. However, I will offer some advice for picking a commercial stand or blind.

Ladder stands come in many styles and shapes, ranging from homemade structures to commercially produced stands. Whether you buy or make your own ladder stand, it truly should be portable. This is, it should weigh about thirty-five pounds and break down for easy carrying. I have one that breaks into three pieces which are then neatly bundled into a back pack. Such a stand should re-assemble in less than five minutes. The stand should be of sturdy construction. The seat should be comfortable. This is very important, since you probably will spend many hours perched on it. Some stands are just about as comfortable as an English bicycle seat! The stand should be painted some color that will blend in well with the surroundings. I prefer earth tones or black. I have had good success with black ladder stands, especially when properly positioned. Quite frankly, I prefer the tripod stands over ladder stands. Ladder stands have one big drawback. They have to be used against a tree. There probably is as much variation in tripod stands as any other type. Again, weight is important and I would keep weight below the thirty-five pound limit.

The best tripod stands, in my opinion, are also take-down models, since they can be erected in less than five minutes. It is the seat that quickly distinguishes the brands now available. Remember again that you probably will be sitting on top of the tripod for a long time. My favorite tripod stand has a fold-down, molded plastic seat that conforms easily to my posterior. The fold-down feature is important so that I do not have to sit down in a very cold puddle of water.

There is an infinite variety of ingenious contraptions offered by self-climbing and hanging stand manufacturers. Most models easily conform to the weight limitations. However, several brands are very difficult to carry in the woods. To be easily transported, a stand

The inside of a blind should be designed to allow movement without making excessive noise. Most noise comes either from kicking the side of the blind or in sliding open the shooting ports.

must collapse into a manageable bundle with back packing straps attached. The K.I.S. (keep it simple) principle never was more important here. Since the stand is located well above the ground, with no legs to support it, camouflage is not critical. However, the type of base used is important. A solid base of plywood or metal will project an unnatural shadow that deer notice, especially when it falls in or adjacent to the middle of a trail. I prefer stands that have a series of bars for a base, as this produces a more natural shadow effect.

Self-climber and hanging stands often are limiting in that, once again, you have to have a tree on which to erect them. I recently ran into this problem while bowhunting. I found a beautiful trail with scrapes and rubs all along it, but the nearest useable tree was better than fifty yards away. Most of the trees present were saplings except for a single old oak tree better than thirty inches in diameter. My self-climber would not even reach around the tree. The one physical feature about these stands that differs from the ladder and tripod stands is the critical need for security. One of the most common factors in hunting accidents today is falling from a tree stand. **Believe me I know what it is like to "take the elevator down," and I do not like it.** You must assume at all times that your stand is capable of falling. You should use a safety belt or harness whenever you hunt.

Blinds, as with stands, come in all shapes and sizes. Most hunters construct their own blinds, but a number of quality models are available for those of you who prefer to spend your off-season time in other ways. Blinds, especially the elevated models, should blend in with their surroundings. Too many blinds are placed on top of hills or in the middle of clearcuts. I recently toured a gentleman's land, where he had hunted deer for some twenty years. All of his blinds were located in places where he could see for long distances, and totally avoided the travel corridors that stood out like "sore thumbs." He was not even hunting the deer habitat!

The inside of the blind is important. Remember that you literally are sitting inside a box which will magnify any noise you might make. The most common source of noise in a blind occurs when you accidentally kick the side of the blind. For this reason, many hunters line the floor and lower one third of the blind with carpet. The shooting ports can also cause problems. Some commercially available stands have sliding glass windows. Try to quietly slide one of these windows open with a ten point buck slipping slowly away! Also, most blinds come with windows on all four sides. This allows total visibility, but deer can see right though the blind. The hunter is silhouetted. I suggest that you close half of one window so you can hide your profile.

Once you have decided on the types(s) of stands or blinds you will use, it is time to consider the proper use of the equipment at hand. Which stands to use, when and where to use them are determined both by the particular set of conditions and the stage of the rut you are hunting. That will be the topic of a later chapter.

THE MOBILITY CONCEPT

Other than perseverance, no other factor will influence the probability of success or failure more than mobility. The successful trophy hunter is a highly mobile creature. Unfortunately, most whitetail hunters have what I call a "river fishing" mentality. This is, a river fisherman goes to the river, sits down on the bank and "hopes" the river brings by a fish. This method produces limited results. On the other hand, there are fishermen who understand the fish and their behavior, opting for the strategy of going to the fish.

Mobility is the key to hunting mature bucks. A self-climbing or lock on stand that can be carried as a backpack will allow you immediately to adjust to an individual buck's movments. (Courtesy of Tree Lounge.)

So it is with successful whitetail hunters. The permanent stand is the enemy of the trophy hunter. You must be able to adjust at a moment's notice to a buck's dynamic activity pattern. It is a cat-and-mouse game when it comes to trophy whitetail hunting. Here's an example:

Last season I hunted with George Chase in New Brunswick. Although I came away empty-handed, it was one of the best hunts of the year. George had patterned a tremendous buck he estimated would gross in the higher 180's B&C. The buck had a sanctuary off of a fairly recent clearcut. The sanctuary was almost stereotypical, positioned adjacent to a drainage in a white cedar thicket. At that point in time (pre-rut), the buck regularly traveled with two other bucks, one a huge nine-pointer and the other a young eight-pointer.

The buck had two travel corridors, each along the drainage, but in opposite directions. He appeared to be concentrating on the upper end of the drainage, leaving his sanctuary in the morning to feed and work his rub line. One day, George was working the upper drainage when he heard a loud thumping sound, followed by a guttural grunt. Since these sounds were accompanied by a vigorous raking, he knew it must be the big buck rubbing one of his sign posts. Sure enough, a three hundred yard stalk put George in a thicket overlooking the drainage. The sound was emanating just below him, but he could not see the buck to save his life.

George looked up suddenly to discover that he was being watched by the nine-pointer! The buck was standing across the drainage, looking straight at him, or so he thought. It turns out that the buck did not see him after all. About that time, the big buck left his densely vegetated post with a loud crash. He was not aware of George's presence, nor was the nine-pointer. The nine-pointer then did a very curious thing!

He walked down to the signpost, which

George had positioned himself to see, walked up to it and licked it. I have seen this behavior before. It apparently is some response to the dominant pheromones deposited by the larger buck.

I hunted that signpost for two days afterward, not once seeing the big buck. I saw both the nine-pointer and the eight-pointer, and could easily have killed both of these bucks, but the big boy was nowhere to be seen. On the third day, George and I expanded our search once again.

We discovered that the buck had moved to the other travel corridor, either in response to my presence or as part of his normal travel routine. Frankly, I think the latter is more likely, as the other two bucks never gave any indication of being aware of my presence; but then again, you never know.

I hunted that buck for a week. Every time I adjusted to intercept the buck, he adjusted to avoid me. Time ran out on me before I could get that one chance. I was convinced that the buck had to leave the sanctuary along a ridge adjacent to the clearcut. A few days after I left for Texas, George was sitting on that same slope when the monster walked easily within gun range. By law, George could not carry a firearm if he was guiding. Unfortunately for him, he **was** guiding on that day. George was sick, to say the least!

Such is the nature of trophy whitetail hunting. The odds always are in the buck's favor. The only way you have to reduce these odds is to use a highly mobile, non-permanent stand or blind. That is why I have had such good success with blinds constructed from natural materials.

GO NATURAL WHEN POSSIBLE

It is not going to make me very popular with the stand and blind manufacturers, but I prefer to go without a man-made blind whenever possible. Naturally constructed blinds are the very best way to hunt mature bucks. Blinds constructed from brush, tree tops, or even leaf litter are readily accepted, even by the wariest of bucks. Remember that deer, especially bucks, memo-

Natural blinds, constructed of materials on site offer much greater flexibility in hunting mature bucks.

Robert Skinner

rize every aspect of their home range. Anything out of the ordinary will immediately draw their attention. Even old does are that wary.

A number of years back, I was hunting in Mexico with some friends. One of these fellows was an avid bowhunter who really wanted to kill a Mexican whitetail with a bow. We placed a tripod stand on a water hole, where we had seen a number of good bucks watering. When we returned, he was eager to relate his experience. He reported that he was sitting quietly on his stand, when a large doe walked out of the brush to drink. She was walking slowly, apparently unaware of his presence. Suddenly, she stopped dead in her tracks and looked right at him. The wind was in his face, so he knew

Bucks quickly pattern hunters, knowing full well where every permanent stand is on the property. That is why the author strongly recommends the use of portable stands.

Mike Biggs

that she had not smelled him. Something obviously was not right! She did a very slow about face and forgot about her drink. There is no way to guess how many times she had come to that same water hole, each time memorizing the surroundings. To her, the tripod stood out like a "sore thumb." If, on the other hand, we had built my friend a brush blind out of natural materials, she probably would never have given him much thought.

PERMANENT STANDS AND BLINDS

There **is** a place for permanent stands and blinds in deer harvesting, but you need to understand how to go about using permanent structures. First of all, permanent stands are very useful in harvesting the antlerless segment of the population, especially when erected at feeders and food plots (where legal, of course). It often is difficult to achieve your doe harvest quota (as discussed earlier), and blinds are especially useful in this unpleasant chore.

Second, blinds can be quite useful in commercial hunting and/or guest entertainment operations. On the Diamond H Ranch in South Texas, and Grassy Lake Farms in Kentucky, we regularly use enclosed blinds for guests and paying hunters. The guide can drive right up to the blind, let the hunter step directly from the vehicle to the blind; and thereby leave little scent on the ground around the blind. Hunters are admonished not to leave the blind to reduce problems with human odors.

There also is an excellent strategy that can be employed when using permanent blinds. I like to rotate use of the blinds so that the deer never have extended experience with hunters. This, of course, requires a large number of stands in order to be successful. I try not to hunt a stand more than once each week.

The reason for all of these precautions will be obvious with a little discussion of my research findings. For years now, I have monitored buck movements in and around stands. As I have noted in several sections of this book, and will continue to discuss throughout, bucks quickly become conditioned to the presence of permanent stands. They adjust their activity patterns and habitat selection to reduce the probability of encountering a human. My experience has shown that bucks quickly learn the location of a stand, and take avoidance maneuvers by the third day of occupation by a hunter. Stands that have been in the same location for years are avoided entirely by mature bucks.

THE SETUP CONCEPT

For all of the above reasons, I have come to the idea that the best way to use stands and blinds is through what I refer to as a **"setup**." A setup is a particular set of conditions, unique to each potential hunting location. These include, but are not limited to, the presence of attractive features such as food or rutting activity, travel corridors or sanctuaries. How you go about developing a plan of attack is dependent on each specific setup.

Before the season ever commences, I know exactly where I will be hunting the first few days of the season, mostly resulting from weeks of scouting the many months prior to opening day. At each setup, I have two or more stand locations pin-pointed, and the approach to each delineated. I like to use reflective pins or flagging to mark the best path to each location.

I never take a stand or blind into a setup prior to opening morning. I carry my stand with me, and take it back out each and every day I hunt a specific setup. The path I take is well-planned and is designed to avoid disturbing the specific deer I am hunting, or leaving human scent where it can later be detected. I will discuss this concept in greater detail later in this book.

Each setup should be carefully choreographed and thought out well in advance. At each location, there are several potential stand locations to allow for the changing wind. Never will I hunt a setup that has the wind in the wrong direction. I am not going to waste months, and perhaps years, of work due to impatience.

HOW TO STAND A STAND

No discussion of stands and blinds would be complete without consideration of how to remain on a stand for a long period of time **without** alerting every deer within a mile. Earlier, I noted that one of the keys to successful trophy hunting is mobility, and that the other key is perseverance. Second only to poor stand placement, inability of a hunter to remain still costs many a trophy buck each season. Here are some hints to improve your stand etiquette.

Over the years I have developed the ability to "turn off my mind" when sitting on a stand. It is difficult to concentrate on what you are doing if you are thinking about what is going on at the office, or other extraneous material. Remember that you are out in the woods to have a good time, enjoying nature. Develop the ability to take in everything that is going on around you. It is surprising to me to hear a hunter proclaim that he becomes bored on the stand. This is impossible! There always is something going on for you to watch and learn.

Many times I have asserted that the successful trophy hunter spends the entire day on his stand. If you develop the ability to watch all that is going on about you, the time passes quickly. A tufted titmouse feeding along a limb, or two squirrels playing all provide adequate stimulation. For those of you that still cannot find amusement, a good friend of mine offers a solution. He attributes several of his better bucks to Louis L'Amour. He carries a L'Amour novel into his stand and reads one page at a time, each time pausing to look about him. He even has a camouflage cover for his books. When I have to spend a particularly long time hunting a specific buck, I also use this ploy.

However, even if your mind **is** in the proper state, your body may have different ideas. One of the worst things you can do is predispose your body to give you complaint! Loading up on coffee before you go out is just asking for trouble. Caffeine is a strong stimulant that has devastating impact on your kidneys. I anticipate these problems by carrying along a glass jar for emergencies. It may be humorous to contemplate the idea of urinating in a jar, twenty or so feet in the air; however, it can be done with finesse after a little practice.

What you eat can affect your ability to sit still. One of the most notable culprits is the simple sugars and carbohydrates. A heavy meal or snack on high carbohydrate foods will guarantee that you will have trouble sitting still. I suggest that you try high protein foods for snacks. These foods take longer to digest and will not make you as sleepy.

There is nothing more frustrating than to have a bad cold or cough and trying to wait out a monster buck. On numerous occasions, I have been convinced that I was choking to death, trying to suppress a cough! No matter how hard your brain tells you to not to cough, your body is going to win out in the end— it is pure reflex action. But, there are some evasive maneuvers you can take.

Since I seldom am without my rattling antlers, I use a gimmick that has served me well for many years. I try to suppress the cough for as long as possible, then rattle like crazy while I give way to the cough. This generally covers up the sound, even though bucks grunt and cough as they fight. Also, I suggest that you carry a small pebble in your pocket, and place it in your mouth to keep your throat moist. Candy usually is not a good idea, as it has an effect on your throat. Cough lozenges can be smelled for hundreds of yards, so unless you are down wind from your target, I suggest you avoid coughdrops.

Cold also is an enemy to remaining still. I have hunted in subzero weather more than once, and it is not easy to tolerate these extreme temperatures. For this reason, I suggest that you acquire the most modern of cold weather gear. Dry chemical hand warmers also are of great value. As far as I know, they do not give off a perceptible odor. Your hands and feet are the most critical to keep warm. Research has shown that if your hands are warm, the rest of your body will remain fairly content.

A final word on being quiet. If you cannot stand to sit there any longer, I urge you to get down and go to the camp. You will do more harm than good if you stay. On many occasions, I have not hunted because of a cold or harsh weather conditions. Why waste months of scouting just to stay in the woods?

SUMMARY

There are a wide variety of stands and blinds from which to choose. Your choice of stand type or blind will be determined by the habitat you hunt and the specific set of conditions involved. The "name-of-the-game" when it comes to trophy whitetail hunting is mobility. The more mobile you are, the more adept you will be at adjusting to a specific buck's change in behavior and activity pattern. No matter which stand you choose, it should be lightweight, and capable of being erected in a short period of time

Stands and Blinds: Effective Use in Deer Hunting

without alerting the deer of your presence. Permanent blinds and stands will guarantee less success than mobile, non-permanent stands.

Ray Sasser

THE HUNTER

It's that time of year,
I must go through all my gear.
Time to pick up the pace,
get everything into place.

When opening day came,
I was back at the same old game.
Trying to outsmart that old buck,
At which I'd had no luck.

I know exactly where he lives,
Not a chance to him I'd give.
With all my camo, scents and lure,
I'd get him this time for sure.

I was on my stand at dawn,
On the highway I could hear trucks drone.
Only young bucks would come and go,
Not a bit of him he'd show.

He was smarter than all the rest,
I knew I was up against the best.
All season long it was the same old way,
He would defeat me every day.

I saw him one morning with my light,
I must say he was quite a sight.
Had ten points-- high, heavy and wide,
Was very big and filled with pride.

At the end he'd won again,
He must have held the upper hand.
He defeated me on his own,
As a hunter I'm not alone.

One thing is clear in my mind,
He's still there and still not mine.
He will spread a lot of genes,
To me he is just a dream.

He has gained all my respect,
Even though I'm a nervous wreck!
...K.S.

Chapter 22

THE SCHOOLING OF A TROPHY BUCK

Early last fall, a friend of mine came by and he was all excited. Earlier, I had helped him plant an excellent food plot on his hunting club. We had limed, fertilized, and planted a mixture of wheat, oats, and arrowleaf clover. By October, the plot was a green oasis in the forest. The vegetation was knee-high and was honeycombed with deer trails.

Now Ben is a pretty rabid deer hunter. He spends more time and money in search of a trophy buck than just about anyone I know. He had built a rather impressive deer stand on the plot-- one with carpeting and a swivel chair. He began sitting in that stand on a regular basis in early spring. The excitement came one October day when he saw a tremendous buck saunter out onto the plot to feed. Ben had just about decided to abandon his vigil because he had seen only does, fawns, and an occasional young buck. But there he was, munching quietly on the lush forage. The buck was a truly magnificent animal of 10 points and, according to Ben, a 22-inch inside spread. For the next few weeks, Ben ate and slept that big buck. It was all he would talk about. "That buck is all mine," he told me. "I've got him completely figured out!"

The buck always arrived about an hour before dark and stayed until just after sunset. He always came by the same route; out of a dense thicket of loblolly pine. He left by following a small stream that meandered through a stand of large water oaks. Ben only had to tolerate the wait until hunting season.

I did not get to see Ben opening weekend. As a matter of fact, it was a good 10 days into the season before I saw my friend. I asked about his monster buck. His face dropped, he looked down, and began to kick at an imaginary object. "I didn't get him. I've hunted him every day since opening day. That %#@$*& has just vanished! I bet some dumb-luck hunter shot him."

I really felt sorry for Ben. The man had worked so hard to kill his trophy and had come away empty-handed. But, he had made an all too common mistake. Despite his zest for trophy hunting, he had not done his homework. He had assumed he was dealing with a dumb animal that was tied solely to instinct. He forgot to ask himself how this old veteran got to maturity in the first place.

I excused myself for a few moments to make a phone call. When I returned, I asked Ben if he would like to see his buck. I felt that the buck was still very much alive. Such a buck would certainly have drawn a lot of attention if indeed it had been killed. In fact, I was willing to bet that the deer was still in the same area. I told Ben I would show him the buck, but he would have to leave all guns at home. Ben gave me a puzzled look and agreed.

It was almost dark by the time we arrived at the gate. Ben had fidgeted all the way out. He was afraid it would be too dark to see anything by the time we got there. I pulled out my Q-Beam from under the seat. Ben quickly understood. The phone call had been to a good friend of mine who was the game warden in the area. We were going spotlighting.

The food plot was located in a little clearing surrounded by forest. As we rounded the forest edge, two greenish discs were shining brightly in the plot. The light caught a massive set of antlers sporting 10 perfectly symmetrical points. He was a good buck all right. A doe and a fawn stood nearby. The big buck ducked his head and darted into the darkness. Ben's mouth dropped open, and he began to suck in air. The excitement had returned to his face.

I told him that he had a slim chance to kill this buck but only if he was willing to change his tactics and abandon the food plot. He looked at me as though I were crazy. After all, this was the only place he consistently saw the buck. He was unwilling to take my advice. He hunted hard the rest of the season and never saw the buck again. To add insult to injury, the buck even constructed a rather large scrape under a small tree in the middle of the food plot!

As part of our cooperative deer management program, we encourage hunting clubs and landowners to keep records on all the deer harvested from their area. One general relationship

The Schooling of a Trophy Buck

Ray Sasser

Although food plots are an integral part of deer management, mature bucks seldom venture out on them during daylight hours. It is best to hunt the travel corridors adjacent to the plots.

---

always shows up; there are far more young bucks in the harvest than older ones. Originally, we concluded that this harvest structure reflected the actual age structure of the herd, and it certainly does in part. Buck mortality is tremendous and very few individuals make it to maturity. At least 85 percent of all bucks die before reaching maturity. However, the number of older deer showing up in the harvest is not a reflection of their actual abundance.

Biologists will tell you that deer are instinctive creatures, responding to environmental stimuli with predictable behavior patterns. This is generally true, but not always the case. Deer have the capacity to learn. Many of the behaviors we have observed on heavily hunted areas suggest that bucks and even does quickly develop various strategies for survival. On an area where we regularly conducted deer drives, I saw a buck crawl on all fours between another driver and myself. The only predictable thing is that, once a strategy is adopted, it remains basically unchanged as long as it works. Take Ben's buck for example. Let's examine how this particular buck came to behave as he did, and then develop a strategy that could have been used to harvest Ben's trophy.

THE SCHOOLING OF BEN'S BUCK

Ben had actually seen this buck before, but there was no way for him to remember it. It was six years previous on another food plot. The buck was just a young fawn then, feeding contentedly and playing around his mother. The nubbin' buck was one of the 60 or so fawns that had survived of the 100 born earlier that spring.

During the first 10 to 14 days of life, the young fawn remained hidden in the grass along the edge of a forest clearing. His only contact with another deer was the two or three times a day that his mother came to feed him. His mother was a matriarchal doe; that is, she was the dominant doe in a social group consisting of several of her daughters and a few granddaughters. She had begun to drift away from the group in May to find her fawning area. She had used the same area for the previous three years, and would defend it against all intruders.

By the time he was three weeks of age, the buck and his mother had rejoined the social group. Some of the other does also had fawns, while others had none. Now a young buck has very little social status; they are about as low as a snake's belly.

During the remaining summer months the young buck learned much about survival. Better than half of the other fawns would die from one thing or another during summer. Instinctively, he reacted to the alarm signals of the older deer. He was also beginning to learn by association some of the cues that meant danger. However, at six months of age he was anything but a

Young bucks learn a great deal from their mothers during the first six months of life. After this time, a yearling is on his own.

Mike Biggs

finely tuned survival machine. He depended heavily upon the matriarch for protection.

By fall, the social group consisted of mature does, a yearling buck who had taken up with the group, our nubbin' buck, and the few remaining fawns. As the forage became scarce, the family group began to feed on a food plot. It was on this food plot that Ben and the young buck first "met."

On a crisp, clear evening in November, the group approached the plot. The matriarch entered first, followed by her fawn, the other does, and finally the yearling buck. He was a nice buck for his age; a six-pointer with a 10-inch spread. Now, at this time, Ben was not so discriminating about the quality of the buck he harvested. The deer had just started to feed when the thunder of a .30/06 shattered the evening air. The six-pointer fell in his tracks. The matriarch flagged and ran, followed by the buck fawn close at her heels. This happened two more times during the hunting season. Another buck that was running the matriarch and one of the mature does were shot from the same plot. This was lesson No. 1. Food plots were dangerous places.

By the following summer, the matriarch had a new fawn to tend to. She had run the yearling off prior to fawning, and he had taken up with a small group of mixed-aged bucks. There was no mistake about his social position with this group. He was quickly put in his place-- at the bottom of the ladder. But, in spite of his lack of social status, he benefited from the relationship. The buck group was comprised of older individuals that in one way or another had survived the previous hunting season. They were much more wary than the doe group. They stuck to the creek bottoms and thickets when they travelled and rarely crossed an opening in daylight. Being a subordinate buck, the yearling never made the first move.

It was during the second fall that he learned his next lesson. The rut was in full play. The social group had broken up, and it was every buck for himself. Some of the older bucks had just left

Yearling bucks often abandon their fawn home range, finding a new home sometimes miles away. This is advantageous to the deer, but spring-summer mortality is highest for these young bucks.

Mike Biggs

Eventually, young bucks join a social group, made up of one or more older bucks. These more experienced bucks teach the "tricks of survival" to the newcomer.

suddenly. He and another buck of similar social status were chasing a doe in estrus. The doe dashed out onto the old food plot. He started to follow, but hesitated just for a brief moment. Something was too familiar. The something was Ben. The brief hesitation saved his life, as the other young buck threw caution to the wind and rushed headlong onto the food plot. It was a fatal move. The remaining yearling drifted off, ultimately ending up several miles from the area.

We have found through our radio-telemetry studies that fully 70 percent of yearling bucks take such trips. Fortuitously, trips are selectively advantageous in that those that change home range prior to the rut are less likely to be shot. I radio-tracked one buck for four years. He was collared as a nubbin' buck. We lost the buck during his yearling season and thought that his collar had ceased operation. To our surprise, we started receiving radio signals again in the middle of March. The next season he again disappeared, but this time we were ready for him. We searched the entire area and found him some four miles away along a major creek drainage. Each year thereafter, the buck made the same pilgrimage, until finally his radio did go out. To our surprise, the buck was killed two years later on his traditional rutting area. The buck had eluded hunters for six years and was killed only when a hunter decided to sit along a creek bottom where he had seen some tracks.

The next time the buck encountered Ben, he was a three-year old. Both had matured considerably. Ben's zest for deer hunting had expanded to the pursuit of a trophy-class animal. He no longer haunted the food plots, as several years had failed to net anything but small bucks. The three-year old had long since learned that the early morning was not the time to be out and about. His normal pattern was to remain hidden in a thicket until around 9:30 a.m., and then travel the ridges above small stream bottoms to check his scrapes. This particular season, the buck had moved his home range some three miles from the old food plot. He had established a line of scrapes along a ridge slope adjacent to a small drainage.

Ben had found his scrapes and had set up a ladder stand about 20 yards downwind. What he did not know was that the buck also ran his scrapes downwind. At 9:45, Ben grew tired of waiting. He decided that the buck was not going to run his scrape that morning. He would try again in the afternoon. As Ben climbed down from his stand, he heard the sound dreaded by every trophy hunter. A buck snorted and vanished over the nearby ridge.

Ben returned regularly to the area until the accumulating pile of leaves in the scrape convinced him that the activity was futile. The buck had learned his final lesson. He shifted his activity to the very early hours of the pre-dawn and after dark. In short, he became nocturnal. By the time Ben saw the mature buck, now a 10-pointer, feeding on the food plot that fall afternoon, the deer had joined a rather exclusive club; the most wary game in North America, the trophy-class whitetail.

FIVE WAYS BIG BUCKS ARE DIFFERENT

I recently attended a party at which deer hunting was the center of conversation. One particularly boisterous fellow proclaimed loudly, "There are deer hunters and then there are *deer hunters!*" I smiled politely, amused by the brashness of the guy, giving the matter little thought at the time. On the way home, however, I began to consider his claim. And, you know, the more I thought about it, the more convinced I became that the man was right. There really are two kinds of deer hunters.

In any hunting camp there is always one individual, possibly two, who is different from the rest. You seldom find him in camp at lunch, and he virtually lives in the woods. November or August, January or September, he is out there searching for something. His hunting partners may view him with great esteem or with great suspicion. Some years he may not even shoot a buck, but he doesn't seem to mind. When he does kill a buck, it is a good one. Why is he so different? Maybe it is because he is hunting a different "species" of deer: *the Big Buck*.

Other than having larger antlers, the Big Buck (*Odocoileus virginianus "giganteus"*) differs little in outward appearance from the smaller variety. The real differences, those that make the Big Buck almost impossible to shoot,

The trophy buck often is different in every way from his younger followers. He is different in disposition, rutting behavior, home range size, daily activity patterns, and habitat preferences. Often, as with this type of animal, the fellow who hunts trophy whitetails also represents a separate "species" of critter.

Mike Biggs

The Schooling of a Trophy Buck

are subtle, but quite striking upon critical examination. He is the premier survival machine, finely tuned to his environment by years of close calls and near-fatal mistakes. Basically, there are five major distinguishing characteristics that set the Big Buck apart from other deer.

Dispostion

There is as much difference physically and mentally between a yearling and a mature buck as there is between a high school athlete and an All-Pro lineman. The big Buck has come up through the "school of hard knocks. " He began at the bottom of the pecking order-- kicked, butted, and bullied by even the lowliest doe. As a yearling, even his own mother turned on him.

Forced out on his own, the young buck drifted randomly until joining a buck social group. His social position once again was well established, at the bottom of the barrel. His first rut came like puberty to a teenager. He was gangly, impetuous, and often downright foolish. It is at this age, or perhaps the following year, that most bucks are harvested by that *other* type of hunter.

Somehow, either by instinct or more likely sheer luck, the buck reached maturity. Each year he had grown larger in body size and antler development. His body weight had stabilized around the age of four or five years, while his antlers continued to enlarge until the age of six or seven years. Peak body weight may be 95 pounds in the Edwards Plateau of Texas or upwards of 400 pounds in Canada and some southeastern states. It is probably more body size and experience than antler size that determines social position. For example, the dominant buck in my biological studies of penned deer is seldom the one with the largest antlers.

At maturity, the buck either has become a loner or may spend the spring and summer with a mixed-age buck group. There certainly is no doubt about his social position now. His only tie to his adolescent days is the agonizing "puberty" that he must endure each year as he approaches breeding condition. Already pugnacious by nature, the Big Buck exhibits all manner of anti-social behavior. In many ways, he resembles a prime pasture bull; he is dominant, and he knows it. Mature bucks even walk differently from younger bucks. A heavy body and well-developed muscles give the Big Buck a slow, almost John Wayne-style swagger. Russell Thornberry, a noted trophy whitetail guide in Alberta, reports that in his area one can easily distinguish the tracks of a monster buck in snow. Big Bucks drag their feet, producing a smeared, swaying trail.

A Big Buck will not tolerate any sign of dominance behavior. Younger bucks cower away from him, head held low and tail pulled close to the body. The Big Buck's unpredictable dominance displays can be as mild as a look or as explosive as an all-out charge. However, all of this power is not without cost. He seldom eats, and spends a great deal of time on the move, traveling at unusual times through *safe zones* (travel corridors). He must never let down his guard. Should he ever become weakened, subordinate bucks will turn on him. I have found large, trophy-class bucks near death, with multiple wounds to the sides and rump. Subordinate bucks are always waiting for their chance.

For example, each fall I tranquilize my penned bucks in order to weigh and measure them, as well as to remove their antlers for safety reasons. As far as a tame buck is concerned, I am just another buck. Each year I warn my students not to bend over in the pen, but each year one does. You can't imagine the sight of a terrified student flying through the air!

On one such occasion I darted a large, dominant 10-pointer. He had spent the entire summer bullying two smaller-bodied bucks. The moment the Big Buck showed signs of the drug taking effect, a smaller 8-pointer hit him broadside, sending him rolling head over heels. The 10-pointer was unable to defend himself, and I literally had to grab a stick and stand between him and the challenger to protect him. Both of us learned a lesson that day.

Rutting Behavior

Mature bucks are not the sex-crazed fools younger bucks are. Oh, they occasionally will fall prey to poor judgment in the face of a pretty doe, but for the most part, they seldom act without caution. The main difference in rutting behavior lies in *where* and *when*. First, Big Bucks have well-established breeding territories. These territories are acquired early in life, and they are not given up lightly. I say "they" because it is rare for a true Big Buck to have a single rutting territory. Our radio-collared bucks often travel in a large circuit, stopping for varying periods of time to re-establish a rutting area used in previous years. One buck in particular lived all summer in a very small area, and then began to drift off in early fall. It usually took him until spring to return to his original area. He was killed some seven miles away.

Each rutting area is extraordinarily similar in appearance. Rutting territories usually include a slope with sparse vegetation, an abundant supply of saplings for antler rubbing, and overhanging limbs for scrape-making. Scrapes usually are established in the same areas year after year, even when the dominant buck is killed. New bucks move in to claim the choice places. Scrapes may be single or multiple, but usually are distributed in a long line. It is interesting to hear hunters say, "The rut is back on; bucks are working their scrapes again." As often happens with hunters, it is the right observation, but with the wrong conclusion.

The purpose of scrapes is probably twofold. First, scrapes are used to advertise the presence of a rutting male to the local doe population. Because doe home ranges generally are fixed (except perhaps in the Mississippi Delta country), bucks have to keep on the move to find new conquests. Second, scrapes also announce the return of the Big Buck, similar to a male dog announcing his presence. It is interesting to watch a small, obviously subordinate buck encounter such a scrape. You would think he was a kid caught with his hand in the cookie jar! He sniffs at the scrape, ducks his head, and hightails it out of there. He may sneak a quick urination, just to show the old boy.

But, why are hunters sometimes wrong about the rut? A scrape line should be thought of as a trotline. The Big Buck works the trotline as an old river fisherman would. He "baits" his "hooks" in hopes of catching a receptive doe. When a particular hook starts to produce, the Big Buck centers activity around that spot. An older buck will concentrate his scrape activity in areas with a history of success, whereas a younger buck may waste time starting and abandoning unproductive scrapes.

Once a particular area stops producing, the Big buck will either move on to another line or rebait old scrapes. It is the visiting of old scrapes that prompts oldtimers to proclaim that the rut is "on" again.

Home Range Size

Home range size generally becomes greater as the buck matures. Yearling bucks generally have some home ranges similar in size and location to that of their mothers, but toward the initiation of the rut, yearling home ranges often deteriorate into a drifting pattern. Big Bucks know every inch of their home ranges, however, including all of the *safe travel corridors* and *sanctuaries.* Big Bucks are well aware of permanent stand locations, usually giving wide berth to the waiting hunter.

The literature is confusing on home-range sizes of whitetails. Some writers say they have a small home range, 500 acres or so, while others claim they have ranges of several thousand acres. Much of the confusion comes from the way in which home ranges are calculated. Some researchers include only the area occupied at a certain season of the year, while others use the yearly or even the lifetime movements of the animal. The seasonal approach makes more sense to me, especially if hunting animal is a prime concern.

Home-range size during the rut is probably regulated by two factors. First, the buck:doe ratio can greatly influence home-range size during the rut. If there are a great number of does and only a few bucks, as on many overhunted ranges, there is no real

The mature buck has a completely different behavior from a younger subordinate buck. He is pugnacious and jealous of his "territory."

Mike Biggs

sense in the buck having a large home range. Why go out for a burger when you can eat at home, especially when you could get run over in the process of going out? On the other hand, on ranges with high buck population densities, Big Bucks will have to travel farther to find receptive does; hence, they have much larger home ranges. On one area I am managing for trophy whitetails, home range has steadily increased as the number of mature bucks has increased. Unfortunately, we now are losing good bucks, because they have to leave the area to find does.

Daily Activity Patterns

There is nothing more frustrating than to watch a Big Buck all summer, plan the kill, and then be disappointed when he virtually disappears just prior to opening day. He has done one of two things: he either has shifted his home range or has shifted his activity period.

Whitetails are diurnal. This means they are active during daylight hours, primarily in the early morning and late afternoon. This certainly is what you read in the technical literature about deer. Unfortunately, however, few deer have read the technical literature. Deer are adaptable to local conditions. Big Bucks especially are quick to learn the best times to be out and about.

Once, on one of my management areas, the local "fence rider" was convinced we had killed all of the deer on the place. We indeed had hunted the area very hard, but I knew we had not killed an excessive number of deer. No amount of talking on my part would persuade the man that there were still plenty of deer, however. So, one night I took him to a large, green, food plot. Under the light of the Q-Beam, we counted 92 deer on the three-acre area!

A Big Buck prefers to run his scrapes just before sunrise and again after dark. If there is not too much activity on the area, he will pay a mid-morning visit to the scrape, as well. It is at this time that he is most vulnerable. Indeed, the majority of Boone and Crockett bucks I have known of have been taken in mid-morning. But, if you do not get him at that first opportunity, he may become totally nocturnal.

I once watched a field at around two a.m., using a starlight scope. There was no moon. During a two-hour period I watched no less than five bucks attempt to mate with a doe. The bucks even spent some time sparring. (There was no clearly dominant animal among them.) Such bucks would be downright hard to shoot legally.

Habitat Preferences

The most interesting difference between Big Bucks and younger ones is their choice of habitats. It has only recently come to light that bucks often have different habitat preferences from does, especially during such stress periods as late summer and winter. If you spend much time studying the movements and behavior of bucks, you quickly will establish in your mind exactly what buck habitat looks like. From a quality standpoint, buck habitat is much poorer than that used by does. Bucks and does have different needs at certain times of year. During the rut, food consumption by bucks often decreases to the point that, combined with the constant activity of the rut, they lose considerable weight. That is why mortality is much higher in bucks during the post-rut period than in does. Toward the end of the rut, this can be turned into the hunter's favor. Bucks will be in great need of high-energy foods then.

Why should a buck deliberately select the poorer habitat? Several possible answers have been proposed, but I favor one in particular. The name of the game, when it comes to perpetuating the species, is getting genes into the next generation. Even if the buck dies in the process, he is successful. One way to ensure that your offspring survive the winter stress is to avoid competing with does and fawns for food.

Big bucks tend to favor poorer habitats than does, giving way to their offspring to better assure survival of their genes.

Mike Biggs

Hence, the theory is that bucks abandon the better habitats so that these areas can be used by their offspring. But, what about the younger bucks that did not have the opportunity to breed? There also is a very reasonable explanation for that. An advantage to "hanging around" with the dominant bucks is that there is the opportunity to better oneself socially. So, for the younger bucks, the chance to climb the social ladder and breed as dominant bucks the following year is worth the chance of dying young. I will discuss buck habitat at length in the next chapter.

USING THIS KNOWLEDGE

Now that we have described this new "species" of deer, what does it all mean to that unique type of hunter? How can this information be turned into an advantage?

The Big Buck is a very difficult animal to hunt, but it is not impossible to harvest such a trophy. The first thing you must realize is that you are dealing with a uniquely trained animal. Each buck has developed his own strategy for survival. The only way to outsmart him is to know him. He has one weakness: once he has found some behavior to be useful in avoiding hunters, he will stick to it as a matter of habit. He will deviate from that habit only after a close call. So, what that special kind of deer hunter is doing in the woods all of the time is *studying* deer. There is no simple answer. It may take a good hunter two years to figure out a buck, but it is worth the effort.

Many trophy hunters say that such a buck is virtually unshootable. I don't think so. It is certainly difficult but not impossible. The hunter has to be willing to change many of his preconceived ideas about deer hunting. Let's take the example of Ben's buck and develop a strategy that will put the odds more in Ben's favor.

First of all, the hunter must decide early in the year which buck or bucks he is going to hunt. Start early, probably during the summer. There is no substitute for time spent in the woods. Concentrate your activities in and around the drainages; that is where the deer activity will center at this time. Upland forage has long since become woody and hard to digest. The bottoms are full of rapidly growing weeds after the spring flooding. Deer use creek drainages as travel corridors, even when the forest has been removed by clearcutting. Sit quietly adjacent to areas where there are signs of heavy deer activity, such as tracks and browsing (leaves and twigs nipped from bushes). But, don't overdo it. Too much human activity in an area will cause a shift in behavior. Follow deer trails backward to find bedding areas. If you see a single deer moving down a trail in early morning, you can safely assume that the animal is coming from its bedding site. Beds are generally situated on the north side of a slope in summer and on the south side in fall and winter.

As fall approaches, look for signs of antler rubbing. Ridge slopes with a fairly closed canopy and sparse brush are the best places to look. Bucks like young saplings in areas where they can see for some distance, and which provide easy escape. Ridge slopes are perfect for this.

If you are going to harvest a truly trophy-class buck, you had better get him early in the season before he shifts his activity patterns. Once you have located the buck you want, work out his travel pattern. You don't have to find his exact bed, but you should find his general bedding area. Next, look for his scrape line. If he is a real trophy, you can bet that he is at the top of the pecking order. Large active scrapes certainly will be his. But whatever you do, *do not* set up a stand on or near his scrapes. Remember that, at the very best, he will run scrapes considerably down wind at mid-morning. The vast majority of Boone and Crockett bucks were killed around 10 a.m.

The best place to ambush your trophy is along the travel path from the bedding site to the scrape line. If you have done your homework you will no doubt have seen him taking this route. Now you're ready. Slip into the area before daylight and find your predetermined vantage point. If you use a portable ladder stand (although I discourage it), carry it in with you. Do not leave the stand in the woods. Believe me, that buck knows every bit of its home range and will recognize strange objects.

Do not move from or leave your stand all day. If you are lucky, or better yet, if you have truly done your homework, it will be a relatively short wait. When you see him, take your time and get your best shot. You will have only one. If you miss, you might as well give up because you probably will never see the buck again.

Late season bucks are exceptionally difficult to kill. The best strategy is to continue your scouting. Scrape hunting probably will be unproductive unless the buck is in one of those rare places with no hunting pressure. Your best chance will come at the end of the rut when bucks are beginning to travel in groups again. Food is getting scarce by this time. The big bucks have been pretty much off their feed for a couple of months and will be in dire need of nourishment. This is the time to return to the travel corridors you found late in summer. Again, mid-morning is the best time to hunt. A student of mine recently tried this technique during the last week of the Texas season. He found a travel corridor along a creek bottom and positioned himself behind some freshly cut pine saplings. In no time, three good bucks came by him. He shot the biggest one, an excellent buck with 18-inch high antlers. Main beam length was better than 26 inches!

SUMMARY

If you are serious about shooting a trophy-class buck, you might give these suggestions a try. I cannot guarantee they will work in every case. You are dealing with an intelligent animal that has arrived at his own individual strategy for survival. You will have to study him and develop a more effective strategy to outsmart him. It can be done, but only after a great deal of hard work and a willingness to change on your part.

Any hunting strategy you develop

must be custom-tailored to the particular buck you are after. I think you will find that it is a lot of fun, and a heck of a lot more challenging. If you don't mind the work, you might consider quitting deer hunting and start *deer hunting*.

Chapter 23

BUCK HABITAT: WHAT IS IT AND HOW DO BUCKS USE IT?

Mike Biggs

This year, I passed a milestone in my career. I finished some fifteen years of intensive white-tailed deer research. As I begin my next decade or so of research, it is interesting to review our progress in the management and harvesting of whitetails. The last decade, in particular, has seen tremendous advance in our knowledge about these elusive animals. Fifteen years ago, the hunter had little to aid in his quest for a trophy buck. There were no grunt calls, no human odor neutralizers, little in the way of sex attractants, and, most certainly, no artificial rattling antlers cast from space age materials. Today, the technology of deer hunting has progressed to a point far beyond anything I ever anticipated. This also is true in regard to our knowledge about the daily lives of deer. In this chapter, I discuss the latest installment in our evolving knowledge about whitetails. I recently have confirmed what we suspected for some time about bucks—they prefer different habitats than does!

RADIO-TELEMETRY

In spite of the vast amount of research on whitetails, we only recently learned anything useful about the behavior of bucks. This is due primarily to the limitations imposed by radio-telemetry and the difficulty in catching mature bucks. The general public, thanks to television, is now pretty familiar with radio-telemetry and its uses in wildlife management. Unfortunately, however, there remain many misconceptions about what this technology will accomplish and how scientists use radio-tracking to learn about animals. Much of the confusion results from television portrayals of radio-telemetry as being capable of pin-pointing the exact location of an animal, as well as telling the researcher precisely what the animal is doing at any time. All a researcher has to do is capture an animal, place a radio-transmitter around its neck and then monitor the animal's every movement from afar. This simply is not so. As one who was in on the beginnings of radio-tracking technology, I am painfully aware of the limitations of radio-tracking systems. For example, a number of years back some researchers undertook the job of radio-tracking whales by satellite, a highly attractive idea on the surface. Yet to the surprise of researchers the high-tech system often showed the whales visiting downtown San Francisco! Now that is a nice place to visit, but I really do not think that whales are likely to go shopping there. Today, many of our telemetry problems have been solved. Advent of integrated circuits, long-lived lithium powered batteries and sophisticated receivers and antennas, evolved primarily for other electronics applications, now allow us the luxury of evesdropping on the day-to-day lives of many species of animals.

In order to accurately predict where an animal is and what he is doing, you must have a transmitter that broadcasts with sufficient power to reach at least a mile, and a receiving system that will present an accurate picture of the deer's location. Simple? Not really, since a radio-signal in the woods is much like a driving a golf ball into a cemetery full of tombstones. Those trees are nothing more than columns of water that will reflect a radio signal in all directions, as well as absorb a good portion of its energy. We spent several years perfecting antenna tracking systems that would give a reasonably accurate prediction of the deer's location. The accuracy of an antenna system is much like the trajectory of a bullet. Reloaders strive for the magical minute of angle that gives supreme accuracy. In the case of radio-telemetry, five minutes of angle is often something to write home to mom about. When the animal is a half-mile or more away, that kind of accuracy puts you somewhere in the same county! It has only been recently that we produced systems that give the kind of accuracy to answer many of the questions asked by hunters, particularly about bucks. That is why we only now are discovering the subtle differences between buck and doe behavior and their habitat preferences.

The last problem faced in studying buck movements and behavior lies in the fact that, since shooting a mature buck is extremely difficult, trapping and radio-collaring a mature animal is downright impossible! That is why some of the early studies on deer movements concluded that deer have small home ranges, which they often do not have, and that a deer dies within a mile of where it is born (again false). These researchers were studying does and yearling bucks. We were faced with either improving our capture techniques or developing a transmitter battery that would last long enough to follow the young buck into adulthood. I have never been able to convince a mature buck to come in for a battery recharge! Fortunately, we solved both of these problems and now routinely track older age class bucks.

BUCK HOME RANGES AND HOW THEY USE THEM

The white-tailed deer does not randomly roam over the countryside in search of its daily needs. Many hunters and landowners believe that a thousand acres of forest, brushland or farmland represents a thousand acres of deer habitat. This is not true. The landscape is broken up into various size patches that may supply all or none of the deer's needs. We learned long ago that it is advantageous for deer to be very familiar, not only with each other, but with the world in which they live. A deer, especially a buck, knows every inch of its home range and quickly notices any changes within it.

We found that does are pretty much concerned with basics of survival, feeding and escape from predators. As a result, does are usually more sedentary and have relatively small home ranges of a few hundred acres. This number is greatly influenced by the nature of the habitat, but the figure holds true for most cases. Bucks, on the other hand, concern themselves with far more than food and survival. It is their responsibility to maintain the genetic diversity necessary to keep the whitetail species healthy and responsive to changes in the environment. Consequently, bucks often have tremendously large home ranges, depending on the time of the year, comprising as much as several thousand acres. They also must face an added dimension to their world, the hunter.

The accompanying computer drawings illustrate the nature of buck home ranges in the pineywoods of east Texas. Although we can draw a nice line around a buck's home range, notice that the animal does not use the entire area equally. There are regions within the home range that, depending on the season, are highly attractive. Such areas have been called "core areas" by many researchers. During the hunting season, core areas may take the form of sanctuaries. Since I first coined the term, a number of hunters have written me for some idea as to how to locate sanctuaries. Until recently, I could only give general descriptions of such areas. Analyses of my telemetry data, however, have given some startling revelations about the nature of sanctuaries.

Not only do bucks have larger home ranges, they move about within their home ranges in a much different way than does. Movements through an annual cycle are more pronounced in bucks, with well established travel corridors and core areas. The accompanying computer drawing gives a good example of the typical movement of a mature buck throughout the year. The striking thing is that core areas for each season occupy different areas within the home range You can imagine the frustration of a hunter who patterned this particular buck during summer, only to discover that the buck had moved away from the area in the fall. This buck shows an all too familiar pattern of splitting of the core area during the rut. The buck has two distinct sanctuaries, one representing a more familiar bedding area from summer, and the other a rutting territory. By winter, the buck has moved again, concentrating his activity in another portion of the home range. Does, on the other hand, tend to maintain some overlap between spring, summer, fall and winter core areas (see attached map). Core areas appear to be expanded or retracted as daily needs dictate. What all of this means is that does remain reasonably predictable, while bucks tend to move their centers of activity each season. The picture becomes even more clouded when we examine the types of habitats preferred by bucks and does. It is a wonder that the two sexes ever get together!

HABITAT PREFERENCES OF BUCKS AND DOES

Perhaps the most startling finding to date is that bucks and does seem to prefer entirely different habitats, with only some habitat types being commonly used. My study took place in the pineywoods region of east Texas, but the results apply throughout the whitetail's range. Deer do not walk about

Mike Biggs

Mature bucks have completely different habitat preferences from does and younger bucks.

and say to themselves, "Oh, this is loblolly pine, I think I'll stay here." If transplanted to the farmland of the mid-west, an east Texas deer would search out a general habitat structure that most resembles its pineywoods home. Deer seek cover and food, and these take many forms. So, the results of my study apply to most areas. In order to give you a better understanding of how differently bucks and does perceive their worlds, let's take a look at how my deer used the various types of habitats.

Openings and Fields

Although openings and fields provide many of the essential foods for whitetails, these areas were used by bucks and does in different ways. Such areas were highly attractive to does in the spring and summer, but bucks showed little daytime interest in them during any season. We did, however, see some use at night by bucks. In the fall and winter, both bucks and does preferred other habitats over this type.

Food Plots

Although does often spent a great deal of time in and around food plots, bucks seldom ventured onto these areas during the daylight hours. In fact, bucks spent very little time feeding on the cool season grains and legumes planted in these plots. Bucks had other things on their minds during the fall, and wasted little time feeding.

Clearcuts

Throughout much of the whitetail's range the forestry practice of clearcutting is highly controversial. Proponents of the practice point to the tremendous amounts of forage produced in forest regeneration areas, and assert that these activities are detrimental to deer in the longrun. Opponents, on the other hand, feel that the short term gains produced by clearing the forest are offset by the conversion of a highly diverse forest to a monoculture of trees. In essence, both sides are right. We found that young clearcuts were attractive to both sexes during the growing season. At first, when the vegetation is quite low, does primarily used the clearcuts during the day, with bucks tending to frequent them more at night. As the young forest continued to grow, however, bucks and does tended to use these areas more and more during the growing season. But, when fall and winter rolled around, deer pretty much avoided clearcuts altogether! Obviously, large expanses of clearcuts would have a devastating impact on deer populations. Later, as we will see below, bucks became highly attracted to these areas.

Dense Stands of Young Evergreens

As clearcuts and forest regeneration areas grow, the stand becomes so dense that little or no forage grows beneath the canopy. If you have ever spent much time in this habitat type, you will understand what the word "dense" means. The briars, blackberries and other vines will literally tear the shirt from your back. And, that is precisely why bucks tend to prefer these areas! We found that bucks were highly attracted to dense regeneration areas, while does showed little inclination to spend time there. Bucks primarily used the streamside management zones (SMZs) to travel to and from these areas. Bucks spent much of the daylight hours bedded in dense stands, venturing out to feed or to visit rutting territories during the fall.

Old Growth Evergreen Forest

This type of habitat is characterized by having mature evergreens, in this particular case pines, with very little understory vegetation. Weeds and small shrubs dominate the forest floor. Bucks significantly preferred this type of habitat only during the fall rut. This habitat type, incidentally, is heavily utilized by does during every season of the year. Hence, the only time that the bucks and does come together in old growth evergreen forests is during the rut. This is completely logical in that, 1) since the does prefer this habitat type, bucks naturally are drawn to it, and 2) the open nature of the habitat and numerous young saplings make a perfect place for a buck to "set up shop." It is also very hard to approach a buck without being seen. Does use these stands as foraging areas, feeding on the numerous browse species and succulent weeds.

Old Growth Mixed Pine-Hardwood Forest

Although highly touted by environmentalists, mixed conifer-hardwood stands were not attractive to bucks, and only seasonally attractive to does. The problem is that the amount of forage produced in a forest is greatly influenced by the amount of shading from the canopy. A hardwood canopy produces more shade than a coniferous canopy; hence, the presence of hardwoods has a negative impact on forage production. However, this is offset in the fall by the contribution of acorns and other mast from the hardwoods.

Old Stands of Hardwoods

Pure hardwood stands were attractive to does during much of the year. Bucks, on the other hand, tended to treat these areas as they did the old pure pine stands. The open nature of the understory, and availability of numerous small saplings for rubbing, provide excellent rutting areas for the bucks. This habitat type also provides good visibility, making it difficult for a hunter to approach without detection.

Roadsides and Rights-of-way

Bucks continually avoided these areas, seldom venturing close to the potential danger. It is interesting to note that many hunters concentrate their activities near roads and rights-of-way. Occasionally, a hunter is successful in such situations, but only because a buck is forced to cross a road.

It is now obvious from my study that bucks and does view their worlds in highly different ways. The doe is concerned primarily with the rigors of daily survival and tends to concentrate her activities where a particular need can be satisfied. In general, does have very stable home ranges of only a few hundred acres, making only minor shifts in use during the changing seasons. The life requisites of does include

Buck Habitat: What is it and How do bucks use it?

Robert Skinner

Openings and fields are used differently by bucks and does.

Robert Skinner

Large expanses of clearcuts would have a devastating impact on deer populations in the long run.

Although food plots are important to deer management, mature bucks seldom venture out on them during shooting hours.

Robert Skinner

Bucks use dense stands of young evergreens for sanctuaries and bedding areas.

Old growth evergreen forests were significantly preferred by bucks.

Robert Skinner
Old stands of hardwoods are excellent mast producers, and were highly attractive to does during winter months.

Robert Skinner
Old growth mixed pine-hardwood forests received little attention from bucks.

Robert Skinner
Older bucks tend to shun roadsides and rights-of-way during shooting hours.

food, water and cover. Cover, particularly dense cover, is not as critical for does as for bucks. Bucks, on the other hand, tend to limit their activities to the more dense regions of the forest. Oddly enough, this is even true during the warmer months when hunters and the rut are far out of mind. The one thing that we do not know is whether or not these sex differences in habitat preferences are learned or genetically incoded in deer. That is the topic of future research. That is what makes the white-tail so intriguing. There always is something new to learn. The technology of deer hunting continues to evolve with the animal. In this section, I will discuss how you can use this information to increase your chances of harvesting that trophy buck during the next season.

DEVELOPING A HUNTING PLAN

Each year millions of hunters take to the field in search of that elusive monster buck. Sadly, most of these hunters will either go home empty handed or with something less than anticipated. Most of the time failure to score can be attributed to the hunter himself. Success or failure depends on many factors, but most important of these is knowing where to find big bucks within your hunting territory. In the above sections, I revealed what we have been finding out about the habitat preferences of whitetails, especially bucks. These revelations explain much about the basic behavior of mature bucks, and how these seasoned veterans go about undetected year after year in the most heavily hunted deer woods. Now I will discuss how you might go about recognizing preferred buck habitats and how you can develop a successful strategy to harvest a wall hanger next season.

The behavior of the white-tail buck is innately different from that of does. In an earlier chapter, I outlined the schooling of a buck. This can be seen very early in life, about six months of age. As part of my trophy buck management program, I often require landowners and hunting clubs to harvest large numbers of does. It happens almost without fail that the first deer to fall are the "nubbin" bucks! This is not because they are less intelligent or wary than their young sisters. Rather, even as fawns, bucks are more aggressive and curious about their world. Consequently, a buck fawn will readily venture into places where no self-respecting deer will normally go. The result is often disastrous! However, if the youngster survives his first year, this aggressive curiosity pays off greatly. It allows the young buck quickly to learn as much as he can about his world—knowledge which has definite survival value later in life.

By the time a buck is mature, he is well-versed in the tricks of day-to-day survival. Does, on the other hand, usually develop a more laissez faire attitude about life. In most of our deer ranges, does are inadequately harvested, receiving reduced hunting pressure. There is absolutely little need to perfect many of the time-consuming survival strategies of bucks. This is not to say, however, that does lack this

The type of habitat selected by a mature buck is the product of his natural innate preferences for cover and the combined experiences of his life. Each buck is unique and should be treated as such.

ability. On the Schwartz Ranch in South Texas, we harvested only does for five or six years, leaving the bucks to reach maturity. A young man who started hunted the first year of the program was riding with his dad one day. They approached a large wheat field filled with bucks. "This place is no good, Dad," he complained, "there's not a doe anywhere to shoot!" We had almost reversed the normal behavior pattern of the sexes. The does were wild and the bucks were relatively docile.

But, even under such conditions, there are still obvious differences in the way that bucks and does conduct business. Some researchers, myself included, feel that deer have adopted a strategy whereby the bucks tend to occupy one portion of the range and the does the other. Why? It appears to have something to do with procreation. The "name-of-the-game" in natural selection is getting your genes into the next generation. There is much confusion about the survival of the fittest concept. Even if the buck dies naturally or is killed by a hunter, he is successful as long as he produced offspring. So, if bucks decide to live in places where does spend little time, they are in fact increasing the chances that their fawns will survive. Neat, huh?

SUMMARY

Whatever the reasons, we now have established that bucks and does might be found in different places for much of the year. My telemetry research has recently confirmed this assumption, and it explains why so many hunters have difficulty in harvesting a buck. This is further supported by two decades of observation of hunters. In fact, hunters are out there doing everything they can not to be with the deer! Hopefully, this chapter will serve to reduce this problem.

Chapter 24

BUCK SANCTUARIES AND TRAVEL CORRIDORS

It is with some degree of trepidation that I write this chapter on the real secret of trophy hunting. In fact, some of our most notable and successful trophy hunters are not exactly thrilled about it, either! Why? Because I am about to give away one of the keys to the kingdom. One of the best-kept secrets of trophy whitetail hunting is about to come to light— a secret I learned years ago by accident as a trophy hunter myself, and later confirmed through my research. Whitetails have learned through years of co-evolution with wolves and man, that there are ways to avoid detection by the ever-present predator.

The 1984-85 season ended as most. I had received my usual quota of phone calls from hunters wanting to know one thing or another about the private life of deer and how to bag that big one. One evening, however, I received a particularly interesting visit from a fellow named Harry. He came to see me in what I considered to be a rather agitated state.

It was the usual story. He had hunted his heart out and had developed a perpetual headache from eyestrain;

yet, a good buck was not to be found. That is the story of hundreds of other hunters I talk to annually. But, one thing really interested me: this guy owned his own land and was the only hunter on the 1,500-acre area! He had the place all to himself, but to save his own life could not kill a buck. I knew it could not possibly be due to an absence of deer, because his part of the county is crawling with them.

Going against my own rules, I agreed to go out with Harry to look the place over. As we drove along, he spoke in a staccato fashion, telling me everything he could think of regarding his land and his hunting techniques. Boy, what a place he had! It certainly was one of the best deer ranges I had seen in the area. The diversity of habitats was staggering. The topography was steeply rolling with many ravines jutting like fingers into the uplands. White oaks, red oaks, and beech were everywhere. The uplands were interspersed with numerous small openings, perfect for summer deer range.

We spent two days looking at the property, Harry showing me every inch of his hunting territory. He had, indeed, spent a great deal of time hunting the area, but he had made one glaring mistake. I asked him if he had an aerial photograph of his property. He did not, so I asked him to draw me a detailed map of his land, showing each hunting spot. I also asked him to show me all trails he used to move to and from these areas.

Slowly but surely, the story unfolded on an old brown paper bag. My grunt of disapproval was met with a look of bewilderment. I asked Harry to tell me what he saw wrong with the map. Unfortunately, he could see nothing.

It turned out that, over the years, Harry had locked himself into a pattern of hunting the same territory over and over again. Paths had been worn clean from his own footsteps. Actual hunting area did not amount to more than a few hundred acres— less than 30 percent of the tract. Harry always had seen deer in these areas, and he had killed many yearling and two-year-olds, so he just naturally assumed that this was the best place to hunt. In spite of the fact that he owned the property, Harry could not tell me what was in some portions of the place.

Hunters basically are lazy. They also are extremely conservative. The average deer hunter is very reluctant to change his hunting methods, for fear of ending the season empty-handed. I can tell a hunter about a good spot. He will agree it looks good, but then go straight back to his own hunting grounds.

The white-tailed buck is an adaptable and highly intelligent animal. We have discussed this through this book. The yearling buck or doe has little in common with him. I have observed mature bucks doing some often strangest things to escape detection. Once, on a deer drive through a 350-acre research pen, I watched a 10-pointer crawl on all fours between me and another driver not more than 30 feet away. The other fellow never saw the buck! I have seen mature bucks, when chased by a research helicopter, go to waterholes, dive in, and stick their noses

Sanctuaries and Travel Corridors

above the surface for air. And, I have observed radio-collared bucks become totally nocturnal under heavy hunting pressure. Yet, hunters continue to treat the mature buck as a dumb animal, incapable of recognizing a wooden box blind freshly placed near a scrape.

For a trophy buck, the best strategy for survival is one that is suited to the conditions under which it lives; however, one common factor can be found in every buck's survival strategy. Mature bucks try to be *where* the hunter is not, and *when* he is not. He spends much of his time in a **safe zone** or **sanctuary**— a place where the buck feels relatively safe from disturbance. This sanctuary may be in the thickest brush, the most wide-open habitat, or even several miles from the summer range. Whatever works best is quickly adopted. After all, if he makes a mistake, it costs him his life!

One day late last season, a 5-year-old buck moved quietly through a thick pine-regeneration area to look for acorns in a nearby bottom. He carefully moved well to the north of a large, green food plot. The big buck often used the plot at night, but he would not go near it during the day.

His luck had run out this day, however. A hunter bored with sitting in his stand had decided to get out and move around a bit before checking in for the morning. The buck fell with a single shot to the shoulder. A nice shot and a happy hunter. But, unfortunately, that shot also made for a most unhappy biologist. The buck was wearing one of my radio-collars, and I had hoped to follow the buck until it died of natural causes.

The buck very early had adopted a good survival strategy. He would spend most of the mornings and late afternoons in a dense growth of blackberry and greenbrier. About mid-morning, he would skirt the green plot to a small bottom. There he would feed on the acorns covering the ground beneath a huge white oak, then rest in the nearby pine thicket. Shortly after noon he would slip carefully back to his bedding spot. He moved through the pine thicket by way of a small streamside management zone left by the logging crew.

Such travel paths are called **travel corridors.** They are like the "seams" in a football team's zone defense. When first introduced into professional football, the zone defense wreaked havoc on NFL quarterbacks. But, it did not take long for coaches to learn that the zone had as many weaknesses as strengths. Quarterbacks have begun to pick apart the best of such defenses, finding the uncovered areas and hitting them. Whitetails have done the same with hunting pressure.

Each hunter in an area exerts a sphere of hunting influence. In response to earlier successes or local peer pressure, hunters quickly develop hunting habits which are as specific as a signature. For example, on one of the areas I manage, the type and position of stand tells me instantly who is hunting a particular area. In order to examine how sanctuaries and travel corridors develop, it is necessary to study the behavior of hunters, not deer.

Recently, I spent a considerable amount of time finding and mapping the locations of hunting stands on one of the national forests in East Texas. As a point of reference, I measured the distance of each stand to the nearest permanent road, power line, or pipeline right-of-way. I also recorded various characteristics of stand placement and overall deer-habitat quality. To my astonishment, the vast majority of stands were less than 1,500 feet from a permanent road! In fact, almost 30 percent of the stands were within 500 feet of the road. Obviously, the stands were placed more for the hunter's convenience than as a good place to hunt. Hunters that I actually observed approaching and leaving stands frequently drove to within 50 yards and left their vehicle within sight of the stand. One hunter had rigged a swivel seat on the back of his three-wheeler and hunted directly from the vehicle. Can you imagine a bright red motorcycle, smelling of gasoline, with a camouflaged hunter parked on top of it?

There were other strikingly similar characteristics of stand placement. The average stand was placed in such a manner as to provide maximum visibility. Average visibility distance was a little over 150 yards. The middle of a clear-cut or pasture was preferred over dense woods. I asked several hunters how they went about selecting stand locations. Few had really concrete criteria. Most offered that they placed stands where they had seen deer during scouting trips. Some said they just "guessed."

Eighty-five percent of the stands I examined had been placed in what I considered to be *poor* fall habitat. Because most stand sites were chosen during late summer or early fall, decisions were being made on what the deer were doing during the wrong part of the year.

I decided to take this analysis further. Acquiring a 7.5 minute topographical map of another national forest area. I marked off a uniform 1,500-feet **hunter influence zone** along all roads and rights-of-way. The result was astonishing. Just as with a zone defense, there were glaring holes in the hunters "defense." I tried area after area, achieving the same results each time.

Then, I tried another test on a friend who is just about the most avid trophy hunter I ever met. (And believe me, I know some rabid, card-carrying trophy hunters.) I knew only that he hunted in a generalized area of the national forest. He is extremely secretive about his hunting territory, but he takes considerable pride in the fact that he kills a trophy buck each year, virtually beneath the noses of the hunting masses on public land.

I narrowed the overall area to about 50,000 acres of prime deer habitat. Then, I applied my hunter-influence scheme to the map, but to my surprise, the entire area showed no sanctuaries, and certainly no travel corridors. Then, I decided to examine the map again. This time I noticed I had ignored one small area midway down a drainage. Marking off the 1,500-feet contour line in relation to roads, I noticed that a small, open patch suddenly appeared. "I've got you, Ron," I thought.

The next day, I was at Ron's business bright and early. I told him I had a new,

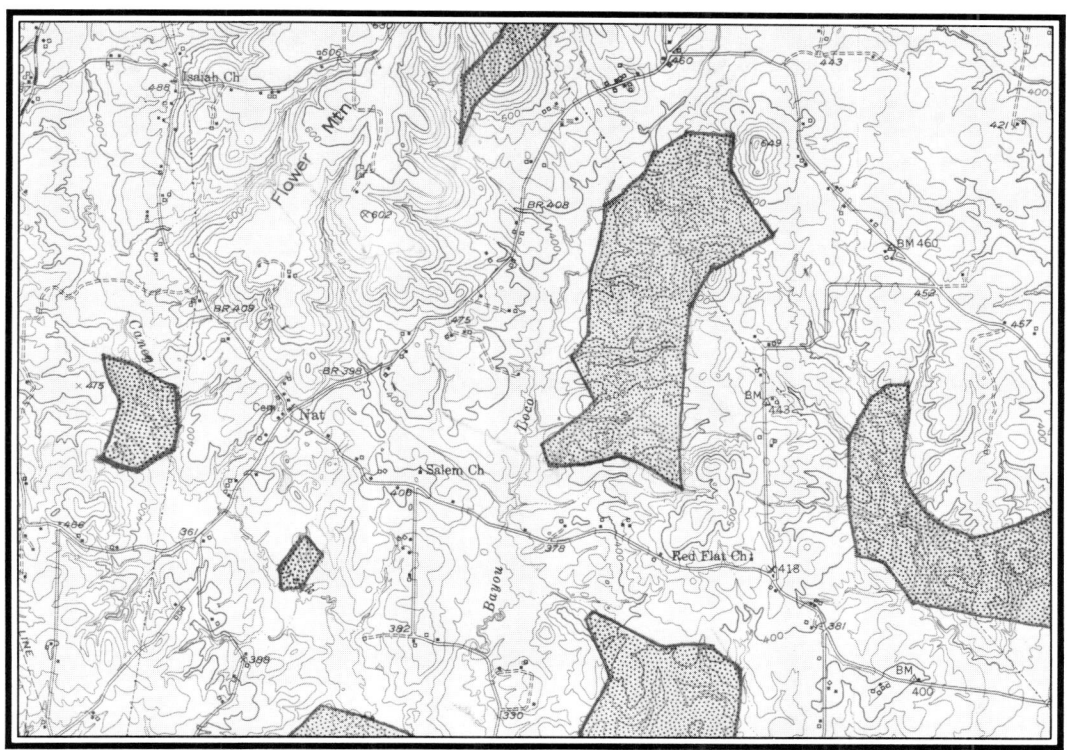

The author has found that, even on public hunting grounds, virtually all stands are within 1,500 feet of roads. The less-hunted areas (shown in gray) are potential buck sanctuaries.

scientifically developed method to determine exactly where to hunt for trophy bucks. He obviously was interested. Producing the map, I told him that I had selected randomly a map and applied my procedure to it. He did not have to say a word—the look on his face told it all. It went from surprise to pale, from pale to horror, and from horror to anger. After I calmed Ron down, I assured him his secret was safe with me, and that if he ever caught me hunting the spot, he was free to issue bodily harm. Reluctantly, he agreed to forget the whole matter and be friends again. I said he was a serious trophy hunter!

I still was not totally satisfied with the test, so I decided to go into the field for another look. We biologists have many ways to determine whether or not deer are present in an area. One of these is the browse survey. I often take unofficial browse surveys as I walk along in the woods. It really is not difficult to learn, even for the layman. All you have to know is about 20 species of plants. During late fall and early winter, deer are becoming quite desperate for something to eat. This is when they turn to the twigs of browse plants for support. The heavier the browsing, the higher the deer use in that area. (For a more detailed discussion of this technique, I suggest you return to the **Record-Keeping** chapter for an explanation.) Each

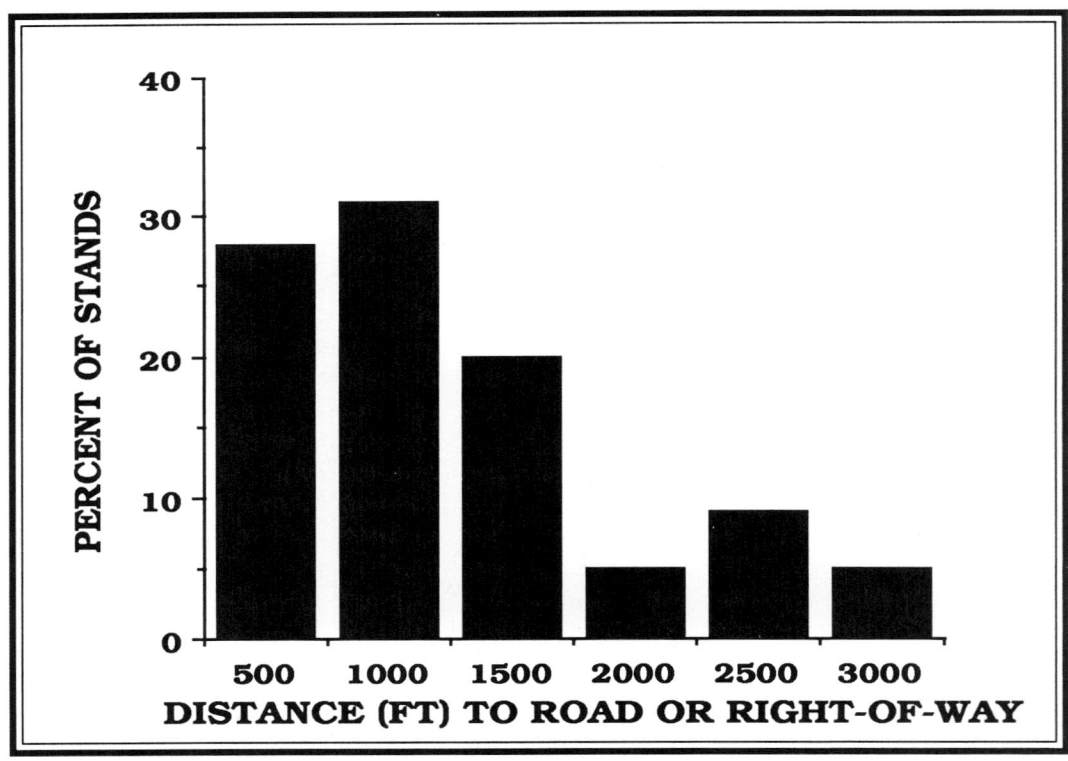

This graph clearly illustrates the author's contention that most hunters simply don't venture too far off the beaten path when hunting whitetails, even in a wide-open and heavily pressured national forest. The author's research with radio-collared bucks indicates that they adjust to pressure by moving into relatively unhunted areas.

Sanctuaries and Travel Corridors

of my mapped sanctuaries and travel corridors showed higher utilization of browse plants than did hunter-influence zones. One more piece of evidence to support the concept.

The next obvious step is to study deer movements under actual hunting conditions. Fortunately, I have been doing just that for several years now, and have accumulated a good bit of data on movements of bucks and their responses to hunter activity.

WHERE DO BUCKS GO UNDER HEAVY HUNTING PRESSURE?

In 1975, I began a research project that was to delve into the innermost secrets of the daily lives of white-tailed deer. The project was aimed at examining the impact of forestry practices on deer behavior and population biology, and I soon discovered there still is much to be learned about the behavior of these creatures.

You could fill up a standard-sized den with all of the publications, both technical and popular, that have been written about whitetails. In spite of this, however, the trophy whitetail buck remains one of the most elusive game animals in the world. Serious trophy hunters may venture far and wide for exotic trophies, but many of them eventually return to spend their lives hunting that trophy buck.

Despite all of the research done on deer, little really is known about the behavior of bucks. If you examine most of the radio-telemetry studies published, the vast majority of the observations reported are of does, not bucks.

Researchers learned the hard way what hunters already knew; it is downright difficult to capture or kill a mature buck. That is precisely why you will read in most technical publications that the author(s) is reporting on the movements of 10 to 20 does and 2 to 3 bucks, most of which are yearlings.

There currently are two comprehensive research projects dealing specifically with the behavior of whitetail bucks: one at Stephen F. Austin State University, in the Pineywoods of East Texas, and the other at Mississippi State University. Dr. Harry Jacobson, who directs the project at Mississippi State, laments that, "The animal that everyone is most interested in is the mature whitetail buck. But, it is %@#& difficult to capture one! Consequently, we know little about their true behavior."

Dr. Jacobson is studying one of the most interesting populations of whitetails in North America. He is observing the responses of bucks in the Mississippi Delta to hunting, management, and periodic catastrophic floods. In my opinion, he is dealing with a unique race of deer. These animals have evolved in an environment that dictates that they be highly mobile as a pre-adaptation to flooding. Some of his bucks have home ranges that include two states!

Whitetails always have used travel corridors to move from one area of suitable habitat or protection to another. The literature is filled with accounts of such deer migrations. Dr. Jacobson feels the travel corridors used by deer in the Delta to move from one

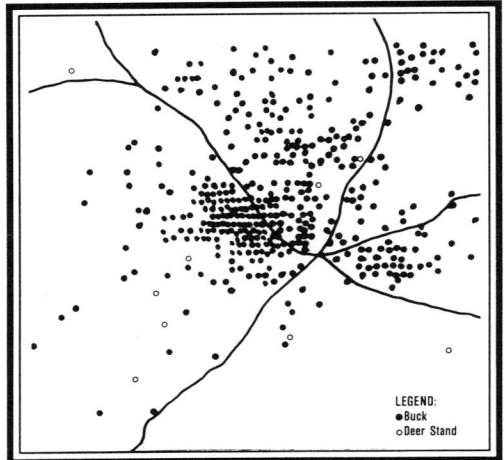

The map above shows plotted locations of radio-collared bucks on North Boggy Slough Hunting Club during the spring and summer. Bucks roam freely over the entire area during these periods of non-hunitng, and frequently are seen by visitors to the club.

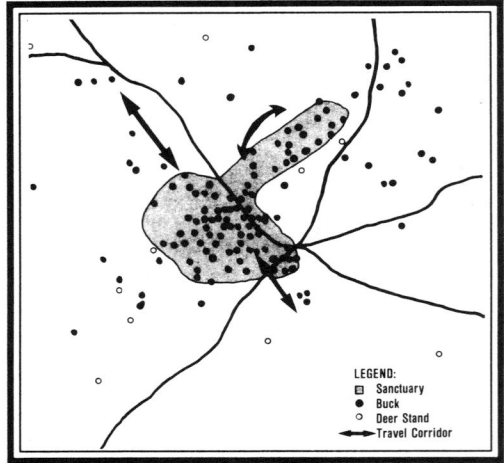

During the hunting season, mature bucks seldom were radio-tracked in the vicinity of established stands (circles); rather, they retreated to undisturbed sanctuary areas (gray zone) and moved primarily along safe travel corridors (arrows).

high spot to another are ancestral. Deer always cross at the same place, utilizing the existing levee system for travel. Likewise, I am working with the Diamond H Ranch in South Texas. Recently, I came upon an old map of the ranch developed by a trapper named Swede Bingamin (sic). He had very carefully drawn all of the "deer runs" on the map. To my delight, these are the same travel corridors used by the deer even today.

But, if we have known about travel corridors for some time now, why is it news to hunters? Previous studies have reported on migrations of populations, not single individuals. Hunters do not hunt populations— they hunt individual deer. Only recently have the highly individualized movement patterns of specific bucks come to light.

In spite of the differences in Mississippi and Texas deer, Dr. Jacobson and I have discovered similar behavior patterns in mature bucks. More recently, I have observed these same patterns in bucks living in Canada, the Mid-West and Mexico. They learn very quickly to

Sanctuaries and Travel Corridors

avoid hunting pressure. "There is no doubt," Dr. Jacobson says, "that deer activity during the hunting season is a direct function of hunter density." In essence, the more hunters you have in the woods, the more deer will change their normal behavior patterns. Such changes are aimed at avoiding human contact.

Methods used by each deer to avoid human contact are unique to the particular situation, and often are related to the hunting history of the area. Bucks are more difficult to kill in heavily hunted areas than are those protected from excessive pressure. That is precisely why some trophy hunters prefer to haunt the more heavily hunted areas. It presents a challenge. Hunting bucks on a large ranch, with little or no hunting pressure, offers little in the way of challenge.

Dr. Jacobson radio-collared several bucks on a private hunting club, and all were killed during the very next season. The club protects its deer, controls hunting pressure, and is generally organized about its hunting. On a heavily hunted public area, however, Dr. Jacobson collared six bucks, all of which survived the hunting season. "I couldn't get one buck through the hunting season on a management area," he notes, "yet all six of those guys made it on a heavily hunted public area. That should tell you something about the ability of the whitetail buck to survive."

I have been radio-tracking bucks for some time now on North Boggy Slough Hunting and Fishing Club and the Cherokee Family Hunting Clubs here in East Texas. Boggy is unique in that it has one of the oldest deer populations in the state. Thanks to Temple-Inland, a forestry-products company, there were deer on Boggy Slough when you would have been hard pressed to find a deer anywhere else in East Texas. Deer on this area have been hunted continuously for 50 years. So, it comes as no surprise that trophy bucks are not very easy to kill there. Bill Goodrum, a second-generation biologist who manages the area, feels that the only way to harvest a trophy is to be aware of the many sanctuaries and travel corridors used by the bucks of Boggy Slough. My radio-telemetry observations fully support his claim.

In order to better understand how bucks utilize sanctuaries and travel corridors, let's examine some of the unique movement patterns we have observed in North Boggy Slough deer. One buck in particular comes to mind. We do not give names to our animals as some researchers do, so let's call him Buck No. 82. We feel giving names to animals over-humanizes them, but old No. 82 surely was a nice buck! We radio-collared 82 when he was a yearling. He was captured by drop net on one of our many green food plots, along with his mother.

During the first year of radio-tracking, No. 82 remained within a few hundred acres of the capture site. The spring following capture showed 82 away from his mother, who by now had another fawn. He became one of the most predictable deer we had. In order to obtain a radiolocation on the buck, all you had to do was drive down the main road. He could be located easily within a few hundred yards of the road. On some occasions, we even saw him before we received a location: he was that dependable.

Buck No. 82 survived his first hunting season in good shape. Several hunters had reported seeing the young spike on nearby green plots, but had refrained from shooting him.

That season was the last time No. 82 could be found easily during the hunting season. By his second year, we researchers were the only individuals who ever could get a glimpse of him. By this time, he was a six-pointer of moderate antler spread for his age. We rarely saw him with any other bucks; he apparently preferred his own company over that of the group— a highly unusual behavior.

Up until October of his second year, No. 82 remained fairly predictable. By November, however, he was gone. He just seemed to vanish. One day he was there, the next he was not. We justifiably assumed that his radio had malfunctioned, and marked the deer off our "active" list after a month or so of searching. But, the following March we were shocked to find his transmitter happily beeping away from the same home range area.

Could the transmitter have reinstated itself? Not very likely. He had to have gone somewhere, and the next October we were ready for him. But the son-of-a-gun did it again! He just disappeared into thin air.

In December, the security man on the area told us of a nice buck he had seen some seven miles away, in a large creek bottom. It was an area nobody hunted, as it lay between two clubs. The exciting thing was that the buck was wearing a radio-collar! We searched for the buck in that region, and sure enough, old No. 82 was down there, all right. We had discovered his secret to survival. He had found the "seam" in our "zone defense." The following March, there he was right back in his old home range. Ironically, it would be some years later that I killed one of my biggest bucks adjacent to this same sanctuary.

Buck No. 82 repeated this behavior every year until he finally was shot by a

Robert Skinner

Permanent stands are quickly located by older bucks, allowing them to "pattern" the hunters.

Sanctuaries and Travel Corridors

fellow who drifted down into the creek bottom to try a new spot. The buck had successfully eluded hunters until maturity. He was killed quite by accident. That is when we really became interested in buck movements.

The literature published on buck movements mostly had concluded that buck and doe home ranges were somewhat similar in size, with bucks having slightly larger home ranges. Our research has shown that, during part of the year, this probably is true. During the rut and hunting season, however, this may not be the case at all. Some of our bucks have remained stationary, while others have adopted No. 82's strategy. Buck No. 5 was one such buck.

We captured No. 5 as we had No. 82— on a small food plot as a fawn with his mother. He was just a button buck at the time, and I really did not give him much chance to survive the first winter. But, I collared him anyway and hoped. The young buck did survive, and remained on the area for many years. He was a dominant buck on the property. Buck No. 5 gave us some more insight into how bucks think.

During his first year, I checked the progress of our radio-tracking program. A computer printout of deer locations showed one lone location way to the north of No. 5's home range. Naturally, I accused my students, who were assisting me in the research, of taking a bogus data point. I was wrong; they had checked it out already, and had confirmed No. 5 indeed had traveled up tot that area for a brief visit. But, what was so special about that area? The only thing we could find different was an absence of hunting pressure there.

During the following season, we discovered exactly why No. 5 had gone to that spot. No. 5 took off suddenly in November. We do not know if the movement was in response to hunting or the rut, but he did take off. And, guess where he went? He traveled directly to that "pre-scouted" spot. From there he drifted far to the East, then South, finally ending up the following spring right where he had originated. He repeated this behavior every year, with the only difference being that he always took different routes.

This buck never was seen by any hunter on the area, and seldom by the resident biologist. I saw him on only three occasions, each time for only a fleeting moment. He was an extremely fine, heavy antlered buck.

But, what about those bucks that stay pretty much stationary? We have been amazed by the fact that even these bucks seldom are seen by hunters. Buck No. 63 was one of these deer, but he was unlucky enough to make a single fatal mistake. He ventured too close to a food plot.

Now that we have accumulated a large number of movement observations (better than 15,000) on bucks at both Boggy Slough and Cherokee, we can begin to make some generalizations about their defensive behavior patterns. Movements of bucks during the spring and summer growing periods are fairly uniform over the area. The two plottings of buck locations from Boggy Slough gives a good explanation to what bucks are doing before and after the season begins. In the spring and summer, hunters often see bucks running in groups; however, the fact that you see a buck in an area during the warm season is no guarantee you will see him there during the hunting season!

When hunting season rolls around, most of our mature bucks retreat to the more inaccessible areas (sanctuaries), and they travel to and from these areas via travel corridors. The plotting clearly shows how bucks use these areas to avoid hunters. The most intriguing thing about these observations is that hunting stands, which traditionally have been used on this area, are avoided like the plague by the older bucks, especially late in the season. Yearling bucks, on the other hand, use the green plots and stand areas with little regard for their own personal safety.

Once we began to understand the survival strategies of mature bucks, we initiated a program to improve our harvest of older-age-class bucks. Area Manager Bill Goodrum had become quite frustrated by the later part of the 1983-84 season, for instance. We all knew he had several top-quality bucks out there, but hunters just were not seeing them. Bill decided to make a very gutsy change. He decided to move his hunters from the traditional stands to temporary blinds along travel corridors and sanctuaries. (The Boggy Slough story is discussed in detail in a separate chapter.)

The result was dramatic. Some of the biggest bucks to be harvested up until that time were taken during that short period. A graduate student of mine, Dr. Bill Wall, killed his first and probably biggest buck during one of these "surprise" hunts: a trophy with 18+ inch tall antlers! The following season, Bill Goodrum repeated his new strategy, but varyied stand placement just a bit. The bucks soon adjusted to this new strategy. Obviously, we had to be as adaptable as are the big bucks in order to maintain a quality trophy harvest on the area.

HOW TO ID BUCK SANCTUARIES

To attempt a description of a typical buck sanctuary is an impossible task. No two sanctuaries are alike. Each buck arrives at his own distinct survival pattern; one which is custom fitted to the particular situation. However, there are some general characteristics that typify buck sanctuaries. First, let's look at these general commonalities and then take a specific look at three different bucks, living in three real-life situations.

The concept of buck sanctuaries is completely logical on close examination. Ask yourself, "If I were a big buck, where would I go and how would I behave to avoid detection?" The obvious answer is a place where hunters seldom venture, and a place which gives you more than one way to escape detection should your sanctuary be violated. Such places exist on almost every piece of property. They may be dense thickets of undergrowth, heavily stocked pine plantations, or even places that are well away form roads and access. They should also be places where the approach of a hunter is easily

Sanctuaries and Travel Corridors

detected, by sight, sound, smell or all three. Sanctuaries should afford protection from the elements as well. By now, you should be thinking about some area on your hunting ground that fits this description. Now let's examine three different real-life bucks, and see how each selected and used his own sanctuary.

Bucky

I knew Bucky for most of his life, first as a whitetail biologist, and later as his death sentence. I do not normally give names to the bucks I study, but this particular buck merited more than a mere number. I first became aware of Bucky's presence when he was a yearling. As part of my research on whitetails, I regularly conduct habitat analyses to determine browse utilization and overall habitat conditions. It was on one of these trips that I disturbed a five-point yearling bedded down in an open pine plantation. It was summer, and it seemed perfectly logical to me for him to be there. There was plenty of shade, and a cool breeze was blowing through the pines. Startled, he jumped up and ran into a nearby stream bottom. Each time I returned to the stand, I found Bucky bedded down pretty much in the same place. But, then fall came and Bucky disappeared.

The next summer, I once again encountered what I considered to be a nice two- or three-year-old buck bedded down in the exact same area. The more I thought about it, the more I became convinced that it was indeed "Bucky." As far as I was concerned, he was a lucky buck to have survived the hunting season, as that is one of the heaviest hunted areas in the county. Since he obviously showed great potential, I decided to watch him and attempt to get a radio on him. My attempts to radio-collar the buck were, unfortunately, unsuccessful, but I did return regularly to study his behavior. One thing I most definitely wanted to know was, where did he go in the fall?

Just like clockwork, Bucky disappeared the next fall. I was determined to find the buck's sanctuary. I made a detailed drawing of the habitat and terrain of the area. The pine stand in

Big bucks like this learn early to avoid "regular" hunters. To bag him, you've got to find his hideout.

which Bucky spent the summer was located adjacent to a large agricultural field, but the field was split in two pieces by a small stream. The stream traveled from the pine thicket, through the field and into a hardwood bottom about a mile away. The stream bottom had been cleared about 15 years previous, and was now an impenetrable tangle of saplings and vines. This was particularly the case in a bend of the stream. This is where I decided to center my search. Sure enough, there in the thickest vegetation, I found numerous rubs during October. Soon, scrapes began to appear along the stream slope. I decided to spend some time watching the two paths leading to and from the area. Before long, I had Bucky pretty well figured out in regard to his daily movements. As the rut developed to its full intensity, he began to venture farther and farther along the stream bottom. By November, he had scrapes all along the ridges above the stream, extending for more than a mile.

Bucky repeated this behavior pattern until the day of his death at 8 years of age. He reached peak antler development at 6 and began to show signs of deteriorating by 7. I decided that his time had come the following season. Since I knew the two established escape routes from his sanctuary, it was simply a matter of deciding which of the two to hunt. One of the paths led to a green food plot, while the other led to an oak bottom. I flipped a coin and the oak-bottom path won. The buck failed to appear. The next day, I repeated the process with the same results. But, the third attempt paid off. I traveled to a pre-chosen site about 40 yards upwind from the trail. Using a backpack stand, I climbed about 20 feet up into a pine and settled down to wait. The buck appeared around 11:30 a.m., walking in a slow, foot dragging gait. Bucky now hangs on my wall in a place of honor; a fitting end to a fine buck. But you know, there is another buck now occupying that same sanctuary. Perhaps, he, too, will adorn my wall or that of a friend. Will Rogers once said, "I never met a man I didn't like." In my case, I seldom shoot a buck I have not known for some time.

Kicker

Many hunters spend a great deal of time hunting the various hardwood bottoms. It is much more difficult to pattern a buck in hardwood country, especially if there is a large tract of land involved. This is primarily due to the highly migratory nature of deer in frequently flooded forests. We have recorded movements of several miles in such deer, some even swimming rivers in flood stage to escape hunting pressure. One such deer was "Kicker" (later dubbed the "The Ghost of Boggy Slough").

This particular buck was around for about 6 years, and, to my knowledge, was never seen by a single hunter, in spite of the fact that there are more than 20 hunters per day in the area. Kicker received his name from the tremendous atypical set of antlers, complete with numerous kicker points. I first noticed Kicker in the early 1980's when he was a yearling. I remember the buck for two reasons. First, he had the most incredibly deformed set of yearling antlers I have ever seen. And second, he lived smack dab in the middle of one of my study plots. To this day I never have known where the buck went in the spring and summer; however, let the rut come around, and there he was right where I saw him last season. I determined that the big buck spent the warm season within the hardwood bottom. I spent a great deal of time there, but never saw him.

The unique thing about this particular buck was that his sanctuary lay exactly in a "no man's land" border between two hunting clubs. Neither club has ever erected a stand there for fear of incurring the other club's wrath. The entire sanctuary area is no more than 50 acres within an extensive bottom of at least 2,000 acres. But, that little 50-acre area receives no hunting pressure, and is an island between two branches of the same stream. When the buck left the island, he usually swam the stream after dark, and returned just at daylight. I even recorded the buck feeding on an oat patch around 2 a.m. The fellow that hunts the oat patch complains incessantly about the lack of good bucks in the area.

Later on, Kicker's sanctuary was disturbed by a timber harvest and he moved to another area. It was in his sixth and final year that I would take his life. The story of the Boggy Slough Monster is given consideration in another chapter (see **The Ghost of Boggy Slough**).

Urbanite

So far, I have discussed two commonly occurring types of sanctuaries— bottomland forest and mixed woodland-agriculture. Now I would like to discuss a most interesting buck I later called "Urbanite." This particular buck was unique in that he spent the entire hunting season within 100 yards of a housing development. There was a small brushy incursion into the development that lies between people's yards and the fairway of a golf course! About three-quarters of a mile away from his refuge was a rather large hunting club, the members of which often saw the big buck all during the summer. The buck had become somewhat of a celebrity among the members. They tried every way possible to kill the buck, short of breaking the law, but no hunter ever got a shot at the buck. Now this may seem highly unusual to you, but let me relate three similar cases that ended in quality bucks being harvested.

Clyde Neeley is a good friend of mine from Eunice, Louisiana. Clyde is an excellent hunter and shot, and has been known to pass up bucks for several years rather than shoot a small one. Just prior to the 1985-86 hunting season, Clyde told me that he had one of his patented feelings about the upcoming season. "I just know it is my year," he said. "It's time to shoot the big one." Clyde was hunting as usual on the South Fork Ranch near Kerrville, Texas. Ranch managers had told Clyde about a great double drop-tined buck seen by helicopter several miles form the camp house. Clyde really wanted that buck and hunted all over the ranch for him. He finally got the buck, but guess where? Clyde shot the buck within sight of the camp house, near an old junkpile. There is no way of knowing how long the buck had been using the area for a sanctuary, but being in the right place netted Clyde the buck of a lifetime.

Harry Jacobson of Mississippi State University reports that a Boone and Crockett record-book animal was taken in the suburbs of Starkville, Mississippi. Harry took semen from the buck and later artificially inseminated some does with the dead buck's sperm.

Finally, the famous Albertson buck of Trinity County, Texas, was killed within easy distance of the Brushy Creek Club House of Champion Paper Co. I wonder how many guests drove past that buck, probably bedded down near the road, without ever seeing him?

HOW TO HUNT TRAVEL CORRIDORS AND SANCTUARIES

It was the end of December, and it was colder than a wrought-iron toilet seat at the North Pole. I was feeling sort of ridiculous, because I was hiding in a small clump of Texas persimmon, smack-dab in the middle of a sheep pasture. I pulled up my collar against the piercing Hill Country wind and settled down to wait. Gazing sleepily at the 100 or so sheep feeding in front of me, I hoped no one would see me there. A few hundred yards away, automobiles were darting back and forth down the highway.

Back at the camp, my partners had little idea as to where I was hunting. It was midday, and by now they probably were all sound asleep in their ritualistic nap. They had come to think of me as being pretty much crazy anyway, and had long since accepted anything I did as normal for me.

Actually, it was really quite simple. We all had been desperately trying for some time to kill a tremendous buck. The monster had been seen on numerous occasions, all at inopportune times, throughout this ranch. He appeared to have no set pattern and no favorite place. I wanted more than anything to kill that buck, so I decided to apply some logic to the situation. The buck had to be somewhere on the ranch, because surrounding landowners and hunters had not reported either seeing or killing such an animal, and they surely would have. He just *had* to be there somewhere.

Now, where was absolutely the least likely place for the big buck to be? The answer came in a flash. The rancher wintered his sheep on a large oat field near the state highway bordering the property. From the road it looked completely flat, but I knew better. During a dove hunt in September, I found a small ridge paralleling the highway. The ridge had about three or four feet of elevation, and I had hidden successfully behind it to surprise the low flying doves as they flashed across the field in a high wind. The ridge would make a perfect travel corridor for a crafty old buck to move from a dense thicket of shinnery oak on one end of the field to a deep ravine on the other.

The bleating of the sheep was becoming annoying when I noticed a small, gray figure moving slowly through the herd. The deer was following the protective relief of the ridge. Through the scope, I quickly determined that the diminutive figure was a doe, picking her way slowly through the white bodies. *They aren't supposed to like sheep,* I thought, and there did seem to be an expression of distaste on her face. She moved on across the field and down into the ravine. Once again, I huddled as close to the ground as possible; there is nothing but a fence or two

---

When hunting pressure becomes more than big bucks care to deal with, what do they do? Their choices are simple: either vacate the area or retreat to the nastiest cover available in the vicinity. Through his radio-tracking studies on hunted bucks, the author has determined that many trophy deer simply abandon their "homes" until the season is over, then return. This can present the hunter with special problems.

Mike Biggs

between the Texas Hill Country and the Arctic Circle. No more than a minute had passed when I noticed another gray figure following the protective ridge. "Another doe," I thought, casually peering through my scope.

I really do not remember much after that, although I do recall saying loudly, *It's the buck!* I just threw the .30/06 to my shoulder and fired instinctively. (I spend a great deal of time practicing just that action.) The trophy went down as if his legs had been cut from under him. I ran excitedly toward the monster, literally wading through half-crazed sheep; after the shot, the woolly beasts had gone berserk. A horrible feeling came over me, and I hesitantly looked around for white carcasses, as it suddenly dawned on me that I had not cleared my shot—something I would scorn my hunters for doing today. To my relief, no dead sheep were to be seen.

The big buck lay on his belly, his legs tucked neatly under his body. His head was outstretched, and those magnificent tines seemed to stick into the sky. This buck was bigger than I ever had imagined. His net Boone and Crockett score was 167 7/8 inches. My success had been the result of a combination of good guessing and a willingness to try something new.

I was a mere lad then, and I knew little about the private lives of whitetails. That probably was to my favor. Today, after years of scientific study, I have managed to ferret out the very secrets of trophy whitetail hunting used by the few truly outstanding hunters on this continent. And, these

This buck was bagged by understanding how whitetails react to hunting pressure. If deer there feel threatened by even a normal amount of hunting pressure, they will adapt their lifestyle to avoid humans at all cost.

techniques differ little from those I used on that cold December day.

Surely, by now, the preponderance of information gathered by me and the many other whitetail researchers has convinced you that old bucks adopt survival strategies which guarantee that the average hunter never will have a chance to bag such an animal. The survival strategy adopted by each buck certainly is unique, but each shares a common secret. Big bucks try to be where the hunter is not, when he is not. **In order to kill one of these magnificent animals, you must stop thinking like a hunter, and start thinking like a deer.** You must decide early on whether or not you wish to become a hunter of mature bucks or a shooter of lesser deer. Once you make the decision to hunt trophy whitetails, heaven help you! You are doomed to a life of frustration, loneliness, and on rare occasions, the ultimate in satisfaction. Noted Houston trophy hunter Mike Tate says, "Trophy hunting is a disease. It is never cured, and is usually terminal." That's only a slight exaggeration.

Trophy whitetails are hunted under one of two basic conditions. First, there is a growing trend toward hunting clubs and leases. This trend probably began in Texas, but it is now spreading across the South and other parts of the country. No matter what you think about leases, they are the wave of the future. The hunting club offers the hunter several advantages, among which are safety, regulated hunting pressure, and often a controlled harvest. Unfortunately, however, many clubs now are under what could be considered highly artificial intensive-management programs, in which even the genetics of whitetails are being manipulated.

The second— and most common— situation is the public hunting area. Although presenting much more of a challenge, public hunting areas are often less intensively managed. That is precisely why I like them! These lands include the public forests, open corporate lands, and state-owned management areas. The intensity of management on these management areas differs with each agency involved.

The trophy-hunting strategy adopted depends upon which of these two conditions you select. Hunting clubs are the easiest to analyze, especially if they have been in operation for some time. Hunters develop habits which are as characteristic as their handwriting. On some of the clubs I manage, I pretty well can tell you who is hunting that area. If you have just joined such a club, the first thing to do is sit down with each of its members for a talk. Get them to show you their individual hunting territories on a map or photograph of the property.

Now, you probably are saying, "Wait a minute! No hunter in his right mind is going to tell me where he hunts!" You may be surprised, though, because on private hunting clubs, territoriality takes precedence over secrecy. Plot each of the hunting stands and areas on the map or photograph. Next, you need to eliminate the influence of roads on deer movements. Because the vast majority of hunters seldom venture more than 1,500 feet from a road, mark off this **influence zone** right from the start. Be sure to include all rights-of-way within the influence zones.

If you are new to the club, you probably will be relegated to what most of the hunters feel are the poorest areas. That assessment may not be correct, however. If some time has passed since the club was formed, what once was considered poor hunting territory now may be just the opposite. These unhunted areas are found quickly by older bucks and are accepted readily as *sanctuaries*. There have been many instances in which a new member, to everyone's surprise, comes in on opening day with the club's biggest buck of the year. This usually is written off to dumb luck, and everyone else returns to their old habits!

The best time to join a hunting club or scout a public area is just at the end of the season, especially when it is of several weeks' duration or longer. This is the perfect time to scout out the best places to hunt the following year. Most of the hunters have become tired of the place by this time, and are turning their interests to the Super Bowl and spring fishing. In late winter, bucks will be doing just about what they were at the close of the season; however, they will be a little less wary and more approachable. Identify the potential sanctuaries as given above. Visit each of these areas and look for the subtle signs of a big buck. A rubbed tree that looks suspiciously fresher than the others, a narrow but well-worn trail from a thicket, or several well-packed beds on the southern exposure of a hillside all demand further attention. Mark all of these observations on your map. Finally, spend a great deal of time in the woods at midday. This is the time when bucks are most active during winter. Their fat reserves have been depleted by the rut, and they now are trying to find nourishment.

By opening day, you should have formulated a season-long hunting strategy. The first few days of the season should find you using tactics similar to those used by the other hunters. But, keep two things in mind. First, direct your hunting efforts to potential travel corridors. As noted earlier, hunting territories are like the zone defense in football. Big bucks will try to pick apart these defenses by traveling in the corridors (seams) between them. **Even at the beginning of the season, trophy bucks will try to limit their movements to the late-morning and early-afternoon hours.** These are the times you need to be out there, times when most of the membership will be back in camp, playing cards and napping. If you are lucky enough to find a scrape along one of the travel corridors, please do not camp directly on it! Instead, find yourself a good vantage point well away form the scrape, preferably down wind, and watch the trail passing near it.

Second, always leave your bucks a sanctuary during the early part of a long season. Such areas should be *sacrosanct*. Stay away from them at all costs. Some of my hunting clubs actually designate sanctuaries into which no hunter is ever allowed to go. If you are caught hunting a sanctuary, your membership can be forfeited.

As hunting pressure increases, bucks gravitate to their sanctuaries, seldom venturing away from them in the daylight hours. On East Texas' North Boggy Slough Hunting and Fishing Club, which I have helped manage for many years, sanctuaries are characterized by small, extremely dense pockets of pine saplings. It is virtually impossible to walk through some of these thickets. The big bucks stay in their sanctuaries during the day, and travel to feeding areas under the cover of darkness. If you try to enter a sanctuary, the bucks have little difficulty slipping out the other side, unnoticed. That is precisely why hunters of the old northern hunting camps used drives and standers to flush out the big bucks. This certainly was not good conservation, but it was effective. Once sanctuaries are violated, however, the game is over. On one of my hunting clubs, excessive hunting pressure and repeated harassment in sanctuaries drove the big bucks completely from the tract— to the delight of surrounding clubs. Years of management work were wasted in one season! Radio-collars proved that some of the bucks even traveled 14 miles to a new sanctuary, returning long after the season was over.

The decision to invade a sanctuary should be made only after early-season tactics have failed, and you are ready to pay the price of making a mistake. There is no room for failure now. The trick is to slip into the sanctuary, kill your buck, and get out with as little disturbance as possible: a not-too-simple task. That is where the scouting you did late last year comes into play. If you have done your homework carefully, you should have a pretty good idea of where the bucks will be. You should know by then where they are hiding, and the travel corridors leading from the sanctuary. Now, the hard part.

If you are not prepared to stay all day, you might as well forget it. Slip in well before daylight, find your vantage point, and wait all day if necessary. Never move during the day. When hunting sanctuaries, I use every trick and gimmick I have at my disposal. I use gray camouflage, a cryptically colored backpack ladder stand, and odor neutralizer. If I fail to see a buck or the one I want, I stay and use the time to plan the next hunt. After dark I pack up my gear and slip quietly out of the woods. Take your time, and make as little noise as possible.

Sanctuaries never should be hunted on consecutive days. Always wait a

Mike Biggs

There is no set description of a sanctuary. Each buck finds a set of conditions that best suit its survival instincts.

day or two between hunts, and always take a different route into the sanctuary. You have to learn to be as devious as a big buck. When the big moment arrives, will you truly be prepared?

Russell Thornberry, famed Canadian trophy-whitetail outfitter and hunting writer, tells me his hunters seldom have more than three or four seconds in which to decide whether or not to

---

The author has found that producing bucks such as this is no simple task, but harvesting them may be even tougher! Once deer season opens, the veteran bucks instantly recognize the warning signs of hunting pressure and go into hiding, usually in the thickest and/or most remote areas available to them. Hunters who continue to "follow the crowd" and hunt the same old places in the same old ways stand little chance of taking the mature bucks. Study a topographic map of the area and correlate it to hunting pressure, and you probably can locate the buck sanctuaries.

Mike Biggs

shoot and then take that shot if they choose to do so. Unfortunately, few hunters are indeed ready to take that shot. How much of the off-season do you spend getting into good physical condition? How much time do you spend practicing shooting off-handed prior to the season? (See **The Art of Shooting Deer** for more details.)

Assuming you are prepared to make that one shot, let me give you a few tried-and-true hints to improve your odds of success. First, if there is any doubt in your mind as to whether or not the buck is a trophy, he probably is not; a true trophy is obvious from the first glance. Second, once you decide to shoot, never, never look at his antlers again. This especially is true for bowhunters. You can do that when he is on the ground.

Your next concern is how you are going to kill him. Because you are after a trophy, not just meat, forget the fancy shots. The neck and head are not good places to shoot a buck. No matter how good a shot you are, there will come a time when you miss— or worse yet, wound a perfectly good trophy animal. A buck who has lived for years dodging hunters and who has grown a magnificent set of antlers does not deserve to be treated like a mere target. Finally, shoot until he is down and out. Many good bucks have been lost because hunters failed to take those additional shots.

When you finally have that big buck down, your job still is not over. I prefer to get my trophy out of the sanctuary as quickly and quietly as possible. This is much easier to do on private clubs than on public lands, as all you have to do is pack him out. There is far less danger of being accidentally shot by another hunter, although you still should exercise caution.

Public-land hunting presents an altogether different challenge. Because it is impossible to talk with each of the hunters who will be sharing the area, you will be forced to resort to indirect methods. As noted earlier, few hunters venture more than a few hundred yards away from the road or right-of-way. Why? I really do not know. Perhaps it is a matter of convenience, or maybe a reluctance to travel into unfamiliar terrain. At any rate, the phenomenon does occur, and you can take advantage of it.

Obtain a map or photograph of the prospective area early in the year. As on private hunting clubs, mark off the influence zones for roads and rights-of-way. The next step is to travel to the area in late winter for the kind of scouting recommended earlier. **On public hunting areas, however, you need to select many potential sanctuaries and travel corridors, as you may find them occupied on opening day.** Always have an alternative area in mind prior to going into the field.

Never drive into the woods. Since other writers and I began authoring how-to magazine articles on trophy-buck hunting, many hunters have adopted the spirit of what we are saying, but their execution leaves much to be desired. The fact that travel corridors and sanctuaries exist does not mean that if you drive deeper into the woods, your success will improve. It is the exact opposite. Last year, the national forests I checked were alive with three and four-wheel all-terrain vehicles. Now, I have nothing against these vehicles; I have used them for years myself. What I do object to is improper use. The whitetail is a very careful animal, and it does not like anything new in its territory. Any unusual disturbance elicits defensive behavior patterns. Can you imagine the impact of a three-wheeler roaring into a sanctuary? Foot travel is still the best way to hunt trophy deer. Leave your vehicle well outside the sanctuary.

The latter part of the season is the best time to hunt trophy bucks on public lands. Harvest records from various wildlife agencies indicate that the vast majority of hunting pressure occurs during the first week to 10 days of the season (in areas where there is a lengthy season). After that, most of the easy bucks have been harvested, and hunters rapidly lose interest. By the last week of the season, you pretty much can have the woods to yourself. I like to keep track of my sanctuaries throughout the early part of the season. I regularly check to see which are being visited by hunters and which are being ignored. By the last week, you may be surprised to discovered how many sanctuaries have received absolutely no hunting effort. These are the places and this is the time I love to hunt. It is a lonely existence, but a most enjoyable one. I try to slip into an area and hunt all day. Often, I will not cover more than a few hundred yards during the 12 or so hours of daylight.

SUMMARY

Hunters too often become stereotyped in their hunting methods, allowing bucks to develop avoidance strategies which successfully allow them to remain undetected even on the most heavily hunted areas. Whitetails are preadapted to seek sanctuaries and to use travel corridors to move to and from these areas. You may feel that all of these recommendations are a lot of trouble, and that this type of hunting is not for you. That is all right; this type of hunting certainly is not for everyone. But, just being aware that trophy bucks are intelligent animals that adjust to your presence is enough to improve your success. If you follow my recommendations, however, your chances of harvesting a real trophy will be enhanced greatly. At least, they will until those big bucks come up with some new tricks of their own. And, I know they will!

Chapter 25

Mike Biggs

UNDERSTANDING BROWSING PATTERNS

A few years ago, a hunting club hired me as a whitetail management consultant. The club lands were owned by a timber company, which planned to do some clear-cutting on the property. The club members objected strongly to these actions, and both the company and the club had decided to hire a consultant for an independent opinion.

I arrived at the property early one morning, and after spending that day and one more walking around the woods there, I filed my report. It simply stated that there was a far greater problem to be dealt with than clear-cutting. The club's deer herd was in terrible shape, hovering close to the brink of a population crash.

You would not believe the reaction of the club members to my report. I received numerous nasty letters and phone calls, some questioning my parentage! One member asked me how much time I had spent on the property; upon hearing I had been there for two days, he exploded in laughter. "You mean to tell me that you only spent two days on our club," he chuckled, "and from that you decided that our deer herd was in trouble?"

Now, in earlier times, I would have hung my head and tried to reason with the man, using all of the scientific know-how I could muster. But, those were the old days. Instead, I looked the man straight in the eye and informed him that he obviously knew little about whitetails, no matter how long he had hunted on the property. We almost came to blows at that point, but after he cooled down, I agreed to visit the property again— with him tagging along.

As we strolled around the forest, I literally could see an awakening sense of awareness on his face. I showed him the most favored deer-browse species, pointing out how each had been eaten to the ground. Then, I showed him species that were eaten only by deer when the animals were in dire need of anything in their stomachs. I really do not know whether or not I won him over then, but later that year the area's deer herd did crash, as predicted. We now are close friends, and you could not find a greater supporter of the wildlife-management profession.

The sad truth is that, as one of my professional friends puts it, "The average whitetail hunter thinks deer can fly and eat barbed-wire!" All of that stuff out there in the woods that deer eat is just a "green blob" to most American hunters. But, in Europe it is a completely different story. Before the nimrod can take to the European woods with his trusty gun, he must pass a very thorough test about every aspect of hunting and wildlife ecology. This includes a review of his knowledge of the favorite foods of game species. Knowing such things not only makes you a more knowledgeable hunter, but also greatly improves your chances of harvesting a trophy animal.

Browse is the basic food of whitetails (see **Nutrition and Supplemental Feeding**). Browse, to those of you brave enough to admit you do not know, is made up of the twigs and leaves of woody plants. This may be small shrubs or young tree saplings. Whether you live in Montana or Georgia, the diet of deer is based upon browse, for it is the one food group to which deer turn when other foods are absent. Such foods as acorns and agricultural crops cannot be depended upon for a sustained food supply. Weeds and grasses often are ephemeral, or seasonally available. Therefore, understanding browse is the key to understanding deer. In this chapter, I will expand on what I discussed earlier about whitetail nutrition by discussing: 1) some basic characteristics of browse in general; 2) the favorite foods of deer in particular; and finally, 3) how you can turn this knowledge into venison on the table.

THE BASICS

As noted, the average hunter looks at the forest as just a green mass of vegetation. "Browse is browse," one hunter told me. But, nothing could be further from the truth. As I noted earlier, browse is like a can of mixed nuts at a party. After an hour or so, all you have left is peanuts! That precisely is what's happening out there in the woods.

Understanding Browsing Patterns

There are species of plants that are "cashews," and there are species that are "peanuts."

It is very difficult to write a generalized treatise about the browsing preferences of whitetails. I listed some of the favorite browse plants by geographic area in Chapter 12. The one sure thing about these animals is their ability to adapt to localized conditions. However, we can set down the basics, using a few examples. Throughout the whitetail's range, there are three basic categories of browse plants. **The first category includes "ice cream" plants, or first-choice browse. These are the plants a deer prefers over all others, and rightly so; these species are the most palatable and nutritious.** Deer have very specific nutritional requirements. They prefer a diet consisting of a minimum of 16 percent protein. Theoretically, a deer always could eat enough food to get this much protein, but there is one small problem. An average deer's stomach (rumen) holds only about 9 to 12 pounds of plant material. So, a deer is faced with obtaining all of the nutrition it needs within that amount of food. You can see why a deer is so particular about what it eats.

First-choice browse plants vary with geography. In the South, such plants as honeysuckle, Alabama supplejack (rattan), greenbrier, and blackberry are relished by deer; in northern forests, such species as northern white cedar, red maple, hemlock, and American mountain-ash are preferred. Unfortunately, however, these are the first plants to disappear from the range when browsing pressure becomes too great. Because many of our deer populations now are at a saturation point, first-choice browse plants usually are found only in small, isolated areas where they have escaped detection.

Most deer are faced with acquiring needed nutrition from plants other than those listed as first choice. **Most of the woody plants eaten by deer come under the category of second choice. These are the species that may not have the concentrated nutrients or**

Smilax, a woody vine, is an important whitetail browse type in many areas. The ability to recognize plants, and a knowledge of which ones are important to deer, will make you a better hunter no matter where you live.

Robert Skinner

palatability of the first-choice species, but make up for it by their abundance. Dogwood, American beautyberry, and red mulberry are commonly occurring southern browse species in this group. Yellow birch, eastern white pine, and serviceberry often show up in a second-choice diet of northern deer. These are the real "bread-and-butter" species of the deer manager.

Although whitetails are highly adaptable creatures, often resorting to extraordinary measures in order to survive, one thing is true throughout the range. Deer must keep their stomachs full of some type of food, no matter what its quality. There are many species of beneficial micro-organisms living in their stomachs that they cannot live without. These micro-organisms digest plant material taken into the stomach and supply much of the needed nutrition for deer. So, deer are obligated to keep something in their stomachs at all times. That is where the last category of browse plants comes into the picture. **The third-choice plants are species that meet few of the animal's nutritional requirements, but provide "stuffing" for its stomach.** These plants are consumed in large quantities under two situations. First, they are eaten when better foods are unavailable. In the northern states, this is particularly true when there is heavy snow on the ground. Plants such as black spruce, aspen, and red pine are readily available when the snow is particularly heavy. Second, deer turn to third-choice browse plants when the deer population becomes so dense that most of the higher-quality plants have been consumed. This was the case with the Texas hunting club discussed earlier. The deer had eaten every reasonably nutritious plant on the place, and had proceeded to work heavily on such third-choice species as loblolly pine, American hornbeam, southern waxmyrtle, and post oak. It was all there to be read by one literate in deer ways! It is a sad sight to see deer with "pot bellies" distended with worthless browse and ribs showing beneath their tightly stretched skins.

The palatability of browse also is determined by the time of year. **Deer prefer, and get the most nutrients out of, newly growing plant parts.** Consequently, many plants are only seasonally preferred. It is much like a can of cheap "no name" asparagus. There is no greater turnoff to me than to take a bite of asparagus and encounter one of those woody stems; good asparagus is soft and easily chewed. That is precisely how it is with deer browse. Whitetails prefer to eat soft, succulent stems and leaves, rather than hardened, woody stems. Numerous studies have shown that deer have the incredible ability to pick out highly digestible plants. Plants basically put on two growth flushes each year— usually spring and fall, depending upon the amount of rainfall. In fact, the most palatable species tend to put on flushes of growth at irregular intervals in response to rainfall.

Preference for a certain browse species also may be influenced by where the plant is growing. For example, it is well documented that soils

Understanding Browsing Patterns

Robert Skinner
Blackberry vines produce not only fruit but plentiful browse during the growing season, making this an important plant in many deer habitats.

greatly determine the nutritional quality of a plant. An American beautyberry growing on poor soil is not as readily eaten as is one on good soil. What makes a good browse-producing soil? Two basic factors are involved: soil nutrients and soil moisture. There is only one place in the forest that consistently has better soil nutrients and moisture, and that is bottomland. Bottomlands and creek drainages, because they lie downhill, receive the most runoff from rains and snows. Water carries the better nutrients downhill with it and deposits them in bottomland areas. My radio-telemetry studies have shown that deer basically are creek-bottom animals. They use drainages not only for feeding, but also as travel corridors.

Deer have evolved a simple seasonal feeding pattern. In the spring, upland areas usually begin producing food first. There is adequate moisture then to support plant growth, and upland plants are highly nutritious at this time. As summer approaches, how-

Dogwood falls into the category of "second-choice" browse species for whitetails, meaning it is among those plants eaten mainly after first-choice species have been depleted.

ever, the upland plants complete their first flush of growth, and deer are forced to retreat to the drainages for the most nutritious browse. In most regions, the early-fall months also are somewhat dry. Hence, deer often are found in the wetter drainage systems during summer and early fall. The fall rut pattern often obscures some of the attraction, but it is there. I have seen many a hunter waste his time trying to kill a buck that he saw regularly on upland range during the spring and early summer, but which long since had moved to wetter portions of the forest.

Man's activities also can greatly affect the quality of food plants. Agricultural practices, forestry operations, and water management all affect deer browse. Woody plants adjacent to agricultural crops often are taken by deer as a spin-off of crop fertilization. I have seen deer feeding on what are usually lesser-quality browse plants bordering corn and soybean fields. High levels of soil nitrogen increase the protein content of these plants.

However, forest management probably has the greatest impact on browse production and quality. Just because there is a forest is no guarantee that quality browse is available to deer. You should understand that a deer's world is only about four feet tall. What goes on above that height, although certainly affecting deer, is of little concern. The amount of light reaching the forest floor is critical to browse production. The canopy continues to close as the forest grows, slowly retarding the growth of understory plants. Such forestry and range practices as thinning and clearing can increase greatly the quantity and quality of browse plants. Clear-cutting, although often unpopular with hunters, also can increase browse production significantly, provided the cut areas are not too big.

No practice does more to increase browse quality than fire, though. Much maligned by the general public (probably due to our friend Smokey), fire often is associated more with destruction than benefits. Nothing could be farther from the truth! My good friend and colleague, Dr. Jim Corbin, recently told me that the American Indian knew the positive benefits of fire, regularly burning the woods to increase game abundance and reduce ticks and chiggers. Studies have shown that fire only temporarily kills back browse. Almost immediately browse plants begin to sprout back, sending up highly nutritious shoots. I have conducted many controlled burns over the years, and have found that deer respond almost immediately. In fact, I have conducted burns during the day and have seen deer flock to the burn area that very night. Obviously, the plants had not sprouted that quickly, but the deer seem to have been attracted to the ashes. Some think deer even lick these ashes for the minerals. At this point, I am uncertain.

Finally, browse production can be influenced by water-management practices. Wet areas are attractive to deer. **Ponds, lakes, streams and marshes are reliable sources of quality browse**. In fact, I have seen deer feeding in the water along lake shores, often "bobbing" for water plants. In the South, such wetland species as willow and American cyrilla are very popular with deer. Pond weeds also are attractive to deer throughout the range. Because whitetails need a readily available supply of water, there usually are higher deer densities around such places. Cattlemen have known this for years, using manmade ponds to spread out livestock grazing pressure.

PUTTING THE BASICS TO WORK

The above discussion on browse production and preferences may be a bit too technical for your tastes; however, a little work on your part will make it pay off big during the hunting season. **The first step is to be able to identify quality deer foods.** As noted, the types of food plants eaten by whitetails varies greatly with geographic area. But, I have found that it is not difficult to learn the plants, even if you are not a biologist; all it takes is a little practice. Although there are hundreds of plant species, you will be surprised to learn how few actually are important to deer in any one area. A particular species may be highly favored by whitetails, but so rare that you seldom see it in the woods. Hence, it is of little importance and concern. In order to be eaten, a species has to be readily available; so, the more scarce species can be bypassed from the outset.

There are numerous woody-plant identification manuals and books available to the general public. The best way to start, however, is to spend some time in the field with a knowledgeable person. I have found few individuals who know more about the native plants in any given area than do Soil Conservation Service field personnel. These folks always are willing to help out, too. State game-department biologists usually are helpful too, welcoming visitors in the field.

The next step is one I find myself preaching month after month: Spend a lot of time in the field. You would be amazed how little time many hunters actually spend in the field in pursuit of whitetails. Any chance you get is the time to be out there, observing deer movements and browsing patterns. But, never go into the field without two things: a notebook and a plant-identification manual. I have found a notebook to be of great importance in my trophy hunting and deer management. I carefully record every observation I make, no matter how trivial it appears at the time. You would be surprised how all of these small individual observations add up to a clear picture of what is going on out there! One of the things I pay particular attention to is what the deer are eating, when and where; no matter where I am.

Hunters often tell me that they have difficulty identifying browsing sign. This usually is not very difficult at all. Excluding domestic livestock, the only other animals that consistently feed on browse are rabbits and rodents. Sign of rabbit and rodent foraging is easily distinguished from that of deer. Deer lack upper incisors, and must pinch off their food, while rabbits and rodents have very sharp upper and lower incisors that cleanly cut the stems from the plant. Therefore, stems that have been browsed on by deer have the overall appearance of having been torn off, rather than cut. Furthermore, any browsing sign above "rabbit height" safely can be considered deer sign. Unfortunately, however, if there are cattle on the range, all bets are off, because cattle compete heavily with deer for browse, and they eat plants in a manner quite similar to that of deer.

Pay particular attention to which species are being eaten during the non-growing season (fall and winter). The most palatable species at this time often are evergreens, such as yaupon in the South and white cedar in the North. But, you should spend your time examining the less-palatable species, too, because these are the species that tell you the most about the herd. If you find high utilization of such species, you pretty well can bet that the mast crop (acorns, berries, etc.) is poor, and/or the herd is at a peak population density. If more than 15 percent of the third-choice plants are being browsed, the range probably is heavily stocked

It is important for both the manager and the hunter to be able to recognize deer browsing sign. On the left is the typical browsing pattern of rabbits (notice the clean cut stem); while on the right is a typical plant browsed by a deer (note the "pinched off" appearance.

Understanding Browsing Patterns

with deer.

You can use this type of browse analysis to determine your chances of harvesting a deer, as well. To the observant hunter, the woods are a marvelous place with many secret cues. First, if your goal is to harvest just any deer, you certainly want to hunt where there is a high population density. A few days in a potential hunting territory during the spring and summer should tell you much about the relative deer density of that area. For example, if you see many species of first-choice browse plants, and absolutely no use of third-choice species, you should know quickly that your chances of seeing a deer are slim. On the other hand, should you want a trophy animal, you may want to hunt such a place. I have found that antler quality deteriorates rapidly after the herd density exceeds a light stocking.

Analysis of browsing patterns also can be used to locate those trails traveled by only a few deer— usually, trophy bucks. **It is interesting to note that deer seldom travel from one place to the next without browsing on the way**. If a buck uses a trail over a period of time, browsing sign increases. With a little self-training you should be able to recognize concentrated browsing along escape trails and travel corridors. It also is possible to locate summer and early-fall buck refuges by examining browsing intensity over the landscape. Again, it all may look alike to the untrained eye, but you will find areas where browsing intensity is greater than others. Concentrate your searches along wetter areas, such as stream drainages and swamps.

The amount of late-fall and winter browsing is directly proportional to the availability of fruits and nuts during this time. In a poor acorn-production year, areas with good supplies of quality browse, such as greenbrier, honeysuckle, and palatable conifers, should be examined for browsing sign. When hunting such areas, remember that these are feeding areas, and you should not hunt right in the middle of them. Locate trails leading to a feeding area, and hunt along these trails. You also may try some stalking.

Over the years, I have tried many strange tactics in order to harvest trophy deer, and now I will give away one of my secrets. I often use what I call "natural" food plots. Here in East Texas, we often plant food plots consisting of a cereal grain-legume mixture. These are good areas for harvesting does and "cull" bucks, but they seldom produce trophy bucks. These deer are just too smart to expose themselves in such a manner. For them, I try something completely different: I apply a balanced fertilizer to the native vegetation! In fact, I am just finishing some research that shows that application of fertilizers to native forage significantly increases some important nutrients and palatability. It is quite a trick to fertilize vegetation right out there in the woods. I select a good, moist-soil area with good sunlight beneath the forest canopy, and then apply as much as 400 pounds of fertilizer to an acre. I am especially attracted to patches of honeysuckle. I usually make such applications in early spring, and I may follow them up with an application of 100 pounds of ammonium nitrate in mid- to late summer. Other hunters probably would not recognize the effect of such fertiliztion on the browse, but the deer certainly do! You would be amazed at the increase in visitations to such areas caused by fertilization. With this method you "build" yourself a natural food plot, which the deer already are accustomed to browsing, and one that cannot be detected by most other hunters. Pretty sneaky, eh? Maybe, but it works for me, both in hunting and management.

SUMMARY

Trophy hunting is becoming more and more difficult with time. Each year, there are more hunters taking to the field in search of trophy bucks; and, the bucks themselves are becoming harder to kill. In order to be successful today, the hunter must arm himself with numerous tools and methods. Likewise, the serious manager must learn to recognize the extent of utilization of the forage on his property. One tool is the ability to recognize areas where deer are concentrating their activities. Understanding browsing patterns and mastering the recognition of preferred browse species can enhance greatly your chances of harvesting a quality buck. It takes time, and it involves a lot of hard work. But, you will become a better hunter and sportsman for it; and, you probably will develop a better appreciation for the whitetail as a marvelously adapted game animal.

Chapter 26

Mike Biggs

HOW TO AUTOPSY THE RUT

Recently, I was reading a report developed by the Texas Parks & Wildlife Department on the chronology of the deer harvest in that state. A meticulously drawn graph clearly illustrated what I already knew. Most of the deer are harvested within the first few days of the season, with only a slight resurgence in harvest during the last days. This trend illustrates two phenomena in deer hunting. First, the deer become increasingly more difficult to kill as the season wears on. Second, hunters themselves begin to lose interest as hunting conditions become more challenging. By the time the season has passed, most hunters have all they want of the whitetail, and gladly put up their guns for more rewarding pursuits. This absolutely is the wrong thing to do, especially during the post-season winter period. The post-season period is the best time to learn about whitetails, yet many hunters still behave as if we biologists pick up the deer at the end of the season, and store them in a closet until the next year! The deer **are** still out there and they have much to teach us about their behavior during the previous season. In this chapter, I offer some suggestions as to how you might effectively develop a post-season scouting plan, and hopefully put this plan to use next year.

The rut is very much like a living creature. It is born, it develops and then it passes. In order to understand what deer were doing during the rut, you carefully must perform a "Quincy-like" autopsy which reconstructs each event as it happened. In order to conduct this autopsy, you will need a few basic tools. By now, you should be aware of the importance of maps and aerial photographs in trophy-deer hunting. If you do not have a set for your favorite hunting territory, they are easily obtained from the Soil Conservation Service, U.S. Forest Service or the U. S. Geological Survey. Some avid trophy hunters even go up into the air themselves to photograph their area. You also will need a notebook. Together, my maps and notebook make up what I call my post-season scouting report. The scouting report is made up of little pieces of information that may seem unrelated on the surface; however, when assembled in my notebook, a vivid story often unfolds. Here is how you go about such an analysis.

I seldom am far from my notebook. During the season, I carefully record all deer movements, no matter how trivial they may seem. On a map of the area, I note the direction, time and sex of each deer's movements. Over the entire season, you would be amazed at the volume of information you will accumulate. But, it is often difficult to do much scouting during the season itself, for fear of disturbing the truly big bucks from their sanctuaries. This is best accomplished after the season.

As I noted in the past, **travel corridors** are like seams in the zone defense of football. The deer quickly learn the safe travel paths to use in their daily movements from one preferred area to the next. Bucks, especially take advantage of the natural vegetation and topography to move undetected from their sanctuaries to feeding areas and rutting territories. The best way to start your search is to locate all roads and rights-of-way. It is a curious thing that roads almost always travel the ridge tops, only occasionally crossing

Diaries, topographic maps and aerial photographs are the stock-in-trade of the trophy hunter. Learning how to autopsy the rut can significantly increase your chances of harvesting a quality buck next season.

creeks and drainages. Creek crossings are expensive, and engineers tend to avoid them when possible. Rights-of-way, on the other hand, tend to travel in a straight line direction across the countryside. I scout roads differently from rights-of-way.

Each drainage system has associated with it one or more doe social groups. A drainage may be only a temporary creek or a large perennial stream, yet they differ greatly from upland areas. Forage is more succulent and the soils often are more fertile in the bottoms. Deer know this and tend to concentrate their activities in these areas, venturing into the uplands primarily during the wetter portions of the year. Therefore, I locate all road crossings of drainage areas on my map, and then conduct a field investigation. In the North, tracking deer is made easy by the presence of snow, while in the South, you must resort to searching for tracks in the soil. Locating a stream crossing, I start at the crest of the hill and walk slowly down the road, across the creek and then up the opposite hill. If the road is paved, it often is necessary to walk the roadside. A little attention to the scale of the map or photograph will enable you to mark the location of all tracks. You will be surprised to discover that the vast majority of crossings occur somewhere between the hill crest and the creek itself. Deer usually like to walk the slope rather than the ridge top or creek bottom. You should also record the relative number of tracks crossing in each direction. Surprisingly, travel corridors are often "oneway streets;"

The best way to begin your autopsy of the rut is to walk out the drainages of your hunting territories.

this is, deer tend to travel to a destination along one trail and return by another. Since there is no way to ascertain the time of crossing by this method, you will have to resort to other means in order to determine whether or not it is a morning or evening trail.

Rights-of-way are more difficult to investigate, but I find them particularly useful, especially if the right-of-way is newly constructed. Pipelines and power lines are often poorly revegetated, and provide quite a bit of bare ground to investigate. Again, I tend to concentrate my activities near creek crossings, but I certainly do not ignore upland areas as I walk over them. In cases where the vegetation is too thick to conduct track counts, I use a little trick. I carry a common garden rake along with me and scrape away the vegetation. This will allow me to investigate the area later.

Once you have located the travel corridors, it is time to work out the detail of each trail. Some trails are very easy to follow, probably representing common-use trails by doe social groups. The more subtle trails, those probably used by bucks, are more difficult to recognize. I generally start with the more prominent trails, and work backwards.

Trails tend to coalesce, and when traced often look like the branches and trunk of a tree. Using a compass, I carefully walk along the main trail and draw in its path on the map. Distance estimates are accomplished by pacing. It is easy to measure your normal pace when walking in the woods. Just lay down a tape and walk down it several times, recording the number of paces in a known length. Calculate the average, and you have your pace standardized. Pacing and mapping is tedious work and cannot be done traveling at a full gallop! I may spend an entire day working out a single trail. Be on the lookout for subtle clues as you walk along. Deer tend to browse more heavily along their trails, so pay attention to the extent of browsing. Deer foraging sign is easily recognized. Since deer lack upper incisors, they have to pinch off the vegetation. Other animals such as rabbits have sharp upper and lower incisors, and cut the vegetation cleanly. The more heavily used trails are easy to recognize. Every type of vegetation has been sampled by some deer during the year.

The greatest problem I have in teaching hunters to recognize trails revolves around perspective. The white-tailed deer is only about three and one-half feet tall. A six feet tall man does not see the world in the same way as a deer. I tend to walk trails in a crouched position, one that is not too comfortable, but puts me at "deer height." At that level, you begin to understand the deer's world a great deal better, and you begin to think like a deer. This also enables you to see the lesser side trails that may lead to a bedding site or sanctuary. I classify trails as either primary or secondary. A heavily used primary trail is drawn in on the map in red, while the lesser secondary trails are colored in blue.

I also use some little tricks to determine when deer use trails. Where the soil is workable or where snow is present, I use my rake to smooth out an area across the trail which is large enough to record a deer's movements. I rake such an area just before daylight one day, return four hours later and record the number and direction of tracks. This is repeated every four hours. In more difficult areas, I use a thin piece of thread strung across the trail.

Once travel corridors have been established, I begin my dissection. As I noted above, trails often are used for different activities. In some areas, there are separate bedding and feeding areas, while in others, deer tend to bed and feed in the same area. My next clues come from beds, rutting sign and direct observation.

BEDS

Over the years, I have been able to reconstruct a general pattern for bedding areas. There is a distinct difference between summer and winter bedding sites. Summer beds tend to be in the more open areas where cool breezes combat insects and heat stress. Grassy slopes and open stands of trees are highly favored in the spring and summer. In the fall and winter, however, deer begin seeking protection not only from hunters, but also from the wind. Beds tend to be located on southern exposures with screening vegetation. Young evergreen thickets are particularly attractive to deer at this time. Beds are very difficult and time consuming to locate, but the work can pay off big! Bedding areas, especially for bucks, used during the late winter are probably in the same area used during most of the season. In order to find them, I use a systematic approach.

Using a compass, I walk in perpendicular lines from the established trail. My path usually extends from the trail upward across the slope and onto the ridge top. These "cruise" lines are positioned about twenty yards apart, but the distance depends on the density of the vegetation. There are two cues for which to look. First, the vegetation is always pressed down in a small semi-circle. Since a deer will remain bedded for four or more hours,

Finding a bedding area during the post-rut period means that next season there may be a new head on the author's wall (Courtesy, R. L. Marchinton).

this imprint of the deer's body will often remain for days. On a recent trip to Wisconsin, I found that beds in the snow were particularly easy to find, even after a light snowfall. Second, deer tend to defecate shortly after rising from their beds. The presence of pellets, especially in large numbers, should signal a more intensive search is necessary.

Once a bed is located, search the vicinity for additional beds. This will give you some clues as to number and sex of the deer. More than two or three large beds usually indicate a doe bedding site. Often, I can tell whether or not each deer was an adult or a fawn by the size of its bed. A large bed with two smaller beds to each side is a sure sign of a doe and her fawns. As with trails, location of each bed is carefully recorded on the map. The next step is to look for rutting sign.

RUTTING SIGN

Long after the rut is over, the woods abound with clues left by rutting bucks. During the pre-rut period, it is almost impossible for a buck to travel along a trail without stopping to rub small trees along the way. I investigate rubs found in my searches. Too little attention is paid by hunters to rubs. Each tells a different story about the buck(s) using the trail. By January, the first rubs will be noticeably aged. Conifers are particularly attractive to bucks, and these trees often will die from the rubbing. It takes most conifers about sixty days to show signs of death (dry or brown needles) in the winter; hence, a dead pine sapling means that the buck attacked it during the pre-rut or early rut period. On trees that remain alive, the inner wood has a tendency to turn gray after a few weeks. Fresh rubbing, on the other hand, is characterized by freshly exposed wood, and in the case of conifers, fresh sap oozing from the wound.

The direction of travel can also be determined by examination of a rub. Bucks tend to rub the side of the tree opposite to the direction of travel. Extensive rubbing only on one side of several trees suggests that the buck uses the trail only during one time of the day, and that the trail is one of those "oneway streets." This is the most commonly occurring rub type. The rarest type is the **signpost**, a larger diameter tree that regularly receives attention from one or more bucks. Signposts tend to be located either in rutting territories or adjacent to bedding sites within sanctuaries. I mark the location of a signpost with a large star on my map. This signals me to later return to the area for a more intensive search.

Scrapes are primarily constructed during the pre-rut and early rut periods; consequently, they are often difficult to recognize during the post season. This especially is true for areas with appreciable snow fall. A primary scrape may go undetected beneath a foot or more of snow. In snow country, however, scrapes often appear as large black "smears" in the snow. Bucks will give themselves away late in the year. They scrape even after antler drop, probably in response to the brief period of testosterone production that initiates development of the new antler. Post-season scrapes are most commonly located near bedding and feeding areas, and are often much larger than typical scrapes. Again, each is carefully recorded on the map.

CAST ANTLERS

Much has been written about searching for cast antlers in post-season scouting. Fact is that I know of no other method that gives you a better idea as to the presence of a trophy-class ani-

Shed antlers tell you a great deal about the location of mature bucks.

mal. This is particularly true for those of us who concentrate on trophy hunting. Since there are only a set number of days in the season, I can ill afford to waste my time hunting a young buck. If I can locate a particularly large cast antler, this tells me two things. First, that the buck is worth hunting. Second, since bucks tend to drop their antlers in the vicinity of a late season sanctuary, finding a monster antler greatly narrows my search. Each year, I record the location of all cast antlers found. The fact that you find a small antler should not mean that it does not receive attention. Over the years, I have collected several series of antlers from the same bucks, and am able to monitor each buck's progress in antler development. Some disappear, presumably as a result of mortality, while others never develop into a true trophy. A few, however, have piqued my interest enough to develop a hunting strategy for a particular buck.

DIRECT OBSERVATION

The last post-season scouting technique I use is direct observation of the deer themselves. This probably is the most enjoyable time of the year for me. There are no pressures to harvest a buck, so I can leisurely study their behavior. I sit for hours along trails, carefully recording the behavior of each deer observed. I coordinate this information with that obtained with other seasons of the year to produce a year-long picture of deer behavior on a particular area. Behavior changes from one year to the next in response to various factors. One year, there may be a particularly large acorn crop; while another may see an acorn famine. A farmer may rotate his crops in such a manner to significantly change deer travel patterns. All of these things are carefully noted.

You may find these recommendations excessive or too time-consuming for your tastes. If you do, that is unfortunate, since you are missing the best part of deer hunting. I feel the whitetail is the most popular game animal in North America not because it is the most abundant, but because it is the most difficult to hunt, bar none! So,

Mike Biggs

Direct observations of deer in the field remains the best way to determine what is going on at any point in time. Pay particular attention to the condition of the coat, appearance of first rubs and scrapes, and increased activity from breeding activity. These indirect cues will tell you a great deal about the nature of the rut on your land.

while those other fellows are back home watching the Super Bowl, you could be laying the groundwork to harvesting that wall hanger next season.

SUMMARY

Several times in this book I have stressed the importance of year-round scouting and study. The short period after the rut is an excellent time to examine in detail what happened during the hectic fall breeding period. This will allow you to better understand what **your** herd is doing, especially if you accumulate several years' observations.

Mike Biggs

Direct observations of deer during the rut cycle may mean the difference between success and failure. The author contends that he seldom harvests a buck he does not know, meaning that it may take two or more years to work out a buck's rutting pattern.

The more you know about your deer, the more consistently successful you will be.

Chapter 27

Mike Biggs

HUNTING THE RUT

Earlier in this book, I outlined the basics of the white-tailed deer's rutting biology. Understanding what is going on in the trophy buck's mind and body is paramount to having him on your wall instead of in the woods. In this chapter, I will discuss application of the basics so you can turn the one time a trophy buck is vulnerable—the rut—to your advantage. Other chapters in this book will address more advanced techniques, but here are the basics on which to build.

RUT STRATEGIES

The strategy you adopt will depend upon many situations and conditions. You may be hunting the pre-rut, or you may be hunting in an area where the hunters literally are falling all over each other. So, let's take a stepwise approach to developing **your** hunting strategy. First of all, there are three basic steps to the rut, each with its own set of strategies and hunting techniques. These steps are: 1) pre-rut, 2) rut, and 3) post-rut. Some other authors have discussed more than these, but I feel that this simply is splitting hairs for the sake of adding verbiage.

THE PRE-RUT PERIOD

The pre-rut period often, unfortunately, occurs before the legal hunting season. The pre-rut period may be as early as August in South Carolina or as late as October and November in Mexico. Those of you who hunt with a bow probably will be most interested in hunting strategies for the pre-rut. I am finding more and more bowhunters in the woods as the hunting pressure and cost of hunting increases, and as bucks become more adept at avoiding detection. The pre-rut is a time when the buck is still spending most of his time in and around his summer core area or sanctuary. The vast majority of these areas occur along creek bottoms

During the pre-rut period, bucks tend to remain close to their summer home range, and are most predictable at this time.

Mike Biggs

and drainages, and usually are in some pretty thick vegetation. The summer core area may only be a few acres in size, and is, therefore, often difficult to locate. I suggest that you spend a great deal of time in the woods. I spend many quiet hours just roaming around the woods during June, July and August. I slip around the woods with no particular destination. If I see a deer moving away from me, I attempt to get a good idea of its sex. The middle of the day is probably the best time to do this. Why? During summer, deer are still pretty much sticking to the type of activity pattern (see **Movements and Home Range**) that most deer hunters know best. They become active just at daylight, and then spend most of the hotter portions of the day lying in their beds. The late evening again shows increased activity until well after dark. So, in the summer, the midday period is a perfect time to catch a buck in his bed. If you are not charging around like a bull elephant, and you are paying close attention, the buck will run just out of sight and then try to slip back into his bedding area. Mark these areas on a map or aerial photograph—you have found a sanctuary!

Since the buck begins his ritualized pre-rut behavior in and around his bedding site, this is also the time to look for sign. As I noted earlier, mature bucks like to have a rubbing signpost near their beds. The bigger the tree, the better. Most of the time, species such as cedar or pine are used, since these species have light-colored underbark which can be seen for some distance. The best time to look for sign posts is early in the morning or late in the afternoon. At these times, the buck is out and about so you will not disturb him as much; and, the light is more parallel to the ground. A signpost located in a thicket that cannot be seen in the middle of the day stands out like a beacon in the early or late hours. Once you find a bedding area of a mature, rutting whitetail, it is a simple matter to figure out his trail system. As the buck leaves his bedding area, he just cannot help but rub every stick of vegetation that will give him some re-

Locating a signpost absolutely is the best way to find rutting bucks. Finding one of these structures assures you that a mature buck is in the area.

Mike Biggs

sistance. These little rubs will be located along each side of his main trail. Again, map out the trails from the bedding area on your map. Now you have the buck pretty well patterned. The next step is to decide how you are going to harvest him. I suggest that you not hunt right on top of the bedding area. Remember that he has more than one trail, and if he detects you, he will simply move out by some other route. Therefore, the best approach is to set up your portable stand along one of the trails. **Never** set up a permanent stand when hunting for trophy whitetails. It will be a fatal mistake. Mature bucks get that way by knowing every inch of their home ranges. The slightest change in a trail will trigger defensive maneuvers. Remember that the rut is not as yet underway, so the buck is still more interested in survival than reproduction. The best approach is to use a portable backpack stand or tripod and carry it in each day before daylight. Always set the stand downwind, at least 30 yards from the trail. Avoid whenever possible walking on the trail itself; just your scent may cause the buck to abandon his trail. I also use an odor neutralizer; most of those on the market will do a fine job. I once had a buck walk downwind from me no more than 10 steps. The wind was blowing about 15 to 20 mph and the buck did not even smell me! I like to use a portable tripod stand to hunt the pre-rut. It takes only about five minutes to set up such a stand, so there is little disturbance.

Should the pre-rut come before the legal hunting season, or if you are more inclined to hunt with a gun, you still need to do your pre-rut homework. Chances are that the buck will remain aorund his summer bedding area until the rut is underway. If you know where bedding areas of several bucks are located, you can make regular inspections of each area in order to determine the progress of the rut.

THE RUT

The first signs of actual rutting will appear around the bedding area. Even

A portable backpack stand is an excellent device for moving in on rutting bucks. Carry your stand in before daylight and back out after dark.

Robert Skinner

before the male hormones take their full impact on the buck's behavior, he will begin to make "practice" scrapes. These scrapes do not really mean very much other than the buck is in the area. But, they do show you that the rut is about to begin in earnest. One of the most common questions asked is: how to tell whether or not the buck you are scouting is a trophy or some yearling upstart. Many a hunter has wasted his time sitting on a scrape, only to discover some spike made it! Again, if you are doing your homework, there is little doubt about the presence of a mature buck. Mature bucks are the only ones that have large signposts. The presence of a well-worked signpost on a large diameter tree (say six inches or more) is a sure indicator that a dominant buck (or at least one that thinks he is) is working the area. Whitetails are often reported to be non-territorial. It is true that their behavior does not totally fit the classical definition of territoriality, but they do mark and defend territories, even before the rut. I recently videotaped a dominant buck on the Sombrerito Ranch, belonging to Bill Carter of Houston. This particular buck has defended his "territory" for several years now. The buck appears to be rubbing his antlers on a large bush, but close examination of the videotape reveals that he is not rubbing his antlers at all. He is rubbing the scent patch on his forehead. After each rubbing session, he carefully sniffs the bush to check the progress of the scent marker. This marker probably is related to territorial marking and serves as an announcement to does of his presence. Earlier I discussed other possible uses for this gland.

Since, as we learned earlier (see **The Rut: A Time of Turmoil**), bucks begin scraping close to their summer bedding area and then extend a line of scrapes along their home drainage, this is precisely the best place to get a shot. Again, the technique is similar to hunting the pre-rut. Use a portable stand, move in before daylight, set up well away from his trail and use a cover scent even if you are downwind. He

A sudden increase in the number of bucks you see is a sure sign that the rut is underway. This is a time to use tactics matched to this stage of the annual breeding cycle.

Mike Biggs

may decide to check out the trail if he suspects something. Bucks will travel off of their trails, downwind, when they suspect danger. Finally, do not hunt directly on top of the scrape! It is an all too common mistake made by hunters. If you have done your homework, you know where his trail is and which direction he will travel to get to the scrape. Ambush him on his way to the scrape, not with his nose in it.

If you do not get your buck during the early rut, you may have difficulty. Most bucks will move to another drainage when the majority of the available does in their drainage have been bred. This is a time when post-season scouting during the previous year pays off. If you paid atttention to those scape lines that suddenly appeared at the end of the season, or that huge sign post that showed up along a ridge in January, you may have some good ideas about where to look for a vagrant buck. Once you find him, do not tarry, as he will only be in the area for a short period of time before he moves on to share his favors with other doe social groups.

I often am asked about rattling up trophy bucks. Most hunters show interest in rattling, especially with the deluge of articles recently about the subject. Hunters also ask if rattling will work in their area, or just in South Texas. I have rattled up bucks all over the country. The trick is to know when and where to rattle (see **Advanced Rattling and Calling Techniques**). The technique is not as important as some authors would have you believe. I have seen bucks rattled up with twisted beer cans!

Mike Biggs

Grunt calls are very effective during the rut, but are of less use during the pre-rut and post-rut periods.

If you are doing your homework, you will know when the rut is taking place. Keep records on each and every deer you see, marking down whether it is a doe, buck or lone fawn. As the rut comes into full swing, there will be more and more lone fawns running around lost. The buck will run off the fawns, especially nubbin' bucks. Also, a larger percentage of bucks in your observations will tell you that the rut is underway. That is the time to go rattling. The best place to rattle is up hill from the bedding area or scrape line. If you find a signpost, you have a gold mine, since the buck is no doubt somewhere near. Slip into the area about daylight, use a cover scent and rattle. You do not have to rattle long, just a few minutes will do. If the buck is in the area, he will come to the "horns." The behavior of a mature buck coming to rattling is highly variable. Some rush in, while others circle. That is when the cover scent comes in handy. If the buck does not respond, just slip out and try again the next day, or later that day. But, *do not* spend too much time in the area.

THE POST-RUT

The post-rut period separates the deer hunters from the crowd. It is a time that will drive you to drink. The big bucks have had everything thrown at them, and they are more wary than at any other time. Some will have become nocturnal in response to intense hunting pressure. I spent some time studying the techniques of the true experts in trophy hunting, the professional guides. I also have monitored mature bucks for many years now by radiotelemetry. The story I get from the guides is substantiated by my research. There is just no way to kill a trophy buck during the post-rut, using conventional means. So, try some pretty unconventional methods.

Understanding the basics helps. Here are the facts. During the post-rut, mature bucks will probably not be moving around during the day. They will also be bedding up in some pretty thick vegetation, which is impossible to slip through undetected. And finally, they will have more than one escape route should you disturb them. But, you can improve your chances.

The best approach is to try to identify as many of the trails used by the buck as possible. Next, narrow down the ones that he is most likely to take in flight. The final step is to make a guess which one of these he will take when you force him to move. On that one I can be of no help. Luck and experience is all that will help you. The best way to get the buck to move at a speed that will allow you to get a shot is the silent drive. Here is how it works.

You should position yourself in a place where you will have a clear shot at the buck. Remember, you will have only about three or four seconds to make the shot. Hopefully, you spent the summer practicing shooting offhand. The best place to set up is a spot where the buck will naturally pause. A narrow opening or a woodland edge are such places. Now, you will need the services of a couple of your friends. You might try using a few more to block other potential escape routes, but that often turns into chaos. Ask your two friends to walk **slowly** with the wind into the sanctuary. There is no need to make noise other than natural walking; the buck will quickly be aware of their presence. If you have planned properly, and if you have luck, the buck should slip slowly in front of the drivers, pausing at your predetermined spot before dashing to safety. Make the shot count. Do not try anything fancy such as neck shots or head shots. A well-placed bullet in the shoulder will break him down and

Mike Biggs

A silent drive, using two of your hunting buddies is an excellent "last resort" method for ferreting out trophy bucks from their sanctuaries.

---

assure that he is not going anywhere. It would be a shame to waste such a fine animal due to a crippling shot.

Other techniques include everything from rocking a canyon to using firecrackers. I really cannot recommend such techniques, but with a little creativity, you may come up with something new that works for you.

SUMMARY

Understanding the rut is crucial to harvesting a trophy whitetail buck. Each stage has its own characterisitics and hunting techniques. Learn to recognize each and master the proper techniques. Each technique should be matched to exactly what is going on during that stage of the rut. Fishermen

Mike Biggs

The rut is the one time that a big buck is vulnerable. The desire to procreate is so strong, a buck even can be tricked by a doe decoy. In these two unique photographs, a buck investigates a decoy, drawn by visual cues to the vaginal area.

use the term "match the hatch," to denote using the proper bait at the proper time. So it is with hunting the rut. Again, as I have said throughout this book, it may seem like a great deal of effort, but it does pay off in the long run. It is fun and it may get you a trophy buck.

Mike Biggs

Chapter 28

Mike Biggs

HUNTING RUTTING SIGN

The rut is a remarkable time for whitetail bucks, especially the big ones. After all, the average buck has spent the summer leisurely enjoying the abundant browse and weeds, plus the company of other bucks. The tough times of winter are over, there are no hunters to worry about, and a doe is nothing more than another deer with which to compete for food.

The onset of fall, however, brings on an entirely different set of situations. The boys are not so friendly any more, the does are beginning to look pretty good, and humans are beginning to show great interest in the out-of-doors. As the rut begins, the truly big bucks are faced with many contradictions. Somehow they must manage to hold their own against potential rivals, accomplish their breeding responsibilities, and avoid being shot by hunters in the process. It is the rut that is the trophy buck's Achilles' heel. Understanding the rut and all of its components will greatly improve your chances of harvesting a trophy-class buck.

I know of very few hunters who are unaware of the rut and its consequences in hunting. But, do you really know the various stages of the rut and how to exploit each?

The rut actually begins during early fall, when bucks begin to prepare for the breeding season ahead. If you pay very close attention to your deer, you will note that it is the bucks which first shed their red summer coats for their heavier, gray, cool-season pelage. During September and October, there will be many bucks running around in gray color, while the does still are red. Why? It really is quite simple. The bucks have to change their coats early on because they have more pressing matters which require energy and protein. The does will shed later, at a more leisurely pace.

PREPARING FOR THE RUT

Let's examine what a mature buck needs in order to be successful during the upcoming breeding season. First, he needs a reasonable set of antlers—the bigger and more impressive the better. Antlers serve a multitude of functions, from a platform with which to engage the "enemy," to an evaporative surface for his territorial scents and love perfumes. But, antlers are not everything. In reality, all he needs for combat is a reasonable set of antlers with which to engage his opponent. Once engaged, he needs the muscles and body size to push the challenger around. For this reason, the buck must go into training very early in the fall. Training takes place in and around his favorite home space, an area researchers call the *core area*. Thus, developing the ability to recognize such core areas is useful to the successful trophy hunter.

My research has shown that core areas usually are quite small, often 50 acres or less. A core area must have two major attributes. First, and probably of more importance, it must provide adequate screening so that the animal is not readily seen by an intruder. Second, it must provide all of the life requisites, such as food and water. During late-summer and early fall, the buck must be able to gain as much weight and store as much fat as

Mike Biggs

Once the buck sheds his velvet, he is obligated to rub. The experienced hunter can put this to his advantage by developing "rub highway maps" for his area.

possible. The coming rut is a time when there will be little time to replenish fat stores. Therefore, high-energy and high-fat foods are essential within the core area. Those of you who are bowhunters, or even serious gun hunters, should learn to recognize the preferred food items within your own particular hunting region. In the South, for example, fruits of the American beautyberry are essential deer food during late August and early September. Fruit production of this plant is highly reliable, and a buck can fatten on it very quickly without traveling far. Other food items include cultivated grains, such as corn and milo (grain sorghum).

During the **pre-rut period,** big bucks will do three things. First, they spend little time moving about. Economy of energy is critical. This is the time that is hardest on the whitetail manager; you see very few bucks, and you begin to wonder whether or not your hunters will be pleased with the coming season. Many states and provinces begin their bow seasons at this time. If you are a bowhunter, you can greatly improve your chances by learning to recognize core areas and by studying your deer year-round. Once you find such an area, your chances of seeing the buck are high, because he certainly is not going to move very far unless disturbed.

Second, a big buck needs to develop his athletic abilities. In so doing, he gives himself away. There is only one way for a buck to develop the muscles needed in combat: sparring with mock opponents. These mock opponents can be anything resilient enough to stand pushing and rubbing with his antlers. This is the time when the first rubs begin to show up. I have spent a considerable amount of time studying where these early pre-rut rubs occur, along with the types of places and vegetation preferred by big bucks, and I have found chances are great that if you find old rubs from previous years, you will find new ones during the current pre-rut period.

RUBS

I have seen areas in which virtually all of the vegetation had been killed by a single buck. In fact, there was one instance in which a big buck lived in a thicket adjacent to a large nursery operation. In one year alone, the buck did over $60,000 in damages to nursery stock! The deer later was killed by a bowhunter, and it scored high in the record book. If you develop for yourself a map of your various hunting territories, each year recording the locations of both old and new rubs, you can pattern your bucks pretty well.

I also have found that specific tree types are preferred by bucks. I have collected a considerable amount of data on such trees, and can characterize them as follows. Bucks prefer two basic types of trees. First, there are the mock-combat trees. These are small (one to four inches in diameter) trees that have enough spring to them to simulate a pushing match with another buck. Evergreens such as cedars and pines often fit this bill beautifully. As a matter of fact, if there are small-diameter cedars in an area, you

It is not always the buck with the largest antlers who wins a fight. Here, a very impressive buck is beaten by a mediocre eight-pointer with much smaller antlers.

can bet that some of them will be rubbed. Other species I regularly encounter as rubs in my region are hollies, such as yaupon, along with willows, sassafras, and elms.

The second type of tree used as a rub— and, I might add, the most important type to locate— is the signpost marker. As noted several times previously, such rubs are the real indicators that a dominant buck is in an area. We are talking really *big* trees here. I have seen signposts marked on trees as large as 12 inches in diameter. Favorite species for signposts are those that will provide high visibility after the bark is rubbed off. In other words, trees with white or light-colored wood are preferred. Again, cedars and pines make excellent markers. I know of one such marker, a cedar, that has been used for over five years now on one of my management areas, and it is almost worn through. You can see the tine marks along the trunk and lower branches, some as high as four feet above the ground!

My research has shown that signposts most often occur in one of two situations. First, over the years a young buck continually will bed in the same area unless otherwise disturbed. Slowly, most of the small saplings become "rubbed out;" that is, they are killed from excessive rubbing. Also, each year the buck grows, and he rubs bigger and bigger trees. By the time the buck is three or four years old, he has found one particular tree within his summer core area that he really likes. Most of this type of signpost marking occurs very near his bedding area. Because most summer bedding areas are in very dense vegetation, I try to look for them in the early morning or late afternoon. At such times, the light is more parallel to the ground, and it more easily penetrates the dense vegetation. It is at these times that the signposts stick out, with their white, rubbed surfaces. If you find one of these early signposts, you have an excellent opportunity to harvest that buck; however, you have to work out his various escape routes from the

Robert Skinner

The signpost is perhaps the best indicator that a mature buck is in the area. Bucks make signposts to advertise their presence, help synchronize the rut, and to suppress subordinate bucks.

bedding area. Hunt the trails leading to the signpost bedding area, *not* right on top of the signpost.

The second type of signpost is one that is worked as the dominant buck moves from one doe social group to the next. This type of signpost is more difficult to find. Again, it is best to locate old signposts on a topographic map of your area, then visit them regularly in order to determine whether or not the buck is courting in the area. Once you find such a signpost you need to move quickly, as he may be in the area for only a short time. Obviously, unless you are spending a great deal of time in the woods, you will have no way of knowing whether or not the signpost you find is fresh or "yesterday's news."

This idea of bucks moving around and establishing various rutting territories is a relatively new one. For years we biologists have hammered the hunting public with the notion that a deer will die within a mile of where it was born. Sometimes this is true, but most commonly it is not, as far as bucks are concerned. The problem was that early on we did not study mature rutting bucks. Does are easier to trap, and the published data are weighted heavily in favor of does. Also, much of the early deer-movement information came from the Edwards Plateau of Texas, an area so densely populated with deer that no buck has to travel very far to find the favor of a doe.

Nowadays, however, the story is shaping up somewhat differently. Several researchers, including me, have learned that a rutting whitetail buck often is a vagrant animal. There is no predicting where he might turn up. For example, a good friend of mine, Clyde Neeley of Eunice, Louisiana, killed a double-drop-tined buck better than 20 miles from where it had been seen during a census! It appears that bucks have established routes they take in visiting various doe groups. Each drainage system has associated with it a group of closely related does. These doe groups have a distinct social structure. Bucks, on the other hand, are adapted to moving about, to spread the genes, so to speak. This keeps the genetic diversity of the deer population high.

SCRAPES

Along with rubbing comes the better known scraping behavior. Although most hunters are familiar with the concept of scrapes, there is some confusion and many myths surrounding them. Just because you find a scrape, still steaming with scent, does not necessarily mean you will kill a trophy buck there. There definitely are some gray areas when it comes to hunting scrapes.

First, not all bucks make scrapes. This has been proved by several researchers. I have seen dominant bucks that never have made a scrape in their lives, while bucks of lesser social stature may make many scrapes. One thing we *do* know about scrapes is that they serve several functions, all of which relate to scent communication. Bucks communicate in three ways: (1) scent; (2) sight; and (3) sound. Rubs and signposts, plus various behavioral

Mike Biggs

Bucks make scrapes for several purposes, among which are advertisement for does, and suppression of other bucks. You can use scrapes to map the rutting territories of bucks on your property.

postures ("body language"), dominate sight communication. Scent communication, on the other hand, is a bit more complicated. The bodies of whitetail bucks are covered with many glands, from the face all the way to the feet. Facial glands are used year-round to mark "territories." Bucks often rub their faces, especially their foreheads, on rubbing trees and signposts to further identify who is in the neighborhood. These may also serve to regulate breeding and to suppress subordinate bucks. Scrapes serve to tell other bucks that a rutting male is in the area, and also, to make does aware of the buck's presence. Now, this may be old hat to some of you, but let's have a closer look at scrapes in order to develop a useful hunting strategy.

Realize that bucks do not just make scrapes in just any old place. My research has shown that they have definite preferences for scrape location. For example, the vast majority of scrapes I have examined occurred on slopes, as opposed to hilltops or bottoms. Because deer are creek-bottom animals, this is completely logical. They use creeks and drainages as travel corridors. What better place to announce your presence than along a highway? Scrapes and rubs are nothing more than billboards! Now, ask yourself, "Where are the best places to have billboards?" Would you want one in very dense bushes? Of course not; you would want the highest visibility possible, in order for it to be seen by more individuals. That is exactly the way it is with rutting whitetails. *The vast majority of the several thousand scrapes I have examined occurred in areas with low understory density.* Areas along streams are perfect for scraping. The dense hardwood canopy shades out the heavy brush, allowing good visibility. Soils also are important in scrape-site selection. Most of the scrapes in my study areas have been constructed in sandy or sandy-loam soils.

You have to develop an ability to read scrapes, but this is more of an art than a science. I have seen many an excited hunter sit on a scrape for days without ever seeing the animal that made it. Unfortunately, there are many types of scrapes. Early in the pre-rut period, bucks begin making false scrapes, if for no other reason than to practice. Such scrapes may be constructed and never revisited.

Several bucks I have been studying during the last few years have led me to some interesting ideas about scrape development. There is one buck in particular that best typifies "normal" scraping behavior. He is a nice four-year-old buck that lives on my farm along a stream bottom. The buck always beds in the same general area during the summer. Early in the fall, numerous rubs appear in the same spot as in previous years. He has destroyed almost all of the saplings in his summer core area. As the pre-rut comes to an end, this buck begins making scrapes within a few hundred yards of his core area. They are always in the same places. One is along a trail that leads uphill from the bedding area, while another occurs along the slope of the creek bottom.

As the buck moves into full rutting behavior, the early scrapes are ignored entirely, but the buck still beds in the same refuge. Each day, however, I find scrapes farther and farther away, always along the creek drainage. By December, the buck regularly is servicing scrapes up and down a two-mile-long trail. Some of these scrapes are given more attention than others. But, sometime late in the month, the buck completely leaves the drainage. He has been seen numerous times several miles away, but he has not yet been killed. My radio-telemetry studies confirm this behavior pattern in other bucks as well.

A scrape line is like a fisherman's trotline. The buck strings out his line and "baits his hooks," hoping to catch a doe. If one or more scrapes starts to produce results, he spends the majority of his time in that area. But, when activity there slows down, the buck either returns to old scrapes to "re-bait" them, or extends his scrape line. In this way, he manages to encounter several unrelated doe groups. These revisits to old scrapes, or construction of new scrapes, generally are interpreted by hunters to mean that "the bucks are rutting again." It is a good observation, but the wrong interpretation. Bucks always are rutting once the rut begins - they just are not always in your area.

PUTTING IT ALL TOGETHER

In order to score on a big buck, you must put all of this information together into a workable hunting strategy. The strategy you select depends on whether you are hunting the pre-rut or rut period. Both rubs and scrapes most commonly occur along slopes of streams, with little vegetation to obscure visibility. With a little practice, and by studying some good aerial photos and topographic maps, you should have no trouble picking out the high-probability areas. Next, you need to put together a composite rutting picture. There are sure signs to a rutting buck truly being active in your area. First, there will be freshly worked scrapes.

These are easy to recognize, because they are pawed out daily and often smell like a pig pen. The presence of hoofprints and fresh droppings is a sure giveaway.

But, the presence of a scrape alone is no assurance that there is a good buck in the area. Look for signposts. They are the single most important clue to finding trophy bucks. A freshly worked scrape line should have a signpost somewhere along its length. *This is precisely the place to hunt.* You literally have found the pot of gold at the end of the rainbow.

But, you must be careful when hunting a signpost. Its presence usually means the buck is bedding very near. Too much disturbance or the wrong move can cost you a great deal of work and a trophy buck. For example, I had a fine 20-inch-plus buck located last season. He had a huge signpost on an old cedar and an incredible string of baited scrapes leading past it. I asked one of my assistants to set up a tripod stand for me along the trail, and he did so. Arriving before daylight, I climbed into the stand seat and waited for dawn.

Just about the time I had enough light to make out objects, I discovered to my horror that the stand had been set up right on top of the signpost. Slowly turning my head, I noticed a thick clump of young pines about 20 yards from the stand. The pine thicket was no more than 50 feet in diameter. Our mistake was made obvious when the buck suddenly jumped to his feet and dashed over a small hill before I even could raise my rifle. I gave up on the buck until this coming year-- but this time, my stand will be in the right place!

SUMMARY

Hunting the rut is much more complicated than most hunters imagine. There is more to it than just finding a scrape and waiting for your buck to come by. You have to do a great deal of pre-season scouting, record keeping, and logical thinking. Try not to fall victim to one set way of figuring out a buck. Use both rubs and scrapes to pattern your deer. It is not easy, and it does take time, but it does pay off.

Mike Biggs

Chapter 29

THE TRICKLE RUT: UNDERSTANDING AND RECOGNIZING IT

It is hard to believe nowadays that the white-tailed deer was once on the brink of extinction. As I noted early in this book, market-hunting and wholesale habitat destruction had reduced the whitetail to less than a half-million animals by this century. Prior to 1950, whitetails existed in small pockets of huntable populations, with very few over-population problems. After 1950, however, several positive events caused whitetail numbers virtually to explode.

Elimination of the screwworm in the Southwest, increasing popularity of the hunting club concept in the Southeast and downright hard work on the part of state game biologists all contributed to the rapid comeback of the whitetail. But, alas, we have done our job too well. Today, we have as many or more whitetails than ever existed. Overpopulation threatens the future of the species in many geographic regions. In Texas alone, there now are more than four million animals; and, the herd is still growing! This overpopulation trend will lead to dire consequences, one of which many hunters even now are facing—the trickle rut. What is it? In this brief chapter, I will discuss what causes a trickle rut and how you can recognize the tell-tale signs of its approach.

UNDERSTANDING THE TRICKLE RUT

In order to understand the trickle rut, it is necessary, once again, to review the normal rutting patterns of whitetails. Each year, bucks and does undergo significant changes in both their physiology and anatomy that prepare them for the coming breeding season or rut. *When* the rut occurs depends on many factors. In healthy herds, the rut usually occurs at a time that enables the does to drop their fawns at the most opportune time in the spring or summer. In much of the

A doe will experience several estrous cycles, if she is not bred early in the rut. However, each time she misses being bred, the probability of a successful conception decreases.

Mike Biggs

Pineywoods region of the South, for example, the peak rut occurs around the first of November. This allows the fawns to be born in the April-May interval when forage is abundant and nutritious. In the Mississippi Delta, on the other hand, the rut occurs much later. Why? There have been two explanations proposed. The first, and I might add less plausible, is that the area was stocked with Mexican and South Texas deer. The second appeals to me more. If fawns were dropped during the traditional spring period, flooding would be disastrous to the young fawns!

The rut is late in South Texas for the opposite reason. It is timed so that fawns are born during or after the hurricane season, the time when much of the region's rainfall occurs. Whenever the rut occurs, it is important that it be synchronized with optimum conditions. In order to do so, deer have to undergo a series of changes whose sequence is critical in maintaining the timing of the rut. Bucks have to molt their old summer red coat, replace it with a grayish winter coat of hollow hair, shed the velvet, increase body weight and muscle development, and finally store up enough energy to last through the rut. Does also have to shed and replace their coat, as well as store up energy reserves for the coming cold season. Does live in well-established social groups of related females (matriarchal groups).

In order to better synchronize the fawning period, related does often show tendencies to come into estrus at the same time. This may be coordinated by pheromones (chemicals used to affect another's behavior), or by the genetic similarity of the doe group. At any rate, healthy mature does usually come into breeding condition at about the same time. The number of estrous periods experienced by a doe depends on whether or not she is bred. For example, Pineywoods does often experience a first estrus in mid- to late October. Hopefully, each doe is bred on the first estrous cycle, so there is no need for a second estrus. If a doe is not bred, however, she will continue to cycle at 25-28 days until either she is bred or the breeding season is over.

Unfortunately, the more times a doe misses conception, the lower the probability of a successful pregnancy. In well-managed herds, there usually are three peaks in the rut. The first, or primary rut, occurs when the mature does come into estrus. The secondary rut occurs when the yearling does come into breeding condition. The third, or tertiary rut, occurs under one or both of two conditions.

First, does not bred during the primary and secondary ruts come into a third estrus. Fourth and fifth estrus have even been reported for some herds. Second, in extremely well-managed herds, or in herds that are growing rapidly under protection, the first-year fawns may even come into estrus. I have seen this on several occasions, usually in herds maintained well below carrying capacity. Therefore, the physical condition of the herd has much to do with the timing of the rut. I have moved the rut forward by a full month by controlling the population and in-

Mike Biggs

In order for the rut to occur in a discrete time interval, both bucks and does have to coordinate an entire series of physiological and anatomical changes, among which are shedding of the summer coat, accumulation of body fat, and mineralization of the antlers.

---

creasing the quality of herd nutrition.

Bucks also come into "season." The cue for timing of the rut is the length of the night. As the days become shorter, bucks begin to produce testosterone at higher levels, which triggers the typical rutting behavior of bucks. Under the influence of male hormone, neck and shoulder muscles begin to over-develop in response to daily rubbing exercises. These muscles are important to the coming combats with potential rivals. As I noted earlier, the rut is a pretty complex series of events, each step of which must precisely be timed in order to assure successful reproduction.

When deer are in poor condition this

precise schedule is thrown off, reducing reproductive capacity and, most important to sportsmen, making the herd very difficult to hunt. When herds have no well-defined rutting period, this is called a **"trickle rut."** Instead of does coming into estrus in a more or less synchronized manner, each doe becomes reproductively ready only after she has managed to satisfy her own physiological needs. As strong as the reproductive urge is, the doe "thinks" of herself before reproduction. If she does not have adequate stored energy to support herself and her developing fawns through the winter, the doe simply will not bother to breed.

LEARN TO RECOGNIZE A PENDING TRICKLE RUT

Since many whitetail herds are now at or above carrying capacity, more and more hunters each season will have to learn to recognize symptoms of a coming trickle rut, and develop strategies for hunting under these conditions.

Now that you are aware of the trickle rut concept, how do you go about anticipating or recognizing it? Since the trickle rut usually occurs in overpopulated herds, you often can anticipate its occurrence by visiting with professional wildlife managers in your area. They can give you a good idea of the population status of your herd; or even better, if you are keeping adequate records on your herd, you already will be aware of the problem. Unfortunately, biologists often know too well that the herd is above a safe population density and are anxious to discuss the matter with any sportsman or landowner. If, however, you are one of those many hunters who absolutely have no idea where the nearest biologist may reside, here are a few simple clues.

Molt Pattern

The first change to take place in deer at the end of the summer growing season is the molting of the red summer coat. Depending on geographic region, this should occur around the first to middle of September. If you are out in the woods about this time, use a pair of binoculars to examine each deer you see. The red coat is shed fairly rapidly, with the deer experiencing a brief period of "mangy" appearance. This is, the red summer hairs begin to fall out to reveal the thick, grayish winter coat growing beneath. The molting stage should be fairly brief, lasting only a few days. Should you encounter groups of does, some with gray winter coats and others still with summer coats, or should you see reddish colored deer well into the fall, you can suspect a coming trickle rut.

However, just because you notice these cues one year does not mean that there will be a trickle rut each year thereafter. Even in overpopulated herds, an exceptionally good summer, an excellent early fall mast (nuts and fruits) crop, or a die-off during the previous year may be just enough to synchronize an overpopulated herd. So, repeat your evaluation annually.

Rutting Behavior

Another cue to a trickle rut lies in the rutting behavior itself. If there is a pronounced rutting period, it will be made apparent by concentrated and agitated activity in your herd. In healthy herds the sudden appearance of several does in estrus will produce a frenzy among the bucks. Consequently, there will be a dramatic rise in activity, with the number of deer seen per outing increasing. There also will be numerous "motherless" fawns, since the buck will drive away a fawn when he is attending its mother.

In a trickle rut, this peak of activity really never occurs. Frankly, the bucks are confused and spend a great deal of time moving about in search of a receptive doe, instead of setting up breeding territories and sticking with them. Therefore, during a trickle rut, one day you may see a single doe pursued by one or more bucks, followed by several days of inactivity. This can be quite frustrating to the hunter who does not understand what is happening.

SUMMARY

The trickle rut probably is the most frustrating situation in which to hunt whitetails. Unfortunately, with ever-increasing populations throughout the whitetail's range, hunters probably will be faced with hunting the trickle rut in years to come. The ultimate solution is to make an effort to control the population density through adequate removal of antlerless animals. But, hunters and landowners alike often are reluctant to remove sufficient females from the herd.

> **If there is a pronounced rutting period, it will be made apparent by concentrated and agitated activity in your herd.**

Mike Biggs

Chapter 30

Does: The Ultimate Bait

It seems nowadays that whitetail hunters are searching for the magic bullet; the one-size-fits-all panacea guaranteed to bring a monster buck running to the gun! But alas, there is no such magic. Yet, there **is** perhaps one exception to this rule. A magic bait does exist that not only drives a mature buck wild, but when properly used can bring even the most battle-scarred veteran running to his end. This wondrous bait is not corn, it is not an "oat patch," and it is not some man-made concoction. Rather, it is the wonder of wonders in the deer world, the whitetail

Mike Biggs

doe! In this chapter, I will discuss how you can use these sweet little ladies to your advantage during the coming season, and hopefully, score on a trophy buck.

In order to understand the concept of using does as bait, let me rehash some of the material presented in the behavior chapters. Much of this discussion cannot be found in the published literature— it is that new to science. For some time now, I have been studying the movements, behavior and habitat preferences of whitetails in the South. I entered into this study with quite a number of pre-conceived ideas about deer. I totally believed what was published about whitetail behavior, and accepted the dogma of science with reckless abandon. But, science is a changing creature. It evolves as more information is gathered and processed on each aspect of our natural surroundings. So it is with whitetails.

I first discovered that the reported sedentary nature of these animals was not necessarily so. Many of the early studies had been conducted in areas where the deer population was so great, that there literally was nowhere for a deer to go. Also, buck:doe ratios were so skewed that even a yearling buck had little need to travel afar in search of receptive does. To my surprise, I discovered that bucks do travel great distances, and that the established concept of home range was faulty. Home range, as with the concept of carrying capacity, often is vague and subject to interpretation. Often, our interpretations relate little to what is important to the whitetail itself. The whitetail buck is a survivor. He has been around for 2.5 million years. Part of his survivability lies in the fact hat he is not predictable. He may be sedentary, traveling only a mile or less during his entire life. Or, he may be a vagabond, venturing as far as 60 miles during his lifetime.

I next discovered that, as often is the case with people, there is a tremendous difference in the way that bucks and does view their world. From the very outset, bucks have different innate behavior patterns that set them apart from does, even in unexploited herds. It has been a common problem among whitetail biologists that excessive numbers of "nubbin" bucks are killed during antlerless harvests. Why? Even at this age, the buck is more aggressive and venturesome. This often puts the little buck in jeopardy, since this diminutive twin sister is more timid and sticks closely to her more experienced mother. With time, the buck expands on this behavior pattern, adapting an individualized behavior pattern which best fits his particular situation.

I only have recently discovered that bucks and does generally prefer different types of habitats. They behave much of the year as if they were two completely different "species," each sex occupying slightly different portions of the habitat available to them. In this way, bucks accomplish two things. First, they give way to the does who often occupy the best habitats. In so doing, the bucks assure that their offspring will survive, thereby passing their genes on to the next generation. Second, the habitat types preferred by bucks are those which better guarantee survival for the bucks themselves. These are the denser regions of the forest-- areas where the secretive buck spends much of its time. The only time this general trend is reversed is during the rut. And, it is at this time that the bucks will abandon their quest for survival to search out breeding does. This is the time when the two sexes share common ground and habitat, and it is the time to use this brief change in behavior to your advantage.

I first came to the idea of using does as bait through my own research and through my long-time association with various guides and outfitters. I have always had a hunting philosophy that revolved around going to the buck, rather than depending on chance to bring the buck to me. The sanctuary and travel corridor concepts arose out of this philosophy. But, as I noted above, science is an evolving creature; and if you are to keep up, you have to evolve with it. The true trophy hunter has a "tool box" that is fully stocked with tricks and tactics that can be drawn on at the proper time. Using does as bait is one such tool.

Successfully hunting a trophy whitetail buck is not easy. Every tactic it seems, no matter how effective, requires a great deal of work on your part. So it is with this technique. Once again, you will have to spend a great deal of time in the woods, studying the individual behaviors of does and doe groups. In the following sections, I will first discuss the tactics necessary to pattern your doe movement and reproductive cycle; and then give you some hints as to how to properly use the **ultimate bait.**

PATTERNING DOE GROUPS

Does spend most of the year traveling in more or less related doe groups. This is a fact that keeps surfacing in this book. They are made up of mothers and daughters, aunts and nieces. There is a tight-knit social order, with a dominant doe (alpha doe) and her subordinates. The fact that the does are usually related, plus the fact that most of these deer are pretty much on the same nutritional plane, dictates that most of the mature does will come into estrus at about the same time. You can also assume that once the estrous pattern of a particular doe group has been established, these deer will stick closely to the timing in future seasons. Therefore, I return to my ever-present note taking activity.

Since does rarely abandon their home ranges as do bucks, a pattern established for does during the summer will pretty much hold true for the fall and winter seasons. There will be difference in the exact portions of the home range in which you will find your does, but the home range will remain pretty static for most of the country. In some northern climates, does may take part in a migration to winter range, yet these areas are pretty predictable. During early September and on into October, I spend my time slipping around the woods in search of deer. These are relatively casual times in which I have the luxury of taking my time. I may sit beneath a tree at a good vantage point

Mike Biggs

Locating and patterning does is one of the most successful techniques used by trophy hunters. If you know consistently where a specific doe will be, you have won half the battle.

for most of the day, recording the number, sex and relative age (adult, yearling or fawn) of each animal I see. How successful you are at seeing and observing deer is directly related to your experience in finding deer.

One of the most commonly asked questions when I talk with hunters revolves around how to find deer. Since I have spent most of my life with deer, the fact that this creates a problem often escapes me. Here are some hints to make the best of your scouting time. As I have noted previously, whitetails evolved in the woods, most commonly in association with creek drainage systems. Their invasion of the more exotic habitats such as South Texas brush country has been more recent, yet even in such areas, deer are associated with wetter portions of the range. Therefore, deer are not distributed just willy-nilly over the landscape. The general annual pattern is for deer to expand their activity into the dryer uplands during the wetter portions of the year, then retreat again to the bottomlands as the summer dry period develops. Hence, you can pretty well expect deer to be intimately associated with streams during the late summer and early fall.

The first thing I look for in potential streamside travel corridors are well established trails. The presence of a heavily traveled trail and unusually high browsing pressure along the trail will guarantee that the trail is a common-use trail. A common-use trail is one that most of the does in the social group use to travel to and from bedding and feeding areas. It also is relatively easy to find the beds of individual does. They usually occur in more open areas such as over-grown fields or young clear-cuts. All of these facts are carefully recorded on maps and/or aerial photographs of the area. Once these trails have been mapped out, I start my daily vigil over-looking common-use trails. Again, I take detailed notes as to the time and direction of travel. This information will give a good indication of the location of bedding and feeding areas; although in the South, bedding and feeding areas may be in the same location.

I grew up in a farming and ranching family in Texas. My grandfather never ceased to amaze me at his ability to identify each and every one of his many head of cattle. He knew at a glance which cow was standing before us, and everything there was to know about her reproductive performance. So it is with deer. Believe it or not, a liberal amount of observation will gain you the ability to identify each doe in a social group. There are little cues such as physical abnormalities and behavioral mannerisms that make each animal distinctly different from the others. As the summer wears on, I try to work out the specific behavior and movement pattern of as many individual does as possible. Those of you that utilize green food plots in hunting deer will find this particularly easy with practice. Don't just sit on the food plot. Slowly work out the doe's travel path by progressively moving away from the food source until you have her normal daily routine mapped out. The importance of this activity soon will become apparent.

PATTERNING THE REPRODUCTIVE CYCLE

Once you have the movement patterns of one or more doe groups worked out, it is time to determine the reproductive cycles of the doe group. If you have taken careful notes and have studied your doe group adequately, you should have by now identified the alpha doe of the group. She is relatively easy to recognize with her constant dominant threats and assertions. A dominant doe will assert herself in subtle and not so subtle ways. She may just look at the other does. Such a gesture will elicit head dropping behavior in subordinate does, a sign of submission. Or, she may be more aggressive when some unwritten rule is transgressed. She may kick, butt or make a charging run at a doe of less social position.

The reason for identifying the dominant doe is that she will probably be the first doe to come into estrus. This is because she is in better condition than the rest, and probably older and more physiologically stabilized. She is the doe to watch, as she will be the trigger to the rutting process.

The timing of the estrous cycle in does can be derived both directly and indirectly. If you have the time to observe your does carefully, there are cues that the doe is about to come into estrus. First, her activity will become agitated and often increased. She will be moving about a little more than the other does. These cues are helpful, but

It is a little known fact, but does as well as bucks use chemicals to communicate their reproductive readiness.

Mike Biggs

if you are lucky, you may get to observe one of the most little known behaviors of does. Few hunters know that does will make scrapes. That's right, they make scrapes. In fact, many of the scrapes so religiously monitored by hunters may actually be made by does! I have seen does make scrapes in both captive and wild situations. Apparently, the doe also feels the need to communicate her reproductive condition by chemical cues. Such behavior in a doe usually means that estrus is either at hand or will be in the immediate future. Also, you can closely examine the hocks of does with a pair of binoculars. Estrous does tend to have dark hocks similar to those of bucks.

Usually, you rarely have the good fortune to make such detailed observations of does. Most hunters lack the time necessary to monitor does in such a manner. If this is so, you will have to resort to more indirect means to pinpoint the normal estrous pattern of a particular doe group. One such tactic is to be at hand when the does begin fawning in the spring. The general pattern is for doe groups to break up during the fawning season. The dominant doe will go to the best fawning site, while lesser does are relegated to less suitable areas. During the first few days after fawning, does rarely move great distances. If you find your dominant doe in an area, you can be assured that her fawns are nearby. She will probably have them hidden in two different areas within her fawning territory. Unless you see her nursing her fawns, you will not be able to tell when she has delivered. However, by ten days she should have her fawns moving about with her, and this probably is the first time you will see them. As soon as you see her with fawns, you can back-date 200 days to the approximate time at which she was bred. This will narrow your search during the coming fall.

I also try to watch the udder or "bag" of my does. In deer, the doe's udder will fill with milk only just before she fawns. Unlike some animals, such as domestic sheep that enlarge the udder many weeks prior to birth, deer tend to limit milk development to a few days before giving birth.

Another commonly used technique revolves around the rut itself. Whenever I see a buck running a doe, I always make a note of the fact. If I can recognize the individual identity of the doe, that goes into the book also. Hence, over a period of several seasons, I can pretty well nail down the estrous cycle of an individual doe social group.

If you detect a receptive doe, you have found the finest bait available. All you have to do is sit back and wait. And you won't have to wait very long! Since a doe is in estrus for only about 36 hours, she should almost immediately attract considerable attention. The trick is to be able to observe her from afar without your presence being obvious. For, it s the doe that you must fear at this time, not the buck. He probably will come in with only the doe on his mind; she, on the other hand, will be the one that gives you away. If you miss the show, don't worry. You have her activity pattern worked out. Although she will probably run from the buck, she will be reluctant to leave her established trail

Mike Biggs

Even the wariest of bucks is drawn to an estrous doe. You can turn this to your favor, provided you do your homework.

system. In fact, it has been my experience that she will return to the point where you first saw the pair, in a manner similar to that of a rabbit pursued by hounds. If you have her home range worked out, you can also limit your hunting to that particular area.

An excellent modification of these techniques is practiced by many commercial whitetail guides. Where legal, keeping your deer on a well-planned feeding program not only improves nutrition, but also allows you to keep track of your does. You would be amazed how often a strange buck will show up with a doe group at feeding time. When a buck shows up, concentrate your hunting on that area, as the buck will be in attendance for the next day or so and there will be other callers in the vicinity.

SUMMARY

These tactics are not the last word in trophy buck hunting, only another "tool for your tool box." As with all trophy hunting techniques, the real trick is knowing when to use the right tool to get the job done. As often has been the theme in this book, the key to success using any technique is spending time in the woods, learning as much as you can about deer behavior and the activity patterns and habits of specific animals.

Chapter 31

TIMING YOUR TACTICS

About ten years ago, about all of the gear that was available to the average deer hunter was a gun, bow, insulated underwear and field clothing. Today, the situation has changed dramatically.

The modern Nimrod now has an incredibly confusing array of technology from which to choose. Grunt calls, plastic rattling antlers, estrous scents, buck scents and enough varieties of camouflage to conceal the hunter in every situation from urban warfare to arctic fighting, are hawked in every outdoor magazine. But, amidst all of the hype, these technologies— when properly applied— do have the potential to increase your chances of scoring on a big buck. The problem lies in knowing how and when to use them. In this chapter, I hopefully will dispel some of the confusion regarding a few of these products (namely grunt calls, rattling horns and scents), while presenting some sound advice on their proper use.

BACK TO BASICS

Although it is probably a rehash of

old information, a short refresher course in basic deer behavior is in order. (Refer back to the initial chapters of this book for a more in-depth analysis.) Even as you read, deer are out there, doing a host of interesting things. Although there is innate worth in knowing about day-to-day deer behavior, hunters are mostly interested in what bucks are doing during the hunting season. Therefore, I will limit this discussion to that period.

Whitetails have an interesting social organization in which the males and females spend much of the year apart. Recent research has demonstrated that bucks and does prefer different habitats during the non-reproductive period. Does remain in well-structured social groups shortly after the fawning period (at approximately 1 year of age). Their mothers force them to leave just prior to fawning; hence, this is a time of dispersal, especially for young bucks. (Studies have shown that orphaning of young bucks actually **increases** their chances of survival!) Once the bucks have joined a social group, they must face years of struggle to attain dominance. Social position is achieved or maintained over the entire year both by covert and overt actions. During the spring-summer period, when antlers are developing, bucks butt, kick and use "body language" to dominate rivals. Every opportunity is taken to assert strength over another buck. You would think that subordinate bucks would do better to leave and establish their own social group, but there is much to be learned and gained by "hanging around with the boys."

Perhaps the best time to improve one's social position is during the early-fall sparring period. During this time, younger bucks conduct ritualized sparring matches, which serve to train them for more serious fights and to demonstrate their increasing strength. Antlers serve many functions, among which are sparring, fighting and scent dispersal. Once a buck has a sufficiently large set of antlers to engage an opponent, body strength becomes more important. That is why I often have seen large-antlered bucks bullied by smaller-antlered bucks with larger bodies and more experience. Bucks fight not only to attain dominance during the coming rut, but also to gain a higher social position in the next year's rut. Coupled with a natural aggressiveness, due to increased hormone levels, bucks always are looking for an opportunity to express their abilities during the rut-preparation and pre-breeding periods. An understanding of the types of fighting is helpful.

There are two basic types of fighting observed in whitetail bucks. First, there are sparring matches, which signal the beginning of the rut-preparation period. These are nothing more than tests between bucks of the same social group. They also can be likened to the blocking session held as part of football practice. The sparring matches are not serious, but they tell of what is to come. The second type—and, I might add, most uncommon— are the true battles. These fights come as the rut nears, and usually take place between two dominant bucks of different social groups. These fights are something to behold! The bucks circle each other with ears laid back and hair on end. Their eyes are turned back in their heads, and at some unseen signal the combatants come together with a force that would make mountain sheep envious!

It also is during the pre-rut that bucks begin to expand their interest in scent-marking. Remember that bucks and does scent-mark throughout the year, but it is most pronounced at this time. The whitetail evolved in the forest; that is an established fact. Being a forest animal, as I have said, it must rely heavily on scent communication. Visual displays, often seen in prairie mammals and many birds, are of little use in the dense forest growth. Furthermore, I feel that deer populations in pre-Columbian times were not very dense, requiring that animals leave "notes" for one another in order to communicate. Several innate behavior patterns are of interest to the hunter. First, it is a fallacy that whitetails use scent communication only during the rut. To the contrary, deer regularly communicate with each other by a whole host of glandular secretions throughout the year. The forehead gland, for example, is used over much of the year, although its exact purpose is still debatable. Does even rub-urinate when they meet an unfamiliar doe in the woods.

The impact of testosterone on buck behavior is unquestionable. Increases in blood-level of this hormone initiates antler-velvet shedding, muscular development and scraping behavior. Muscular development is attained, under the influence of the steroid, by the rubbing of antlers against anything that presents resistance. Glandular secretions often are deposited on rubs as a means of identifying the perpetrator of the signpost. Scraping, although considered by most hunters to be an activity exclusive to bucks, as I noted above, is done by both sexes. Which hormone(s) produces this behavior in does is not known, but the fact remains that a percentage of the scrapes found in the woods were initiated by does! However, the general message is that there is a receptive doe in the area, awaiting attention. Whitetails have an uncanny ability to trail another deer from scent left at these "communication centers." I have seen bucks trailing an estrous doe like a hound on a hot scent trail. However, this trailing probably is related to the interdigital

Bucks have the ability to trail estrous does like a hounddog on a blood trail.

Mike Biggs

glands as much or more as estrous scents. Deer recognize differences in odors produced by another deer. The complex combination of interdigital gland scent and the estrous scents probably are the cues used by bucks in trailing does.

The timing of scraping is important. Generally, most deer begin scraping during the pre-breeding period, reaching highest intensity just prior to the peak of the rut. At that time, the air must be permeated with a confusing array of odors, signifying all sorts of physiological conditions. This is particularly true in herds that are in good physical condition, because synchronization of the rut is pronounced in such herds. Overpopulated and poorly managed herds seldom show a distinct peak in rutting activity, and consequently are very difficult to hunt. Once the pronounced peak rut is completed, rutting activity subsides for about 23-26 days. During this time, bucks either move to adjacent territories or lie low in an effort to conserve energy.

A second, less-pronounced peak in the rut (often called a "secondary" rut) usually occurs about a month after the initial, primary rut. By this time, some bucks have lost libido, from reduced testosterone production. Younger bucks tend to begin socializing by this time, while older bucks remain pretty much loners until after the second rut. It is very rare to see two bucks square off in a sincere fight. Social position is well established, and it would be a waste of energy to engage in such behavior. Understand that the buck is primed to participate in a single, pronounced rut early in the season, and is generally worn down by the end of the reproductive period. In some herds, a brief third rut occurs in which a few young does, and even fawn does, are bred. However, this rut is so seldom seen, or, if occurring, so minor, that there is little need to consider it a plus in your favor.

The post-breeding period finds bucks, no matter their social position, trying to recover from the rigors of the rut. Bucks lose as much as 35 percent of their body weight during the rut. They spend more of their time in the post-rut "worrying" about escaping detection by hunters and replenishing food stores, rather than about mating. Scraping activity now is primarily one of habit more than necessity, and no buck in his right mind would be caught fighting. The time for that is well past.

Now, the question arises: How do you make sense out of this complex activity, in order to put venison in your freezer and a bragging-sized rack on your wall?

DEVELOPING A PLAN OF ATTACK

Technologies available to the hunter are of no use unless they are applied in the proper manner and at the proper time. In spite of my purist tendencies, I have come to use many of the available "gimmicks" to help me harvest trophy bucks. It appears that the whitetail is now co-evolving with technology, in a way similar to largemouth bass coping with new lures, to the point that the hunter must engage in a "cat-and-mouse" game if he is to be successful.

Over the years, I have been lucky enough to produce some pretty fine bucks as a whitetail biologist. Unfortunately, however, I soon discovered that producing a trophy buck was only the first step. If he could not be placed on the hunter's wall, my job was not completed. Hence, I too, have evolved with the deer. Here are just a few tips in using existing technology to your favor. (Reasons for the above discussion soon will be obvious.) In order to make things more clear, I have included a timetable of the rut and suggested use of appropriate technology.

Early Season

Because many hunters now begin the year bowhunting, there are numerous opportunities which previously were unavailable. Bucks in most areas rub out of the velvet during early September (October in the Mississippi Delta). After the antlers are clean, they rub everything in their path, as they travel to and from feeding and bedding areas. Bucks also mark trails with frontal scent and make rudimentary scrapes.

This is a good time to begin making mock scrapes and rubs. To make a mock scrape, all you have to do is take a stick (or shed antler, if you are a purist) and scrape a place beneath an overhanging limb by an established trail. Mock rubs are made in similar fashion, by rubbing an antler against a sapling until the shiny underbark is exposed. Some type of scent then should be applied, although it not always is necessary, to the mock rub or scrape. Now, this is as good a place as any to discuss commercially available scents. Frankly, I have some real problems with these products.

The chemicals produced by deer for communication probably are short-lived, volatile fatty acids. Their life-expectancy and range probably are quite limited. This creates the basic question: What is in the bottle of scent you

Robert Skinner

Mock scrapes are useful in bringing bucks to you during the pre-rut period. Mock scrapes can be constructed, either using commercially available rutting buck scent or left untreated. The simple visual cue of a "pawed out" depression appears to be adequately stimulating to a rutting buck.

Mike Biggs

When properly timed, rattling during the period just prior to the rut can be quite rewarding, provided you are patient and allow the bucks time to respond to this calling technique.

---

purchase? At this point, we really do not know what is in that bottle! It seems logical to me that, once a chemical of this nature is placed in the bottle and stored on the shelf, there surely is some serious degradation of chemicals occurring. By the time the product reaches your hands, it may simply be water and ammonia. But, in spite of all this, you may surprisingly elicit a behavioral response with these products. Dr. Larry Marchinton and Dr. Carl Miller, at this very moment, are methodically analyzing these compounds for the answers.

There are two basic types of suitable scents on the market. The first is a buck rutting scent, usually taken from the tarsal glands of rutting bucks— or at least, that is where it should come from. These scents probably have more validity than the others. The second type is an estrous scent, derived from does supposedly in heat.

When and how you use each of these scents greatly will determine your success. During the pre-breeding period, it is best to apply rutting scent to both mock rubs and scrapes. Use of an estrous scent is inappropriate at this time. (Which brand you use is up to you, as I have found most to be similar.)

During the rut-preparation and pre-breeding periods, limited rattling can be productive; however, how you rattle is critical. Refer back to my discussion of the types of fights between bucks. The pre-rut finds many young bucks sparring with other bucks from the same social group. This is too early for all-out fights. If you bang your antlers together in a terrible commotion at this time, all you are going to do is run every self-respecting buck out of the county! Set up along a rub line, so that you have a good advantage on an approaching buck. Just "tickle" the antlers together for small bursts of 10-15 seconds. Wait 15 minutes and try again if no response. This also is not the time to use rutting-buck scent. The bucks are not rutting yet, and the smell of a rutting buck will serve only to frighten away a potential trophy. Likewise, the use of a grunt call now may bring some deer, out of curiosity, but it seldom will get you a good buck. Save the grunt call for later.

My good friend and whitetail outfitter Bob Harris and I have had a running disagreement for several years now about rattling. Fact is that his technique and mine are different. But, it also is a fact that both of us enjoy a certain amount of success. The main difference is in when we do what we do. The time to make a terrible commotion is just prior to the peak of the rut. This is the time when bucks are the most stirred by high blood-hormone levels. This also is the time that big bucks begin to roam and to establish rutting territories. Because this also is the most likely time for "strange" bucks to meet, most of the fights occur just prior to the rut.

The time period involved is only a few days, so make the most of it. (Several portions of this book outline techniques for determining the peak of the rut.) By this time, the chosen area should be covered with active scrapes and rubs. Pick your spot carefully. I like to find an active scrape along a trail leading from a buck sanctuary, and concentrate my rattling uphill and upwind from the scrape trail. I use a liberal amount of rutting scent on the downwind side of me, as this is the direction from which a buck is likely to approach. Austerity should not be an issue; use two or more bottles if necessary.

The rattling sequence is simple. I begin with a ground thump made with the butts of the antlers, followed by a resounding crash of the antlers. Make as much noise as possible, even thrashing the bushes nearby. The whole sequence lasts 20 to 40 seconds; then, I put down the antlers and wait for at least 15 minutes. If a buck does not respond, I repeat the process on and off for as long as an hour in the same spot. To add to the show, I also blow a grunt call, using the word "ahhhhh," repeated several times to simulate effort. Remember, the buck may not respond right away. I often am concerned that hunters will buy a set of rattling antlers, try them once and, if they do not work right away, toss them into the closet. Have patience, and give them time to work.

The Rut

Once breeding has commenced, all of the rattling in the world probably is not going to work. This is the time to use the grunt call and estrous scents. You will be attempting to simulate the following events. First, a buck finds a doe either by trailing her or airborne odors

This shows a "typical" rut for many parts of North America. (Shift times to fit yours.) Gray areas are periods of greatest success with most methods.

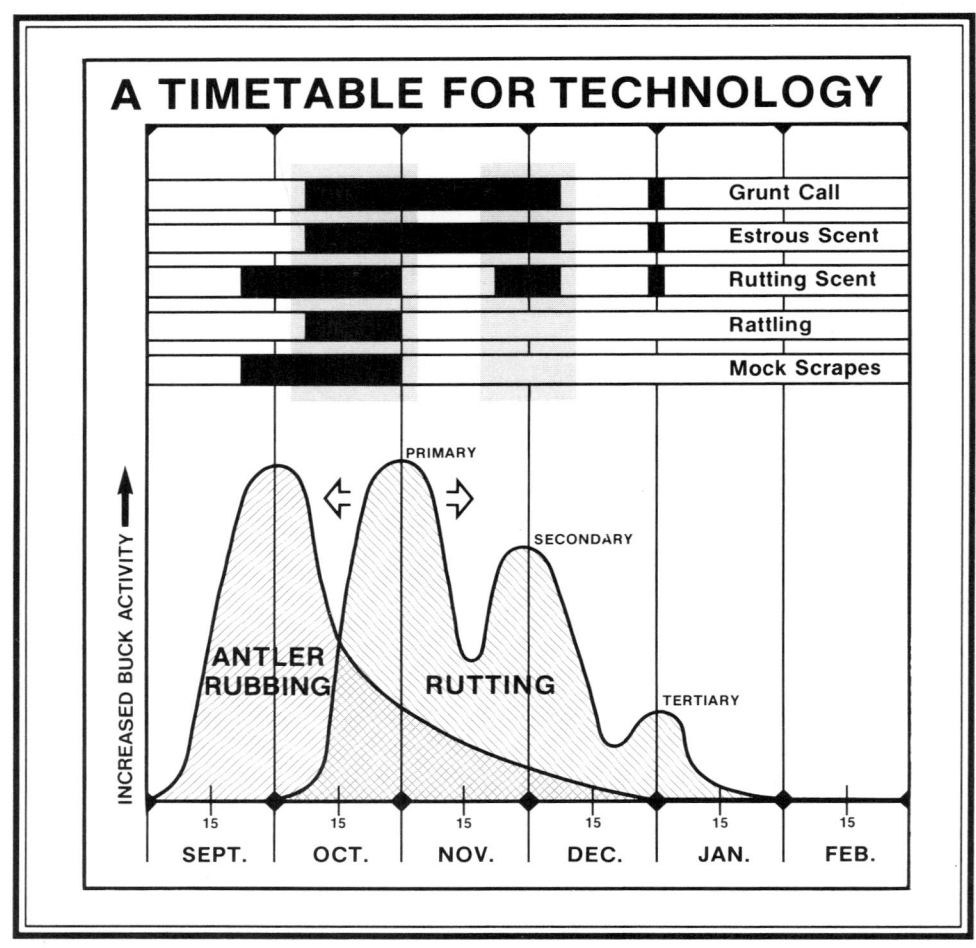

from her body. As he approaches, he issues a series of small grunts, similar to those used in the doe:fawn nursing relationship. The grunt is variable in pitch, depending on the age of the buck and the conditions. Several bucks may be attracted to the estrous doe at the same time, each buck emitting his own grunt version. A dominant buck takes the grunt sequence of a subordinate buck or stranger as a direct affront to his social position, and often will challenge the intruder. Now, how do you go about using this to your favor?

The first thing I do is find a likely location. The best place for calling, as in rattling, is in an area that has a high probability of harboring a dominant buck. An active scrape adjacent to a sanctuary is the best possible place. Areas adjacent to doe feeding areas also are very productive. I apply a liberal amount of estrous scent to the scrape itself, then make several scent stations 20 or so yards downwind from me. I also apply an adequate amount of rutting-buck scent in the same locations. Remember, you are trying to simulate the attendance of a receptive doe by another buck.

Once the scent stations have been deployed, I find a good vantage point and let the grunt call do its magic. Most of the available brands will work, but I use Eli Haydel's call— mostly because he was one of the first to develop such a call, and partly because I have killed a 190-point non-typical buck using it! I make a short series of calls using the word "who" as I blow the call. The call is made by a buck as he runs behind or approaches a doe, so put some emotion into it. A slight variation on this technique involves using the word "whoah" blown into the call, to simulate a subordinate buck's grunt. Personally, I prefer to use the dominant version. If the buck does not respond immediately, I give him another chance after about 20 minutes. He well may be with a doe already, and as with turkeys, no amount of calling will lure him away from a sure thing.

I also am compelled to make a comment in regard to calls. Several outdoor writers have produced articles extolling the virtues of the "tending doe grunt" call. This is utter nonsense, as does do not make grunts while the breeding ritual is taking place. As I noted in the chapter on spring and summer behavior, does do grunt, but only as part of the maternal behavior pattern. It is a shame that some companies tend to invent deer behaviors, just to sell their products.

I also have had reasonable success with estrous scents during the rut, by establishing scent trails leading from active scrapes. A doe urinates in an active scrape when she is receptive. As she leaves the scrape, she leaves an identifiable trail, arising from several possible sources, for the buck to follow. This is not to say that the doe also finds the buck simply by hanging around the scrape area. Returning to check his "baited line," the buck picks up the trail and follows. Using estrous scents, I treat the scrape and then deposit an easily followed trail to a good vantage point for an ambush. Manufacturers sell all sorts of gimmicks for depositing such trails, but just dripping the bottle behind you is as good as any other method, in my opinion.

After The Rut

After the primary rut is completed, you can put away your grunt calls and rattling horns for at least a month. During this time, it is better to use other techniques, such as hunting travel corridors and sanctuaries. The rut is less pronounced from now on, so do not over-state your case. Whatever seems unnatural to a mature buck will be avoided. He knows better than you what should be going on at that time. The next time to strike is during the secondary rut, a little less than a month after the first.

Taking advantage of the secondary rut requires a little finesse and a whole lot of homework. Bucks by this time are wiser than during the primary rut. Safe within their sanctuaries, big bucks seldom venture forth except for a sure thing.

The post-breeding doldrums bring the most frustrating times for the trophy hunter. No amount of technology will work during this time. Occasionally, a distress call will elicit some response, but this is rare. The only technique that seems to work is to "tickle" my rattling antlers lightly in a broken-record fashion. This performance, used entirely without scents, is repeated over an hour or more in hope that a buck will respond, mostly out of curiosity. But, to be honest, I find that other post-rut hunting techniques are more productive. Techniques such as silent drives and "rocking" (throwing or slingshotting stones into buck sanctuaries) have produced more post-rut bucks for me than rattling, grunting or scents.

SUMMARY

Hopefully, this primer on the use of modern whitetail technology has removed some of the guesswork. When asked by hunters whether or not these "gimmicks" work, I always give the same answer: "Does a purple worm work in bass fishing?" The answer, of course, is "yes." In the right hands and at the right time, high-tech gimmicks do work, but only if you have done your homework. Always remember that your greatest weapon is your mind, and when it's used properly, the result may be a real wallhanger.

Chapter 32

ADVANCED RATTLING AND CALLING TECHNIQUES

Mike Biggs

I recently gave a couple of presentations at the Dixie Deer Classic in Raleigh, North Carolina. It was the same presentation I have given many times over the country. And, just as with many such talks, a fellow came up afterwards, hat-in-hand. "I know just about everybody knows how to rattle and call deer," he confessed, "but I just can't get the hang of it." I asked him about his experiences with rattling horns and deer calls. An all too familiar story developed. It seems that he had little faith in the reliability of these techniques in his area. He only tried them in moments of desperation. Unfortunately, he is no different than most of the hunters I know. Here is how the average hunter rattles or calls deer.

He goes out just before daylight, climbs into his stand and fidgets until about 8:30 or 9:00 a.m. Since he knows that these "gimmicks" don't really work, he pulls out his antlers or call just before abandoning the stand, rattles for about thirty seconds, looks around for maybe a minute, and then gives up. His rationale is that, since he is going into camp anyway, what can it hurt? Over the last decade there probably have been about as many articles written on rattling and calling deer as there have about the rut! But, before you flip over to the next chapter, not everything on the subject has been said. Although rattling and calling bucks now are common techniques, few hunters really know the ins and outs of calling deer. Most of the hunters I know have absolutely no idea how to use the equipment, where and when to use it, and what to expect from the deer in return. In this chapter, I will discuss some of the time-tested advanced methods I have found useful in luring bucks into bow and rifle range, both before and during the rut.

THE BASIC PRE-RUT BEHAVIOR PATTERN

Pre-rut Period

I already have given you a detailed discussion on the basic behavior of whitetails. But, there are some specific points about which I should remind you. For, a good understanding of rut behavior is important to using **rattling** and calling to your benefit.

Once bucks shed their velvet, the uncontrollable urge to rub something manifests itself. Prior to the rut, bucks tend to isolate themselves in preparation for the rigors of combat and courtship. With the passing of each day, the buck becomes increasingly aggressive. Many of my articles on patterning bucks have centered around the use of rubs in working out the travel corridors of bucks. Since bucks are obligatory "rubbers" during the pre-rut period, a single buck may rub a hundred or more

trees and saplings. We now understand that there is more than one function for rubbing. First, under the influence of the steroid, testosterone, the constant rubbing action serves to provide intensive workouts for the neck and shoulder muscles. Second, rubs serve as signposts on which various chemical communicators are deposited. As I noted earlier in this book, these chemicals come from a variety of places, including the forehead gland and the tarsal glands. Scents deposited during tarsal rubbing-scraping behavior are picked up on the forehead

Bucks are obligatory "rubbers" during the pre-rut period. The sounds of rubbing are highly atttractive to bucks, especially older individuals.

Mike Biggs

and antlers. As the buck rubs his antlers and forehead against a tree, these chemicals are deposited, producing a chemical message to other bucks.

Later, the rubbing behavior becomes quite pronounced, especially among older bucks. Mature bucks tend to choose larger trees for signposts. It is not uncommon for extremely large bucks with massive antlers to select trees, ten or more inches in diameter! This rubbing sequence is particularly impressive. The big buck will approach his favorite signpost, often shortly after rising in the morning. Bracing himself a few feet away from the tree, he slams forward bringing his brow tines in sudden contact with the tree's surface. A resounding "thunk" often is heard for a great distance. The buck then rubs his brow tines briskly up and down, working his neck muscles severely. He may also push with all his weight against the tree. In so doing, he leaves a characteristic depression in front of the tree. Obviously, rubbing serves two functions. First, it prepares him for serious combat with an equally matched opponent. Second, the sound produced by this activity can be heard for great distances. It is pretty intimidating, even for a whitetail biologist who certainly has no prospect of taking this fellow on!

Along with the sounds and sights of antler rubbing, there also are many vocalizations. The most common one emmitted during antler rubbing by truly big bucks is the **effort grunt**. Along with the tell-tale sound of brow-tines hitting wood, the buck often makes a deep "uuummmpf" in conjunction with the effort of striking and rubbing the tree. Again, this sound can be heard for quite some distance.

All of this work pays off during the combat period. The big bucks are spoiling for a fight during the few days leading up to the rut. All reason has left them. They are fully muscled and extremely aggressive. Anyone who has ever owned a "tame" buck knows full well how dangerous such an animal is! Although there are very few records of bucks attacking humans in the wild, a tame buck is perhaps one of the most dangerous animals on the earth. My penned bucks can usually be bluffed during their first two years. But, come the third rutting season, they quickly learn that I am nothing to worry about. That precisely is why I remove their antlers before this time.

Two mature, keyed up bucks coming into contact is a sight to behold. The bucks approach each other in stiff-legged fashion. There is no doubt what is about to happen, only when. As they near each other, each buck appears to change color before your eyes! What actually is happening is that the hair is raised in an attempt to appear much larger than reality. It is body size, not antlers, that will determine the outcome of the confrontation. The bucks then begin to circle, eyes turned back in a peculiar fashion.

One of the most interesting sounds made by bucks is the snort-wheeze. It is an aggressive vocalization, pure and simple. It only is made by bucks. I never have heard a doe make such a sound. The snort-wheeze is difficult both to describe and to make. Here is

As a buck approaches a doe, he often "struts his stuff," with antlers in prominent display. Grunting also is used at this time.

my best attempt at describing the sound.

Open your mouth ever so slightly, and draw in four or five rapid breaths. Each should be as deep, but as staccato as possible. Then quickly exhale with a loud hissing sound. The exhale should be protracted as long as you have the breath to make a sound. Unfortunately, there is no call on the market today that simulates this sound.

Eli Haydel (Haydel's Game Calls, Bossier City, LA) and I have worked for more than a year now attempting to duplicate the snort-wheeze mechanically, but we still are not satisfied with the call. He has a commercially available tape made at Mississippi State University of actual bucks making the snort-wheeze and other sounds. I highly recommend it, especially if you wish to make these sounds yourself.

At some hidden signal, the two bucks come together with an awful crash. The typical sparring "tickle" of younger bucks does not even compare to this sound. Then all thunder breaks loose! I have seen truly big bucks fight for thirty or more minutes, until one either was killed or severely punished for his transgressions. During the fight, however, dirt, rocks and trees all are thrown into the air. In addition to the clashing of antlers, stomping of hooves and assorted debris flying through the air, both bucks will emit several effort vocalizations. These sounds, called **effort grunts**, are similar to the sounds made by men lifting heavy objects. They are not unlike the sound made by a big buck when he works out on his signpost. Often, the grunts are long and protracted, and similar to a drawn-out breeding grunt.

The Rut

After the combat period, bucks tend to settle down (if you can call it that!) to the problem at hand— finding a suitable doe to court. Most hunters now understand how the buck and doe come together. Through a series of visual and chemical cues (see **Deer Senses**), both the doe and buck seek out the opposite sex. Once together, the buck begins a courtship ritual, every bit as interesting as those of the showiest of birds.

The buck really struts his stuff, coming toward the doe with head held high and the "full glory" of his muscled physique on display. Lesser bucks may forego this formality and rush in with their heads down and neck extended. In both cases, the bucks emit a deep grunting sound, now familiar to many hunters. It is amusing to me that I never heard a hunter report hearing a buck grunt until grunt calls came on the market. Yet, bucks were out there, grunting themselves silly year after year. My friend, Dr. Jim Corbin, tells me that diaries of earlier East Texas explorers report that the Caddo Indians were very proficient at calling in deer by grunting with their voices. Seems there is little really that is new!

Whether or not the grunt serves any really stimulatory function is uncertain. It may only be an unrelated sound made as part of the display or "begging" phase. Personally, I feel that the grunt does serve an important function in courtship. But, it does have one negative point. It immediately draws the attention of other bucks! The sound of a buck grunting is a sure bet that courtship is taking place. This may not be any real concern to a dominant, mature buck, but to a younger buck it only invites trouble.

Recently, some individuals have asserted that the doe makes a grunt in response to the buck's call. In my many years of deer research, I never have heard such a sound, although I am willing to be proven wrong.

A Word About Sounds in the Woods

Whitetails evolved in a woodland situation. As with many woodland species, dense habitats dictate that elaborate mechanisms be developed to aid in getting the sexes together during the breeding season. Many mammals have developed unique calls and chemicals for this purpose. Whitetails are no ex-

Mike Biggs

Many of the sounds produced by whitetails are low-pitched in nature. A buck often makes low grunts as he walks. These sounds are perfect for communicating through dense vegetation.

ception. Although whitetails have several senses at their disposal, two seem to play an important role in buck:buck and buck:doe communication— scent and sound.

In spite of what you may read, we still know very little about the chemical communication of deer. As one who has studied the chemical communicators (pheromones) of everything from army ants to deer, let me assure you that such chemicals more often than not are highly complex systems, whose formulations are difficult at best to determine. Even when we identify a specific chemical involved in animal communication, there are two problems. First, a compound known to elicit some fixed behavior may elicit quite another if present in the wrong concentration. For example, my research with ants showed that attractive pheromones became repellents when present in too high a concentration. Second, and perhaps even more important, a single chemical may not be involved. There may be several compounds involved. Do you see the problem? Consequently, I spend little time worrying about eavesdropping on the chemical communication of deer, or using it to my advantage. But, when it comes to sounds, that is quite a different story.

Whitetails have evolved a sound communication system which lends itself to communicating in the woods. Most of the sounds made by deer are low-pitched in nature. This is due to the physics of sound. Low frequency sounds tend to travel better through substances than high pitched ones. Higher frequencies are useful when there is little vegetation to block the transmission of sound, such as open prairie.

When one considers the spectrum of possible sounds to be made by deer, the grunt and its derivations is the most likely candidate. The higher pitched alarm calls are suitable for short range communication. In addition, there are non-vocal sounds that can be made by deer. The antler rubbing and impact sounds discussed earlier are perfect examples.

PUTTING IT ALL TOGETHER

What all this boils down to is that **you** can use these characteristics of deer communication to your advantage. Here's how.

Antler Rubbing

Last October, I was fortunate enough to hunt New Brunswick with my friends Gordon Whittington and George Chase. Gordon and I have been close hunting buddies for years, but George was relatively new to me. I am very picky about who I hunt with. But, George and I hit it off fine from the start. It seems that George was one of the few people I have encountered who had discovered a calling technique I have used for years. He uses antler rubbing to call in big bucks!

The bowhunter often is at a disadvantage in that the rut most commonly occurs **after** the bow season. Consequently, bowhunters rarely have the opportunity to call in a good buck; rather, they must rely on traditional techniques such as patterning and trail sitting to harvest a good buck. But, this should not be the case. Bucks can be called in during the pre-rut period, using antlers.

Remember that, as with every technique used in trophy buck hunting, you want to simulate as closely as possible what is going on out there at that point in time. The flyfishermen call it "matching the hatch." It surely makes little sense to go clashing antlers together during the pre-rut period. It only will serve to run off the bucks. But, it makes a great deal of sense to use antler rubbing to accomplish the same thing. Remember that big bucks daily take part in the rubbing ritual. If you can simulate this sound within a big buck's territory, he may just come in to investigate.

The technique is simple. As with George, I use a single antler; either side will do. Take the antler in both hands and strike it firmly against a good-sized tree. Then slowly rake a tine up and down on the tree. I even make an effort grunting sound just shortly after striking the tree.

Bucks respond to antler rubbing in a much different way from antler rattling. Most commonly, a big buck will come in very carefully, usually downwind. He is not sure who has violated his territory, and since he is not as yet overly aggressive, he really would rather not fight. Don't overdo the rubbing. Just rub a minute or two and wait. It may take a buck a half-hour or more to respond, so be patient. Try to position yourself so that the buck must give you a clear view as he passes downwind. This also is a good time to use a partner, especially if you are a bowhunter.

Antler Rattling

As I already noted, much has been written about antler rattling. However, here are some hints seldom discussed. In rattling, there are two rules to live by. First, it does you absolutely no good to rattle where there are no rutting bucks. Although hunters occasionally kill a good buck by just randomly selecting a spot and banging two horns together, the consistently successful hunter is very selective about his rattling location. I always rattle near active rutting buck sign— rubs, signposts and scrapes. I also try to make the buck come uphill, if possible. Since most travel corridors occur adjacent to drainages, I position myself upslope from the path of travel.

Second, and possibly foremost, it does you no good to rattle one time and go to the camp! You should decide to use rattling on a specific day and stick with it the entire day. I use the bass fisherman analogy to describe my rattling technique. The bass fisherman goes out with his assortment of lures and begins working a predetermined series of likely looking spots. He uses structure and has a strategy matched to the time of day and type of structure being fished. So it is with the hunter. I suggest that you have a pre-determined rattling course established. Start at daylight, rattling for short periods (once every fifteen minutes), for one to two hours at each location. Remember that you may not catch a buck in the right mood to have him just come rushing in on you. He may sneak in for a peek.

Here's a little hint for your rattling routine. Just prior to rattling, I try as much as possible to simulate the events leading up to a fight. I make a loud snort-wheeze call, followed by a ground thump with the butt of my rattling antler. This simulates the stamping of hooves and the aggressive calls of bucks. Then I clash the antlers together with great force. Too many hunters are timid about making noise. They have spent a lifetime trying to be quiet in the woods. Somehow it just does not seem right to make so much noise! But, the more noise the better. Sound does not carry well in the woods, so make yourself known. I break limbs, stomp the ground and blow my grunt call in an effort grunt simulation. Although I probably look quite ridiculous, it has worked countless times for me; and, I have some mighty nice heads on my wall to prove it.

Grunt Calls

Quite a bit also has been written about grunt calls, since these vocalizations were first discussed by Mississippi State researchers. Grunt calls work very well during most of the rutting period. Again, the success of this technique lies more in **when** and **where** than in how. Once again, grunts are best used where bucks and does are most likely to meet. We now know that bucks try to position themselves adjacent to doe feeding areas, so as to intercept the ladies on their way to and from feeding. Areas adjacent to fields or mast producing areas, especially those with many active rubs and scrapes, are perfect setups for grunting.

A short time back, Gordon and I grunted in a nice young buck from several hundred yards in Mexico. Since deer and humans have similar hearing abilities, I conducted some tests to see just how far you could hear a grunt call. In a wooded habitat, I was able to detect the sound for more than 400 yards; while in the open, this distance extended only an additional 100 yards. These distances probably are conservative since, although deer hear very similarly to humans, they have those rather large cones (ears) on their heads for trapping sound more efficiently. Hence, I believe deer can hear a low pitched sound for at least a half mile.

The Mexican buck was so cooperative that I decided to play with him. Several writers have given detailed advice on the techniques of grunting. I tried every variation of the call I could think of, yet the buck was undeterred in his approach. At one point, I must have sounded like Bozo the Clown! On more than one occasion, this has been the case. Apparently, if you grunt at the right time (during the active rut), bucks will respond even if you do mess up a bit. So, don't be afraid to try grunting.

The one mistake hunters make in using a grunt call centers around the length of time they wait after grunting. Too many times I have seen a fellow go out in the woods, pull out his grunt call, grunt three times, wait five minutes, shake his head and go home. My experience has shown that bucks sometimes take up to an hour to respond. The Mexican buck, although deliberate in his approach, took several minutes to span the distance between us. The only reason we saw him coming was that he was in open brush country. If he had been in dense woods, we might not have seen him at all. So, be patient.

SUMMARY

Rattling and calling are two techniques which will work throughout the whitetail's range. However, in order to make these techniques work for you, it is important to match what you're doing with what the bucks happen to be doing. These are just two additional "tools" for you to add to your box of tricks.

Mike Biggs

Chapter 33

Ray Sasser

LUNCH-TIME TROPHIES

How would you like to hunt a place where there are few other hunters, and where, when you see a deer, there is a high probability that it will be a buck? Furthermore, where any buck you see will be the best buck on the property?

Sound pretty good? Well, before you grab your gear and rush out the door to be first in line, you'd better wait a minute. You probably already are hunting there! More than likely you are missing out on some of the best trophy-hunting opportunities only because you don't understand big bucks.

As a whitetail biologist and manager, I often have said that the hardest job I have is getting the hunters together with the deer— especially the bucks. It often seems hunters are doing everything in their power to keep from harvesting quality animals! The average deer hunter goes out well before daylight, endures an often prolonged pre-dawn wait, sits on his stand until around 8:30 a.m., and then returns to camp, either to complain about the poor pickings or lie about what he saw. He then returns to the woods around 3 p.m., to have another sittee until after dark.

But, while he is in camp taking a

midday nap, a totally different whitetail world emerges. The really good bucks, partly due to hunting pressure and partly due to the rut, usually do not start moving around in earnest until about 9:30 a.m. In fact, the majority of known Boone and Crockett bucks have been taken between 10:30 a.m. and noon! By shifting *your* activity period to coincide with that of the mature bucks, you can greatly increase your chances of success.

RESEARCH ON DEER MOVEMENTS

My students and I have been radio-tracking whitetails in the Pineywoods region of East Texas for almost twenty years. Now, radio-telemetry work is *not* as exciting as it is portrayed on television, but our results and computer analyses are indeed exciting. Unfortunately, much of the information you see written on whitetail movements was divined from studies involving primarily does. Mature bucks are difficult to trap, and even more difficult to radio-track. However, after several years and a great deal of effort, we have managed to put together some startling facts about mature hunted bucks and their behavior. Recently, several other researchers, working in such diverse habitats as the Brush Country of South Texas and the Delta country of Mississippi, have corroborated much of what I reported in several of my articles for *North American Whitetail*. The fact is that mature whitetail bucks are different critters indeed from the other segments of the deer population.

Most hunters view the general activity pattern of whitetails as crepuscular; that is, they are active in the early morning and late afternoon. And, in fact, deer pretty much stick to this general behavior pattern during most of the warmer months of the year. Does and younger bucks also may adhere to such an activity pattern even during the hunting season. During the cooler months, however, many deer -- especially mature bucks -- shift their primary activities to the *warmer* portions of the day. I have tried to correlate whitetail movements to such factors as moon phase, barometric pressure, and air temperature. To date, we have found temperature to be the best indicator of deer movement of all environmental variables.

Deer are very sensitive to temperature. During the warmer months, they try to maximize movements during times when temperatures are rather cool. During the hotter portions of the day, they often seek shady places with a good breeze blowing. In East Texas pine forests, for example, our deer prefer the more-open pure pine plantations during the summer, where temperatures are more moderate and there always is a cooling wind. In the fall and winter, however, deer shift activity to areas where there is a good southern exposure, in order to maximize the warmth of the sun and have protection from chilling north winds. Such places are where you are more likely to find a mature buck basking in the midday sun come hunting season.

Lunch-Time Trophies

Mike Biggs

Bucks like this one can only be killed by using unorthodox methods. One method is to hunt all day. The average hunter only hunts during the early-morning and late-evening hours, primarily due to misunderstanding the mature buck's activity pattern.

PROBLEMS WITH HUNTING THE MID-DAY

There are some problems associated with hunting the midday, however. Whitetails depend heavily upon their acute sense of smell for protection. We have noticed that there are certain conditions that work in favor of the deer, and others that work against him.

During the early-morning hours, there usually is less wind and cooler temperatures. Because many of the chemical compounds perceived as odors by deer are volatile in nature, warmer, windier conditions are very much in the buck's favor. But, this is not always the case. Relative humidity has much to do with scent dynamics. This really is nothing new to quail hunters, who have known for years that their dogs are better able to find birds under humid conditions. The early-morning and late-evening hours often are more humid, but they are also cooler. Midday, on the other hand, usually is warm, with the highest winds of the day. The chances of being detected by a buck, therefore, are much greater during a midday hunt.

It also is much more difficult to stalk a deer in the middle of the day. Again, humidity has a lot to do with the problem. Litter on the forest floor has a strong affinity for moisture. Leaves and twigs are less brittle when moist, and are less likely to crack and snap beneath your feet. By midday, however, it is almost impossible to walk on litter without giving yourself away to an ever-wary buck.

DEVELOPING A MIDDAY STRATEGY

Now, let's put all of this technical stuff into an understandable set of tactics that will help you to get that trophy buck. First of all, it ought to be pretty obvious to you by now that, in order to kill a trophy buck, you are going to have to be somewhere besides your camp. My radio-telemetry studies showed that there is no single time in the midday period when you are most likely to harvest a quality buck. The time of day a buck chooses to move about is dependent not only upon temperature and rutting activity, but also upon the buck's own personal experience with you and your fellow hunters. Chances are that if he has been around for any real length of time— and he probably has, if he is a true trophy animal-- he has figured you out pretty well. He knows where each hunter is and his favorite hunting times. Consequently, there are two strategies open to you.

First, if you are the type of hunter who just cannot stand the idea of the other hunters being out there while you are cooling your heels back at camp, go ahead and hit the woods before daylight. But, go out with the full intention of staying *all day*. This tactic really is the best, because moving about during the pre-dawn and post-dusk hours greatly reduces your chances of disturbing the buck. Spending the day on a stand can be similar to sitting on one of those English bicycle seats for 12 hours - especially if you are a veteran hunter who has lost some of that youthful zeal. But, if harvesting a trophy buck were easy, everyone would have trophies on their walls.

If for some reason you cannot stay on the stand all day, you will have to plan your hunt even more carefully. I have outlined strategies in other chapters on how to find those special places (sanctuaries) where bucks hide from hunters. Choose your path to and from your stand carefully, because you do not want to blunder upon your trophy buck while he, too, is out and about.

It is important to understand the above discussion on scents. Scenting conditions often are prime during midday hunting hours, so it will be necessary for you to take every precaution to avoid being detected. I often am asked about the use of the many cover scents available, and whether or not these products are worth using. Here is my answer: *The white-tailed deer has three basic senses with which to detect you: sound, sight, and smell. If you sit still and don't wave your arms like a chicken, there is only one way a buck can detect you, and that is smell. Most of us can sit still; so, to answer the question, yes, I use a scent cover-up.*

I never have been one to recommend specific products, but I can give some advice on the subject. The best cover scents are those that mimic natural smells. Some hunters have had success with compounds that are derived from skunks and foxes, but I now shy away from such products. You just never know what experience or lack of experience a buck has had with scents. I prefer the more natural plant scents available. I use my own concoction of various plant products and chemicals. It has a pleasant smell, and it can be worn directly on the body. As one who started out using skunk scent, I have found this most enjoyable! Does it work? Well, I had a 7-point buck walk 15 yards from me, downwind in a 20-mph wind, without even showing a sign of detection. That is good enough for me. Most of the "odor neutralizers" on the market work equally well.

In order to ensure that you do not leave a scent trail on your way to your stand, I suggest that you do two things. First, you can treat the soles of your boots with one of the cover scents. Some hunters even use doe scent, and claim they have had bucks follow them to their stands. I have had no such experiences, but I never would dispute such claims. The second approach, and one I use often, is to wear rubber boots. I must agree with well-known bow hunter Gene Wensel that rubber usually leaves little if any human scent. I even have used hip waders on colder days to prevent scent from my pants from rubbing off on thick vegetation.

I also might add to my earlier comments about sitting still. During the last few years, I have made a somewhat perverted habit of sneaking up on hunters on my deer club and watching them in operation from a safe, protected position. You would be amazed how many of them could not sit still if their lives depended upon it! They wriggle and thrash around in a manner that would be detected by even the most naive of yearling bucks. Sitting still is critical in midday hunting. Remember that the deer has everything going for it: sight, smell, and sound. One imprudent movement could ruin an entire year's work. There is, however, one way to reduce the probability of detection, should you just have to move. Over the years, I have tended to climb higher and higher into the trees with each succeeding season. I am not one who loves heights, but I have found that a higher perch minimizes detection by sound and scent. Deer often do look up, but they are less likely to look above 45 degrees.

Camouflage likewise is important in midday hunting. I prefer the more muted colors, such as greens and grays. I learned this a number of years ago from European hunters who never have owned a piece of camo-pattern clothing.

Midday hunting tactics do work; I

have many trophy-class heads on my wall to prove it. Most of my best trophies were taken between 10 a.m. and noon. For example, I spent much of the last two years working out a pattern on a very good buck on one of my management areas. The big buck's behavior had not changed for the entire study period. He had found himself a sanctuary in a small creek bottom near an agricultural field. That bottom was so full of briers and vines that there was no way you could approach the deer without being detected. But, I pretty well had figured out his pattern by last opening day. It seems the old buck always spent the early-morning hours leisurely lying and standing within the safety of his sanctuary. About 11 a.m., he would leave the sanctuary by one of two paths, each traveling along a creek bottom-- one trail east and one west. The eastern trail led to a green food plot, while the western one traveled circuitously toward an oak flat.

Because I had no idea which trail he would take, I just flipped a coin. It turns out that I was wrong on my first and second tries. However, I knew that sooner or later I would win. On the third try, I donned my rubber boots, covered myself with cover scent, and headed to my chosen spot. Using a backpack tree stand, I climbed about 20 feet up into a large pine, 40 yards downwind from the trail. It was about 8 a.m., and I knew there would be a good wait. By 10:30, my feet had fallen asleep, and my bladder felt as though I had been to an all-night party, but I tried to hang on for another hour. Like clockwork, the big buck showed himself at 11:15. It was a mistake he did not survive.

SUMMARY

Midday trophy hunting is not easy. It takes hard work and the ability to stand long hours of boredom without moving. But, such tactics can pay off in big dividends to those willing to pay the price. If you try it, I cannot guarantee you that you will kill a record-book buck, but your chances of harvesting the best buck on the property you now hunt will be greatly improved.

Whitetail hunting should be an enjoyable experience-- one which the hunter looks forward to being in the woods throughout the day. Unfortunately, however, many hunters miss out by spending only the early and late hours in the woods.

Ray Sasser

Chapter 34

Mike Biggs

HUNTING NOCTURNAL BUCKS

Dick Idol and I recently were having dinner together, and naturally, the topic of conversation was trophy deer hunting. "You know," he said, "I honestly believe that there are mature bucks out there that are impossible to kill!" I agreed wholeheartedly, since independently I had come to the same conclusion long ago. There is absolutely no animal more difficult to kill than a battle wise, mature whitetail. I honestly believe that there are two "species" of whitetails— those that are hunted by the average hunter, and the "Rambo with antlers" that continues to frustrate hardcore trophy hunters. Even in areas where eighty to ninety percent of the bucks are harvested annually, some bucks grow to maturity, successfully dodge hunters year after year, and finally die of old age. Some of the highest scoring bucks have been incidentally found dead in some of the nation's most heavily hunted regions. But, is the mature whitetail totally infallible? Can the seasoned survivor of countless seasons be taken, even with the odds in his favor? I would never say that there is no such thing as a buck that cannot be shot, but I do feel that many of those hard to hunt bucks can be taken with the proper techniques. In this chapter, I discuss some of the proven, and often unorthodox, techniques used to score by the most successful trophy hunters.

WHY ARE MATURE BUCKS SO DIFFICULT TO KILL?

First, let's examine what it is about trophy whitetails that makes them so difficult to kill. In several chapters of this book, I report on my telemetry research on responses of bucks to hunters. It seems that bucks, if they live past their first season, quickly learn the activity patterns of hunters and each hunter's "signature." This is, a hunter over the years develops techniques that seem to work well, and is very reluctant to change. Techniques are freely shared with other hunters on the club or hunting territory; hence, most hunters in an area use pretty much the same techniques. This may also be true throughout the whitetail's range. Bucks quickly recognize these hunter activity patterns and adjust their own schedules accordingly. Most trophy hunters, on the other hand, spend the entire day in the woods, with the average trophy being taken in late morning. Since I first began writing about midday hunting, suggesting that hunters shift their own schedules to that of mature bucks, many hunters have written me testifying to the success of this technique. Recently, however, these sportsmen are learning the hard way what Dick and I already knew. The mature whitetail buck is the ultimate survival machine. He will adjust his schedule and even his habitat preferences to avoid detection. His repertoire of survival tricks include moving to inaccessible places, and even hiding upon approach by a hunter. I once observed a buck dive into a pond when pursued by a helicopter capture crew, and stick just his nose above the water. At this point, I make it a point never to argue with a sportsman about any odd observation of buck behavior.

By the time most bucks reach maturity, they have become nocturnal, making them very difficult to kill. In order to be successful, you will have to add some "new tricks" to your repertoire of hunting methods.

Mike Biggs

I have been proven wrong too many times! If all of these tactics are not enough to worry about, the mature buck can always resort to the ultimate survival tactic, he can become nocturnal.

I first discovered that old bucks become nocturnal under heavy hunting pressure as part of my radio-telemetry project here in the Pineywoods. I have spent a great deal of time studying buck behavior in relation to that of hunters, and developing legal hunting strategies to harvest trophy bucks. The result of this work, in part, is this book. Legal is the keyword here, since unfortunately too many of the record-book heads have been obtained by less than scrupulous means. A good friend of mine once asked an old indian in Saskatchewan what was the best way to kill a trophy buck in the Province. The old man smiled knowingly and replied, "Hunt night!"

PROVEN TACTICS FOR NOCTURNAL BUCKS

I have the greatest respect for the few professional whitetail guides who annually enjoy success in obtaining their clients the finest trophies possible. In my search for proven tactics, I turned to these men for tried and true methods. One of these men noted with a grunt, "It is hard enough to kill a trophy buck when you are by yourself," He went on to explain, "but, it is quite another to do it with another hunter at your side." I have developed several unusual techniques that can even the odds. Perhaps most successful of these techniques is the silent drive.

Most mature bucks have become totally nocturnal by the late season post-rut period, retreating to their sanctuaries by day and making brief sorties for does under the cover of darkness. My studies have suggested that some bucks even become nocturnal from day one. The survival tactic is brilliant. A dominant buck will travel to a pre-selected area to search for receptive does. Instead of running "willy-nilly" over the countryside as would a younger buck, the old veteran sets up house in a pre-scouted sanctuary. The buck may have found the sanctuary during an exploratory trip as a yearling. Sanctuaries vary considerably in appearance, but they all share one common trait. It is virtually impossible to approach the area without being detected. The buck develops several alternative escape routes, and is long departed when the hunter violates the sanctuary. Most hunters would be shocked to see the monster bucks that routinely move away just out of sight.

Nightly excursions yield a receptive doe, which the buck herds back to his sanctuary. In the relative protection of the sanctuary, the buck attends the doe over the next twenty-four to forty-eight hours. The doe herself is a hedge against hunters. She represents another pair of eyes and ears. Since a buck would rather hide than run, a hunter is more likely to see the doe, as she flits through the thick vegetation with tail flashing, than the buck slipping away in quite a different direction. Once mating occurs, the buck loses interest and the doe drifts off on her own. That night, he again travels forth in search of still another doe. The silent drive can be used to short-circuit this cycle.

I prefer to wait until all else fails before resorting to the drive technique. One thing is for sure, if you don't get him on your first try, you will never get a second chance at him! The technique is simple, but requires considerable advanced work. First, you have to identify a sanctuary, and this is no easy task. In order to do so, you have to apply some creative thinking and downright good logic. In this book, I outline several techniques for locating sanctuaries. The best logic to apply would be to ask yourself one basic question: *Where would I go if I did not want to be detected on this property?* This approach is surprisingly productive. Once you have identified potential sanctuaries, you should locate the most likely escape route(s) to be taken by the buck. This is often difficult to accomplish without spooking the buck in advance. A return to basics is in order. Bucks will use travel corridors to move to and from their sanctuaries. Although rubbing occurs primarily in the early pre-rut period, a dominant buck cannot resist the temptation to leave a few of his calling cards around. If you are hunting the pre-rut and early rut periods, he may even make a few scrapes for you along his travel corridor. The sudden appearance of rubs or scrapes along a trail should alert you that a big buck has set up shop in the area.

Once a travel corridor is located, the key is to pick the right moment to conduct the drive. If you are going to have only one chance at him, you might as well put everything in your favor. For this reason, why not conduct the drive when adequate light is available? The period mid-morning to mid-afternoon is an excellent time for silent drives. These are times when the buck probably will be bedded down, and is more likely to be surprised at your approach, especially in areas where most hunters are in the woods during early morning and late evening hours. The shooter should approach the travel corridor from the downwind direction and *quickly* obtain a suitable vantage point. Use of stands is probably not a good idea, as you want to remain as quiet as possible.

At a pre-determined time, the drivers begin to *slowly* walk with the wind along the travel corridor toward the sanctuary. Although I discourage it, drivers may carry guns should the buck try to double back. The pace should be casual. Remember, this is not a tiger hunt, so there is no need for excessive noise. The buck will be aware of your presence in due time. As to the number of drivers, I prefer to have two when it is possible. I have each man walk parallel to the travel corridor. I ask them not to carry on conversations as they walk along, since I want the buck to attempt to slip out, not dash past the shooter.

One mistake often made by the shooter is to have his attention diverted by a doe. Be deliberate, but do not tarry in identifying the sex of the fleeing deer. If the buck is indeed attending a doe, he probably will move just behind her, so be alert once she has passed. It has been my experience, that you will have only three or four seconds to make the i.d. and then shoot. Remember that this is no time for fancy shots. Take a shoulder shot whenever you are given the chance. If your bullet hits this spot, you can rest assured that the buck will not travel far.

I have used the silent drive method on numerous occasions to harvest trophy-class bucks. I also have had success using a modification of this technique, especially when the number of drivers is limited. I dab a bit of cotton with predator scent and stick it to the driver's hat. The odd mixture of predator, especially if dog urine is employed, and man scents really sends the bucks scurrying for safety.

As interesting as is the silent drive tactic, two other whitetail guides have used a "David and Goliath" trick for years to consistently harvest trophy whitetails. Jon Ducharme and John Finnegan of Dolan Creek Ranches are famous for their unorthodox hunting techniques. I have been hunting with these men for several years, and remain amazed at their knowledge about mature buck behavior. They hunt in the canyon country of Southwest Texas, where the tallest thing is often a javelina! But, in this country, heavy trophy hunting has forced the truly good bucks to become nocturnal. I had a particular interest in killing one of these canyon monsters, so I teamed up with Jon and John during a recent season. One canyon held a tremendously large buck for several years; and, in spite of everyone's efforts, the buck had successfully survived numerous attempts to ferret him out of his canyon sanctuary. The buck had the typical nocturnal activity pattern. He would travel away from his canyon in the dead of night, find a receptive doe, and then return with her to his sanctuary for a couple of days. On approaching the canyon, John produced a long leather thong and began looking for a rock. Selecting the right sized projectile, John began hurling these little cannon balls into the canyon. The technique worked beautifully. First a

The author has found that slingshots are quite useful in rooting out nocturnal bucks from their sanctuaries. Here Jon Ducharme demonstrates the proper technique.

doe, then a buck emerged from the canyon. Although I had to "stretch my barrel" a bit, this technique yielded a marvelous thirteen point buck with twenty inch spread.

I have used a similar technique here in the forested Southeast to shake trophy bucks from their sanctuaries. Since I am not very good at leather work, and the pineywoods is pretty much devoid of rocks, I use a commercial slingshot and rocks picked up in my driveway. This technique works particularly well in thick pine plantations and swampy areas. The technique is simple. First, I identify potential sanctuaries on my hunting territory. Next, as discussed above, I find escape routes the buck may take when startled. It has been my experience that bucks using thick pine plantations as sanctuaries tend to use the stream-side management zones (hardwood stringers left along drainages) for travel corridors. I position myself in such a manner which affords a good view of the drainage and then shoot rocks into the plantation. Sometimes I even dip the rocks in predator scent to add to the effect. But, do not expect the buck to emerge instantly. He may wait several minutes to make his escape attempt. He did not mature on rash decisions, so be patient. As to likely travel direction, I feel that the buck will travel into the wind if it parallels his trail or up the drainage if the wind is crossing the travel corridor.

The one thing that typifies an experienced trophy hunter is that he will try *anything* to harvest a good buck. There is a considerable amount of technology currently available to the hunter. Although I am not normally a fan of technological gimmicks, feeling that your brain is the best gimmick, there are some of these products which can be used when all else fails. Since Dr. Harry Jacobson first studied the vocalizations of whitetails, a number of commercial manufacturers have produced grunt calls. What a grunt call is or what exactly it does is debatable, but they probably simulate the low call a buck makes on approaching a doe. Bucks will resort to all manner of tricks to win the affections of a receptive doe, among which are to give a call similar to that made between the doe and her fawn at nursing. He appears to be appealing to her maternal instincts. Several species of mammals and birds use this technique to woo the female of the species. Grunt calls can be used to lure nocturnal bucks from their sanctuaries.

The technique I use with grunt calls is to approach the sanctuary from the downwind side. I never walk on the trail itself, rather I walk parallel to it. Finding a vantage point some fifty to seventy-five yards from the sanctuary, I give just a few calls in succession. There is a tendency of hunters to overcall, so resist this temptation. If the buck is within hearing range, he will think that another buck is herding a doe nearby. The response is highly variable, and often similar to responses to rattling. The buck may come rushing in or he may circle to get downwind. As a precaution and to further establish the scam, I use a liberal amount of "doe-in-heat" on the downwind side. If the buck does circle, he may thereby encounter one added cue that what he thinks is going on indeed is! I also use an odor neutralizer to reduce my odor.

There are times when you have done everything right, but the buck fails to respond. Should he be with a doe at the time, there is no way you are going to call him away. Therefore, I often return to the same calling point day after day until I get a response. If this technique does not work, I resort to plan B. Plan B is the last in my repertoire of tricks. By late in the season, there is little need to worry about making mistakes. When all else fails, I will try anything.

There probably has been more written in the last five years about rattling than any other topic. Unfortunately, most articles are written from a narrow perspective. What works in one place often fails miserably in others. With the advent of several synthetic rattling horn products, I am concerned that hunters will try this technique, fail and give up on it forever. Although some hunters speak of horn rattling almost as a religious experience, the techniques you use are not as critical as knowing when and where to use them. I once took an examination intended to test the individual's knowledge about whitetail behavior and hunting. I will never forget missing one of the questions about timing of rattling. The question was worded, "When is the best time to rattle, pre-rut, rut or post-rut?" My answer was, of course the pre-rut. To my surprise, the author maintained that the rut was the best time to rattle, and happily marked my answer wrong! But, **he** was wrong. Experience has taught me that it is very difficult to call a trophy buck away from a receptive doe using rattling. The best time to rattle is anytime you find fresh new scrapes. This means that bucks are either in the pre-rut stage, or that they are once again looking for receptive does during the declining stages of the rut. The technique you use will depend on which stage of the rut is occurring. I have devoted an entire chapter to advanced rattling and calling techniques, but here is a primer.

During the early pre-rut, or even just prior to this time, bucks are really not in the mood to fight. They spend most of their time rubbing saplings and sparring with other bucks. These sparring matches are usually not serious encounters. If you clash your antlers together at this time, all you are going to do is frighten the animal away. I borrowed a phrase from the trout fishermen-- match the hatch. This is, try to simulate what is going on out there at any one point in time. If the bucks are just sparring, try a very casual rattling technique. I just "tickle" the antlers together at five to ten minute intervals, and then wait. I wait for very long periods of time, perhaps as long as three hours. If a buck hears you, he will make an effort to locate the two fellows that are sparring. He will be casual about this and will approach cautiously downwind. This is a time when movement and scent are critical. I use an odor neutralizer, but no deer scent. If it is not the rut, why use rutting scents?

As the pre-rut develops, serious combats occur. This is a time not to be bashful about rattling. Very few hunters have ever seen a real buck fight. Some report seeing fights, but most are just sparring matches. I have been lucky enough to see a half dozen honest to gosh buck fights in my life, and they were impressive to say the least. When two mature bucks come together, it is a sight to behold. They circle each other with their hair raised like two dogs preparing to fight. They actually seem to change color from grayish to dark brown. Suddenly and by some subtle cue, the bucks come together with a terrible clash. The fight that ensues would rival any Hollywood stunt fight. The fight may last only a few seconds or several minutes. The longest I have seen two bucks fight is forty-five minutes. Suddenly, one buck will break away and run with its tail

---

Often, rattling is a good way to lure nocturnal bucks out of their sanctuaries, provided you match your technique to what is going on at that point in time.

Robert Skinner

between its legs, the other buck in hot pursuit. Bucks will snort, grunt, paw the ground and rake the vegetation during one of these fights. So, in order to simulate a real fight, you will have to do all of these things. A dominant buck cannot resist coming to such a commotion during the early rut. He may come rushing in or circle. I once had a buck jump right over my shoulder, run about fifteen yards and turn and face the startled rattler. Needless to say, I quit rattling!

In order to add to the effect, I use liberal amounts of buck rutting scent; doe scents are not appropriate at this time. Contrary to popular belief, the bucks are not fighting over the attentions of a doe. They are simply fighting for dominance. The idea of a demure little doe standing by while the two boys fight it out for her affections is ludicrous.

During the post-rut, bucks can be lured from their sanctuaries by rattling; however, it must be done carefully. The buck knows good and well that the time for fighting is over. In fact, some of the bucks are getting back together. This is also a time when bucks are likely to spar. So, I return to my sparring technique. Do not expect the buck to roar into action, however, as it may take two hours for the buck to respond. I have rattled in the same location for a week before getting a response, but that is the difference between a trophy on the wall and disappointment.

SUMMARY

In spite of all of these tricks, Dick Idol is right, there **are** bucks that will never be taken, and that is what trophy hunting is all about. The true trophy hunter does not sit out there for hours in the cold to kill a buck that is bigger that that of another hunter. There is too much of that nowadays. He hunts the mature buck for the challenge. And it is some challenge! If it were possible to kill every buck, I think deer hunting would lose its universal appeal. The thought that there always is a buck that is better than you is very appealing. Hopefully, some of the techniques discussed here will make you a better trophy hunter and help you achieve that ultimate goal-- the trophy whitetail.

Ray Sasser

478   *Producing and Harvesting Whitetails*

Mike Biggs

Chapter 35

Mike Biggs

HUNTING CLEARCUT BUCKS

There was a time when an article on hunting clearcut bucks would have been limited to certain southern states. Today, however, the forestry practice of clearcutting is common throughout most of the whitetail's range. Whether you are talking about Pennsylvania hardwoods or southern pine forests, clearcutting is now an integral part of both timber management and deer management.

Few other land-management practices have stirred more controversy than has clearcutting. The subject of countless lawsuits and appeals from environmental groups from Texas to Washington State, this common forestry practice is both friend and foe to whitetails. Let's examine some of the basic principles involved.

BASIC TERMINOLOGY

The term **clearcutting** conjures up all sorts of images, ranging from total devastation to rebirth of a forest, depending on which side of the issue you take. *By strict definition, clearcutting means the removal of all merchantable timber from a site.* Once an area has been clearcut, all that remains is residual trees that have little value in today's market. It seldom is a pretty sight to behold, but it does mark the beginning of a process in which man takes advantage of some naturally occurring phenomena.

For millions of years, nature has been in the clearcutting business. Whether it be by hurricane, wildfire or tornado, nature continually reaches in and "stirs the pot," so to speak. Nature hates stability, and takes infinite delight in "messing up" what ecosystems have spent years trying to stabilize. Many species of animals take advantage of these periodic disturbances.

After a disturbance, a series of predictable steps take place. As I noted earlier in the book, ecologists and wildlife managers call this occurrence *succession*. Each plant and animal community developing after a disturbance becomes increasingly complex, until most of the nutrients and energy are tied up in living material. Consider the large amount of vital nutrients tied up in a large red oak. Weeds and grasses lead to woody plants, which in turn are replaced by more permanent and long-lived trees. Likewise, for every stage of succession there are species of animals that are benefitted by that particular set of conditions. After the clearing of a forested site, the weeds and grasses that develop early in this process are home to seed-eating songbirds and game birds, such as quail and doves. However, as the weeds and grasses are replaced by more permanent, woody vegetation, the conditions conducive to these species disappear, along with doves and quail. One by one, animal species thrive and decline as succession proceeds to a final *climax forest*.

Whitetails are commonly considered by modern hunters to be creatures of the forest. The more forest you have, the more deer you have, right? This is not always the case. To understand where the whitetail fits into all of this, we have to return to the above concepts.

Whitetails, although highly adaptive to varying situations, thrive on disturbance. Their whole breeding biology is designed to take advantage of natural disturbances within seven years of occurrence. My research, and that of other scientists, has shown that whitetails have the ability to saturate their range within this time period--believe it or not. Deer feed extensively on two basic food types during the growing season: browse and forbs (weeds). Erroneously, many hunters and landowners think deer commonly eat grass. With only a few minor exceptions, grasses are seldom a mainstay of whitetails.

As far as a deer is concerned, his world only includes the thin band of vegetation between the ground level and about 4-1/2 feet above the ground. To the deer, if it is not happening in this layer, it might as well be happening on the moon. A deer's needs have to be satisfied within this layer of vegetation. And, that is where disturbance comes into the picture.

Within seven years following a dramatic disturbance of the forest, be it manmade or natural, forage plants grow well beyond the reach of deer. Radio-tracking studies have shown that most whitetails *will not move* their home ranges to new food sources unless something really dramatic happens. This means that a deer is in for some pretty tough times unless regular disturbances are experienced within a mile or two of where he lives.

That is where man's forestry activities can be beneficial to deer, despite popular opinion. By properly scheduling timber-harvesting activities, the modern wildlife manager can do a much better job than nature can in providing essential foods to deer. Rather than waiting for unpredictable, random acts

One of the most important clearcut features visible in this photo is the streamside management zone (SMZ), which bucks use to travel into and across the clearcut. Timber has been left along the various arms of stream channels; however, some of these do not provide bucks with an escape route, and offer poor hunting during early stages of regrowth.

Robert Skinner

Shortly after a clearcutting operation (left), there is little cover for bucks; but within a few short years (right), there is both forage and cover for bucks. Clearcuts of this age are very difficult to hunt.

of nature, man can plan both the distribution and timing of disturbances. This is not to say that all timber harvesting is beneficial to deer. Unfortunately, in our zeal to provide wood products to people, we take a perfectly good management concept and apply it over too much of the landscape. Nature seldom destroys more than a few acres of habitat with a single disturbance. Man, on the other hand, has a tendency to paint with a broader brush. Clearcuts of several hundred acres or more most commonly have a detrimental effect on whitetails, depending on how such timber harvests are conducted.

So far, this discussion has been limited to only one component in a whitetail's world: summer and spring foods. Deer have other needs, such as water, winter feed and cover. Utilization of weeds and browse greatly diminishes throughout much of the whitetail's range during the colder portions of the year. High-energy foods, such as acorns, agricultural crops and soft fruits, often are critical during these times. Protection from the weather and hiding places from hunters and other predators also are important requirements, especially for bucks.

Bucks behave in very dissimilar ways to does in most areas. Seldom do bucks venture into openings during daylight hours, preferring to remain in the more dense vegetation. But this is a "Catch 22" for bucks, in that the more densely vegetated areas also have the least food. Consequently, bucks either must move longer distances to feed or reduce their feed intake. Most long-distance moves are conducted either through well-screened travel corridors or at night.

This is where the environmental

conscience of the landowner comes into play. If the company or private landowner just clears a large expanse of timber *without* paying attention to the topography and watershed involved, there is little benefit to deer or the deer hunter. One company that **does** pay attention to these kinds of environmental details is International Paper.

I have worked closely for many years with IP's Mid-South Region Wildlife Biologist, Tom Bourland. "The nature of modern silviculture is such that we must pay more and more attention to the retention of what we call streamside management zones," he asserts. Many companies pay lip service to SMZ retention, but IP "puts its money where its mouth is." An SMZ should include the area from the crest of one hill to the crest of the other. Within the SMZ, hardwood species important to deer, such as oaks, should be managed.

Bucks will use SMZs to cross even the newest of clearcuts *if* adequate screening is provided. Adequate screening would be present if you could stand on one side of the SMZ and not see through it. Often the nature of the topography involved provides adequate screening, even when the SMZ is quite thin. Bucks tend to move just below the crest of the watershed.

Now, it is time to return to the clearcut itself. You must ask yourself one basic question: "Why would a deer want to be in a clearcut?" Well, there really are only two reasons. First, a deer may venture into a clearcut in search of forage, the type depending on the time of the year. Second, the clearcut may provide dense cover in later growth stages.

By the time deer season rolls around in much of North America, frosts and leaf-fall have reduced the forage quality of most clearcuts. Only early-fall weeds seem to be attractive at this time. Now, paying attention to the type of site-preparation used becomes important.

Site-preparation is, as the name implies, the preparation of the site for the planting of trees, much as you prepare your garden for planting. Several site-preparation techniques are used by timber managers. First, there are those methods that push natural successional processes back only enough to allow tree planting and to reduce competition for those trees. These methods usually promote the growth of browse species. Second, there are the more intensive methods that reduce the site to the very earliest of successional stages, and which inhibit browse production. These methods favor the growth of weeds and grasses.

Early in the season, especially before acorn fall, deer seek out areas with high weed production. Weeds characteristically are high in protein and energy, which prepare deer for the rigors of the coming winter. Weed production is dependent on fall weather. An early, cold fall will produce little in the way of weed production. A mild, wet fall, on the other hand, will tend to produce large quantities of nutritious food. Later, during the last part of most hunting seasons, deer either feed on residual acorns (provided adequate acorn fall occurred) or on the starchy stems of browse plants. Hence, *when a* deer uses a clearcut for feeding depends on the type of forage being produced and the nutritional needs of the deer.

There is a "kicker" in all of this, however. Bucks tend to be off-feed during most of the rut, paying little attention to meeting their basic physiological needs (other than reproduction). The only exceptions to this are in the older, more experienced bucks, which tend to seek cover more than they seek mates. Romantic forays often are limited to the night. Bucks are highly attracted to the dense growth, especially of conifers, provided in 7- to 18-year-old plantations. These impenetrable thickets of vegetation not only provide cover from inclement weather, but also make it virtually impossible for you to approach the buck without him being aware of your movements.

Bucks often move from one dense cover patch to another via SMZs. Again, this points out the critical importance of these habitat features to deer, especially bucks. SMZs also provide varying amounts of high-energy foods that can be picked up "on the run," so to speak, as the buck travels from cover to rutting grounds.

Now it is time to discuss how you can turn this information into venison and a trophy on your wall.

DEVELOPING A PLAN OF ATTACK

How and when you hunt a clearcut depends on several factors, among them the time of year, age of clearcut, type of site preparation and extent of SMZ development. In order to begin developing a hunting plan, you have to consider the basic ecological principles of *edge* and *corners*. Remember that *edge is the point where two habitat types meet*. This can be the edge between the clearcut and the SMZ or the interface between the clearcut and an adjacent forest. Also, remember that *a corner is any place where three habitat types come together*. A corner is almost a sure thing in deer hunting!

From ground level, I find it difficult to make much sense out of a thickly vegetated clearcut. For this reason, I either acquire aerial photographs or go up into the air myself to study the area. This may sound excessive, but the return usually justifies the cost of a flight. The average cost of most of my flights seldom exceeds $120, including photographic development and printing. In the U. S., aerial photographs

A good place to locate your stand in a clearcut is at a corner, a place where the SMZ, clearcut and adjacent forest meet.

also are available at a relatively inexpensive rate from the U. S. Geological Survey, Eros Pata Center, Sioux Falls, SD 57198. If you consider ordering a specific aerial photograph, have the necessary information, such as county, township, etc., ready *before* you contact this agency. It makes for better relations and gives you faster turnaround time. Large-scale photography is available for almost any area for no more than $65.

Once you have a photograph, identify all possible travel corridors, edges and corners. This is the time to apply a little logic to the analysis. For example, an SMZ that juts out into a large clearcut but does not connect to adjacent cover probably will not be used as much as one that completely crosses the clearcut.

The width of SMZs also is important to note. Wider features generally are more attractive than thin, lightly covered ones. Ask yourself what you would do to travel across the clearcut if you were a buck. This also is a time to consult a topographic map. Often hunters have problems thinking in a manner that allows overlaying two different types of maps of the same area, but with a little practice you can learn to interpret more than one level of information. for example, a saddle is a slightly depressed area that connects two different drainages. This low point between the two watersheds is a natural funneling feature for bucks. Hence, if you have an aerial photograph that shows two SMZs located parallel to each other, examine your topographic map to see if a saddle occurs between the two. Using this reasoning, I recently located an impressive buck that would score around 160 Boone and Crockett points. He was using a saddle to move from one doe group inhabiting one watershed to another. There was a rub-scrape line extending along the slope of one drainage, across the saddle and into the midslope of the adjacent drainage. Bucks use structure just as bass do!

You also need to take into account the current needs of bucks, as well as the successional state of the clearcut. As noted, bucks do not use clearcuts uniformly over time. No mature buck in his right mind would venture by daylight into a freshly cleared area! Most commonly, bucks make the most use of clearcuts when the trees are 10 to 20 years of age. At this point, the densely packed vegetation represents an impenetrable jungle that cannot be entered without the buck knowing about it. such areas are primarily used as cover.

One exception to the above would be a situation in which few SMZs are available and/or a buck simply *must* cross a clearcut. In this case, bucks tend to favor clearcuts that either have sufficient topographic relief to hide their movements or have been site-prepared by shearing and windrowing of residual trees. Windrows are constructed along the topographic contours, and bucks use them as natural screening features. In fact, the periodic breaks in the windrows provide a funneling effect a hunter can use to his favor. Bucks will use SMZs to cross even the newest of clearcuts *if* adequate screening is provided.

One question I am consistently asked by clearcut hunters is, "Where do I put my stand?" The tendency is to position a stand so that the hunter has visibility in all directions. Too many times I find stands positioned right in the middle of a large clearcut! A more reasonable strategy would be to locate your stand along a natural travel corridor. This is particularly true when hunting the more densely vegetated, older plantations. You pretty well can count on a buck using an SMZ to move from his bed (probably in the thickest vegetation) to a scrape line or feeding area in the adjacent forest. He will travel along the slope of the SMZ, just below the ridge line, generally downstream as he leaves his bedding area. Therefore, the best place to position your stand is either well away from the bedding area along the SMZ, or at the point where the SMZ enters the timber (a corner). It is my experience that the buck generally will bed at the head of the drainage, especially if there is a saddle connecting to another drainage system. In these cases, he either will travel downstream along the SMZ or across the saddle and then down the adjacent drainage. Proper stand placement to intercept him in his travels can pay off.

When you hunt a clearcut also is important. You must be aware of the current stage of the rut and the physiological needs of deer at any point in time. For example, the presence of large numbers of fresh rubs along SMZs is a sure indicator that the bucks are making regular trips up and down these features. Trips are likely to occur any time of day. All-day hunting is in order in this situation.

If, on the other hand, the rubbing period is long past, bucks are more likely to make their moves under subdued light, especially on young plantations. After the rut, bucks are in need of high-energy foods to replenish lost stores. If there is an abundant acorn crop, you need to concentrate hunting along travel corridors that lead to oak stands and flats. Likewise, if there is a poor acorn crop, areas with abundant quantities of weeds will be more attractive to bucks. Agricultural crops will be visited regularly during these times. Unfortunately, however, most of these visits will be nocturnal. Your best bet is to intercept the buck late in the day. This requires the ability to make an accurate shot under low-light conditions.

I have written several times about methods that are effective during the post-rut period. Young plantations lend themselves to silent drives and using slingshots to move bucks. In these cases, bucks will tend to use their old SMZ travel corridors as escape routes. Position a hunter at the junction between an SMZ and a forested area. Unless pushed too strongly, bucks will be reluctant to flee across open country.

SUMMARY

As we move into the next millennium, clearcutting as a forestry practice will become more the rule than the exception. Clearcutting can, if properly conducted, be beneficial to whitetails. The whitetail hunter likewise can make use of manmade habitat features to harvest trophy bucks. Trophy hunting is a constantly changing scene in which bucks and man co-evolve to cope with a changing environment. Developing good clearcut hunting skills is just one more "tool" you need to add to your "tool box" of tricks.

Mike Biggs

Chapter 36

Mike Biggs

FIVE STEPS TO A LATE-SEASON BUCK

It is late in the season, and the trophy buck you have been dreaming about all year has not materialized. No doubt desperation has set in, and you are just about ready to pack it in for the year. Right? Well, whatever you do, *don't give up yet.* Unfortunately, many hunters think that if they do not bag a good buck by the end of the first week, they might as well go home. Nothing could be further from the truth.

It is true that the vast majority of bucks are harvested during the first few days of the season. But, what kind of bucks are these? Most of the bucks killed early are younger, less experienced bucks that easily fall to the gun. That is precisely why some areas with very heavy hunting pressure have as much as 80 percent of the yearlings harvested during the first week. But, the older bucks still are out there-- wiser and much more difficult to harvest. The fact is that, if you truly are interested in harvesting a trophy buck, your chances actually *increase,* not decrease as the season progresses. In order to be successful, you need to adopt these five tried and true steps to late-season hunting.

ANALYZE YOUR HUNTING TECHNIQUES

It never ceases to amaze me how hunters become stereotyped in their behavior patterns; the behavior of each actually is as unique as a signature. Early in each hunter's life, whether by accident or by learning through association with others, a hunting behavior develops which is seldom modified to fit new situations. Just because you once harvested a good buck by doing things a certain way, it is no indication that repetition will gain you anything but frustration.

You need to ask yourself some basic questions. Do you always hunt during the same times of the day? Do you hunt the same deer trail time and time again? You would be amazed at the large percentages of "yeses" I get when I ask that question at hunters' meetings. Most hunters are caught in a rut. But, it is time to change if you really want that monster buck.

You should ask yourself another question. How hard do I hunt? Oh, I'll bet you say that you really hunt hard. But, do you really? I have a good friend who tells me every year that he hunts hard with little or no success. I have watched him for some time now; and, what he calls hard hunting is sitting on an oat patch from just before daylight to around 9:30 a.m. He then goes into camp for breakfast, takes a nap, goes back out around 3 p.m., and stays until dark. That is not hunting hard, that is hunting lazy! He thinks that, for some magical reason, a monster buck is going to be stupid enough to blunder by him like an old elephant going to the elephant's graveyard to commit suicide before his gun. He has hunted the same oat patch for the last 10 years and seldom has killed anything better than an eight-point, two-year-old!

My radiotelemetry work in deer research over the last several years has pointed out clearly the foolishness of such a hunting strategy. The average mature buck becomes active around 9:30 a.m., and with minor breaks in between, remains so until about 3 p.m. The hunters and the big bucks simply are not getting together. Most of the Boone and Crockett bucks have been harvested between 10 a.m. and noon; yet, I have a great deal of trouble convincing hunters to venture into the field at this time. I seldom hunt before 9 a.m. -- a strategy most perplexing to my hunting companions. There is something wrong in their minds about my standing on the porch with a cup of coffee as they walk off into the darkness!

An oat patch (green plot) or permanent stand is *not* a good place to harvest a monster buck. Although you occasionally will kill a buck off one of these stands, your chances of harvesting a truly good buck are slim. Again, my radio-tracking studies substantiate this. Mature bucks will avoid permanent stands and food patches like the plague. I have had mature bucks move between hunters like an NFL veteran receiver exploiting the zone defense. On one occasion, a rather large buck moved within 20 yards of a hunter without being detected. That buck knew good and well that the hunter was there. After all, the guy hunted the stand every day for two solid weeks!

Bucks also will move completely out of a heavily hunted area. Some of my bucks spend all summer and early fall within sight of a stand (one even regularly bedded down beneath one) and then move out to an unhunted area just prior to the opening weekend.

ANALYZE THE HUNTING PATTERNS OF OTHER HUNTERS

One thing is certain. If you are doing something wrong, just about everyone else is, too. So, take heart. The mistakes of others can be used in your favor. You probably have been hunting so far under one of two situations. You either belong to a hunting club or lease or you hunt the public lands. In the first case, the hunting patterns of others are easily established. On most clubs, each hunter has his territory that is virtually sacrosanct. No one would dare venture into another's hunting territory. Hunters make no bones about it; you know where they hunt and they do not expect to find you there. And, you probably are the same way with them.

The successful trophy hunter cannot function without good maps and aerial photographs of his area. It is time to get these maps out and to develop a hunting profile for your club. My research has shown that most hunters seldom venture more than 1,500 feet from a road or right of way. The big bucks know this and avoid these **hunter influence zones.** Mark off the 1,500 feet hunter influence zone along all roads and rights-of-way. In addition, mark off an equal zone around all permanent hunting stands. I will bet you that the resulting map will reveal exactly where you need to hunt to encounter hunter-wise bucks.

The number of unhunted areas on a hunting club or lease often is amazing. Some clubs hunt as little as 10 percent of their area. Over a period of years, the big bucks have learned precisely where the non-hunted *sanctuaries* are and gravitate to them at the first sign of hunter activity.

On public lands, you will have to use a little finesse to determine typical hunter activity patterns. The best way is to keep track of where you see hunters on the area. In addition, you can count on the 1,500 feet influence zone rule more on public lands than on private clubs. Most hunters frequenting public hunting grounds come there unprepared and reluctant to venture far from the security of a road. Hopefully, you already will be very familiar with these areas and feel comfortable moving about the less accessible portions. If not, I suggest that you adopt a tried and true technique. Use the creek drainages in the same manner that the bucks do-- as **travel corridors** -- to and from your hunting area. These corridors may not be the most direct route, but they most definitely are the surest. Streams always are marked clearly on topographic maps and show up nicely on aerial photographs. Streamsides also are usually less dense in vegetation than the uplands are, and walking is easier.

ANALYZE THE BEHAVIOR OF YOUR DEER

A man was once asked what he would do if he found out that he only had 10 minutes to live. "Well," he said, "I'd sit down and think about it a minute." In trophy hunting, it is often time to sit down and think about your deer. You do not have to have a Ph.D. to understand the behavior of deer. But, you do have to be observant and logical.

Looking at your hunter influence zone map, ask yourself what you would do, if you were a buck, to avoid detection. Like a field general, work out various movement strategies on your map and mentally test the feasibility of each. Bucks do learn very quickly how to avoid detection. They may change their time of movement or where they move. The trick is to be where they are when they are there. The one catch to the system is that each and every buck is unique in its survival strategy.

Buck survival strategies usually are derived by accident. Something a young buck did or did not do allowed it to live into its second year-- a critical period. Just like the hunter's routine, something that worked early on was kept in the buck's behavioral repertoire. For example, we radio-tracked a rather nice buck we called Buck 82 for some time on North Boggy Slough Hunting and Fishing Club (Houston County, Texas). As a yearling, we never had a more predictable animal. Every day, the buck was in exactly the same place at the same time. We thought we had the buck pretty well figured out, until his second year. He had managed to survive his first hunting season undetected by hunters.

Most of the hunters on North Boggy are committed to the trophy management program, and although several had seen the little buck, no one would think of doing him in. That season was the last time we ever saw that buck until he was a mature, trophy-class animal.

The following rutting season came and Buck 82 disappeared. Search as we would, we simply could not find him. We finally gave up, concluding that he had been taken by some poacher or that his collar had failed in some way. Up until that time, we were convinced fairly well that the scientific literature was right: a buck would die within a mile of where he was born. Since then, we have learned better. And, several other researchers working throughout the South have observed similar phenomena.

In March, we were shocked to find that the buck was once again right there in his old home range, transmitter beeping merrily along. But, where had he gone? Had he been there all along? The following year, we answered these questions. It turns out that the now big buck was traveling seven miles to a sanctuary area deep in a swampy bottomland. His strategy worked every year, until he was shot by a fellow who just happened to hunt that area. That sanctuary still is there and still is being used by big bucks (see **Sanctuaries and Travel Corridors**). I never have told anyone where it is either. Bucks have killed just about all the saplings in that area from their rubbing. In fact, the area probably has one of the highest buck densities I ever have seen in the Pineywoods. And, some of those bucks are real wallhangers.

During the late-season, bucks tend to be more nocturnal, and stick pretty much to their sanctuaries. That is when you should pit your logic against a buck's wits, in order to score. Study the area carefully, applying logic to work out potential travel corridors and escape routes.

Mike Biggs

Bucks learn every inch of their sanctuary. They know when something new is present, and they usually flee without investigation. Escape corridors are well thought out and established early in life. Another one of our radio-collared bucks gave us insight into how this is done. A nubbin' buck was collared near a large clearcut during late winter. The young buck spent the following spring and summer with his mother, leaving her only during fawning. It was during the following fall that he gave us a little bit of knowledge about how bucks think. For some strange reason, he just took off one day and traveled a goodly distance to the north. As I noted earlier, I thought the movement was not real, probably a bogus data point in our computer.

But, it was not a bogus data point. The buck appeared to be checking out the area. This was confirmed later on during the second hunting season, when the buck went directly to this spot by way of the same route. Each and every year thereafter, the buck revisited the sanctuary, but he added a twist. He always would take a different route to the sanctuary. This must be a pretty good strategy, since the buck was never harvested.

DEVELOP A NEW HUNTING STRATEGY

Armed with basic knowledge about your hunting area, and the behavior of bucks, it is time to develop a successful hunting strategy.

The ideal situation is for you to have developed a season-long hunting strategy. We now know that trophy bucks use travel corridors to move to and from their sanctuaries. The best time to locate these is just after the hunting season ends. Late winter is a time when the big bucks are a little less cautious, and consequently are observed more easily. Mature bucks do not eat much during the rut and may lose as much as 30 percent of their body weight. They are very hungry and are trying desperately to replenish depleted energy reserves at this time. Most of the hunters also are out of the woods by this time, so you probably should have the place to yourself.

Deer are creek-bottom animals, whether you are in South Texas or the Piedmont of Alabama. They have evolved to be associated with the wet, fertile soils of drainages. A buck's movement (see **Movements and Home Range**) strategies are tied carefully to this fact. Drainages are used as highways. The big bucks like to move just below a ridge, an effective military tactic. The vegetation is less dense in these areas and escape is just a few steps away in the denser upland brush.

I once had the privilege of watching a buck do exactly that. On one of my many trips to some national forestland, I was walking down a small drainage system. About midway down the creek, I noticed a hunter sitting on the ground against a tree. I decided not to walk past him for fear of being shot, so I settled down behind a large downed treetop. It would be interesting, I thought, to just sit and watch a hunter in action. About 45 minutes had passed when I noticed a nice nine-pointer walking slowly down the edge of the creek. He obviously was looking for a place to cross, as the creek bank was quite steep there. I was located above the hunter so I could view the entire show. I settled back against the stump to watch.

As far as I could tell the hunter remained totally unaware of the buck's presence. And, the buck certainly was unaware of the hunter's presence, but not for long. The buck suddenly stopped dead in his tracks and sniffed at the air. The wind was not in his favor, but it was an unpredictable wind. The buck stood perfectly still for some time. The only movement I could detect was a slight ear twitch. Then, the hunter made a fatal mistake. He coughed.

I was surprised to see that the buck did not bolt at the obvious presence of man. Instead, he just lowered his head and vanished in the brush adjacent to the stream. It was amazing that something that large could just slip away so quietly. The hunter probably went home thinking that he had chosen a bad spot. He had made a mistake and never knew it. But, the biggest mistake he had made was in choosing the wrong place to sit. He was sitting smack dab on the buck's trail! If he had been where I was, he would have had venison in the freezer and a fine trophy on the wall.

A good season-long hunting strategy should include leaving some of these travel corridors unhunted. The bucks will find them soon enough and will grow to feel that they are safe for daytime use. Only after all other tactics have failed should you begin to hunt these areas.

If you have done your homework, you will have spent a considerable amount of time investigating potential travel corridors. The trick is to locate those that are used to move to and from sanctuaries. That will not be easy, but a little time expended sitting and watching deer move in late winter will help. **Never, never enter a sanctuary**. Locate them by indirect means. If bucks always are seen coming from a thicket about mid-morning, the chances are good that the area is being used as a sanctuary. By moving carefully, you will be able to work out the current escape and movement patterns associated with the sanctuary. I concentrate my hunting efforts adjacent to travel corridors.

But, suppose you have not done your homework. It is too late now to get out and scout the area. Too much activity probably will get you into trouble. The best thing to do is sit down and think a minute. Get out your map of the area and mark off the hunter influence zones. They should be well established by late season. Try to identify several potential sanctuaries. Ask yourself how you would use each area if you were a buck. Work out alternative hunting strategies.

In those rare cases where the entire area has been saturated with hunting pressure, the best strategy is to change the time of day that you hunt. My telemetry studies have shown that bucks try to move when the majority of hunters are not in the field. If you are like most deer hunters, you probably have been hunting from dawn to mid-morning and again in late afternoon (see **Lunchtime Trophies**). It is time to try something new. Use the early-morning daylight to slip into one of your selected spots. The light will allow you to move more quietly, since you will not be stumbling over every log and rock on the way. Find yourself a good vantage point and stay there!

Whatever you do, do not move. If you see nothing, use the time to plan your next hunt. Always change your approach to an area and never walk an existing deer trail. The scent trail you leave will cause a buck to shift to another trial.

Lastly, do not become discouraged. Remember that the big bucks frequent areas where deer densities are very low. You cannot expect to see mobs of deer and kill a good buck; the two are mutually exclusive. But, remember that you only have to see one deer— the right one— to be successful.

ADAPT YOUR HUNTING STRATEGY

The last step often is the hardest thing for a hunter to do, especially in the late season. You feel you only have a few days left in the season and, if you make the wrong decision, what little chance you had is lost forever. This is not necessarily so. If you have been doing the same old tired things all season, you pretty well can bet that you never will see that good buck that way. You really have nothing to lose.

Deer hunting is a battle of wits and logic: your logic against the buck's wits. If you proceed with hunting in a logical and planned manner, there is no reason why you should fail. The bucks are out there. They have not been transported magically to some other planet.

SUMMARY

If you have planned a truly workable late-season hunting strategy, you should be able to methodically eliminate areas until you score. After thoroughly covering one of your potential big-buck areas, mark it off on the map and proceed to the next likely spot. Keep at it. Slowly but surely, you will locate your trophy. But, the key is patience. You have got to be willing to put in the time to assure your success. The only characteristic shared by the best trophy hunters is that they spend a lot of time in the woods. One thing is for sure, you cannot kill a trophy buck at home or in the deer camp.

There actually should be a sixth step. *Do not let yourself get into this situation next season.* If you make hunting a year-round activity, you not only will enjoy deer hunting more, but you also will increase your chances of success greatly.

Chapter 37

TWELVE-MONTH DEER SEASON

It's summer-- time to think about fishing for that hawg bass, water-skiing on your favorite lake, or the family vacation. Deer season is long-past and is but a dim memory, and next season is far, far away. But, is it really? The whitetail is still out there in the woods, doing the things it needs to do in order to survive each and every day. There is a great deal to be learned about deer right now, each and every month, but unfortunately, most hunters miss out on these experiences. Ask yourself some basic questions. Were you truly ready for that season? Did that "monster buck" turn into a yearling six-pointer? Could you have planned better? These are questions you should be asking yourself right now. Deer hunting truly can be a year-round activity.

FOUR HUNTING SEASONS

There are three basic hunting strategies for whitetails— early season, mid-season, and late season. We begin our twelve-month season in reverse order with the late-winter. Few seasons tell us more about the secretive habits of the whitetail than this time. January and February are months when most hunters are sitting home in front of the fireplace. Sometimes I feel that hunters think we biologists pick up all the deer as soon as the season is over and store them in a closet until the following season! The deer are out there, fighting for survival and pretty much doing the same kinds of things they were doing at the end of the season.

Late-Winter

Late-winter is the time to study deer. Bucks will adhere to the movement patterns adopted in late-season well into winter. The advantage you have is that at this time there are no other hunters in the woods. The big buck slowly but surely, due probably to hunger, begins to make mistakes he would not have dreamed of making during the season. Bucks became a little less wary, and they are more likely to move in search of diminishing food during the daylight hours. The rut has taken its toll in weight loss, and the big buck is desperately trying to replenish depleted fat stores.

Spend a great deal of time in the woods. Forget about the old trails watched during the season. Have some fun; there is no pressure to kill a buck now! Get out and explore your range. Truly big bucks still will be frequenting the harder-to-hunt areas. Try to locate bedding areas and trails leading to and from them. There are two ways to do this. Recently, I awoke to a rare East Texas snow. I immediately grabbed my field gear (always kept handy) and drove out to my farm. Very carefully, I recorded every deer trail encountered during a systematic search of my property. They stood out like sore thumbs. There were trails I never had seen before, and I know my farm pretty well. These trails were the ones established during the late season to take advantage of a particular food supply and to avoid detection.

You can find late-winter trails even if it never snows in your area. Most of these trails have not been used enough by late season to be detected. A single deer leaves little evidence of its move-

Mike Biggs
Late-winter is an excellent time to scout. One of the tell-tale signs of travel corridors is a heavily used trail. By late winter, trails have been used repeatedly by bucks and are worn deep, and should be located on your map of the area.

ment. However, by February, a deer will have worn a substantial trail to and from its bedding site. Travel corridors usually will be located along minor drainages, especially at the head of a watershed. I like to sit above such a drainage and record when and where the deer are moving. Foul weather and fair weather are treated separately--each goes into my notebook for the coming season.

Late winter also is the time to prepare your wardrobe for the next season. That worn-out jacket or lost pair of gloves needs to be replaced now, not on the way to the hunt. Most of the mail-order houses offer late-winter clearance sales on cold-weather gear. They know how sportsmen think and aim their catalogues in this direction. I like to have three different sets of hunting clothes for use here in the South. Each is directed to the specific foliage and typical weather conditions unique to each of my three hunting strategies. I call these my green, brown, and gray outfits.

The green outfit, as the name implies, is aimed at early-season hunting. It includes a pair of tough, green camouflage, non-insulated gloves for negotiating thick vegetation, and light-weight, green camouflage jacket, pants, and a cap. For a possible early-season cold snap, I include a pair of insulated long underwear.

During mid-season I change to my brown outfit. It includes a heavier brown camouflage, waterproof, insulated jacket; insulated gloves; and heavier boots (preferably waterproof). I also have an insulated jumpsuit for those

The author keeps various boxes, each with the appropriate gear for that particular time of the year. This allows him to quickly change to the appropriate equipment and camouflage.

quick trips to the field. You would be amazed to know how many bucks I have harvested while I was wearing a three-piece suit! There are a number of brown camouflage hats to choose from, depending mainly on your own tastes. Insulated long underwear and heavy socks are also included with this outfit.

Late-season calls for the heavy "artillery." My gray outfit is a very heavily insulated pair of gray coveralls worn over the best insulated long underwear I can find. I prefer the softer materials, as nothing is louder than some of these synthetic materials on a cold winter morning. I also have a pair of heavily insulated waterproof (rubber) boots. This time of the year demands that you spend a great deal of time in the woods. The amount of time you spend is directly proportional to success, unless you are extremely lucky. The more comfortable you are, the more likely you are to stay with it. Of course, in states where required by law, each of the three outfits include the appropriate amount of blaze orange.

I keep each of my hunting outfits in separate footlockers, regularly checking and maintaining each. *Do not* fall into the temptation to mix outfits. Boots ruined in the early season are of no use in late-season outings. This may seem like a lot of trouble, but believe me, it is worth it in the long run.

I may have been assuming quite a bit when I advised you to scout your hunting territory during late-winter. Unfortunately, many hunters have absolutely no idea in January where they will be hunting the following season. You have three options available, depending on your particular geographic area, economic status, and local customs. So-called "free hunting" is becoming about as scarce as dinosaurs. If you opt to hunt on public lands, your best bet is to start with a biologist or local game management officer. January and February are usually slack months for these men, if there is ever such a time. Make an appointment and spend some time visiting with them. Do more listening than talking; these men have little patience for "one time I . . ." stories. Be sure to ask some questions about local deer biology, especially when is the peak of the rut and if there usually is a "second rut." Your advisers probably can give you some information about hunter success and hunting pressure for each area considered.

The two remaining options revolve around hunting for a fee. This trend began in Texas a number of years ago and continues to gain acceptance across the South as less and less land becomes available. The fact is that people now are willing to pay for exclusive hunting rights. Memberships in hunting clubs and leases are available in many states. Most contractual agreements between landowners and sportsmen begin in either January or September, but most landowners and hunters know by mid-season whether or not they will be leasing the following year. An excellent place to start your search for a lease or club membership is with a local agriculture extension agent or Soil Conservation Service representative. These people usually know most of the landowners in the area and quickly can narrow your search to hotter prospects.

As the white-tailed buck becomes worth more and more to the sportsman, the number of day-hunting operations will continue to increase. The typical operation usually offers varying accommodations and fee-schedules, depending on services rendered and the quality of bucks harvested. Some individuals now are offering "management" hunts for does, spikes or "inferior" bucks.

An entire book could be written on day-hunting horror stories (see **Guided Hunts for Whitetails**). Current opportunities range from high-dollar, resort-type hunting to cheap, shot-out confidence-man operations. The amount of money paid often does not indicate the quality of the hunting experience. Since most of the smaller operators develop their clientele from advertising, you might check the various outdoor magazines and newspapers. You probably will find very few advertisements this time of the year, so I suggest you acquire some back issues of these periodicals. Your best bet is to obtain some old newspapers from your area. Select a few prospects and give them a call— never write a letter. They probably will be pretty surprised to receive an inquiry so early in the year. Be sure to ask the important questions such as how many hunters do they take at one any one time and how much land do they have? Ask for some references and check them out. Finally, take the time to go and visit your prospects. Once you decide on an area, make arrangements and agreements as soon as possible. Give the operator a deposit and schedule the best times to hunt.

Spring

By spring green-up, you should know pretty well what your deer are doing at late-season. Remember the food habits of whitetails. They prefer browse (leaves and twigs of woody plants), weeds (forbs), and mast (acorns, nuts and berries). Each of these food items is utilized and becomes available at different times of the year. In the spring, the warmer weather and early rainfall usually produce an abundance of weedy growth in the uplands. Browse plants will be leafing out at this time and providing highly nutritious foodstuff for body growth and antler development. Deer become more visible during this time of the year. The pressures of the hunting season are long behind, and there are other things to worry about now. This is the time to locate your buck. You may not be able to recognize him yet but he is there.

Does usually break up their matriarchal groups during spring to find the best fawning sites. The pregnant doe becomes more and more territorial as birthing comes near. Bucks, on the other hand, are now becoming more and more social. They are running in groups of three to seven or more, and they are more concerned with establishing social dominance. After all, there are some individuals that did not make it through the previous season, and their social position is now open.

Summer

By mid-summer, bucks become more obvious as their antler buds develop. Pick out one or two groups and stay with them. I have a close friend who harvests a trophy-class buck every year. Some say he is lucky while others speak of his fall hunting prowess. Neither is the case. He simply locates one or two candidates during the summer and spends a great deal of time studying the habits of each. By opening day, he can tell you every move the big bucks make. He has established contingency plans for hunting each, and usually he has his buck on the ground by opening-day evening. Hunting, as in Hollywood stardom, seldom knows instant success.

Summer also is the time to sight yourself in. Hunters often spend their summer evenings developing loads for their favorite caliber. Each load is tested carefully on the range for its merits in accuracy and killing power. But what about the hunter? What is he doing for his accuracy and killing power? The average buck is not shot from benchrest! It is shot offhand and under a great deal of duress. It is very difficult to place a high lung shot when your rifle moves two feet with each beat of an overtaxed, excited heart.

A few suggestions are in order. First, the average whitetail is killed at a distance considerably less than 100 yards. Hunters often tell me of their extraordinarily long shots in areas where I know good and well that such shots are impossible. So, practice at a 100-yard range. Next, you seldom shoot a deer while you are wearing a short-sleeved, lightweight shirt. Don each of your three outfits and learn to shoot with each. Practice shooting offhand until you obtain a good grouping with each.

But, what can you do about the excitement? Two things will help in this case. First, the excitement of seeing a buck cannot be described. Any man who becomes cold-blooded about shooting a big buck should stop hunting deer immediately. But, you **can** lessen the impact of seeing the buck. If you have been doing your homework, you will have become familiar with the deer on your area. The excitement of seeing that big buck will have been experienced many times before the season starts. In the case of deer hunting, familiarity breeds sanity.

Lastly, you need to get into good physical condition now. One friend of mine, who guides for part of his living, takes a refresher course regularly in CPR (Cardiovascular Pulmonary Resuscitation). He has already seen three heart attacks on his place from hunters who were out of shape and excited. Running and weight training are excellent ways to prepare for the coming season, and besides that, they are good for you. I have a one-mile course set up on my farm that ends at my rifle range. I run the course, pick up my rifle at the shooting bench and

Good physical conditioning will mean the difference between making an accurate, killing shot on a trophy-class buck.

Ray Sasser

immediately begin shooting offhand. The first time I tried this, my grouping was an impressive 12 inches! Not very good to say the least.

Fall

Fall is a time for scouting and a time when the deer traditionally shift to mast for sustenance. But, do not count on it. Acorn crops often are sporadic and cannot be counted upon. First, check the availability of acorns. If there is a good acorn crop, that is where the deer will be. If not, look somewhere else. Bucks will be frequenting these areas only during pre-rut. Once rut begins, do not plan on their return-- they'll be more interested in does than acorns!

I like to combine hunting activities in the fall. In my area, there is a squirrel season which begins about the same time as bow season. Now, I really do not enjoy squirrel hunting that much. I grew up in an area where one just did not shoot squirrels-- they were animals that lived in parks. As a matter of fact, I once got a spanking for killing a squirrel. But alas, when in Rome . . . Squirrel hunting does two important things. First, it puts you in the woods in a hunting situation. Second, it is best accomplished in a slow and methodical manner. Hence, squirrel hunting affords the perfect opportunity to scout for rubs and scrapes, as well as, to see that big buck. Again, all information obtained is carefully recorded in my notebook.

THE HUNTING SEASON

Next is hunting season itself. By this time, I have done my homework, and I know exactly where I will hunt and how I will go about it. Simple? Not really, because you may have had the woods to yourself most of the year, but now, all those people who did not do their homework are invading the woods. For this reason, I try to develop contingency plans. Since I concentrate my activities toward two or three bucks, there always are options in case some-

Ray Sasser

A good pair of binoculars can tell you a great deal about the coming acorn crop. The author regularly checks the status of food crops as he walks around his hunting territory, stopping periodically to examine the limbs of oaks for acorns.

thing goes wrong.

I suggest that you make every attempt to accomplish your goal early in the season. As time passes, it will become harder and harder to harvest that big buck. That is where all that late-winter study pays off. With time, there will be fewer and fewer hunters in the woods. Once the easy pickings are gone, most hunters will lose interest and turn to other things. Now is the time to start hunting those areas you carefully have avoided during the early season. Purposely leave your bucks some safe zones, especially the areas you found heavily used last January and February.

You probably will have only one or two chances at your buck. If you miss or make a mistake, he quickly will adopt a new strategy, even becoming totally nocturnal if necessary. Slip in, set up, and do not move until you have him.

SUMMARY

Deer-hunting is a year-round activity. In these days of heavy hunting pressures, the hunter who does his homework and truly prepares for the coming season will be rewarded with a fine buck and venison on the table. The hunter who fails to prepare adequately will only see continued frustration.

If you follow these recommendations, I cannot guarantee that you will harvest a trophy-class buck. But, I can guarantee you that your hunting enjoyment will be increased greatly. It may seem like a good deal of trouble, but give it a try. What do you have to lose? Become one of the few— the twelve-month deer hunter.

Monster bucks are only taken consistently after many hours of complex study of your hunting territory. But, this work not only pays off, but adds a great deal to the hunting experience.

Mike Biggs

PART III: SOCIO-ECONOMICS OF WHITETAIL MANAGEMENT AND HUNTING

Chapter 38

PEOPLE MANAGEMENT

Each fall, I am beset with a large number of prospective wildlife students, each hoping to realize their dreams of managing large herds of elk, antelope and whitetails. I always ask each Nimrod why he or she wants to study wildlife. "Cause I don't like people!" most commonly is the reply. Then I explain the sad realities of the profession, **wildlife management is people management**. If you cannot get along with, nor do you like people, you might as well try some other profession. They usually go away saddened, yet disbelieving, what I have told them. Unfortunately, too many of our modern-day wildlife biologists never got this lecture— it would be a much better world if they had!

It is ludicrous for any whitetail manager to think that he truly is the one managing the herd. Biologists do not manage deer, people do! Every time a hunter pulls a trigger, he is making a management decision. Every time a landowner or hunting club fails to harvest the recommended number of antlerless deer, that is a management decision. Learning to manipulate (and I mean this term ethically) people and their attitudes is a trait few biologists share. Most of the biologists I know are well-equipped to manage a deer herd, but are seriously lacking in their people management and communication skills. In this chapter, I will discuss ways I have found useful in changing the opinions, attitudes and actions of hunters and landowners to best benefit whitetails.

HOW KNOWLEDGEABLE IS THE HUNTER?

Obviously, if I thought hunters were totally educated about deer, I never would have written this book! But, honestly, I have found over many years of working with hunters, that the average guy knows more about his weapon than about the animal he is hunting. Even as recently as ten years ago, most of my audience at a talk did not know that bucks re-grow their antlers annually! Fortunately, thanks to magazines such as **North American Whitetail** and **Deer and Deer Hunting**, the American hunter is much better informed about the basic behavior and biology of deer. However, there still is much dogma and fantasy being perpetuated in the barber shops and cafes of this country.

I recently read a biography of Aldo Leopold, the Father of Wildlife Management and of the Wilderness Concept. Leopold lived and worked primarily in Wisconsin, where he made the state's deer herd his prime concern. He was on the state wildlife commission, and was instrumental in changing many of the harvest regulations for whitetails. His main concern was over the periodic loss of deer to winter-kill, stemming directly from overpopulation. Yet, judging from the articles written about him in the 1930's and 1940's, Leopold was not a popular individual. One prominent newspaper even referred to him as the "egotistical Mr. Leopold," and questioned by what authority he had come to know so much about Wisconsin's deer. Obviously, his strong assertions that antlerless deer harvest was critical to proper management of the deer resource fell on deaf ears. The great deer die-offs of the first half of this century in Wisconsin should forever be a condemnation of those who questioned Leopold's authority.

But, that was more than 40 years ago, right? Well, I recently sat in on a meeting of "concerned" landowners in Leon County, Texas, in which the recommendation to remove antlerless deer was ridiculed and our authority questioned. Nothing has changed! The problems encountered by Leopold are those we deal with today on a daily basis. Yet, the solutions to those problems remain the same. We in the whitetail management profession have seriously neglected our people management skills.

The average American is now highly educated, urban or suburban, and extremely ignorant about nature. Most of what the average person knows comes from television nature shows and hearsay. Not being scientists, trained to look at the world in analytical terms, the layman makes a single observation, and draws far-reaching conclusions from them— most of which are downright fallacious!

A recent survey indicated that most

citizens obtain information about wildlife from three sources: outdoor magazines, television and by word of mouth. State game agencies and biologists were not even in the top two-thirds of the list! But, how credible is this information? Unfortunately, much of this information is flawed or presented from an angle to confuse or mislead the reader. Some is downright wrong! For example, I recently read an article in one of the most prominent outdoor journals in this country. The "authority" writing the article presented information about the rut behavior of deer. He discussed how bucks inhale the urine of does, raise their heads, and curl their lips in a "slaymen" behavior. Sadly, he was trying to describe *flehmen* behavior. There were two other articles in the same issue with similar mistakes. In spite of the great public demand for credible information, the wildlife profession seriously ignores this need.

Even in these modern times, resource management decisions are made, not by professionals, but by interest groups. One federal forester recently exclaimed in despair, "We no longer are managing trees by silviculture, we are managing them by *liticulture*!" He was referring to the many lawsuits filed against the U.S. Forest Service over the cutting of timber on the public domain. Clearly, it is time we all become involved in public education, from the school level to the media. But, how can you become involved, and how can the attitudes of sportsmen, landowners and the general public, concerning white-tailed deer management, be manipulated to benefit both the animal and man?

EDUCATING THE PUBLIC

There are three basic target groups for whitetail education: hunters, non-hunters and anti-hunters. The first two categories are perhaps the easiest groups to deal with; the anti-hunting group seldom changes its mind. I will discuss techniques for dealing with the anti-hunter in the next chapter. I feel that our efforts are best spent educating the hunting and non-hunting groups, making up about 90 percent of the general populace.

Since hunters generally are a coherent group, they probably are the easiest to reach. Over the last 15 years, I have taken an active part in hunter education. I have been very successful in changing both the level of knowledge and the attitudes of many hunters and landowners. My education program is modeled after one of the most innovative and effective hunter education programs in the nation.

Many years ago, Drs. Harry Jacobson and David Guynn of Mississippi State University, hit upon the idea of organizing a two-phase education program. They reasoned that the best way to get people to make the right decisions about resource management, was to involve the public in the management process. Up to that time, the dogma among whitetail management professionals was that the public was too "ignorant" to understand complex management principles. Yet, we deal with individuals daily who, in their day-to-day jobs, are lawyers, doctors, mechanics and technicians, each of which

The ability to work with the public is an important trait for the modern whitetail manager. Public workshops and short courses are some of the most effective methods to educate the hunter and landowner.

having expertise about which wildlife biologists know very little.

The first phase of their program centered around organizing and training hunting clubs to collect data from their own herd. If the hunter distrusted state biologists, they reasoned, then they certainly cannot question their own records and findings! Workshops and short courses were organized around Mississippi, bringing together the state's biologists, private consultants and university researchers. Care was taken to incorporate only those biologists who enjoyed working with people. There is nothing more boring than some introverted biologist trying to talk to 500 people. The workshop series periodically was moved around the state in order to reach more people. Today, they have reached several thousand hunters and landowners, and I believe Mississippi to have the most knowledgeable group of deer hunters anywhere.

Second, hunting clubs were identified through these workshops which showed a sincere interest in quality deer management. Technical assistance was provided in the initial establishment of goals and record-keeping systems. Data from clubs was sent to the state game department where, working in coordination with Drs. Jacobson and Guynn, an annual report and management recommendations were prepared for each cooperator. Mississippi now is a model state for quality deer management.

My program here in the Pineywoods has seen identical results. We have done our job so well that it is difficult to attract large numbers of people to our programs. We have reached so many people that it is "old news" to most of our constituency! "We would like for you to come speak to us about deer management," invited one club, "but, please don't talk about shooting does." My initial impression was that there was strong anti-antlerless harvest sentiment involved. "Don't get me wrong," added the fellow, "we all agree about doe harvest. We just want to hear something new." Other portions of the state do not fare so well. The Post Oak Savannah Region of Texas has not received this education program, and is the source of many of the state game department's most vocal critics.

Coupled with a state-wide touring deer shortcourse, there also should be public service announcements regularly playing on television and radio about the principles of deer management, especially antlerless harvest and protection of young bucks. We need to initiate the equivalent of the "catch-and-release" philosophy of many fishermen's groups. Although I do not always agree with this philosophy, it has been quite effective. In the South, a fisherman who habitually keeps every fish he catches is looked upon by his peers as an unethical sportsman. Likewise, it would be nice to foster a "let 'em walk" philosophy in deer hunting, in which the idea of killing a yearling buck is unacceptable. Peer-group pressure is the real key to changing human behavior. That is the topic of the next section.

USING PEER-GROUP PRESSURE

One of the most effective methods in changing the behavior of hunters on a club, or even public lands, is the effective use of peer-group pressure. I have significantly altered the average age of bucks harvested on a club, solely by manipulating the attitudes of the hunters, not the age composition of the herd. Here's an example.

Earlier, I talked about the Boggy Slough Hunting and Fishing Club (see **The Boggy Slough Story**). This is a very old club which is owned and operated by Temple-Inland Inc., a large southern timber company. Temple uses the club primarily for customer and political entertainment. The type of

The author has used peer-group pressure as an effective means of achieving his management goals on many hunting clubs. Here is the "famous" shoot-don't shoot bulletin board he has used on many clubs to protect the younger bucks.

hunter coming to Boggy first of all is a guest, and secondly is not used to being told what to do. So, it would be very difficult to just go in and order the guests to kill or not to kill a certain type of deer. Frankly, we knew that the guests were the key to achieving our goal of quality buck management. Managers Gene Samford, Darryl Stanley, Bill Goodrum and Don Dietz needed some tool to get the hunters to do what was needed. We decided to use peer-group pressure. It would be a two-part program.

A large bulletin board was set up in the club house. On one side of the board we placed the words, **DON'T SHOOT,** and on the other we placed,

SHOOT. Beneath these headings, we regularly placed the photographs of guests with their bucks. We never said anything about the correctness of a guest's harvest decision, we just took a picture of every hunter with every buck harvested! In a very short time, you would be amazed at the change in attitude of the guests. "I hope this was the right buck to shoot," a noted politician told Bill, "I sure as &@*% don't want my picture on the wrong side of that board!" We also placed photographs of the types of bucks we preferred to be harvested, along with mounted examples.

In addition, we regularly presented a well-planned and entertaining program each evening before a hunt, on the goals of our program and the progress of our work. In no time, the hunters began to feel that they were indeed part of the program, and took pride, not only in being invited to hunt Boggy, but also in their individual contribution to the success of our program.

Since that time, I have used these techniques successfully to change the behavior and attitudes of hunters on many clubs and properties. An informed hunter, in most cases, will make the right decisions about management. We, unfortunately, have underestimated the hunter and have neglected his needs.

DEALING WITH THE NON-HUNTER

Studies have shown that, given adequate information, the general public will support deer hunting. But, do not become too smug over this news. These same studies indicate that although this group is not totally opposed to hunting, they lean heavily toward the anti-hunting sentiment. In order to assure that the average non-hunter understands and supports deer hunting, I feel we should address two areas.

First, **we need to clean up our act!** Frankly, there are far more "slob hunters" in the woods today than we ever would admit to. I deal with thousands of hunters annually, and I am afraid to say most are less than acceptable in their behavior. Here are some notable examples.

How many times in a season do you wear your camouflage outfit into a public place, as if it were a "badge of office?" As I will discuss in the next chapter, the general public equates camouflage with the military and/or paramilitary, and fears anyone so dressed. I have seen fellows come into a store not only decked out in camouflage, but with face paint, and even blood smeared on their faces. What does this say to the non-hunter? Are the anti-hunters right about this being a "blood sport?" How many states require the hunter to display his kill prominently on his vehicle? What does this say to the non-hunter? This practice should be abandoned as it creates the wrong image, and ruins a whole lot of venison in the process.

The behavior of hunters in the field, especially on public or open lands, often is deplorable! **Hunting is not a right, it is a privilege.** There are no guarantees for hunters in the Constitution. And, it should be treated as such. Each fall, more and more landowners post their lands, not because they are opposed to *hunting*; rather, they are opposed to *hunters*. Litter strewn over the landscape, fences cut, gates left open, all say one thing: Hunters are slobs! Again, peer-group pressure is the key to changing this deplorable behavior. Whenever one of your hunting buddies behaves inappropriately, make it painfully obvious that you do not want to associate with someone who behaves in this manner. It takes courage to stand up for what is right. But, do you love deer hunting enough to stand up for it?

We seem to continually apologize for our pastime. We should stop trying to justify what we do, rather discuss openly our feelings and the benefits of hunting. You should take every opportunity to speak with non-hunters, explaining in logical terms why you hunt. And finally, it is time to put away the term "sport hunter." It gives the wrong impression, and besides, **we do not hunt for sport**. We hunt because we enjoy it and it allows us to express our inner instincts to behave as human beings in a natural world. The instinct to hunt still is very strong in each of us, and is manifested in many ways. The bargain-hunter at the shopping center, the stamp collector and even the bird watcher all are expressing this innate desire. Take time to explain not only the biological reasons for deer hunting, but your inner-most feelings about your favorite pastime.

SUMMARY

Wildlife management is people management. The ability to manage people and to effectively communicate is an important asset for the whitetail manager and hunter. In order to do so, you must develop your communications skills, and gain insight into how people think and what motivates them. Peer-group pressure is the single-most effective means to change the way hunters and landowners do business. I have used this technique effectively to achieve quality buck management goals, even on properties where hunters are invited guests.

The non-hunters will determine the future of deer hunting in this country. Current data suggest that, although the average non-hunter is in sentiment with the anti-hunting faction, he will support deer hunting when given the correct information. One of the best ways to gain support from the non-hunting public is to present a positive image. Wearing of camouflage in public and other hunter rituals have to be curtailed. It gives a bad impression of what deer hunting really is about.

Take every opportunity to talk with the public about your feelings and the benefits of hunting in your life. It is the benefit not the justification that will sway public opinion. No one buys a product because they justify its purchase in their mind. The benefit of owning it is the real justification. Likewise, the best approach to gaining public acceptance of hunting is to emphasize the benefits it brings to the hunter and society.

Chapter 39

IN SUPPORT OF DEER HUNTING

It was one of those perfect New England fall mornings. The night had seen a gentle frost settle over the landscape, and the little prisms of solid-state water were producing thousands of tiny rainbows in the early morning light. Sitting beneath a maple, a hunter quietly surveys the scene, in hopes of spying his quarry. Suddenly, the stillness is shattered by a small army of blaze orange clad "protectors" of wildlife. With air horns roaring, they descend on their unsuspecting prey to prevent him from shooting a deer. After an ugly confrontation, the hunter gives up and moves on, hopefully to better days. In a courthouse in Rusk, Texas the walls reverberate with an outcry of public sentiment against shooting does. The poor biologist standing at the front of the room must endure insults and subtle intimations of bodily harm, all as a result of recommending a heavy doe harvest.

Two seemingly unrelated events. One involving radical animal rights activists, the other conservative hunters. Yet, they reflect identical pervasive attitudes about white-tailed deer; viz., deer populations, if left alone by man, can control their own destiny. Hopefully, by this point in the book, you have come to realize that both are irrevocably wrong! In this chapter my intent is to arm you, the hunter, with enough ammunition to take on the anti-hunting forces with a sane, articulate argument in favor of deer hunting.

The white-tailed deer is perhaps one of the most resilient species inhabiting the western hemisphere. In spite of wholesale damage to old growth forests over the last four hundred years, whitetails have fared well. They are an ancient species, probably inhabiting North America for 2-3 million years! During this time, the whitetail has endured countless changes in its habitat, plus the onslaught of hundreds of predator species. The saber-toothed tiger and cave bear were contemporaries of the whitetail. Yet, deer have outlasted most of them. Man, it seems, is only another in a long line of predators harassing whitetails. And, ironically, they probably will be around long after we are gone. What makes these creatures so flexible and ecologically successful?

Prior to the coming of man, the ancestors of whitetails had bridged the gap between Asia and North America, as had so many land mammals. Whitetails quickly spread southward into Central and South America. They thrived in the constantly changing forest. Wild fires, tornadoes and hurricanes wreaked havoc across the land, yet only served to encourage deer populations. For, as I noted earlier, deer are well suited to take rapid advantage of disturbances.

In old growth forests, most of the nutrients and sunlight are intercepted and held captive by the large trees and mid-story vegetation. Yet, a catastrophic disturbance can greatly change the situation. Suddenly, nutrients once tied up in large trees, are released and made available to weeds, grasses and shrubs. The abundant sunlight and moisture made available after a disturbance can produce a hundred fold increase in deer foods. But, this increase is only brief, lasting 7 to 10 years.

Whitetails are marvelously adapted to rapidly responding to optimum growing conditions. A doe has the capability of producing 19 or 20 offspring in her short life-span. Consequently, in only 6 or 7 years, a habitat can become saturated with deer.

The common myth among both hunters and anti-hunters is that deer populations have the ability to control themselves. This is utter nonsense! They never have, nor will they ever be able to control their own population growth. This is but one of many myths perpetrated by anti-hunters. Let's take a look at these myths and develop a logical argument against each.

Myth. Deer populations have the ability to control themselves.

In the chapter on population growth, I outlined the basics to population growth in whitetails. In summary, they primarily are a K-adapted species, responding quickly to habitat disturbance and optimum growing conditions. In the pristine world, such disturbances were commonplace, so there was little

In Support of Deer Hunting

Mike Biggs

The price of letting "nature take its course" often is disease and starvation!

concern for adequate habitat for deer. But, alas, it is a different world we live in. Man in his wisdom has exerted a considerable influence on the natural world— few can deny that! Modern man does not understand the basic rules by which mother nature operates. Fire and disturbance is viewed as a catastrophe, rather than a blessing. Consequently, man often has taken it upon himself to "protect" the natural world from itself. Whenever there is a forest fire, we run to put it out. Whenever forests are slated to be cut, we run to the courts. As I noted in the last chapter, one modern forester recently offered that the U.S. Forest Service does not practice silviculture, they practice liticulture, meaning that decisions about resource management are made in the courts, not by professionals.

Faced with what I now perceive as a very much unnatural world, we no longer have the luxury of "letting nature take its course." We are locked into management, and management includes both habitat and population control. As I have said many times, Daniel Boone is dead! This is an irrefutable fact. And, no amount of wishful thinking is going to change it.

Deer populations do not have the ability to control their own growth. The common arguments are that, at high population densities, whitetail does either re-absorb their embryos or do not conceive in the first place. Also, bucks under stress produce less viable sperm. These are ludicrous arguments at best. First of all, although there are reductions in *in utero* embryo counts at high densities, I never have seen these counts go to zero! This means that fawns are being born, even when the population has saturated its environment. The control comes through the miserable deaths of these fawns after birth, usually during the first two to three weeks.

Second, the fact that some does do not conceive at all is an indication of very poor physical condition. What it boils down to is quality of life. How much quality of life is there for an individual that is so starved for nutrients that she cannot even support a fetus? Is this any less cruel? Anti-hunters rather would like to see deer go off in the woods and tastefully die out of our sight so that we do not have to deal with the realities of the situation.

Third, I know of no data which substantiates the claim that bucks adjust sperm production to population density. I would hate to see the herd that ever achieved this physiological state. Yet, many anti-hunting groups firmly believe that these phenomena occur. I suggest in all cases that you ask a simple question. Where are the scientific data?

Myth: If predators are left alone, they will control deer herds.

Hunters often put forward the argument that they benevolently have taken over the job of predators in controlling the population. Anti-hunters say that predators should be allowed to perform their natural role in life. But, what predators? Which ones can step forward to control deer population growth? As I noted earlier, whitetails have been coping with predators for millennia, and have survived to tell the tale. The only predator that appears to have had a significant impact on deer populations was the wolf. Wolves and deer are brothers. The deer and the wolf have grown up together, each intimately dependent on the other. However, the wolf was obligated to a co-dependency relationship. Although wolves had the ability to switch to alternative, smaller prey, the welfare of wolves greatly was influenced by the abundance of deer.

The deer-wolf relationship marvelously adapted deer to respond to man. Under constant wolf predation, deer learned to occupy the refugia and sanctuaries lying between wolf territories. This behavior pre-adapted deer to seek similar sanctuaries under heavy hunting pressure by man.

Therefore, wolves were the primary predators of deer during the last several thousand years, serving not to control, but to dampen the population over-shoots periodically experienced by deer. But, when was the last time you saw a wolf running around the woods? Sadly, there are no wolves to work their magic on deer. And, no matter how much we desire them to return, wolves never will be allowed to exist in the heavily developed and urbanized world of today. Recent attempts by the U.S. Fish & Wildlife Service to restore Red Wolves to certain areas has met with increasing resistance by the local inhabitants. Even some of the most ardent anti-hunters will support professional predator control!

Studies on the impact of other predators such as coyotes have given mixed results. In some areas, and under some conditions, coyotes can exert influence on herd growth. But, not one study has substantiated that coyotes are a consistent control agent to whitetails. So whether we like it or not, man now is relegated to the role of the wolf. The role of predators in deer population control always has been questionable, but today is not even a reasonable alternative.

Myth: Deer populations can be controlled by alternate means.

In Support of Deer Hunting

Occasionally, anti-hunting groups reluctantly will admit that something has to be done about deer population growth. Alternatives to hunting include: 1) use of professional hunters, 2) relocation, and 3) birth control measures. Let's look carefully at each of these.

The whitetail now exists at somewhere between 15 and 20 million animals. Annually population growth amounts to approximately 35% in many areas. In order to keep the existing populations healthy and ecologically productive, we would have to annually remove some 5 to 7 million deer. As a professional whitetail manager, I have found that a good hunter can kill perhaps a dozen animals a day under ideal conditions. Consequently, this would require paying some 500,000 man-days of professional hunting, at an approximate cost of $50 million!

The few extant whitetail predators have little effect on population growth.

Mike Biggs

Yet, there are a large number of citizens out there that are more than willing to do the job for us free of charge. But, even if we had this kind of money to invest in deer management alone, would the deer be better off? Not at all. In much of the range, deer exist only because they represent an economic resource (see Chapter 43) to the landowner. One Texas Hill Country rancher once told me, "If I did not make money off of deer, there would not be a single one on the place!" Banning of hunting does not protect a species. Rather it works against it. In Kenya, elephant populations have been seriously depleted since a ban on elephant hunting was imposed by that country. It is naive to think otherwise.

Relocation of deer is not even a viable alternative. The debacle that took place in the Everglades during the early 1980's is a perfect example. Flood waters from two tropical storms had forced deer to be crowded into a smaller portion of their range. The herd was deteriorating rapidly, so the State of Florida decided to have a special hunt to reduce the population. The resulting furor brought national media attention to the problem. A court injunction halted the hunt in the northern portion of the region, where protectionist groups proposed to capture and "relocate" some 2,000 deer. Where these animals were to be relocated was never clearly explained. The proposed hunt in the southern portion took place as planned.

Protectionist groups removed only 18 deer from the northern portion, at a cost of $8,000 ($444 per deer). Within a year, only 6 deer had survived the capture ordeal, and better than 60% of the remaining wild deer had died from starvation. On the southern portion, where 723 deer had been harvested, the herd fared much better. Including hunting mortality, only 23% of the deer were lost from the southern herd. It is interesting to note that, given the cost for the protectionist approach, it would have cost more than $300,000 to accomplish this task! After the flooding had subsided, the herd once again returned to normal healthy levels. The northern herd, however, quickly destroyed the remaining habitat, guaranteeing that recovery of this herd would take many years. Yet, in spite of these facts, the news media never reported the ultimate outcome of the Everglades deer disaster.

Finally, use of birth control devices is almost too ludicrous to discuss. Chemicals have not been perfected which can serve to control reproduction in deer, and if they were available, how can we deliver the proper dose to each deer? Will deer experience some of the same carcenogenic effects as humans under hormone therapy? The cost alone of this approach would be incredible.

Myth: Hunters have an advantage over the deer.

It is sad to say that this statement is the most commonly used argument against deer hunting. Anti-hunting forces take pleasure in portraying the hunting of deer as a slaughter or a "war on wildlife." The fact is, however, that managers seldom are able to talk hunters into killing the number of deer necessary to control the population. Also, anyone who has hunted deer will tell you that the advantage lies solely with the deer! The average success rate for deer hunters in most states is quite low, and the incredible amount of time expended per deer harvested would never stand up to an efficiency analysis.

WHY DO WE HUNT DEER?

Faced with the facts, there is little alternative to hunting in order to control deer populations. But this aside, there is a better reason why we hunt deer. Man has developed an intimate relationship with whitetails since first coming to North America either by land (Indians) or by sea (Europeans). **The whitetail is the real symbol of the American spirit— adaptable, resilient and hardy.** He is the ultimate game animal; capable, after millennia of coping with a vast array of predators, of thwarting even the most skilled of hunters. Under modern sport hunting regulations, there is no way that deer populations ever will be reduced to the low levels seen at the turn of the century. However, deer **are** threatened by over-protectionism, by both pro- and anti-hunting forces. After more than 50 years of regulated hunting, whitetails continue to increase their numbers at an alarming rate. This fact cannot be refuted by anyone. The salvation of the whitetail lies staunchly rooted in the hunter, not the protectionist. But, what are you doing to assure that whitetails continue to enjoy their role in life? Do you shrink from anti-hunters rather than taking them on in a well thought out debate of the real issues? Sadly the answer too often is a resounding NO! If you love whitetails, it is time to make a commitment.

THE HUNTING DEBATE

Unfortunately, most hunters are quite introverted. In spite of the fact that they feel very strongly about what they do, hunters are slow to become involved in public controversy. It takes a major defeat to rally the forces. Immediately after the television program *Guns of Autumn*, we saw a flurry of activity in support of hunting. But, in no time these activities fell off dramatically. The battle will be fought and won in the field of education, both through the school system and the public media. Yet, the North American Wildlife Conference recently abolished its conservation education committee! What insanity is this?

It is instructive to examine the fate of the average dollar spent on licenses by hunters. The vast majority goes to law enforcement, in spite of the fact that poaching is not the major problem we face today. In Texas, less than twenty cents goes to information and education, and most of this is spent on a slick state magazine. Hunter education programs center more on safety than they do on ethics and wildlife management. Clearly, there is a need for some serious changes!

What can you do? Well, to start off I suggest that you become as informed as you can about wildlife management and the anti-hunting philosophy. You have to understand the enemy and how he/she thinks. Read every article written against hunting. Clinically analyze the points presented and find out the true facts. Then, develop a sound argument against each. Studies have shown that the average American will make the right decision about wildlife management when given the facts. So, it is up to you to get the facts to the public. Welcome the opportunity to debate the issues whether publicly or through the print media.

However, you must be careful not to fall into the trap posed by anti-hunters. Remember that they are portraying the hunter as a drunken slob, who thinks with his fist. So do not punch one of these guys out! That precisely is what they want. They would like nothing better than to have a television camera record a hunter beating some poor guy to a pulp.

The proper approach always is to give the appearance of a sane, articulate person who has given his position considerable thought. Dress properly. One of my pet peeves is the use or misuse of camouflage. Every time I give a talk on a Saturday morning at some sport show, half the audience shows up dressed from head to toe in camouflage! I can just hear it now.

"Hey Joe, wanna go down to the deer show?"
"You bet, let me go get my camouflage on!"

The average American views camouflage as para-military, and you know how we Americans feel about military types running around in our neighborhoods. So, avoid fitting the stereotype at all costs.

Always have your agenda established before you go into "combat." Decide on two or three keys issues and, no matter how often your opponent changes the subject, repeat your stand on these issues. Be logical in your presentation, making the material easy for all to understand.

Never lose your temper, no matter how insulting the position taken. As I noted above, that precisely is what they are trying to do. A simple smile, a touch on the arm and the friendly admonition, "Now, you know that's not true," will go a long way. Then re-state your pre-established positions. But, what are some of these positions?

Most anti-hunting groups have offensive programs, meaning that they never have had to defend **their** position. You would be surprised how quickly they become disoriented when you put them into a defensive position. I have some one-liners which are quite effective.

If anti-hunters have their way, it will mean the end of wildlife. Every time hunting has been banned, wildlife has fared poorly.

This is a hard-hitting statement, yet it is true. Hunting is the salvation of wildlife species, not the end. Look at what happened to elephants in Africa. Bans on hunting in some countries have meant the virtual extirpation of the species. Kenya had some 75,000 elephants prior to the ban. Now, there are less than 7,500!

Non-hunters do not have a track record in paying for wildlife management and protection of habitat.

Again, this is a highly defensible statement. No one can deny the incredible impact hunters have had on wildlife throughout the world. The amount of money spent on wildlife annually dwarfs anything spent by protectionist groups. Attempts by states to support non-game programs have not met with success. Where are the acres of habitat set aside by anti-hunting forces?

The vast majority of money raised by pro-hunting groups generally is spent directly to benefit wildlife, yet 30-85% of dollars raised by anti-hunting groups goes into someone's pocket. The anti-hunting, animal rights movement is big business.

Perhaps the greatest weak point of the animal rights-anti-hunting forces lies in the area of fiscal responsibility. Funds raised by these "non-profit" organizations are difficult to track, and in some cases, downright fraud is involved. Many of the groups have impressive stock portfolios, including some of the major polluters of our environment.

Hunters love animals!

No statement has as great an impact on the audience as this one. I have used it many times, with interesting results. The average anti-hunting supporter honestly thinks that hunters are blood thirsty savages, who want to see the last member of the species die. Yet, we do love animals. What hunter has not had his heart lightened by a new born fawn sniffing at a flower, or taking its first steps? Who has not rejoiced in the call of a woodpecker or a squirrel? Nothing is more effective than a hunter telling what his way-of-life means to him. I like to talk about the beauty of nature, the joys of just being in the woods, and most importantly, of being one with nature. Man always has been a hunter in the natural world. **We do not hunt for sport, we hunt because it is our nature.** Everyone is a hunter in one way or another. The berry picker is a hunter. The wilderness enthusiast is a hunter. And, yes even the housewife looking for a bargain at the discount store is a hunter. Play up the experience, not the kill. After all, is killing a deer the only reason you go to the woods?

My dietary preference is venison.

The recent defeat of anti-fur interests in Aspen, Colorado, proved that Americans staunchly believe in the right of choice. You can take advantage of this by stressing that, in these times of concern for health and the environment, the taking and eating of venison is both ecologicially and physiologically sound, since it is documented that venison is low in fat and cholesterol.

SUMMARY

I hope this short chapter has given you reason for thought. How committed are you to deer hunting and whitetails? If you truly are, you will become actively involved in social and political issues. Become knowledgeable about the basics of deer ecology, learn as much as you can about how non-hunters think and perceive the hunter, welcome opportunities to talk about deer hunting, and always give a good impression. There is still time, but it is running out. If we lose hunting, we and the whitetail will suffer.

Chapter 40

TO BE A TROPHY HUNTER

Although I do not remember the name of the movie, the plot forever will stick in my head. It seems the "heavy," played by Richard Boone, was a millionaire trophy hunter who financed a time-travel expedition to the days of the dinosaurs. He successfully duped the hero into believing that he was interested solely in the scientific nature of the project. The story became dramatic when the hero realized, to his horror, that Boone only wanted to add to his collection of trophies!

This is an all-too-familiar theme in the movies and on television nowadays. The image of the trophy hunter is one of a person who is out to get the last remaining specimen of the species, no matter what the cost. The Humane Society of the United States is adamantly against hunting, but is particularly vociferous about "trophy" hunters, who are portrayed as mere collectors of animal heads. In the opinion of many, the trophy hunter is a deplorable creature who sits in his trophy room, surrounded by evidence of his prowess. Even among hunters, I often hear comments about trophy hunters that are so preposterous that I decided to put this nonsense to rest once and for all. In this chapter, I will define the term "trophy," as well as, explore the true nature of the trophy hunter and his motivations. In the process, I think you will find that the modern trophy hunter actually is the epitome of conservation.

WHAT IS A TROPHY WHITETAIL?

A trophy buck is one that is mature — often referred to by hunters as a "prime" animal. To qualify as a true trophy, there are several reasons why the buck must be mature. First of all, it is biologically sound to harvest only the mature individuals. In many species, the older-age-class individuals already have contributed to the genetics of the population, and their further contributions are limited. Reproduction is primarily an activity of younger individuals in prime physical condition. Most top-end trophies are harvested within a year or two of the time when they otherwise would die from natural causes. Second, and most important, mature animals have survived years of natural and man-caused mortality agents. I am convinced that the whitetail buck is almost unkillable by legal means after he reaches 4 years of age. Hence, he represents a challenge that cannot be matched by any other game animal. Admittedly, I am prejudiced toward whitetails, but the fact remains that the mature whitetail buck is the most difficult animal to harvest. I often am asked to visit the homes of successful trophy hunters. They show with pride their record-book kudu, eland or sable antelope. Yet, when asked about their whitetail, most hang their heads and point apologetically toward some hidden niche, in which resides a most pathetic specimen. The whitetail is the great equalizer, attainable with only the greatest of difficulty no matter the social or economic status of the hunter.

In many states and provinces, the probability of a buck reaching maturity is very slim. Heavy harvest rates of

Mike Biggs

A "trophy" certainly is different things to different people. The author feels that a trophy is one that is a mature whitetail, which best represents the type of quality deer available in that specific geographic area. This Texas Hill Country deer certainly meets these criteria.

70 percent or more on bucks are not uncommon. Unfortunately, the likelihood of a hunter experiencing the joy of harvesting a *true* trophy in such places is even more remote. Clearly, if we do not allow our bucks to mature, the challenge of harvesting the most difficult game animal will remain out of reach. Too often I hear hunters say, "Well if I hadn't shot him, some other guy would have!" That is poor logic to me.

MAKING OF A TROPHY HUNTER

Individuals who become trophy hunters do so for a variety of reasons, but most seem to follow a predictable evolution, unlike other hunters, who reach a certain plateau and stay there. Social scientists have noted for years that the hunter can pass through several steps during his lifetime.

First, there simply is "the need to kill something." We all have seen this in the young boy with a brand-new air rifle. Just the idea that the gun will kill an animal is enough to motivate the young Nimrod. Later, when he acquires a more powerful arsenal of weapons, he may or may not pass out of this stage. Unfortunately, we all know of individuals who never have graduated from the "kill everything that moves" syndrome.

Next comes "the need to kill a limit of game." There is a feeling of accomplishment in achieving the legally imposed harvest limit. Hunters proclaim with pride that they "limited out." The goal is solely to acquire a limit, rather than a quality hunting experience. This attitude has produced hefty fines for game-law violations, because some don't know when to quit. Again, many hunters find this level all too comfortable and never change throughout their lives. I once met a 70-year old man whose claim to fame in that particular area was that he killed two bucks every year for 50 years. Obviously, I was not around for many of those hunts, but I did observe him over a 10-year period. He killed two bucks every year, all right, but they always were yearlings. The age of the buck or the difficulty in harvest meant nothing; the goal was to fill the limit.

The third stage is "the need to harvest more game or bigger game than anyone else." Hunting is viewed as a competitive sport, in which one expresses his prowess over another. An acquaintance of mine does not consider a hunt a success unless he has bested his hunting buddies. Asked if he had a good hunt, he is likely to respond, "Naw, I didn't even limit out, and Joe shot more than me!" This type of hunter is not very likely to graduate to the next stage.

The technologist is a hunter who feels "the need to be concerned with the techniques used in hunting." Bowhunters often fall into this category. The techniques and equipment used to harvest game are just as important to them as the kill is. If it cannot be done "properly," according to established rules and methods, the technologist would just as soon come home empty-handed. These hunters are a joy. I have seen bowhunters, for example, get just as much fun from a prolonged yet unproductive stalk as from killing a buck. The kill was only secondary to the experience for them.

Now, we come to the final category. The last stage in the evolution of the trophy hunter lies in "the joy of the experience itself." These hunters go to the field more to learn and observe deer in their natural state than to kill a buck. The kill is not necessary for a successful hunt. In fact, many of these hunters harvest bucks only infrequently. One such individual, Bob McElroy of Houston, probably has not killed a buck in several years, yet he is out there every year, hunting for that trophy. And, he is one of the best trophy hunters I know.

THE TROPHY HUNTING EXPERIENCE?

Hunting as we know it today is a form of recreation, and recreationists tell us that there are several steps to a quality recreational experience. The first is in **making the decision to participate**. Few hunters have trouble with this one, and there certainly is no lack of enthusiasm for the sport.

Next comes **the planning phase**. Unfortunately, few deer hunters spend any appreciable amount of time in this activity. Many of these chapters have preached the necessity of doing your homework when hunting trophy whitetails. It not only increases your chances of success, but also broadens the experience. For example, Texan Bill Carter, a recognized authority on both trophy-deer production and hunting, asserts that the whitetail hunter should spend much of the year practicing his shooting skills and developing reliable loads. Bill contends that most big bucks are lost because of lack of preparation by the shooter than any other reason. But, something else is lost without planning: a great many experiences in anticipating the coming season. We used to poke fun at the old-style outdoor articles, the ones we called "me-and-Bob" stories. You probably remember them well. They all started out the same way: The author is about to pull the trigger on some monster animal, when he cannot help but remember back six months or more, when he and Bob decided to make this hunt. That plot was used to excess, but it did have merit. A large portion of a quality hunting experience lies in the anticipation.

The actual **recreational experience**-- in this case, shooting a buck-- lasts only a brief moment. Many times I have shot a big buck and then lamented that the experience was over too fast! That is where the next and final stage comes into play. The **recollection** of the trophy-hunting experience is the most important phase. As far as I am concerned, if a trophy hunt does not produce these lasting memories, then it was a fruitless endeavor, no matter how big the buck was. That is where that much maligned head on the wall comes into play. It reminds us of pleasant memories, pure and simple.

Now that you're armed with this information, let's listen to what some trophy hunters have to say about their activities.

To Be a Trophy Hunter

RAY SASSER

Ray, a resident of Dallas, is one of today's best-known outdoor writers, producing material for virtually every major outdoor magazine. I have known Ray for many years and have profound respect for his abilities as a writer and as a trophy hunter. I caught up with him recently and sort of turned the tables on him, asking him about his views on hunting trophy whitetails. He is more accustomed to being the interviewer than the interviewee, but once he got his wits about him, he had some very interesting things to say.

"Well," he said, "you know as well as I do that trophy-whitetail hunting is a strange thing indeed. It is a disease!" Ray spent his early years just trying to

Ray Sasser is one of the premier writers and trophy hunters in the country today. Ray feels that trophy hunting is a "disease," from which you seldom recover.

kill any buck, and he certainly killed his share. But, over time, it became unnecessary for him to kill a buck. Ray remembers well the first time he passed up a buck. "It was a weird feeling," he notes, "one which left me confused, then proud of myself." For the first time, he began to watch deer and to learn more about their habits. The average gun hunter spends about three seconds watching a buck-- that is the amount of time it takes to sight in and pull the trigger.

There also is a mystical nature to what Ray had to say about trophy-whitetail hunting. "You know, I passed up dozens of bucks this last season without popping a cap," he said. "I seemed to derive pleasure in 'counting coups' on a buck. Just knowing that I could have killed a particular buck was as good as actually doing it."

I never had given that angle much thought, but Ray was correct. If you can outsmart an old buck and bring him into killing range, you really do not have to kill him to have a successful hunt. Besides, as Ray puts it, if you shoot the deer, "Then, you would have to field dress him, and that's a whole lot of trouble!" In short, Ray considers the trophy hunter to be one who has evolved to a higher plane of hunting enjoyment.

NOEL FEATHER

I caught up with Noel in his office in Illinois. He is just about as personable a fellow as you would wish to meet. His ability with a bow is legendary, for he has taken a number of record-class bucks. Noel has feelings that are in some ways similar to, but in other ways different from, Ray's. "I hunt trophy whitetails for the challenge," he proclaimed. "I've killed my share of young bucks, the first of which was a yearling 3-pointer that I got with a running shot with a bow. But, later I came to the idea that there was no challenge to hunting young bucks." He went on to explain that hunting trophy bucks is the ultimate hunting challenge, in spite of the fact that he also has harvested an incredible number of bears with a bow. "You don't have to kill a buck to enjoy the hunt," he continued. "Just getting close enough to kill him with a bow is enough." Interestingly enough, Noel enjoys competition, both with other hunters and the game itself.

In spite of the fact that Noel is a committed trophy hunter, he had some words of caution for others looking to elevate their standards. He is particularly concerned about young sportsmen. "I see too many young guys take up bowhunting nowadays and immediately go into trophy hunting. This is not a good thing." He noted that the young, inexperienced hunter quickly will tire of the hours of unproductive hunting needed to harvest trophy bucks. Further, many areas just do not have the type of buck most consider a "trophy." He suggested that instead of rushing into it, hunters take their time about becoming trophy hunters. There is no reason to jump from a Stage 1 hunter to a trophy hunter. Take some time to enjoy hunting and outwitting game. Besides, Noel asserted, "The novice hunter lacks the skills necessary to outwit and successfully kill a true tro-

Noel Feather of Sterling, Illinois, is highly competitive when it comes to deer hunting, and this buck will compete with anyone's.

phy buck."

DICK IDOL

Dick is perhaps the best-known trophy hunter in North America today. His contributions both to our knowledge about whitetails and whitetail hunting are considerable. Dick is about as hard to nail down as I am for an interview, but I recently was lucky enough to catch him in his Seeley Lake, Montana, office between conducting hunting seminars.

Dick noted that he came to trophy hunting in pretty much the same way as most hunters. His first buck was very small, but at the time he felt that it had to be the biggest buck in the world! Soon after, he killed a doe, and that left him pretty flat. Now, Dick is not against shooting does, but the thrill of killing a "trophy" doe is just not there for him. Later, he was lucky enough to

Dick Idol is perhaps America's best-known trophy whitetail hunter. He has contributed a great deal to improve the image of the American trophy hunter.

harvest larger and larger bucks, until he harvested three or four in the 125-130 Boone & Crockett class. Then, he was hooked; killing a big buck became a personal challenge. Dick put it clearly. "Once you kill a few 16- or 17-inchers," he confided, "your standards increase dramatically. At least, mine did."

He further noted that the growth of a trophy hunter is something like a learning curve, with hunters falling out at different levels along that curve. Where you fall out on the curve depends on your individual personality, experience and, perhaps most important of all, opportunity. "The guy who harvests a 14-inch 6-pointer in some parts of Pennsylvania has reached the epitome for that country," Dick explained. "That's just about the best he can do, no matter how hard he hunts."

Dick suggested one of the best definitions of trophy buck: one that is exceptional for the resource at hand. It is the highest goal attainable for any particular geographic area. "I certainly have different standards when I hunt Alabama than when I hunt Alberta," he noted.

In conclusion, this noted expert offered a comment that is most profound. He said he believes trophy hunting is the salvation of the whitetail as a species. Shooting a big whitetail offers more to the hunter than, say, shooting a quail or a pheasant, because there is no obvious way to measure quality in those species. "The meat hunter can never appreciate the whitetail for itself," Dick claims, "or the quality of its habitat, or the experience of hunting it. It is just a package of meat!" Also, Dick is concerned about the "bum wrap" taken by trophy hunters from the non-hunting public. To criticize the trophy hunter because he kills for the antlers is totally off base. The fact that he is not killing the animal strictly for meat is difficult for a non-hunter to comprehend. Trophy hunters have more reverence for the animal itself than any pure meat hunter ever could have.

AS FOR ME......

Finally, it is only fair that I consider my own motivations in trophy-whitetail hunting. Unlike the above sportsmen, I came to deer hunting for unusual reasons. Yet, I have come to the same opinions. My early days were spent not in killing whitetails, but in producing trophy bucks for others to hunt. Early on, I was frustrated by the fact that growing a trophy buck is relatively easy, but harvesting that buck is very difficult. Consequently, I became interested in effective techniques for harvesting mature bucks. So much for my scientific point of view!

I now have become "infected" by the trophy-whitetail "disease". The "sickness" has progressed to the point where I really wonder if any buck can reach my lofty standards. Each year I am invited to hunt with several whitetail outfitters. After several years of my looking but not shooting, many a poor outfitter has thrown up his hands in disgust and proclaimed there is no way to please me! Perhaps Noel Feather is

The author came to trophy hunting primarily out of frustration with hunters! It seems that it was one thing to grow a monster buck, but yet another to kill one.

W. Alex Wall

Mike Biggs

right in saying we sometimes become so driven by the challenge that we forget to have the experience.

But, there is one positive point about all of this. I have come to appreciate each and every buck for his own merits. As Dick noted, we judge a trophy on a floating scale. I always try to harvest an example of the top class of buck a particular place has to offer. I came close this past season in Mexico to pulling the trigger on a 6-pointer, sporting 12-inch tines and a 24-inch inside spread. Perhaps there is hope for my recovery yet.

Hopefully, if you aren't a trophy hunter, you have come to understand him better through this chapter. As you see, he is not the bloodthirsty creature portrayed by the movies. He is a stickler for technique and a quality experience, and his "success" is not measured in Boone and Crockett or Pope and Young points. He is an elite purist, who understands the meanings of the words "quality" and "trophy."

Chapter 41

Organizing a Hunting Club

A cloud of dense cigarette smoke hovered ominously over the crowd of 300 or so people attending the state wildlife association's annual meeting. The tension was so thick you literally could cut it with a knife—and I was on the menu! The theme of the meeting was "leasing and hunting clubs." I swallowed hard in anticipation of what was about to confront me and began to speak.

Somewhere in the middle of the talk, I began to sense that there was a growing agreement among the audience, and my confidence substantially increased. "These are not the good old days any more," I declared. "The day of the mountain man is gone. If you want quality hunting experiences, you are going to have to make your own. And, hunting clubs are the best way I know of to do just that."

With that declaration, I thanked the crowd and asked for questions. Sentiment was pretty much divided among the attendees. One man noted that he was sick and tired of having to deal with the growing number of hunters and decreasing game quality. Another rose, red faced, and exclaimed, "I've hunted for 20 years on an area, and this year there are hunting-club signs posted all over the land; they want $125 for a membership! I'm gonna sell my 4-wd pickup and take up fishing." I chuckled to myself regarding the economics of that statement. "I'll bet he spends more than that on cigarettes," I thought.

The fact is that hunting clubs are growing substantially in popularity, even in regions that are the very bastions of open-land hunting. The reasons for these changes are quite simple. The good old days **are** gone. Quality hunting opportunities are becoming increasingly more rare as the North American population continues to increase. When it comes to hunting, the demand far exceeds the supply. Faced with this situation, many sportsmen and sportsmen's groups are acquiring land and forming hunting clubs.

A hunting club is an organized group of sportsmen who either lease or purchase lands for exclusive sport hunting and recreation by its members, and who actively participate in the management of wildlife on that property. No one is really sure how many hunting clubs there are in the U.S. today, but in East Texas alone there are more than 2,000! The average size of these Pineywoods clubs is a whopping 2,000-plus acres.

Hunting clubs are not a new idea — they are as old as game management itself. The early hunting clubs often were called "preserves" and were the exclusive domain of the aristocracy. As far as we know, Kubla Khan formed the first hunting preserve more than 600 years ago. Sportsmen's clubs are a tradition in Europe, one brought to the New World by the pioneers. Hunting preserves and clubs soon were common throughout New England and the Deep South. They were places where gentlemen gathered for sport and camaraderie. Such names as Southlands, Burnt Pine and Bostick Plantation today have become synonymous with quality hunting experiences.

Hunting clubs declined in popularity for a number of years following the turn-of-the-century, probably due to the growing success of state game and fish agencies at restoring game populations. There still was plenty of land to hunt, and the growing game populations were there for the taking. But, by the 1950s the American population was growing at a phenomenal rate, and the pickings no longer were easy. It seemed that everywhere the hunter turned there was someone else hunting the same animal. Sportsmen once again turned to the hunting club to improve the quality of the experience. Starting in Texas, the trend soon spread to Mississippi, then to Georgia, Louisiana, Alabama and Florida. Now, hunting clubs are flourishing along the East coast and creeping slowly into the Midwest. California recently has passed legislation aimed directly at aiding hunting clubs and preserve operators.

Whether you like it or not, the trend is here to stay. This chapter is aimed at those of you contemplating forming hunting clubs, and it hopefully will get you around some of the obstacles and pitfalls I have observed over the years. In order to give you some pointers on organizing and running a hunting club,

Organizing a Hunting Club

I will draw on experiences from working with the several thousand clubs around the country.

THE PEOPLE

Wildlife management is people management. The choice of sportsmen for your general membership will mean the difference between many years of hunting success and feuds rivaling those between the Hatfields and McCoys. I have said on many occasions that I can tell more about a man by hunting with him for one day than by living around him for years. Hunt-

The choice of sportsmen for your hunting club is the single-most important decision in forming a hunting club. It will mean the difference between many years of hunting success and feuds rivaling the Hatfields and McCoys! After all, the purpose of forming a club is to enjoy the fellowship of the hunt.

ing brings out the best and the worst in people. I have seen preachers turn in frothing-at-the-mouth poachers under such conditions. So, choose you membership wisely.

You should select your initial membership on the basis of: (1) people you enjoy and trust; (2) demonstrated sportsmanship; and (3) commitment to wildlife-management principles. *Every* member should fit these criteria. Do not make the mistake of selecting someone just because he is a good friend or a relative. Inviting someone to join a club is like getting married; you are stuck with him for a long time.

Next, you and your membership should establish a system for the addition or replacement of members. Vacancies should be filled under written guidelines, not through the "buddy" system. Several of the hunting clubs with which I work require letters of recommendation and a background check for game violations. That probably is a good way to eliminate "bad eggs" from the outset.

Every organization needs goals, and hunting clubs are no exception. There are several decisions that need to be made by the membership. The first of these is the type of club to be organized. Will the club be for members only, or will provisions be made for guests? Also, is the club to be a family enterprise, or just for its members? These are questions that have to be answered early on. Often, clubs are formed by relatively young guys who give little thought to the toddlers back home, but those toddlers soon become teenagers who also want to hunt. I have seen otherwise well-managed clubs break up under the demands of growing families.

You probably are saying to yourself right now, "Wait a minute! You've got us organized and a system set for getting new members, and we don't even have a place to hunt yet." That is true, but first things first. I learned a long time ago that you do not get your hamsters *before* you get your cage.

Now that you have an organization, you need to decide on the specific goals of your hunting club. Is it being organized primarily for deer hunting, or is there equal demand for other game species? This will determine the focus of your management program, as well as how you run your club. My experience has been that, with the exception of southern quail-hunting clubs, most clubs are organized primarily for deer hunting. Other game species are taken only incidentally.

In deer management, there are three options open to the club. It can be managed for trophy-deer production, quality-deer production, or simply for deer hunting, regardless of animal quality. Each one of these goals carries with it a different set of activities and attitudes. For example, genuine trophy-buck management is a costly business, often demanding fewer club members. The number of members you have will dictate the type of management program. If you have 50 members and you plan on obtaining 2,500 acres of land, you can forget about true *trophy* management. My experience has shown that, under a trophy-management program, you will be able to harvest only one trophy buck per 1,000 acres. (Total acreage required could be even greater in some regions.) Faced with this reality, most clubs soon retreat to the quality-buck management option. Under a quality-buck program, you can expect to harvest one good, mature buck per 150 to 300 acres, depending upon the quality of the habitat. If you just want to shoot deer, and do not care about the quality of the bucks harvested, you can have one hunter for every 75 to 100 acres in most habitats. A higher hunter density will guarantee problems.

Whatever goals you establish, write them down for all the members to see. That brings us to the next step.

THE BASIC ORGANIZATION

A good friend once said that verbal agreements, even among the closest of friends, always will end in disaster. This certainly is the case with hunting clubs. I recommend that bylaws be established, *unanimously* agreed to by the membership, and a printed, signed copy distributed to each member as soon as possible. The bylaws should include procedures for amendments.

I also recommend to clubs that they incorporate as non-profit organizations. Incorporation carries with it many advantages in these times of legal mania. Formation of a club implies the collection of money, and money means taxes. Also, there is the liability question that seems to be ever-present. It will be far easier to obtain a lease or landowner agreement if the club can show adequate liability insurance. There are three areas of liability to consider. First, member-member conflicts should be considered. This means that if one member injures or kills another, adequate coverage is available. Second, if members are allowed to entertain guests, they also must be covered. And lastly, there should be coverage for uninvited guests, even poachers. At this writing, the National Rifle Association provides such coverage at reasonable cost. You should be able to secure liability insurance for around $500; however, do not hold me to this, as the insurance picture changes daily.

ACQUIRING THE LAND

Every July, my phone begins ringing off the wall; hunters are calling, looking for land to lease. There could be no worse time of the year to begin such a search. Now is the time to start looking.

First, however, members should decide what type situation they want. There basically are two options open to the club. First, the club may be able to secure exclusive hunting rights to land without paying a fee. This situation is more likely to occur in the Midwest and West, as landowners in these regions are more accustomed to allowing free hunting access to their lands. But why would a landowner agree to such a thing? The advantages are obvious. By allowing exclusive access by a hunting club, the landowner can reduce both his headaches and liabilities. Granting exclusive rights assures that he will know exactly who is hunting on his land and that those who do are adequately insured for recreational activities. Furthermore, hunting clubs can help maintain the security of the land, as well as, making improvements to roads, fences, gates, etc.

The next option open to your club is a lease agreement. Leasing is becoming very popular throughout the U.S., especially with the current state of the agricultural economy. It is not new, however, the Europeans have leased hunting lands for centuries. However, leasing probably has generated more game-management "people problems" during the last several years than in any other period. Areas in which landowners traditionally have allowed the general public access to their lands are now the focus of such conflicts. Citizen's groups in Louisiana and Arkansas recently have filed legal proceedings concerning the leasing of private lands and gating of private roads. I do not intend to argue either pro or con on this issue; however, I will point out that the proportion of lands being leased for hunting is growing at an incredible rate— and there is no indication that the trend will be reversed. State agencies lack the funding to develop free-access agreements with private landowners.

THE RIGHT PROPERTY

I always am amazed at how little thought hunting clubs give to the selection of their club property. Many groups are so glad to find an available tract that they will take anything. The wrong choice will be disastrous, however. I suggest that you secure the services of a professional wildlife consultant. Their fees are not very expensive, and their knowledge is worth every penny you pay them. Here are some general guidelines to follow.

The No. 1 problem in hunting-club management is *control of the land*. This is especially true for lands that traditionally have been open to the public. Careful consideration should be given to the configuration of the club property. The ideal property is perfectly square. A long, narrow piece of property, or one that is very irregular in shape, is a nightmare to protect. Also, if there are public roads transecting the land, you are in for some real problems— especially if they're non-paved community roads. Such roads often are "playgrounds for poachers." Thought also should be given to the surrounding landowners and adjacent hunting clubs. What are the attitudes and management philosophies of these parties? Find out— it pays off.

Although you will be hunting wild animals, you must remember that *wildlife is an agricultural crop*. Just as the potential production of corn is determined by the quality of the soil, game quality and quantity also are determined by the soil. Bottomland soils usually are the most productive in terms of game, although some of our prairie soils also are known to produce fine animals. However, I usually recommend an equal mix of upland and bottomland types. The problem with bottomlands is that they often do not produce the amount of forage necessary to sustain a good herd. Further, bottoms may be subject to periodic inundation from flooding. **The ideal property would be one that has about 50 percent of its area in bottomland forest, and 25 percent each in cropland (preferably grain) and upland forest.**

HOW MUCH LAND?

The amount of land you acquire for your hunting club will depend upon several factors, among which are the number of hunters, the management goals your club sets, and surrounding land-use. Normally, I recommend that the average deer club control at least 1,000 acres and no more than 5,000 acres. The reason for the high minimum figure comes from my telemetry (radio-tracking) studies, which repeatedly have shown that it takes at least 1,000 acres to control a whitetail population. Any lesser acreage would put you at the mercy of surrounding landowners. However, in Texas there is a growing trend in which smaller landowners are consolidating their properties into larger management units. Should you be lucky enough to find such a situation, grab it fast!

The maximum figure is proposed because it is physically impossible to control anything larger than 5,000 acres. Some managers have had success with as much as 10,000 acres, but they also have experienced some real problems. The idea of forming a club is to have fun, so why set yourself up to headaches?

LANDOWNER AGREEMENTS

No matter whether you obtain your hunting club property by free-access agreement or by lease, a written document should be drawn up for both parties to sign. This is where a lawyer can be of great service— especially one with experience in such contractual arrangements. Several agencies currently have model-lease agreements which are available to hunting clubs. Most of these are well written, and their use could save you some money. I suggest that you contact your local resource-management agency for a model-lease agreement. The USDA Soil Conservation Service often has been of considerable help to hunting clubs, too. There also is an excellent model lease available in the publication, *Guidelines for Increasing Wildlife on Farms and Ranches*, which can be purchased from the Cooperative Extension Service of Kansas State University. (Contact F. Robert Henderson, 113 Umberger Hall, Kansas State University, Manhattan, Kan. 66506). I have attached a model lease to this chapter.

Tom Bourland, Wildlife Management Consultant, notes that, "The lease agreement is one of the most critical aspects of hunting-club management. Without it, the club never can hope to have security or accomplish its goals." Tom should know, as he is responsible for the leasing and administration of several million acres of corporate lands. He suggests that a lease agreement contain the following considerations.

First, it should state exactly who is

involved in the lease. It should state clearly who the lessees are and the landowner from whom they are leasing. This should be followed by an *exact* description of the land, including a map and location. The purpose of the lease agreement should be stated clearly, followed by the term of the lease and the established price (if any).

A very critical portion which covers the rights of the parties involved should follow. This should include any hunting rights retained by the landowner and his/her family members. I have seen numerous conflicts develop over the family and friends of landowners hunting on club lands. I suggest that you try to include the landowner if possible, as it will make for a more friendly relationship. Such provisions also protect the landowner.

I often am called in to provide expert testimony in lawsuits between hunting clubs and landowners. One such case is particularly vivid in my mind. The landowner decided to clear some timber, a decision to which the hunting club objected strongly. The club sued and lost both the case and its lease, because there were no provisions in the lease agreements to cover landowner restrictions.

The general conditions of the lease should be presented in detail. Such aspects as the use of permanent stands, clearing of foodplots, and especially the construction of a clubhouse should be considered. Futhermore, the disposition of any improvements if and when the lease is terminated should be given. One of the most important aspects is the conditions for forfeiture of the lease.

This will protect both parties, reducing the possibility of arbitrary cancellation of the agreement.

Returning to the ever-present liability question, the lease agreement should include an indemnity section. This section should explain clearly the current condition of the land and who will be liable for damages to property and/or people. It often is a good idea to include the landowner in your general liability policy. Most policies can be adjusted in such a manner.

Lastly, it should be clearly stated who is allowed to hunt on the lease. A list of members should be attached, so that there will be no problems related to who has access to the property. If guests and/or family members will be allowed to hunt on the club, this is the place to make such a provision. A guest-registry system should be established here, as well.

After reading all of this, you may be asking yourself why you even considered the idea of a club in the first place. Actually, there is very little hassle to establishing a lease, and the extra work done up front will pay off in the long run— and it is the long run that is important. In order for a hunting club to be successful, you need to be assured that your management work will pay off for years to come.

ECONOMIC CONSIDERATIONS

I often am asked what is a fair market price to pay for a lease and/or club membership. There is no set fair price; it depends on exactly what you are getting for your money. Again, this is where a good wildlife manager can be of considerable service. He will evaluate the property, based on its game-production capability, and weigh that against the local market.

As recently as 5 years ago, good quality leases could be obtained for about $1 per acre per season. That is no longer the case in many areas. At this point, it appears that—depending upon quality — leases should stabilize at around $3 per acre per season. That means that a 3,000-acre tract is going to be facing an annual lease payment of $9,000. Depending upon the management goal (trophy, quality or simply deer management), there can be 10 to 30 members on a club of that size. This computes to an annual per-member fee ranging from $300 to $900, or $25 to $75 per month, as the finance companies put it. Even at the upper price, this seems quite reasonable for an entire year's hunting recreation, not to mention camping and other outdoor pursuits. However, I recommend to my clubs that they increase the membership fee by about $100 per man to cover other expenses, such as foodplots, gates, signs, etc. *Even if you work out a free agreement with the landowner(s), you should charge the membership a fee to cover management expenses.*

GETTING STARTED

The old saying, "There is no such thing as a free lunch" never has been more true than when it comes to hunting clubs. Because wildlife management is a form of agriculture, it will take a great deal of work and money to produce the quality hunting and other recreational experiences you expect from a good hunting club. Let's take a typical new club and develop a plan of attack for management.

I cannot emphasize enough the importance of involving professionals in the establishment and management of your club. A shopkeeper cannot run his business without knowing his inventory or working capital, and so it is with a hunting club. The first thing a professional biologist will do is an overall census (inventory) of the currently existing resources. This usually will include a game count and a habitat-quality evaluation. Second, he will recommend that you get control of the property. This means such activities as posting, fencing and gating to control access. It also is a good idea to establish a good working relationship with the surrounding landowners and clubs. A well-organized group of sportsmen and landowners can do much to accomplish long-term goals.

The results of deer protection are fascinating to watch. Depending on the initial condition of the herd, perhaps three to five bucks will be harvested on the club the first year. With proper protection, the herd could build up to a point that would allow approximately 20 bucks to be harvested by the sixth or seventh year.

At the point, the number of bucks harvested will level off, and in a few years, quality of bucks will begin to deteriorate. *Deterioration in quality is due primarily to lack of population control.* It is quite difficult to get club members to harvest the proper number of does, especially after they have been protecting them for years. But, quality-buck management is doe-management. Due to differential mortality between bucks and does, you will always have to harvest about twice as many does as bucks, especially if you want to harvest as many bucks as possible. However, the harvest system you adapt, again, will depend upon your management goals.

Whatever goals you set for your club, there is one thing that cannot be overlooked: keeping records. *There is absolutely no way to determine your progress without keeping records on each deer harvested from your club.* Measurements such as dressed body weight, age, antler characteristics and whether or not the does are producing milk when harvested will tell the biologist much about your progress and the status of your herd.

That brings us to a final point: No organization can operate efficiently and harmoniously unless each and every member is actively involved. I recommend that you schedule meetings at least twice a year to discuss club business and to evaluate progress. These also are times for consideration of applications for new members. Many of my hunting clubs invite speakers to give presentations on the latest findings about deer management and biology. Some clubs even have a newsletter through which the membership is kept informed about changes in game regulations, and there are even news items about members. A hunting club is a social entity, and the more you keep it that way, the better.

What makes some clubs fail? Nothing can guarantee the failure of a club more than lack of: (1) goals; (2) adequate democratic structure; and (3) communications. Clubs fail due to the last two reasons more than any other. For example, I worked for some time with a club that was doomed from the outset. It had no formal bylaws or goals, and the only time the members talked was in small groups of dissent in local bars. The "leader" of the club was the type of individual I see all too often. He had acquired the lease himself and then had populated the club with several of his friends. He referred to himself as the "lease captain," and he ruled the club with an iron hand. He felt that all of that deer-biology stuff was just a waste of time; he knew how to manage a herd. After about 3 years, small feuds broke out regularly and most of the membership left in disgust. Unfortunately, this fellow is still in charge of his little empire, and he rules over a new group of subjects. Avoid such clubs like the plague!

THE FUTURE

There is every indication that hunting clubs will continue to grow in popularity. In Texas, where much of the concept was developed during the 1950s, there recently has developed a new type of organization. Individual clubs are going together to form "super clubs" to make up larger management units. These units are uniformly managed, and they have experienced considerable success in improving not only buck quality, but also the quality of deer hunting itself. In areas where the average club landholding is only 200 acres, it is not uncommon to see management units of a combined 10,000 acres! Each member club functions separately, but it does so under a common set of management goals. In these times of declining land-base and increasing hunting prices, this concept shows promise to assure that the average deer hunter, not just the millionaire, will continue to have the opportunity to harvest a bragging-sized buck.

So, if you're a serious whitetail hunter and you haven't looked into joining or forming a deer club, perhaps it's time you did. Clubs aren't the only answer to today's hunting problems, but for many people in many situations, they're the ticket to a productive future.

HUNTING LEASE

THE STATE OF   )(
COUNTY OF   )(

1. **PARTIES:**

    This agreement is made between _____, herein referred to as Lessor, and _____, herein referred to as Lessee.

2. **PREMISES:**

    Lessor herby leases to Lessee, and Lessee herby leases from Leasor, for the term and upon the terms and conditions hereinafter set forth, all that certain tract of land situated in _____ County, ____, more fully described in the attached Exhibit A, reference to which is herein made for all purposes, hereinafter referred to as "leased premises."

3. **TERM:**

    The term of this Lease shall commence on the ___ day of _____, 19__, and shall terminate on the ___ day of _____, 19__.

4. **RENT:**

    Lessee agrees to pay to Lessor, at Lessor's place of business at _____,

_____ County, _____, on _____ 1, 19___, the sum of $_____, as payment in full for this lease.

5. **USE:**

    5.1 Lessee shall use the leased premises solely for the hunting of deer and other legal game and none other.

    5.2 Ingress and egress to the leased premises shall be through private roads belonging to Lessor. Lessor shall designate, from time to time, which roads Lessee shall use for ingress and egress.

    5.3 All gates across roads shall be kept closed and locked (if Lessor has provided a lock therefor) at all times.

    5.4 Lessee shall permit only the hunters named on Exhibit A attached hereto, and no others, to hunt upon the leased premises. Each hunter shall carry the I.D. card, issued by Lessor, at all times while on the leased premises.

    5.5 Lessee agrees to use due diligence in the prevention and suppression of fires on the leased premises and agrees to promptly report the existence of any fires to Lessor.

    5.6 Lessee shall properly post the leased premises so as to adequately warn the general public that the premises are leased for hunting.

    5.7 Lessee shall not, nor permit anyone else to, kill, injure, trap or in any other way take any fur-bearing animals for profit.

    5.8 Lessee shall not litter the leased premises and agrees to remove Lessee's garbage and trash from the premises.

5.9 Lessee shall not cut any trees on the leased premises without the written permission of Lessor.

5.10 Lessor reserves the right to lease the premises for grazing and mineral production, to conduct timber and farming operations thereon, to remove rock, sandstone and gravel therefrom and to go upon the premises for inspection thereof.

5.11 Lessor reserves the sole right to determine the number of deer to be killed on the leased premises.

5.12 Lessee shall comply fully with all recommendations made by the wildlife biologist.

6. COMPLIANCE WITH LAWS:

Lessee shall fully and promptly comply with any and all applicable and valid laws, rules, ordinances and regulations of Federal, State, County, Municipal or other lawful authority, including the Parks & Wildlife Department pertaining to hunting and leasing of land for purposes of hunting.

7. ASSIGNMENT AND SUBLETTING:

Lessee may not assign or sublease the whole or any part of the demised premises.

8. ATTORNEY'S FEES:

If suit is brought to enforce any covenant of this Lease or for the breach of any covenant or condition herein contained, the parties hereto agree that the losing party shall pay to the prevailing party a reasonable attorney's fee, which shall be fixed by the Court, and Court costs.

9. DEFAULT:

9.1 In the event Lessee defaults in the performance of any of the terms or provisions of this Lease, then in such event, this Lease shall immediately terminate, and Lessee shall immediately vacate the premises. Any unused portion of the rental paid hereunder shall be retained by Lessor as liquidated damages.

9.2 The remedy provided for herein shall be cumulative and in addition to all remedies provided by law.

10. INDEMNITY:

To the fullest extent permitted by law, Lessee shall HOLD HARMLESS AND UNCONDITIONALLY INDEMNIFY Lessor, its officers, agents, employees, parent and affiliated companies from and against all claims, actions, damages, losses, liabilities and expenses (including, but not limited to, all expenses incurred by Lessor in the investigation, handling, defense, settlement and/or payment of same, including reasonable attorney's fees and court costs) based upon or arising out of injury, including sickness, disease or death, without regard for suddenness of onset, to persons or damage to or destruction of property, including the loss of use resulting therefrom, directly or indirectly caused by, arising out of, or incidental to this Lease, Lessee's use of the leased premises, or the presence of Lessee, its agents, employees, licensees, sublessees, assigns, invitees, customers, or any other persons upon the leased premises, with Lessee's consent, regardless of whether such persons are or are not acting within the scope of their permission, or the condition of the leased premises, regardless of whether or not caused or claimed to have been caused by active or inactive negligence or other breach of duty by Lessor, its employees, officers, and/or agents of any other person, EXCEPT ONLY where Lessor's negligence is the SOLE cause of such injury or damage. Lessee shall at all times PROTECT, HOLD HARMLESS AND UNCONDITIONALLY INDEMNIFY Lessor from or against any loss, cost, damage, charge, fine or expense whatsoever which Lessor might suffer or sustain or become liable for by reason of any failure on the part of Lessee to comply with Federal, State or local laws.

11. LESSOR'S RIGHT TO TERMINATE:

In the event the operation of this Lease should result in the extreme and unforeseen hazards to the ownership of the leased premises by Lessor, particularly with respect to damage from fires, but not confined solely thereto, Lessor reserves the right, in that event, to cancel this Lease immediately and refund the unused portion of the rental provided for herein.

12. REMOVAL OF LESSEE'S PROPERTY:

Lessee shall remove all personal property placed upon the leased premises by Lessee upon the termination of this Lease, and any property not so removed shall, upon the termination of this Lease, become the property of Lessor.

EXECUTED this the ___ day of _____, 19__.

_____ - Lessor

By: _____

_____ - Lessee, for myself and the other hunters named herein.

NOTE: This document is printed solely as an illustration and does not constitute legal advice. It always is best to consult an attorney in such matters.

THE CAMP

The cooling nights of early fall,
Is the greatest time of all.
Soon we will ready the hunting camp,
Where we all will try to be the champ.

Tales are told that may not be true,
No one knows for sure, not even you.
About the one that got away,
We'll have to wait another day.

Its not the actual kill that counts,
Its really the life of a hunting camp.
An opportunity to slow down the pace,
From the everyday business race.

A chance to watch nature's creatures at play,
On a nice, clear, crisp fall day.
The warmth and glow of a big campfire,
Is a lot for anyone to desire.

Surrounded by friends that mean so much,
Its a very nice way to stay in touch.
                                        ...K.S.

Chapter 42

GUIDED HUNTS FOR WHITETAILS

The aging wildlife biologist took a long sip of coffee, leaned slowly back in his chair, and began to speak with unquestionable authority. "The American hunter is not ready for trophy hunting," he said, "and our hunters will never be willing to pay the kind of fees they pay in Europe!"

Such disdain was being aimed at a comment made by a Hungarian-born wildlife manager who had just predicted that the American hunter soon would be facing, 1) a smaller land base on which to hunt, 2) higher license fees, and 3) higher fees for hunting rights.

The argument ended right there; neither man wished to carry it further, but each deeply felt he was right.

At about this same time, I was in the Hill Country of Texas on my first "pay hunt" for whitetails. For some reason or another, I had failed to get onto a hunting lease that year, and because virtually no public hunting was available in Texas at that time, I had decided to try one of those new day-hunting deals.

Upon arrival, we were told that all hunters would meet at 3:30 a.m. the following morning for general orientation and guide assignments. That all seemed pretty peculiar to me, because I knew good and well that it did not get daylight until around 6:30. What in the world could take so long?

The answer was to come with harsh reality. Upon arriving on time at the designated area, I discovered (to my horror) that there were about 350 to 400 hunters clustered around a large platform! It looked more like a rock concert than a deer hunt. A man soon appeared and climbed atop the platform with a great deal of authority. "Now, listen up men," he said. "When I call out your name, you are to go with your guide." For the next hour, I listened patiently as name after name was called. The longer it went on, the more it sounded like mail call at a military camp.

My name finally was called, and I dutifully followed a "guide" to his pickup truck. In the back were two rows of wooden benches. Six men sat on each side of the truck, guns between their legs and eyes staring into those of the opposite hunters. *This truly must have been what D-day was like,* I thought to myself. We each hung on as the truck lurched into the darkness.

On arriving at my stand, the "guide" showed me a reflector-lined path. "Whatever you do, don't leave the stand!" he admonished. I nodded and meekly followed the path to the enclosed tower blind. Climbing up into it in the darkness, I settled down to await the coming dawn and, hopefully, a good buck. However, at this point I was beginning to have my doubts.

As dawn began to break, I was shocked by the sight of dozens of similar stands scattered across the landscape. I literally was looking into the eyes of another hunter some 600 yards away. I was stuck there, because the guide's warning and the sight of so many hunters convinced me that my life was in jeopardy if I got down from the stand. I resigned myself to wait until noon and the guide's return. On arriving back at camp, I packed my belongings, as did many other terrified hunters, and left for home. *No one ever will be able to convince me that pay hunting is the way to go,* I thought as I drove off.

Some 20 years have passed since these two events took place, but things have changed substantially since then. The old biologist and I have been proved wrong. Many then-unforeseen things have taken place in the world of whitetail hunting. Twenty years ago, there were many deer hunters, but there was not the avid, widespread interest of today. I dare say that a magazine such as *North American Whitetail* scarcely would have made it at that time. Today, deer specialty magazines are sold out before I can find them on the newsstand. And, the old Hungarian just sits there, drawing quietly on his pipe, with one of those "I-told-you-so" looks on his face. American hunters **are** being faced with a decreasing land-base on which to hunt; license fees **have** increased substantially; hunters **are** intensely interested in trophy hunting; and they **are** willing to pay higher fees for a quality experience. Because more hunters are turning to fee-hunting for whitetails, I would

Trophy bucks such as this fine buck harvested by Stan Christiansen often, unfortunately, are out of the reach of many hunters. A pay-hunt can be the once in a lifetime experience, even for the fellow with an average income. (Courtesy, Stan Christiansen)

like to outline some of the basics in selecting a pay hunt and maybe help you avoid some of the pitfalls. This chapter should be particularly useful for those of you who, although genuinely interested in deer management, do not have the opportunity to participate in this aspect.

WHY A PAY HUNT?

Twenty years ago, you hardly could find a whitetail hunter who did not have a place to go hunting. The average hunter at that time not only had access to quality hunting experiences, but also had a reasonable expectation of harvesting a trophy or quality buck in many areas. Most of the deer herds were in a recovery phase, following some 75 years of declining numbers. State game departments, using Pittman-Robertson funds, had done an excellent job of restoring the whitetail over much of its original range— in some cases, even *expanding* the range. These booming herds provided some of the top trophy-class bucks you read about in today's outdoor articles and record books.

Today, however, most whitetail populations have peaked out under a system that provides *too much* protection for the overall herd. A true trophy buck now is almost a mythical creature unattainable by many hunters in many places. I feel sorry for many of the hunters with whom I talk deer hunting. Each and every one of them is thoroughly convinced that there is a trophy buck on his hunting club or public hunting ground. Sadly, this often is not the case, because overpopulation of deer and overshooting of bucks eliminated most prospective trophies years ago.

The average deer hunter has changed, as well. Hunters certainly are more affluent than before, but they have little free time in which to scout for, locate, and harvest a trophy buck. Finding a good hunting territory also is a time-consuming and frustrating business. The solution to this dilemma is a pay hunt, utilizing the services of a professional. If this tends to turn you off, remember that elk hunters and many other big game hunters have been doing it for years.

SOME BASIC DECISIONS

Once you decide you are interested in pay whitetail hunting, some basic decisions have to be made. Ask yourself early on whether or not the quality of the experience is tied to actually harvesting a trophy buck. Are you seeking a memorable hunting experience, a head for your wall, or both? These are very important questions, as their answers will dictate the type of hunt you need to select.

Because the whitetail is spread across most of North America, from Canada south to Mexico, it is a pretty good idea to decide on one or two geographic locations from the outset. A good friend of mine owns some 7,000 acres in the Pineywoods of East Texas, with some pretty good bucks living on his land. Yet, when it comes time to hunt a trophy buck, he always goes somewhere else. One day I asked him why he does this. The answer was simple: To him, part of the whitetail-hunting experience was traveling to new and interesting places. You might give this some thought when you select your hunting spot.

Hunters usually pick a particular geographic area because they either have visited the area in the past or have read about it in some hunting article. You can use either method, but I would suggest that you try talking with several recognized experts in trophy whitetail hunting too. There really are not that many true experts. You probably have seen most of their names crop up in magazine articles, or you've heard them speak at outdoor shows. Most of them are quite willing to give you sound advice about picking an area.

Once you have decided on a geographic area, you need to think about the type of hunt you want. There are two basic types available. First, there is the day-hunting operation. Now, I am not talking about the type of hunt discussed at the beginning of this article. Such operations as that one still may exist, but most of them have fallen by the wayside. (The whitetail hunters of today did not just come in from the farm!) Per-day hunting services are called day-hunting operations. You usually are charged by the day, with a minimum number of days hunted. Minimum number of days ranges from two to three. For a fee, you are provided with a guide (usually not more than three hunters per guide) and the opportunity to harvest a quality animal. There also are some operations which offer antlerless hunting in this manner.

Next comes the package hunt. For a predetermined fee, the hunter may spend three or more days hunting with a personal guide. The hunter-to-guide ratio usually is two to one. Such hunts provide more personalized hunting experiences than do day-hunts. Package hunts often include such features as transportation while on the property, meals, lodging and other amenities.

You should decide whether or not guaranteed success is important to you. You would be surprised at the number of hunters attracted by the advertisement, "Guaranteed Kill." Day-hunting operations seldom guarantee success, while package hunts commonly do so. However, it has been my experience that your chances of harvesting a true trophy buck lie more in your choice of area and outfitter than in the exact type of hunt structure. My good friend, George Chase of Canada, offers no guarantees with his package hunts, yet his are some of the finest whitetail hunts I ever have experienced.

Now, let's turn to the all-important question: How much should you expect to pay? **Ironically, the average hunter will pay about the same amount per trophy buck harvested, no matter which type of operation is selected.** Remember from the outset that trophy whitetail bucks are not produced cheaply. Most pay-hunting operations are under intensive management programs, and such programs, as we have seen earlier, do not come cheaply. As a whitetail manager, I am well aware of what it costs to produce a trophy buck, both economically and ecologically. It takes a lot of land, often expensive deer-proof fences, and always expensive habitat management to produce a big buck.

On the average, you can expect to pay from $1,750 to $7,000 U.S. for a trophy buck. Now, get up off the floor and think about it a minute! How many trophy bucks have you killed in the past ten years? I am not talking about some 5-pointer with a 10-inch spread; I mean a real, honest-to-goodness trophy buck. Also, how much money have you spent on deer hunting in the last 10 years to harvest that 5-pointer? An honest answer might surprise you. The average hunter in North America pays about $650 per year in license and hunting-privilege fees. On your own, you normally can expect to harvest a trophy every 3 to 5 years. So, you see, you probably already are paying those kinds of prices without really knowing it. Furthermore, have your past hunting experiences been of such high quality that you hope to relive them in your last moments of life? Your answer probably is "no." That probably is why you are reading this chapter. The fact is that many hunters could afford a quality pay hunt every two or three years.

QUESTIONS TO ASK

If you decide to lay out the kind of money it takes to book a trophy hunt, you surely do not want to end up in the same sad state I did on my first hunt-for-pay experience. There are some definite pitfalls, but they can be avoided. In researching this chapter, I asked some of the most notable trophy-whitetail hunters and guides which questions they would ask if they were picking a pay hunt. Their answers were remarkably similar.

Bill Carter of Houston is a well-known sporting-goods dealer, trophy-whitetail hunter, and trophy-whitetail outfitter. He also is a pretty fair whitetail manager, as well. He owns the Sombrerito Ranch near Laredo, Texas. "In considering a pay hunt," Bill says, "be sure to get as many references as possible. Make sure that the references are from the last hunting season, not 5 or 10 years ago." That is a very good point. Some outfitters acquire a piece of property that literally is crawling with trophy bucks, then shoot it out over a few seasons. The hunters who bought hunts early on are very pleased, while later hunters might give less-than-glowing reports.

But, references often are deceiving. You certainly would not expect an outfitter to provide names of people who had bad hunts, even in well-run operations. Harvest records, however, are not deceiving. I would be very wary of any operation that could not provide harvest records for all bucks taken from the property. The old line, "statistics don't lie, only statisticians," never has been more appropriate. Average numbers of points, spread, beam circumference and average Boone and Crockett score of bucks harvested quickly will tell you what your prospects are for harvesting a trophy buck on that place. In picking a pay hunt, I often recommend asking for: a list of hunters who have hunted for more than one season; pictures of bucks harvested; harvest records for all bucks to date; and then, what I call little "giveaway" questions.

The best giveaway question I have found is, "How will we hunt?" The best answer is, "Whatever it takes to help you legally harvest a quality buck." This tells me right off the mark that the outfitter is willing to work himself to death to help you be successful. Another giveaway question is, "How big a buck can I expect to harvest?" If the outfitter hedges or makes exorbitant claims, watch out! The best answer is "We average bucks with X qualities, and the biggest buck harvested last season was Y big." Your chances of harvesting such a buck will depend on many factors, but he will do his best to get you the best animal possible. Finally, ask, "How long will it take to harvest a good buck?" Without hesitation, the outfitter should be able to tell exactly how long the average hunter can expect to hunt before being successful. It is an important question, especially if you are paying by the day. A good example would be Johnny Hudman of the Nail Ranch. He not only can tell you the average measurements for bucks harvested during the last several years, but how long you can expect to hunt before harvesting a buck. He is straightforward and clear about these points.

Now, we return to the ever-present discussion of price. I have found that there is no consistent pricing structure for trophy-whitetail hunts. For this reason, you need to be very careful to find out exactly what such a hunt will cost you. Package hunts often are better in that everything provided is laid out in black-and-white; you know exactly what you are paying for, and how much it will cost. Day-hunting operations clearly should state what services are provided with the daily hunting fee, plus what extras are available. On the average, you can expect to pay $200 to $350 per day.

If you are not careful, you can have some pretty shocking surprises. I visited one operation that advertised trophy bucks for a modest fee of $800 per buck harvested. It sounded pretty good on the surface, especially when I viewed some impressive harvest records. On closer examination, however, I discovered that the fee did not include guide fees, lodging, or meals. There also was a game-cleaning fee. Because the property was miles from the nearest sizable town, the hunter almost would be forced to stay with the outfitter. My calculations indicated that in order to harvest a trophy buck, the hunter would have to spend around $2,000. The "bargain" hunt was no bargain after all.

There are some elaborate pricing structures in operation for trophy bucks, most of which are tied to the quality of the buck harvested. It is my advice to shy away from such operations unless you can have *in writing* the maximum amount you can expect to pay. The most common system now in use revolves around antler points and spread. The average trophy-hunting operation using such schemes charges $50 per mensurable point (tine) and $50 per inch of antler spread. Thus, a 20-inch wide 10-pointer will cost you $500 (points) plus $1,000 (spread), or $1,500. Be sure to ask whether or not spread is measured outside spread, a difference of about $100. Because you no doubt are after the biggest buck you and your guide can find, be prepared to pay for the largest buck possible.

These pricing schemes can be rather bizarre. One operation charges $75 per inch of outside spread, $75 per antler point, and 75 cents per pound of weight! In considering such a pricing scheme, I was amused by the thought of a guide, trusty calculator in hand, telling a hunter that the buck rapidly disappearing in front of him would cost $1,587.75 to shoot. That (the idea, not the price) is a bit much for me. I would recommend going with a fixed daily rate or package price, no matter how big the buck killed.

MAKING THE MOST OF YOUR DOLLAR

The hunting experience takes in more than just shooting a big buck. Scientists tell us that the recreational experience involves many parts, of which the actual activity is only a small part.

The author dropped this superb buck on a guided hunt on Dolan Creek Ranch in Texas, showing that big bucks can be the reward for those who do their "homework."

Who has not spent many a reflective hour recalling a quality hunt that may have lasted only a few days? Because you have decided to invest a great deal of money in a trophy-whitetail hunt, why not make the most of it?

Bill Carter, who has hunted trophy whitetails, as well as, other big game all over the world, recommends that you begin your "hunting experience" months in advance of the booked dates. Even the selection of the rifle can be a pleasurable and memorable experience. Bill recommends regular practice sessions with a light-caliber rifle for at least six months prior to the hunt (see **The Art of Shooting**). In so doing, you not only extend the planning and anticipation phases of the hunt, but also improve your proficiency with a firearm. The fact that you will be paying for a trophy hunt does not guarantee you that you indeed will *kill* that big buck. The guide can find you the animal, but you are the one who will have to shoot it. Russell Thornberry, noted Canadian whitetail outfitter, points out that on the average, his clients have about three seconds in which to make a killing shot on a trophy deer. My experience has been that the average hunter is not prepared to make such a shot. Why spend a great deal of money and time trying to harvest a trophy buck, only to blow it at the big moment, due to lack of preparation?

I might inject here an admonishment to the prospective client. You are paying for the experience of the guide, as well as, a trophy buck. One of the advantages of pay-hunting is that the guide is out there for you all year, studying the movements and behavior of "his" bucks. Therefore, listen to your guide. Outfitters will tell you that the number one problem in getting a client a good buck lies in the unwillingness of hunters to do what they are told. This especially is true if the client has hunted the area before; repeat hunters often make the mistake of thinking that because something worked there before, it will work again.

A PERSONAL EXPERIENCE

In conducting research on this chapter, I decided to become a member of the trophy-hunting public. Now, as a trophy-whitetail manager, I have more than enough opportunities to shoot quality bucks. But, if you are going to write about something, you need first-hand experience. So, I booked two hunts, using the criteria outlined in this chapter. As far as my outfitters were concerned, I was just "John Q. Deerhunter." I felt it would be more realistic that way, as outdoor writers and biologists have been fooled in the past (because of preferential treatment).

My time is at a premium, so I decided to limit my hunting to my home state of Texas. I traveled to Del Rio to hunt with Dolan Creek Ranches, owned and operated by Jon Ducharme and John Finnegan. As I noted above, I was just another hunter to them. Dolan Creek charges a flat fee and makes no promises for a successful kill; i.e., you pay your money, and you take your chances.

My guide, Larry Coleman, met me at my hotel the evening before the hunt. He was an amiable fellow. We had a drink and agreed to meet at 5 a.m., because the ranch was some 50 miles away.

The next morning, everything fell apart. Larry arrived on time and picked up me and two other hunters. Just outside of town, his Blazer began to fill up with smoke. It gave a chug and died right there on the highway, transmission blazing. I would have fallen apart in such a situation. Here was Larry with three paying hunters, miles from the ranch, with a vehicle that was not going anywhere. Larry obviously was worried, but he quickly got control of the situation. He made sure we were comfortable and then took off down the road in search of help.

Just as the sky was beginning to get rosy in the East, another Blazer roared up beside us. Help had arrived in the nick of time.

We arrived at the ranch in plenty of time to hunt, but the bucks just were not moving. We were facing a full moon and mild weather, a situation difficult to fight. However, Larry remained unshaken. Over the next two days, we tried every trick he knew. *I wouldn't have his job for anything,* I thought.

We finally decided to try rattling one more time in an area where Larry had seen a pretty good mature buck. On our very first rattle, the buck came roaring in on us, and I dropped it with a single shot. I was amazed at the obvious excitement Larry felt when I killed the buck. Later, my guide confided in me that he had been extremely tense ever since the vehicle breakdown. An unhappy and unsuccessful hunter meant failure, and he very much disliked failure.

Much of the pressure faced by trophy-whitetail guides comes from the expectations of the hunter. Many hunters feel they are paying more for a trophy animal than for a trophy-hunting experience. "The very best you can do with a client is go away friends," remarked one outfitter. "If you get a man a 20-incher this year, he will want a 21-incher next year! Sooner or later, you aren't going to be able to satisfy him."

SUMMARY

In the modern whitetail hunting environment, limitations on time and access to hunting lands may prevent some hunters from experiencing the thrill of harvesting a braggin-sized buck. One alternative may be the pay-hunt. Pay-hunting may not be for every hunter. You may object to attaching a dollar value to game, or you may not be able to afford the cost of such hunts. But one thing is for sure, pay hunts **can** provide some hunters with the kind of quality trophy-hunting experiences only dreamed about by others.

Mike Biggs

Trophy bucks like these are only dreamed about by most hunters. They do not come cheaply. Management is an expensive business. However, saving for a "once-in-a-lifetime" hunt can bring lasting memories.

Chapter 43

THE ECONOMICS OF WHITETAIL MANAGEMENT

There is an old saying, "There's no such thing as a free lunch!" And, never has this been more true than with wildlife. I was amused a few years ago, when I saw a cartoon of two hunters holding a limit of pheasants. "Boy, it sure is nice to live off the land and harvest these free pheasants," was the cut-line. In the background was the poor farmer who obviously had invested a great deal in time and money in those pheasants. Seldom does the landowner or hunter realize the cost of wildlife management.

Landowners always ask two very embarrassing questions: *How much will it cost? What will I get in return?* Unfortunately, few wildlife biologists can answer either question. Yet, it is important to be able to analyze any wildlife management operation on an economic basis. Whether we are discussing a commercial whitetail hunting business or endangered species, there are economic realities which must be considered.

Too often I hear some wildlife biologist proclaim with, I might add, a great deal of authority: "That's not economically feasible!" However, such statements usually are made without the benefit of sound economics data, or an understanding of the landowner. It is the ethical responsibility of the whitetail manager to inform the landowner, hunting club or agency about the costs and benefits of any management activity. But, it is for the user to decide whether or not some strategy is economically feasible. Here is an example.

A good friend of mine once managed a ranch for a very wealthy landowner. This fellow loved deer, and enjoyed inviting his friends over for a trophy hunt. Among them, no doubt, were individuals who could benefit the landowner financially and/or politically. The annual food plot budget for this operation alone was a whopping $44,000. Now, there is no way that the few bucks taken from the property return this amount of money; yet, the landowner was more than happy to spend it. Deer, friendship and business were worth a great deal to the landowner.

On the other hand, I also have known guys who attempted to make a profit from commercial deer hunting. Many of these men knew little about business and economics, and failed to show a profit from their operations. They did not understand the economic feasibility of such ventures. In this chapter, I will outline the basics for making financial decisions for your management program; be it a commercial hunting operation or a private operation for personal enjoyment. I also will examine the hunter's side of the economic equation. One way to assure pure competition is to have both an informed producer and an informed consumer.

MARKETING WHITETAILS

There are three marketing approaches available to the landowner:
1. **give-it-away;**
2. **wholesale;**
3. **retail.**

Many landowners, especially in states where public hunting long has been a tradition, opt for the first approach. Why? There are differing motivations, but most center around "good will." One timber company here in the South reserves a significant portion of their lands for public access hunting. They assert that this generates good will among the local people. But, does it really?

In Old England, there once was a practice of maintaining a common grazing ground (The Commons) for all villagers to use. The concept was based on the idea that each farmer keep the number of livestock grazed at some pre-arranged level. Yet, this seldom was the case. Soon, one farmer would add another cow to his herd, thinking that just one cow could not possibly hurt. Then his neighbor, seeing this, would add a cow of his own; and, before too long, the Commons was destroyed. A wise man once said, "Something belonging to everyone, belongs to no one!" It is sad to say, but this certainly applies to public lands. Uncontrolled properties traditionally have lower deer populations, and more management problems than private, controlled access lands. In the South, poaching and dumping are major problems on uncontrolled lands.

The fact is that few benefits accrue to the landowner from allowing free public access. In fact, there are more liabilities than assets. Now, this may be a "hard pill to swallow" for some of you, but **the truth is that the wildlife resource no longer is a free commodity for the taking**. When I was a teenager, I walked out my Grandfather's back door, grabbed up my gun and started walking. I stopped hunting when I got tired. The idea of fences and property rights never entered my head, nor did it occur to any of our neighbors. But today, we are faced with more than twice as many people, few of whom have grown up on the land. Landholdings are becoming increasingly fragmented. Farms seldom are owned by individuals who depend on their land for a livelihood; rather, they have purchased the property for financial or aesthetic reasons. Couple these realities with an ever-increasing problem with "slob hunters," and you have a considerable number of problems.

The next approach is to **wholesale** access to the game. Wholesaling involves selling a commodity to someone, who in turn sells the commodity to the ultimate consumer. A hunting lease is an excellent example of the wholesaling approach to wildlife-recreation.

There are several advantages to the landowner who chooses the wholesale approach. The wholesaler only deals with a few individuals. He does not have to invest a great deal of money in facilities and services. But, his profit per commodity unit is much lower than the retailer. He makes his money on volume. Hence, the wholesale approach might be attractive to the: 1) absentee landowner, 2) landowner who really does not enjoy working with people, 3) landowner with little discretionary capital, and 4) large landowner.

There are disadvantages to wholesaling. The amount of money earned per commodity unit is much smaller than for a retail operation. The wholesaler depends on large volume sales. A small landowner may see little advantage to leasing a 100-acre parcel for $3.00 per acre; yet, one who owns 10,000 acres may think this is a fine arrangement!

The final approach is the **retail** operation. The best example would be the commercial whitetail hunting resort. There seem to be more and more of these operations annually. The retail operation must invest large amounts of capital in order to develop the habitat, services and amenities required by paying guests. The retail operator also must deal with large numbers of people, requiring good people management skills. The advantage to such a marketing approach is a higher return per commodity unit, making this approach often attractive to the small landowner.

HOW DO WE MAKE FINANCIAL DECISIONS ABOUT DEER MANAGEMENT?

Public Hunting

As I noted earlier, even when hunting

opportunities are "free," someone must pay the bill for deer management. "But," you may assert, "if we do not charge for deer hunting, surely there is no cost." Boy, are you wrong! Deer thrive because private landowners allow them to co-exist with man. Deer are available on state and federal lands because these agencies expend effort and monies to protect or augment the herd. In the case of the private landowner, there are opportunity costs to maintaining deer. Every acre of woods that is not managed for agricultural or timber purposes has lost opportunity associated with it. The private landowner who leaves grain, or plants cover crops pays for deer management. The government biologist's salary and expenses are paid from funds either produced by taxation or by direct user's fees. These costs are real, and should not be discounted in considering the economic cost of whitetails.

It is estimated that the average deer hunter spends $500 annually in pursuit of whitetails. I think this is a very conservative figure, since hunting in Texas alone is a $3 billion industry! But, even using these very conservative figures, that amounts to some $850 million annually spent on deer hunting. Hence, the whitetail conservatively is worth more than $10 billion to the American economy.

The Wholesale Approach

The leasing of hunting rights is a growing phenomenon. Once purely a Texas idea, we now see hunters leasing lands from Florida to New York. But, what is a lease worth? And, how do you determine what are the costs and values of a leased property? Before we can answer these questions, it is necessary to offer a short primer on financial analysis. Terms such as *present value*, *guiding rate* and *net present value* have to be defined.

Present Value.— Suppose I were to give one of my students a contract, guaranteeing that I will hand over a crisp $100 bill 20 years hence. What is this contract worth today? It certainly is not $100! Over the next two decades, inflation alone will see to it that the true value of this money decreases. Would you pay $75, $50 or $25 for the contract? Economists long ago developed methods which will allow you to make the right decisions. But, in order to calculate this value, you must establish the **guiding** or **discount rate.** Guiding rate can be defined in many ways, but is most commonly considered to be the return available on an alternative investment; hence the additional name of *opportunity cost.* For example, if the rate a bank might pay on a passbook savings account is 6%, then the guiding rate would be 6%. Some financial analysts add in a certain percentage for risk. After all, I could very well not live another 20 years! What good would the contract be then? But, for our purposes we will use a simple 5% guiding rate.

Given this information, we can use the present value equation:

$$PV = (FV)/(1+d)^t,$$

where **PV** is the present value of a future income (**FV**),

d is the guiding rate, and **t** is the amount of time. Therefore, at a 5% guiding rate, the $100 contract would today be worth $100/(1+.05)^{20}$ or $37.69. If you pay more than this amount, you lose money. If you pay less, you make a good deal!

We can apply this same analysis to costs, as well as, incomes. Suppose we anticipate an expenditure of $100 in ten years. What is the value of that expenditure in today's dollars? Again, we use the present value equation, finding that our future expenditure of $100 is worth $61.39 today.

Net Present Value or Worth.— If we reconcile the present values of costs and incomes for a particular venture, we can calculate the **net present value** of that project. This is accomplished easily by subtracting the present value of costs from the present value of incomes. Here is another example.

We develop a project from which we plan to receive $500 of income at the end of a ten year period. But, we will have to make a capital investment of $300 at the outset of the project. Is this a profitable venture? First, we calculate the present value of the cost. Since the investment is incurred today, the present value of our cost is $300 $(300/1.05^0)$, or $300. But, the income from the project does not materialize for ten years! Hence, we must calculate the present value of the income, in order to compare it realistically with the investment cost. Using the 5% guiding rate, we learn that the present value is $306.96, yielding a net present value of $6.96 above our guiding rate return. This means that we earn our 5% plus an additional $6.96.

Economics of the Wholesale Approach.—What does all of this have to do with determining the cost of deer management? *It has a great deal to do with deer management.* Too often, lease fees are derived more from the landowner's "best guess," than from sound financial reasoning. Each management activity not only must be properly scheduled, but the anticipated cost of each activity must be considered before arriving at a fair market value. Here is another example.

A landowner has 320 acres of mixed woodland. A group of hunters approaches the landowner, requesting to lease the property for deer hunting. How much does he charge for the lease? His neighbor charges $3.00 per acre; should he charge the same amount?

The first step is to analyze all of the costs attributable to his deer management program. He has read this book, and has decided to manage his habitat on an intensive basis. Following my suggestions, he has established two 160-acre management units, each with a pond and a two-acre food plot. In addition, he plans to burn 40 acres in each management unit annually.

Initial costs for each management unit would be:

1. **pond construction** $2,000
2. **food plot establishment** $200
3. **40-acre burn ($5/acre)** $200,

bringing his total first year investment to $2,400. But, each year he will have to maintain food plots and conduct additional prescribed burns. Hence,

annual maintenance costs might be:
1. **40-acre burn** $200
2. **food plot maintenance** $150.

The hunters have offered to lease the property for a five year period. Consequently, we will use a five-year planning horizon for our calculations. The landowner wishes to receive a return equal to a certificate of deposit which earns 8% annually. Now we have all of the information we need to make a decision on the correct lease fee.

Since each of the five years will see an anticipated cost of $350, we must discount these costs back to present dollars. We already have a total initial investment of $2,400. We must add to this the present values of each successive year's expenditures. Since the first maintenance cost will occur in year two, we substitute the appropriate values in the basic present equation:

$$PVC = \Sigma(FVC/(1.08)t),$$

where,   PVC is the present value of all costs, and FVC is the future value of costs.

Solving this equation for each successive year, we see that year one has a present cost value of $2,400, year two $300, year three $278, year four $257 and year five $238, giving a total present value of costs of $3,473.

The hunters have offered $5 per acre for the lease, amounting to a total annual lease fee of $1,600. Again, we can use the basic equation to obtain the value of the five-year lease:

$$PVI = \Sigma(FVI/(1.08)^t),$$

where,   FVI is the future value of incomes.

The first year's income would be $1,600. The present value of income for year two would be $1,372, year three $1,270, year four $1,176 and year five $1,089, giving a total present value for incomes of $6,507. Now, we subtract the present value of costs from incomes, yielding a net present value for the project of $3,034. Therefore, leasing for $5 per acre is a very good idea. Of course, most financial analyses would have considered the value of the ponds at the end of the project. But we are assuming in this example that the ponds will be paid for by the end of the lease period; and, that the landowner then can make additional financial decisions about them. If the hunters would have offered only $2 per acre, the net present value would have been -$799. Since the idea is to make money over and above the 8% guiding rate, this would be a very poor idea.

There are many potential costs to consider in evaluating a lease fee. Some of the commodities that have value to hunters are:
1. **management,**
2. **food plots,**
3. **security,**
4. **housing,**
5. **shooting range,**
6. **fencing,**
7. **fishing,** and
8. **utilities.**

Each of these must be added into an overall financial analysis of a hunting lease in order to obtain a true idea of an acceptable lease fee.

Present Worth of a Lease.— My good friend and colleague, Dr. Gary Kronrad, and I recently conducted a financial analysis of hunting lease for the purposes of assigning *ad valorum* taxable values. Gary is one of the best resource economists today, and was very helpful in evaluating the actual per acre worth of a deer lease. "Suppose you want to make $5 each year from a passbook savings account offering 5% interest;" he explains, "then you would have to deposit $5/.05 or $100 in the bank." Gary goes on to explain that a $5 per acre per year lease is no different. If we earn $5 per year, then the per acre worth of that lease must be $100, based on a 5% guiding rate. Unfortunately, few real estate agents, and even fewer landowners, look upon a lease in this manner. But, suppose you pay $400 for an acre of land that has an existing $5 per year hunting lease. If the seller has not considered the true worth of the lease in his selling price, you have obtained an acre of land for $100 below its true market value. No one ever would consider selling this same acre without valuing standing timber or the cattle that come with it; yet, hunting leases seldom receive attention.

Wholesaling and the Consumer.— If you are a hunter, you may be pretty nervous at this point. *This guy is telling landowners how to get even more money out of me!* But, before you get upset, let me explain an important point. I noted earlier that good competition involves both an informed producer and consumer. The type of analyses discussed here allow the consumer (hunter) for the first time to determine whether or not he is getting a fair deal. You may be paying $5 per acre for a lease on one side of a road, and your buddy may be paying only $3. Yet, in his situation, a camphouse, gates, and food plots are provided. You only get access to an unmanaged parcel of land. Which of you has the better deal? Why don't you calculate the answer using the above equation. The valuation approach outlined in this chapter allows you the opportunity to evaluate what you are getting for your

Trophy bucks certainly bring the highest retail prices, but what must the operator charge in order to justify carrying bucks to maturity?

Mike Biggs

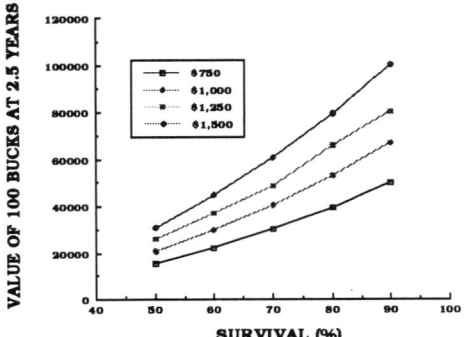 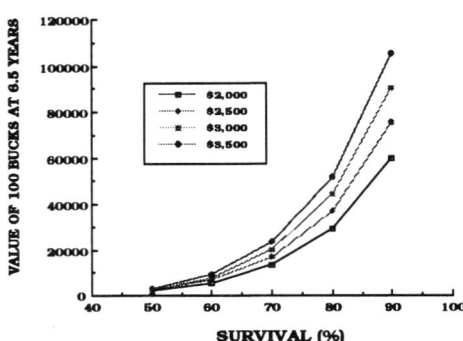

Two options for selling 100 buck fawns in a retail operation. On the left is an analysis of a strategy which sells the same bucks at 2.5 years. Fees range from $750 to $1,500. On the right is an analysis for the same bucks sold at maturity (6.5 years). Note that the present value of bucks in both analyses is significantly affected by survival rate. Also note that, at a 70% average survival rate, the best decision may be to sell the bucks at 2.5 years! If the operator desires to sell trophy bucks, then he will have to significantly increase his trophy fees.

money.

The Retail Approach

During the last decade, the demand for trophy-class whitetails has reached an all-time high! Outfitters are asking, and certainly receiving, $3-7,000 for a trophy buck. This high demand has seen many landowners investing in trophy management programs, in the hope of taking advantage of this high demand. But, are these prices realistic? Is the operator actually making a profit? At what age should a buck be harvested to maximize economic return?

Few landowners have taken the financial analysis approach to decision-making in commercial whitetail management. But, let's examine some of the realities of this approach, hopefully leading you to a better understanding of the retail operation.

Retail operations must offer a host of services and amenities to the paying client; among which are:
1. **guides**,
2. **lodging**,
3. **meals**,
4. **transportation**,
5. **entertainment**, and
6. **game care**.

Each service or amenity must be handled as given above for the wholesale operation. In this regard, there is very little difference, only the size of the capital investment. But, when it comes to the type of animal being harvested, we must examine the operation in a much different way.

In order for a buck to reach trophy size, he obviously must survive to maturity, say five or six years of age. But, not all bucks live to maturity. Even if they did, it is a number of years before we can realize a return on our investment. A buck born this spring will not earn you money for at least five years. All of these things have to be factored into a financial analysis.

Returning to the present value calculations discussed earlier, we can perform some very interesting analyses. For example, suppose we plan to sell bucks at 6.5 years of age. The suggested trophy fee is $2,500. That means that 100 bucks born this year will be worth $250,000 in six years! But, what is the present value of these bucks? Using a guiding rate of 8%, their present value would be $151,595, still a pretty goodly amount of money. But, before you run down to your local bank to borrow money for a trophy deer hunting business, I suggest you read further.

If you have read most of this book, you no doubt realize that mortality rates often are high for bucks— as much as 30% annually in some areas. At that rate, 100 fawns born this year would be reduced to only 12 mature bucks! The present value of these animals would only be $18,191. Lower mortality rates, due to more intensive management would increase survival, but also increase costs.

The same 100 buck fawns could be harvested at an earlier age, reducing the loss of animals. If we charged a modest $750 for a 2.5 year-old buck, the present value of these bucks would be $619 each or $30,318, almost $12,000 more than the trophy buck situation. In fact, we would have to charge $4,170 for a mature buck, to justify carrying them to that age!

This rather simple approach becomes even more interesting when we consider bucks as a perpetual series of harvestable products. In one such analysis, in which Dr. Kronrad and I examined 100 buck fawns sold as a perpetual series of incomes at 2.5 years ($750 each) versus 6.5 years ($2,500 each), yielded a present net value of only $137,887 for the mature bucks and a whopping $312,643 for the younger bucks! Clearly, in order to justify the marketing of mature bucks, the operator must seriously increase the amount charged for the older animal.

SUMMARY

The economic realities of deer management are that there truly is "no such thing as free lunch!" Whether it be public hunting or private whitetail management, someone must pay for the cost of management. These costs can be lost opportunity or direct capital investment. With increasing demands on our lands, the whitetail-hunter increasingly will have to be willing to pay for his pastime.

There are three options available to the private landowner for marketing whitetails: give-them-away, wholesale and retail. The approach taken will depend on the landowner's individual desires and goals. The "free" approach often is selected to generate good will, yet seldom achieves this goal. Problems with public access lands include increased dumping and littering, poaching and game law violations. The wholesale approach is attractive both to the consumer and the producer, in that various services and commodities are valued and charged to the consumer. An informed consumer and producer is important to establishing healthy competition in hunting. The true cost of each valued commodity must be determined over the lease period, using present value analysis, developed by resource economists for such purposes. A wholesale lease adds value to land. A $5 per acre annual lease increases the per acre value of a property, using a guiding rate of 8%, of $62.50!

The retail approach generates higher gross incomes, but must be accompanied by higher initial capital investments.

Trophy deer hunting operations should carefully examine the present value of bucks at various ages, in order to establish trophy fees. Often, younger bucks bring more present value than mature bucks, due to longer carrying time and higher mortality rates.

Mike Biggs

Bucks like this, as the author has noted many times, are expensive to produce. An understanding of the real costs of production is important to a commercial operation.

Chapter 44

POACHING

When asked what is their most important problem in deer management, most landowners or hunting clubs say "poaching;" yet, this seldom is indeed the most important problem. It is the nature of folks to think that the woods literally are crawling with illegal trespassers, who are out to shoot every deer on the property! This chapter is designed to inform you about the impact of poaching, as well as, to offer suggestions how you might reduce any impact these illegal hunters may have on your herd.

There are two situations in which poaching poses a major problem. First, there is the situation where a piece of land is just coming under protection. Such properties characteristically have low deer populations, resulting from years of unregulated hunting. Poaching on these lands often keeps the population from reaching the exponential growth phase discussed in the chapter on population processes. The second situation involves a management program which is aimed at producing large numbers of trophy-class animals. Under this scenario, a new breed of poacher emerges— the trophy poacher. This fellow usually is an accomplished hunter who, for one reason or another, chooses to operate on the wrong side of the law. Some say that it is the thrill of breaking game laws that motivates such men. Others claim that the trophy poacher cannot afford to hunt quality animals, choosing rather to steal his game. For whatever reason, a trophy poacher can do serious damage to your management program. Let's take a look at common poaching methods, in order to develop an effective strategy to combat these criminals.

POACHING METHODS

The average poacher really is a lazy fellow, preferring to kill deer from a road. Here in my home state of Texas, it is amazing at the number of rifles that appear in the windows of pickups around the middle of September. (In Texas, it is legal for someone to carry a rifle in such a manner, provided he/she is driving to a "sporting event.") The technique used by these guys is simple. They just drive the back roads until they see a deer cross, then either shoot the animal from the vehicle, or stalk it from the road, ignoring the trespass law in the process.

A second method involves the use of a spotlight. Spotlighting, "jacklighting" or "jacking" has been used for many years to illegally harvest deer. It began, I am told, in the early days of hunting in America. Southerners often used longleaf pine knots as torches to "shine" deer. These technique developed after most of the deer had been extirpated by year-round shooting and the use of hounds to ferret out the last deer from a particular area.

The trophy poacher, as I noted above, is a completely different critter indeed! They usually are quite the opposite from the road shooter, preferring to work alone. He may remain in the woods or brush for many days, sleeping by day and hunting by night. One famous trophy poacher was recently captured in the Brush Country of South Texas. He had three 150 inch (B&C) deer in his possession at the time, and a notebook full of photographs of equally impressive animals. It turns out that his wife would drop

Spotlighting or "jacking" deer is perhaps the most popular means of poaching in the United States.

him off at some point along a road, then pick him up in two weeks at the same spot. This guy was a significant problem to the local ranchers, and his capture was viewed as a major event.

Since the days of old England, poachers have been using snares to catch deer. Today, some poachers still use this method. I am aware of one man in New Brunswick who used snares set in the middle of scrapes to catch and kill bucks. This not only is illegal, but downright cruel!

In addition to the professional poacher, the landowner or club must deal with a whole host of trespassers. These are hunters who may, either purposefully or by accident, wander on the property. Some hunters simply ignore posted signs, feeling that they have a right to the game wherever it travels.

WHO OWNS THE DEER?

The laws and attitudes towards wildlife in America stem from experiences our forefathers had in Europe. Coming from a system where the landowner or "lord" owned all of the resources, including timber and wildlife, early colonists strived to create laws which clearly state that wild animals belong to the people. This is both good and bad. It is good in that it establishes public responsibility for wildlife; and, it is bad in that it takes the responsibility for the welfare out of the hands of the landowner, placing the onus directly on the shoulders of society. But, this often places the responsibility in no one's hands! The best compromise is to recognize that the landowner holds the game in the public trust, and has the right to determine who has access to his/her lands. Hence, from a commercial standpoint, the landowner "owns" the recreation, while society owns the game.

DEALING WITH POACHERS AND TRESPASSERS

Trespass Laws

As I travel about the country from state to state, I am constantly amazed at the variety of game laws imposed on its citizens. In one state, the landowner is "all powerful," dictating when and how a hunter is to use the land. In another, the landowner is powerless to defend property rights.

In considering this dilemma, some definite trends have emerged. My studies within various states have confirmed that the lowest population densities occur in states with weak or nonexistent trespass laws, and are highest in those with strong trespass laws. This observation is significant. It seems that deer are not safe in the public's hands. A society-landowner partnership is required in order to have reasonable numbers of deer. Hence, the first step to dealing effectively with poachers is to establish reasonable trespass laws in every state and province. Of course, this can be carried to the extreme. In one state, no one can enter another person's property without *written* permission, even if directly accompanied by the landowner! This is a bit excessive.

Even in states with good trespass

laws, there remain problems with poaching. It is ludicrous for any landowner to think that a law will stop the problem. Laws, without enforcement, mean little to the criminal. Landowner organizations have been quite successful in some states by exerting pressure on local judges and law officials to enforce existing laws. It makes little sense to pass a strict trespass law, then have the local justice-of-the-peace levy a $50 fine on the guy!

Control of the Land

The first, and by far the most important, strategy is to gain control of the property. Often, hunting clubs are formed on lands leased from owners who never controlled access to their property. In these situations, it is very

---

One of the best ways to get control of your land is to close non-public roads. This often leads to ill-will between the landowner and the local hunters. One of the best solutions is to communicate with your neighbors about your plans.

difficult to convince a person who has hunted the property all his life that it now is closed to public access. The usual response is for the local hunters to cause a great deal of problems during the first two to three years of operation. You should not let these problems deter you, however, as they usually are short-lived.

The first step in gaining control is to close all roads that are not public. This really creates problems, since many private roads are deemed public by the local residents. Indeed there are common use statutes that may enter into gaining control. I have successfully used gating to regain control. Unfortunately, however, the presence of a gate seldom is a deterrent to some individuals. I would hate to calculate the cost of all the gates I have had torn down over the years. But, I also have found that, if I continually replace gates and lock them properly, transgressors generally tire of the trouble and move elsewhere. Locks seldom are an impediment to a determined trespasser. It is a simple matter to use a bolt-cutter or to shoot the lock. I have found an effective way of locking a gate. I use a **lock safe** made of heavy gauge iron pipe to protect my locks. A sliding bar is attached to the gate which allows it to be locked to the gate post from inside the lock safe. By properly choosing the proper diameter pipe, you can thwart any bolt-cutter on the market today. Also, no one in his/her right mind would shoot up into the pipe! Gate posts should be anchored in cement to prevent them from being pulled up by trespassers.

Using a lock safe on your gates will eliminate a great deal of problems from those that resent the posting of your property.

In addition, it is important to mark the boundaries of the property in such a manner as to make it clear that the property is closed to public access. Several commercial interests sell signs designed for this purpose. I suggest that you erect the signs on a 100 feet interval (accept in states requiring differently), so that anyone crossing the property line clearly can see them. You may need to space them closer together in hilly terrain. The sign should state, not only that the property is posted to trespass, but also the identity of the landowner or hunting club. To prevent these signs from being torn

Robert Skinner

Posting signs should be easily read at a distance and clearly state who is posting the land. Signs should be placed at least every 100 feet along the perimeter of the property.

down, I erect them at least ten feet above the ground on a tree. An added trick is to spread heavy grease on the back side of the signs. This is very effective against vandalism. They may shoot the sign, but they will think twice about pulling it down!

There is nothing more effective than a fence. It states without a doubt that the land is being actively managed. If the trespasser crosses a fence, he obviously has made a conscious decision to do so. There is no room then for the excuse that he did not know the boundaries. If a fence is impractical, I suggest you have the property line blazed with paint. Some state forestry agencies offer this service at a nominal fee.

Security

There is a growing small industry around hunting clubs. Individuals, usually law enforcement officers, can be contracted with to provide security. They often have printed signs which state that the property is being patrolled by contract security. I have found these signs and services quite effective. Some clubs may hire a specific person to serve as a "fence rider." Usually a retired peace officer, a fence rider often lives on the property in housing provided by the landowner or club. His salary is modest, considering the provision of lodging, a vehicle and general expenses. Some fence riders are truly "riders," patrolling the property by horseback.

If you cannot afford security, there is another approach. Since poachers really are no different from any other criminal, they surely think twice about entering a property which is regularly used by its owner or tenants. Just maintaining a presence often is adequate to deter most poachers.

Dealing with the Poacher

Any experienced game warden will tell you that poacher is a very dangerous creature. We have a wildlife management area in Texas named after a fine man named Gus Engling. Gus was

Robert Skinner

A fence is an excellent way to mark your property boundary. If a hunter crosses the fence, he is consciously making the decision to do so, and cannot claim that he just wandered onto the property.

a biologist who made the mistake of coming upon a poacher. He paid for it with his life. Unlike other law breakers, the poacher almost always is carrying a gun. There is no way of knowing what the poacher will do with that gun when cornered. The best approach is just to locate the fellow, and try to get some form of identification without endangering yourself. A license plate number, hunting license number (in states where it is mandatorily worn on the back), or just a good description often will be sufficient. When you encounter one of these individuals, remain cordial and give the appearance of just being another guy in the woods. You would be amazed at what you can learn

Some Novel Approaches

Over the years, I have seen some amazingly innovative techniques for controlling poaching. One of these methods involves the use of reflective "eyes." A friend takes green reflective tape and sticks it on a cardboard silhouette of a deer's head, to simulate the animal's eyes. A jacklighter certainly does not want to shoot anymore than he has to, for fear of being discovered. My friend places these fake deer around the perimeter of his property. Even a biologist cannot tell the difference between the fake and a real deer. In no time, he had the poachers so exasperated that they left the area altogether.

A modification of this technique has been used successfully by game wardens in several states. They use a mounted buck (often named "Bucky") to lure road-shooters. It usually is placed in the bend of a road so that headlights are reflected by its eyes. In one state, they had a one-third response rate by law enforcement officers! One county judge jumped from his car, assumed a defensive shooting position, and began firing away at the stuffed animal. Obviously, he was surprised to discover his mistake. These methods smack of entrapment, but most cases have stood up to the appeal process.

Yet another approach is "Operation Fire Fly," used for some time now in Texas. This very effective program takes advantage of local pilots who are willing to donate time to the cause of

Robert Skinner

Since he probably is armed, it is not a good idea to confront a poacher. It is better to get some form of identification such as a license plate number.

from a poacher by just carrying on a conversation with him. A good friend of mine is a security man on a large hunting club. I am constantly amazed how he has the knack of getting a poacher to tell everything about himself, without ever suspecting that he is dealing with a security agent.

game protection. The procedure is simple. A pilot and spotter fly over the area at night at an altitude that escapes notice. Any spotlighter is easily seen from the air. On sighting, the spotter calls in the location to a ground crew of game wardens, who are in turn guided to the offender by the spotter.

Lastly, I have found that placing three electric wires along fences, one at the bottom about six inches above the ground, and the remaining two at the top of the fence, has a dramatic impact on the number of trespass cases. Although there may be liability problems, proper posting of warning signs may alleviate this problem.

SUMMARY

In most cases, poaching is not a serious problem to deer management. A problem arises either when the population is in a building phase, or under a trophy management situation. The best approach to controlling illegal entry and poaching is to have strong state trespass laws, with adequate enforcement. However, it is incumbent on the landowner, just as in any property situation, to protect the resource.

The best way to reduce trespass is to gain control of the property by closing common use roads, gating, adequate posting and by maintaining a presence on the property. Over the years, landowners and law enforcement personnel have developed novel ways of dealing with the poacher-trespass problem. The approach you use will depend on the particular situation and your management goals. Direct confrontation with a poacher is not a good idea; more subtle methods are encouraged.

Mike Biggs

AFTERWORD

What makes the white-tailed deer so special? As you've seen in the preceding chapters, many factors contribute to this unique game animal's "personality." But, for most of us, it is the whitetail's incredible adaptability which makes him so remarkable. While many other species-- grizzly bears, elk, wolves and caribou, to name but a few-- fled northward and/or westward as the American frontier approached, the whitetail simply dug in and made himself at home, almost literally among our houses. Perhaps only the coyote is his equal among "large" animals in this regard.

Even those of us who work with whitetails and whitetail hunting on a daily basis find ourselves continually amazed at this animal's ability to overcome the odds. Most of the world's wildlife species occupy small, well-defined niches in the environment; few could be called "widespread" in a global or even continental sense. Among those which have managed to occupy multiple niches, virtually none is as large an animal as our whitetail. Yet, this species can hold his own in terms of geographic coverage. Today's whitetail occupies probably more than 50 percent of the temperate and tropical Americas, to which he is native. And with the number of whitetails at what probably is an all-time high, there's little wonder why he is our most popular game animal.

The fact that whitetails are quite common and only becoming more so is the good news. However, it also is the bad. The line between too few deer and too many is a thin one easily crossed, and it is being crossed in new places every year. Whereas there once was a legitimate need to protect breeding stock almost universally, we now realize that overprotection and overpopulation go hand-in-hand when dealing with these animals. Given a choice between too few deer and too many, the prudent game manager would take the former. As Dr. Kroll has pointed out through his extensive population research, whitetails have the ability to become their own worst enemies. It takes years for overbrowsed range to recover from the ravages of too many deer, if it can recover fully at all. When whitetails overpopulate, they and everything around them are the losers. That is why today's deer manager needs to keep his finger on the pulse of the herd from the start, so that he is not continually trying to catch up to a snowballing population. Doing so is difficult, expensive and not always successful.

As we near the end of the 20th century, how can we balance the needs of man and nature in regard to whitetails? Hunters always seem to want more deer, even though deer size and deer numbers are generally in direct conflict with each other. Non-hunters want deer to be plentiful in areas where they can be seen and appreciated, which includes suburbia. Yet, these same people and others have a well-founded fear of Lyme disease, which is often carried by deer ticks. Everyone wants low auto-insurance rates, but a large deer herd in close proximity to people means a high incidence of auto-deer accidents. And finally, whitetails are all too willing to accept free handouts of food, whether offered in feeders or in cultivated rows (including the family garden). How large a price should the farmer-- and ultimately, the consumer-- be willing to pay in order to allow whitetails a visible place in society?

There are no easy anwers to these questions. But, through the work of researchers such as Dr. Kroll, we are developing the machinery of change. His efforts have helped us to gain a better understanding of the whitetail's world and how we impact it. In so doing, this exceptionally talented biologist has pointed out clearly that "letting nature take its course" is NOT the answer in whitetail management. We must work to keep deer numbers within what the habitat will support in harmony with other species and uses. To do anything less is to turn our backs not only upon the whitetail, but upon ourselves as well.

Gordon Whittington, Editor
North American Whitetail Magazine

INDEX

Aging 180
Anthrax 12
Antlers
  and age 237-238
  and social position 238-239
  yearling 237-238
  casting 44, 47, 70, 73, 404
  composition 67-70
  conformation 247-248
  heritability 238-242 (see Genetics)
  hormones 69, 73
  mineralization 72, 84
  nutrition 236-237, 241
  pedicels 68
  potential 76
  rainfall 236
  spikes 237-239, 241, 243
  supplemental feeding 237
  velvet 31
Behavior
  activity patterns
    diurnal 348
  alpha doe 39, 136
  breeding 40
  deer-deer interactions 136
  deer-predator interactions 137
  fawning 19-21
  fighting 37-38
  rub-urination 42
  social Groups
    does 24
    bucks 22, 32
  rutting 424
  fawning territories 18-19
Beds 403
Blue Tongue 24 (see Hemorrhagic Disease)
Boggy Slough 247, 263-275
  antlerless harvest 267
  antler rating 268
  browse utilization 268
  buck harvest 267
  ghost of 269-275
  population trends 266
  people management at 266
  optimum sustained yield 269
Bottleneck Effect (see Population)
Browse (see Nutrition)
Browsing (see Nutrition)
Camouflage 60
Carrying Capacity 11-12, 149-150, 214-215
Census 161-176
  change-in-ratio 172
    calculating 172
  economics 175-176
  guesses 175
  spotlight counts 163-169
    accuracy vs. precision 164
    conduct of 165
    calculating density from 168
  track counts 169-172
    conduct of 170
    aerial counts 173

Checkstations 183
Chemical Communication (see also
    Behavior and Glands)
  scent patch 413
Clearcuts (see Hunting Techniques)
Corner 111
Coverts (see Corner)
Culling (see also Genetics)
  brood bucks 246-247, 249
  principles of 243-245
  selecting brood bucks 247
  slot limit approach 245-247
Deer Range Appraisal (see Habitat
    Management)
Deer Ownership 573
Depredation (see Predation)
Dick Idol 531-534
Diseases
  hemorrhagic Disease 12
  Lyme Disease 12
Does
  alpha doe 39, 136
  as bait 435-442
  patterning doe groups 437-439
  patterning reproductive cycles
    439-442
  social groups 41
Doe:fawn Ratio (see Record-keeping)
Edges 107-110, defined 108
  induced 108
  inherent 108
  soft 109
EHD (see Hemorrhagic Disease)
Fat Deposition (see nutrition)
Fawning (see Behavior)

Fences 251-261
  braces 256
  economics 260
  justification for 252
  origins 251-252
  posts 256
  specifications for 256-260
  types of 252-256
Flehmen 62, 65-66
Food Plots 85-86, 357
  clover 95
  costs of 93
  recommended varieties 99-100
  management 92
  protein levels 92
  selecting 97
Forbs (Forbaceous Vegetation) (see
    Nutrition)
Forage
  categories 80
  protein content 82-83
Forest 28
Forest Management
  basal area 117-118
  D+ thinnings 118
  rotation age 118
  site index 113
Genetics 233-249
  genetic role of does 242, 243, 245
  Gregor Mendel 242
  heterozygosity 242, 249
  Kerr Wildlife Management Area
    Study 236, 240, 245
  Medelian genetics 242
  Mississippi State Study 238-241, 243

Glands 35
  commercial scents 63
  frontal 63
  interdigital 62
  masking scents 63-64
  metatarsal 62
  mock scrapes 63-64
  neutralizing scents 63-64
  preorbital 62-63
  rutting scents 63-64
  signpost marking 63
  tarsal 62
Grunting (see Vocalizations)
Habitat 101-132
  brush 101-102
  components 101
  cover 101, 106-107
  disturbance (see succession)
  edge (see edge)
  food plots (see Food Plots)
  water 101-107
Habitat Management
  corner 484
  deer range appraisal 187
  edge 484
  fertilization 120
  fire 12, 112-114, 394
    backfires 113-114
    headfires 113-114
    firebreaks 114-115
  herbicides 112, 119-120
  intermediate treatments 116-117
  intensive management 225
  mechanical treatments 112
  old growth evergreen forest 358
  openings 111
  preferences 356
  recommendations 130-132
  structure 485
  site preparation 116
  wildlife stand improvement 119
  windrows 485-486
Hemorrhagic Disease 24, 187
Home Range
  and habitat preferences 356
  basic home range 129-130
  bucks 23, 355
  estimates 124-128
  core area 125, 355
  sanctuaries 355-356
  size 128-129, 347
Hunter Behavior 490
Hunters
  education 509
  knowledge 508
  non-hunters
  peer-group pressure 511-513
Hunting
  anti-hunting 515-523
  choosing a pay-hunt 554-558
  guided hunts 551-560
  hunting debate 520-522
  justification for 553-554
  making most of 558-559
  myths 516-520
  why hunt deer? 520
Hunting Clubs 535-549
  acquiring land for 539
  choosing the right property 540
  definition of 536

economics of 542
future of 544
landowner agreements 541
lease agreement 545-549
organization 539
size of 541
Hunting Patterns 491
Hunting Techniques
  analyzing deer behavior 497
  antler rubbing 459-460
  clearcut bucks 357, 479-487
  early season 447-450
  grunting 460-461
  hunter influence zones 491
  hunting the pre-rut 410-412
  hunting the post-rut 415, 452
  hunting the rut 409-417
  late season hunting
  late-winter strategies 498
  mock scrapes 35
  pre-rut 454-457
  rattling 55, 414-415, 460
  rubs 421-424
  rut 457
  rut strategies 409, 450-452
  rutting sign 426-427
  scrapes 413-414, 424-426
  signposts 423-424
  timing tactics 443-452
  year-long scouting 497-504
Interspersion 107, 110-111
Jacobson's Organ 65
Kerr Wildlife Management Area (see Genetics)
Kidney Fat Index 46-48

Lactation (see Record-keeping)
Sanctuaries (Safe Zones) 33, 355-356,365-388,410-411,415,495
  and hunter influence zones 368,383
  and hunting pressure 371-376
  hunting 380-388
  identifying 376-377
Management (see Management Strategies)
Management Strategies
  baseline data 227
  quality buck management 10-11, 219
  blueprint for 219-233
  goals of 213, 219
  herd management 227
  hunting clubs 14
  man's needs 13
  management subunits 222
  numbers management 11, 219
  open lands 13
  state wildlife management areas 13
  trophy management 9-10, 211-219
  type-mapping 221
Mast
  age 119
  crown diameter 119
  density of trees 119
  fertility and site index 119
  fruiting habits 119
  production 119
Metabolic Rates 47-49
Mid-day Hunting
  problems in hunting 465
  strategies for 466-468
Minerals 97-98

supplemental analysis 97
Mississippi State University (see Genetics)
Travel Corridors 329, 365-388, 400, 482
   hunting 380-388, 491
Mock Scrapes (see Hunting Techniques)
Movements
   circadian Rhythms 134
   crepuscular 54, 58
   deer-deer interactions 136
   deer-predator interactions 137
   extrinsic factors 136
   feeding times 142
   intrinsic factors 134-135
   light 134
   moon 139
   nocturnal 41
   snow 144
   tapetum Lucidum 134
   weather 137
Noel Feather 530
Non-hunter (see Hunter)
Nutrition 89
   and hunting 385-398
   browse 102-103, 480, 483
   browsing 389-398
   commercial feeds 89
   costs 91-92
   dietary constituents 87
   fat reserves and energy stores 45-46, 49-50
   feeding patterns 393
   food contamination 90
   forbs (Forbaceous Vegetation) 102, 480, 483
   high-energy foods 482-484
   mast 82, 85
   nutrients 103
   preferred species 391-392
   supplementation 87
Observations 405
Pelage 31
People Management 507-514, 537-539
Pheromones (see Senses)
Poaching 571-579 (see also Trespass)
   controlling 578-579
   dealing with poachers 576-577
   methods 572-573
Population
   and quality management 230
   and trophy management 230-232
   boom-crash cycles 147
   bottleneck effect 12
   densities 29
   density-dependent factors 147, 244
   density-independent factors 147, 244
   effective population density 158
   effective population size 156-158
   growth 145
   growth equation 146
   harvesting 232-233
   intrinsic rate of increase 147
   J-shaped growth 146-147
   K-strategists 149, 153-155
   lag-times 150, 154
   limiting factors 103, 147
   logistic growth 148
   maximum sustained yield 152
   optimum sustained yield 153,

160-214
  overpopulation 39
  r-strategists 147
  recruitment rate 149
  relative size of effective
    population 158
  role of disturbance in 151
  role of predators (see also Predators)
    155-156
  S-shaped growth 148
  sustained yield 146, 151-153,
    219-233
Post-rut (see Rut)
Predation 11, 53
Pre-rut (see Rut)
Public Education 14-15
Public Hunting 563
Radio-telemetry 48, 354
Ray Sasser 529-530
Record-keeping 199-210
  antler quality 203
  antler measurements 183-184
  antler rating 203
  average age of bucks 202
  browse utilization 203
  buck:doe ratio 201, 213
  doe age structure 201
  doe:fawn ratio 178
  dressed weights 183
  fawn crop 200
  lactation 178-180
  parasite loads 185
  sex ratio 183
  spike rate 202
  yearling buck dressed weight 203

Reproduction
  estrus 37, 41-42
Reproductive Performance 177
  (see Record-keeping)
Rut
  autopsy of 359-407
  copulation 43
  courtship 42
  full scrape sequence 40
  hunting techniques 400-407
  neck swelling 34
  post-rut 43-44
  preparing for 420-421
  pre-rut 29, 32 (defined)
  rut 27, 39, 49
  primary 41
  scrapes 35, 40, 42
  secondary 41
  tertiary (third) 41
  trickle rut 429-434
    and molt patterns 433
    recognizing it 430-433
    techniques to autopsy 400-407
  sign 404
  sparring 34
  secondary rut 41
  third rut 41
  understanding it 430-433
Rutting Sign (see Hunting Techniques)
Scouting
  agricultural areas 315
  big buck areas 302
  bigwoods 313
  edges 310
  finding the best tract of land 306

Index

    finding the right buck 312
    hunter influence zones 309
    late-winter 498
    mast crop 503
    narrowing choices 311
    on the ground searching 316
    reading the woods 316
    reliable sources for 300
    river bottoms 314
    site index 302
    soils 310
    spring 501
    summer 501
    trophy hotspots 236
    using rubs 316-318
Screwworm 8, 236
Senses
    conchae 62
    Jacobson's organ 65
    hearing 55
    secret sense 65
    sight 58
    smell 61
    sound 54
    tapetum lucidum 60
    taste 65
    ultraviolet light 60
    visual cues 42 (rut)
Sex Ratio (see Record-keeping)
Shooting 279-298
    calibers 283-285
    decisions in 290-296
    equipment 280
    firearms 280-283
    practice 286
    rules for followup on shot 296
    shot placement 289-296
    sights 285
Signpost 34-36, 40, 238, 329-330, 411, 413-414
SMZ (see Streamside Management Zones)
Snort-wheeze (see Vocalizations)
Stands and Blinds 52, 321, 335, 412
    ladder 323
    lockon 324
    natural 330
    permanent 332
    tripod 324
Streamside Management Zones (SMZs) 121-124, 483-485, 225-227, 357
Stress
    late summer 24
Succession 103, 480
    climax 105
    climax forest 480
    climax species 105
    disturbance 102
    old growth 105
    pioneer species 103, 105
Summer 29
Teeth (see Aging)
Trespass
    control of 574-576
    laws 573-576
    locksafe (gate) 575
    security 576
Trophy 526 (definition) 212
Trophy Hunting 521

Velvet (see Antlers)
Venison 28 Vocalizations 29, 42
   grunting 455, 460-461
   snort-wheeze 37
Vocalizations
   grunt 42, 455, 460-461

Vomeronasal Organ (see Jacobson's Organ)
Wildlife Stand Improvement (see Habitat Management)
Winter 43
Yarding 47-49

SUGGESTED READINGS

Ardrey. R. 1976. The Hunting Hypothesis, A Personal Conclusion Concerning the Evolutionary Nature of Man. McClelland and Stewart Ltd., N.Y. 214 pp.

Berryman, A. A. 1981. Population Systems, A general Introduction. Plenum Press, N.Y. 222 pp.

Brothers, A., and M. E. Ray, Jr. 1975. Producing Quality Whitetails. Wildlife Service Publ., Laredo, TX. 245 pp.

Burger, G. V. 1973. Practical Wildlife Management. Winchester Press, N.Y. 218 pp.

Caughley, G. 1977. Analysis of Vertebrate Populations. John Wiley & Sons, N.Y. 234 pp.

Giles, R. H., Jr. (ed). 1971. Widlife Management Techniques. The Wildlife Society, Washington, D.C. 633 pp.

Halls, L. K. (ed). 1984. White-tailed Deer, Ecology and Management. Stackpole Books, Inc. 870 pp.

Hunter, M. L., Jr. 1990. Wildlife, Forests, and Forestry: Principles of Managing Forests. Prentice-Hall, Inc., N. J., 370 pp.

Leopold, A. 1966. A Sand County Almanac, with Essays on Conservation from Round River. Ballantine Books, N.Y. 295 pp.

Mattis, G. 1969. Whitetail, Fundamentals and Fine Points for the Hunter. World Publishing Co., OH. 273 pp.

McCullough, D. R. 1979. The George Reserve Deer Herd, Population Ecology of a K-adapted Species.

Poole, R. W. 1974. An Introduction to Quantitive Ecology. McGraw-Hill Book Co., St. Louis. 532 pp.

Rue, L. L., III. 1979. The Deer of North America., Outdoor Life-Crown Publishers, Inc., N.Y. 463 pp.

Wegner, R. 1984. Deer & Deer Hunting, The Serious Hunter's Guide, Parts I-III. Stackpole Books, Harrisburg, PA.

NOTES

NOTES

NOTES

NOTES

NOTES